A (

A Critical Cinema 3

**Interviews with
Independent Filmmakers**

Scott MacDonald

University of California Press
Berkeley / Los Angeles / London

University of California Press
Berkeley and Los Angeles, California

University of California Press, Ltd.
London, England

Library of Congress Cataloging-in-Publication Data

MacDonald, Scott, 1942–
        A critical cinema.
        Includes bibliographical references and index.
        1. Experimental films—United States—History and
criticism.   2. Motion picture producers and directors
—United States—Interviews.   I. Title.
PN1995.9.E96M34   1988   791.43'75'0973   87-6004
ISBN 0-520-05800-3 (v. 1 : cloth)
ISBN 0-520-05801-1 (v. 1 : pbk.)
ISBN 0-520-07917-5 (v. 2 : cloth)
ISBN 0-520-07918-3 (v. 2 : pbk.)
ISBN 0-520-08705-4 (v. 3 : cloth)
ISBN 0-520-20943-5 (v. 3 : pbk.)

Printed in the United States of America
9   8   7   6   5   4   3   2   1

For Hollis Frampton,
Jackie Shearer,
Margie Keller,
and Warren Sonbert

For Chuck Roche

And for my mom,
Evelyn May Messinger MacDonald

And my dad,
Frederic LaMonte MacDonald

Contents

Acknowledgments

Because the critical cinema developed in the margins of the film industry and because it remains marginalized in most academic settings, those individuals and organizations that have committed themselves to the maintenance of this extensive cinematic arena are all-the-more precious, as I've realized again and again during the ten years I've labored on this project.

For helping me find my way to films I needed to see, I am particularly indebted to Jonas Mekas, Amos Vogel, John Hanhardt, Richard Herskowitz, Steve Anker; and to Anthology Film Archives (and Robert Haller); Canyon Cinema (Dominic Angerame and David Sherman); the Film-makers' Cooperative (Leslie Trumbull, M. M. Serra); the Robert Flaherty Seminars (Sally Berger, Michelle Materre); the Museum of Modern Art (Larry Kardish and Jytte Jensen at Cineprobe; William Sloan in the Circulating Film Library; Charles Silver in the Film Study Center; and Mary Lea Bandy); the Black Maria Film Festival (John Columbus); the American Museum of the Moving Image (David Schwartz); Light Cone (Yann Beauvais); the Millennium Film Workshop (Howard Guttenplan); Third World Newsreel (Ada Griffin); and Women Make Movies.

For useful advice, assorted leads, and other forms of support, I am grateful to Martin Arnold, Erik Barnouw, Cathy Belson, Jean-Michel Bouhours, Deirdre Boyle, Ruth Bradley, Ed Dimendberg, Jane M. Gaines, Louise Greaves, Ada Griffin, Kathy High, David James, Bruce Jenkins, O. Funmilayo Makarah, Louis Massiah, Christine McDonald, Roanne Moore, William Moritz, Marc Nichanian, Marie-Noëlle Little, Chon Noriega, Jonathan Rosenbaum, L. Somi Roy, David Taffler, Jackie Tshaka, Ludmila Tsivilyova, Maureen Turim, Aruna Vadusev, Johan van der Keuken, Marcia Vogel, Linda Williams, and Lise Yasui.

I have also been fortunate to have the regular financial and institutional support of Utica College, as well as the timely support of the National Endowment for the Humanities, in the form of a Fellowship for College Teachers I held during 1993.

I am grateful to the following journals for permission to include (sometimes revised versions of) interviews and introductions:

Film Quarterly, for "Cinema 16: An Interview with Amos Vogel," vol. 37, no. 3 (Spring 1984): 19–29; "Sp . . . Sp . . . Spaces of Inscription: An Interview with Martin Arnold," vol. 48, no. 1 (Fall 1994), 2–11.

The Independent, for "Sunday in the Park with Bill: William Greaves' *Symbiopsychotaxiplasm: Take One*," vol. 15, no. 4 (May 1992): 24–29; and "The Axeman Cometh: An Interview with Raphael Montañez Ortiz," vol. 17, no. 8 (October 1994): 26–31.

Wide Angle, for the sections of "Quote/Unquote" on Peter Watkins, Ken Jacobs, Nick Deocampo, and Mani Kaul, vol. 17, nos. 1–4 (1995): 115–123, 135–144, 152–156, 157–164, respectively.

My wonderful typist and ofttimes transcriber, Carol Fobes, has allowed this work to proceed, despite my academic schedule and my computer illiteracy.

And finally, for all kinds of intellectual, emotional, and practical support, I am deeply grateful to Frank Bergmann, Patricia Zimmermann, Su Friedrich, Ray Carney, Larry Platt, Bryan Cressy, Don Tracy—and, as always, to Ian MacDonald and Patricia Reichgott O'Connor.

Introduction

That films can provide viewers with in-theater critiques of their conventional film and television experiences is the burden of this volume and of the previous two volumes of this series. When viewers are faced with forms of film that cause them to wonder, "Is *this* a movie?" they have the opportunity to recontextualize their previous filmgoing experiences and to expand their understanding of what film and film history is, has been, and can be. The inevitable conventionality of the popular cinema—"inevitable" because without established conventions, movies cannot be popular enough to return a profit on the financial investments necessary to produce them—continually re-creates an audience with a set of predictable expectations *and*, therefore, with a considerable potential for surprise. If the achievement of the American film industry has been its ability to maintain its economic viability for nearly a century by continually reenergizing a narrow range of filmgoing pleasure, the achievement of the critical cinema, which has been evolving at the margins of the popular cinema, has been the continual proliferation of critical film forms—that is, forms of cinema capable of surprising viewers and catalyzing critique—by filmmakers with limited economic means. Indeed, this proliferation has been so extensive that even naming it has been an endless cause for debate: what I am calling "critical cinema" includes "avant-garde cinema," "revolutionary film," "poetic film," "film as art," "the New American Cinema," "film as a subversive art," "expanded cinema," "alternative cinema," "visionary film," "structural film," "punk film," "trash film," "experimental film," "abstract film," "the new narrative," "materialist cinema," "independent film," "third cinema," "transnational cinema," and "queer cinema."

It is precisely because the wide world of critical cinema confronts conven-

1

tional expectations in so many different ways that I have been emboldened to offer readers a third volume of conversations with accomplished critical filmmakers. Of course, filmmakers' understandings of their own work must always be qualified: as Hollis Frampton said in the first interview I did, "I believe it's obvious that there are things that spectators can know about a work, any work, that the person who made it can never know" (*A Critical Cinema*; Berkeley: University of California Press, 1988, p. 57). Nevertheless, their comments about their work in response to an interested and informed viewer's questions can serve as a bridge across which viewers can walk to a more thorough engagement with the full range of cinema.

Inevitably, each volume of the Critical Cinema series reflects my limited awareness of critical cinema at the moment when the volume is compiled, but each volume has been informed by my commitment to an expanding awareness of the full range of critical-cinematic contributions. *A Critical Cinema 3* enlarges the coverage of the Critical Cinema project in several ways.

Even a cursory glance at the table of contents for *A Critical Cinema 3* reveals an expansion in the geopolitical range of this project, in two senses. First, for this volume I have interviewed filmmakers residing in many nations. In addition to interviews with filmmakers from the United States (William Greaves, Jordan Belson, Charles Burnett, Ken Jacobs, Aline Mare, Elias Merhige, Christine Choy, Cauleen Smith, Peter Hutton, and Craig Baldwin), this collection includes filmmakers from Canada (John Porter), England (Sally Potter), France (Patrick Bokanowski, Rose Lowder), Austria (Valie Export, Martin Arnold), Italy (Yervant Gianikian and Angela Ricci Lucchi), Sweden (Gunvor Nelson), Armenia (Arthur Peleshian), India (Mani Kaul), the Philippines (Nick Deocampo), and Japan (Hara Kazuo). Second, as one might guess from the preceding listing, there is a range of ethnic, cultural, and linguistic traditions, even for filmmakers grouped within a given nationality. William Greaves, Charles Burnett, and Cauleen Smith embody three generations of African-American filmmaking; Ken Jacobs is Jewish-American; Elias Merhige, Lebanese-American; Christine Choy is originally of Korean-Chinese extraction, though she has been living in the United States since the late 1960s; Raphael Montañez Ortiz is a Puerto Rican American (though his roots go back not only to Puerto Rico, Spain, and Portugal, but to Ireland and to the Yaqui of northwestern Mexico). Yervant Gianikian lives in Milan with his native-born Italian partner, Angela Ricci Lucchi, but he himself is of Armenian extraction; Patrick Bokanowski's roots go back to Poland and Russia; Gunvor Nelson is a native Swede, currently residing in Sweden, who lived and worked in San Francisco for more than thirty years; Rose Lowder was born of English parents and grew up in Peru, but has lived in Avignon since the early 1970s. Peter Watkins grew up in England but has lived and worked for extended periods in Sweden, Canada, the USA, New Zealand, and Australia; he currently resides in Lithuania. Amos Vogel is an Austrian Jew who emigrated to the United States to es-

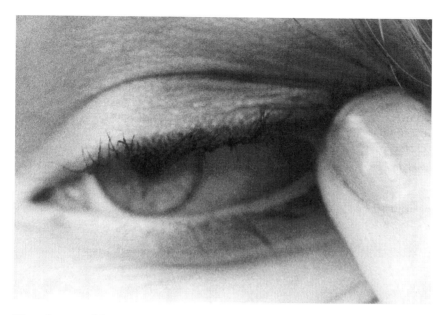

The aging eye of Gunvor Nelson's mother, from *Red Shift* (1984).

cape Hitler. *A Critical Cinema 3* sees the history of critical cinema as simultaneously multinational and transnational, multi-ethnic and inter-ethnic, not simply in the sense that various filmmakers identify themselves with a considerable range of locations and heritages, but because all the filmmakers see their
work as a product of many and varied interests and influences.

Volume 3 also reflects an expanded sensitivity to the institutional surround
of critical cinema. As in *A Critical Cinema* and *A Critical Cinema 2*, the filmmakers interviewed here have worked primarily in 16mm, 8mm, and Super-
8mm (exceptions include Arthur Peleshian, whose complex montage films,
like all officially sanctioned films made in what was the Soviet Union, were
shot in 35mm; Patrick Bokanowski and Mani Kaul, who have worked primarily in 35mm; and selected 35mm films by William Greaves, Jordan Belson,
Charles Burnett, Nick Deocampo, and Sally Potter) and have profited from a
wide range of efforts at alternative exhibition and distribution, including those
of Amos Vogel, the first interviewee, at the New York film society Cinema 16,
from 1947 to 1963. Vogel created an audience for a wide range of cinematic
forms, inspired a nationwide network of film societies, and, in order to supply
these film societies with a range of critical films, became the first American
distributor to specialize in avant-garde film. His *Film As a Subversive Art*,
which grew out of his experiences at Cinema 16, has been and remains an inspiration for this project.

While none of the other interviewees in this volume have provided a level of institutional support for alternative cinema comparable to Vogel's (of course, Jonas Mekas, interviewed in *A Critical Cinema 2* and discussed by various filmmakers in all three volumes, is an exception), many have made noteworthy contributions. Ken Jacobs was instrumental in the establishment of both Millennium Film Workshop and, indirectly (through his students), of the now-defunct Collective for Living Cinema in New York City; Christine Choy played a central role in the development of the producer-distributor Third World Newsreel; Martin Arnold has worked with Vienna's SIXPACK to provide alternative screenings and an international audience for critical film-making; Rose Lowder, in collaboration with Alain-Alcide Sudre, founded the Archives du film experimental d'Avignon, which has accumulated a collection of films and which sponsors screenings of a range of critical films; and Nick Deocampo has established a film school in Manila, open to a range of film-making approaches, and was instrumental in the creation of a week-long festival during which Philippine alternative cinema is screened in commercial theaters. Even those interviewees who have not played a substantial role in efforts to expand the audience for critical cinema frequently discuss the efforts of those who have.

One other institution, the annual Robert Flaherty Seminar (sponsored by International Film Seminars), has played a substantial role in this volume. The "At the Flaherty" chapter includes post-screening discussions with Peter Watkins, Ken Jacobs, Nick Deocampo, Mani Kaul, and Craig Baldwin that took place at various annual seminars. Two full-length interviews (William Greaves and Hara Kazuo) originated with Flaherty discussions and were expanded later in one-on-one conversations. And still others were inspired by screenings at Flaherty events (the interviews with Arthur Peleshian and Raphael Montañez Ortiz). While the Flaherty's historical relationship with critical cinema has been somewhat troubled, it remains one of the oldest organizations in the world to provide regular opportunities for the exhibition of a range of critical cinematic forms (see the special issue of *Wide Angle* on the Flaherty Seminar [vol. 17, nos. 1–4 [1995–96], edited by Erik Barnouw and Patricia Zimmermann).

Several of the interviewees also discuss another form of institutional surround: the historical margins of cinema itself. In some instances, filmmakers have returned to early cinema, and even to pre-cinematic motion study, for inspiration, or in an attempt to explore and/or revise the implicit politics of the earliest cinema and the commercial industry that grew out of it. Ken Jacobs uses various homemade devices (the most elaborate is called the "Nervous System") to explore and transform 16mm and 35mm imagery from prints of early films in live performances often reminiscent of the entertainments of nineteenth-century illusionists. Yervant Gianikian and Angela Ricci Lucchi collect early films and interpretively reprint the original images so that viewers can simultaneously *see* and (in a sociopolitical sense) *see through* the ideology encoded in the original frames; and Peter Hutton's films are often purposely reminiscent, in their simplicity and directness, of the Lumière brothers' original single-shot films. Even when filmmakers do not consciously return or allude to the earliest cinema or to pre-cinematic history, their explorations of imagery-in-motion suggest the motion-study photography of Eadweard Muybridge, Etienne-Jules Marey, and others whose work led finally to the kinetograph, the kinetoscope, and the cinématographe. In one sense or another, virtually every filmmaker I've interviewed has focused on the study of motion, whether it's the physical motion of bodies in space (in films by Rose Lowder, John Porter, Arthur Peleshian) or in previously recorded film imagery (in the "recycled cinema" of Martin Arnold, Yervant Gianikian and Angela Ricci Lucchi, Raphael Ortiz, and many others); the psychological and sociological motion of people in relation to one another (in William Greaves's *Symbiopsychotaxiplasm: Take One* [1967, 1995] and works by Charles Burnett, Christine Choy, Gunvor Nelson, and Sally Potter); or the motion of the spirit (in films by Jordan Belson, Patrick Bokanowski, Arthur Peleshian, and others).

The contemporary "margin" of film history, cinema's current evolution and especially its convergence with video, is also more fully a topic of the interviews in *A Critical Cinema 3* than in earlier volumes of this series. Many of the interviewees make both films and videos; and the increasingly tenuous distinction between the two media is discussed by Jordan Belson (and his collaborator, video pioneer Stephen Beck: their film *Cycles* [1975] was one of the first works to attempt an equal amalgam of film and video), and by Amos Vogel, Craig Baldwin, Aline Mare, Sally Potter, and Raphael Ortiz (who recycles classic film imagery into deconstructive videos).

Of course, the most fundamental issue for the filmmakers whose work is the subject of the interviews in *A Critical Cinema 3*, and for those who have labored to provide a support system for this work, remains the institutions of commercial film and television, especially as those institutions are encoded within the narrative entertainment they produce. Each of the filmmakers included in this volume means to develop a new kind of imagery, a new definition of narrative (or a new, nonnarrative structure), and a new sense of cinema and its actual and potential audience. I've collected these interviews, not with the idea of defining the critical cinema as a rival to the commercial film and television industry (critical cinema is, by definition, dependent on the industry, for both its technology and its history), but in the hope that a broader critical sensibility can recognize *both* the power and the pleasures of the conventional *and* the excitements of learning more fully to understand, through the experience of cinema itself, what the industry is and is not. While the industry remains one of the most broadly prestigious instances of the corporate mentality and its narrow financial goal, the expanding world of critical cinema represents a diverse set of individual and tribal sensibilities and goals excluded from the industry's drive toward "success."

There is at least one important dimension of my choice of interviewees that is not covered by the foregoing discussion, though it is, perhaps, implicit in my comments. I choose to interview filmmakers who make work I admire. Of course, I cannot interview every filmmaker whose films strike me as "great"— or at least as "great for me"—and, indeed, on this level of response I make no distinction whatsoever between the commercial and the critical cinema; I am as "blown away" by Jonathan Demme's *Silence of the Lambs* (1991) or Spike Lee's *Do the Right Thing* (1989) or the Coen brothers' *Fargo* (1996) as I am by Andrew Noren's *Imaginary Light* (1995) or Peter Hutton's *Landscape (for Manon)* (1987). Wherever they stand on the political spectrum, whatever societal or psychological tendencies they can be said to represent, particular films either have the magical quality that for most of us is the catalyst for our film-going, or they do not. As difficult as this "magic" is to define and as outré as enunciating such a concept seems to be in most academic frameworks, I simply cannot proceed—as a moviegoer, as a teacher, as a scholar—without it. Some films strike me as works of "genius," and, more than any other single factor, it is my commitment to these films—and to the filmmakers who manage somehow to produce them, despite whatever compromised economic circumstances they find themselves in—that drives me through the often tedious process of compiling a book such as this one. Essentially, I believe the willingness of so many critical filmmakers to place themselves at risk economically to make their work is evidence of a spiritual commitment to their films and to Cinema. Indeed, a number of interviewees in this volume—most obviously, William Greaves, Jordan Belson, Arthur Peleshian, Mani Kaul, Peter Hutton, and Raphael Montañez Ortiz —see their filmmaking as a form of, or as an adjunct to, psychospiritual evolution, and many of the interviewees speak to the spiritual dimension of their work.

In recent years much has been made of the problems of canonization, in particular of the apparent elitism involved in defining *these*, and not *those*, filmmakers as "great." And there is no doubt in my mind that questioning the canons of cinema and the other arts, and interrogating the process of canonization itself, has been a healthy process, especially in revealing the gender and ethnic biases of the traditional canons and the histories constructed to support them. And yet, to argue that films (or other art works) are merely articulations of social-political forces and that the canonizing of some works and the rejection of others represents nothing more than an attempt to narrow and control the cinematic discourse is to impoverish both our thinking about cinema and cinema itself. While we live in a very wide world of various and multivalent

Catskill Mountain skyscape, in Peter Hutton's *Landscape (for Manon)* (1987).

aesthetic accomplishments and failures, whose theoretical terms continuously evolve, our moment for experiencing cinema and other art forms is quite brief. Except for professional reviewers of commercial features, virtually no one makes a living by looking at films. Even academics devoted to film studies must find time for exploring new and old developments in film history. Given the brevity of those moments we have for seeing films, we have no alternative but to make choices: we must decide to see, and show our students and colleagues, this and not that. In other words, whether it is a conscious process or not, we must inevitably select a "canon" of works we judge are not to be missed.

Some would argue that such choices can be evaluative in different senses: one might choose to show a particular film, not because it is "great," according to some ambiguous, "personal" aesthetic standard, but because it is simply a useful instance of a set of sociopolitical factors, with no particular intrinsic value of its own, *all* films being instances of sets of such factors. But then, all art works, indeed all phenomena of any kind that occur within a society are, equally, sets of such factors. One can in fact study *any*thing. As a result, to choose to focus a substantial portion of one's energies on the production or the exploration of cinema in particular is, by implication, to admit that within the cinematic discourse itself lies something "worth our lives" or, at least, a considerable portion of our time and energy, and of the time and energy of those we serve as scholars and teachers. Since all experiences are "deconstructable," and since our time and energy are finite resources, our choices of films to see, show, and write about must compete with the myriad experiences, in and out of the arts, that surround us. In the end, my decisions on which filmmakers to include in the *Critical Cinema* books do not mean that these filmmakers, and only these, are *the* great filmmakers; my choices do mean that, in my experience, these filmmakers and at least some of the work they've made can compete, in terms of what they have to offer us personally and professionally, with William Faulkner's *Intruder in the Dust*, Willa Cather's *O Pioneers!*, with a show of Edward Hopper's paintings or Spalding Gray's new performance piece, with *Seinfeld, My So-Called Life*, the NBA finals, and a hike in the Adirondacks.

Having confessed the above, I should add that the films and filmmakers represented in the Critical Cinema project tend to move me in at least two distinguishable ways. There are films that, to put it crudely, thrill me—for reasons I can never quite enunciate. I feel this way, for example, about Peter Hutton's *Landscape (for Manon)*, Charles Burnett's *Killer of Sheep* (1977), Martin Arnold's *Pièce Touchée* (1989) and *Passage à l'Acte* (1993), Ken Jacobs's *Two Wrenching Departures* (in various versions since 1989), and Sally Potter's *Orlando* (1992). Second, there are films that I cannot teach without, that generate experiences for students that have the potential to reverberate for years. Try as I might, I cannot organize a serious introduction to cinema without Larry Gottheim's *Fog Line* (1970), Laura Mulvey and Peter Wollen's *Riddles of the Sphinx* (1977), Hollis Frampton's *Zorns Lemma* (1970), Alfred Hitchcock's *Psycho* (1960), Gunvor Nelson's *Take Off* (1972), J. J. Murphy's *Print Generation* (1974), and Stan Brakhage's *The Act of Seeing with One's Own Eyes* (1971). Virtually all the films and filmmakers featured in all three volumes of the Critical Cinema project are included because they've made films that fall into one or both of these categories.

My method in preparing the interviews included in this and previous *Critical Cinema* volumes has remained roughly constant. I examine a filmmaker's work as thoroughly as is feasible, and arrange to talk with the filmmaker about this work in as much detail as possible. While most of the interviews are recorded as in-person conversations, and are subsequently transcribed and edited, I have made it a practice to use whatever interviewing procedure seems most comfortable for the filmmaker. In a few cases, interviews have been conducted entirely by letter, including the Andrew Noren interview in *A Critical Cinema 2* and the interviews with Patrick Bokanowski and Valie Export in this volume. My discussions with Jordan Belson took place entirely on the phone (and were recorded on my answering machine).

The international emphasis of *A Critical Cinema 3* did necessitate two modifications of my usual procedure and suggested a third. Limitations on my access to some filmmakers required that I interview them when they were available, rather than when I might be most fully prepared: I spoke with Arthur Peleshian, for example, when he made a brief stop at Cornell Cinema on a rare trip to the United States; and, as mentioned earlier, I used Flaherty Seminar discussions as raw material for several interviews. Since several of those interviewed for *A Critical Cinema 3* do not speak or write English with enough facility to sustain an in-depth interview, and since I speak and write only English, translation was essential (the details are included in the individual introductions to these interviews). The intermediary of translation—and even the wide variety of English dialect variances in the conversations I recorded—problematizes my concern with providing some sense of the nature of the interviewee as a conversationalist and as a person. My hope is that in my attempts to suggest something of each interviewee's delivery, I do not inadvertently caricature the speaker. Finally, my commitment to representing the internationality and the multi-ethnicity of critical cinema also suggested the formal device, used at various points in *A Critical Cinema 3*, of including more than a single interviewer. For example, the "At the Flaherty" chapter adapts large-group discussions (in each case, the several people who speak are part of a group of more than a hundred); and for the Hara Kazuo interview, I asked Laura Marks to collaborate with me.

From time to time, a colleague will ask me if more is involved in moving from a recorded conversation to a printed interview than careful transcription plus some basic editing for continuity and clarity. I'm always a bit amused by the question. Since in-person conversations involve complex kinesics and subtle vocal signals and usually take place within an environment that provides unforeseen modifications of the conversation's trajectory, syllable-by-syllable transcriptions are at best awkward and at worst incoherent and confusing—and thoroughly unrepresentative of the conversation that actually occurred *as it was experienced*. In every interview included in the Critical Cinema project, I have seen the recorded conversation and its transcription as raw material out of which to fashion a printed interchange that captures, as fully as is possible for me, the essence of what I believe the filmmaker and I communicated to one another, along with my sense of the interchange as an experience. In other words, each interview is to some degree a fabricated illusion of a conversation that is only the final stage in a process that, in many cases, involves years of refashioning the original interchange between the filmmaker and myself. There have been instances during my work on particular interviews when I have invented questions and responses that, under other circumstances, might have occurred during our conversations, but in fact did not. In all instances, I have asked interviewees to sign off on every interchange in every interview (I do make minor stylistic changes for the sake of clarity); nevertheless, what each interviewee agrees to is a conversation we have collaborated to fabricate.

Given my method, readers should not be surprised to find that the interviews tend to make the filmmakers "look good": that is, their comments will gener-

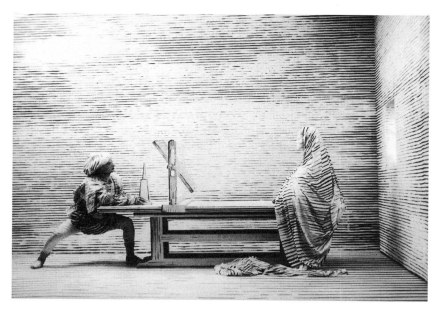

Artist and model, from Patrick Bokanowski's *L'Ange* ("The Angel," 1982).

ally seem intelligible and reasonable, at least within the context of our conversation. I make no apology for this. I am drawn to each interview by my admiration for the work we discuss, and it is this admiration that fuels the process of preparing to talk with a filmmaker and of rendering this conversation into a finished interview. I mean to honor efforts and accomplishments too often ignored by the public at large and even by those who consider themselves specialists in cinema history, rather than to provide anything like an exposé—though my hope is that aspects of interviewees and their work that I may be less than enamored with will be at least subtly evident in both the introductions to individual interviews and within the interviews themselves. That there are grounds for denouncing some of the films discussed in the interviews will be obvious to anyone familiar with the films; but, at least in our current moment, critical cinema must fight for the recognition it deserves, unlike industry filmmaking, which often seems to affect our lives without our interest or our approval.

How many interviews are included in a particular *Critical Cinema* volume and their organization within the volume are functions of the practicalities of publishing, of my current sense of the history and geography of critical cinema and, if the reader can forgive the pretension, of my "aesthetics." Each volume of the Critical Cinema series has been structured differently, as a means of emphasizing somewhat different issues and approaches (see the introductions to *A*

Critical Cinema and *A Critical Cinema 2*), and as a means of suggesting the overall evolution of this interview project and of my own awareness. Like a good many film scholars of my generation (I was in graduate school from 1964 to 1970), my training was in literature, and when I decided to commit my research energies to film, I needed to find ways of utilizing as much of my training as seemed relevant. From the beginning, I have understood the Critical Cinema project both as a reasonably scholarly act of research *and* as a nonfiction novel, formally indebted to two particular literary influences: James Boswell's eighteenth-century chronicling of the life of Samuel Johnson; and the development of forms of storytelling that proceed almost entirely by means of conversation, by the American writers Henry James, Gertrude Stein, Ernest Hemingway, Erskine Caldwell, and Richard Wright.

In my position as a young teacher and budding literature/film scholar, in central New York State, a region not characterized by much conventional film activity, I was fortunate to discover that what I now call "critical cinema" was all around me: Hollis Frampton lived nearby in Eaton, NY; Robert Huot, just to the south; and the State University of New York at Binghamton was building a reputation as a center of alternative filmmaking (Larry Gottheim and Ken Jacobs were full-time teachers in a department that, during the 1970s, included, at various moments, Peter Kubelka, Ernie Gehr, Saul Levine, and Taka Iimura). For me, entering and exploring this unfamiliar cinematic world was an adventure, and it has remained an adventure to this day, as the terrain covered by my cinematic travels has developed from the local to the national to the international. Fundamentally, the Critical Cinema project is the story of one viewer's expanding consciousness of the full spectrum of cinematic inventiveness. That the project has produced a series of volumes—and threatens to produce at least one more—is a tribute to the sensual, intellectual, and spiritual complexity of critical cinema history and geography.

A Critical Cinema 3 begins with an interview with Amos Vogel about Cinema 16, a prologue to the diverse critical filmmaking accomplishments of the past fifty years represented by the twenty-five interviews that follow. The filmmaker interviews are arranged so as to suggest something of the historical impact of each filmmaker's contribution *and* to reflect something of my own personal history in coming to grips with these contributions. For example, the Belson interview occurs early in the volume not only because Belson began making films in the late 1940s, but because his films came to my attention (in the late 1960s) before any of the other films discussed in the interviews; and the Ken Jacobs interview is presented near the end of the volume (despite the fact that Jacobs and I discuss his work of the 1950s in detail) because my experiences with his recent Nervous System works have been more important to me than my earlier experiences with his earlier work.

Within the rough, overall historical arrangement of the interviews, I have placed each interview in an implicitly dialectic juxtaposition with the interviews that surround it. For example, the opening triad of interviews includes Amos Vogel, a European immigrant New Yorker whose hallmark as a programmer was his openness to every kind of interesting film available in 16mm; Jordan Belson, a Californian who devoted his career to the development and refinement of a very particular form of abstract imagery; and William Greaves, a native New Yorker, well known as a chronicler of African-American history, whose one foray into experimental cinema, *Symbiopsychotaxiplasm: Take One*, seems to some of those who know his other work almost inexplicable. Implicit within these dialectically conceived juxtapositions, however, are a set of relationships: Vogel was the first to publicly present Belson's work; and as disparate as their work is, Greaves and Belson share a fascination with Eastern spiritual teachings, which have played a formative role in their filmmaking. And while the three men have shared a commitment to providing alternatives to Hollywood, all three have, at one time or another, been involved in commercial filmmaking. Vogel hosted Alfred Hitchcock and Stanley Kramer at Cinema 16; Belson did special effects for Philip Kaufman's *The Right Stuff* (1983); and Greaves was executive producer of *Bustin' Loose* (1981, directed by Oz Scott, and starring Richard Pryor and Cicely Tyson). All in all, the organization of the interviews is meant to emphasize both the geographic, historical, philosophical, and formal diversity of critical cinema *and* the many connections and continuities within this diverse cinematic tradition.

My "adventure" in exploring critical cinema in these Critical Cinema volumes has become something of a quest. Ignored by mainstream viewers and by the overwhelming majority of film reviewers, critics, and scholars, and endangered as a history and as a set of current practices by each new economic setback, the remarkable world of critical cinema remains as marginalized as it has ever been; this remains true despite its incomparable value for teachers of film and cultural studies and despite the pleasure and enlightenment it offers those viewers lucky enough to find their way to it. If the interviews that follow can attract an expanded viewership toward a body of work that exists only because of a remarkable combination of cinematic ingenuity, economic self-sacrifice, and psychological, political, and spiritual commitment, this author-interviewer and devotee will feel himself well rewarded.

Two textual notes. Titles of films are given in italics in their original language the first time they're mentioned, followed by the English translation (in quotation marks). The English title (in italics) is used consistently after that—except in the Rose Lowder interview and a few instances when a title does not lend itself to English translation (Patrick Bokanowski's *Déjeuner du Matin*, for example): in those instances, the original-language title is used. The year when a film was finished is included after the first mention of the film in each chapter, whether this is in the interview or in my introduction to it.

Amos Vogel

Amos Vogel is the only non-filmmaker I have included in the Critical Cinema project. My decision to use our conversation as the lead-off interview in this volume is an implicit recognition of his major contributions to the history of alternative cinema in the United States, most especially his establishment and development of New York's Cinema 16. Cinema 16 was the longest-lived and most successful film society in American history (at its height, it boasted seven thousand members and inspired a nationwide network of smaller film societies) and was the first organization to specialize in the distribution of avant-garde film. But my decision to begin with Vogel is also a tribute to his unusually creative approach to programming.

During each year of Cinema 16's operation, Vogel would preview hundreds of films—avant-garde films, documentaries of all kinds, animations, foreign or independent features not in distribution in the United States—and, with the assistance of Marcia Vogel and Jack Goelman, he would choose the films he was most interested in presenting to the Film Society membership. Having chosen the films, Vogel would then "edit" them into a series of feature-length programs characterized by a dialectic sensibility: that is, within any given program, each film was almost sure to be followed by a film so different that it could scarcely fail to surprise viewers into a consideration not only of the film itself, but of its juxtaposition with the preceding and succeeding films. Further, since this kind of surprise was recreated by each new film, and each new program, making sense of what Eisenstein might have called the "collisions" between films and programs (Vogel was an admirer of Eisenstein) could be counted on to catalyze at least some portion of the audience into rethinking their narrow sense of film history and of cinema's potential.

Vogel's commitment to an unusual breadth of film forms and to dialectic programming was evident even in Cinema 16's earliest presentations. The first program included five films: *Lamentation* (1943), a dance film with Martha Graham (produced by the Harmon Foundation); *Monkey into Man* (1938), an entertaining documentary on primate behavior, directed by Stuart Legg and supervised by Julian Huxley; *The Potted Psalm* (1946), an avant-garde "psychodrama" by James Broughton and Sidney Peterson; *Boundarylines* (1945), Philip Stapp's polemical cartoon about boundaries between people; and Douglas Crockwell's animated abstract painting-on-glass, *Glens Falls Sequence* (1946). The second program included nine films: the National Film Board of Canada's *The Feeling of Rejection* (1947), which traced the case history of a young woman who learned during childhood not to risk disapproval by taking action and her subsequent crippling fear of failure; James and John Whitney's *Five Abstract Film Exercises* (1943–44), abstract animated "visual music"; *And So They Live* (1940), a documentary portrait of an Appalachian family by John Ferno; and Norman McLaren's *Hen Hop* (1942) and *Five for Four* (1942), animations incorporating imagery drawn directly onto the 35mm filmstrip in conjunction with music, and originally used to publicize Canadian wartime savings programs.

The films in each of these programs not only represent different film histories—documentary, animation, avant-garde—but different traditions within each history (scientific documentary, sociopolitical documentary, documentation of a performance; cartoon animation, abstract animation, direct animation) and quite different formal approaches (the documentaries are in black and white, the animations in color; the documentaries use conventional narration and music, the animations, both prerecorded music and synthetically generated sound). And yet, as varied as these two programs are, Vogel's selections also reveal certain fundamental attitudes: all the films in both programs can be seen as supplying evidence about what might be called individual personal expression. From the very beginning, Vogel was determined to demonstrate that there is an alternative to industry-made cinema that is more in touch with the practical and spiritual lives of individuals, whether these lives are documented by committed filmmakers or expressed in abstract or psychodramatic imagery. For Vogel, filmgoing was more than a process of experiencing, over and over, the particular codes of commercial genre film, or worshipping the physical beauty or the dramatic ability of the stars; it was a means of getting in touch with the immense and fascinating variety in the way people live and with the myriad ways in which individuals express their inner struggles. There is also an economic dimension to Vogel's selections. It is most obvious in *And So They Live*, in Ferno's respect for the dignity of the impoverished Appalachian people he documents, but it is also implicit in the relatively inexpensive level of production used in making all the films. One aspect of 16mm that particularly interested Vogel—it helps to account for the focus on 16mm reflected in Cinema

The Cinema 16 audience at the Central Needle Trades Auditorium.

16's name—was its potential for democratizing the cinematic representation of individuals and social life, and for expressing the problematic realities of class. Of course, 16mm cameras and film weren't cheap, but from Vogel's point of view, the smaller gauge was at least a step in the right direction.

By the time Cinema 16's final programs were presented (in May 1963), the diversity of Vogel's programming was under pressure from a variety of sources. Television was beginning to broadcast some forms of documentary; theaters specializing in foreign-language features were proliferating (Cinema 16 had been among the first, and in many instances *was* the first, to import films by Luis Buñuel, Nagisa Oshima, Roman Polanski, Robert Bresson, Yasujiro Ozu, Agnes Varda, and many others who were to become the darlings of the art-house circuit); and Jonas Mekas and the New American Cinema group were offering a challenge to Vogel's programming and distribution policies vis-à-vis avant-garde film.

In the years following the demise of Cinema 16, Vogel remained active as an organizer (with Richard Roud he founded the New York Film Festival), as a programmer (at the University of Pennsylvania, where he taught film history and theory until 1990), and as a writer. His *Film As a Subversive Art* (New York: Random House, 1974) is a remarkable international survey of films that can be understood as morally, politically, and formally subversive; it provides commentary on many of the films shown at Cinema 16, as well as on newer films that were products of the turbulent 1960s and early 1970s. If Vogel's dialectic approach to programming was rendered out-of-date, at least in the public sector—in part, ironically, as a result of an expanded film awareness he himself helped to instigate—echoes of his approach remain evident in many contemporary alternative screening spaces. And Vogel's remarkable courage and energy, his interest in exposing viewers to the full range of film history remains a model for what *should be* occurring across the country, at least in those academic institutions committed to film studies.

For a more detailed discussion of Cinema 16 and an extensive selection of documents related to the film society, see my *Cinema 16: Documents toward a History of the Film Society*, a special two-part issue of *Wide Angle* 19, nos. 1 and 2 (January–April 1997).

I interviewed Vogel in February and March 1983. An addendum was recorded in September of 1995.

MacDonald: Tell me about your background, especially as it relates to film. Were you involved with film before you got to New York?

Vogel: I lived in Vienna from the beginning of my life (in 1921) until age seventeen. At age seven or so, I got a laterna magica, complete with color slides—just like Ingmar Bergman. I was entranced. Later (I must have been ten or eleven) my father bought me a home movie projector, 9.5mm. It came from France. It was hand-cranked, not motorized. With that projector came not only the ability to make and show home movies (my father filmed family trips and so on) but also the possibility of buying films available in 9.5mm: Krazy Kat and Mickey Mouse, Charlie Chase, Chaplin. I enjoyed running the comedies backward as well—the magic of transforming, subverting reality.

It seems to me that at a very young age I was already an avid moviegoer. I must have been, because I remember many films that I must have seen in Vienna, judging from the way the dates work out. I went to see a lot of American films as a kid, the typical Hollywood exports. I was also able to see not only Austrian films, but German films. We're talking about the period prior to 1938, so that included films made during the Nazi period, not just the German films of the late twenties or early thirties.

Furthermore, there was a film society in Vienna. It's hard for me to believe, but I must have joined at around the age of twelve or thirteen. The programs were held in a beautiful theater at the Urania, a miniature Lincoln Center in Vienna. There must have been five hundred to a thousand members per performance. And I remember all the films I saw there, and I saw quite a few: early German cinema, Russian cinema (well, in 1934, it became illegal to show Russian films, but I did see Russian films prior to that, so that must have been even prior to age thirteen). One film I remember specifically and very strongly is *Night Mail* [1936], the collaboration of Harry Watt, Basil Wright and, on the sound, W. H. Auden, Cavalcanti, and Benjamin Britten. The whole notion of documentary became important to me because of that film. And simultaneously I realized that this was really a poetic film, and I was amazed that such a boring subject—the workings of the British mail system—could be made interesting. Wright's *Song of Ceylon* [1934] was also tremendously important to me.

MacDonald: Did the film society show a variety of kinds of film?

Vogel: They showed mostly feature-length films, but they would accompany the feature with one or two offbeat shorts not available in regular theaters. I don't remember any "social" aspects to that film society, and I have no recollection of who organized and ran it. I was a kid, and I went on my own. I guess I was only interested in the films. I enjoyed going to the movies almost as much as reading books. I read extensively: American, British, and French literature in translation—Dreiser, Dos Passos, Sinclair, Twain, Whitman, Wells, Walpole, Sinclair Lewis, Gide, Zola—and German literature, in the original.

MacDonald: When did you leave Vienna?

Vogel: In the fall of 1938, six months after Hitler took over Austria. I'll never forget what I experienced during those six months. I was very lucky to be able to leave. If I had waited, undoubtedly I would be dead by now. It was very traumatic and has stayed with me all my life.

MacDonald: Did you have any money when you got here?

Vogel: No. Whatever money we did have in Vienna (my father was a lawyer and my mother a teacher; they couldn't get those jobs here) was taken by the Nazis. We even had to leave Europe on a German ship so the Nazis would get the money for the tickets.

Anyway, an uncle of mine had settled in America during the First World War and had become quite rich. This uncle sent a statement—it was called an affidavit—to the effect that he would support us for a period of time. And with that it was possible to get a visa to the United States.

MacDonald: The whole family came?

Vogel: My father, my mother, and I came. My father's sisters and my mother's mother and brothers could not come. Most of them were subsequently killed.

It was also very educational, that experience. Because America did not say, "We will accept anybody who is in trouble." They did just the opposite. America probably let in less than 3 percent of the people who wanted to come. There were quotas based on country of origin. My father was born in Poland, so we were part of the Polish quota. I don't know what the actual figures were. With the affidavit from my uncle in America, my father went to the American Consulate in Vienna and got a number. And they gave him a visa, and told him we'd have to wait six months. If he had come one day later, he would have been told that he would have to wait approximately ninety years. In that *one day*, the Polish quota for the next ninety years was exhausted. That's how small the Polish quota was.

MacDonald: Did you come directly to New York?

Vogel: I had to go to Cuba to wait the six months before we could get in here. Another strange experience. Beautiful country, beautiful people. I love Cubans. But under Batista, the Cuban government was totally corrupt. I spent my time there learning English. I saw many American films during that six-month period.

MacDonald: You finally got to this country in 1939. And you started Cinema 16 in 1947. What did you do in the intervening years?

Vogel: I was not working in film at all. During my last three years in Vienna, I had become involved with a Socialist-Zionist youth group, boys and girls who wanted to go to a kibbutz in Israel—though it wasn't Israel then. We wanted to build a communal settlement where nobody would own land or private property, and all the income would be shared, a real participatory democracy. Part of that group's ideology called for a bi-national state, an Arab-Jewish state. It was *not* to be a Jewish state. I was very happy about that.

At that time, the British decided who could go into Palestine and who could not. In Austria, there had been a program, limited to young people between the ages of fifteen and seventeen. At a certain point, my entire group, including my girlfriend, got permission to go. And many of them did go; those who didn't were subsequently killed. As it turned out, I couldn't go because I was three months too old—a severe blow. When I was in Cuba, and also when I got here, I still had the definite intention to go to Palestine and rejoin that group. I tried everything; I even tried to get myself adopted by someone there. Impossible. The British wouldn't allow it. During this period, in order to prepare myself for that life, I was able to get a scholarship at an agricultural school in Georgia, one of the National Youth Administration colleges that had been started under Roosevelt to bring college level education to the sons and daughters of farmers, primarily in the Southern states, though some of the people who came from Europe were also let in. So I found myself at Haversham College in Georgia, for two years. A very strange introduction to America. I had left a country in which the park benches said, "Jews and dogs should not sit here." Here I saw drinking fountains that said, "For whites only." Later, I moved to the University of Georgia and took agriculture plus general courses in civics, history, whatever. And after that, I worked for two years on farms in New Jersey.

During this period, I became more and more disturbed about the way in which the Arab question was being handled by the Zionists. I did a lot of reading and talking to people. Finally, I came to the conclusion that not only was I *not* a Zionist and didn't want to go to Israel, but I realized I was becoming an anti-Zionist because of the Arab question. I'd prepared myself for a life I now knew I wasn't going to pursue. And I was not interested in being an agricultural laborer in the United States. The point had been a communal kind of living, not simply working on a farm. So I got a degree in economics and political science at the New School for Social Research in New York.

MacDonald: This was 1943–44?

Vogel: Right. We didn't have any money, but I got a scholarship and took all kinds of odd jobs.

During the war I worked in defense factories as an assistant tool-and-die maker. The interest in politics I had developed in Vienna continued to be very strong. I wanted to find some left-wing movement with which I could work, but I couldn't really find one. I was drawn more towards Trotskyites than Stalinists. In Vienna, I had known about the huge concentration camps in the Soviet Union, about the purges, and the trials at which leaders of the Revolution were falsely accused of being Nazi spies. It's amazing to me now that *I* knew of all these things by age fifteen, and at the very time these things were occurring, while many American "radicals" only discovered them from Khrushchev's speech in the sixties!

MacDonald: When did you meet Marcia?

Vogel: In 1942, through a cousin of hers who had come from Europe on the same boat I was on. Marcia and I didn't particularly like each other. A year later, however, I met her again, and we immediately got involved—one of the best things that has happened to me in my life. Three years later we got married. The morning after our wedding night, I walked down to the hotel newsstand and saw this great big headline: NEW TYPE OF BOMB DROPPED OVER HIROSHIMA. So it's easy to remember the date of our wedding! Bad jokes have been made about that, believe me.

At the time we got married, Marcia was doing market research. She'd graduated from Queens College with a degree in sociology.

MacDonald: At what point did you two get involved with film?

Vogel: After I got my degree. I was interested in learning through film. At a certain point after I came to New York, I had become aware that here were a lot of films around, in 16mm, which were not being shown publicly, and which were not available anywhere for me to see. I'm *not* talking solely or primarily about avant-garde films. There were always two main components to Cinema 16: avant-garde films and what might be called nonfiction films (documentaries, scientific studies, psychological studies, informational and educational films). I'd read about these films in a local newspaper, or somebody (not a film person, but a member of a union or a teacher) would mention a film to me. Once in a while I'd go to see such films at local universities. I began to find out who the distribution companies of the films were; I'd go to them and ask, "How can I see your films?" I learned it would be very expensive to rent them and that I'd have to get my own projector. I didn't have the money to do this.

It occurred to me that if I was interested in such films and couldn't see them, there must be other people in a city the size of New York who would be equally interested. Maybe I should get some of these films together and attempt to show them publicly. Maybe enough people would come to see them to pay for the film rental, and the whole thing would take care of itself.

MacDonald: How did you first learn about avant-garde film?

Vogel: I was always very interested in modern art and the avant-garde, particularly in the visual arts. I had been tremendously affected by Meyer Shapiro's magical lectures on modern art. I began to hear things about such films and to look out for them. There was a film magazine (it lasted for only three issues) called *Cinema*, run by Eli Wilenski. (I think that's what his name was in those days; years later, under the name of Eli Wilentz, he became the owner of what was the best and by far the most important bookstore in New York City: the Eighth Street Bookstore.) That magazine mentioned Sidney Peterson and James Broughton as having made one or two films that sounded very interesting: surrealist films, poetic films. It may also have mentioned Kenneth Anger. And, of course, there was Maya Deren. She had begun to show films in New York and to write. I saw her films and was very impressed.

As a spare time activity Marcia and I, and a couple of our friends, decided to see if we could get a little money together and rent the same theater that Maya Deren had rented, the Provincetown Playhouse, and put on a program of films. Next step: I went back to film distributors and convinced them to let me look at films for free on their premises because I was going to try to show them publicly afterwards, which would help them. Many agreed.

I chose a first program and put ads in the papers. The Provincetown Playhouse had two hundred seats. We announced showings for six o'clock and eight o'clock one evening. It was a huge, smashing, immediate success. We had to repeat this first program for *sixteen* evenings! With two showings per evening! My naive but logical supposition was immediately proven correct. I have no doubt that if I had chosen other films, I would have done just as well, so long as they made for a well-rounded program. This idea worked, not because of my excellence as a programmer or anything like that, but because historical circumstances allowed Cinema 16 to fulfill a real social need.

Very quickly, we realized that planning to show films on a one-shot basis, on one evening, was not a very good idea. For the second program, we decided to expand and add weekend shows and really build the audience, so Marcia and I spent the thousand dollars we had received as wedding presents a couple years earlier on expanded advertising, including an ad in the *New York Times*. Well, that second program took place on the evening of the worst blizzard in New York history. Four people showed up at the theater: the projectionist, myself, Marcia, and some crazy person who came through the snow. We were faced with an immediate catastrophe because we had absolutely no other funds. Then my father, who knew about business, told us we could try to keep going on credit, hoping that income from the next shows would pay for what we spent and leave us with a little surplus. We were so naive that we had never even heard of doing business this way!

A second problem we ran into was even more serious, and more interesting. It started on the first evening. A somber representative of the New York State Censorship Office came to the theater and said, "You can't show this program, because your films have not been submitted to the censors, and have not been approved." I said, "I don't know anything about that. I know there's some kind of censorship for Hollywood films, but what's this got to do with me?" He said, "Every film that's shown publicly in New York has to be okayed by us. You have to have a censorship seal." He could see that I wasn't a conniving businessman, but some kind of naive young guy who really didn't know. And he said, "OK, you can show this program, but after this, you have to submit all your films to us."

I was very unhappy about this. When I began to submit films to the Censorship Office (with our second program), we ran into impossible problems. Example: part of the censorship law was that you had to submit a copy of the script. I wanted to show a French animated film for children which had a nonsense language soundtrack; I *had* no script. We had to hire a stenotypist at some fantastic sum, who came and took down "baba, booboo . . ." Can you believe this? We didn't have the money to do that kind of thing. Secondly, we had to rent the films from the distributors earlier to submit them to the censors, who sat on them for at least a week. (And the censors were doing me a favor by looking at the films so fast!) Thirdly, some films (Peterson's and Broughton's, for example) used nudity; sometimes there was some sexy business. Well, the censors applied the same standards to us that they applied to Hollywood films. There was a film by Maya Deren and Alexander Hammid, *The Private Life of a Cat* [1945], a beautiful documentary of their cats at home, including birth sequences, which made the censors reject the entire film as "obscene." Unbelievable!

We decided that we couldn't possibly continue this way. I'm a total enemy of censorship in all of its forms. Period. Without any reservations. To me this process was absolutely obnoxious—"obnoxious" isn't strong enough. By submitting the films to the censors, I was betraying something. We had some discussions with a civil liberties lawyer and decided that we were going to start a private membership club.

MacDonald: Did your troubles with New York State censorship end once you'd become a club?

Vogel: There's pre-censorship and post-censorship. We eliminated pre-censorship completely by becoming a film society. However, with post-censorship, the police can go into a place and say, "You *have shown* something obscene." Had I desired to show hard-core porno films at Cinema 16, I certainly would have had access to them, but we would have been closed by the police, even if we were a club. In any case, I had no desire to do that, not because I'm against porno—it just wasn't what I was interested in showing.

However, if you're a club, you're not subject to blizzards, because you collect the membership fees in advance for an entire year. If the member doesn't come, for whatever reason, you've still been paid. Of course, it also meant that we could not sell individual tickets, and later we had programs where we had to turn hundreds of people away. But you could join the night of the performance, if you paid for the entire year. The fees were very low, ten dollars a year for sixteen performances plus two free guest tickets.

I started showing films in 1947 and six months later we were an official membership film society, nonprofit and tax-exempt. The government checked us out to see that we were not putting a profit into our pockets. What we were allowed to do, of course, is pay salaries. The amount of money that came in simply paid the cost of the operation, plus very reasonable salaries. In the beginning we had nothing: Marcia and I worked for weeks or months for nothing or very little. But ultimately, when it got to be good, Marcia and I together made maybe fifteen thousand dollars a year.

Projectionists were another interesting problem. The union came after us immediately. They said, "This should be unionized," and I was in favor, I've always been in favor of unions. I said OK, despite the fact that they insisted on *two* high-priced union projectionists per show. But it was a unionized operation from the very first performance to the very last. I'm proud of this.

Marcia was in charge of memberships. We hired ushers, who got paid two dollars an hour, or whatever it was in those days. Very little. It was a minimal operation, always determined by the yearly budget.

MacDonald: How long were you in the Provincetown Playhouse?

Vogel: Very briefly. We grew too fast. Why have sixteen nights for two or four hundred each? It wasn't economical. Actually, the very first showing of the Cinema 16 Film Society took place at the Fifth Avenue Playhouse, also an art theater; the film was the premiere of Hans Richter's *Dreams That Money Can Buy* [1947]. After that we went to a place called the Central Needle Trades Auditorium, a huge space. And later, when we had five to seven thousand members, we had additional showings at other art theaters. A member would simply sign up for the Wednesday evening series at the Central Needle Trades Auditorium or for the Sunday morning series at a regular theater.

MacDonald: Did you have a sense of the sorts of people who came to the screenings?

Vogel: We did questionnaires, things like that. There were a lot of artists and intellectuals, and would-be intellectuals and artists. The gamut ranged from the movers and shakers on the cultural scene to school teachers and secretaries, people who wanted to widen their horizons. I'm continuously surprised by the well-known people who say to me, "Ah, Cinema 16, how wonderful it was!" It would be an interesting research project to go through the lists name by name and try to find out who these people are now. All the Beats came—Ginsberg and the rest. All the film people came: people who were teaching film and making films. And there were many liberal bourgeois people. It was the only place to see such films.

MacDonald: Could you apply for state or federal grants?

Vogel: There was a totally different situation in those days in respect to funding: there *was* none. No private foundations were interested in this sort of activity. And what really amazes me, in retrospect, is that this project ran for sixteen years without *any* outside support, dependent 100 percent on membership fees.

MacDonald: What was the process of putting the programs together?

Vogel: I looked at thousands of films to select the programs. I began to go through the catalogues of whatever distribution firms existed, and there were many. It wasn't as though I had to go into barren territory. I had more films than I could handle. But the avant-garde field had to be developed. Sidney Peterson would tell me he knew so and so who had made a little film, and I'd get in touch with this person. Or, having heard of Cinema 16, people would write to tell me about their films. Tens, hundreds of films began to drift in. Any film submitted to us was looked at. I had very good help with this—Jack Goelman, who worked with me. We had a rapport in questions of aesthetics, originality.

I made a folder for every film I saw, regardless of its length. While I was watching a film, I took notes, and the notes went into the folder. As of now, at age sixty-two, I have between twenty and thirty thousand folders.

An entire year's programs, sixteen different events, would be put together in advance. It might consist of two hundred or fifty films, depending on length.

MacDonald: Did you have particular things in mind when you were deciding on programs, or did you just program the films that knocked you out?

Vogel: The latter would be an honest way of putting it. I wanted films that would disturb you in some way, would add to your knowledge and make you change. The whole notion of change was very basic to Cinema 16. I've always been very involved with the idea of creating a world different from the one in which we are living. I'm very dissatisfied with *this* world. I have always considered myself to be a radical socialist, and I have always had the curious notion that even a film on cosmology or a psychological study or an avant-garde work can serve a positive function in improving the world, because it takes us away from where we are now and opens us up to new possibilities.

There was inevitably a strong subjective factor in all these decisions. Essentially you choose in terms of who you are, and who you are is, in turn, the end product of a very long prior development, including your environment, all the influences that have worked on you: your parents, your children, your school, the books you've read, even your genetic constitution. My experience with Hitler was important to me. All these things entered into the picture, obviously.

There were definitely films I did not feel were good enough to be shown. At the same time—this is an important point—there was never any attention paid to what might be called Box Office. I think Box Office is poison. Many times in my life I've had the possibility of starting a commercial theater, but I never wanted to do it because I *knew* that if I did, I would become the prisoner of what the box office requirements were. That was another wonderful thing about having a membership setup. I was able to present programs which I knew in advance would antagonize most of the audience. But that was OK; there were other programs they would like. People soon learned that when they went to Cinema 16, they had to expect to be displeased sometimes.

MacDonald: If you showed a program that offended people one week, was attendance down the next week?

Vogel: No. When people were offended by a program, there was usually a very small percentage who would be extremely upset. They would write us letters, or call us up and say, "How dare you show this piece of shit!" If they said, "Give us our money back," we were delighted to do so. We wanted to get rid of them. We weren't going to have them tell us what to show. I showed one of the worst (that is, most powerful) Nazi propaganda films ever made, a film that to this day cannot be shown publicly: Franz Hippler's *The Eternal Jew* [1940], which I imported from the Dutch Film Museum. The film was stopped at the border here. They wouldn't have let it in, except that Siegfried Kracauer, himself a Jewish refugee from Germany, wrote a letter to the customs people and told them I was going to have a very educational evening for which he was going to write program notes. It was allowed into the country for one showing only. There were many Jews who felt that I had done the worst possible thing by presenting that film: I'd shown a film which said Jews were as evil as rats. Those who objected could not understand why I, myself a Jewish refugee from Hitler, would want to show it.

In some instances I chose films with sex in them. In those days that alone was more than some people could abide. Kenneth Anger's *Fireworks* [1947]?! It was a scandal in those days to show a film with a gay theme. The censors didn't allow it. And even though we had a private club, there were people who felt gay issues should not be talked about. I felt, why not? And I would show the films more than once. I'm a strong believer in showing essentially anything that has human and aesthetic validity and relevance. Maybe it's obnoxious to some, but there's a fighting element in me which rebels against authority and constraint.

From Georges Franju's *Le Sang des Bêtes* ("The Blood of the Beasts," 1949), which Cinema 16 subtitled, presented, and distributed in the United States.

That has been true throughout my life, and it came out in my choice of films. People would come to me and say, "You know those films you showed yesterday with the red, blue, and green dots? They gave me a headache." I'd ask, "What did you take?" They'd say, "You *really* gave me a headache!" So I'd say, "If you get too many headaches, maybe you shouldn't come."

MacDonald: Did filmmakers appear with the films?

Vogel: Rarely. We did not have that tradition in those days. At every showing we did have four, single-spaced pages of program notes which we produced ourselves. Even now there are not many places with program notes. I believe in program notes. I think they have to be done very carefully; you have to be very objective. You shouldn't try to impose something on the audience by having some critic say, "This film is marvelous!" But on the other hand, a lot of interesting information can appear in program notes. But, no, we did not have filmmakers come in person. It wasn't that they came to me and I refused to let them appear; the filmmakers weren't interesting in coming. Filmmakers did attend our Creative Film Foundation events. But even then they were only available for questions. In retrospect, I think it would have been better had we had such programs. We did have well-known film critics and scholars from time to time, people like Parker Tyler.

MacDonald: It must have been very exciting to explore all those films and learn what people would like and how they would respond. What moments stand out?

Vogel: It *was* exciting. And it was a continuing process of feedback. Sometimes, of course, what stands out are not the high spots, but the difficulties. We had huge difficulties with the Hans Richter film, because the distributor was a very crass businessman; he gave us such a hard time. I learned so much about the film business from him. One day we had the film, the next day we didn't. Then we had sent out mailings that we were going to show the film and there was a signed agreement; then they'd tell us we don't have an agreement, we don't like this arrangement. It was a very tough experience for us, but we came out OK in the end and showed the film. Richter and I became good friends. He was a great guy.

The avant-garde was very exciting. When I saw Peterson's films and Broughton's at the very beginning of Cinema 16, I can't convey to you how I felt. They were just marvelous for me. *Why* is an interesting question, because as it turned out, my enthusiasm was shared by only a small portion of the audience. The majority were either against the avant-garde or totally indifferent to it.

MacDonald: Do you have a sense of the reasons?

Vogel: A very simplistic way of putting it would be to say that the most difficult thing for people to take in or absorb or appreciate is a new way of seeing. There's something very comforting about dealing only with the conventional, and, of course, something extremely conservative, if not reactionary. Hollywood and television are constantly giving us things that we've already seen, both in terms of content and in terms of style. The most interesting and important avant-garde films are precisely those films that have never been done before—in content, in style, in form—and therefore are extremely difficult for most people to accept. I prefer to be upset, and one of the main criteria I use when I look at films and write my notes is unpredictability. If I can say that I don't know where a film is going or how it's going to get there, that's one of the greatest assets. I had hoped that by showing these films at Cinema 16, and by making audiences more and more familiar with them, I would develop more tolerance in the audience. I'm sure I succeeded, but only within certain limits. Always there was the complaint, especially with abstract films, "I got a headache from looking at it." They said it then; they say it now. It's obviously an ideological headache.

The main reason why I personally liked these films has to do with what I'd call "visual sensibility." I believe each person involved with culture has either a verbal sensibility, or a visual one. I was so entranced with visual modern art—paintings, photography, anything visual—that it carried over, of course, into film. When I see a Peterson film or an Andrew Noren film or an Anger, I am transfixed; I get acute sensual/sensuous pleasure from it, a pleasure I want others to feel as well. That's why I showed those films.

We had at Cinema 16 two different audiences, at least two. We had an audience that preferred documentary and nonfiction, social and political films, re-

Panelists at the Cinema 16 forum, "Poetry and the Film," held in October of 1953: (from left to right) Dylan Thomas, Arthur Miller, Willard Maas, Parker Tyler, Amos Vogel, Maya Deren.

alistic films; and we had an audience that preferred avant-garde and experimental films. There were instances where the documentary group would say to me, "What the hell are you showing these avant-garde films for! Obviously they're frauds." "Fraud" was popular, like "It gives me a headache!" On the other hand, the avant-gardists were saying, "What the hell are you showing these documentary films for? They're hackneyed. 'Realism' doesn't exist." I was in the middle. For me the films all had a common denominator; they created a disturbance in the status quo.

MacDonald: I'm often surprised by the way in which people who are savvy about contemporary art, poetry, and music are still not able to accept parallel developments in film. In this sense there seems to be a gap between film and the other arts.

Vogel: Well, I'll give you one reason. When you look at a very advanced kind of modernist painting, you can decide whether you want to look for one minute or for half an hour, or just turn away. A few seconds is as much time as some people look at modern art, even when they're *interested*. Maybe I'm exaggerating: maybe it's half a minute or two minutes. With film you're a captive. The abstract or surrealist film that someone has made cannot be conveyed to you in an instant. If you've got a film that goes on for fifteen, thirty, fifty minutes . . . or an hour and a half, there's a kind of domination by the filmmaker over the audience.

Secondly, in other art forms—literature and painting, for example—not only has modernist work been known and accepted for a long time, but in fact modernism has been dominant; we call it *serious* literature or *serious* art. This is not true of film; in film you have the total domination of Hollywood, and Hollywood was not, is not, in the twentieth century.

But don't think for a moment that because the majority of members said in our polls that they didn't want to see avant-garde films, that I showed fewer of them. I used the polls just to get a feeling of where people were.

MacDonald: The time element is important; the audience is captive. But still it seems strange to me. I've routinely used *The Sound and the Fury* in my American literature classes, and students struggle with it, but there's never any feeling that I'm doing something terrible by assigning it. Most students admire the book. But if I show *Serene Velocity* [1970]—and it's a class period, so it's clear that the film can't possibly be longer than thirty minutes or so—they usually react as though I've purposely tortured them. Of course, *The Sound and the Fury* includes a narrative; reading it is largely involved with finding the conventional narrative beneath the complex form and language . . .

Vogel: And that gets you involved. But you can't do that with so many avant-garde films.

Now, I want to make another point. I have come to the conclusion that we are not uniformly open to new trends in all media. Let me be quite personal about this: I love avant-garde film, but I have definite difficulties with very advanced modern music. Why? There are differences between human beings and inconsistencies within us, and that's good too. I think most human beings do not represent a particular viewpoint across all media. There may be such people; if so, they are closer to a true avant-garde. But there aren't many of them. I think some of the resistance to avant-garde films is—I hate to use the word—genetic. I'm absolutely convinced that if you gave me one hundred undergraduates for two years, two courses per year, I could develop in half of them a real appreciation for what's being done in those films. But only in half.

MacDonald: A related question. I've found in programming my own series that when I program a film, I almost always get a fairly sizable audience, but when I program a film *and filmmaker*, I get a smaller group. In my head, having the filmmaker present is an advantage, but not to most people.

Vogel: Maybe they've already had experiences with some of the filmmakers as speakers! They aren't always so wonderful. For you and me they add something (not always!), but for a more general audience, I'm not too sure.

There's only one way in which a more general audience loves the filmmaker, and that is the way we used to do it, and the way it's still being done at the New York Film Festival. If at the end of a film which has been well-received, the filmmaker is there to receive the applause, a wonderful rapport takes place between the audience and the filmmaker. But if that continues into a discussion with the filmmaker, only a certain proportion of the audience will stay, and the questions that come from the audience, I'm sorry to say, are not terribly good. As a result, the filmmaker doesn't open up sufficiently, either. But there have been exceptions, very fruitful interchanges, even with general audiences.

MacDonald: I don't remember seeing any other film programmer present scientific films, though it seems like an obvious idea. Even now, I'm not sure I'd know how to locate quality scientific films.

Vogel: To me, it was the most natural thing in the world to show scientific films, but it took a lot of spadework to find my sources. There was an outfit called Psychological Cinema Register which had a very large collection of films primarily by medical people, psychologists, scientists. It was unusual for them to get a request from somebody on the outside. They didn't even know how to deal with it; suddenly they had to establish a policy. There was often a problem with sex. Should Cinema 16 be allowed to show a bunch of rhesus monkeys fucking?

I always went by what interested me and what involved me, feeling that there had to be others who'd be interested. I even programmed films that were only interesting for their content—films that weren't well-edited, well-photographed, but were absolutely marvelous in terms of what they showed. One such film—I'll never forget it—was called *Neurosis and Alcohol* [1943]. It was about rats that were made drunk, and then presented with extremely frustrating situations. It was hilarious, and extremely revealing and informative about the connection between neurosis and alcohol. On the other hand, we had a film called *Monkey into Man* by Stuart Legg, who came out of the British documentary movement, a scientific (and poetic!) film about evolution, beautifully photographed and edited.

Another good example involved the work of Roman Vishniak, a famous scientist and a famous photographer. The International Center for Photography here in New York had an exhibition of his photography, which ranges from the definitive images of Polish Jews to microcinematography—some of the most marvelous imagery I've ever seen. I spent wonderful afternoons with Vishniak, preparing for the screening. All he had was footage; he did not have finished films, and we had to add the soundtracks, which he spoke on tape. Presenting his work to the public is one of the best things I've ever done.

One quote that has had a tremendous influence on me, maybe the basic one, is, in English (I first heard it in German): "Nothing human is alien to me." Marx used it. It came from the Roman philosopher Seneca, I think. It has allowed me to be tolerant of everything "because it's human." In relation to Cinema 16 this meant there was no such thing as a film that, because of its genre, let's say, would not be of interest to me. I remember Andy Sarris saying that animation is not really film, and explaining why (and I've heard others say it, too). That's harebrained. I've seen some very great works of cinema art in the animated film. The same with scientific film. A few months ago I saw a film on TV, one of the *Nova* series I think, about spiders. I've never seen anything more fascinating, or more visual. How can you possibly ignore such work? I'm delighted that it's there, and I've always wanted to show it. And it's always worked very well, in terms of audiences.

MacDonald: Those sorts of films are on TV a lot now, but it's a shame not to see them on a big screen.

Vogel: That spider film would be wonderful in a first-run theater.

MacDonald: Did Cinema 16 do anything with modified forms of film, 3-D or film installation?

Vogel: Very little. We showed *The Door in the Wall* [1956] based on an H. G. Wells story—a film with variable-size screen images. Had there been a system that would have allowed me to show 3-D in 16mm, I would have definitely wanted to do it. I'm extremely interested. I bought a 3-D still camera recently and I go to the Museum of Holography regularly—what a great (and mysterious) place! Cinema 16 ended before performance art and happenings, which came in during the Sixties. Oh, I do remember an exception. When we premiered Willard Maas's and Ben Moore's *Narcissus* [1956] (we premiered all of Maas's films), he arrived on the evening of the premiere and said, "Where's the door to the projection room?" I said, "Over there, why?" He says, "I gotta do something." He had brought different colored gels with him which he put in front of the lens at certain points so that the film was tinted. Very amateurish, but beautifully done.

MacDonald: When Cinema 16 was developing, were you traveling in Europe to look for films? I know you're a regular at the Berlin Film Festival.

Vogel: Not at the beginning. Later, I traveled to film festivals, and I would go to Paris and London to meet filmmakers, producers, distributors. As time went by, I brought in more and more films from abroad. I remember Agnes Varda asking me if I wanted to distribute *L'Opera Mouffe* [1956], one of her shorts. In those days she hadn't made features yet. I dealt with Georges Franju in Paris, and got *Blood of the Beasts* [*Sang des Bêtes*, 1949]. I dealt with Argus Films, a fascinating commercial outfit that made hundreds of shorts and also features, many of great interest.

Oh, let me tell you a story. There were supposed to be some fabulous student films being made in Poland, at this famous film school. People told me about them, or maybe I read something somewhere. I sat down and wrote a letter to Jerzy Toeplitz, the director of the school, with whom I subsequently became good friends, asking if we could get those films here, and sure enough we got them. (I had to learn about "diplomatic pouch" and about the censorship involved when you import films.) And who made these films? Roman Polanski! *Two Men and a Wardrobe* [1957] and five or six other titles. Also, I was in correspondence with Makavejev when he was making student films in Yugoslavia, but I could never get them out. And I had all kinds of contacts with Japan. We premiered Oshima's *The Sun's Burial* [1960]. So Cinema 16 was an international enterprise.

In retrospect, I sometimes wonder what would have happened if we had had real press support. In those days the *New York Times* not only had no policy of reviewing independent films, they had a critic who was an active, hostile opponent of independent cinema: Bosley Crowther, a very powerful and ignorant man. I'd invite him to every show, but he wouldn't come. Even without much press support, we had seven thousand members. Imagine what could have happened if we'd had it!

MacDonald: Just at the time when Cinema 16 was winding down, between 1959 and 1963, there was a move by a number of people—Jonas Mekas, centrally—to form a filmmakers' distribution cooperative. Your relations with Mekas at this time weren't friendly.

Vogel: No.

MacDonald: When I talked with Jonas, he said that the first day he was in the United States, he came to a Cinema 16 screening. And he was a regular after that.

Vogel: He came to all the showings. He had no money, and we always let him in. We knew of his love for film.

MacDonald: How did the rift between you occur?

Vogel: Well, first of all, there was never anything on a personal level between me and Jonas. It wasn't a situation where two friends had a falling out. I think he will verify that.

When I think back on that period, there is a very definite start to the developments you're asking about, which were for me, to be quite frank, totally unexpected. I learned that a group of people, filmmakers and other people (Dan Talbot [Talbot founded and runs New Yorker Films, a leading distributor of feature films from a variety of nations] was among them), had met in New York. I can't tell you whether they met once or several times. I assume, several times.

MacDonald: You were not invited?

Vogel: Absolutely not. This group then published the first manifesto of the New American Cinema. I got the manifesto in the mail, and I was astonished. Why? Two reasons. First, here was a new organization in New York, which had a point of view I was totally in agreement with: they were radical, anti-Hollywood, anticommercial, committed to independent, avant-garde forms of cinema. What else had I been doing all these years except showing that kind of work? In our original "Statement of Purposes" (which uses fancy language I now find a bit stilted), I make clear that Cinema 16 is against the "empty tinsel of Hollywood," and for free cinema, and so on. What astonished me was that I was *not* invited. I couldn't understand it. The second thing that astonished me was the list of the people involved: they were all people I knew well.

I was so naive about what was happening that I went so far as to investigate why I hadn't been invited. And it became clear very quickly, that the reason I had not been invited was because I would have been precisely the *last* person to be invited. There was an attempt being made to start a new center for independent film in New York, and they didn't want the person who was the head of the other center to be in that organization. It was as simple as that. Obviously, I realize that if a new center is started, there must be a dissatisfaction with the existing center. These activities were based on dissatisfaction, even though the manifesto didn't address that question.

One thing certainly had to do with the fact that Cinema 16 did not have programs devoted to the work of one filmmaker. And I didn't have regular programs devoted entirely to avant-garde film, though there were such programs

American avant-garde filmmakers in Berlin for a 1960 event organized by Cinema 16
and Literarisches Colloquium: (left to right, first row) Stan Brakhage, Carmen
D'Avino, Stan Vanderbeek, Ed Emshwiller; (second row) Bruce Conner, Shirley
Clarke, Walter Hoellerer (of Literarisches Colloquium), Amos Vogel.

from time to time. There must have been a feeling on the part of some people
that I should not have the power to decide which films should be shown or not
shown, and later, distributed or not distributed. That's a very logical feeling.
When you run an organization of exhibition/distribution, you are a gatekeeper:
you open doors for certain people and close them to others—because you don't
show their films.

Anyway, that was the beginning of the whole thing. We all have our interpretations of events, but I'll make the following rash statement: in my opinion,
Jonas was more interested in building a Jonas Empire than I was in building an
Amos Empire at Cinema 16. I was never a very sophisticated person about
power relationships. And I was not very involved with wanting to push myself
or my name. To me, Cinema 16 was a great idea, and it was wonderful that the
idea gave me enough of an income so that I could continue to pursue it. And to
see new films, to find new films—I loved that.

MacDonald: You don't remember any particular incidents previous to that
announcement, where people approached you to do something different than
you were doing, or . . .

Vogel: Honestly, no. I'm sorry that if people had such things in their minds,
they didn't come to me. It's possible that they were afraid to. Maybe filmmakers felt that if they came to me and discussed things that ought to be changed,
they might have less of a chance to have their films selected for Cinema 16.

From my point of view, that would have been a ridiculous fear (my allegiance has always been more to ideas or to artistic creations, than to people; I'd reject the films of people I knew and choose films by people I'd never heard of), but in retrospect I can see how someone might not feel confident about talking to me about such things.

MacDonald: Cinema 16 and the New American Cinema group both distributed films, some of them by the same filmmakers. Did you have meetings about distribution arrangements?

Vogel: That question didn't come up immediately as far as I remember. At first they were simply proclaiming an intention. So far as I remember, there were no negotiations. There was nothing. They absolutely didn't want to deal with me. They were out to do something on their own and the hell with me.

There was an incident much later, toward the end of Cinema 16. Ely Landau (he later produced *King: A Filmed Record, Montgomery to Memphis* [1969] and other films) was trying to build himself up in the film world in those days, and he had heard about my difficulties at Cinema 16. He called me in and in the course of saying that he wanted to help me make my organization work financially, he told me that he was also in touch with Jonas, because Jonas and his group were in financial difficulties as well. This must have been around 1962, 1963. He wanted to bring us together. Jonas and I got together, and there were some talks about Landau's idea, which failed, fortunately. I don't mean "fortunately" in relation to Jonas—not at all—but in relation to Landau. Joining with him would have been a disaster. I'm not being very diplomatic. The man had very good intentions and has done some very good things, but that idea would have been an unholy marriage of commercial interests with two nonprofit, noncommercial institutions. It wouldn't have worked. He would have taken both of us over.

MacDonald: The Film-makers' Cooperative, which grew out of Jonas's efforts, is at 175 Lexington Avenue. That was Cinema 16's address.

Vogel: After Cinema 16 failed in 1963, Jonas decided to establish the office of the Co-op on the former premises of Cinema 16. I thought it was not entirely in good taste. Jonas did a lot of things I can't forgive him for, including certain terrible things he wrote about me in *The Village Voice* at the time when we were both trying to help avant-garde cinema. One that comes to mind right off the bat was a column that began something like, "There are many people who are entirely opposed to avant-garde films because they think that they are the creations of madmen or psychotics. Such a view is represented in this country by Amos Vogel." [Vogel is referring to Mekas's comments in *The Village Voice*, April 18, 1968, subsequently included in *Movie Journal* (New York: Collier, 1972): " 'Experimental Film is synonymous with mental delirium and the escape from reality,' writes French movie critic Marcel Martin. . . . This kind of attitude is still very typically European. In the United States this mentality is represented by Amos Vogel (see his *Evergreen* article). . . ." That Mekas's attack is unfair seems clear from the *Evergreen* article cited: "The Angry Young

Filmmakers," published in November-December 1958.] That was terribly hurtful to me. There's no way one can possibly defend such a statement. I sent Jonas a note and asked him to retract it, or to explain what he had in mind. Or to give me a chance to talk about it in his column. Something! No answer. No retraction. No explanation. Nothing. Jonas was important at that time. Such statements meant that anybody who didn't know me would assume I was totally opposed to avant-garde cinema, and for ridiculous reasons.

I think that while we are doing things in life, we're not always aware of what these things really mean. Ten, twenty, thirty years later, the meaning sometimes becomes obvious. When I started, almost nobody cared about avant-garde films. There was no interest in showing them or distributing them. So I got something started. When I was having my programs, people from all over the country would write to us—a little film society, a labor union, a library—asking if they could show Sidney Peterson's *The Lead Shoes* [1949] or whatever. We would sit around and say, "What should we do? Why don't we send them the film and make up some kind of rental figure; we'll keep some and send the filmmaker some. How about that?" We became distributors because no one else wanted to do it. And we had contracts with these filmmakers that called for a fifty-fifty split of the income. An ACLU lawyer who worked with all kinds of progressive causes gave us the idea of a fifty-fifty split. In those days that was standard in any kind of film distribution arrangement. If somebody had said to me, "Split it ninety/ten, eighty/twenty," whatever, it would have been the same. I didn't know anything about it.

Then, along came the Co-op idea and a split more favorable for the filmmaker. An entirely possible idea. Of course! The intermediary, the middleman, should be cut out, right? I was a middleman. I didn't *make* the films; I only made them available. Although, remember, Cinema 16 was a nonprofit institution: it wasn't that I was putting money into my own pocket; it would be plowed back into the institution. So the Co-op comes along and says, "Let's eliminate even this nonprofit middleman. We'll do everything ourselves. And, *every* film that a filmmaker makes should be in our catalogue. And every filmmaker who wants to be in this catalogue *should be in* this catalogue." It was a very different idea. In some ways, it was a good idea—in retrospect, an obvious idea; but in the long run, it's raised as many questions as the kind of distribution that I ran, questions that to this day haven't been resolved. A co-op confronts the consumer with a huge catalogue, with hundreds of names, and hundreds, if not thousands, of films. How should the consumer choose? The fact of the matter is that avant-garde film distribution is in a very bad way. Between 1975 and 1989, the New York Co-op didn't even have an up-to-date catalogue and may still be in financial difficulties.

Don't get me wrong. Jonas has done very important things for the American avant-garde. How could anybody deny that? He called a movement into being, pushed it, worked his ass off to make it successful. And it's had impact all over the world. But I think of him as a mixed blessing for the American avant-garde.

Because while he was doing all these things, he was simultaneously doing things that, finally, prevented this movement from becoming as powerful or as influential as it should have been.

I would say that the historical catastrophe of the American avant-garde movement is precisely the fact that Jonas and I were not together, that Jonas excluded me at a time when I was doing a very big and very successful project in New York. Despite the fact that the American avant-garde cinema movement became known worldwide, it could not, after a while, sustain itself. And I think that could have been avoided. And a real movement could have been built.

Addendum

MacDonald: When you ran Cinema 16, the film society model was the most standard way of presenting alternative film. During the sixties there was an avant-garde or "underground" movement or at least the illusion of one. Then in the seventies came government support for venues for alternative cinema. I'm wondering how you see the alternative film scene at this point.

Vogel: Of course, to begin with, you always have to look at the overall social scene, because avant-garde film only exists embedded within the larger scene. When we were showing films at Cinema 16, our activities coincided, roughly, with the period of the Beats, which eventually developed into the movement of the sixties. Of course, we started in 1947, 1948, before the Beat era, but the very fact that films like *Pull My Daisy* [1959] were premiered at Cinema 16 shows that there was an atmosphere beyond Cinema 16, if not in the whole country, at least in the urban centers, an attitude, an atmosphere that began to be friendly towards the kinds of experimentation we were concerned with. It's also true that by virtue of showing such films at Cinema 16 we helped to prepare the groundwork for such a situation. It didn't fall from Heaven. But there was a larger social situation that allowed us to develop and be successful.

I don't find this to be true today, or even in recent years. We're in an extremely retrograde and retrogressive atmosphere at the moment—politically, culturally, in every respect—which has very serious consequences for cinema, and certainly for avant-garde cinema, since it's more oppositional than some of the other independent cinemas that are around.

MacDonald: There's an irony here, though, because Cinema 16 thrived at a moment when American culture was especially conservative: the late forties and the fifties. You used the word "experimental"; do you think avant-garde cinema profited from the culturewide ideal of experiment in the sciences and in technology?

Vogel: Well, I *don't* think that the general cultural situation in the forties and fifties was worse than it is now. That's not my memory. There are many factors operating here. At the moment, there's a very tiny audience for avant-garde film, even in an urban center like New York, and there are very few places to see avant-garde film. But you have to be careful not to generalize too much. When I started, there were *no* such showings in New York, but when I did start, almost immediately I found a lot of people who were anxious to see such material and who came to screenings.

It's always a direct interaction between some kind of social agent, and the surrounding social situation at the time. Frank Stauffacher [founder of the Art in Cinema series in San Francisco, and a resource for Vogel at Cinema 16] and I were such agents.

The point is that it would be a mistake to say, "Well, hardly anybody is interested in this kind of film nowadays," period. That's not the case. I can *see* various things that could be done.

MacDonald: Like what?

Vogel: It's very possible for me to sound old-fashioned, particularly as I get older, and the solutions I come up with aren't all that new. There were certain things done at the time of Cinema 16 that are simply not being done now. The first thing would be to try these things again and see what emerges. I'm certain that there could only be an improvement in the situation.

MacDonald: Can you be specific?

Vogel: In terms of programming, the Cinema 16 formula, in my opinion, could be used successfully now. When I say "successfully," I mean it would be more successful than the formulae used today, which include two options: number one, you put together a number of avant-garde films by various avant-garde filmmakers and make a program out of that; or number two, you show the work of one avant-garde filmmaker as the program. As you know, at Cinema 16 there was a *mix*, an eclectic mix of documentaries, scientific films, more conventional narrative shorts, animations, and avant-garde films. When I attend the few programs available now, where you see only avant-garde films, in one of those two formulae, I notice two things. First, there's hardly anybody there; I'm one of maybe ten or twenty people. Of course, there are exceptions, but I'm speaking generally. Second, after seeing five avant-garde films, I myself get fidgety.

Don't get me wrong. While the backbone of Cinema 16 were the more general screenings of various types of short film by various filmmakers, I believe there *also* ought to be separate series where you concentrate on the work of particular avant-garde filmmakers. That's something I didn't do at Cinema 16, though I remember thinking of it frequently. But always I came to the conclusion that given my own personal resources, I just couldn't bring it off in addition to what I was already doing. That was done by Jonas; he was right about that. *But* he did it exclusively. He *only* went in that direction, which in the end created very serious questions about whether such programming can hold or build an audience. In my experience in those days (because I attended his screenings at the Charles Theater and wherever), this method did not work. Instead of an audience being developed, I noticed a decrease in the number who attended, even then.

If we had said to the Cinema 16 audience, we're now going to present an entire program to you of one avant-garde filmmaker (whoever that might be: Oskar Fischinger, Michael Snow), and if I had done this again and again over the course of a year, I would have lost my membership. It was and is difficult for me to sit through an entire program of avant-garde film—and I *love* avant-garde film. Why would it be different for those who have not developed a strong interest in such work?

There's another issue, a very mundane-sounding issue. I'm firmly convinced that whatever kind of programming you do must have a very strong publicity component, a publicist and a promotional set up that reaches out into the general population. Programmers must insist on adequate publicity, even if it means making a pest of yourself at the newspapers. Believe me, I know how difficult this is. I'm not a utopian. But I'm also convinced that this is not being done adequately now.

At Cinema 16, we had very attractive brochures, with a lot of information, and these were very widely available. We printed very large runs of these brochures.

MacDonald: How large?

Vogel: Maybe a hundred thousand.

MacDonald: Really? A hundred thousand!

Vogel: Of course! It was *only* out of that that we got the attendance we did.

MacDonald: What did you do with these brochures?

Vogel: Mailed them; it was very expensive. The one great privilege we had was that we were able to work with first-rate, commercial artists. I was very interested in the visual design of these brochures, and I wrote the texts. If we'd sent out ten thousand brochures, the membership would have been five hundred. All these promotional efforts, unfortunately, are absolutely necessary.

MacDonald: One of the ironies of the seventies and eighties is that once federal and state grant support kicked in to support not just filmmaking but venues for exhibiting film, it took the pressure off many programmers to build audiences. The money would keep coming in, as long as we presented intelligent programming, even if nobody showed up to see the films. I hate making this argument, but, in fact, your success in building audience was at least partly a product of necessity. If you *didn't* build an audience, you couldn't show films.

Vogel: Well, that's true, but on the other hand, I am much in favor of government support for the arts, so long as there are no conditions attached to the money. At Cinema 16 our lives would have been much easier and we would have been even more successful (we might have continued to exist!) had we had outside support. In many other countries, as you know, there's much greater governmental support for the arts than there is here. Anyone who studies this comes to the conclusion that in America we're like paupers when it comes to the arts. And, of course, even the tiny amount now being given will probably be cut further. But as I said, governmental support must be *entirely* without strings or any kind of censorship. Otherwise I would reject it. The ide-

ological, political, aesthetic independence of the project is much more important to me than any support I could be getting from any outside source.

There are many exhibitors now, as then, who don't particularly care about
building an audience. They're in a safe little oasis and they're showing the films
to their friends and everybody likes each others' films. But it is also true that
we find ourselves in an extremely negative general cultural situation, which is
very hostile to the avant-garde and to new ideas, both in terms of style and in
terms of content. Some of this has to do with the suffocating consumerism
under which we are all suffering now. Television has been a horrendous
influence—not because of what television is inherently, but because at the present time, it's owned by business interests. This leads to a kind of national in-
fantilism, cultural idiocy, stupefaction, which has become an international process. American television is dominant across the world, and it has led to the
destruction of national cinemas in most of the existing production centers. So
we also have to look at the question of the avant-garde in that context.

Another point: a very essential point. What *is* the avant-garde? *Who* is the
avant-garde? I think there was an interesting conceptual error made by the New
American Cinema Group in the early sixties: namely, they excluded, either
were not interested in or were opposed to, the commercial avant-garde. They
even questioned whether these people *were* avant-garde. From the very beginning I had always included in my own definition of "avant-garde" people like
Antonioni, and Bresson, and the early Bertolucci. Oshima. Fassbinder. You
could go on and on with these names. It's a very serious error to exclude these
filmmakers. I'm against commercialism as much as the next person, but at the
same time, you have to realize that there are people trying to find new styles,
approaches, content, even in the commercial arena, and they must not be eliminated. Sometimes their achievements—in terms of experimentation—are as
important, if not more important, than those of the strictly noncommercial "experimental filmmakers" you and I love.

If I ran a Cinema 16 now, I would show the works of such people, along with
all the other kinds of "experiment." Certainly this would attract more of an audience.

MacDonald: I think I would go further than you. Most of us get into film,
not through avant-garde work but through popular film experiences. I go to the
movies all the time. I have never seen my interest in avant-garde film as destructive of my interest in the movies. Even at Cinema 16, you scheduled visits
by Hitchcock and King Vidor.

Vogel: Commercial directors can give *us* ideas sometimes. After all, they
have access to production budgets that allow them to try things no other filmmakers can.

Another controversial point—at least for some people, not for me. Video.
There's much greater technical proficiency with video now than there was at
the beginning, and the projection facilities have improved greatly. When the av-

Alfred Hitchcock and Amos Vogel at Cinema 16. In
1955 Hitchcock presented *The Man Who Knew Too
Much* (1955) before that film's release.

erage audience sees good video work well-projected on a large screen, they
can't tell the difference between video and 16mm film, or even 35mm. Certainly, there's interesting avant-garde work going on in video. As a programmer, am I supposed to say to people who only want to work in video, I will not
show your work because it's not "pure cinema"? I don't even know what "pure
cinema" means. If you want to build audiences, you have to include the best
videos, which can range from advanced avant-garde work to wonderful documentaries to music videos.

As we know, the MTV-style, one-image-after-another cutting, accompanied by a very strongly rhythmic soundtrack of rock 'n' roll or rap, or what have you, has entered the commercial cinema: Oliver Stone is an example, both in *JFK* [1992] and *Natural Born Killers* [1995], as are current movie previews—we used to call them "trailers." Much of it is mind-numbing. On the other hand, there are some people who are doing very interesting things in music videos. You can't throw the baby out with the bathwater and say all music videos are commercial and not to be taken seriously as art. What do you do with Zbigniew Rybczynski? And there are many others. *All* of these things should be part of the mix of the programming of this ideal exhibition showcase we're talking about here.

You once raised the question of whether the field would have been better off had Jonas and I been able to work together.

MacDonald: Yes. What do you think?

Vogel: Generally speaking, the split was not helpful to the cause of the American avant-garde. Jonas might disagree, but in my view, had it been possible for us to work together in those days, it would have been to the advantage of the field. But, of course, it's easier to see this looking back.

MacDonald: I think we need to learn from the other visual arts. For me, it's a question of where the dialectic takes place. At the major modern art museums, we can see the history of very diverse approaches that were established originally in opposition to each other; and the public, which is considerable for any major show, often goes to the museum to experience the interplay of these various approaches. In the history of avant-garde film, the situation is very different. On could argue that the New American Cinema model of exhibition and distribution was a healthy response to what Cinema 16 had done. The problem is that these two approaches were set up as mutually exclusive. The Collective for Living Cinema was established in opposition to Anthology Film Archives [the archive and exhibition space developed by Jonas Mekas and others], rather than as a collaboration *within* a growing, larger institutional framework. Each new institution has been built on the ashes of the previous institution—and so at the end, all we have is a lot of ashes.

Vogel: I understand what you mean, but I must tell you that no matter what the present situation is, despite the social factors that are operating against us and the narrowness of the existing showcases, I have a very optimistic attitude. In my opinion, the avant-garde will never die; it *cannot* die. There will always be people who want to go against whatever the current orthodoxies are, who want to strike out in new directions and find new ways of expression. When people ask me how I can be optimistic now about the possibilities for progressive politics or for subversive art, I have a saying: "I have more confidence in my enemies than I have in my friends." I'm convinced that my enemies will continue to do the most outrageously repressive things and therefore will again, inevitably, evoke a revolt on the part of those who are being kept out or kept down artificially and by force. The power of the artistic impulse that creates what we call the avant-garde *cannot* be overcome; it will always rise again.

William Greaves

In general, the filmmakers who produce critiques of conventional cinema and television have tended to define themselves in one of two ways: either as *artists*—painters, photographers, dancers who happen to have turned to cinema as a way of formally extending their other art activities, sometimes in the hope of attracting a more popular following to their work—or as *avant-garde film-makers*, that is, "specialists" in the production of critical forms of film art. But these definitions certainly do not account for all the major contributions to the ongoing discourse of critical cinema. A case in point is William Greaves, whose long, diverse, prolific career has included songwriting, dancing, acting on the Broadway stage and in commercial films (Greaves shared the Actors' Studio's first Dusa Award with Marlon Brando, Robert DeNiro, Sally Field, Jane Fonda, Dustin Hoffman, and Rod Steiger), teaching acting (at the Actors' Studio); producing, directing and co-hosting a television show (National Educational Television's Black Journal; co-host was Lou House); producing, writing, directing, and distributing dozens of documentary films on a wide range of topics (including many on African-American history), and, in a single instance, conceiving, writing, and directing one of the landmark "underground film" projects of the 1960s: the Symbiopsychotaxiplasm project, which was shot in 1968. Greaves envisioned a series of films as the result of the project, but only one film was completed, *Symbiopsychotaxiplasm: Take One*, and that not until 1971.

The Symbiopsychotaxiplasm project was Greaves's attempt to explore the filmmaking process and, in particular, to put the usual film production hierarchy into crisis. Greaves wrote a single scene—a candid argument between a man and a woman about their relationship: she complains about the abortions he's pressured her into and claims he's a homosexual; he denies and temporizes—and asked several pairs of actors to perform the scene in a variety of ways. The crew were given directions to film not only the scene, but themselves filming the scene, and even the activities in their surround in Central Park, where the shooting took place. Unbeknownst to his collaborators, Greaves was consciously acting the role of an incompetent film director, in an attempt to discover how far he could push the cast and crew before they rebelled against him. As the experiment turned out, little overt rebellion took place, but the finished film documents the public process of the shoot, as well as a secret meeting held by the crew (and filmed by them) to discuss the "disaster" of the production. *Symbiopsychotaxiplasm: Take One* (the other films were to be entitled *Symbiopsychotaxiplasm: Take Two, Symbiopsychotaxiplasm: Take Three*, etc.) deconstructs the process of creative collaboration in general, and the cinéma vérité approach to documentary in particular. Few films do as good a job at capturing the mood of the sixties as *Take One*.

In the following interview, I talk with Greaves about his overall career as a means of providing a context for our in-depth discussion of the Symbiopsychotaxiplasm project. The extent and productivity of Greaves's career could, of course, sustain a much more extensive interview, but for the purposes of this volume, it seems sensible to focus on the most extravagantly "critical" film of Greaves's career and on related experiments. Our discussion of *Symbiopsychotaxiplasm: Take One* originated at the 1991 Robert Flaherty Seminar (programmed by Coco Fusco and Steve Gallagher), where Greaves, the final filmmaker guest, was questioned following a screening of *Take One* (I have incorporated many of the participants' questions, along with the self-identifications they provided). In the years since the Flaherty Seminar, I have supplemented that original discussion with a series of one-on-one conversations with Greaves.

In 1994 Greaves revised *Take One*, adding four minutes of material not included in the version discussed here, in order to provide contemporary viewers with a clearer sense of the original project.

MacDonald: I'd be grateful for some general background about your career.

Greaves: I became interested in art very early in life. I used to paint as a kid. In fact, I won a scholarship as one of the five best child artists in New York State, a scholarship to the Little Red Schoolhouse in Greenwich Village. I used to go there every Saturday morning and paint. *My* art was very impressionistic and free-form, but I was still conservative at that time about modern art. I thought Picasso was a disaster. Today I can look at a Picasso and see it's about fracturing reality, like modern jazz.

I was always surprised that people thought I had talent. Do you know the jazz musician Bill Dixon? Well, he and I grew up together, and Bill was an artist, too. He could mimic artwork of any kind. He could reproduce a Rubens, a Turner, to the letter. And he would draw cartoons and other kinds of images he saw in magazines. I couldn't do that. All I could do was paint as I felt. Bill went on to become a fantastic musician in the tradition of Pharoah Sanders and Cecil Taylor. He broke entirely out of the conventional idea of reproducing reality in a traditional way. Bill Dixon's music is *wild*. He did a marvelous score for my film *Wealth of a Nation* [1964], which is about individual freedom of expression.

My career on stage began with dancing. I started out as an African and modern dancer with Pearl Primus. I danced with her at Carnegie Hall, Town Hall, and the Roxy Theater. And then I got into acting. And while I was doing theater, I was writing popular songs. Eartha Kitt, Arthur Prysok, and others recorded my songs [Kitt recorded "African Lullaby," as did Percy Faith; Prysok recorded "Baby, You Had Better Change Your Ways," as did Al Hibler and Donna Hightower]. Between the ages of seventeen and twenty-five, I wrote a lot of songs, maybe as many as a hundred.

When I first started acting, I was a "natural": the first play I did, *Garden of Time*, got rave reviews from the New York critics. They said I was so natural I would "out-cotton Joseph Cotton"! Hell, I was admiring the other actors in the production and here I walked off with all the reviews! I remember thinking, "I wasn't even acting—wait 'til they see me really act!" I was just responding to anybody who talked to me on the stage. Of course, when I actually started *acting*, I was horrible! I got some pans in my next production, and then I settled down and worked at appreciating simplicity in acting and eventually found myself getting hired. I was not only acting on the stage, but in film, in radio, and in early television.

Fritz Pollard, who had been a football star years before with Paul Robeson, had a place called Suntan Studios, and I was one of the actors he was always casting in his films. And also, the Army Signal Corps was doing films on Long Island. I acted in some of those, and I played the lead in a documentary called *We Hold These Truths*, though I never got a copy of it. I've always wondered what happened to that film. During those years I remained very active in theater. I was in *Lost in the Stars, Finian's Rainbow* and in an all-black production of *John Loves Mary* at the Music Box Theater (Tom Ewell, William Prince and Nina Foch were in the white production; I had the William Prince role and Ruby Dee, the Nina Foch role). And I did summer stock. I was probably the most active young black actor in New York between 1945 and 1952. I didn't have great roles for the most part, but I was all over the place. Looking back on it, I'm amazed.

MacDonald: There is so little information about the underground black cinema. You had your first film roles as part of the underground.

Greaves: I have the honor of being featured in the last two black-cast films

William Greaves (in middle, lying on bed) in Powell Lindsay and William B. Alexander's *Souls of Sin* (1949).

of that era, *Souls of Sin* [1949] and *Miracle in Harlem* [1948]. It's a curious experience to have been present at the tail end of that history. I feel like a relay racer, taking the baton from William Alexander and the others. I did two films with William, *The Fight Never Ends* [1948], with Joe Louis, and *Souls of Sin*. He was a role model in a way, not the only one, but certainly one. I saw him function in what was an entirely fascist state. It was a horrendous period.

MacDonald: Even on the most mundane level! In my junior high school, there were regulations about how far from the floor girls' skirts could be. And of course, no one was allowed to wear jeans.

Greaves: You know, Brando and I were at the Actors' Studio together, and he always used to wear jeans. At that time, everybody used to think, me included, that if we didn't wear suits and ties, God would strike us dead. Everyone knew that if you went on a casting call, you showed up with a shirt and tie and a suit—cleaned and pressed— and you were deferential to the producer or the director or the casting agent. You grinned from ear to ear and did all the things that Uncle Toms do, whether you were black or white. And here comes Brando, sauntering into the producer's office in his jeans, and if he didn't like the producer, he wouldn't shake his hand. He had this marvelous instinctual radar. It decoded phonies. He wanted to be himself, and he worked hard at it. He realized the polluting effect that American society had on consciousness, so he was very defensive of himself, which everyone decided was him being an asshole—not realizing that the man was in a very nurturing state with respect to his talent and his consciousness. All this was part of this fascism: the hemline, the demands of authority in the theater business . . . and yet it came to pass that Brando became the preeminent actor of that era.

MacDonald: What was it like working on the black-cast films?

Greaves: *The Fight Never Ends* was my first real film role. Joseph Lerner was the director and William Alexander the producer. We got along very well. Lerner was a good director, I thought, and a savvy guy. He was smart enough to just keep me relaxed. I found that in those days the film directors gave me my own head. They must have felt there was no sense trying to push me out of joint.

MacDonald: *Souls of Sin* seems barely directed. The acting isn't bad, but cinematically it doesn't work at all.

Greaves: Well, Powell Lindsay was a stage director; he didn't have a sense of the cinematic the way Jack Kemp did [Kemp directed *Miracle in Harlem*].

MacDonald: How do you understand the demise of the all-black cinema? There had been some production, even through the thirties, when nobody had two pennies to rub together. And then at the end of the forties, when you would think there might be a market, it disappeared.

Greaves: It collapsed for several reasons. American apartheid, as it had been practiced, was collapsing. The black film industry was a creature of that apartheid system. Black people did not want to be discriminated against in the white theaters downtown any longer. They hadn't been able to get into some of the theaters, and when they did get into them, they had had to sit in the balcony. Very dehumanizing. So they went to the black independent films. But change was happening. All the post–World War II rhetoric about Democracy and the New World and the United Nations and so on was having some impact on white America, which was relaxing some of its neurotic need to oppress black people. The horrors of Nazism, Hitler, the Holocaust—what a racist propensity on the part of a large population can lead to—was having an effect on the American psyche.

And don't forget, Jews were major players in Hollywood. The Jewish community had come out of this horrific experience and had, at that particular time, a much greater sensitivity to humanity, and a strong empathy with oppressed people. Recently, much of the Jewish community has become increasingly conservative. But at that time, I remember distinctly that most of the progressive white people I knew were Jewish. Sure, there were conservative Jews, but there was this progressive group in Hollywood, and they had an impact. I'm thinking of Dalton Trumbo and the people who were active in writing *Back to Bataan* [1945], *Gentleman's Agreement* [1947], and *Pinky* [1949], and in bringing Sidney Poitier to the fore. As a matter of fact, both Sidney and I were up for the role in *No Way Out* [1950]. I didn't get it because I had done *Lost Boundaries* [1949]: Zanuck didn't want to use anybody from one of Louis de Rochemont's films [de Rochemont produced *Lost Bound-*

aries; Alfred L. Werker directed it]; he was feuding with de Rochemont at the time.

Anyway, to get back to the original question, these new Hollywood films began to attract black audiences, and the segregation began to break down. Brown versus the Board of Education was decided in 1954. There was an attenuation, or a dilution—whatever you want to call it—of racism. Finally, black people could go to any theater they wanted, and they were looking at lots of films not made by blacks. There were a few black-cast films made, but the bulk of the films we were looking at were white films coming out of Hollywood.

MacDonald: At the point when you were in *Souls of Sin* and *Miracle in Harlem* were you conscious of a history of that kind of work? The last ten years or so have seen the reconstruction of the history of African-American underground filmmaking since Oscar Micheaux.

Greaves: No, I didn't know that history. I was a young actor gratifying my ego, seeing myself on the screen. I didn't think of the historical. I'd started studying acting when I was thirteen or fourteen, but it wasn't until I was eighteen or nineteen that I started becoming aware of the processes of history. And I didn't think about *film* history, just history in the larger sense. So I was part of it, but didn't even know about it!

I used to see Micheaux walking around with film under his arm. I lived right across the street from where he had his office: I lived at 203 West 135th Street and 7th Avenue in Harlem, and he had his office at 200 or 202 West 135th Street.

I was only about ten years old, but I do remember two bars—The Big Apple (as a matter of fact I wonder if that's where the term "the Big Apple" came from), on the corner of 135th Street and 7th Avenue; and I think the Bird Cage—where they showed films on a screen. We used to peek in and see it was a black film and say, "Let's go see that." We didn't know where it came from. We assumed it came from Hollywood.

Did I tell you that I studied film production at City College with Hans Richter?

MacDonald: No!

Greaves: And Lewis Jacobs was one of my teachers. Jack Knapp was there. I think Leo Seltzer was there, a whole crew of people. Richter was the head of the department. I also studied at a place called the New Institute for Film and Television, in Brooklyn. I'd go to one place during the day and the other at night. I was still a kid.

MacDonald: *Lost Boundaries* was one of a half a dozen Hollywood films of the late forties and early fifties that broke through in terms of dealing with race. Did the cast and crew feel as if they were involved in a breakthrough production?

Greaves: Oh, very much so! We felt we were involved in something very important. Hollywood was doing all these horrible Uncle Tom things—Mantan Moreland and the rest. This film was different: there were classy black people in it . . .

MacDonald: And a lot of variety, too: there are wealthy blacks, working-class blacks, black doctors, black cops . . .

You shot on location for *Lost Boundaries?*

Greaves: Yes, in Keene and Portsmouth, New Hampshire.

MacDonald: Both *Lost Boundaries* and *Intruder in the Dust* [1949, directed by Clarence Brown] were shot on location about events which took place locally. And in the case of *Lost Boundaries*, the events had actually occurred. What was the public surround of the shooting?

Greaves: Keene was very New England, WASPy, but I didn't find the people inhospitable at all. They were cool, as New England types often are, but I don't remember feeling any racial pressures. Of course, you have to understand that by then I was an actor and so full of myself that I didn't have time for racism. I didn't like it when it revealed itself and could be very angry, but I had no problems in Keene.

A few years ago, we had a big reunion in Keene. Larry Benequist, head of the film department at Keene State University, thought it would be a good idea to bring the cast and crew, and the townspeople who had been involved, together for a fortieth reunion. It was a *very* emotional coming together, a wonderful evening.

MacDonald: I assume you met the actual family who had passed for white?

Greaves: Oh yes.

MacDonald: There's a photograph of the Johnston family in Donald Bogle's *Blacks in American Film and Television* [(New York: Fireside, 1989), 139] . . .

Greaves: The actual family was not that white!

MacDonald: It seems remarkable now that they *could* pass.

Greaves: According to some of the townspeople, the family had deluded themselves into thinking they had passed. To some people they may have, but not to others. It was just that some of the white people didn't think it was important enough to make a fuss about. They just took the guy the way he was. But Johnston himself was apparently very uptight about the whole thing. Of course, the kids would think of themselves as white because up there in Keene they didn't have anything to do with black kids.

In going to de Rochemont's place during the *Lost Boundaries* period, I began to chat with Lou Applebaum, the composer for *Lost Boundaries* and the principal composer for the National Film Board of Canada. Lou was delighted that I was interested in the NFB. Louis de Rochemont had allowed me to be an apprentice on *Lost Boundaries*, to observe in his editing rooms, and so on; but even he didn't have any black people working there, and there were no black people with the necessary skills for the work anyway. Even Bill Alexander hired white cameramen and technicians. The unions were entirely racist. The McCarthy thing was happening here, and I was having some trouble getting work, not because I was a member of this or that, but because the whole climate of the industry had begun to change: they wanted to screen out *en masse* a whole group of people. America was locked up.

MacDonald: Had you actually tried to go into production here?

Greaves: Sure. But in 1951–52, in America, it was absolutely unthinkable. It was laughable. Sidney Poitier and Harry Belafonte and all those guys used to tell me, "You're crazy. They'll never give you an opportunity to direct!"

MacDonald: How did you know Canada would be different? How did you get to the National Film Board?

Greaves: I got to Canada partly as a result of reading *Grierson on Documentary* [London: William Collins, 1946; New York: Harcourt, Brace, 1947]. I thought it was a sensational book, exactly what I needed to give me guidance as to how I might approach this whole business of film. I wasn't interested in just making movies, I was interested in social issues and corrective social action. I was particularly interested in the denigration of black people on the screen, and I realized I could make films that would counter some of this adverse propaganda. I heard about the National Film Board in Grierson's book: he had set up the Film Board.

I applied for a grant from the John Hay Whiting Foundation to go to the NFB. I had recommendations from Elia Kazan, who was my teacher at the Actors' Studio; Rouben Mamoulian, who had directed me in *Lost in the Stars*, and Louis de Rochemont—and the bastards turned me down! They could give money to black dancers and singers, but apparently couldn't conceive of a black in control of films. I thought, "Fuck you!" and went to Canada on my own. For a while I lived on nothing but water and sugar cubes, but it was the smartest thing I ever did. Lou Appelbaum helped me get taken on as an apprentice, and after three months Guy Glover wrote a letter on my behalf, and I was taken on formally, with a salary.

I came back from Canada in 1960, because I thought the climate was changing, that the country was becoming more civilized. I had worked on seventy or eighty films and was a full-blown filmmaker. I figured I would get into the industry at some point, but then I had the wonderful opportunity to direct at the United Nations. And then, when I was ready to stay at the United Nations, I got the opportunity to make films for the US government. I did films for the USIA [US Information Agency] during the whole Kennedy period. George Stevens, Jr. was the head of the film department. Willard Van Dyke, James Blue, and a lot of other good filmmakers were making films for the USIA. Apparently George Stevens, Jr. had said to Shirley Clarke, "Gee, it would be great if a black filmmaker could do some of these films we're doing," and she mentioned me. They asked me to send them *Emergency Ward* [1958], which they flipped over, and that's when I started doing films for the USIA. I did four altogether, and out of that came the other film production work.

The path I took, and there may be others (I guess there's crime and prostitution!), was to develop a multiple front, to develop three or four projects I'm interested in, and keep myself available for other kinds of production work that might interest me. I've always tended to turn down commercials or industrials, but education interests me. I've done a lot of educational films for the US government. I've done films for the American Cancer Society, Exxon (a film having to do with minority businesses)—all with interesting subject matter. These sources have provided enough money to put my children through school and to have something resembling a decent life, although at times it's been very stressful, financially. When you commit yourself to independent filmmaking, no matter what level you're at, you've taken a vow of poverty. You keep putting your money into your films because you need to enhance the quality of what you're doing. That's why you *are* independent, because you want to do something that's very pristine, something that's precisely the way *you* want it to be. But it's quite a burden.

On the plus side, that kind of reinvestment does result in a qualitative improvement of your product, which then makes it much more viable and attractive. *From These Roots* [1974] is considered a high-quality film. It won twenty-two awards. Recently, when people contacted Bill Sloan about the history of American documentary for a show in Paris, he mentioned *From These Roots* to them. But *From These Roots* practically bankrupted us, in terms of the energy and the time we put into making what we felt would be an interesting cinematic experience.

MacDonald: Which leads to an obvious question: how were you able to finance *Symbiopsychotaxiplasm: Take One*, a feature-length film experiment?

Greaves: I'd been a member of the Actors' Studio since 1949, and knew the Stanislavsky system—the Method, Strasberg, that whole approach to theater and acting. I began teaching actors in Canada, and one of my actors there was extremely adroit at business ventures and became very successful. He wanted me to make a feature and said, "Anything you want to make, just tell me." I began to realize I could put a feature together using some of the actors at the school, and so I went ahead.

Jackie Tshaka (coordinator, National Black Programming Consortium): Where has *Symbiopsychotaxiplasm: Take One* been shown?

Greaves: We showed it at the Brooklyn Museum retrospective [April 1991]; we also showed it at the Federal Theater and in Paris at a retrospective of black American film. We've had only a few public showings to date [August 1991]. The film was never released. We shot it in 1968 and then had difficulty getting anybody to finish it. We finally got the money for a blow-up in 1971, but then we had the problem of trying to get it launched. I thought I could get it into the Cannes Film Festival, and I flew over to France. The problem was that Louis Marcorelles, the influential critic, went to a pre-screening of the film and the projectionist got the reels all fouled up. *Take One* is already chaotic. It's so fragile that if you mix it up even a little, you lose the film. Marcorelles and I had dinner after the screening, and he said, "I couldn't understand what the film was about!" I was surprised at his reaction, and then later, too late, I discovered that his projectionist had screened the reels out of order.

William Greaves in *Symbiopsychotaxiplasm: Take One* (1968).

I like to think of that incident as a divine intervention: it has kept this film buried for almost twenty-five years. I was so interested to show it tonight because almost no one here has seen it.

Bill Sloan (chief, Circulating Film and Video Program, Museum of Modern Art): I saw *Symbiopsychotaxiplasm* when it was still in a rough cut back in the sixties, and I couldn't believe what I was seeing! What did you have in mind at the time?

Greaves: I had a whole range of concerns. The term "Symbiopsychotaxiplasm" is a take-off on "symbiotaxiplasm," a concept developed by philosopher/social-scientist Arthur Bentley in his book *An Inquiry into Inquiries* [Boston: Beacon Press, 1954] as part of his study of the processes of social-scientific inquiry. Bentley explored how various social scientists went about the business of approaching "civilization" and "society." The term "symbiotaxiplasm" referred to all those events that transpire in any given environment on which a human being impacts in any way. Of course, the most elaborate symbiotaxiplasm would be a city like New York. I had the audacity to add "psycho" into the middle of Bentley's term. I felt the longer term more appropriate to my idea, which was to explore the psychology of a group of creative people who would function as an entity in the process of making a film.

I called it *Symbiopsychotaxiplasm: Take One* because the plan was to make five Symbiopsychotaxiplasms. But we couldn't even get the first one off the ground, and never developed the others.

MacDonald: The thing that used to be said about a certain generation of experimental films—I guess mostly in the late sixties, early seventies—is that they taught you how to watch the film as you were watching it. *Symbiopsychotaxiplasm: Take One* does that, in an unusual way, because you have your surrogates on the screen reacting in the way that the audience is reacting.

Greaves: Well, the function of that first scene, when all hell breaks loose and you are suddenly seeing three separate images on the split-screen—and all the ambivalent craziness that surrounds this kind of location shooting—was to push the audience into a state of annoyance. When spokespeople (people in the crew) appear on the screen and say, "This is not the way you make a movie!" and "What the hell is this all about?" the audience begins to relax and say, "That's right!" They find themselves looking for that clue on the screen that articulates what they've just experienced. The crew says, "This is a piece of shit. He doesn't know what he's doing. I read the script; it doesn't mean anything. It's just bad writing." And the audience thinks, "Yes, it *is* bad writing."

MacDonald: Did you write the basic scene?

Greaves: Yes.

Of course, the actors will suddenly take hold and sometimes have a moment of truth, which takes what is purportedly bad writing and moves it to another level. The nature of acting is that you can put Shakespeare into the mouth of a horrible actor, and it's just a disaster, but with a superb actor, Shakespeare takes off. And you can take very neutral dialogue and by varying the basic circumstances of the dialogue entirely change its impact. For example: "Hello. How are you? What's new? Nothing too much. Have you seen so and so? No, I haven't" means almost nothing. But if one person is a killer and the person he's talking to is a potential victim, the same dialogue is entirely different. Suddenly, the person coming away from it says, "Gee, that was well written." It's in the configuration of motivations and basic circumstances that the full reality of the scene emerges.

Anyway, in the film you find yourself moving back and forth among all those kinds of realizations. One minute the thing is lousy, the next minute it's interesting.

MacDonald: And the different levels are often mutually referential. What the man and woman are saying to each other within their story can be interpreted as reflecting our feelings about the film, but even the struggle they're having getting along is analogous to our struggle as audience with what's on the screen.

Greaves: Also, for a variety of reasons I felt it was necessary to factor into the equation of the film the whole issue of sexuality. I was certainly mindful of the fact that sex/love makes the world go round, and it makes Hollywood go round. It's the easiest way to capture the attention of the average American audience. Failure to address the issue of sexuality has dire implications in terms of the marketplace. During the opening credits we see the maturation of the child in a series of *Family of Man*-type images. And then at the end of that sequence, you're focused on the behind of the black girl with the bike; the cycle is starting all over again. And then, the film focuses in on this couple in a relationship opposite to what has been projected as the normal cosmic cycle: two people getting together and procreating. This relationship threatens that possibility.

Also, in *Symbiopsychotaxiplasm* the sexual issue has more than one level of meaning. It has to do with birth and life versus nonbirth and nonlife, the abortion issue. And in 1966 the abortion issue was (for me) a metaphor for the Vietnam War, where many babies were killed. I also felt that the discussion of sex—especially homosexuality, which was considered unorthodox or unconventional sex at that time—would be controversial and would elicit audience interest and attention. Using sex as the focal point of the scene, I could then orbit the rest of my concerns around it.

MacDonald: Nowadays, abortion is rarely dealt with so directly in films. I don't remember ever seeing characters debate the issue in a film, either in recent years or in the sixties.

Greaves: Abortion was an issue moving up on the wheel of time. It's interesting that in my film *she* wants a child, *he* does not, whereas in Roe versus Wade, it's more an issue of a woman having the right to say she doesn't want this life. What I like about the scene today is that it prevents the film from seeming like advocacy for a particular issue. It creates an interesting tension.

MacDonald: At one point, I thought you were indirectly using homosexuality and abortion as metaphors for the idea that this particular film is not what Hollywood would consider a creation: in other words, that the industry would consider *Symbiopsychotaxiplasm* an "abortion," a "perversion."

Greaves: For me, the homosexuality was more involved with the simple fact that people change, people become homosexual, and people become heterosexual. People have the right to go in whatever direction they want.

MacDonald: So it fits with this film as a production process, as an open system?

Greaves: Sure.

MacDonald: About the choice of Central Park as the location. I assume that on one level, it was just the practical availability of having a space in New York that you could control in certain ways. But it also strikes me that there's an Eden-esque quality to the landscape you use . . .

Greaves: Oh, absolutely! I mean we *could* have shot the scene inside an apartment. Central Park was an absolutely pregnant Eden. The park was appropriate for the traditional Family-of-Man cycle, and it had opportunities for uncontrollable events taking place, like the policeman coming in and asking, "What are you doing?" And in the wider social environment of Central Park, there were so many opportunities for an interaction between our creative nucleus, the cast and the crew, and the public surround.

MacDonald: If we think of the layout of New York City, Manhattan is geometrically arranged for efficiently doing business (at least in theory). It's all about doing things in rigorously structured ways to make money. Central Park is one of the few public places in the city that creates a sense that you can escape (even if that escape is an illusion). It's interesting that this film, which rebels against all the standard assumptions of the movie business, ends up being made in this space. It takes part in the whole tradition of the park as a form of therapy.

Greaves: Absolutely.

MacDonald: Did you shoot material for all five *Symbiopsychotaxiplasm* "takes" and just edit one?

Greaves: Yes.

MacDonald: The original plan was to have each *Take* center on a different couple?

Greaves: *Take One* was going to be an omnibus version, a kaleidoscope of the couples. And then *Take Two, Three, Four*, and *Five* would have been focused on individual couples. We decided to abandon the omnibus version during the original editing; it looked like it was going to be too much.

MacDonald: Did you decide to start with the Don Fellows/Pat Gilbert "take" because their performances were the strongest?

Greaves: No. Originally, we were going to start with the interracial couple you see at the very end of *Take One*. But it didn't matter where we started; we were going to make all five of these anyway, so we decided to go with what was available financially and get started. It was a pragmatic decision, but I felt comfortable with Pat and Don who had done fascinating work.

MacDonald: If you had the money now, would you finish the other four "takes"?

Greaves: Oh yes, I'd love to. We've got great stuff, including, by the way, some wonderful material with Susan Anspach. Susan and the young fellow who played opposite her sang some of their lines. In fact, each pair dealt with the scenario in a different way. The interracial couple made it a psychodrama. We drew on the works of J. L. Moreno, a student of Freud, who conceived psychodrama as a psychotherapeutic tool, a way of accessing and objectifying the subconscious, and brought it to this country. We had a psychodramatist, someone who had been trained by Moreno, come onto the set and work with the actors.

MacDonald: So there's the psychodrama; there's the version with elements of a musical . . .

Greaves: And then there are two other straight-ahead efforts by actors not as experienced as Pat and Don were.

MacDonald: Is there much more material of the crew meeting among themselves and responding to the project?

Greaves: Oh yes, but not as much as I originally thought I would get. I had thought the crew would challenge me *on* camera, and that that conflict would be central to the drama of the film. My thinking was that if I made the crew sufficiently angry by certain types of redundancies and repetitions, they would begin saying, "What the hell's going on? Why are you doing this? What's this all about?" They'd rebel. But they didn't do that, and it was a source of grief, frustration, and depression for me during the course of the shooting.

Similarly, I thought that the actors would periodically have trouble with their lines or with me and that we'd get into these debates over the relative merits of this passage of dialogue or that, of this particular psychological adjustment versus that motivation—that kind of thing. But the actors and the crew were so professional that they couldn't cross that boundary; they were too accustomed to situations where the director is god.

MacDonald: There's a difference though, in that the crew sneaks away to have their own discussion about you and then presents you with the results, while the actors seem to assume that if something is going wrong it's because *they're* not good enough.

Greaves: Well, actors tend to be like that.

MacDonald: I assume it's also because they knew you and your reputation as a teacher of actors.

Greaves: That may have had something to do with it, but typically actors are such an oppressed community, such a desperate community. They have so few opportunities to work that the last thing an actor wants to do is get a reputation for confronting directors.

So I didn't get what I wanted, except for that moment at the end where I say, "Cut!" and Pat says, "This is not working out," and I say, "Yes, it is," and she yells, "It's *not* and you *know* it!" I thought, "Oh boy, here she comes," because Pat was an intelligent, talented, sensitive actress with a volatile personality. She had radar about when something was truthful and when it wasn't. I figured that once she decided to confront me, she'd pull out all the stops. And I assumed that the crew would catch the whole thing. Well, by that time the crew were so pissed off with me that they'd become sloppy in their camera reloading and, wouldn't you know, just at that moment they didn't have any film in the fucking camera! So when I walked across the bridge after Pat, they didn't follow. And then once they were loaded, they felt it was too private a moment to interrupt. They fell back into the conventions.

MacDonald: Was this Pat Gilbert's first film? Don Fellows mentions acting in advertisements.

Greaves: I think it was her first film.

MacDonald: Because there's that added dimension of thinking you may be screwing up because the process of doing takes over and over wastes film. Fellows talks about that.

Greaves: Well, he was not accustomed to cinéma vérité as a methodology for filming. When you do a commercial, you sit down, you've got a slate, you've got a scene number, you've got a script clerk. Everything is all set up. Of course, cinéma vérité doesn't adhere to that and even in the moments when we were filming in a more or less structured and conventional way, Don was surprised that we would do so many takes and that we would do improvisations. Up to that point there really weren't many incidences of improvisation being done in feature films. Cassavetes, but not much else.

Lazar Stojanovic (Yugoslavian filmmaker): In 1970 a Yugoslavian writer came back from the United States and told me about Bill Greaves and this film. He knew that I was very interested in what I call self-analytical movies, movies that consider the medium. I couldn't really get a clear picture of Bill's film— only that it was related to some of Godard's work. Now that I have finally seen *Symbiopsychotaxiplasm*, I think it's a milestone in the history of the sixties.

Michelle Materre (then, associate director, Women Make Movies; subsequently, executive director of International Film Seminars): You must have had your ego in a great place to be able to allow the crew to think about you the way they did.

Greaves: It was a calculated risk. In general, my livelihood turns on people's perceiving me as a director, and yet, for this particular film to work, a flawed, vulnerable persona was essential. I must say I feel very good about my relationship with the crew. Even when they spoke about me at their meeting, they didn't speak in anger. They were six characters in search of an author.

Maria DeLuca (filmmaker): I have a mundane question about the sequence of the crew at their private meeting. Did I miss something? It's one thing for them to say, "Let's get together and have a conference," but film is expensive. How did it happen that they were shooting film?

Greaves: We were well-endowed with raw stock. They saw I was burning it up with these three cameras rolling at once, and I guess they figured I wouldn't miss two or three thousand feet!

MacDonald: Certain ways of critiquing conventional film happen in many places simultaneously. In the sixties there were a number of different attempts to critique cinéma vérité: Shirley Clarke's *The Connection* [1961], Jonas Mekas's *The Brig* [1964], and Peter Watkins's *The War Game* [1965] and *Punishment Park* [1971] are distinguished instances. The one that strikes me as closest to this film is Jim McBride's *David Holzman's Diary* [1967], which itself was inspired in part by the work of Andrew Noren. I'm curious as to whether you had any contact with McBride or Noren, or if they had contact with your work.

Greaves: I've heard of *David Holzman's Diary*, but I've not seen it. I've been involved in *making* films, and, you know, you stay in an editing room until you're exhausted, then you go home and collapse, and get up and do it again. There was a period in my life when I used to go to the theater a great deal, and to the movies. But that stopped after I left Canada in 1960.

Richard Herskowitz (then, director, Cornell Cinema; currently, director, Virginia Festival of American Film): *Did* you think of *Symbiopsychotaxiplasm* as a satire of cinéma vérité in particular?

Greaves: At the National Film Board of Canada, I was in the unit that pioneered cinéma vérité on the North American continent. Terry Filgate (the English cameraman in *Symbiopsychotaxiplasm*) and I were together at the National Film Board at what was called Unit B. We worked on *Lonely Boy* [1961, directed by Wolf Koenig and Roman Kroitor]. The process of learning to do that kind of shooting made me very attuned to the spontaneous capturing of reality and certainly laid the groundwork for this film.

But I should tell you some of the other thinking that I had in mind while making *Symbiopsychotaxiplasm*. I went to a science high school in New York City and was in general pointed in the direction of science. I broke that off in college, but I continued to be interested in various scientific theories. The Heisenberg Principle of Uncertainty, in particular, fascinated me. Heisenberg asserts that we'll never really know the basis of the cosmos, because the means of perceiving it alters the reality it observes. The electron microscope sends out a beam of electrons that knocks the electrons of the atoms being observed out of their orbits.

I began to think of the movie camera as an analogue to the microscope. In this case, the reality to be observed is the human soul, the psyche. Of course, as the camera investigates that part of the cosmos, the individual psyches being observed recoil. Behavior becomes structured in a way other than it would have been had it been unperceived—a psychological version of the Heisenberg Principle. In this sense, my film was an environment in which movie cameras were set up to catch the process of human response.

Another scientific law that interested me was the Second Law of Thermodynamics, which describes the distribution of energy in a system. In *Symbiopsychotaxiplasm*, the cameras were to track the flow of energy in the system I had devised. If the cameras looked at one person and the level of spontaneous reality began to recede as a result of their being observed, that energy would show up somewhere else, behind the cameras in the crew, for example. The cameras were set up to track the flow of energy from in front of the cameras to behind them and back to the front.

Alan Rosenthal (author, director): Did you look at the rushes in between the filming, or did you just continue shooting?

Greaves: Well, we had to look at the rushes to see whether we were getting things on film, but I didn't see the rushes of the crew at their secret meeting until after the shooting was over. Bob Rosen came to me and said, "Bill, we have a little present for you."

Patricia Zimmermann (professor of film, Ithaca College): In documentary and in certain narrative forms, there's a long history of self-reflexive filmmaking as a political intervention to disengage the traditional power of the director. It's evident at least as early as Dziga Vertov. In the sixties, self-reflexivity became an international movement: Godard, Dusan Makavejev, Lazar Stojanovic, many American and European avant-garde filmmakers, you. . . . In all these instances, self-reflexivity functioned as a way of disengaging from certain authoritarian power relations to make way for more utopian ways of working in the world. The scene where you're sitting with your multiracial, mixed-gender crew seems to encapsulate this. And you're an African-American director. Could you situate your method within the politics of the time?

Greaves: Well, clearly we were working in a context of the urban disorders of the sixties and the rage of the African-American community against the tyranny and racism of the American body politic. Plus the more specific struggles: the Civil Rights marches and the other strategies that were being employed by the African-American community. And there was the whole Vietnam problem and the growing dissent over it. There was the emerging feminist movement. And Woodstock. There was an unhappiness of massive dimensions over the way in which society had been run and about the covert authoritarianism that was evident everywhere. True, America was no dictatorship, but there certainly were mores, local and federal laws, social structures in place that inhibited the flowering of the human spirit.

This film was an attempt to look at the impulses and inspirations of a group of creative people who, during the making of the film, were being "pushed to the wall" by the process I as director had instigated. The scene that I had written was fixed, and I was in charge. I was insisting that this scene would be done by the cast and crew, even though it was making them very unhappy. The question was, "When will they revolt?" When would they question the validity, the wisdom, of doing the scene in the first place? In this sense, it really was a reflection of the politics of the time.

Maria Agui Carter (associate producer, WGBH, Boston): The issue this film raises for me is individual power versus collective power. At one point in the film, you say, "I represent the establishment." I find that when I'm directing a mixed crew, particularly a gender-mixed crew, I have power relationship problems because of my gender and race. When you as an African-American director said, "I represent the establishment," how did your crew respond?

Greaves: I had an excellent relationship with the crew. You have to think in terms of the sixties, when there was a breaking out of a whole lot of ossified thinking. The people who worked on *Symbiopsychotaxiplasm* were Age-of-Aquarius-type people, who were in many respects shorn of the encumbrances that many white Americans are burdened with. If you investigated the psychology of these people, you wouldn't discover racism or prejudice. They had a very collaborationist approach.

John Columbus (director, Black Maria Film Festival): Did you expect a counterculture audience for the film? Or did you hope for distribution through commercial theaters?

Greaves: When we first had a blow-up, we did show it to a couple of distributors, and their eyeballs went around in their sockets. They just couldn't figure out how to categorize and package it. One of the critics from *Time* had come by my studio in the sixties and said, "Gee, this thing is not going to be acceptable for twenty years." Right now, more than twenty years later, I have the film with some of the so-called leading lights in innovative distribution, so we'll see.

The arguing couple (Don Fellows and Patricia Ree Gilbert) in
Symbiopsychotaxiplasm: Take One.

The audience here at the seminar represents a high level of appreciation.
You're all cinema people: filmmakers, cinema scholars, and so on, and that's always an unusual situation. I think that the film will make its way into art theaters
and through the college circuit and to whatever film societies are out there. But
it will probably get wider consumption in the twenty-first century because of its
increasing archival value: there were few films made in the sixties that so effectively tracked the psychological and emotional mechanisms of young people.
From a sociological or anthropological perspective, it will have some utility.

Steve Gallagher (programmer): What was the reaction of the cast and the
crew when they saw the film?

Greaves: Only three or four of them have seen it. Bob Rosen saw it, and he
reacted the same way Muhammad Ali did to the film I made about him [*Ali, the
Fighter*, 1971]. That film was shot cinéma vérité, too, and while we were
filming, Ali wouldn't cooperate, for legal and other reasons, I suppose. So we
used a telephoto lens, hidden mikes, and so on. About a year later, after the
fight was over and the film was finished, I got a call from Ali saying, "Listen, I
want to see that film you did." So we set up a screening for him, and he sat in
the theater saying, "How did you get this shot! How did you do *that!*" He was
amazed. Rosen's reaction was similar; I don't think he anticipated the film that
he saw. I think (I hope) he was surprised in a pleasant way.

Jack Churchill (videomaker, musician): Did you always know what you
were doing while you were shooting?

Greaves: There were certain constants that I tried to predetermine as much as possible, and then I released the human consciousness into this field of determinants. It was similar to the way we come into this room. We have all agreed to be here to talk about the film, but what happens takes its own direction.

The interesting thing to me is that if you take a filmmaker, or any artist or writer, and throw them into any milieu, any situation, they will probably land feet first, if they've had enough experience. If you sit a pianist at a piano, even though that person has no music in front of him, even though he may not even decide to play any particular piece, he can still improvise. I used Miles Davis music [from *In a Silent Way*] in *Symbiopsychotaxiplasm* as a metaphor for the film, which is a form of audiovisual jazz. It was improvisational within a certain structure.

MacDonald: One of the things I noticed when I looked really carefully at *Take One* is that while it has this feeling of informality and spontaneity, it's very rigorously composed.

Greaves: Well, the finished film did not develop overnight. There was a lot of agony in the editing room—a *lot*. I had sixty or seventy hours of film. I can't tell you how many editors I burnt out. The film had to be chaos, but chaos of a very special character: *intelligible* chaos. It had to hold your attention, even though it was supposed to be a lousy film.

MacDonald: From the opening minutes it's evident that the film is precise in what it does. During the preface, we no sooner start to get engaged in this argument about abortion, than you flip us out of it by switching to a split-screen image of two different angles on the two characters. And the minute we're starting to become accustomed to the split-screen, you flip us out of that and into candid shots of bystanders observing the shoot. The switch from one level to another in the preface sets up the overall rhythm of the film.

And the following credit sequence confirms the film's precision. Often credits are little more than throwaways, but as you've said, you move through a whole cycle of life, while this sound that was identified as an error during the final moments of the preface gets louder and louder so that we know that even if it *was* an error then, it sure as hell is conscious now. The film is loaded.

Greaves: It *is* loaded, and that took a lot of time. It flows very easily now, but obviously there was a time when nothing flowed. In a way it comes out of my own background as a filmmaker. I began as an editor; I edited maybe sixty or seventy films as a sound editor, as a picture editor, and as chief editor. I was counseled at the Film Board by some marvelous people that the editing room was the best possible place to get a good grounding in filmmaking. And for that I will always be grateful. Some people were trying to get me to become a director very early in the game.

MacDonald: One last question about the film's subtlety. The first time we see you in the film, you're listening to the sound and saying, "This is terrible, this is terrible," but you don't look like you feel it's terrible; you look amused.

It's a kind of foreshadowing, as is your statement a moment later, "Don't take me seriously."

Greaves: I *was* very happy with the fact that there was error and confusion. If you notice me with Victor, the homeless guy at the end, I have the same kind of private smile. That emotion comes out of the fact that the thing was going my way: there was confusion, and conflict, and an unpremeditated develop-ment that was important for the life and success of the film. That's on one level.

Now on the second level, there's a paradox. I wanted to harness the paradox of doing failure, of *using* failure and error and confusion and chaos and un-happiness and conflict! The film is a tour de force. You are drawn inexorably through this cosmic flux. At the end you say, "Wait a minute, what was *that* about, and why was I so transfixed by it?" Well, life is like that, life keeps you totally absorbed from moment to moment to moment and yet oftentimes you can't tell what it's about. I like that paradox. My filmmaking always goes for paradoxes, ironies, contradictions.

You know, it's like Zen: here we are on this earth, this ball, suspended out in space; we're all tied in with the gravitational forces of the sun and yet we're speeding and trying to go off in another direction. Cosmically, we're caught in this equilibrium of paradoxical forces.

John Columbus: Today some people might be a little troubled by the way you handle the homeless man who walks into the shoot near the end. Did you have mixed feelings then or do you now about that scene?

Greaves: We were confronted with that individual, and we said, "Do we want to let this survive as a sequence or not?" I made a determination at the time that we were going to go with it, because though he was intrusive, this was reality—and reality was what the film was all about. I decided to stay open to it, and I'm so glad I did. As you saw, I did take the precaution of getting the guy to sign a release.

There's a mystical element to this film. We certainly recognized that he was drunk and homeless, but in his confrontational nature, he articulated what I was trying to get at in the film. Over the years, Victor has been in different sec-tions of the film, but he works best at the very end: you can't go beyond *that* level of truth. Even though we were all being very spontaneous up to a point (I was probably the least spontaneous of anyone), he was even *more* spontaneous. And that's the nature of film truth: the closer you come to it, the less permissive it is of artificiality following it.

MacDonald: How many versions of the film are there? I understand it's changed over the years.

Greaves: We went through many permutations of the material until we ar-rived at what we have. After he saw the film tonight, Steve Gallagher asked me if I'd cut something out of the film since he saw it a short time ago. The answer was yes. Over the years, every time I've looked at the film, I've thought, "Shit," and I fiddle with this and that.

MacDonald: I understand that you've been considering a *Take One and a Half* and a *Take Two*. What do you have in mind?

Greaves: Well, *Take One and a Half* will be what it sounds like: a halfway point between *Take One* and *Take Two*. Actually, I decided to do a *Take One and a Half* because we were caught in a logjam at a festival in Austria. They were supposed to send *Take One* to France for another event, and they didn't do it, so we had to scrounge around and pull together all the answer prints of *Take One* and assemble a film. In the process of making this emergency film for the Amiens Festival, we used a few things we liked that weren't in the original *Take One*, so you can call that version *Take One and an Eighth*. It's the same as *Take One*, with a few additions [This is the new version of *Take One* mentioned in the introduction to this interview]. But *Take One and a Half* will use sequences of couples who were left out of *Take One*. We'll use the interracial couple you see and Susan Anspach and her partner. I'm not quite sure how we'll weave their story lines into the larger situation, though I did sketch out one outline we might follow. *Take One and a Half* will probably be about ninety minutes, as opposed to the seventy minutes of *Take One*.

MacDonald: And *Take Two*?

Greaves: It occurred to me, when I was in Germany recently, that since the actress [Audrey Heningham] in *Take Two* has lived in Germany for almost twenty years and since the people at the Munich Film Festival like *Take One* so much, it might be interesting to have a look at some of the concerns in *Take One* within the context of that lapse of time. The actor who plays her partner in the original shooting [Frank (now Shannon) Baker] is still in New York at the Actors' Studio, and his craft has developed. So they would interact on several different levels: on the level of the basic screen test (the argument between them), *and* on a psychodramatic level (they did have a relationship with each other in real life); *and* on a third level, in terms of their here-and-now professional and personal realities and whatever has happened to them in the interim. I'd like to bring the actress's German reality into the film—especially the Munich beer halls. I love the energy there, which is kind of ironic because Dachau is only a few miles away. It's hard to conceive of those horrors. For me, it only underscores that, as an old professor of mine used to say, "Genius and gentility, stupidity and savagery are not the private preserve of any one group or race of people."

We would have *Take Two* unfolding in Central Park in the original footage, and then there'd be this abrupt cut into this new recent material. Or we could start off in Germany and intercut between present and past. Those are some of the thoughts I've been playing around with. How much of that I will be able to get to, I don't know.

MacDonald: Which of your other films do you see as particularly experimental?

Greaves: The film I did in Africa called *The First World Festival of Negro Arts* [1966] is experimental in the sense that it uses poetry in conjunction with cinéma vérité in an unusual formulation.

From These Roots is all still photographs. To make a documentary that was dramatic in its impact with only still photographs and sound was experimental then. Today you have Ken Burns's *The Civil War* [1990] and so on. *Ida B. Wells, A Passion for Justice* [1989], which also came out before *The Civil War*, combined sound effects, still photographs, and interviews overlaid with graphics. I think that film was innovative.

And *Ali, the Fighter* was experimental in the sense that it was shot cinéma vérité, but has a progressive, dramatic story line. Certainly the chronology of the event itself was helpful—the events leading up to and including the fight between Ali and Joe Frazier. But apart from that, there was character delineation and a development of dramatic themes. Up to that point in American filmmaking I don't know if there were any films that used cinéma vérité in such a dramatic way. I could be wrong, of course; I'm looking at this through my own tunnel vision.

You know, *Ali, the Fighter* became the basis for *Rocky* [1976]. If you analyze *Rocky*, you'll know that Rocky is a white Joe Frazier. Joe Frazier was in my apartment about four months ago, and he said, "Goddammit, they ripped me off." They used his public persona as the basis for Rocky and Muhammad Ali as the basis for Apollo Creed. They even purchased sequences from our film to use as crowd reactions during the fight. The *Raging Bull* [1980] people also studied our film. There are echoes of our way of shooting in both films. *Ali, the Fighter* was an experiment that went on to become conventional.

MacDonald: Your work on the *Take One* project is ongoing, but you're now [autumn 1995] shooting a film about Ralph Bunche. Is the Bunche project the biggest thing you've done?

Greaves: Well, yes and no. I was executive producer of *Bustin' Loose* [1981], a twelve or thirteen million dollar production. But an executive producer is a glorified baby-sitter. You just hover while this thing is being done, trying to keep harmony on the set and to stay within the budget. In terms of real hands-on direction, the Bunche project is the most expensive I've done.

I was thinking recently about the American ethos, and about Hollywood setting up the guidelines for our expectations and responses. As you've said, we see hundreds of hours of film, TV, and so on, and *then* we *may* see an avant-garde film. There's a related development in Europe. At least a couple generations of Europeans were largely raised on their own films, films from their cultures, in *their* aesthetics, films about what concerns them. Then here comes the American film invasion, wiping their screen culture—and as a result, their actual culture—off the map. I've been to France, Italy, Spain, and Sweden recently, and Europeans look less and less like Europeans to me and more and more like Americans. And European films are mimicking American action films. The American motion picture and television industry and print media are the engine that's driving the cultural transformation of the world.

At the Goethe Institute this past Saturday, I saw a German action film with lots of blood and guns, all these phony film conventions—the stock-in-trade of an American Hollywood product. Europeans figure if they make these films, they'll be able to access the American market. At least some of them think that. Another group makes these films to recapture their own marketplace—not to preserve their spiritual or cultural integrity, but for business reasons. In Germany right now, as I understand it, 12 percent of the market share is controlled by the Germans. Eighty-five percent is controlled by Americans, and about 3 or 4 percent by the French and people from other parts of the world. This breakdown is pervasive throughout Europe.

As a juror at the San Sebastian Film Festival recently, I saw a lot of films from different countries: all were clones of American films and not as good. I mean we do our films very well. That's what we *do*. They're trying to emulate our films in order to recapture their market share, but in the process they lose whatever values and identity they have. I hate to see all these amazing worlds disappear.

Two years ago I was in China and, to my utter amazement, when I'd talk to Chinese filmmakers about the aesthetics of film, about cinema language, they'd talk to me about *Rambo*: "Where do you get the money? How do you make a deal?" Unhappily, the world seems progressively oriented to the bottom line, and the impact on cinema is devastating. It sure plays havoc with *my* truth. When you've got X-hundred thousand dollars of debt to pay off, you have to watch what you say. Unfortunately, I don't know any way around it.

Jordan Belson

(and collaborator Stephen Beck)

By the mid-1960s, the film society movement had run its course, at least in the United States, though a limited public awareness of alternative cinema was maintained and developed in a variety of ways. In New York, San Francisco, and a few other major cities, an avant-garde film movement was in full swing. Alternative screening spaces introduced audiences to a wide variety of young filmmakers, as well as to the achievements of the 1950s, the 1940s, and earlier decades. But for those of us living away from major cities, awareness of the full range of filmmaking was harder to come by. We had increased access to feature-length "foreign film," and we knew from Jonas Mekas's "Movie Journal" column in the *Village Voice* that there was a lot going on that we weren't seeing. But our experiences with what was then called "underground film" were at best sporadic.

For me, the most memorable moment of access to a wider range of critical film forms in the late 1960s came by way of a set of programs assembled and distributed by Janus Films, called "New Cinema" (perhaps to evoke Mekas's "New American Cinema"), which premiered at Philharmonic Hall at Lincoln Center, and subsequently went on tour. New Cinema was a diverse, international collection of films—short melodramas and documentaries, animations, avant-garde films—more reminiscent of film society programming than of the then-contemporary programming at underground screening venues. For me, the two most startling revelations in the New Cinema programs were Chris Marker's *La Jetée* (1963) and Jordan Belson's *Allures* (1961).* Marker's film

*The other "New Cinema" films: *Act without Words* (1964) by Guido Bettiol; *Actua-Tilt* (1960) by Jean Herman; *Al!* (1964) by Yoji Kuri; *All the Boys Are Called Patrick* (1957) by Jean-Luc Go-

Design used in Jordan Belson's *Allures* (1961).

remains widely known, but *Allures*, and Belson's work in general, has moved
out of the public eye, in large measure because Belson himself withdrew his
films from circulation in 1978. More than any other film in the New Cinema
programs, *Allures* sang the excitement of the future, and of the potential of
what Gene Youngblood would call "expanded cinema," while simultaneously
enticing viewers in the direction of the long history of Eastern spiritual
thought. Indeed, the combination of visceral pleasure and spiritual energy in
Allures and in Belson's other films of the 1960s—*Re-entry* (1964), *Phenomena*
(1965), *Samadhi* (1967), *Momentum* (1968)—were crucial in the thinking of
both Youngblood (see "The Cosmic Cinema of Jordan Belson," in *Expanded*

dard; *The Apple* (1962) by George Dunning; *The Concert of M. and Mme. Kabal* (1962), *Renaissance* (1963), and *The Games of Angels* (1964) by Walerian Borowczyk; *Corrida Interdite* (1958)
by Denys Colomb de Daunant; *The Do-It-Yourself Cartoon Kit* (1961) by Bob Godfrey; *Enter
Hamlet* (1965) by Fred Mogubgub; *The Fat and the Lean* (1961) by Roman Polanski; *Les Mistons*
(1966) by François Truffaut; *The Most* (1962) by Gordon Sheppard and Richard Ballentine; *The
Running, Jumping, and Standing Still Film* (1959) by Richard Lester; and *Two Castles* (1963) by
Bruno Bozzetto.

Cinema [New York: Dutton, 1970], pp. 157–177) and Sheldon Renan (see "The West Coast Abstract School" and "Jordan Belson," in *An Introduction to the American Underground Film* [New York: Dutton, 1967], pp. 93–96, 116–118), along with Mekas, the two most influential American critical-cinema chroniclers of the decade.

Belson's 1960s films were instantly identifiable, and remain memorable, because of certain characteristic visual gestures that, in a wide range of particular films, provide metaphors for a cinematically distinctive sense of human existence. As William C. Wees suggests, "The single most common shape [in Belson's films] is the circle, whose center corresponds with the center of the screen and whose peripheries become concentric rings or spirals with radiating dots and lines. Sometimes these mandalas of light are geometrically precise constellations of tiny glittering dots; at other times they are pulsing discs and halos of misty, glowing colors"; and at still other times this shape looks like pupil and iris and suggests a "cosmic eye" (Wees, *Light Moving in Time* [Berkeley: University of California Press, 1992], pp. 131, 133). That the imagery suggests outer space one moment and atomic particles the next is a way of suggesting that, basically, the macrocosmic and the microcosmic are one and that the means for understanding this unity is the "inner eye" of the spirit.

Originally (and still) an abstract artist in the tradition of Kandinsky, Belson recognized the potential of film as an extension of "nonobjective art" at the "Art in Cinema" screenings, a series of programs organized by Frank Stauffacher and Richard Foster and presented, beginning in 1946, at the San Francisco Museum of Art. (The early "Art in Cinema" programs are listed in Stauffacher, ed., *Art in Cinema* [New York: Arno, 1968].) Belson began his filmmaking career as an abstract animator, making "visual music" akin to the films of Hans Richter, Oskar Fischinger, and Norman McLaren. From 1957 to 1960, in collaboration with musician Henry Jacobs, Belson wowed audiences at San Francisco's Morrison Planetarium in nearly a hundred "Vortex Concerts." Belson and Jacobs used the planetarium's visual and sound systems to create evening-long presentations of abstract sound and image—ancestors of the current laser shows so common to planetariums and sports arenas. Working with real-time motion at the Vortex Concerts changed Belson's way of approaching film. By the 1960s, he was no longer an animator, but had begun to use "a special optical bench . . . essentially a plywood frame around an old X-ray stand with rotating tables, variable speed motors, and variable intensity lights" (Youngblood, p. 158), though Belson has always refused to reveal the particulars of his method.

Increasingly unhappy with the reception and exhibition of his work, and with the difficulties of maintaining first-rate prints, Belson finally withdrew his films and himself from the public sphere, preferring to make films, graphic work, and paintings in private. He has been able to support himself and his film-making during this retreat partially as a result of his contributions to Philip

Kaufman's *The Right Stuff* (1983) and other commercial film and video productions. Selections from his films remain available on *Samadhi and Other Films*, a 1989 Mystic Fire video, accompanied (unfortunately) by a soundtrack composed by John Luther Adams; but the excerpts on this video provide merely an evocation of the experience of seeing Belson's work projected in 16mm. One can only hope that Belson's films will at some point reenter theaters and the consciousness of new generations of filmgoers, before the processes of decay do irretrievable damage to the few prints that remain and to the originals.

I have not had the pleasure of meeting Belson in person. Our interview began as a phone conversation in San Francisco in early December 1992; and continued in subsequent phone conversations in 1993–94. In January 1994, I supplemented our discussion of *Cycles* (1975), Belson's collaboration with video artist Stephen Beck, with a phone interview with Beck.

MacDonald: I'd be interested to know what you remember from the period of the late forties and early fifties, when you were starting to make films.

Belson: I'll do my best, though memory is not my strong point.

MacDonald: Where was your film work first shown?

Belson: At Art in Cinema, I think. I got very turned on by Art in Cinema. Even though I was a child of the motion picture era, it had never occurred to me to make movies. I thought of myself only as a spectator. But when I saw the Art in Cinema series, particularly the hands-on type of films that Norman McLaren made, the possibility of combining film and what I considered Art intrigued me. I guess I saw some Fischinger there too, and the very earliest Whitneys [*Five Abstract Film Exercises*, 1943–44].

MacDonald: There are interesting relationships between your early work and some of Fischinger's films, *Radio Dynamics* [1942], in particular.

Belson: Well, yes. Fischinger was one of my heroes. But I think the real similarity is that we both belonged to the school of non-objective painting. I don't know if you're familiar with that term, but at one time the Guggenheim was called the Museum of Non-Objective Art. It was dedicated to a certain type of modern art: Kandinsky, Rudolph Bauer mainly, kind of an Art Moderne with spiritual overtones. Fischinger was part of that movement, too. In fact, I believe the Guggenheim supported Fischinger for a while to get out of Germany and settle in the United States. The director of the museum was a formidable lady by the name of Baroness Hilla Rebay. On the basis of my paintings, she also partially supported me—put me on a monthly stipend for a couple of years.

MacDonald: When was this?

Belson: 1949–1950. Looking back, I now have the greatest respect for her and what she accomplished. She is entirely responsible for commissioning the present Guggenheim Museum, designed by Frank Lloyd Wright. She had enough money to encourage people to work in that non-objective style, and she did. She exhibited some of my paintings in their annual shows. Harry Smith was very desirous of connecting up with her, so when she came to California, we both met her at the airport and took her first to my studio in Berkeley and then to his wretched little room over a bebop nightclub in the Fillmore district of San Francisco. When he wanted to move to New York, she provided the means for him to do so and also allowed him to stay in a studio in the old Guggenheim Museum itself, where he lived and worked for his first few months in New York—or so he told me.

MacDonald: When she came to San Francisco, had you both started to work on film?

Belson: We were painters, but both of us had made some films. I remember I was about to show her one of my films, when she grabbed the reel and started unwinding it onto the floor, looking at it with her naked eye. She told me that this was not advanced filmmaking, compared to Oskar Fischinger. I suppose I was a little hurt by it, but I realized she was right. I was just starting out. I'd done two animated films: one unbelievably crude—*Transmutation* [1947]—and then *Improvisation #1* [1948], which was a little more polished. They were still just black and white drawings on cards. The title, "Improvisation," was typical of the non-objective artists, who aligned themselves with music. Those films are lost now.

Few people even know that I am also a graphic artist, but to me it's as important to my creative development (and my sense of self) as my film work. It's been my main activity since I stopped making films in 1989. Of course, even before I started making films, the paintings I made seemed to call out to be animated. Actually, I thought of them as animations-in-painting. These early paintings contained sequential imagery where a form would be shown going through some type of metamorphosis. Logically, the next step was movement. All those early graphic works were pre-cinematic. The early film works were really paintings animated. Looking back now, it seems pretty inevitable that I would flip over into film, though I certainly had no conscious intention of making films early in my life, except maybe when I was a child and had fantasies about being a Disney cartoonist. In many ways abstract films were the "cartoons" of art film programs.

Art in Cinema was started by Frank Stauffacher, who helped me shoot *Transmutation*. He had a camera and I asked him if he would help me film the animated drawings I had made. Stauffacher was a graphic designer, but he didn't start making films until after he had founded the Art in Cinema series. Then he made some films that have become classics in their own way: *Sausalito* [1948], for example. Tragically, he developed a brain tumor and died shortly thereafter. But he was very instrumental in stirring up interest in films and filmmaking in this area.

Hy Hirsh was very helpful, too. He was a professional photographer and on the staff at the Palace of the Legion of Honor [a San Francisco art museum]. He was in charge of photographing the exhibits and the individual art objects for their files. He had his own darkroom at the museum and he was very skillful with cameras, and he also had a motion picture camera. He was a little older than most of us and very generous with technical assistance. It was only after Harry Smith and I were working on films for a while that he actually started making his own. He made oscilloscope films at first: *Come Closer* [1952] and *Eneri* [1953], which is "Irene" spelled backwards. He helped me film my scroll paintings, and he took me downtown to a camera shop and helped me buy my first camera, a used 16mm Bell & Howell: thirty-five dollars. He took the start button apart so I could take single frames with it, and showed me how to frame and focus with a mirror (there was no through-the-lens viewer).

MacDonald: What about Smith? What films had he made at that point?

Belson: I met him in Berkeley in 1946. At that point he had not made any films, but as I remember, we both started making films after seeing the Art in Cinema programs. He had a rather scornful attitude towards artists. He preferred to think of himself as an anthropologist. However, he was a considerably skilled and talented artist himself, and he did produce some extraordinary works of art. In fact, I think his paintings, his drawings, and other graphic works are where his real genius shows through. He did some remarkable paintings around 1950 in which every shape was synchronized, note-for-note, to Dizzy Gillespie recordings. Two of these are reproduced in *American Magus, Harry Smith* by Paola Igliori [New York: Inanout Press, 1996].

MacDonald: Texturally I find what he called *Early Abstractions* [completion dates unclear] stunning.

Belson: You mean the paintings-on-film?

MacDonald: Yes.

Belson: When he started to do those, he was still in Berkeley. I remember seeing him working on them. Though he was scrupulously neat *in* the films, he worked on the floor, on a rug, and the rug was all sprayed with colored dyes and inks. He had a method of using pressure-sensitive tape, pre-cut into dots like they use in office filing systems: "Come Clean Gum Dots" they were called. You could buy them at stationery stores. He made a special effort to contact the manufacturer and actually went to Los Angeles to get their entire selection of graduated-sized dots and circles so he could animate without having to cut them himself, though he did cut strips and other shapes of masking tape which he would put onto the clear 35mm film stock. After he put the "Come Clean Gum Dots" and the other shapes onto the filmstrip, he would spray colored dyes onto it with a mouth atomizer. Then, before he took the gum dots off, he'd coat the whole thing with Vaseline or something of that sort. Then he'd pull the dots off and color the uncovered sections. He called these films "batiks," because that is essentially what the batik method is: designs are painted with wax on cloth, dyed, and then later the wax is melted off. Those films were very vital. They had a raw, *brut* quality because of the way they were done.

I remember he then tried another technique. He borrowed a camera, made a lightbox, put cutout forms on the lightbox so that everything was blacked out except perhaps a circle with the light behind it, and at night with the lights out, playing a phonograph record, he would dance around his room and film the lightbox from various angles. Then he'd wind the film back, put the record on again, and film another cutout, say a triangle. And so on. The record would give him cues as to when to bring things in, when to take things out. He improvised a couple of little films in that way [see Smith's *No. 4*, on the *Early Abstractions* reel at Film-makers' Cooperative in New York]. In one night he could do a whole abstract film and have a synchronized soundtrack as well.

Later, he tried to interest Hilla Rebay in the idea of his doing a three-dimensional film in the non-objective style that she favored, by sending her a series of paintings he had made for viewing with a stereoscope, which he also included. He had worked out the stereoscopic principles of what made things look in front of or behind other things. He also did a series of small, impeccable paintings in that perfect non-objective style and tried to interest her in financing a film in which those compositions would appear. I've got slides of those paintings, which I hope someday to see published.

MacDonald: When I was doing research on Amos Vogel and Cinema 16, Carmen D'Avino told me that the fact of Cinema 16's audience for unusual forms of films was the instigation for his filmmaking. He might not have made any films, had Vogel not created that audience. Would you say the same for your work and the Art in Cinema programs?

Belson: Probably, yes. I could list artists whose work we saw during those showings that inspired us in some way. People like Douglas Crockwell. Most people have forgotten him. He was a successful illustrator in the Norman Rockwell style and used to do *Saturday Evening Post* covers. In fact some people confused his work with Norman Rockwell's: Rockwell, Crockwell. Anyway, he did weird, surrealistic, spooky little films. I'd love to see them again. And I was turned on by *Rhythmus 21* [1921] by Hans Richter. Something there gave me a clue as to how I might get started, as did the early surrealist films, and [Georges] Méliès, and the early films by the Whitneys. And McLaren. I got a big kick out of *Begone Dull Care* [1949] and *Fiddle-Dee-Dee* [1947] and remember studying them on rewinds to see how some of the effects were achieved. I suspect that's where Harry got the idea of painting on film, too. I tried to follow McLaren's career as best I could. McLaren did a 3-D film in 35mm called *Now Is the Time* [1951], which was shown in regular movie theaters (you used Polaroid glasses). I found some of his other techniques intriguing, though I never used them.

Smith and I, and Hy Hirsh spent a lot of time together. Occasionally we would go to a downtown theater that showed nothing but cartoons—on the marquee they'd have, "20 CARTOONS 20." This was before television, where they now have cartoons twenty-four hours a day, it seems. I think we were looking for anything that was visually dynamic and animated. In those days animated cartoons were about the only creative things going on in the commercial film world.

MacDonald: At a certain point, your films began to reflect your interest in Eastern metaphysics. What led you in that direction?

Belson: That's a big question. I was always on the fringe intellectually: Jung, Aldous Huxley, Thielard de Chardin, magic, the occult, et cetera. When I was about thirty-five, I had I won't say a mid-life, but a one-third-life crisis. I was profoundly dissatisfied with everything about myself and my life, and I decided to see if there wasn't another level or dimension to life that I could turn to as a way out. Gradually, I got into hatha yoga, which seemed like a perfect method for tuning the mind and the body to be more receptive, to understand more than just the brute facts of existence. This led to studying other Eastern philosophies.

Up until that time I was a complete agnostic. I had always found religion and religiosity repulsive, actually. I had a friend [Dorsey Alexander] who became very religious in a proselytizing, Bible-quoting way, and whenever I saw him coming down the street, I'd hide in doorways. But eventually I was able to think about spiritual things without cringing.

Yoga was the key to it all. Hatha yoga gives you a system and a very clear, precise technique for developing the spiritual side to your consciousness. It does this through physical exercises, and by various precepts and codes of behavior. I stopped eating meat and became a vegetarian, an extremely important step—but unfortunately, especially at that time, a step out of society. My theory was that if I could refine and perfect myself, I would become a better artist.

MacDonald: When I was looking at your early scroll films, I noticed that at first you were creating these animated *surfaces*, but by the time of *Allures* you've begun to envision virtually infinite space—levels beyond levels. In a sense, this change charts the spiritual development you're talking about.

Belson: That's a good observation. Of course, *Allures* was also a reflection of what was happening in the world at large—in outer space. *Allures* was probably the space-iest film that had been done until then. It creates a feeling of moving into the void. *Re-entry* was also very influenced by the exploration of space.

MacDonald: Recently I re-read Gene Youngblood's description of the Vortex Concerts in *Expanded Cinema*. I had always identified them with mid-sixties psychedelia, and was surprised to find that the Vortex Concerts came before that. They were related to space exploration in a different way: they took place in a planetarium.

Belson: Right. By the time the sixties came around, Vortex was all over. The culmination, I suppose, was taking the show to the 1958 Brussels World's Fair. I don't think we ever recovered from that.

Vortex started in a straightforward way. Back then, San Francisco had a very new and attractive planetarium, Morrison Planetarium, in Golden Gate Park. It had a lot of specialized lighting, and projectors which simulated all kinds of astronomical phenomena in a very smooth way, probably state of the art (Henry

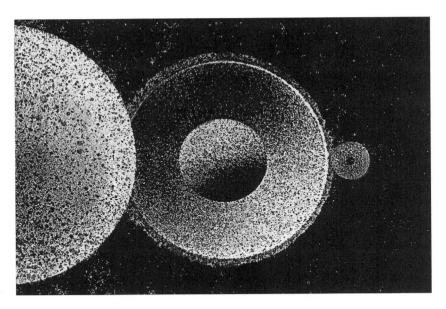

Horizontal Mandala (1952) by Jordan Belson, used in *Mandala* (1953).

Jacobs and I found out when we went to Europe how primitive planetariums over there are, compared to what we have here).

The people at the Morrison were, and I assume still are, quite clever from an engineering point of view, having built their own star projector and other specialized projectors, and they were also quite polished in their performances. They used the full color spectrum in house lighting with a dramatic flair. But for the most part it was all pretty dry, the astronomy lecture kind of thing. Henry Jacobs, who was a composer of electronic music and very informed about what was being done in that field throughout the world, told me in glowing terms that he had discovered what a wonderful theater the Morrison Planetarium was, with a multidirectional sound system, and it would be great if we could put on an electronic music concert there. At first, the idea of using the visual possibilities of the theater was secondary, but when I saw all those great projectors, I changed my mind. We decided to work together and make it an audiovisual concert: electronic music *and* abstract imagery. Henry is a bit of a con man, and he sweet-talked the planetarium people into letting us experiment with their auditorium. They were open to the idea: they were proud of their facility and thought this might be a prestigious way to use it, a way of displaying their smooth astronomical effects and their multidirectional sound equipment, and a way of making more people aware of the planetarium.

MacDonald: Were you well known at the time as a filmmaker?

Belson: Maybe in a very small circle of aficionados my name stood out, but the planetarium people didn't know us from Adam. Henry got them interested. We started out rather modestly with just performances of electronic music over their good speaker system. They gave us a few nights when they weren't putting on their usual show. They'd provide the personnel: the ticket takers, the ushers, and the people who keep the building lit up . . . and parking. The Morrison is right in the middle of Golden Gate Park, easy to get to. It was a rather attractive event. Audiences came, and the program became more and more elaborate. Our demands on the planetarium's engineering department became more time-consuming. They were building special equipment for us. At first, they rather enjoyed the challenge.

MacDonald: How long did it take for the audience to develop?

Belson: It was surprisingly fast. People were ripe for it apparently. This was just on the brink of the era of the light shows and the happenings. The audience was a real cross section of the population. In fact, some of the people were a little too colorful for the planetarium's staff! We had good advertising. We had posters in the streetcars and the buses, and TV newscast coverage—Henry, the PR man once again! It doesn't take much to get the news people out to cover an unusual creative event. The highly respected art and music critic, Alfred Frankenstein, came to one of our early shows and wrote rave reviews in the *San Francisco Chronicle*. It just snowballed, and pretty soon we were getting huge crowds. We had to put on two or three performances a night, when only one was scheduled. People would wait for the hour or the hour and a half it took for a performance, and we'd do it again for them.

In fact, we were so successful that we destroyed the whole thing for ourselves. The planetarium eventually came to feel that *they* were working for *us*. I suppose they felt we were using everything they had developed and stealing their glory. Actually, we weren't just using their effects. Henry went down to Stanford and got the chief engineer at a think tank there to build a special rotary-controlled mechanism which allowed us to whirl the sound around the room smoothly, hence the name "Vortex." The planetarium had the speakers arranged in a circle, but they weren't being used in a rotational way. In those days the effect seemed miraculous.

It was a very important period of discovery for me. Up until that time, all of my films had been animations. This was the first time I used imagery moving in real time, blending images together from various projection sources and creating multiple superimpositions. The house lighting there allowed you to flood the whole dome with any color you wanted, in deep, saturated colors. I remember a simple effect where we made the whole dome very dark red and then we introduced the full starfield into the dark red and gradually faded the red out, leaving only the bright stars against absolute black. It was very dramatic.

The audience would always break into spontaneous applause when they saw it (which never happened in the planetarium's regular shows). And unfortunately, we upset the planetarium's lecturer when we accidentally left the star projector on and rotating overnight and set them back 2,000 years! Then they accused us for the death of some fish in the adjoining aquarium.

Anyway, we used their equipment, but not the way they originally intended, and the star projector was the least of it. We added devices that projected interference patterns over the entire dome, which allowed us to create effects that had people screaming as if they were on a roller coaster. Interference patterns are created when you have two visual patterns that work against each other. I don't think anybody had seen those particular effects at that time. I still have some of the paraphernalia.

I used the effects carefully. I wasn't just blasting the audience psychedelically. It was all carefully composed, and synchronized with the music, so that there was form and shape to each piece. I suppose we would do about eight compositions on a program. For some of the compositions I might do only a mood setting, and for others, something more elaborate. During the two or three years of Vortex Concerts, I did about fifteen full-blown synchronizations to electronic compositions from all over the world—composers such as [Toru] Takemitsu from Japan. Also, I had learned to time images, to fade in and fade out, dissolve, to compose in ways that were very different from anything I had done on film so far. As you know, animation is pretty much one frame at a time. With animation you tend not to think in terms of multiple exposure, dissolves or fades; you don't even need a camera, you can do it all on cards or directly on film. After those synchronizations for the Vortex Concerts, my films started to have a different look, I had found new and more sophisticated ways to produce controlled abstract imagery.

MacDonald: Was *Allures* the first film you finished after that period?

Belson: No. There was a shorter film, called *Seance* [1959], which was done to a composition by Pierre Shaeffer, who taught at New York University, I think. At the Vortex programs we performed a composition of his that I decided would be a perfect soundtrack for a film. I took some of the imagery that I was already working with from the Vortex Concerts and made a film out of it. I recently sent a copy to Anthology Film Archives.

Allures was an expanded version of the same sort of thing. It used imagery I'd been working with for Vortex, and an electronic score that Henry Jacobs and I produced together.

MacDonald: The individual Vortex compositions were eight to ten minutes long?

Belson: Right. Somewhere I've got the programs stashed away.

MacDonald: Do you still have the scores?

Belson: I may have saved my notes on what images to bring in at what point, but I don't think they'd make much sense to anybody else. I made my notes with a fluorescent crayon and read them during the performances under an ultraviolet light so I could see without lighting up the room. It was very complicated because I had to remote control twenty to thirty different projection devices.

MacDonald: I assume no direct records of the performances were ever made.

Belson: No. In fact, filming was not possible because of the extremely low level of light used. If you had walked into the darkened chamber during a performance and looked up, you would have seen absolutely nothing. But people who were already in there, whose eyes had become accustomed to the dark, might be seeing a very vivid, brilliantly lit display. And we could make it very, very dark in there, rock-bottom black, absolute void!

It was such a subtle and beautiful arena for these experiences to take place in, a perfectly smooth hemisphere to project on, perfectly silent projectors that worked by remote control. No smoking, so no beams of light revealed the source of the images. You could create some beautiful and terrifying sensations and feelings there.

I guess we were the first to use planetariums for something other than astronomy.

MacDonald: Tell me about the Brussels World's Fair.

Belson: Vortex in Europe was really very funny. We found out that there was a planetarium on the fairgrounds, and we persuaded some rich people here in San Francisco to give us the money to go. We had been invited to participate in a week of experimental music events. John Cage and other avant-garde composers were there. The planetarium director was under the misguided notion that we were rich Americans. He didn't know we were just penniless opportunists. He seemed to think our presence was going to bring prosperity and attention to the planetarium. The planetarium was already there before the fair was built. It turned out to be an old, neglected, decaying, dingy, art deco building, in the middle of this modern glitzy world's fair, a leftover from an earlier fair in the thirties.

MacDonald: How many shows did you do?

Belson: Two or three, I think. They were a total disaster. We had made the false assumption that we could pick up a lot of the equipment we needed right there in Belgium. But we couldn't even find a roll of electric tape. We had to get some things from the Bell & Howell Company in London because we simply could not find them in continental Europe. And then to make the situation even more absurd, the planetarium gave us an assistant who didn't speak English, and we didn't speak anything but English.

The planetarium itself was very primitive. It didn't have any of the niceties the Morrison had. There was no fade in or fade out, no dimmers. Snap, the lights go on; snap, the lights go off—like in a kitchen! The equipment was all very clunky and antiquated. Instead of knobs that would turn, they had levers that you had to slide up and down. It was like Frankenstein's laboratory. And a deplorable looking cloth dome, all stained. And wooden folding chairs!

To add to the comedy, Henry was out on the Zeiss star projector, rigging up some pieces of our equipment for that night's performance, when I innocently pushed a button on the control panel, and all the lights suddenly went off and I heard this crash. Henry had fallen off the star projector and had hurt himself badly. We had this wild ambulance ride, like out of a Mack Sennett comedy, to the fair hospital, where they taped Henry up—he'd cracked or bruised a rib.

MacDonald: Did you show at other European planetariums?

Belson: We contacted two (Paris, Moscow), but we never got a nibble; actual disdain from Paris.

MacDonald: I first saw your sixties and early seventies films other than *Allures*, when Sheldon Renan presented them at a summer institute at Hampshire College. He made clear to us that the films were more precisely structured than I had realized, though there wasn't time for him to go into the details. Could you talk about how the structures of these films developed?

Belson: In the films I made in the late sixties and early seventies there were specific reasons why I put images together in the particular ways that I did. The films may seem abstract, but if you are familiar with the kinds of subjects I was dealing with, you might see aspects of the images not otherwise evident. However, I wouldn't want to burden viewers with thinking that they have to understand precisely what these images mean to me.

For example, *Re-entry* was based to some extent on John Glenn's first flight into orbit. If you listen very carefully to the soundtrack, you actually hear John Glenn's voice mumbling something about passing over Perth, Australia. The structure of the film begins with leaving the Earth, then goes out into orbit and beyond, glimpsing some aspect of the universe not visible here on Earth—a glimpse of Heaven perhaps—and then comes back to Earth, reenters. At the same time, that voyage is a simile for the transmigration of the soul. *Re-entry* is like a birth experience. In *The Tibetan Book of the Dead* birth is described as a reentry into the world, from outer space, through the mother's womb.

Sometimes I would choose a subject that I was not only interested in, but wanted to know more about. It would take maybe a year to produce a film. During that year, I would study as much as I could on the subject, and eventually the images would arrange themselves in an order appropriate to the subject. *Samadhi* is a good example. I hoped that somehow the film could actually provide a taste of what the real experience of *samadhi* might be like [The definition of *samadhi* varies: in Hinduism, it is a state of deep concentration resulting in a union with, or an absorption into, ultimate reality; in Buddhism, it is the meditative concentration that is the final step of the Eightfold Path].

Usually the subjects I chose to build images around had some kind of traditional form of their own that I found useful in constructing my film. Take *Chakra* [1972], for instance. If you study the chakras (the psychic centers in the body), you find that there are seven of them (there's some disagreement about how many there are, but the general consensus is seven). They're usually depicted as arranged along the spinal column and described starting from the bottom, going to the top. Each chakra has its own unique characteristics, and centuries of elaboration and analysis have accumulated around these characteristics. Whether or not you believe the chakras exist, this tradition and literature do exist and many intelligent people have taken them quite seriously. In *Chakra*, I was able to transfer the traditional order of the chakras into a film, starting with the first (lower) chakra and working up to the seventh (top) chakra.

I based *Light* [1973] on the electromagnetic spectrum: infrared light on one end and ultraviolet light on the other; visible light is in the middle. The order of the spectrum made a perfect storyline—a solid, almost scientific basis—for me to follow in placing my images.

Music of the Spheres [1977] was based on our solar system, the sun in the center and the planets at different distances around it.

MacDonald: Did sound develop in analogous ways?

Belson: Sometimes, yes. While I was doing the soundtrack for *Chakra*, I came across a list of the sounds people have reported hearing when in deep meditation, traditionally about ten sounds. The first is what they describe as the sound of the honey-intoxicated bee. Then there's the sound of a motor and the sound of a bell, the sound of a flute, and the sound of thunder. I just went right down the list, exactly as listed in the book, and put those sounds on the soundtrack to accompany the chakras.

I worked that way for ten or fifteen years, but eventually I did stop. During that period I felt the need to put images together in some meaningful order. In a way, I'm in the opposite camp now. I don't want there to be *any* ideas connected to my images, and if there *are* any there, if anybody sees any, those are entirely in the eyes of the beholder. There is meaning in my newer films, certainly, but if *I* were to speculate on what they might mean, it would be no better, no more accurate, than what *you* might speculate. I have no inside information about them. Even in the earlier films, when I did have specific meanings in mind, I *never* insisted that anybody else see them that way. The films were always meant to stand on their own. Actually, the films are not meant to be explained, analyzed, or understood. They are more experiential, more like listening to music.

People are always asking me how I make my images. Actually, I derived my imagery from many different sources. When I was working on the films, I was always experimenting with anything I thought might produce the kind of imagery I was interested in, anything from lasers, optical printing, liquid crystals to the facilities of an entire TV broadcasting studio. I tried everything. It probably doesn't show, but I didn't want it to show. I tried to be pretty ruthless about eliminating any images where the means by which the imagery was obtained was obvious. I didn't want the viewer to be more aware of the process than of the event taking place on the screen. That's one reason I've never cared to dis-

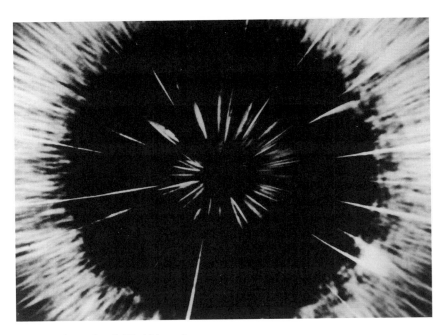

From Jordan Belson's *World* (1970).

cuss my techniques in any detail. I like a convincing illusion. Idle curiosity about how I produce the images can only spoil the experience of the films, as far as I'm concerned. But I will say I used a lot of different source material, there was no *one* way. Although there is a dominance of a certain kind of imagery, I've always tried to include as many different elements as possible. Mine is a composite imagery.

MacDonald: Many viewers probably think you make your films with high-tech procedures. That was certainly the sense I had when I first saw *Allures*.

Belson: Well, *Allures* was no-tech, but I have used some electronic technology. When I worked with Stephen Beck on *Cycles*, his synthesizer was advanced for that time. While I am generally antagonistic to high-tech methods, I admit I would gladly use all that technology if it were conveniently available to me, but high-tech image-making equipment is so outrageously expensive and goes out of date so quickly that you have to be part of a commercial enterprise to use it at all. Many fine artists and technicians are doomed to work only on commercial projects that someone else wants, which is not the same thing as producing works of art on your own.

I remember the first time I was invited down to Silicon Valley to some big research center, a huge operation with rooms full of gigantic computers, each the size of a refrigerator. As I walked down the aisle, I could actually feel the computers sucking information out of my mind. I subsequently realized that that's what they're built for, to draw information to themselves. The operators tend to become extensions of the machines. They don't realize it, but they're like robots. You have to think like a machine, you have to *become* a machine to some extent.

It's not that I don't like computers. In fact, I consider computer art to be the wave of the future. God knows where it's going to go from here. It's hard to believe what they can do already. But those areas were closed to me. My best bet was to work with simple mechanical and optical means that I could handle myself, and to stress individuality, creativity, and artistic finesse. That was the only way I could justify making films. Of course, you can't ignore the course of events. As a matter of fact, I feel somewhat obsolete: the drive of history just keeps moving on, and pretty soon you realize that you're outdated, old-fashioned, technically archaic, when at one time, not so long before, you might have been "state of the art." The avant-garde becomes the rear guard.

MacDonald: I wonder if that combination of Op Art and spirituality that became known as psychedelic art at the end of the sixties, an approach synonymous with San Francisco, wasn't to some extent inspired by your work, *Allures* in particular, which was widely seen.

Belson: Probably it was just the zeitgeist. The Beat era, which here in San Francisco was centered in this neighborhood [North Beach], had already established a tradition of performances of jazz and poetry in the various local bars. Films were shown on occasion, in the bars or on the glass fronts of the bars, and sometimes out in the street. Some events would be well-publicized, and a big audience would show up. Poetry would be read, jazz would be played, and films would be projected. I personally never organized such events, but I allowed my films to be shown.

Allures came along a little later though, and by that time I shied away from the bohemian life around me. I needed to earn a living.

MacDonald: How did your collaboration with Beck on *Cycles* develop?

Belson: Steve was a brilliant young electronics engineer, who I met when he was an artist-in-residence at the Center for Experiments in Television here in San Francisco. I found him to be a compatible personality. And I was particularly interested in his synthesizer. We decided to do a film together. *Cycles* is without a doubt 50 percent his, if not more: he's entirely responsible for the soundtrack. To pay for *Cycles*, Steve made a grant application to the AFI [American Film Institute]. At that time, as recent as it is, film and video were still separate mediums. There was almost no crossover. Our intention was to make a film that was equally film and video, that would combine some of the unique qualities of both.

Cycles is comprised of one sequence repeated twelve times, each time with electronic and cinematic variations. For me, it was another film in which I took an already existing metaphysical concept and tried to illustrate it. The text that we based our continuity on was a book by Sri Yukteswar, the teacher of Yogananda. Sri Yukteswar was a disciple of traditional Indian teachings, but well aware of modern science. His book, *The Holy Science* [Los Angeles: Self-Realization Fellowship, 1974], gives the physical universe a philosophical context. In that book, Sri Yukteswar has a graph of a grand cycle containing all the different periods that human development on Earth goes through. It's been too long since I read this book to tell you the specifics, but I do remember the graph divides history into periods of ten thousand years, each of which has a different level of spiritual development. According to this system, we are in a very low period right now in terms of spiritual development, though we are presumably coming out of it. In *The Holy Science* the characteristics of each individual cycle are explained.

Here, again, truth is not the issue, only the use of an attractive metaphysical concept. Each segment of *Cycles* represents a period in the cycle of human development. I would never tell anybody to look at one of my films for any kind of precise information or spiritual teaching, even though I, myself, may have derived inspiration from sources like this. So to whatever extent it is useful to know where I got my inspiration from, I pass that along.

MacDonald: Your films are more expressions than teachings.

Belson: Exactly. Expressions of ideas and experiences that were meaningful to me. I am neither teacher nor scholar.

MacDonald: How long did you and Beck work together on *Cycles?*

Belson: About two years, I think. It was a rather complicated process. Back then, Steve Beck's direct video synthesizer was one of the few instruments with which you could actually generate images, and it could also do many things to images fed into it. That instrument is what attracted me to Steve in the first place. I've always been attracted by electronic imagery, but it's been my downfall in many ways. I've done a lot of work that hasn't aged very well, because I couldn't resist working with electronic imagery before it was really perfected (although I haven't seen these films for a long time; they may be better than I remember). *Cosmos* [1969] has a lot of early electronic imagery in it that I went through an inordinate amount of trouble to get. I had to rent the facilities of an entire television broadcasting studio in order to get the "key-in" effect I wanted.

MacDonald: The imagery of *Cycles* seems very familiar from your earlier films. Is it fair to say that you suggested the particular type of images, and Beck helped you articulate those with new sound, and new video texture and color?

Belson: If I recall correctly—it's almost twenty years ago now—I put together about a forty-five-second film sequence: there was a ring of fire, and a wave that breaks, and droplets that descend, et cetera—a basic sequence. We took that sequence and other film material and Steve's synthesizer to the film lab that I worked with, where they could film (kinescope) from a video screen. The synthesizer is, or was, about the size of a small piano, so taking it was no simple matter. We ran my forty-five-second continuity through Steve's synthesizer and he would transform it in various ways, while we were looking at it. Using the lab's camera, we recorded as many variations on the sequence as we could. We ended up with twenty or thirty really interesting versions of the original composition. Then we chose twelve versions appropriate to the *Cycles* concept. We were able to augment the electronic variations with representational film imagery, whatever seemed required. For example, there's a forest fire, some electric sparks, some imagery of my street with the TransAmerica pyramid building in the background. We added in those images in the proper places, using a long scroll-like chart to keep track of what we were doing.

Cycles has a rather spectacular ending, the dance of Shiva. Steve had taped a dancer previously and had electronically enhanced the imagery to represent Shiva as Creator, Shiva as Sustainer, and Shiva as Destroyer. I thought the merging of his imagery and mine at that point in the film was particularly effective.

MacDonald: How have you supported yourself over the years?

Belson: Well, usually in a commercial art capacity of some sort. All during the Vortex years, I worked half-time as an engraver at an old-fashioned factory called Bemis Bag Company. I loved that job. I engraved rubber plates for printing on difficult surfaces like burlap. I was so good at it that they allowed me to work there half-time instead of full-time, which the labor unions for some reason always insisted upon—enslaving you for a whole day and ruining your life entirely. So that helped. Previous to that, I had worked in an advertising agency, as an idea man, or "whipping boy," as they called it. They fired me for sadistic reasons, nonconformity or something of that sort. I teamed up with Henry Jacobs: we formed a production company to produce television commercials. People were willing to pay for motion graphics.

MacDonald: Do you remember commercials you did?

Belson: Not really—oh, there was one commercial for MJB Coffee—but it was so off-the-wall that they only showed it a few times. Later, we and a third partner tried to hire ourselves out as graphic designers. Eventually we gave it up and after Vortex I got a job at an envelope company designing letterheads and logos. I did that for two or three years. In fact, I was working there when I got my first grant from the Ford Foundation, and I was seriously torn between wanting to stick with the job, which I'd worked hard to get and keep, or taking the grant. Making films was becoming a bit of a nightmare as far as earning a livelihood goes.

MacDonald: How much did you make from your films?

Belson: In those early days, there was no market for films of that sort. There still isn't actually, certainly not enough to live on. Except for grants, I always had to support myself. After the grants started coming, I did finally give up working at regular jobs and devoted myself entirely to the films, but it was a marginal existence at best. I gave up my last regular job around the time of *Samadhi*.

I lived simply and didn't cultivate any gross materialistic needs. An ordinary person probably couldn't live on what I managed with. I didn't really need too much, but even that was hard to get. Eventually I got to the point where I was earning a fairly steady amount of money for my film work. I had a number of films out, and the distributor, Pyramid, had a wide circulation in schools and universities. They used to send me monthly computer readouts of rentals and sales, and some of those readouts were four or five feet long! There'd be unexpected names, like IBM, buying or renting the films. That went on for about ten years, so I had a fairly steady income, though it never exceeded four or five thousand dollars a year—barely enough to scrape by on. Occasionally I would sell some material to producers making educational films or scientific films. I never really promoted my work. The promotion was pretty much generated by the films themselves. For a while there I did think I was the focal point of the World's consciousness. I was getting letters from all over. People were writing articles, dissertations, lectures, and books about my films. Now I'm looking back and wondering what happened.

MacDonald: You've also done special effects work for commercial films.

Belson: Yes, commercial producers bought some of my material for the science-fiction films *Journey to the Far Side of the Sun* [1969] and *Demon Seed* [1977]. I don't know if you know it, but I *am* the Demon Seed!

MacDonald: How did your material get into that film?

Belson: I don't know much about the director, Donald Cammell. He's British, I believe. He co-directed *Performance* [1970] with Nicholas Roeg, and I remember seeing a picture of him as Osiris in a Kenneth Anger film, possibly *Lucifer Rising* [1974]. Somehow he managed to get a shot at making a Hollywood film. I didn't actually work on that film (although I did design a sequence they didn't use), I just gave Donald permission to go through my footage and use what he wanted. He and his team made a valiant effort to use my material to express the developing emotional states of a giant computer out of control. Of course, it was very hard for them to do the film they wanted; because of the financing, they had to succumb to influences from other powers in the studio— a standard Hollywood story, I guess.

My most important experience of working commercially in special effects was for *The Right Stuff*. I was included in the crew very early in the production—practically right from the start. The entire film, which was made in San Francisco, took about two years and forty million dollars to complete.

MacDonald: How much material did you make for *The Right Stuff?*

Belson: I shot twenty thousand feet of film, about the length of an ordinary feature. Of that, they used about three minutes.

MacDonald: What happened to the rest?

Belson: I have a lot of it here. I had an understanding with Philip Kaufman that when the film was over I could have the workprints or what was left of them. They are in deplorable condition, all chopped up and gummy with tape and crayons and stuff, but there are long sequences in perfect condition that have probably never been projected. Someday I hope to put that material in order. It's a big headache because 35mm takes up a lot of room, which is something I don't have very much of. But it was rather unusual for me to get the material back because that's not the way they do things in Hollywood. Usually when a film is over, everything—workprints, originals, audio—is put in storage in Los Angeles. I don't know what happens to it after that. It all burns up in some big conflagration later, I suspect. But Kaufman was decent about it, let me have my material before they hauled everything away.

MacDonald: Did you have much say in how they used what you did for them, or did they do what they wanted with it?

Belson: That's pretty much it. I was kind of a wild card. The main special effects for the film were done at a place here in San Francisco called Colossal Films. A special division called USFX there was created to do nothing but effects for *The Right Stuff*. Kaufman brought me in as a separate artist, and I suspect Colossal resented that. They weren't very cooperative, and there was a lot of internal friction between the director and the effects department.

It all started when a few years earlier Kaufman had come over to my studio. He was being considered to direct the first *Star Trek* movie [*Star Trek—The Motion Picture*, 1979]. When he came over, that project was in the developmental stage and he was collecting ideas. I showed him my films, and we had a very enjoyable conversation. As it turned out, he did not direct *Star Trek*, and I didn't hear from him again until he was developing *The Right Stuff*. When he first brought me into the project, they hadn't acquired the financial backing that they needed to actually go into production. The producers had put up the money to get the script written and developed, and they were waiting for someone else to come in with the *big* money.

I suggested to Kaufman that I make a 16mm film with a lot of my effects mixed with *Right Stuff*-type material, so he could see if my work would be useful or not. I made the film quickly and called it *The Astronaut's Dream* [1981]. I used a lot of NASA material, rockets taking off, things of that sort, mixed with my material. It came out quite well. I even got a soundtrack together. Kaufman would show it to people who came by the office at Zoetrope. It was a big hit. If nothing else, it entertained the visitors and made them think that something really interesting was happening there.

By that time I was pretty solidly in with the movie, and I was at the office when the word came that financing had been finalized. Everybody gave a big cheer, and Kaufman said, "We're rich!" It turned out to be true. I imagine everybody connected with the film made a lot of money. I made more money than I'd ever made in my life—eventually, a thousand dollars a week, and those weeks would go by so fast that I almost didn't have time to cash the checks! For me, making the money was one of the most exciting parts of the whole experience, and I imagine this is true for most people working in commercial film, because in other ways the process is very frustrating.

MacDonald: What exactly is your contribution to the finished film?

Belson: There's a sequence when John Glenn is in outer space for the first time.

In orbit he saw a phenomenon NASA named "the fireflies," and Kaufman wondered whether I could simulate that. I gave it a try and managed to come up with an effect that worked, so Kaufman was inclined to keep me around to do other effects. By the way, it turned out, as I discovered when I finally saw NASA footage of "the fireflies," that what I had imagined was exactly what the real fireflies actually looked like. I also did most of the views of Earth from outer space. Also, Mach one, Mach two, and rushing effects outside the XI cockpit, and starfields.

Filming in 35mm and seeing my work on the big screen was a surprisingly important experience for me. 16mm was always a little too small. I wouldn't want to make too much of it, but coming as it did towards the end of my film career, I regard it as a peak experience. I still think about it. I suppose in some respects it has something to do with the movie mystique conditioned into me since childhood, but it's odd because when I was making my own films, I was never aware of any connection to the movies. I had even stopped going to the movies.

MacDonald: When?

Belson: In the mid-sixties. I've never been back. Well, I did go back once to see *2001* [1968] and later to see *Demon Seed*. Both terrible experiences, with rowdy, noisy audiences, popcorn, et cetera.

MacDonald: In your recent work—and the more recent, the more true this seems—you've become less involved with focus and concentration within the frame and more involved with the *field* of the frame. Sometimes you hint at circularity: something will be moving through the frame in an arc that implies a much larger cycle, but it's not your focus anymore.

Belson: Right. Eventually I abandoned the intense centralized imagery for more of a spatial landscape-like sensibility. Central and noncentral seem to alternate; the most interesting is when they combine.

MacDonald: When you did *Northern Lights* [1985], did you study the northern lights?

Belson: Not exactly, though I had certainly seen the aurora borealis in photographs many times. I don't remember what inspired me to do that film. After I put it together, I saw that it seemed to be alluding to the aurora borealis all by itself, so I gave it that title. Since finishing the piece, I've seen new aurora footage that makes me realize how close I was to what the northern lights actually look like.

MacDonald: As I studied the *Creation* compilation [an anthology of effects compiled for a PBS documentary, *Creation of the Universe* (1985)], and *Samadhi and Other Films*, it struck me that each of your films is a single, complete work, but it's also raw material for the next work.

Belson: Sure. That's the way I've always worked. I would add, subtract, recombine and constantly reshape and transform the material. Seven or eight layers of imagery is not unusual. Sometimes a complete transformation is possible, electronically or otherwise. An example of what I mean: I was looking at one of my films (on tape) through a crystal ball the other day. Everything was transformed. Because of the curved glass, forms that moved from side to side on the screen now moved from the bottom to the top. There were very dramatic, three-dimensional-looking arches in space, and movements curving and diminishing off into the distance quite convincingly that were not there before. It was, essentially, a new film.

The same thing is true with soundtracks. I'm constantly trying to find the most effective combination of sound and picture. Images that don't look good with one kind of music might look very good with another. Recognizing that all these possibilities exist leads to a certain amount of indecisiveness and inconclusiveness, but on the other hand it leaves the process open for improvement. The imagery is more malleable than you might think. All along, I was constantly tearing my films apart and rearranging them.

Actually, it is a bit confusing because I grew up thinking that a work of art, once it's finished, is sacrosanct, and should not be touched or altered. I used to believe that, but it's definitely no longer true for me.

MacDonald: In fact, we realize now that even if you don't go back and revise films, they're decaying anyway; they're changing on their own.

Belson: Oh, thank you for *that* comforting thought!

MacDonald: In your most recent films, *Fountain of Dreams* [1984] and *Thoughtforms* [1987], you create a strange composite energy in the frame. Things are moving from right to left *and* from left to right *at the same time*. It's as if forces are pulling in opposite directions even though they're part of a single frame of experience. Instead of separating out the yin and yang, it's as though you show them intertwined.

Belson: Yes. One of the electronic experiments I'd like to try involves having those opposite forces meeting and then twisting around each other into a single shape.

MacDonald: I've often thought that films that center the image—whether it's Chaplin being in the very center of the frame, or Griffith centering actors within a symmetrically masked frame, or Fischinger causing circles within circles to come toward you from the center of the frame, or the circle mandalas in *Allures* changing color—are about the spirit (or, at least, reflect a belief in the spirit) while films that use the frame as a kind of porous space through which things move—the Keaton films, for example, where Keaton is often moving through the frame or things are moving toward and past him through the frame, and *Thoughtforms*—are more fully about the material world. Obviously that's a problematic reading . . .

Belson: But you are definitely on to something. I do believe centered, symmetrical imagery pertains more to the spirit.

MacDonald: But your later work is just as spiritual as your earlier work, don't you think?

Belson: Well, what I'm reaching for in these recent films is a combination of the two, an equal degree of inner and outer. I am essentially an artist of the inner image and have been for a long time, even before I realized it. Eventually, I began to have experiences where I could actually see visions with my inner eye that you could legitimately call an *inner image*. This imagery *was* centered, circular, symmetrical—although there are amorphous inner phenomena as well. Most primary forms in nature and in the universe are symmetrical and circular. The planets, the solar system, a galaxy—they're all circular, spherical, and symmetrical.

MacDonald: Although as you move through them, you realize that there are layers upon layers. Your later works' complexity and multi-layeredness is like a different perspective on the same mystery.

Belson: Right. I'm involved with the kind of imagery that has been dealt with in Tibetan art and in some Christian art of the Middle Ages: the windows in Gothic cathedrals, for example. Such circular and symmetrical shapes have always been associated with the quest for spirituality, even to the extent that some people believe that such shapes, mandalas or the designs inside Moorish mosque domes, can precipitate spiritual feeling. It's probably true. There is something magical about circles.

After seeing one of my films, a psychiatrist and professor at one of the local colleges sent me an essay about the soul by the Renaissance astronomer Kepler, who speculated that human consciousness was circular in nature and is derived from the spherical form of the universe itself. If you slice through a sphere at any point, you get a circle. That circle is derived from the sphere, but it doesn't have the dimensions of the sphere itself. In Kepler's view, human consciousness is like a slice of the cosmic consciousness. Kepler maintained that the human soul has retained that circular nature: he calls it a *punctum* (*punctum* means "centerpoint" in Latin). I'm not sure whether he thought of it as a physical organ or whether it was something insubstantial, but real nevertheless. He describes it as circular with a small opening in the center.

MacDonald: That sounds like a lot of the imagery in your earlier work.

Belson: I've known about the *punctum* since around the time of *Samadhi* and have consciously made it a part of my work. The first time I actually saw a *punctum* inside myself, I knew I was dealing with something very real. There *is* an inner sun and it *can be* perceived, but you have to take the time, and you have to have a method. You cannot just say, "I'm going to see it now." You've got to learn how to reverse the senses so that essentially you're looking "in" instead of "out." Meditation, done regularly, is one of the ways of doing this.

Actually, Kepler went further. He explained that the glow, and other phenomena connected to the outside edge of the *punctum*, pertain primarily to physical life, outer life. And phenomena connected with the inner perforated center of the disc are a function of the inner consciousness. This has informed a lot of my thinking. In my life and my art I've always hoped for a perfect fusion of those two realms.

Astronomy has been another of my main influences. Back in the sixties I had this photograph of a beautiful galaxy, perfectly shaped, seen on edge—a dark ring with a glowing nucleus. I put this photograph where I could see it frequently, and as a result I entered into many, many meditations on this galaxy. It taught me a lot about the universe and human life. A galaxy seems to be a living organism of some kind, with a nucleus and vital organs—spherical star clusters that are slightly separate from the main body—which may be vital organs, though you may not recognize them as organs because of their gigantic size. It is also possible that some galaxies are male, and some female. Somehow they're in communication with each other, and they mate in some way, give birth to smaller galaxies which eventually grow larger. Galaxies seem to have individual personalities and temperaments. There are wild and crazy galaxies, and there are peaceful, serene galaxies. Teeming with life of every kind, they appear to be spinning through space like frisbees, perhaps laughing as they go, with us along for the ride. Not necessarily *true*, but thinking about them has provided me with a galaxy-based consciousness instead of an Earth-based awareness, some sense of the Big Picture.

[During the process of interviewing Belson, I spoke with Stephen Beck about *Cycles*.]

MacDonald: I'm curious about your memories of the *Cycles* project.

Beck: I moved out here to San Francisco in 1970, to be an artist-in-residence at the then new Center for Experiments in Television, which was associated with KQED, the public television channel in San Francisco. They had started the center with support from the National Endowment for the Arts, which was a fairly young organization in those days, and the Ford and Rockefeller Foundations. They offered me an incredible opportunity to continue developing my direct video synthesizer.

At KQED, I did TV shows, and I did performances and installations with my synthesizer. Not being in New York, I didn't get early recognition with the first wave of video people, like Nam June Paik, but before long I got invited to do shows and be part of MoMA events. It was an exciting time for me. Later, I gained access to videotape and started working with video as a compositional form.

While I was still at the University of Illinois, I had become a fan of the underground movies that were shown at the campus during the late sixties, usually on Friday and Saturday nights.

MacDonald: Are there particular films you especially remember?

Beck: The underground film shows had quite a mixture of things. There was the poetic work of people like James Broughton. And there were the visualists, as I called them at the time: James and John Whitney—I remember *Lapis* [James Whitney, 1966] and *Permutations* [John Whitney, 1967]—and the films by Oskar Fischinger, Len Lye, Scott Bartlett, and Jordan Belson. It was pretty exciting. A couple hundred people would show up, and for a dollar or fifty cents we'd see two or three hours of fascinating independent film.

I saw a lot of resonance between the non-objective films and the visual experiments I was doing. I made some films of my own at Illinois, filming imagery generated on an oscilloscope screen by an audiotape. Ronald Nameth, a film professor there at the time, and I filmed thousands of feet of oscilloscopic film. I'd sure love to get my hands on a few of the films today. I think they wound up in India.

Recently, I've been very interested in Mary Ellen Bute and her film *Abstroniques* [1954], which was also made with an oscilloscope. Of course, at the time I didn't know about Mary Ellen, and I didn't realize I was following in a tradition.

Before I left Champaign, I had started to do light shows and performances using the oscilloscope films and other optical devices. Those were the days when our technology led the world, and we were doing beautiful things with technology, like going to the moon. But conversely the very same technology was being used in a very destructive and negative way in Vietnam, for which we're still paying.

Being at that time totally in love with technology (and being a musician as I was, and still am), I felt there ought to be some way of using technology in the service of art and beauty. I was formally an electrical engineering student, but I worked my way through school at Illinois by helping to build the electronic music studio, and I hung out with artists and musicians, and started collaborating on performances with some of the musicians there. The idea of the video synthesizer developed out of light shows and the music synthesizers I was building.

Before there was such a thing as computer graphics, the question was, "How could you make an image without a camera?" For my own aesthetics the question was, "I've seen these things inside my mind's eye since I was two or three years old. How do I visualize them?" Later I learned there were such things as phosphenes and eidetic imagery, and wanted to recreate those images using optical light as a medium. And I was fascinated and astounded by what television was technically, and yet how limited it was conceptually. I got the idea to develop a video synthesizer technique and invented circuits that let me modulate the light on a color television screen. I proceeded to build circuitry, mostly analogue circuitry (this was still the precomputer, predigital era), rewiring a color television set so I could feed it my own signals. At first, I fed music into the circuitry to see what it would look like. Friends would come over; we'd get high, and watch the stuff and everybody would go, "Wow, this is great!" And then we'd show it to other people, who weren't high, and they'd also go, "Oh wow, this is great!"

Of course, John Whitney was doing work with the digital computer at IBM, but that wasn't a real-time process. It was essentially point and line graphics generated out of vector display, like an oscilloscope, and filmed one frame at a time. Even those big IBM computers could take a long time to generate the next frame of an animation. I wanted to do more work with color and surface and form, texture and chiaroscuro, and I wanted to do it in real time—just put my hands on these controls and produce images, like playing an organ or piano.

About a year after I came out here permanently in 1970, Jordan Belson called me up. I was delighted. Of course, I had seen Jordan's films and was quite impressed with their composition and flow. I went over to his apartment, and we struck up a friendship. I'd visit him often, maybe once a week. We'd have long conversations about all kinds of subjects. He shared his library with me, a considerable library on mystical subject matter. I was very excited and influenced and motivated by what I saw in his films, and he was eager to try and work at KQED. He came over to the studio and I showed him some of my early compositions: a piece called *Point of Inflection* [1970] and another called *Cosmic Portal* [1971]. And he really liked them. Since I was doing electronically very similar things to what he was doing filmically, it was as if we had a rapport already established.

I think the real reason we hit it off was because we were both less interested in *how* you made these images, than in what they mean, where they come from, and what their psychological and metaphysical implications are. When I used to present work, the question that irritated me the most was, "How did you do it?"—instead of "Why did you do it?" or "What is this all about?"

At a certain point, we started saying, "Wouldn't it be great if we could do some sort of collaboration." I was intrigued with film as well as video, because in working with video you learned right away that there were horrendous limitations. You just couldn't control brightness and contrast and color in video, and there was really no such thing as a VCR. And editing videotape was still tedious and expensive. You had to go into the studios and work with the big equipment and the technicians. It was difficult to create even a simple fade. With film you could just sit there with your little Moviola and there was your film, all gorgeous and beautiful, laid out so that you could vary your approach and work at your own pace.

Jordan and I started speculating about how you might permute and mix film and video images. He was very eager for me to run some of his films through the video synthesizer. I could hook up video cameras to the synthesizer and scan photographic imagery, process it in various ways, and then record it on videotape. So we did some experiments like that. I've still got a couple on one-inch videotape (we did them on two-inch videotape and later I dubbed them to one-inch). We were both very interested in a work that would be a true combination of electronics and optical cinema *and* a blending or balancing of our egos. Directing had been very personal for each of us.

It was suggested to me that if I were to apply for the AFI independent filmmaking grant in 1973 with a good project, I might be lucky enough to receive the award. So we put together our idea for the project, and in fact they awarded us the grant. I think it was the first of their projects that ever involved video. Video art was a radical idea at the time for funding organizations. Our project was unusual in another sense also. In 1973, MoMA invited forty or fifty video artists to the Open Circuit Conference to talk about what was happening in this new medium. I outraged people at that conference by showing film as well as video. It was like heresy. The film people were suspicious of video, and the video people didn't want to have anything to do with film. Of course, I was interested in breaking down those barriers, and this project was a blow to these separatist camps.

So the AFI funded the project on a conceptual basis, and then we had to come up with the actual project. About that time, a good friend of mine, Howard Klein, the arts director for the Rockefeller Foundation (and a wonderful human being: he personally helped dozens of individual artists by giving them grants to pursue their work), and a student of Yogananda, presented me with *The Holy Science* by Sri Yukteswar. It was serendipity: the message finding the messengers.

On page twelve of the introduction to *The Holy Science*, there's a chart on the yugas, the cycles of life—and boom! There it was: the script for the film, all diagrammed!

Of course, the concept of cycles in the film relates to the film reel, which itself is a powerful icon. In video there's also a circular form: the spectroscope displaying the color signal. All in all, there are a number of aspects to this theme of cycles.

MacDonald: Were you and Jordan equal partners in all phases of the process?

Beck: It's very complex. I was bringing Jordan knowledge of electronics and physics, and he was bringing me knowledge of metaphysics. He was exactly twice my age at the time and while some might assume there was a master/teacher relationship, it wasn't like that. We were synergetic, that's all.

From the start we had agreed that the final work would be as much of a fusion of film and video elements as we could possibly make it, and that when it was finally done, we would release it both as a 16mm film print and as a videotape. The process developed like a board game. We'd each put our image down on "the board" and wait for the other's "next move," slowly building up a sequence. And there were hours and hours of conversation and exchange. One day I went over to Jordan's place. We had been struggling with the problem of theme and variation, the nature of the motifs we would use. Jordan showed me twelve icons that would represent the key elements of the basic theme. This led to seven or eight pages of drawings. We drew on musical staff paper, to reemphasize the concept of musical approach. These basic icons were edited together on 16mm positive, and we would modify each element, evolve it with successive passes through the video synthesizer.

One element that was of particular interest to me was the human form. We used the video synthesizer to transform it and reveal its other dimensionalities. Jordan was known for purely abstract, non-objective imagery. You would rarely see anything representational in his work. So our collaboration also involved a combination of representational and photographic elements within a larger non-objective context.

DIAGRAM

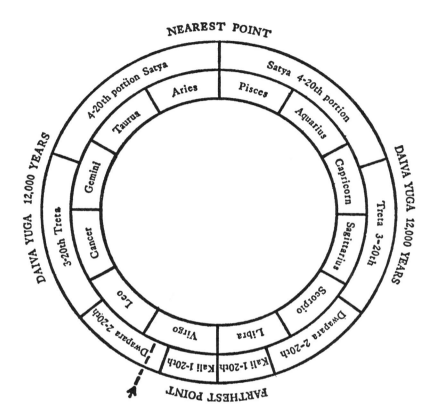

Virgo is the sign opposite Pisces. The Autumnal Equinox is now falling in Virgo; the opposite point, the Vernal Equinox, is perforce now falling in Pisces. Western metaphysicians, who consider the Vernal Equinox to have chief significance, therefore say the world is now in the "Piscean Age."

The Equinoxes have a retrograde movement in the constellations; hence, when the Equinoxes leave Pisces-Virgo, they will enter Aquarius-Leo. According to Swami Sri Yukteswarji's theory, the world entered the Pisces-Virgo Age in A.D. 499, and will enter the Aquarius-Leo Age two thousand years later, in A.D. 2499. — (*Publisher's Note*)

The diagram of the *yugas* in Swami Sri Yukteswar's *The Holy Science*.

I composed the soundtrack after the film was edited visually. The sound-track was a collage of elements. It's hardly what you would call a musical track, although there are musical passages within it: a few bars are lifted from one of the movements of Holst's *The Planets*; and there are phrases of local musicians, and various electronically synthesized sounds. The overall sound structure is based entirely on the visuals.

MacDonald: How long did it take you to put the visuals together?

Beck: We worked on it for well over a year, pretty intensely most of the time. One of the advantages of personal filmmaking is you can take as much time as you like, though you don't want to take too much time because ideas need to be hatched and born before they become overripe. *Cycles* took longer than we thought it would and longer than the budget covered. Altogether it was probably eighteen months from the official formal start of the project until the final prints were released.

Arthur Peleshian

In September of 1990, I had the good fortune to travel with a delegation of American film/video makers, critics, and scholars to Riga, Latvia, where we met with a corresponding delegation from various film centers in the already-crumbling Soviet Union, for a week of screenings, papers, lectures, and discussions. The focus of the meeting (jointly sponsored by International Film Seminars, the organization responsible for the annual Robert Flaherty Seminar; the Latvian Cinematographers Union, the Union of Cinematographers of the Soviet Union, and the American-Soviet Film Initiative in Moscow) was "The Legacy of Vertov and Flaherty in Soviet and American Documentary." It was clear from the films presented by both delegations, however, that for this event, "documentary" had been defined broadly enough to include a wide range of approaches, including some that, at least in the West, would be considered part of the history of avant-garde filmmaking. The Riga event revealed at least one notable irony: the younger Americans tended to admire the formal inventiveness and political commitment of Vertov and to see Flaherty as comparatively reactionary, while the "Soviets" tended to see Vertov as a puppet of the now-discredited Communist regime and to admire Flaherty's individualistic spirit (see Patricia Zimmermann, "Strange Bedfellows: The Legacy of Vertov and Flaherty," *Journal of Film and Video* 44, nos. 1–2 [Spring/Summer 1992], a special issue devoted to the Riga event). And for me, there was one major surprise: that recent "Soviet" filmmakers, working in 35mm in established Soviet film studios, had produced a number of films that, in the United States, could only have been produced by avant-garde filmmakers working in 16mm outside the industry.

I was particularly impressed with the films of Victor Kosakovsky (who presented his 1989 film, *Losev*), Andrei Zagdansky (who presented *Interpretation of Dreams*, also completed in 1989), and Arthur Peleshian, who did not attend the Riga meeting, but whose films, *My* ("We," 1969) and *Vremena Goda* ("The Seasons," 1975) were presented, inspiring a demand by the American delegation for a special trip to the main television station in Riga, where a print of a third Peleshian film, *Nash Vek* ("Our Age," now in two versions: 1982, 1990) was available. From a Western vantage point, all three filmmakers provide critical alternatives to the montage school of Soviet editing, which continues to dominate Western thinking about Russian and Soviet cinema. In *Losev*, Kosakovsky uses extended, rigidly composed, meditative shots to honor the persistence of the Russian Orthodox theologian Losev, who was ordained just before the October Revolution and was able to maintain his faith and integrity through seven decades, until the regime collapsed. In *Interpretation of Dreams* Zagdansky recycles archival imagery to create a skeletal history of Russia and the Soviet Union from the time of the czars until the collapse of the communist regime, accompanied by readings from Freud. While both Kosakovsky and Zagdansky use editing strategies very different from those of Eisenstein or Vertov in order to chronicle the demise of the world that dialectic materialism, and dialectic montage, had helped to construct, the editing of Peleshian's films is in the montage tradition, though he defines his approach as "distance montage," in contradistinction to the collision montage polemicized by Eisenstein.

Peleshian arranges individual shots and sound bites so that while no narrative or polemical continuity is immediately apparent, an overall vision gradually evolves. Images and sounds are repeated, always in new contexts, until the entirety of Peleshian's sense of a subject—whether it's the day-to-day life of farmers and herdsmen in his native Armenia (*The Seasons*) or the global fascination with the exploration of space by Soviets and Americans (*Our Age*)—can be comprehended. Peleshian's films are simultaneously visions of human societies and personal expressions. *Our Age*, for example, is about "our age" of space exploration—and I know of no film that more powerfully communicates the excitement and the terror of sitting in a tiny capsule as mega-thrust lifts a rocket into space—and about human "age." Peleshian turned fifty as he was making *Our Age* and embeds within the film his sense that as we grow older and come to grips with age's relentless "countdown," we desire to "blast off," whether it's in space travel, which allows us to rise above our national identities and see the Earth in all its global expanse and limitation, or in our individual struggles to transcend our limits and our particular historical moment.

I was able to speak to Peleshian (with the assistance of translator Elena Dubrovsky) when Richard Herskowitz arranged for him to visit Cornell Cinema in Ithaca, New York, in June of 1991. The edited transcript was sent to Peleshian, whose corrections were translated into French by Marc Nichanian, and subsequently into English by my colleague at Utica College, Marie-Noëlle Little.

MacDonald: I notice from your biography that you did appliance design before you went into filmmaking. What got you interested in making films?

Peleshian: I was a draftsman and an artist and I liked film very much. I felt that what I wanted to say could be best expressed in film.

MacDonald: Did you see a lot of film when you were young?

Peleshian: Yes. In Russia people go to the movies a lot.

MacDonald: At what time did you see the revolutionary films of the twenties? Eisenstein, Vertov, Pudovkin . . .

Peleshian: I didn't see them until I entered the film institute in Moscow.

MacDonald: *Nachalo* ["The Beginning," 1967] is the earliest film you show now, but I noticed in your filmography that there is also a film entitled *Gornyi Patrul* ["Mountain Vigil," 1964] and another called *Zemlya Ludei* ["Country of Human Beings," 1966]. What kinds of films were they?

Peleshian: *Mountain Vigil* was my first film. I made it when I went back to my home town on vacation. The institute proposed that I do this project and they gave me a theme. In Armenia there's this unusual job: people sit on the mountains and their duty is to see that rocks don't fall onto the train tracks. They maintain the safe passage of the train. The film is about these people. I took this theme and translated it into my own visual language. I made a decision that if this film didn't work, I wouldn't continue at the institute. But it was a success. At the student festival I received a prize.

During my second year I made the film *The Country of Human Beings*, in Moscow.

MacDonald: What was that about?

Peleshian: Everything: such large questions as, "What is this planet?" That film also received a prize at the student festival.

MacDonald: In this country it was very unusual, and still is, for a student filmmaker to be able to make a 35mm film.

Peleshian: At the time it was normal for us, but I do not know what changes have occurred since, though as far as I know students still work in 35mm.

MacDonald: We saw *The Beginning* last night and if I understand it correctly, the title has several layers of implication. It refers to the beginnings of social movements, and to the beginning of a new kind of film history where montage becomes important, and to the beginning of your film career.

Peleshian: It is my beginning, and the beginning of our modern history—a beginning that has no end and that ends with a new beginning.

MacDonald: One could say that in society there is always continuous revolution of one kind or another.

Peleshian: But in this instance, I was referring specifically to the October Revolution. In various instances I incorporated other processes of liberation. Of course, everyone has his own beginnings.

MacDonald: *The Beginning* is about social revolution, but it is also, I assume, your declaration of independence from the history of montage editing.

Peleshian: I didn't realize it at the time, but in that film I was already developing the principles that I was later to call "distance montage," the theoretical explanation that I understood and started to write about after the film *We*. Those principles were inherent from the very beginning, though I was only able to completely recognize them later.

MacDonald: *The Beginning* is more like Vertov and Eisenstein than your other films, and yet very different.

Peleshian: Superficially, on the surface, it's similar, yes. But in the way that everything is organized, it is very different. In fact, this film led some people to believe that my principles were the same as theirs when in fact they weren't. When I began to explain the difference between my style and theirs, the term "distance montage" was born. None of them did what I do.

MacDonald: There's a very unusual technique used in *The Beginning*. We see what is essentially a still photograph, which then goes into motion. That gesture is done over and over during an early passage of the film. It's almost like looking at the beginning of cinema.

Peleshian: I was thinking of my own visual language. I was making an analogy to the way a train starts, gets going, and then stops. The film has its start, slowly it stops and starts, and then eventually the motion is continuous, like a train's.

MacDonald: When you made *The Beginning*, which is almost entirely archival footage, were you inventing that form so far as you knew or did you know of other films made entirely of archival footage?

Peleshian: It's *mostly* archival footage. There is a little bit of my own footage. I used archival footage because it has the impact of fact.

MacDonald: But did you know of earlier filmmakers who had worked with archival footage?

Peleshian: No. I came to the idea myself. People had used archival material, but not in the way I used it. The people at the institute were very shocked, surprised that I had actually used the footage that was available there. It wasn't the thing to do. Furthermore, to try to tell, in ten minutes, fifty years of our history was already a risk, and a first in our film history.

MacDonald: There was a version of *We* that you apparently finished. Then it was shortened. Why was it changed? And by whom? Are there different versions?

Peleshian: I was asked to shorten it.

MacDonald: If you were told to do something, was it required that you do it? Were they asking, or demanding?

Peleshian: Nobody forced me to do anything. There were episodes in the first version that just didn't work.

MacDonald: Were those episodes a problem politically or artistically?

Peleshian: Perhaps both. I don't know. For me it was an artistic problem; for them, perhaps, it was political. I know they were fabulous episodes, but I don't feel I lost anything by cutting them because even in the shorter version, the film expressed what I wanted to say. The editing expresses me.

MacDonald: Once you took out a particular episode, did you reconstruct the film?

Peleshian: Yes. I had to rearrange the entire structure. Because of my method of distance montage, when you take something out, you have to reorganize. If you change one element, you've changed everything.

MacDonald: A question about the title. I assume you are referring to Armenians in particular, but also to everyone, and that the idea is that if you get to the heart of what is most particular about a people, you get to the part of them that unites them with all people.

Peleshian: Yes. The Armenians are simply an opportunity that allows me to talk about the whole world, about human characteristics, human nature. One may wish *also* to see Armenia and the Armenian in that film. But I have never talked about a specific nationality. I would never have allowed myself to do it then, and would not now. If I had meant only the Armenian people, I would not have had the guts to call it *We*. The Armenian people are a "we" that is just a piece of the larger "We."

MacDonald: The form of the film suggests the same thing because we look at separate details but come up with a general response.

Peleshian: Yes. Every specific element, every frame has the genetic code of the whole film. There are no accidental shots or frames. Every particular element has been thought out and is representative of the whole.

MacDonald: How long does it take from the time you have footage for a film until you are finished editing?

Peleshian: I started *We* in May and by November the long version had been finished. And because they asked me to shorten it, I lost another half-year in editing.

MacDonald: Do you work full-time on the editing?

Peleshian: During that film I don't remember sleeping. I stayed at the studio and worked when no one was there. I'm doubtful I could do the same now; I was young then.

MacDonald: Was it widely seen?

Peleshian: By professionals, by my instructors, at festivals. People in the field knew about it, but it wasn't screened much. Right after that film I received my diploma from the institute. Many people liked it, but at the same time, they were doubtful about it because it was so unusual.

MacDonald: All your films are about people and the environment, but *Obitateli* ["The Inhabitants," 1970] and *The Seasons* seem particularly focused on that issue. What led you to make *The Inhabitants*, your film about animal life?

Peleshian: Many people were offended or insulted by *We*. After that experience, I was mad at mankind and decided to make a film about animals. Animals don't get upset, but at the same time, by focusing on them, I could say the same things as I was saying about people.

MacDonald: Am I correct that both *We* and *The Inhabitants* are partially archival footage and partially shot by you?

Peleshian: There is very little archival footage in *The Inhabitants*.

MacDonald: You are one of the very few filmmakers I have ever seen who uses the whole screen. Often you cover the entire screen with a particular kind of design.

Peleshian: I'm always very aware of composition. It's a very important component of putting the whole film together. There shouldn't be any extra compositional elements. Compositions should be detailed, specific—like soldering, or like the things a jeweler does with pieces of jewelry. The images had to be very full, but very carefully composed, without anything superfluous.

MacDonald: I assume the title of *The Seasons*, like *We*, has multileveled implications. It can mean the seasons of the year, but also the seasons of life: youth, middle age. I assume that since you were getting toward middle age, you were becoming more conscious of the whole life cycle.

Peleshian: Again, I was thinking of *everything*. It's not specifically the seasons of the year *or* of people: it's *everything*. One should not forget that this film's main "heroes" are not the people, but the seasons and nature. It is not man who imposes himself upon nature, but rather nature that imposes itself upon man. The film is about the interrelationship between man and nature.

MacDonald: Do you think of your films as, to some extent, a map of your own personal experience, as gauges of where you are in your life during certain periods?

Peleshian: Automatically, they probably are, yes. I don't specifically want to talk about myself, but inevitably it happens.

MacDonald: You mentioned last night that in your process of constructing a film you begin at both ends and work towards the middle. Do you always do that?

Peleshian: Yes. Even if I don't set up a beginning *and* an end, when I do the beginning I have the end in mind. I always begin thinking of the ends, and I slowly build into the center from both ends.

MacDonald: Do you always wait until you have all the visuals and all the sounds before you begin to edit?

Peleshian: It'd be best if I had everything; it'd be the ideal. Ideally, all the details, all the aspects, both sound and picture—everything should be in my pocket. Then if I do have to make changes, they're very small. If I don't like what I have when I start editing, if it doesn't work the way I'd ideally like it to, then I look for other things. To create the sound for *The Inhabitants*, I put together thirty different tracks.

MacDonald: The sound seems as fully layered and montaged as the imagery.

Peleshian: Even more than the image. A lot more. At times, the sound takes on the role of the picture. The picture takes up space; the sound works but takes up no space.

MacDonald: You mean the sound is an environment within which the image is a graphic space.

Peleshian: Yes. In my films the image can take the place of the sound, and the sound can take the place of the image.

MacDonald: You use many different techniques in every film, but in *The Seasons* in particular, you do mirror-printing. Is that because you want to emphasize the verticality of the mountain region that's the focus of the film?

Peleshian: It's the verticality *of the film* I'm most interested in, not the verticality of the mountains. It's a symmetrical film. Mirror printing gives the film a center. If the viewer should incline in one direction, the mirror image then balances from the other direction. The film creates a center of gravity for the viewer. If you build an architectural tower, it always has a center of gravity. Any skyscraper in New York has a center of gravity; that's what keeps it from falling.

MacDonald: Don't you think that it's particularly appropriate in *this* film since gravity is so central for these people? There's a scene where the mountain people use gravity to pull the haystacks down the mountainside.

Peleshian: Yes. Their duty is not only to drag the hay down but to stop it before it goes too fast. But that principle is not specific to this film. It is in all my other films. It only happens that one notices it more in *The Seasons*.

MacDonald: More and more as we talk, I realize that all your films are simultaneously about people and also about film itself. And what you're saying about people is, on another level, what you're saying about film. For instance, in *The Seasons* we see, over and over, the shot of the man and the sheep going down rapids in a river. On one level, the shot reveals something about life in Armenia, but it also seems a comment on the editing process itself, which produces "rapids" in the "stream" of the filmstrip.

Peleshian: Yes and no. For this very reason I was doubtful about this interview, because we need very specific, technical vocabulary, terminology, to be able to really get into the films. It's hard to talk about them in plain language. For me, distance montage opens up the mysteries of the movement of the universe. I can feel how everything is made and put together; I can sense its rhythmic movement. I believe that the solar system is based on the same principles as distance montage. I'm convinced about this. I hope I don't sound pompous, but that's what I think.

We all know time. It's like a bacteria and it's killing us. I feel that my distance montage destroys this bacteria and approaches absolute time.

Armenian farmers bringing a haystack down a mountainside, in Arthur Peleshian's *Vremena Goda* ("The Seasons," 1975).

MacDonald: Which is clearly the subject of *Our Age*.

The first time I saw *Our Age*—it was the long version—I was overwhelmed. Last night the shorter version created the same experience: I realized that the film affects me because in a sense it's about me. One of the central motifs is the rhythm of the 10, 9, 8, 7, 6, 5, 4, 3, 2, 1 countdown that leads up to the launch of the rockets. Often, this rhythm dissolves into the sound of a heartbeat. I assume one implication is that the pressure of our personal time running out as "our age," our physical age in years, increases, leads us to "launch" projects that may seem beyond us. As our time runs out, we want to transcend "our age"; and the nature of "our age" is determined by the kinds of transcendent "launches" we tend to instigate.

Peleshian: Yes, we want to go to absolute time. At first, I wanted to give this film a different name—a name that would suggest a foreign or strange territory where there is no time. But finally I decided to give it a title that is about us, about me. It's about what I'm striving for, what we're all striving for—every person, humanity. But the wishes and desires of the people to ascend, to transcend, are literally carried out by the astronauts. That's the role they play in society.

MacDonald: Why are there two versions of the film?

Peleshian: I don't know why. I just wanted to have two versions.

MacDonald: Last night you were talking about distance montage and how, after a certain point, the spectator hears things that aren't there. I know what you mean: I hear that heartbeat and the time counting down throughout the film, even when it's not actually on the soundtrack. And sometimes I can't tell whether I am really hearing it or remembering it, imagining it.

Peleshian: Yes. The power of distance montage is that even if something that's part of the whole isn't there at a particular moment, you feel its breath. Distance montage is capable of making what is absent present.

MacDonald: How much of the footage in *Our Age* is archival?

Peleshian: I shot most of it. The shots of American astronauts are archival, but I shot all the material of the Russian cosmonauts. I became very close friends with the cosmonauts. They liked me very much, and they liked the film very much also. For some reason they believed in me, and I know that *Our Age* is their favorite film about them. It accurately portrays the cardiogram of their lives.

MacDonald: *The Seasons* was made in 1975 and the first version of *Our Age* was finished in 1982. That's a seven-year break. Were you working on other people's films during that period?

Peleshian: Film is difficult to make. There are so many things involved. You get this idea and, if you want to make a film about astronauts, you have to develop a plan, you have to organize what you're doing. Filmmaking takes so long because there are inherent problems that go along with it, especially with what I do. Some animals give birth every nine months and others give birth every seven years. I happen to be of the second sort.

MacDonald: Maybe you're getting to be a larger animal as you grow older.

Peleshian: It's fate. I prefer to make fewer products but to make them better.

MacDonald: In the United States people who make films that are formally ingenious, "experimental," are often considered a little crazy or at least impractical and "elitist," not only by audiences but by other filmmakers. Is the filmmaking community in the Soviet Union supportive of your work?

Peleshian: Yes, they have always defended me. I don't know about America, but in our country, nobody has ever considered an experimental filmmaker "crazy."

MacDonald: What are you working on now?

Peleshian: Two films: one is called *Konets* ["The End"], the other, *Zhizn* ["Life"].

MacDonald: *The End* is about death?

Peleshian: No. This film too is about life. It is about man, time, what is eternal and what is temporary; it is about change.

Before we finish, I want to try to be a little clearer about distance montage. Distance montage and the effects that it creates evolve like a sphere. It's not linear, it's spherical. It's in continuous motion. If I find the system, if I construct it correctly, it will go, it evolves, and two processes will occur: you will go from the beginning of the film to the end *and* there will be a mirror effect; you will also go the other way. Central elements may never meet each other; they run parallel to each other, always looking for each other, but they never meet. But they exist together constantly, independently. They love each other and they look for each other, but they can never be together. They are always striving toward each other, but the territory changes constantly.

MacDonald: D. W. Griffith increased the pace of editing to excite and engage the viewer. In the Soviet Union in the twenties, montage became a way of emphasizing Marxist ideology: a montage like the Odessa Steps sequence in *Potemkin* could become a central metaphor for the ideology in the film. You've gone further. You've elevated montage into a complete film. It's not *in* a film, it *is* the film. In Eisenstein there is story, a montage, story, a montage, story, a montage. A Peleshian film *is* montage.

Peleshian: Eisenstein's montage was linear, like a chain. Distance montage creates a magnetic field around the film. It's like when a light is turned on and light is generated around the lamp. In distance montage when the two ends are excited, the whole thing glows. Sometimes I don't call my method "montage." I'm involved in a process of creating unity. In a sense I've eliminated montage: by creating the film through montage, I have destroyed montage. In the totality, in the wholeness of one of my films, there is no montage, no collision, so as a result montage has been destroyed. In Eisenstein every element *means* something. For me the individual fragments don't mean anything anymore. Only the *whole* film has the meaning.

Distance montage allows you to defeat time. Take *The Beginning* and *The Inhabitants*, for example. Both films are ten minutes. To see *The Beginning* you have to watch ten minutes from the beginning to the end, so you've lost ten minutes. But in distance montage when you reach the end, you're also back at the beginning. That which would have taken twenty minutes, you have done in ten. The experience develops spherically and the speed was twice what it seemed. This is very important for distance montage. You go from this point to that in ten minutes, but at the same time, you're going from that point back to this without losing a moment. And the effect is that the film *revolves*; it is "revolution" in a new sense.

This is a primitive explanation. In fact, distance montage is much more complicated. Orbits are created. Sound and image cross each other, intersect each other, switch, change territories. The sound enters the territory of the picture and the image enters the territory of the sound. You start to *see* the sound, and you *hear* the picture. Physically, a particular image or sound may no longer be perceived, but because of your memory and distance montage, it *is* still there. It's like water boiling in a kettle: you see that the water boils and turns into steam, and you feel the warmth on your body; you no longer see the water, but you feel its presence. The same thing happens with the picture; it boils, boils, boils until it turns into steam.

If we're being clever with our metaphors, I would want to say that whereas

Eisenstein saw editing as a means to get from *here* to *there*, I see editing as a means for seeing *where we are*. In other words, with Eisenstein there are two bodies with only one head, whereas with me there is only one body that has two heads, very far from one another, and looking in opposite directions.

MacDonald: Thank you for your patience with my questions.

Peleshian: I've tried to simplify things to get ideas across. But my films are precisely *not* about language, about verbal communication. The difficulty is that one cannot express with words what one finds in my films. If it were possible to say it with words, the films would be useless. Words *cannot* express it. One should not talk about films, one should watch them. This is why I have always been against interviews.

Charles Burnett

The denigration and exclusion of black America has been so central and so public a part of the history of the American film industry that when African-Americans have had anything like an opportunity to respond, they have usually used this opportunity to offer competing products to the largest audience available to them, which has usually been the underserved African-American movie audience. The earliest attempts to develop a cinema representative of black America—the trilogy of projects conceived by Booker T. Washington and Emmett J. Scott: *Lincoln's Dream, Up from Slavery*, and *The Birth of a Race* (this one film was completed in 1918)—were aimed at raising the consciousness of the huge audience that had made D. W. Griffith's *Birth of a Nation* (1915) a household name. But the black underground cinema that developed following the failure of *The Birth of a Race* at the box office aimed its products at the network of theaters that was developing to serve a population excluded from the white mainstream (see chapters 3 and 7 of Thomas Cripps, *Slow Fade to Black* [London, Oxford, New York: Oxford, 1977]). In general, while the black underground cinema was, at least in some cases, financially independent of Hollywood, it did not offer critical alternatives in terms of style and structure: in general, these films seem to have echoed many of the themes and plots of Hollywood film and its visual rhetoric. Their critique seems to have been primarily at the level of peopling films with black actors and actresses. Of course, there may have been exceptions, particularly in the films of Oscar Micheaux, whose work sometimes seems to reveal a campy self-awareness of the inevitable results of his limited financial resources, an awareness prescient of the "trash filmmakers" of the 1960s and 1970s.

In any case, the demise of the black independent cinema in the late 1940s and the limited integration of a black presence, first in a series of Hollywood "problem pictures" and subsequently in Hollywood commercial filmmaking in general, did little to change this basic pattern. Indeed, nothing changed it until the 1980s, when the emergence of an expanded African-American audience and a determination in the industry to exploit this audience brought a group of young African-American filmmakers, many of them graduates of major film schools, into prominence: Charles Burnett, Julie Dash, Charles Lane, Spike Lee, Robert Townsend, John Singleton, Mario Van Peebles, Carl Franklin, Bill Duke, and others. While these filmmakers have been dedicated to narrative feature film and are schooled in mainstream film rhetoric, they have often used their opportunities to attempt new approaches to the representation of American society. The two most notable directors in this regard are Spike Lee and Charles Burnett.

While Lee and Burnett are very different filmmakers, both have achieved a measure of commercial and critical respect, while simultaneously seeing some of their more inventive accomplishments widely misunderstood and underrated. Lee's films are so energetic and his public persona so visible that the subtlety of his hip-hop expressionism, especially in the films where he deals directly with tensions between ethnic groups—*Do the Right Thing* (1989) and *Jungle Fever* (1992)—has been generally ignored. In each of these films, Lee's expressionism is a means of drawing viewer attention to the production process in order to keep viewers aware that Lee's experience in *making* the films (a constructive, economically productive, multi-ethnic activity) models an answer to the inter-ethnic hostility that regularly destroys economic opportunity and human life in the worlds depicted *in* the films. If Lee can work with a multi-ethnic cast and crew to create viewer sympathy for blacks *and* whites (indeed, my informal polling of my classes has consistently revealed that in both films, Lee creates at least as much sympathy for white characters—for Sal and Vito in *Do the Right Thing*, for Angela and Paulie in *Jungle Fever*—as for black characters), why can't other filmmakers do the same?

In *Killer of Sheep* (1977), Burnett devised a strategy related to Italian neorealism: he used his own neighborhood as his location and his friends and neighbors as cast and crew to create an effective and memorable representation of an aspect of LA life—and implicitly an ironic critique of American society. Roberto Rossellini and Vittorio DeSica were forced to resort to neorealist tactics as a result of the economic devastation of war; Burnett is forced into the approach through the economic devastation of "peace"! At the same time, Burnett creates both a sense of the deprivation in the lives he reveals and a demonstration that this deprivation is continually being transcended. Virtually every incident in *Killer of Sheep* can be read on several levels simultaneously. One of the most memorable moments in the film occurs outside a grocery store just before Stan (Henry Gayle Sanders) and Gene (Eugene Cherry) arrive to cash a check. We see four adults sitting in a car, filmed from directly in front of the car. The two men and two women, who seem in high spirits, appear ready to drive away, except for the fact that a can of beer is sitting on the hood of the car. Burnett extends this shot just long enough so that viewers have time to wonder if these people are going to drive off with the beer in full view on the hood, when the person sitting in the driver's seat reaches through what we have assumed is a windshield and takes a drink of the beer. The action transforms our sense of the shot entirely: what was a vehicle with passengers ready to leave on a pleasure trip becomes an abandoned wreck that, like so many of the people we meet in *Killer of Sheep*, is going nowhere. And yet, as disheartening as this recognition is, there is also an upbeat dimension to it: these people have managed, at least for a moment, to turn deprivation and immobility to their advantage—they are enjoying themselves in the car, albeit not in the way they might choose. Further, Burnett has created a memorable moment of magic and humor that undercuts any desire on the viewer's part to indulge in merely feeling sorry for the people living in this neighborhood.

The implications of this incident and many similar incidents are reconfirmed near the end of *Killer of Sheep*, when Stan and his wife (Kaycee Moore) and daughter (Angela Burnett), Gene and his wife Dion (Dion Cherry), and their friend Bracy (Charles Bracy) pile into Gene's car to go to the racetrack. Their excitement is infectious (it is their, and our, first trip out of the city during the film) but short-lived: a flat tire and Gene's lack of a spare brings the trip to an end, and the car hobbles back toward Los Angeles. But the very inability of these people to get where they want to go is transformed when Bracy bawls Gene out for not having a spare: Bracy's frustration (exacerbated by his confidence that he has a "nag" that's "sure to come in") expresses itself this way: "Man, I'm out here singin' the blues, got my money on a horse [that] can't lose. You out here on a *flat*. I always told you to keep a *spare*, but you's a *square*; that's why you can't keep no spare. Now, how we gonna get there, huh?" The rhythm and rhyme of Bracy's speech is made particularly emphatic by Burnett's decision to accompany the speech with a passage of music that synchs together with Bracy's words. Throughout *Killer of Sheep*, Burnett accompanies the seemingly endless round of day-to-day activity with a history of African-American contributions to American music. The "synching" of Bracy's complaints with the soundtrack, following what at first seems the film's most optimistic scene, is a way of demonstrating that the blues, pop, jazz, and classical music we've been hearing are not only appropriate accompaniments to the actions we've watched, but that the frustration in African-American life caused by the lack of social mobility (and represented by Gene's flat tire and lack of a spare) has created, *has necessitated*, these musical contributions.

Killer of Sheep is Burnett's response to the frustrations of his world, and in particular to the limitations he is confronted with as an African-American filmmaker interested in depicting and interpreting what he has experienced. Like

Bracy's speech, it is both an index of the societal limitations that Burnett has faced, an explicit and implicit critique of these limitations, *and* a transcendence of them. That it is the first film by an African-American filmmaker to be accepted into the Smithsonian Institution's film preservation program, and that it was accepted the same year as Griffith's *Birth of a Nation*, gives particular poignancy to this transcendence.

In the twenty years since he completed *Killer of Sheep*, Burnett has finished four features—*My Brother's Wedding* (1983), *To Sleep with Anger* (1990), *The Glass Shield* (1995), and *When It Rains* (1996)—and he has collaborated with other filmmakers in a variety of ways. If none of his subsequent features is the equal of *Killer of Sheep, To Sleep with Anger* is very close, especially in its demonstration of Burnett's willingness to see the psychological and emotional complexity of African-American life and, implicitly, to critique the tendency, even of African-American filmmakers, to exploit the drug trade. *The Glass Shield*, Burnett's first attempt at a more conventional film, is an intense but confusing film noir about a young black cop lost in and finally betrayed by the moral vacuum of an otherwise white Southern California police station (the film is based on a real incident). Like the main character, Burnett seems trapped in *The Glass Shield* between the demands of his personal commitment and the expectations of him on the part of the white "precinct" of Hollywood filmmaking. Indeed, it is tempting to see *The Glass Shield* as Burnett's psychodrama, the way we can now read Buster Keaton's *The General* (1926) and *The Cameraman* (1928) as psychodramas of his loss of power in Hollywood.

I spoke with Burnett in April 1992 in New York, and again in August 1994 in Los Angeles, just as he was seeing *The Glass Shield* into distribution.

MacDonald: When I first saw *Killer of Sheep*, I liked it, but I also patronized it. I thought it was a pretty good film—neorealism applied to new territory. Later as I used it in courses, I realized it was more subtle than I had noticed. Now, there's hardly a moment I don't find pretty amazing. I'd be interested to know the background of the film.

Burnett: I was at UCLA at the time. *Killer of Sheep* was my thesis film. I had been in a political study group that was making films about working-class people, about exploitation in the workplace, things like that. And most of the films were very formula-like: the shop management exploits workers, the workers get together and form a union, they strike, and so on. Some of the students wanted to make films about resolving problems within the workplace, as if that's all that was necessary. Most of the kids who were making the films were from the upper middle class, and some were rich kids playing at film with no idea how the working class lived. I come from a working-class environment, and I wanted to express what the realities were. People were trying to get jobs, and once they found jobs they were fully concerned with keeping them. And they were confronted with other problems, with serious problems at home for example, which made things much more difficult.

Then I realized that even though you're from the community, once you go to the university, your whole outlook changes, and you wonder if you can still say that you speak for the community you came from. I remember I was in the barbershop I still go to. There was a Paul Robeson Day coming up, and I was thinking that everyone in his right mind would be sympathetic to what Paul Robeson did, particularly people in Watts because of how things were there economically and how people suffered because of the Watts riots and the fact there were no major stores—department stores or food stores—in Watts at the time. So I was talking to the barbershop owner about Paul Robeson, and I found he admired Robeson for his art, but not for his politics. I was surprised. I came to realize that there are a lot of conservatives living in Watts.

MacDonald: They thought Robeson was too leftist?

Burnett: They thought he shouldn't have said anything negative about his country. There was a generation of people, an older generation, who had a notion of "not making waves," people who had been involved in the Civil Rights movement, including some of the shop owners in Watts. They thought of the American flag as the symbol of freedom. For them it was bad to disrespect the American flag and to renounce the government.

Another time, a friend of mine was involved in a murder and was being sentenced; he could have gotten the gas chamber. I was with his family and a bunch of us kids who had all grown up together, and they were thinking that he was going to be let out because, even though he had robbed the store, he had already left the store when the store owner came out with a gun. The store owner was killed in an exchange of gunfire, and it was my friend's belief, and his family's and his friends', that he shot in self-defense. If the store owner hadn't come out with a gun, he would not have been shot. *I'm* saying, "Yeah, but *he* started it, he robbed the store." There was this chasm, this split, between me and the others. So even having had direct experience with the working class, going to UCLA changed my outlook. I no longer represented the people I'd grown up with.

There was this big notion in the sixties and seventies that if you're out in public, you have to represent the "Black People," to speak for the "Black People." We found out how untrue that was because in different communities people had different realities and agendas. People in the South Bronx and Harlem live differently, and so the best you can do, and there are problems with this too, is to speak in terms of regional realities. A film can't do everything for everybody.

MacDonald: How early did you know that you wanted to make films? Did you have support from your family and friends, and in school?

Burnett. No. Maybe because I had a speech problem—I still have it, more or less [Burnett stutters]—I never really felt part of the gangs. In the long run, that

had a lot to do with my taking a different road. My grandmother *was* supportive, but the schools I went to were just *awful*. When I was in junior high, instructors would point out the students who weren't going to be anything:
"*You're* not going to be anything, and *you're* not going to be anything!"

When I got to high school (Freemont High), the freshman class was assembled in the auditorium, and I remember the principal explaining how many people were going to drop out. It was horrible, but it turned out to be true. Our freshman year, the auditorium was packed, but when my class graduated, there weren't
enough of us to fill the *stage*. The dropout rate was incredible; and in many ways,
the school encouraged it. There was nothing there for a student to do; and in general, the people at the school made you feel that they were doing you a favor.

The only people who got respect at that school were athletes, and Freemont
had great athletes, the best in the country. And, strangely enough, there was a
good debating department.

MacDonald: So what gave you the idea you could be a filmmaker?

Burnett: Well, I'd always wanted to play with cameras, but never had the
chance and didn't think much about it. I guess I was ready to go to Vietnam,
like everybody else, and was waiting for the draft. A friend of mine, Charles
Bracy, was planning to go to LACC [Los Angeles Community College]. I visited the campus and liked the way it looked; it was quaint, with ivy and old
buildings, really nice—not the way it looks today. We went up there to enroll,
and they said, "OK, come," so I went.

I was interested in electronics and was thinking about becoming an engineer, but I got disenchanted with that. You had to specialize, which I didn't like;
and, added to that, I met some engineers who came in to take refresher courses;
their biggest concern was security and having, after twenty years on the job, a
three-week vacation. It just didn't seem like an attractive life.

I started taking creative writing classes. I don't know how I got into that, but
there was a wonderful teacher at LACC, Isabel Ziegler, who edited a magazine
called *Ante*. She was well known as one of the best teachers around; the way
she taught class just pulled me in—at that time, I had *no* idea of becoming a
writer. I took her course, then I audited it, like everyone else did. Most people
there were auditing the class.

One of the good and important things about a city college, as opposed to a
university like UCLA, is that you get working-class people of various ages and
varied experiences.

At the time, I was working at a library downtown and going to the movies a
lot, and I got interested in making movies. I inquired about studying at USC,
but it was too expensive; you had to *have* money before you could get a loan.
When I applied at UCLA, they said, "Sure come on over!" So I did. I'm glad I
went to UCLA because the program developed you as a total filmmaker.

MacDonald: Did you take film history as well as film production?

Burnett: Oh yeah. Not so much because it was required, but because I was trying to extend my stay at UCLA; it was the cheapest place to make movies. At the time, it was like eighty dollars a quarter to enroll, and you had access to everything for eleven weeks. It would have cost many times that outside of school, so I just exploited the system. I really got my money's worth. A lot of film students there were doing pretty much the same thing. It was a good time to be a filmmaker.

MacDonald: Recently, the term "LA Rebellion" has been applied to you and other black independent filmmakers during that period. Was that term used at the time?

Burnett: Well, no. You know scholars: they have to unify everything and give it a name. But those times in the sixties *were* rebellious times. The Civil Rights movement led to the ethno-communications program at UCLA, which was a reaction to the film department's not including minority groups. The ethno-communications program brought in minority people who were trying to make films that dealt with *their* world and *their* vision, as opposed to entertainment. I think everything we did was an attempt to respond in our own way to this previous outsider status and lack of participation.

I know I got into doing films because I wasn't happy with the people I saw on the screen. I just couldn't identify with the stories or the characters. A lot of us were trying to develop our own cinema in reaction to the conventions. It *was* conscious to a certain extent, but it wasn't like we were wearing T-shirts and carrying banners saying, "We're the LA Rebellion!" We did try to form an organization a number of times, but it never worked out. I personally didn't think of us as a solid front. We were a bunch of individuals who wanted to go in our own directions. It's only looking back that you can find a pattern, and something of a movement.

MacDonald: Your first film, *Several Friends* [1969], was made at UCLA?

Burnett: All the films up through *Killer of Sheep* were made there. *Several Friends* was a class project. Generally we had to work together and share equipment, especially because of the number of minorities coming into the department. It wasn't just Julie Dash and myself and the Black Rebellion. Visual Communications, the Asian group, came out of that period, and the Chicano Coalition. Haile Gerima, Clyde Taylor, and Teshome Gabriel came a bit later and injected a lot of energy. A theoretical approach began to emerge and the whole idea of black film aesthetics. The study group I mentioned was reading Ian Watt and Georg Lukacs and the Russian critics. But in terms of having a real "renaissance," where a group of filmmakers sit down and work out problems through discussion and filmmaking—like the Harlem Renaissance writers did—we're still seventy-five years behind, and we get further behind by the day. Filmmakers don't have the kind of community novelists and poets have sometimes had.

MacDonald: And there hasn't even been a journal where black filmmakers seriously debate issues over a long period of time.

Burnett: Right. Critics do the talking, and we do the listening! I remember Teshome and I getting into an argument. I disagreed with him about an interpretation of my film, and he said that once a film is done, it's no longer the film-maker's: it's up to scholars to interpret and tell the filmmaker what he means. I said, "Oh yeah?!" I definitely disagreed with *that*.

MacDonald: I understand that *The Horse* [1974] was adapted from a Faulkner story.

Burnett: No. I *was* into Faulkner at the time, and *The Horse* was an attempt to do something in the Faulkner vein. I was waiting for another project to develop, and I had a little money to do something while I was waiting.

MacDonald: It feels so different from your other work—because of the country location, I guess.

Burnett: Believe it or not, it won a little prize at Oberhausen. I took a chance on the actor who plays the owner; he was from Canada and had nothing to do with the South. I'm not sure he works for me. The other actors were just friends.

Did you notice, there are *two* horses? We had to go back up to the town, where we were shooting, *every day* because this actor couldn't stay over-night—I don't remember why. Anyway, we had to drive two hundred miles back into town, then get up in the morning and drive back out there. It was so dumb. We used this broken-down old horse for the first couple of days of shoot-ing. We left as usual, and the lady thought we were finished and sent him to the glue factory! To finish the film, we had to borrow the only horse available, a young colt, black and frisky. It was ridiculous, but those are the kinds of prob-lems you have making independent shorts.

MacDonald: The film is a little surreal for me. The landscape is so Califor-nia, but all the accents are Southern.

Burnett: I was hoping people didn't know too much geography.

MacDonald: When you began work on *Killer of Sheep*, which uses the neo-realist tactic of placing actors within a real environment, how much of the film was scripted?

Burnett: It was *all* scripted. *All* of it. Because of economics. I wanted it to look like a documentary, or as close to a documentary as possible. Realism was an issue then. UCLA had a sort of radical stance toward conventional filmmaking. Anything that was "Hollywood" was suspect. The idea was to come up with something new. We talked a lot about the idea of Truth. How can you do a film that represents the real experiences of real people? The only way I could find to give a sense of reality was to film so that it looked like you were just there with the camera. If you had a plot, it had to be something other than some simple situation that was resolved at the end of the film. But it wasn't until after the film was already written and shot that I got interested in Italian neorealism. I think you gravitate towards things that have similar concerns to your own.

MacDonald: There were a lot of scenes where you cut to kids playing in these vacant lots. Were those all set up?

Burnett: Yes. We didn't have the money to just ramble about and look for material. We had to have a very small crew, too. Local kids worked on the sound, things like that.

MacDonald: Was this your own neighborhood, and were these people from your neighborhood?

Burnett: Yeah. All the characters, except for Stan, Bracy, and Gene were nonprofessionals.

MacDonald: How much was shot that you didn't use? How much did you want to shoot that you couldn't find the money for?

Burnett: Just about everything that I shot I used. I didn't shoot the middle of that little trip where they get the flat tire. And we didn't shoot a section where Stan goes to fix this nail in the roof, but falls down and injures himself. He stays home on sick leave and begins to like it. He doesn't want to go back to work, but finally his situation demands it.

MacDonald: You create a sense of narrative development, but within it, people aren't getting anywhere.

Burnett: Yes. I wanted to have a sense of story, and a sense of movement forward. But also, I wanted the film to go in a circle so things end up where they begin. One of the themes is that there is no end to struggle. In order to survive, you are always going to be resolving some issues while new issues begin, so that in the end there's the feeling of a cycling or spiraling. There's no conventional plot, but there *is* a structure.

MacDonald: From the opening seconds, the imagery is very subtle: things are happening on multiple levels at once. There are subtleties of composition and editing and subtleties about the way the music on the soundtrack works with the visuals. I'm particularly struck by the bizarre, almost-surreal moments where the kids crawl out of the crevices in a house or play near that building that has no bottom floor. Usually, one talks about surrealism *versus* realism but in these images, reality *is* surreal.

Burnett: Yeah, though I don't know if you can use the word "surrealism" because surrealism is a conscious attempt to go beyond reality. These things are *there*. They are *part of* reality. They're not metaphors.

MacDonald: Maybe one person's reality is another person's surreality.

Burnett: Remember the guy who has the motor in his house? I knew a guy who actually had the whole front end of a car in his house. I was thinking to myself, "Wow, this is really weird. I live in this community, but this goes beyond what I could have imagined." But when he explained that he couldn't leave it outside because someone would steal it, he seemed very logical.

These other guys had a bad generator in their car, or something was wrong electrically, and it would burn the battery out every day. Instead of getting the electrical problem fixed, they would go out and steal two or three batteries every night to keep the car going. It was too much trouble to get the darned thing fixed; it was easier to steal batteries, though it was more dangerous; they could have gotten shot. I went over to their house one morning, and they were peeking out

Stan (Henry Gayle Sanders) in Charles Burnett's *Killer of Sheep* (1977).

of the window. The guy on the other side of the fence was mad. He had his hands in his pockets, like he had a gun. So these guys just went out and put some stuff in the trunk of their car, and they were about to drive off, when I said, "What's he mad about?" Someone said, "Someone stole his battery!" They had stolen his battery. The guy suspected that they had done it, and he was talking indirectly at them about what he'd do if he caught somebody in his backyard, in his car. They just said, "Let him try it," almost like a challenge. It was madness, you know?

Another guy didn't have a regular radio in his house. He had a car radio powered by some batteries in his closet.

I mean people just do what's convenient, what seems practical. From the outside, it may look weird, but it's what works. I wanted to show that kind of thinking in the film.

MacDonald: It reminds me of the moment when the two young guys are stealing a television set and an old guy calls the cops. The thieves are outraged that anybody would interfere with what they're doing—as though what they're doing is perfectly legitimate.

Burnett: People in those neighborhoods look at life, and what they're reduced to, in a strange way.

MacDonald: Maybe the most memorable composition in the film is the one where the viewer is looking at the front of a parked car, with the people sitting inside and a beer on the hood. It's an amazing moment that dramatizes a fundamental difference between the way the film audience sees things and the way these neighborhood people see them.

Burnett: My brother used to have a Buick, and he and his friends had this thing about driving everywhere. It wasn't a gang type of thing; they were just into going places. One time, they went down to Long Beach and got in a fight and someone knocked all the windows out of the car. But that didn't stop them from driving it. They would get in the car with their overcoats on and just drive around. Nothing stopped them. That shot came from their experience. In a sense, a lot of what's in the film was just a matter of picking up on reality.

MacDonald: The importance of editing in *Killer of Sheep* is signaled in the opening sequence. First, you hear a child and an adult singing a lullaby, followed by the shot of a father bawling out his young son for not standing up for his little brother. Then the mother walks over and slaps the boy, and you cut on the slap to a close-up. Then we hear Paul Robeson singing the same song. You go from childhood to adulthood in one quick, brutal moment. The timing of that cut dramatizes the shock to the boy's—and our—sensibilities, and may suggest that, as a filmmaker, you've developed your sensibility from experiencing such shocks, just as Paul Robeson did.

Burnett: At least as I grew up, about every kid experienced that kind of thing. There's the whole issue of survival, the literal survival, of the family. If you have a brother, you can't let him get beat up, no matter how wrong he is. I think for many kids it presented a problem. It really affects your sensibilities and your moral outlook. You have to protect your own, the family ties and all that sort of thing, in spite of the fact that members of your family can be *wrong*. And the whole film is about that, about how in order to survive, you destroy the child inside you. In the scene with that kid the adults are the models of what the kids are going to be, but from a kid's point of view, it's an invasion by the adult world. Religion was a very strong element in the black community where I grew up, but it didn't go much further than the Old Testament, eye-for-an-eye kind of thing. What one was taught on Sunday was often in conflict with what one saw all week.

MacDonald: Early in the film, in the scene where Stan and Bracy are sitting at the kitchen table, you move from day to night or night to day in the space of a direct cut. At times, viewers are not sure where they are in the cycle of the day. Was this another version of the idea that the characters move around without really going anywhere? Are they lost in time, as well as in space?

Burnett: Well, time was a concern of the film. How do you get a sense of time? You mention that scene at the kitchen table. I find I'm more aware of time because I have to do so much *in time* these days. I have goals and things to worry about. My family and friends are oblivious to this. They can't understand why I can't do things with them, *be there* with them. I'm always saying, "I have to work; I can't do it, I just don't have the time."

The time sense of that neighborhood, at least of many people, is very different. They sit down early in the afternoon and end up chitchatting all day until it's time to go to work. Even when we were filming, some of the guys in the film had no feel for the usual filmmaking sense of time. They had a sense of time, of course; let's say we looked at time differently. I'd tell them, "We have to start shooting at a certain time," but it was very difficult for them to be there, or to understand the importance of being there on time. When I was younger, going to school with one of the guys (the guy on the apartment floor with a bandage around his head [James Miles]), I had to go by his house to wake him up in the morning, and invariably he'd be asleep. He wouldn't want to go and I'd have to wait for him and *I'd* be late. And when it'd get *really* late, then he *really* didn't want to go to school. He'd want to hang out someplace else, around some other school—stand outside the fence and look at the girls, whatever. Finally, I stopped going by his house.

Time is a peculiar thing in the black experience. I can't put my finger on it psychologically. It all has to do with interests, goals—where you're going.

MacDonald: The most obvious commentary in the film is the intercutting between the slaughterhouse where Stan works and the characters' daily lives. I often show Georges Franju's *Le Sang des Bêtes* ["The Blood of the Beasts," 1949] on the same day that I show *Killer of Sheep*. Franju also cuts back and forth between the slaughterhouse and everyday Parisian life. Do you know that film?

Burnett: No.

MacDonald: How did you decide to have Stan work in a slaughterhouse?

Burnett: Actually, I was looking for some symbol that would create nightmares for this man, that would seem to push him toward becoming insensitive. He has to strain to hold onto this thing of being human. I ran into a kid who I used to ride the bus with to school. He told me that he was working in a slaughterhouse. At the time they were killing animals with this cylinder where a rod came out and punctured the animals' brains, or they'd hit them in the head with a sledge hammer.

All day long there would be this thump—this continuous thump. I couldn't imagine anyone bearing that, so I thought that would be a good job to have Stan do. And the irony of it, the paradox, is that in order to live, you have to kill. You slaughter the animals for sustenance, whether food or money. I didn't want it to be simply a symbol of people going to the "slaughterhouse" of society; that would be too obvious, too heavy-handed.

And there's the whole thing of the Judas goat, who leads the other goats to the slaughter and is, momentarily, spared. That also gets at an aspect of the way society is.

MacDonald: The irony is that Stan's is actually a relatively good job.

Burnett: It pays the bills, but what it does to you internally is the problem. There are few jobs one can have, I suppose, that are conducive to making a good life, whatever that is.

MacDonald: This is the kind of question that comes from looking at too many films, I suppose, but there's a place where Stan and his pal go to the apartment house where the guy is trying to get his sunglasses back from the woman who has the gun. Some kids are playing on a nearby roof. At the end of that sequence, one kid's arm has been hurt, and he's standing there crying. And right at that moment you're at the end of a roll of film and there's a bit of flare-out. I assume that you wouldn't have wanted to throw the shot away because it's an otherwise good shot, and I know you didn't have a lot of money to work with. But the fact that we see the flare and know that it is a flare—it's just long enough to be recognized for what it is—seems a way of saying that what's true economically of this neighborhood, for the people *in* the film, is also true economically for you as a filmmaker, coming out of this neighborhood. It suggests that these are parallel hurts, parallel setbacks.

Burnett: I was trying to make the film look unslick, documentary-like. But in that particular shot the flare was unintentional. I was using an Arriflex and I took my eye away from the camera several times and didn't bring down the eye piece and light got in. I needed the end of that shot, and the overexposure didn't bother me, because it helped give the film an immediate, unpolished feel. Probably I should have had a really good original and then experimented with the material, made it grainy, added scratches, whatever. Trying to do everything in the camera on the original was always difficult. The same thing was true with the sound. The kids helped with the sound, so there were problems, but generally the problems fit with the nature of the film.

MacDonald: One of the themes of *Killer of Sheep* is that Stan, and people in general, do the best they can with what they have. All through the film, there's a motif on the soundtrack of African-American contributions to American music. Was this a way of suggesting what has been accomplished despite limitations?

Burnett: A lot of the music in the film is music my mother used to play, though at the time I wasn't aware that this was unusual. In my neighborhood, people used to play one record over and over and over again until the record wore out. It would seep into your unconscious and surface years later. For example, in the opening scene of *To Sleep with Anger*, the sister is singing "Precious Memories." I remember walking down the street, humming that tune, and trying to remember where I had heard it. And then I remembered back to childhood days, and that record; I started remembering bits and pieces of it and getting the lyrics. I finally pieced it together and realized where I'd first heard it. It was the same with the music in *Killer of Sheep*. Most of those records were the ones my mother played, except the Gershwin. And not only my mother, but the other people in our neighborhood. It was like stereo; everyone would have the same piece on, and you'd walk around hearing it from every direction. I wanted to preserve that element of the music, and of course it's also music that tells stories about life that relate to Stan's experiences.

MacDonald: Often, the music is simultaneously part of the life we're seeing *and* an ironic comment on it. Robeson's singing "This Is America to Me" works on several levels at once.

Was the soundtrack part of the original concept for the film?

Burnett: Yes.

MacDonald: In addition to the recorded music, there are other suggestive bits of music in the environment—the kid's toy that periodically plays "Yankee Doodle," for example. It's another of the film's repetitive cycles.

Burnett: Actually that's an ice cream truck—one of the things you hear in the community a lot, and get used to. Ice cream trucks always came around and the kids would run out. That song repeats itself over and over. There are some really nice sounds in the community. Real nice.

MacDonald: Often, you have an action happening within the frame, accompanied by sounds that suggest very different activities going on outside the frame. I assume this had something to do with economic limitations—it's a way of getting two things done in the same shot. But it's often very suggestive. When Stan is sitting at the table at night, first we hear the dogs barking and later, someone trying to start a car.

Burnett: I wanted to get inside Stan, but I didn't want to use flashbacks or dream sequences. I wanted to find other ways of commenting on Stan's inner life and problems. What is happening outside reflects on Stan. It's a part of him, a different side of him.

MacDonald: Is Angela Burnett, who plays Stan's daughter, your daughter?

Burnett: My niece.

MacDonald: You seem very quiet, as Stan is. How fully did you relate to Stan? How much are you like him?

Burnett: Not a lot I hope. I mean Stan is sort of a hero in the sense that he's trying not to let his situation destroy him. He's trying to maintain his self-esteem and dignity and hold his family together and give his kids values. I don't think you can do more than that. It's not a question of giving a kid a brand new car, or sending him off to Harvard or Howard, or wherever he wants to go. It's like the old saying in the Bible: if a man is hungry and you give him a fish, he will eat today; but if you teach him how to fish, he'll eat every day. I think what's important is these lessons you learn that will carry you through life. That's what Stan is trying to instill in his kids: the importance of persisting and enduring and looking out for your family. You can't ask a father or a family to do anything more.

MacDonald: Given your limited means as a filmmaker, you seem in a struggle similar to the one Stan is in.

Burnett: That's true. It is a continuous struggle. There's always another hurdle to jump—if you're *lucky*, if you have something to challenge you.

MacDonald: You said that when you were making the film, you really didn't have a sense that there was much of an audience for it.

Burnett: At that time there wasn't any distribution for independent films. *Killer* was basically a film made to respond to a lot of things I was concerned

Stan's daughter (Angela Burnett) in mask and a friend, in Charles Burnett's *Killer of Sheep* (1977).

about. I knew it wasn't going to get shown except in schools, and for friends. Just through word of mouth, it has gotten around over the years. Today, film-makers know there's most likely going to be some venue where a film will get shown. There are film festivals that have sections for black independent films, Latino films, whatever. In the sixties, there were "underground movies," exper-imental films you'd have to see at midnight. The big distributors of independent films specialized in educational films; if your film wasn't a documentary, there just wasn't any means of distributing it.

MacDonald: How much was *Killer of Sheep* seen?

Burnett: Outside of UCLA, I think Howard was the first place where it was shown. And then Oliver Franklin put together a successful tour of black Amer-ican film. It went to five or six different cities, and ended up at the Flaherty Seminar [in 1979]. After that, *Killer of Sheep* took off, though basically, it's been seen mostly in classroom situations and museums.

MacDonald: Is it shown more now than it was in those first years?

Burnett: There's been a surge recently because of the Smithsonian's selec-tion of the film.

MacDonald: Did that surprise you?

Burnett: It certainly did! I got a call from a friend in Philadelphia, who knew it was selected before I did. Our two kids were making a lot of noise, and I couldn't understand what she was saying. She asked me, "Why do you think they chose your film?" And I thought she meant for some film festival—I didn't know what was going on. Later, someone else called and said, "You know, your film has been selected to be preserved by the National Archives." I was shocked: it must be one of the cheapest films they've selected. In fact, the biggest cost was trying to get a release print.

MacDonald: What did *Killer* cost altogether?

Burnett: Probably less than ten thousand dollars.

MacDonald: Did you pay actors?

Burnett: No. I used a lot of friends who owed me favors.

MacDonald: Do you still live in Watts?

Burnett: Actually, I lived a couple of blocks away from Watts proper. Watts is a very particular place, with definite boundaries. Some of the film was shot in Watts, the rest just outside of Watts. Now, I live on the west side of Los Angeles.

MacDonald: The last few years there have been a number of films about South Central LA. Any feelings about these other films?

Burnett: One problem I have is the fact that you don't see balance or diversity in these films. If one Hollywood film does well, they just look for similar scripts.

MacDonald: Scripts that focus on drugs and gangs.

Burnett: Yes. It's very strange because most of these producers don't interact with anybody other than producers like themselves, but they dictate taste and perception to the rest of the country and decide how the rest of the country thinks about such places, and it's very difficult to change the attitudes they create. The producers think, "This is what the public wants," but most of them haven't read much of anything outside the trade papers. They're probably Yale or Harvard law or business guys, vice presidents of production, things like that—most of them haven't made film. So you have a combination of factors that works against making decent films. It's frustrating. You go to them with a script, and they say, "Well, this isn't *Boyz in the Hood* [1991]. Why don't you make it like *Boyz in the Hood?*" There's a lot more to life in South Central than *Boyz in the Hood*.

MacDonald: You've made two films about LA neighborhoods that are very different from *Boyz: My Brother's Wedding* and *To Sleep with Anger*. There was a gap of four or five years between *Killer of Sheep* and *My Brother's Wedding*, which is your first 35mm film. How did *My Brother's Wedding* develop?

Burnett: I was at the Berlin Film Festival, and ZDF [Zweites Deutsches Fernsehen, German television's Second Channel] approached me after a screening of *Killer of Sheep* and told me they had a small fund called "Camera Money," and if I had a project, they'd like to go into co-production with me. I said, "I do have a project!" And once we started negotiation, *My Brother's Wedding* was right there. Then I sold *Killer of Sheep* to Channel 4 in England and got some grants. Anyway, I put the money together—about eighty thousand dollars—and got favors from places like MGM and Lorimar. There was a strike at a lot of studios at the time, and cameras were just sitting around, so I got a really good deal on cameras, and on film—good short-ends from *Dallas*.

I wanted to do a story about young men who hadn't made up their minds about what they wanted to be and do, who find themselves in a kind of vacuum. And I wanted to do something with the concept of "brother's keeper," about what it means to be responsible: it takes more than just having a good feeling; it takes a commitment, someone with an idea and a plan, someone who knows how to say, "No."

MacDonald: *My Brother's Wedding* seems very different from *Killer of Sheep* in terms of structure and action. In *Killer of Sheep*, things are going nowhere. Here, there is some of that feeling, but you mostly work toward the big moment of Pierce being caught between the two crucial commitments in his life. Were you conflicted about how to put the film together?

Burnett: No. I was trying to do a film that would have a larger, and younger, audience. *My Brother's Wedding* is very conventional in a certain way: there's a beginning, middle, and end; there's a problem that begins to emerge at the very beginning and you can see that there's going to be a major conflict, and you wonder how it's going to be resolved. Basically, it was *clear*. And I remember being conscious of trying to infuse it with more humor than *Killer of Sheep*.

I wanted the characters not so much to represent Reality, which is what I *was* striving for in *Killer of Sheep*, but to be obvious caricatures, *not* real people. The whole film was seen from Pierce's point of view. His resentment of the middle class was distorted, and so the middle class characters seem very exaggerated, and his romanticizing of the poor was naive and childlike. Anyway, I *didn't* want people to think this was real.

MacDonald: There are some powerful scenes—when Sojer comes home from prison, for example—but there are other things that seem preposterous, like the grandmother's wig . . .

Burnett: Oh god, that wig! I didn't get a chance to really edit the film. Not to make excuses, but it came down to myself and a sound person making the movie, and just going at it the best we could. I'm trying to re-edit it on video now, just to see what I can do with the film. There's a large chunk of what you saw that I'll be glad to take out. Some things seemed to work on paper, but I didn't execute them well. I *hate* the whole robbery scene. It could have worked, and I need to recut; if it still doesn't work, I'll just take it out. And the chase down the street takes forever! It should be long, but it's ridiculous.

Another problem was this one actor—the guy who comes into the laundry looking for work. He was crazy, an A-1 troublemaker. He would disappear for months! And in the meantime, the funders are saying, "Charles, where's the film!" And I'm saying, "I have to find the *actor*; we have these scenes to shoot, and he's gone!" Finally, I find him in Louisiana where he's been ordained as a minister! He says if I give him plane fare to LA, he'll come back. He's a really smart guy, very talented—if he'd just stop being selfish.

We'd started having problems earlier. Right after we got enough film of him so that we were committed to using him, his manager called and said, "He wants more money." I said, "You're joking! We have *a contract*. I only have so much money." He says, "But he's the star of the movie!" I say, "*No one's* the *star* of this movie! It's a *film*." We get in this big argument and I say, "Look, I can give him all of his money up-front, rather than paying him by the week, but that's all I can do." So I did that. We start up and then something else happens: he needs a loan. So we do *that!* It went on and on, and the last thing was that he disappeared and turned up in Louisiana.

When the film was finally shot, I made a rough assembly, and shipped it out to ZDF. I was hoping I'd get a chance to recut it, but I never had the money or the opportunity.

I think it could have been a *relevant* film. I like what it was trying to say. It was a portrait of the early eighties, just before crack turned the community wild and the shootings started.

MacDonald: *To Sleep with Anger* seems such an unusual portrait of an African-American family, at least compared with everything else I've seen in movie theaters.

Burnett: I think that's one of the problems it's had. How do you market an unusual portrait of realistic people, when the audience has come to expect a certain kind of portrayal of black life in films that continue to confirm the prejudices and the filmic conventions that have developed from them? When *To Sleep with Anger* was screened, a lady asked me, "Why did you avoid showing drugs? Black people take drugs, don't they?" And I said, "A small percentage." One person told me that she didn't know black people had washing machines! You'd be amazed at what people's perceptions of other cultures are. Hollywood remains a culprit. It's very dangerous, too, because one of the problems you have in trying to do films that deal realistically with people of color is to try to create self-esteem. A lot of kids have just given up. It's very difficult to write a script that shows a strong, positive black male character. To do a decent story about a family is very difficult. And if it's a black and white situation and there's a black and a white main character, it's so difficult to have them on an equal footing. There's almost always either an obvious or a subtle dependency.

MacDonald: There's also a tendency to avoid the idea that men can be sensitive. That moment in *Killer of Sheep* when Stan holds the cup of tea to his face and talks about the sensation of the heat being like a woman's breath during lovemaking—that's very unusual.

Burnett: It's strange how the possibilities and the realities are reduced to a formula. One of the biggest problems about this business is trying to create complex, subtle images. If it's hard to verbally explain an image, that becomes a stumbling block. Like the pigeons in *To Sleep with Anger*. I used to raise pigeons, and pigeons are tumblers and rollers . . .

MacDonald: Tumblers and rollers?

Burnett: Yes. Pigeons are bred to tumble. They fly around and roll backwards and flip. You can breed them to the length of the roll you want. You can
create pigeons that do three flips or ten or that tumble all the way to the ground.
They can't fly without tumbling: it's genetic. So kids sit around all day, watching pigeons fly and tumble. It's really neat.

So they didn't know anything about pigeons, and said, "How do you get
these pigeons to tumble?" I said. "They do it naturally." It became a thing. They
kept complaining, "We don't understand how these pigeons are going to tumble!" I kept saying, "Don't worry about it!"

And the fire thing—where Gideon's [Carl Lumbly] feet are on fire—"What
does that mean!" They couldn't understand it; and it was very difficult to translate. So, the first thing they want to do is cut it out, and you have to fight for it.
"Well," they'd say, "why *do* you need that? Do you *really* need it?" I'd say,
"Yeah, we really need it." Money is involved, and there's this notion that you
don't make the audience work. So they want to cut anything out that creates
questions. But if you don't try, then there's no growth, either in the audience or
in you as a filmmaker. What they want runs counter to what art *is* in film. You
were talking before about images as metaphors. If you break a strong image
down, it loses its meaning. It's like trying to explain a joke. The thing that
makes the joke work is the fact that two things come together and create a crazy
thing that you really *can't* reduce to words or formulas.

Of course, films made according to a formula are often very successful,
financially.

MacDonald: Was it much easier to work with an experienced cast in *To
Sleep with Anger?*

Burnett: It's easier on one hand, but one of the bad things about these low-
budget films is that only a small percentage of the time is spent dealing with the
actors. It's all politics, keeping people happy . . . doing everything except what
you're supposed to be doing. And time! You have just so many days. There's a tendency to underbudget these films, and promises don't get kept, because of "reality," so the actors don't have enough rehearsal time. When (finally!) you do get a
few minutes to work with the actors, it does help to have experienced people.

MacDonald: It was great to see Julius Harris again. I remember him from
Nothing But a Man [1966].

Burnett: Oh yeah! All those guys—Julius Harris and David Roberts (he died
last year in Chicago) . . . —were *so* professional! They really taught *me* something. David was *so* sick during the shooting, but he did an incredible job. What
a trooper. None of those guys complained. They were *right there* all the time.

MacDonald: One of the great pleasures of your films is the subtle moments
of humor. The motor falling off the truck in *Killer of Sheep* is really sad, and yet
there's this Scott Joplin song playing in the background, and for a moment it's
Laurel and Hardy moving the piano in *The Music Box* [1932]. It's both funny

and painful, as is the corpse lying on the floor during the last fifteen minutes of *To Sleep with Anger*.

Burnett: I think life is like that. There's a relation between humor and tragedy. The further you are away from a death or an accident, the more you can see the humor. This lady had come to shoot her husband in my old barbershop in Watts, and the way the barber described the scene—everyone ducking and jumping to get out of the way of this woman—was hilarious. But a few moments before, when she was *there*, it wasn't funny at all.

Parts of *To Sleep with Anger* were structured around black folklore that has elements of both tragedy and humor.

MacDonald: You work on other people's films to make ends meet?

Burnett: Yeah. I just got back two weeks ago, from working with Dai Sil Kim Gibson on a film we're trying to do together about blacks and Koreans. We shot ten minutes from her screenplay (which is forty minutes or an hour long)—so that we can use it to raise money to finish her segment of the project. Then we'll do my segment. And I just worked on a documentary with Mary Brown about Ted Watkins.

MacDonald: And your part in these films is?

Burnett: It varies. I wrote part of the screenplay for the black section of the black/Korean project. Dai Sil wrote the screenplay for the Korean section, and I directed her ten-minute segment. I was doing camera and co-directing on the documentary on Ted Watkins. And I help people write things. Stuff like that.

MacDonald: Is *To Sleep With Anger* your most successful film financially?

Burnett: No, it's not been successful at all, at the box office. A lot of critics liked it, but insofar as people seeing it, no.

MacDonald: I guess I'd assumed it's done well because I've seen it on TV.

Burnett: Goldwyn did a real bad job distributing the film. It barely made a million. They didn't spend a penny on promotion. Julie Dash's *Daughters of the Dust* [1991] made much more money—not that I'm knocking her film. But we had well-known actors—Danny Glover, Mary Alice—and well-known critics gave the film good reviews, so *To Sleep with Anger* could have and should have done as well as *Daughters of the Dust*. But Goldwyn didn't want anyone to tell them what to do, and yet, they didn't know what to do with the film. There were signs that it was going to flop, and they didn't care. We tried to get them to help us do things that were free, the kinds of things Haile Gerima has done with *Sankofa* [1993]. The distributors didn't want *Sankofa*, so Haile took it out himself, and has made a fortune four-walling it.

We're trying to keep the same kind of disaster from happening with *The Glass Shield*. It's based on a true story about this cop, Johnny Johnson, a young black guy who integrated the Signal Hill Police Department (Signal Hill is near Long Beach). The police department there was notorious for beating people up, particularly blacks and minorities, "long hairs," anyone who wasn't straight and reactionary looking. One young kid with a promising football career was found hanging in the jail, and the police said it was a suicide or an accident, whatever. His mother had the coroner investigate, and he said, "No, he died at the hand of another." While that case was going on, they tried to appease the public by having the police department hire a minority person, who found out what had happened and told what happened, and was hated for that. *The Glass Shield* is partly about him, and also about what happens in police departments around the country.

It premieres in October, I think. I've just told Miramax to get off their cans. First, they were going to open it in eighty-five theaters, and now distribution is becoming a rush job; there may not be enough time left to do the film justice.

Hara Kazuo

To people in some sectors of the world, Americans have often seemed prone to public self-exposure, a people oblivious to modesty and privacy. And yet, even in the United States, it has been possible, and remains possible, to shock film viewers simply by revealing the inevitable realities of human experience. Even in the 1990s, a screening of Stan Brakhage's *Window Water Baby Moving* (1959) or Gunvor Nelson's *Kirsa Nicholina* (1969) can create consternation for American college students simply by offering them a clear look at the experience of birth. Indeed, as "open" as we may seem, the number and complexity of American visual taboos have instigated various forms of response within each of two film-critical traditions. In American avant-garde filmmaking there have been many forms of self-exposure within what is usually called "psychodrama," the dramatization of disturbed states of consciousness (Kenneth Anger's psychodramatization of the excitement/terror of homosexual desire in *Fireworks* [1947] is a particularly good example). There is also the Brakhage-inspired tradition of liberating perception itself, which is evident in the two birth films mentioned above as well as in Brakhage's *The Act of Seeing with One's Own Eyes* (1971), a perceptual exploration of the Pittsburgh morgue, and Anne Severson's *Near the Big Chakra* (1972), a close-up meditation on women's genitalia. And there is the "diary film," which in many instances—in Carolee Schneemann's *Fuses* (1967), Andrew Noren's *Huge Pupils* (1968), Robert Huot's *Rolls: 1971* (1972), among others —has included candid revelations, shocking to many viewers. A second set of confrontations of taboo is part of the tradition of documentary, especially cinéma vérité, where some filmmakers have exposed and explored the operation of American institutions (Frederick Wiseman's prolific career has been devoted to such revelations) and others have carried the synch-sound cinéma vérité apparatus into their own homes to reveal the workings of their personal relationships: Amalie Roth-schild in *Nana, Mom and Me* (1974); Ed Pincus in *Diaries* (1976) and *Life and Other Anxieties* (1977); and, more recently, Ross McElwee in *Backyard* (1984), *Sherman's March* (1986), and *Time Indefinite* (1993).

But what of societies where privacy and modesty are more jealously guarded than in the United States? In some cases, these societies have produced few filmic confrontations of the hidden. In two instances, however—Austria and Japan—the extreme power of taboo has energized particularly emphatic responses. Perhaps the most visceral of all cinematic confrontations of taboo have come in the films of the Viennese avant-garde "Actionists"—in particular, Otto Mühl and Kurt Kren (in their many "materialactionfilms") and Valie Export (in, for example, *Mann & Frau & Animal* ["Man & Woman & Animal"], 1973)—whose immersions in bodily process remain at least as shocking in the 1990s as they were in the 1960s and early 1970s. However, if one thinks in terms of the *social experience* of using filmmaking as a means of stepping through the barriers between private and public, it is hard to imagine a more confrontational filmmaker than Hara Kazuo in his feature films *Sayonara CP* (1972), *Kyokushiteki Erosu Koiuta* ("Extreme Private Eros: Love Song," 1974), and the film known in the United States as *The Emperor's Naked Army Marches On* (1988).

Of Hara's features, *The Emperor's Naked Army Marches On* is easily the best-known. Hara's documentation of the activities of Okuzaki Kenzo, the Japanese anti-imperialist World War II veteran—or fanatic, depending on your point of view—who caused an international incident by shooting lead pellets at the Emperor, is consistently gripping, and sometimes shocking (for instance, when Okuzaki beats up another elderly veteran who refuses to cooperate with him, in the man's own home). While Hara's original goal was simply to record Okuzaki's activities in general, their filming became increasingly focused on Okuzaki's discovery that several officers who had served with him in New Guinea had cannibalized fellow Japanese soldiers. Okuzaki and Hara drag these long-hidden, now "private" crimes into the public eye, as we watch. The English translation of the film's title (*Yuki Yukite Shingun* in Japanese) is unfortunate: a better translation is "God's Army Marches On," which suggests both the divine inspiration Okuzaki claims and the relentlessness of his (and Hara's) pursuit of his own sense of truth and justice.

Extreme Private Eros: Love Song is, if anything, more gripping than *The Emperor's Naked Army Marches On*. It chronicles Hara's own relationship with Takeda Miyuki: first, when they are lovers (in one instance, Hara is filming as he and Takeda have intercourse), and later during the break-up of their relationship and Takeda's subsequent personal and political activities in Okinawa (where she conceives a child with an African-American GI stationed in Okinawa and delivers the child, unassisted, as Hara and the viewers watch). More fully than *The Emperor's Naked Army Marches On, Extreme Private Eros* exposes Hara's own pain including his personal humiliation in being confronted by Takeda with what she sees as his personal weakness.

The earliest of Hara's films, *Sayonara CP*, documents the activities of a number of seriously handicapped Japanese as they, and Hara, publicly confront their fellow citizens with the realities of their physical limitations. Though the film has never been in distribution in the United States (I have seen it only in an unsubtitled video version), it became—like Hara's subsequent features—well known in Japan and, perhaps, had a progressive impact on Japanese society's response to the handicapped.

This interview with Hara began at the 1992 Flaherty Film Seminar, first, in the post-screening general discussions of *The Emperor's Naked Army Marches On* and *Extreme Private Eros: Love Song* and, then, in an interview, during which Laura U. Marks (a critic, with some facility in Japanese, who was doing research on Japanese independent film) and I talked with Hara. The discussions and the interview were supplemented in 1995 when Stephen Schible, who had been Hara's translator at the Flaherty Seminar, agreed to ask Hara a series of questions about *Sayonara CP* and his newest project (released in 1994 as *A Dedicated Life*). My thanks to Schible for his considerable efforts on behalf of the interview. As in the interview with William Greaves, I have identified those who queried Hara during the Flaherty post-screening discussion by both name and occupation (using the participants' self-descriptions for these identifications).

In Japanese culture, given names follow family names (that is, Hara Kazuo, Okuzaki Kenzo, Takeda Miyuki). Since the Flaherty discussion with Hara took place in English (as translated by Schible), I use Western order from here on.

Laura U. Marks: I'm going to start with a couple of film history questions to try to situate *Extreme Private Eros: Love Song*. We're curious about its relation to other Japanese documentary films, in particular Shinsuke Ogawa's Narita Airport films [seven films, 1968–1973, including *Daini Toride No Hitobito,* "The Peasants of the Second Fortress," 1971] and Shohei Imamura's *Nihon Sen-goshi* ["The History of Postwar Japan as Told by a Bar Hostess," 1971].

Hara: I saw Mr. Ogawa's films about the Narita Airport events when I was a high school student, in the sixties and seventies. We are both from the same era and I was influenced by Mr. Ogawa in the sense that by watching his films, I realized that I must make films as well.

Marks: Both of you seem to have an obsessive relationship with your subject. As I understand it, Ogawa and his film crew lived in Furuyashiki-mura for three years.

Hara: There are many similarities in the way we think. In fact, at one time I thought I would like to join Mr. Ogawa's production company. But I realized that once I joined, I would be a member of Ogawa Productions. I decided to work not in the village but in the city, and to be in charge of my own productions.

Marks: You worked with Shohei Imamura, and obviously there are connections between your filmmaking and his. But I see particular similarities between *Nihon Sen-goshi* and *Extreme Private Eros*. Both of you seem interested in outsiders who tell alternative histories.

Hara: I am often told about that similarity between Mr. Imamura and myself. Because Mr. Imamura and I deal with similar issues—postwar Japanese history, the relationship of documentary and fiction, women who are outside conventional morality—people tend to see us as similar filmmakers. But I feel we are very different, though it *is* true that, like Mr. Imamura, I like lower-class women, as a filmmaker.

Marks: Could you explain why?

Hara: No.

Marks: When I write about you I'm afraid I'll be making up reasons why. I'd be grateful for some help.

Hara: There's a way you can look at postwar Japanese history through the relationship between men and women. Men have made Japan a less interesting country. It's not that I feel that women have moved Japanese history only in a positive direction either, but I do feel that women have been a progressive force in the history of postwar Japan.

Usually, you can tell if a filmmaker likes men or women, can't you? When I look at Mr. [Nagisa] Oshima's films, I don't think the women portrayed in his films are sexy at all. But in Mr. Imamura's works they're always sexy.

Marks: I'm interested in how you portray masculinity in your films. It seems to me that you, yourself, by being so open in your films, infringe on traditional Japanese masculinity.

Hara: Traditionally, men in Japan do not cry. Usually one cannot even consider allowing them to cry on screen. When the student movement was occurring in the seventies, there was also the feminist movement, and in response to the feminist movement, there were people who said that if females can become more free, then men should be allowed to express their feelings, too—that men should be allowed to cry. I was not acting when I cried on screen in *Extreme Private Eros*. But I *was* trying to be part of that new mode of living as well as I could, and my crying reflected that desire. Some people would consider it effeminate [*memeshii*]. In a broad sense there are three types of men in Japan: there is the male chauvinist Japanese man, who will work only with men and believes that women are to stay at home; there is the man who will try to listen to what women have to say and try to bring the women's points of view into his thoughts and actions; and there is also a perverted type of man—"perverted" in a pejorative sense—who has a mother complex, a desire for a mother figure. I am like that.

Marks: In your films you are willing to put yourself in the position of being so obsessed by your subject that it's as though you are not complete by yourself, but need the individuals you film in order to grow.

Hara: As a filmmaker, I try to understand what I want to do, not so much by *confronting* my subject, but by trying to become "empty inside myself" and letting my subject enter me. The subject becomes my opponent and I become the receiver of the opponent's action and development.

Before I made my first film [*Sayonara CP*, 1972], I spent five years with handicapped people. And it took five years to understand what kind of situation those people were living in. Then I thought, how can I change the situation that handicapped people live in? My answer was to collaborate with the two characters in my first film.

Similarly, when Miyuki Takeda [the focus of *Extreme Private Eros*] and I first met, she had just come into the city from the countryside. She didn't know what she should do or how she should act. I was important to her. In *Extreme Private Eros* she criticized me by saying that I'm good with words and for that reason shouldn't be trusted. But she started moving towards the feminist agenda because of my influence, and that agenda changed our relationship and the film. Once I've instigated my collaborators, they find a target and fly towards it, and *I* follow *them*. The relationship (between the man and the woman, in *Extreme Private Eros*, and between the handicapped person and the nonhandicapped person, me, in *Sayonara CP*) reverses. I want to film the process of that reversal.

MacDonald: It's the opposite of much traditional documentary where the filmmaker begins with a thesis and in the filmmaking fleshes it out with the necessary information.

Also, traditionally, the documentarian is a "masculine" presence and the subject is rendered "feminine." In *Extreme Private Eros* the subject is a strong woman and you are the "feminine" presence.

Hara: Yes. I like to be the one who receives—for the duration of making a film, say one or two years. Sometimes the subject becomes depressed, passive. In that case, there is nothing I can do but start attacking, until the subject becomes active again.

Jesse Lerner [filmmaker]: Many of us have this image of Japan, a stereotypical image maybe, as a place where the pressure to conform is very strong. The woman in *Extreme Private Eros* and Mr. Okuzaki in *The Emperor's Naked Army Marches On* really break that stereotype.

Hara: *Extreme Private Eros* was made twenty years ago, so you're looking at Japan in the seventies. That was a very active time, a very liberal time. It was not just Miyuki Takeda who acted as she did. She was a member of a group. Of course, Mr. Okuzaki is a person who goes beyond generations and time and everything else.

As a filmmaker it is not interesting for me to portray subjects who are "normal." It is easier for me to follow somebody who is aggressive, who is living an interesting life. As an independent filmmaker, I don't have much money, and I don't have all the time I would like to spend making films. Therefore, I need a subject that really makes me want to jump into a project and work.

MacDonald: In any period similar things may be going on in different places in the world simultaneously. In the early seventies in North America there were also people bringing cameras into personal experiences this way. Have you seen North American films with a related approach?

Hara: I haven't seen any American films of that sort. I *have* become interested in the difference between Japanese and American documentary. I've spoken to some filmmakers and critics in Japan, and those people and I agree that there is a difference and I'm wondering why. I'm not talking about all American documentaries. I haven't seen that many myself, so I can only say very generally that I feel there is this difference: American documentaries often criticize something, whereas the films of Shinsuke Ogawa and Noriaki Tsuchimoto (for example, *Minamata: Kanja-sans to Sono Sekai* ["Minamata: The Victims and Their World," 1972], a well-known exposé about a village whose inhabitants got mercury poisoning from factory waste) do not criticize, but seem to move along with the subjects. I'm not saying one approach is better than the other, but I always feel that difference.

MacDonald: When you say, "move along with the subject," do you mean they literally live with the subject, or that they create a kind of synergic relationship with the subject?

Hara: In Japanese there is a phrase, "eating rice from the same bowl." There's a sense of community that is born from a close relationship, and conflicts develop from that closeness as well. A working relationship involves a kind of kinship. Of course, American filmmakers become very closely involved with their subjects, but I feel they tend to leave space between themselves and the subjects.

Also, there is a tendency in recent American documentary filmmaking to rely too heavily on interviews, and to feel that you can edit bits and pieces together to make a documentary. Many recent works use interviews in a very superficial way, and they put too much trust in the words spoken by the subjects. In Japanese there is a phrase, "peeling pickled garlic" [pickled garlic (*rakkyo*) is often eaten in Japan]. You peel a pickled garlic one layer at a time and you peel another layer and there is still another layer beneath it—there is no core in a pickled garlic. When we have a relationship with reality and explore it, we peel one layer of reality, and we think we can see another world. But the trouble with that level of reality is that if we peel *it*, we see still *another* layer. The third or fourth layer is not exactly the real truth either. What is interesting about making documentary films is peeling those layers, and it is difficult to do that simply by relying on the words you record, on the interviewing process, where you only face the first level of reality. There is a difference between what a person is saying and what a person is feeling. So I try to peel the expression on a person's face, and go to other levels of truth.

Margarita de la Vega Hurtado [director, Latina/Latino Studies, University of Michigan]: In *Extreme Private Eros*, how much control did your subject have over the final film? There are a couple places where I see Miyuki Takeda objecting to being filmed and yet you continue to film.

Hara: *Extreme Private Eros* began at the point when Miyuki Takeda decided to go to Okinawa and asked me to come to Okinawa and film her. I think she still had feelings towards me. She was not pregnant yet, but she had told me that she would like to become pregnant and deliver a baby on her own, to prove her existence as a woman, and that this should be part of the film. I asked her if she was serious, and she answered, "Yes." I decided to do the project. She did not have a final say about the content of the film. I saw it as my film (and I believe *she* saw it as my film).

Lise Yasui [filmmaker]: I have complex feelings about Miyuki Takeda: I liked her sometimes and I hated her sometimes. What I understand about the attitudes toward the black GIs she expresses in the pamphlet she passes out in Okinawa is disturbing. She accuses the black GIs of using the women in Okinawa and yet she, as an independent woman, seems to be using you *and* the black man *and* her baby.

Hara: What I wanted to do in this film was to express my feelings as I lived through and filmed the events, and that is very difficult to do. When Miyuki Takeda was going out with the black guy, Paul, I went to film them, and I became very jealous while I was filming. When you operate the camera, you have to worry about the aperture, the focus, the distance between the subjects and yourself—you have to be very logical. But I was very emotional. For some reason, during that one time a friend of mine was there, and I asked my friend to film for me because I could not continue. That's why I'm in only part of that scene. I was crying.

Later, I thought about what to do next. I thought, "I cannot shoot like this anymore." And so instead of filming in a one-on-one situation, I begged my current wife [Sachiko Kobayashi] to come into the project.

MacDonald: Were you upset because the man was black? What were your feelings about the interracial situation in Okinawa?

Hara: I would have been equally jealous if the man were Japanese. At the time, there were ideas about Black Power in Japan, as well as in America. Okinawa was segregated into a white area and a black area. Miyuki Takeda and those other girls intentionally went to the black area because they were interested in the American Black Power movement.

Marks: What was in the pamphlets the woman was passing out in Okinawa, and who were the gangsters who beat you up? Were the women beaten also?

Hara: Only I was beaten. The Okinawa gang was local and Miyuki Takeda was from the mainland. In the seventies, within Japan, Okinawa was considered a Third World area, and many people who were challenging the Emperor's Japan went to Okinawa, including Miyuki Takeda. Since she was not from Okinawa, most likely the gang misunderstood her act of distributing the pamphlets.

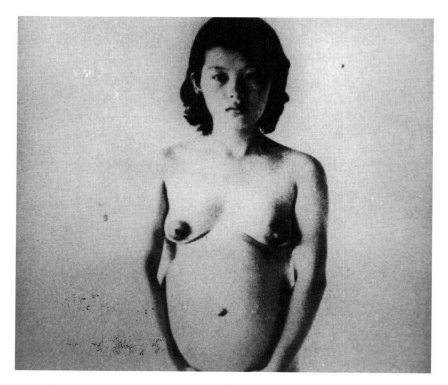

Miyuki Takeda in Kazuo Hara's *Kyokushiteki Erosu Koiuta* ("Extreme Private Eros: Love Song," 1974).

It may be very hard for the viewer to understand the content of the pamphlets in the English subtitles. For most of their stay in Okinawa, Miyuki Takeda and the other woman, Sugako, were staying in the black section. In that area there were many couples, Japanese women and black men. In the pamphlet, she wrote about those relationships. It may have seemed to the Okinawans that she was looking down on Okinawa, but that wasn't the case. She respected Okinawa very much. She loved Okinawa.

Yasui: Feeling about Miyuki Takeda as you did, was it difficult to portray her bad side, as well as her good side?

Hara: Well, I don't think she has a "bad side."

Towards the end of the film, Miyuki Takeda was part of a commune, and when that commune ended about three or four years later, she raised her two children on her own. But it is difficult in Japan for black-Japanese children. Miyuki Takeda decided it might be better for Yu, the half-American half-Japanese girl, to live in the United States. Two or three years ago, Yu was adopted and moved to America.

Generally, our lives have gone separate ways.

Marks: Both *Extreme Private Eros* and *The Emperor's Naked Army Marches On* explore some sort of racial mixing. There's the interest of the Japanese women in black American soldiers in *Extreme Private Eros*. And in *The Emperor's Naked Army Marches On*, we learn that even when there was cannibalism at the end of the war, there were racial taboos about who could be eaten. Are you interested in attacking the idea of racial purity in your films?

Hara: A politician has said that Japan is a homogeneous country. In our generation we laugh at that.

Marks: But even in my own experience I have seen the great prejudice in Japan against Koreans and people of color, and the difficulties that mixed race children have.

Hara: That's true. But I mean that there are differences even among Japanese. Okinawa has been returned to Japan, but the people living in Okinawa feel they are Okinawan. They believe they are a separate race.

MacDonald: How did you decide that *Extreme Private Eros* was finished?

Hara: My experience as a documentary filmmaker is that when I am filming, I will suddenly get a feeling that I can end this project now. I obey that feeling. Sometimes it takes me three or five years to make one film, because I will continue until that feeling comes.

Yasui: Can you talk about how your relationship with Miyuki Takeda affected your editing decisions?

Hara: I shot the events one by one, chronologically, and what I did during the editing process was compress the information I had gathered. I didn't change very much. I feel that when you edit this kind of film, it's most natural to just connect everything the way it was shot.

Phred Churchill [videomaker]: How do you see your own presence as a character in your films? How do others in Japan see you?

Hara: One Japanese film critic said that I must be a very masochistic person, since I like to film strong subjects and am often dragged around by them. But I consider myself normal. I *am* drawn to strong characters and it's interesting that when you confront a strong character and work face-to-face with this person on a film, you become confused within yourself. In that state of confusion the world starts to look different—and you have the opportunity to show your audience something special.

What's important is that the subject and the filmmaker get together, energize each other, and develop a process. I never intend to step out of that process and film objectively. I'm not only following what is happening, I try to set up a situation where the tension between filmmaker and subject is energetic. Miyuki Takeda did what she did and Mr. Okuzaki did what he did, but I do things *with* the subjects. We become parts of each other's living and developing.

MacDonald: What's it like to make personal films in your society? There's a saying that "It's the nail that sticks up that is beaten down." How is it as the nail that sticks up, *you* have not been beaten down?

Hara:What you need is the power to bounce back at the hammer that is pounding on you. That's what Mr. Okuzaki did and what Miyuki Takeda did. They acted *their* way no matter who was hammering, or how much they hammered.

Portia Cobb [film- and videomaker]: I have a question about the birthing scene. How come no one was there in the room with Miyuki Takeda, other than you shooting? And how come you and the person with the mike [Sachiko Kobayashi] did not put the equipment down and help?

Hara: Miyuki Takeda had told us not to help at all. We did plan to call an ambulance if we figured there was a threat to the baby's life. In Okinawa, Miyuki Takeda had worked for a midwife, so she had experience and was confident that she would be able to do it on her own.

Alan Rosenthal [filmmaker/writer]: But at what point do you stop being a filmmaker and become a human being? Several times in the film we hear the words, "Is the baby choking? Is the baby choking? Is it swallowing some blood?" As far as I can understand, there is no reaction from the person with the mike or from you. Was there in fact no problem at all, or were you simply avoiding the problem in the interest of your work?

Hara: As a documentarian, I like to become involved in a relationship with my subject, and see how I myself am changed by the relationship, but I don't want to become directly involved, except by holding a camera. It's not that I didn't feel any emotions during the birth scene. I felt many things. But I also felt it wouldn't be appropriate for me to say something, or to add a voice-over later on and express my emotions then. At the time, I was very nervous and didn't know what I would do if something did happen to the baby.

I was sweating so much that my glasses became foggy and I couldn't see. I was using two cameras, one with a wide-angle lens. With that camera it's sometimes hard to tell if you are in focus. Being nervous is no excuse for my shooting the footage out of focus, but I feel I couldn't have displayed my emotions in a more effective way.

When Miyuki Takeda was asking me if the baby was moving or not, I was responding. My voice is in the film.

Rosenthal: How come it's not in the subtitles?

Hara: I was whispering and decided not to have the whispers translated.

Yasui: There's a Japanese tradition of women choosing to give birth like this, isn't there?

Hara: Yes, but in our time birth has become an industry. Miyuki Takeda wanted to express herself through the act of giving birth to a baby, and she felt she wouldn't be able to do that if she gave birth in a hospital. In modern Japan she is a very rare case.

One more thing. I promised her I would show the film to her and the child after ten years. And after ten years I did get a call from Miyuki Takeda, and I set up the screening. During the film, Yu watched very attentively. Afterwards we went to a restaurant, and I asked her, "What did you think?" She answered, "It was very good." When I heard those words, I felt the film was worth the effort.

Maria DeLuca [filmmaker]: So often I feel repelled by films that seem voyeuristic, especially when the camera seems fixed on an intense emotional scene. I did not feel that way about your film. The sex scene was very disturbing at first, but almost immediately I felt very involved, in an unusual way.

Hara: I wanted to do something that could be called voyeuristic but would not repel the audience.

In Japan there are many social systems: the system of the imperial family, other cultural systems. There are many restrictions—you cannot do this or that. But the biggest restriction is privacy. What I want to do is not to intrude on *other* people's privacy, but to reveal my own, and to see how far I can go in that revelation. I want to drag my audience into my life, aggressively, and I want to create a mood of confusion. I am very frightened by this, and by the things I film, but it's because I am frightened that I feel I must do these films.

Richard Herskowitz [then, director, Cornell Cinema; currently, director, Virginia Festival of American Film]: What attracted you to Mr. Okuzaki and to *The Emperor's Naked Army Marches On* project?

Hara: It was "love at first sight." [laughter]

Mr. Imamura introduced me to Mr. Okuzaki. That was the very beginning of the project. After Mr. Okuzaki shot lead pellets at the Emperor and was going through his trial, Mr. Imamura was considering making a film about Mr. Okuzaki, using money provided by Toho, a film company in Japan; but he decided that Toho would not want to get involved with such a controversial subject. For about ten years after that, Mr. Okuzaki wrote Mr. Imamura letters, pleading with him to make a film about his ideas. During those ten years—between the time of Mr. Okuzaki's trial and the time I met Mr. Okuzaki—Mr. Imamura gradually lost interest in making documentary films. And during that period, Mr. Imamura approached several young filmmakers about making a film about Mr. Okuzaki. All of them refused. One day, when I was meeting with Mr. Imamura, we discussed Mr. Okuzaki's activities, and I decided to go to Kobe and meet Mr. Okuzaki. We talked for about seven hours: I say "we," but during six and three quarter hours Mr. Okuzaki did the talking. I was impressed and decided to make the film. I put the credit "Conceived by Shohei Imamura" to show how grateful I was to him for introducing me to Mr. Okuzaki.

When we started to work on the project, Mr. Okuzaki would introduce people to me, and *every* time he made an introduction, he would say, "This is Mr. Hara, who was introduced to me by the famous film director Imamura; he is going to make a film about me." At that time, I was not known.

In the beginning, we got along very well. The first trouble began when we shot the scene where Mr. Okuzaki goes into somebody's house and punches him. I was rolling the camera, not getting involved in the activities. After that scene was shot, Mr. Okuzaki was very angry at me, claiming that he was almost murdered and that I refused to help him. He had wanted me to become involved when he was assaulting the other person. I was the cameraman for the film, and the eyepiece for a 16mm camera is not easy to see through—things look dark—and I had enough to do just to follow the activities. I was not able to see enough even to decide whether or not I should intervene. But Mr. Okuzaki felt that I must get involved. That was our first confrontation.

MacDonald: Did you and he have rules about what you could or couldn't shoot? Did he dictate what he wanted you to shoot?

Hara: Usually. At first, Mr. Okuzaki was very cooperative. He was more than willing to give me ideas, and usually would call at 6 A.M. to talk for at least an hour about these ideas.

But, of course, I knew that in order to portray Mr. Okuzaki's character and his ideas, it wouldn't be enough just to follow what Mr. Okuzaki said. So I got a list of Mr. Okuzaki's war buddies, and I visited each of them. And during *those* visits, I heard about the story of cannibalism that I tell in my film.

But to get back to the question. At first, Mr. Okuzaki tried to dictate rules to me. He even insisted that there should be two edited versions of the film. He would edit one version and I would edit the other. Of course, I refused.

Mr. Okuzaki also said, "You must film *everything* I do." My reply was, "If I film everything you do, I will run out of money very quickly." I suggested, "Why don't you buy an 8mm camera and film everything yourself?" And Mr. Okuzaki replied, "I want to be covered in 16mm."

MacDonald: How did you get to film in the various private homes?

Hara: None of those people gave me a simple yes as an answer. Every time I went to film, there was a big argument about my filming, and I would run the camera even during those arguments. For the finished film I cut out the arguments. Shooting the film was never easy. But to answer your question: the people I filmed knew what kind of person Mr. Okuzaki was. They were afraid of him, and therefore *couldn't* refuse because they knew what kind of trouble they'd get into with *him* if they tried to refuse *me*.

The person who Mr. Okuzaki hit at the beginning of the film didn't know who Mr. Okuzaki was—that's why he acted the way he did. The second time he appears in the film, he has changed his attitude. People who know Mr. Okuzaki refer to him as *sensei* [an honorific term used for people of status]. When people use that word to Mr. Okuzaki, he becomes very pleasant.

I had a crew of five, and they gradually became involved in a debate about who to follow, who to respect: Mr. Okuzaki or me. They tended to follow Mr. Okuzaki's wishes—he's that kind of man.

MacDonald: In America, you have to get releases from people you've filmed or they can sue you. Is that true in Japan?

Hara: No. That's one of the differences between America and Japan.

MacDonald: How was the film received in Japan?

Hara: It was screened in a rather small art theater in Tokyo for quite a long time. Later, it was more widely seen. For a documentary film in Japan, it is said to have been very successful. There are many "top 10" lists published in Japan and my film was considered the best film, or at least second best, on many lists that year.

There is a big difference in the reactions to that film by people who have actually been to war and by the younger generation, who do not know about war. My young audience was shocked by my film, but at the same time the theaters were often engulfed with laughter. Among the people who are older, who have experienced war, there are two major opinions: first, a sense of thanks to Mr. Okuzaki for saying the things they couldn't say themselves; and second, a feeling that the violence Mr. Okuzaki uses in the film is not acceptable. In the confrontation between Mr. Yamoto and Mr. Okuzaki, many older people side with Mr. Yamoto, who was against violence, and who did not want to reveal everything.

Currently, Mr. Okuzaki is in Kyoto jail. He gets quite a few fan letters.

MacDonald: Was there any rehearsal for the film, any advance planning with the people filmed?

Hara: We didn't rehearse at all. It was all done on the spot. There was one part where Mr. Okuzaki decided to rehearse on his own—the scene where they visit a restaurant and then go to another location to discuss the topic of cannibalism. After I shot that sequence, I learned that Mr. Okuzaki had gone to the restaurant before me to set things up!

MacDonald: But in general, when you walked up to the house with the camera crew, nobody knew you were coming?

Hara: I did not speak to the people before filming (except for some of Mr. Okuzaki's war buddies, as I mentioned earlier), because Mr. Okuzaki said I shouldn't. Mr. Okuzaki felt that if we announced we were coming, the people would hide or run away.

Jackie Pardon [artist/programmer]: What was the impact on the Japanese public of the revelation that officers and soldiers had been engaged in cannibalism?

Hara: The information about cannibalism was out in the print media before it came out in my film, but this was the first time Japanese people saw people actually speak about their experiences.

The biggest impact the film had was not due to the cannibalism, but to the fact that Mr. Okuzaki accused the Emperor of causing the war. In Japan it is very difficult to openly accuse the Emperor for the war, and the fact that Mr. Okuzaki did so in this film was a very big incident in Japan.

Tom Johnson [filmmaker]: I want to go back to Alan Rosenthal's question about *Extreme Private Eros*. When would you stop being an observer and participate in the situation? Okuzaki later shot the son of one of the men you interviewed; would you have intervened in that incident?

Hara: While I was shooting, I thought constantly about this issue. I wondered what I would do if Mr. Okuzaki committed a crime in front of the camera. Should I continue shooting and not do anything, or should I continue shooting while trying to convince Mr. Okuzaki not to commit the crime? As it turned out, Mr. Okuzaki went to shoot the commander-in-chief's son without telling me, so I never really had to make that decision.

Ken Jacobs [filmmaker]: Why did he shoot the son? And why were people in the audiences for the film laughing?

Hara: Once Mr. Okuzaki decides to commit a crime, he goes into action. Only after he commits the crime and is imprisoned will he relax and be satisfied. That's the kind of person he is. For Mr. Okuzaki, whether it was the commander-in-chief or his son made no difference: it was the action itself. You understand, I'm explaining on his behalf right now; I'm not sure if he would agree with me.

In general, Mr. Okuzaki is a very well-mannered man and very kind. But when he decides to do something, he will sometimes become very aggressive, though he uses his aggression in a very calculated manner. That is because his opponent is the government. Authority is a very big opponent. Mr. Okuzaki cannot always be aggressive because he will run out of energy. He mentions the word "God" very often; in his thought structure, God provides the energy for him to continue fighting. Mr. Okuzaki receives God's energy, holds it inside, and saves it until the appropriate time to be aggressive.

About why the young people laughed: maybe Japan is known, from the outside, as a free country, but in reality there are all kinds of things that tie down the younger generation; they are under a lot of stress. So when they see Mr. Okuzaki having an argument with the police, they tend to see a man doing whatever he wants to do. That excites them and allows them to release their anxiety.

MacDonald: Apparently, Mr. Okuzaki has been involved in a number of issues and incidents. How did you decide to focus on this one?

Hara: First, I met Mr. Okuzaki and decided to do the film. Then, I started to do research on my own and I learned about the cannibalism incident, and I talked to Mr. Okuzaki about my desire to cover it in this film. At first he refused, but later agreed, and I began to shoot.

Originally, Mr. Okuzaki was more interested in doing something about issues relating to the future, whereas I wanted to so something about the past, about the war. Then when I went to each of Mr. Okuzaki's war buddies with Mr. Okuzaki, he started to realize that something terrible may have happened and he became very aggressive in his pursuit of the truth.

Michael Grillo [medieval historian/Flaherty projectionist]: What was most difficult in making the film?

Hara: While I was editing, I was very depressed, very gloomy. I didn't support everything Mr. Okuzaki did. I mentioned that it was "love at first sight," but gradually I started to think of Mr. Okuzaki as an enemy, at least at times. And Mr. Okuzaki criticized me so often during the filming that by the time I was editing I had no idea that the film would turn out well. When you look at the film, you may think that Mr. Okuzaki's logic has a sense of continuity, but during the shooting there seemed to be no such thing.

Kenzo Okusaki in Kazuo Hara's *Yuki Yukite Shingun* ("The Emperor's Naked Army Marches On," 1987).

The act that Mr. Okuzaki committed, shooting the lead pellets at the Emperor, is a very important part of Japanese postwar history, so I wanted to portray Mr. Okuzaki's feelings about that issue, but I felt that not many people would see the film. I also felt that 80 percent of the audience who did see it would dislike it. The best I could hope was that 20 percent of the audience would understand Mr. Okuzaki's feelings about the slingshot incident, and would like the film.

There was so much trouble that I almost gave up.

MacDonald: How did you support yourself during the years when you were shooting and editing?

Hara: In Japan there are no real funding sources for the type of films I make, so during the five years that I was in production, I worked as an assistant director for other filmmakers in Japan. At first, I didn't think the project would take five years. My wife (she's the co-producer of the film) felt that if we borrowed 200,000 yen [about nine hundred dollars, when the film was produced] from one hundred of Mr. Okuzaki's fans, we would have enough money to shoot the film. That's what we did.

During the shooting, I eventually ran out of money. I borrowed from my parents. And I also got contributions from Mr. Imamura.

MacDonald: Did Mr. Okuzaki see the film?

Hara: During Mr. Okuzaki's trial, arrangements were made to show my film in court, so he did see the film. I received a letter from him after he was in prison. He said the film was not very interesting for him, because it only shows what he did, rather than what his ideas are. But I think he was lying. In one of the "top 10" lists that year, Mr. Okuzaki was the number one actor of the year. He was very happy about that and felt it was because of God.

Right now, I cannot write letters to Mr. Okuzaki because in Japan there's a law that a convicted prisoner can send letters only to family members. But before he was in prison, I received a letter from him saying that he would very much like to make a sequel. This time, Mr. Okuzaki wants to be the producer, writer, main character, *and* director. [laughter] I asked him what *I* would do, and Mr. Okuzaki said, "You'll operate the camera."

MacDonald: Has the film been on Japanese television?

Hara: No. Japanese TV stations still cannot break through the taboo about dealing with the Emperor.

MacDonald: How did you decide on the title?

Hara: In Japan the title is *Yuki Yukite Shingun*. The English title is not a very accurate translation. "God's Army Marches On" would be better. Mr. Okuzaki claims to be a part of "God's army." The "Marches On" part comes from seeing how relentless Mr. Okuzaki is in what he does.

MacDonald: What kind of reaction did the officers who confessed in the film have to the film?

Hara: Most likely my film did not affect their lives at all.

I was told the right wing might make trouble for me. But the right wing in Japan now operates for a profit. It is not like in the past when they really had a belief system. When the right wing people see Mr. Okuzaki with his car [the car is covered with slogans], they decide what he does will not lead to any kind of a profit and so they do not respond. Some right-wingers did say that they understood what Mr. Okuzaki was doing, and that he might be a right-winger himself. The issue of right wing and left wing is a complex one. Personally, I cannot decide whether Mr. Okuzaki is left wing or right wing.

MacDonald: I may be mistaken but I had a sense that you particularly enjoyed Ken Jacobs's films this week.

Hara: I thought *Cherries* [in various versions since 1980; the full title of Jacobs's Nervous System performance is *XCXHXEXRXRXIXEXSX*] was the most interesting work I saw at the Flaherty Seminar. Ken Jacobs makes what I would call "Another Cinema." A lot of people here criticized him for using pornography in *Cherries*. And the close-ups of the characters having sex, especially as projected through his system, were something entirely new for me. I was extremely shocked—but amazed as well.

The movement of the people having sex, as controlled by Jacobs and his apparatus, made me think of many things, not just sex; it became extremely mysterious and surprising. And that surprise was much larger inside me than any thoughts about the political issue of pornography. I think it is wasteful to decontextualize the pornographic element of the work. Pornography is made to make men have a hard-on, but watching *those* images of sex doesn't give me a hard-on: it makes me think of other images, other issues.

Marks: Jacobs's method allows us to read the imagery in many ways and to read many kinds of pleasure into it. *Cherries* allowed me, as a woman, to read the pornography in a way that was subversive of its original intent. But I *did* get a "hard-on." Actually, for me the pleasure was both mental, aesthetic, *and* physical, sensual. For me, the one *is* the other.

Hara: Looking at *Cherries*, I felt that people are very strange and also very lonesome and tragic.

I think that social restrictions become built-in restrictions in our consciousness, which are impossible to free ourselves from. There are many social restrictions that only women face. And the more restrictions there are, the more energy the restricted person builds up, often as anger.

MacDonald: You mean that the people who object the most to *Cherries* get the energy to object from feeling excessively restricted in their own lives?

Hara: Yes.

MacDonald: Is there Japanese work that relates to Ken Jacobs's work?

Hara: There is one filmmaker who has explored the fundamental idea of motion in Japan, but he uses only a standard projector.

MacDonald: Do you mean Taka Iimura? [See *A Critical Cinema*, the first volume in this series, for an interview with Iimura.]

Hara: Yes, though I don't know Mr. Iimura's work very well.

Marks: What other developments in Japanese film interest you now?

Hara: Today Japanese films are at a low point.

MacDonald: What are you working on now?

Hara: If you live for a long time, many things happen. I have two children by my current wife. The second child, a boy, committed suicide when he was thirteen. And as a filmmaker I want to think about why this happened, by making a film. Recently, I've begun filming a little. I myself am the reason for my son's suicide.

MacDonald: If you'll forgive me for asking, how do you mean? I'm curious because my son attempted suicide when he was fifteen.

Hara: My son went to kendo lessons every day, and one day I returned home and he had not gone to a lesson. I became very angry and hit him. My son started crying, ran out of the apartment, up to the roof, and jumped off the building. The reason for his death is clear: I hit my son.

At that time I thought it would be better if I expressed my anger at my son. I'm not saying this to avoid responsibility, but people in my generation, born after the war and influenced by the ideas and movements of the seventies, have all raised their children in rather similar ways. They tend to feel that they should express their feelings towards their children at full force. But our children are not always strong enough to receive all of that energy. My son couldn't bear it, and he committed suicide. So what I feel I must do in the new film is to try to redefine the values of the postwar generation.

MacDonald: In the United States, until the advent of TV talk shows, it was virtually taboo to talk in detail in public about the pain and problems in one's own family. I assume it's even more taboo in Japan. Is that the taboo that you mean to confront in this new film?

Hara: No matter what subject I decide to film, I always face the same thing: Japanese family imperialism. That's the similarity in all my works. The system of Japanese family life developed as part of the Emperor's political system. So "the opponent" in my films is very large.

MacDonald: That opponent is not only Japanese. Whenever fascists gain power, they often do so in the guise of "family values," which usually means a decision to romanticize the family.

Hara: I agree.

Marks: About your relationship to your audience: do you have a political end you wish to effect? Or do you simply want to communicate more personally?

Hara: Basically, I have political themes in my films, but I am very weak at heart, easily frightened. I don't really have the desire to organize other people politically. The generation previous to mine was very influenced by the Japanese Communist party and was interested in organizing. My generation shuns organization.

I have many twisted emotions within me. Everybody has those kinds of feelings inside them in Japan because it's a very conservative society: there are many systems and restrictions, many taboos. Everybody holds in pain, fear, and dissatisfaction. My great desire is to clearly identify those taboos, those restrictions, and then destroy them. The political message in my films is to say my feelings directly; my films are about self-liberation.

Addendum

Early in 1995 Steven Schible made contact with Kazuo Hara in Tokyo on my behalf, so I could ask him about his earliest film, *Sayonara CP*, and the project he had just completed, *A Dedicated Life* (1995). Schible met with Hara and Sachiko Kobayashi, Hara's wife, discussed my questions with them, and transcribed and translated their answers. I reworked the material and returned it to Schible and Hara for corrections.

MacDonald: I have only seen *Sayonara CP* in the original Japanese, but it seems clear that your method in that earlier film is consistent with your later films. Could you talk about the origin and evolution of that project?

Hara: Now, in the nineties, it is common to see people in wheelchairs in public. Perhaps it has been this way for a long time in New York, but in Japan it is only recently that handicapped people go outside. *Sayonara CP* was shot in 1971. Until the end of the sixties it was almost unheard of, in Japan, for handicapped people to leave their homes. There was no opportunity for handicapped people to take part in society. If they weren't confined in their homes, they stayed in larger facilities designed for the disabled. The vitality of the handicapped, their *life* in every sense, was confined. I felt that I wanted to change this situation somehow.

In our society things are valued in terms of their usefulness in labor. This includes the body. Hands are more important than feet, since at the workplace the hands are usually used more often than the feet. Those people with so-called major disabilities are considered of little use.

At that time, it was a new idea that a change in the relationship between those who were physically handicapped and those who weren't was called for. I felt that something needed to be done about the confinement of the handicapped, and about the inability of the non-handicapped to reach out to them. I felt that the first step would be for the non-handicapped to see the handicapped in the most frank, honest manner possible. I felt that seeing them in this manner would lead to a questioning of the way in which these people were treated, and that ultimately this would lead to a changed relationship between the handicapped and their surrounding environment.

So first there was a need to *look* at the issue of physical disability. The first scene in *Sayonara CP* shows the protagonist refusing to use his wheelchair, getting off, and going outside on his knees. A wheelchair is a very useful tool for a person who cannot walk. But from the perspective that there is a need to transform the attitudes toward the handicapped, it was necessary to remove the wheelchair. At least that's what we figured back then. In the film, we wanted to study the public view of physical disability, by actually forcing the viewer to focus on the "handicapped" body and carefully scrutinize the physical nature of disability.

MacDonald: Is there personal background for your interest in the handicapped?

Hara: Personally, I didn't know much about the disabled. I moved to Tokyo when I was twenty, to study photography and become a photojournalist. The first subject I dealt with in school was the handicapped, though I couldn't continue as a photographer for long: through photographs, I could only know the people superficially.

Then, soon after starting school, I ran out of tuition money, and had to support myself by delivering newspapers. I couldn't continue my studies while at the same time maintaining my relationship with the handicapped, so I quit going to school.

I began to frequent facilities for the handicapped. There were many organizations trying to deal with the issue at that time, and I met with people in each of them. All in all, it took about five years for me to learn my way around. Around the third year, I began to work at a school for physically impaired children as a member of the staff. I worked there for fourteen months, and while there, I took photographs of the children I was responsible for. These photographs were later exhibited at the Nikon Salon Gallery at Ginza. Sachiko Kobayashi came to see the exhibit, and moved to Tokyo with the desire to make a film about the issue. She asked me if I could shoot the film for her. What we eventually made was my first movie. She produced it, and I shot it.

Sachiko Kobayashi: All of the money for the film was borrowed. We borrowed twenty to thirty thousand yen each from interested friends and acquaintances, and got a few contributions of about ten thousand yen from people interested in the disability movement.

Hara: It took us six months to shoot the film, though the total number of shooting days was only fifteen or sixteen. It took six months to edit.

During the shooting, the two protagonists (Hiroshi Yokota and Koji Yokozuka) and I talked after each shooting day. If we felt OK about what we'd done that day, I'd ask, how about doing this or that next? We held discussions and made adjustments throughout the shooting.

Schible: There were many other handicapped people in the film. Did your discussions include them?

Hara: Those other people were members of the same organization as the protagonists. I didn't work as intimately with them as I did with the two main individuals in the film, but they were important in several ways. *Sayonara CP* includes a section of interviews regarding sex. During the discussion of sex, people other than the film's protagonists speak in front of the camera. When the film came out, this shocked the public, since they didn't think the handicapped *had* sex, or were even capable of having sex. It became quite sensational. The controversy probably made many realize that the handicapped were human.

These other people were also important when Hiroshi Yokota's wife decided he could no long be involved with the film. She didn't want Hiroshi Yokota to make *any* film. And when she realized that the film wasn't going to be a visually appealing film about the handicapped—it isn't beautiful to see a person who normally uses a wheelchair try to do everything on his knees—she was even more upset. Understandably. But we kept shooting. Hiroshi Yokota and I were very clear that we needed to shoot in the manner that we did. For his wife this was shameful. It led to the scene where she asks, "Why do you have to do something which is so embarrassing, something which makes you look so low?" The wife wants to live an ordinary life with her husband; she wants an ordinary family. To her, her husband's walking on his knees is nothing more than an embarrassment. As the shooting went on, her emotions became stronger. Things developed into an argument. Of course, I filmed all of this as it was going on. Hiroshi's wife became hysterical, and I wound up filming her saying, "Stop!" straight to the camera. Finally, she told him, "Stop shooting or I will have to divorce you."

Later, Hiroshi called me to say he couldn't continue with the project. I contacted the members of his group and suggested we all go over to his place and try to convince him to continue. His friends asked him why he had to stop. Of course, he wanted to continue; he was only quitting because of his wife, though in the end, because of the insistence of his friends, he decided not to quit. So he continued, and his wife continued to confront him.

There were other incidents also. Toward the very end there is a scene at a *hokoshya tengoku* [literally, "pedestrian paradise": on Sundays and holidays, some city streets in Japan are closed to vehicle traffic in order to allow people to use the streets for recreational purposes]. At that time a *hokoshya tengoku* was still a very new thing. Hiroshi Yokota is a poet, and he wanted to express his feelings as a handicapped person at the *hokoshya tengoku*. We decided to go and shoot on the street, where we attracted a crowd. It was a satisfaction to Hiroshi Yokota to be able to express himself to the crowd. As I was reloading the camera, the cops came and said we shouldn't do this. They said that a *hokoshya tengoku* wasn't a place to put on a show, that it was a place where people had to keep moving, to keep walking.

Since Hiroshi Yokota had a speech disability, the cop couldn't understand what he was saying, and of course, he didn't try to listen. He took Hiroshi Yokota away. We rushed to the police station and negotiated with the cops on his behalf. We tried to explain what we were doing, but they weren't very accepting. Eventually, we became his guarantor and got him out.

To Hiroshi Yokota, all this was a very positive development: he felt that his act of self-expression had communicated so strongly that he had put the police in the position, first, of having to arrest him and, then, of having to free him. When he said this to me, I said, "In the first place, it wasn't your self-expression at all, since we carried you here. And you were only released because we became your guarantor. You say you accomplished this with your own strength, but that's not true."

He and the others in the group had an illusion about their ability to express themselves. They thought that, given a chance, they could do things just like anyone else. Upon hearing what I said, he realized I was correct. He was shocked, and he became disillusioned. He was able to understand the nature of mainstream society, the society of the non-handicapped, for the first time. He had come to a new starting point, and was able to recognize the meaning of his handicap, and where he stood in relation to the rest of society. He became empty inside. When he told me that he no longer had the energy to continue, I said, "We have to continue! There are more things to shoot." But he insisted on stopping, so I went to his house with the members of the group again. We eventually convinced him to come out with us.

The last scene was shot early on Sunday morning, in an industrial area with no pedestrians around. We got into an argument. He wanted to stop. I wanted to continue. The argument became heated, and she [Hara points at Sachiko Kobayashi] said, "If this is the end, at least do one last thing: strip in front of the camera and do a handstand or something!" He took this literally. He stripped and tried to do a handstand.

MacDonald: How did you go about distributing what must have seemed a shocking film? And how did other handicapped people respond?

Hara: The film was independently distributed, and at the time, this meant that it could not be screened at an ordinary theater. It had to be shown at universities and town halls and so forth. The first screening was at the Department of Education at Tokyo University. We passed out flyers to organizations involved with the handicapped. At that screening, we were strongly criticized. We were asked why we had to do such a miserable, non-humanitarian film. They felt sorry for the people in the film.

But the two protagonists were at that screening and *they* criticized those who criticized the film. They said the film was a collaboration between themselves and the filmmakers: "Your attacking Hara implies that you think we are incapable of taking initiative. Something's wrong in *your* thinking."

Those who were criticizing my position realized their misunderstanding, and that the many films which were made about the disability issue were not made by filmmakers who saw themselves on the same level with their subjects, who confronted their subjects as equals. On the contrary, films prior to ours had had a very patronizing attitude toward the handicapped: they merely felt sorry for them.

When a non-handicapped person saw our film, he was shocked. But when people with cerebral palsy saw it, they became very interested. They felt we were doing something interesting, not something shocking. Eventually, a screening of the film was considered a good way to cultivate a new kind of thinking about the issue.

As far as I can see, the handicapped members of the audience did not go though the same sort of disillusionment that Hiroshi Yokota did. On the contrary, I think to them he was doing something cool, by going outside and drawing people's attention to the issues. In the end, the film became a positive form of agitation: more handicapped people went outside and some of these people started to organize their own movements. Things certainly changed.

MacDonald: Did Hiroshi's wife accept the finished film?

Hara: No. I didn't have her permission to use the material of her, and she was quite angry. She said we were wrong for doing this, and her anger was written up in *The Asahi* [a Tokyo newspaper]. The headline was "It's Nothing But a Show." The article itself was objective and very understanding, but the headline was unfair.

MacDonald: Could you tell me something about *A Dedicated Life* [1994], your new project?

Hara: The protagonist, Mitsuharu Inoue, is known as an avant-garde novelist of the postwar era, but I didn't want to film him because of this. I became interested in him when I went to hear his lecture on the changing nature of human relationships, and the relationship between fact and fiction. I was very moved by his lecture. As a documentarian, I cannot avoid dealing with relationships and with issues of fact and fiction.

Also, Mr. Inoue is a person with a lot of impact. He speaks loudly, and he gave me the feeling that he would instigate things for me, as Kenzo Okuzaki did—my documentarian's sixth sense. So I decided to make a film about him.

It took me five years to complete the film. I thought it would take about ten years, because Mr. Inoue is a prolific novelist, and it was my intention to study his works as I shot. My original intention was to make a film about him confronting the issue of fact and fiction. I wanted someone who could elaborate on this issue through his actions. As I was doing research on Inoue, I gradually noticed that the biographical description that accompanied his books included many fictional elements. Later, I realized that this could be the main thread of the film.

The project changed after it was underway, when Mr. Inoue became afflicted with cancer. I was able to capture his battle with the disease. First, he was diagnosed with cancer of the intestines, then it was liver cancer, and then it spread to his lungs. The footage I was able to make while he was alive covers the process of how he learns that he has cancer, and how the illness progresses. He had an operation for the liver cancer, and I was able to film that. I also filmed his conversations with his doctor. He died three years after the shooting began.

At the Flaherty

In 1987, Richard Herskowitz asked me to attend that summer's Robert Flaherty Seminar, which he was programming, as a representative of *The Journey* (1987), Peter Watkins's $14^1/_2$-hour, meta-critique of mass media, which Herskowitz had decided to present, in toto, during the seminar week. It was my first Flaherty, though I had been hearing about the Flaherty's sometimes volatile post-screening discussions for years. And as the mid-week discussion of *The Journey* approached, I was increasingly aware that a considerable number of seminarians were hostile to the Watkins film. The evening before the discussion, and despite the fact that I knew I wouldn't be representing the film alone (Watkins was present for the discussion, along with several others who had worked on the film in various capacities), I broke out in welts, from shoulders to knees—something that had never happened to me before and has not happened since. I am hard-pressed to understand this reaction; I had (and have) no doubts about the quality and importance of Watkins's work and did not think I cared what the Flaherty Seminar thought of me. In retrospect, it seems obvious that the intensity of my reaction was a function of my unconscious recognition that the Flaherty is one of the longest-lived (in 1995, the Flaherty celebrated its fortieth anniversary), most influential organizations in North America devoted to critical forms of cinema.

Francis Flaherty, Robert Flaherty's wife, began the Flaherty Seminars soon after Robert Flaherty's death in 1951 as a memorial to his life and work. Beginning as an intimate get-together of (mostly documentary) filmmakers, the Flaherty evolved into an annual, week-long gathering of around a hundred film- (and more recently video-) makers, programmers, critics, librarians, academics, and other film-interested people, a kind of ongoing community of newcomers and returnees. Documentary has remained the focus of the annual seminars but avant-garde film has been a relatively consistent subtext (see MacDonald, "The Flaherty and Avant-Garde Film," in *Wide Angle* 17, nos. 1–4 [1995–96], edited by Erik Barnouw and Patricia Zimmermann, a special issue on the Flaherty Seminar and the best source of information on the institution's history). Indeed, I first became aware of the Flaherty not through standard documentary channels, but in Jonas Mekas's *Lost Lost Lost* (1976), during which Mekas, Ken and Flo Jacobs, and several others attempt an invasion of the 1963 seminar, in the name of Jack Smith's *Flaming Creatures* (1963) and Jacobs's own *Blonde Cobra* (1963).

For many Flaherty seminarians, the discussions with film- and videomakers immediately after screenings are the heart of the Flaherty experience, the melodrama that energizes the seminar week and instigates the confrontations of personality and ideology that become the stuff of Flaherty legend. The discussions, which are usually moderated by the year's programmers and/or members of the Board of International Film Seminars, generally last around an hour. Usually, a single maker responds to questions and statements (when necessary, with the assistance of a translator); sometimes several makers field questions. Seminarians are urged to attend all the discussions and be an integral part of the group process, which distinguishes the Flaherty Seminars from film festivals and most other film gatherings. The discussions are always voice-taped and the tapes become part of the seminar's archives—implicitly, a resource for future scholars.

At their best, the discussions elicit interesting, and sometimes brilliant, insights from the filmmakers, many of whom see a Flaherty invitation as an honor and have clearly readied themselves for the seminar audience. Again, at their best, the discussions are an open forum where attendees can declare themselves about individual works and their makers, and voice their general cinematic concerns of the moment. By and large, attendees deal with each other with respect and good humor; and as the Flaherty week evolves, the group's interchange reflects the bonding that occurs not only during screenings and large-group discussions, but during smaller-scale interchanges at meals and between events.

At their worst, the large-group discussions function as punishment for makers whose works or whose attitudes offend the shared sensibilities and ideologies of seminarians, whose "questions" are meant to goad the guilty makers for the pleasure of their colleagues. The fact that some invited film- and videomakers spend only a short time at the Flaherty, while attendees are together morning, noon, and night, day after day, tends to exacerbate an us versus them atmosphere—as does the reputation for "toughness" of Flaherty discussions. Of course, even within the most "brutal" Flaherty interrogation, there are widely varying attitudes. Indeed, when I listened to tapes of several legendary "trashings" of makers, I heard a good many positive comments about the works being discussed.

I have excerpted five Flaherty group discussions; they were chosen and are arranged so as to provide some sense of the Flaherty experience. The first two discussions are instances of more volatile discussions. I had direct involvement with both (I represented *The Journey* and arranged for the other representatives of the film to be present; I programmed part of the 1992 seminar and invited Ken Jacobs to present his Nervous System piece *XCXHXEXRXRXIXEXSX* ["Cherries," performed in various versions since 1980]). In both cases, the presentations discussed were conscious confrontations of the Flaherty audience. In making *The Journey*, Watkins's goal was to demonstrate a new approach to media making, one that defied our conventional, "professional" sense of media time (*The Journey* is as "slow" as the slowest "structural film") and of who gets to be the focus of media attention (much of *The Journey* centers on the comments of everyday families from fourteen nations around the world, presented uncut in as close to real time as possible). Further, in presenting the entire film (some of it during scheduled screening times, the rest late at night or outside the Flaherty's formal screening schedule), Herskowitz knew he'd test the seminarian's patience and stamina. I invited Jacobs to present *XCXHXEXRXRXIX-EXSX* because I knew his two-hour exploration of a bit of French pornography was sure to create something of a ruckus: I wanted Jacobs's appearance to be reminiscent of the mood of 1963's attempted Mekas/Jacobs "invasion."

If the Watkins and Jacobs discussions are instances of Flaherty discussions at their most cantankerous, the discussions with Filipino filmmaker Nick Deocampo and Indian filmmaker Mani Kaul, who were invited by programmer L. Somi Roy to the 1994 seminar, and with American Craig Baldwin, invited to the 1995 seminar by programmers Bruce Jenkins and Marlina Gonzalez-Tamrong, are instances of Flaherty discussions at their most harmonious. The Kaul and Deocampo discussions represent two very different approaches to film history that have always played a role at the Flaherty: film history as the creation of individual works of film art and film history as a set of institutional structures. In a long, distinguished career, Mani Kaul has made 35mm experimental narratives and documentaries in one of the world's major film industries. Deocampo has made a good many films, but at the seminar his primary commitment was to discuss his involvement in developing institutional structures for a broad range of filmmaking and film exhibition in the Philippines.

The discussion with Craig Baldwin about his most recent film, *Sonic Outlaws* (1995), raised the issue of media piracy, which, in a period of shrinking funds for the arts, seems sure to become an increasingly important film-critical trend. Baldwin (and those his film documents) defies established media institutions altogether by stealing from them and by ignoring governmental regulations aimed at protecting these institutions.

Each of the five discussions is preceded by the titles (and completion dates) of the films discussed, and the date of the discussion. When possible, I have identified each questioner by name and by occupation/affiliation, using the seminarians' self-identifications as a guide (I identify speakers by occupation and affiliation only once, the first time they speak during this set of discussions). When I have not been able to identify a speaker, I have used the term "seminarian." In the more extended discussions with filmmakers elsewhere in this volume, I have sometimes played fast and loose with the specifics of what the filmmakers and I originally said to each other, always, of course, subject to the filmmakers' subsequent approval. In these Flaherty discussions, when I have identified a speaker other than myself, I have stayed as close to the specifics of the taped recording as coherence allows.

Peter Watkins: *The Journey* (1987), August 12, 1987

[At the large-group discussion, *The Journey* was represented by Watkins, and by several of those who had participated in the production: Manfred Becker (editing and sound editing), Vida Urbonavicius (sound editing), Joan Churchill (graphic design), Don Tracy, Scott MacDonald, and Patricia O'Connor (producers of Utica/Ilion, New York shooting), and John Campbell (assistant camera, Portland, Oregon shooting). Nearly all the questions were directed to Watkins.]

Seminarian: Could you share with us your thoughts about the length? Was it part of your original concept?

John Columbus [director, Black Maria Film and Video Festival): And do you think it's appropriate to confine people to chairs? I was trying different ways of staying with the film. One way was to lie on the floor and not look at the image, and, if I did not go to sleep (and a few times I did, and I'm certainly not the only one [laughter]), but if I did not—and in fact most of the time I did not—there were times when something that was said intrigued me and I'd pop up and look. Sometimes, I thought, "Why didn't he just make a sound tape and intersperse visual imagery?"

Watkins: The point about sound and visuals is a very strong one, and I thought about it a great deal. I haven't measured this exactly, but in 5 to 7 percent of the film there's no image at all—and I have wondered why I didn't do that more.

As to the length, we're going to propose that community groups and other groups work with the film in a very stretched-out process, so that people can look at a couple of hours and either talk about what they've seen or leave. Then sometime later, a bit more could be shown and discussed. The film should be only one part of an expanding social process, against which the film's profile is gradually diminishing.

I'll be writing a teaching guide this fall [this guide was not completed until 1992]—a bad expression because the "guide" is going to be as open as possible. I'll be exploring places in the film where I feel I've been able to get out of the conventional traps and where I feel I'm still stuck in them. I'm going to try to be as frank as I can. Of course, one can set out to be tough with oneself, but actually it's very difficult: during filming, decisions are made very fast, and very intuitively and deep. But I'm going to write about those decisions as openly as I can.

When I started *The Journey*, I'd been thinking about the questions it raises, since before *The War Game* [1965] was banned back in 1965. Over the years, I've been part of many discussions in schools and with public audiences. At first, those discussions often focused on the question, "Why aren't we told information? Why are governments hiding information from us?" This was a common theme in many countries, and for a while *The War Game* was a good way of getting that discussion going. But by the seventies, discussions were focusing more on, "What about the material we *are* getting? How is *that* affecting us?" We're all feeling our way in the dark, and many of the public (I would guess) now have an enormous concern, but no easy way of talking about it. Many people feel they can't verbalize effectively about the control of information, because they've had no practice in such verbalizing. In most schools, it's never been the practice to talk in any detail about the ways we get information; and our profession, to put it mildly, doesn't talk about such issues very much with the public. I don't mean only the forms into which information is structured, but also our relationship as professional media people, or lack of a relationship, with the public.

I've recently been in Australia and New Zealand, where *The Journey* opened with the help of core groups, like the one here with me tonight. Something we discussed a great deal there, in secondary schools and universities and publicly, is that if you look at the whole social matrix, or whatever you want to call all of us when we interrelate, where exactly *is* the media? Are we *inside*? Are we *outside*? Most seem to assume the media is apart from the social matrix, and many people vocalize the distance now.

So to come back to your question about the length, I suppose originally I thought the film would be about three hours or so, but you know what happens: we shot a lot of material and then more countries became available to film in and by the time I got back to the National Film Board of Canada [where *The Journey* was edited], I had about a hundred hours of material. I felt that a lot of it was going in very strong directions, and I did not want to do the usual chop chop chop, which I would have had to do, even to reduce what I had to four or five hours.

In any case, the length is absolutely irrelevant, because (I don't have to tell you good people, you *know*) it doesn't really matter these days whether something is six hours, sixteen hundred hours, or six minutes. If they're not going to show it, they're not going to show it. And these days they are not showing most broad challenges to the system.

Michael Grillo [medieval historian, Flaherty projectionist]: I did not have any trouble with the length (granted I was the projectionist, so I could get up and pace around). I don't think you have to see the whole film with studied, staring attention, and I'm willing to bet none of us did. I would suggest that by its duration *The Journey* reinforces the fact that one cannot devote even an hour

Peter Watkins directing the Hendricks family in Utica, New York, during the production of *The Journey* (1987).

a week to any serious issue, without changing the principle of one's life, the very details of one's day-to-day experience. The film has much redundancy. By the fifth time we've seen the Hiroshima photographs, there's a certain amount of tuning out; but this points to the whole necessity of dealing with such issues regularly and in the banal, rather than during special moments apart from everyday life.

Sally Berger [then director, International Film Seminars; currently, video curator, Museum of Modern Art]: After a while, I began focusing on the body language of the people being interviewed, and more and more, I noticed that there was someone in each group who seemed tense. There seemed to be a lot of tension among many of the families.

Watkins: I suppose it's because we're dealing with *people*. I can't really tell you exactly what relationship each person had to the camera; you'd have to go back and ask the families. I didn't have the luxury of working as much as I might have liked with all of them. As it was, the film necessitated three trips around the world: to meet the families; to go back and see them a few months later; then, to shoot. But whenever possible, we did try (and without being patronizing) to talk about the equipment and the process. After awhile I think most people grew more accustomed to the shooting than they thought they would—even to looking into the camera, which I asked them to do. As you said, in the shots when a person is talking, the camera is often showing more than one person: we were trying to broaden the reference by showing the children fidgeting, for example, and the various other dynamics that are occurring between members of each family.

Seminarian: A long film, and extended shots, don't necessarily get people to question media. During a lot of the film I felt that the only action it would encourage people to take is to leave the room where the film is being screened and get some fresh air! There is powerful stuff in the film, but it could be collapsed a lot. Did you consult peace groups and educational institutions to try and figure out the best way to structure the segments so people could really work with the film?

Watkins: No. I've been with about twenty audiences in five countries, and their responses have been very varied. Sure, some people don't like the length. Roughly speaking, maybe 40 to 50 percent of the audience stay through; the others leave at various points. Many of the positive reactions have come from teachers.

Seminarian: It's just *too long*. [laughter] I sat through most of it, and enjoyed a good bit of it. I tend to agree with your positions in the film so you're preaching to the converted. But I'm assuming you want to make some change, and I question seriously whether those you want to change are going to sit through 14 ¹/₂ hours of film, regardless of the content.

Also, I question the simplistic assumption that if the governments of the world don't spend money on arms, that money will be available for social welfare. I know of no instance where that's been the case.

Watkins: As far as I know (I may be wrong here, but as far as I know), none of us made that assumption. I certainly didn't, and I don't remember any of the families doing so. Of course, many of the families would be aware of the irony you have raised—that, of course, if the money weren't used for arms, it would get absorbed somewhere else—but the purpose of the film, nonetheless, is to raise the point, not as an assumption, but as an enormous tragic irony that we live under now.

MacDonald: A point about the length. I teach American literature as well as film, and I routinely ask my students to read major novels, some of which take many hours to read. I realize that given the conditioning we have, it doesn't seem practical or comfortable to deal with a 14 ¹/₂-hour film, but even in the mass media there are long works. Virtually every regular series on TV is watched an hour a week for a whole season.

David Taffler [media educator]: I think the film should be even longer than it is, so that it could deal more thoroughly with even more of the relevant issues. My relationship with the families continued to grow throughout the entire film, because the information we receive between the family sections continually recontextualizes these people.

Seminarian: I could learn from the survivors of Hiroshima, and even from the woman who lives near the tracks where the "white train" [the "white train" disperses nuclear bombs from their final assembly point in Texas to nuclear submarine bases and other delivery systems around the country] passes, but when the camera arrives in the homes of the families, it takes on this messianic quality. I feel the families were put in an extremely difficult position of having to respond to these transcendent questions and having to reveal their ignorance about so many things. I agree we should all be aware of these issues and should talk about them. But I also feel an invasion of those homes.

And *nobody* knew anything. There are millions of people all over the world working on these issues. *Somebody* is aware, *some* people know, *some* schools deal with these things! Where were *they?*

Watkins: Maybe our perception of people is different. Of course, there are peace groups working with these issues, but the problem is that, nonetheless, the arms race has been escalating out of control. Sure you find people who know about such things, but the large majority don't.

Juan Mandelbaum [film- and videomaker]: I came to feel that this was just another form of media manipulation, of forcing people into a situation. I know they agreed to participate, but they didn't know what they were agreeing to . . .

Watkins: Excuse me! Here, I must interrupt. You've made an assumption there, which to be fair to us, to me, is incorrect. Wherever possible, and it nearly always was, we spent a considerable amount of time with each family that had agreed to be in the film, discussing the questions we would ask and our filming process. Obviously, that's not the same thing as doing it—I agree with that—but we absolutely did not do the more traditional thing of just rushing in with a camera.

Seminarian: It just seemed so set-up! They're always sitting there, very gloomy [laughter], saying how they never knew *anything* [laughter] . . .

Watkins: Well, excuse me, everyone, I must say here that I don't think this is funny. Maybe we have a different sense of humor . . .

Seminarian: But his point is very well taken . . .

Watkins: Possibly, yes, I just don't find it amusing.

Maria DeLuca [filmmaker]: I don't think the laughter was meant as disrespect to anyone who made the film. It's just a breaking of tension. We're all really tense, at least *I'm* really tense.

Watkins: It *is* difficult to talk about things you don't know, but most of the families, once the process was over, said they felt glad to have shared what was essentially an educational process.

There was a German family—a well-educated farming couple in their mid-thirties—who had a hostile reaction to our process. They took what I would call a conservative position on these issues, and I thought it would be good to include them. This family was very disturbed by the information, particularly by the Hiroshima pictures, and they said, "You are trying to manipulate us!" I thought, "Well, I hope we'll get through this because it'll be very useful for the film." But they became more and more hostile to the process, and did not want their children to participate in the filming, even the sixteen-year-old daughter, because as they said (and this is a quote): "We're already angry about the way teachers manipulate them; we don't want anyone else manipulating them. That's *our* function." We did what we could to continue, but it just went from bad to worse, and finally everyone was so uncomfortable that we stopped filming.

I didn't know what to do with the material we had. On one hand, I thought it would add something to the film, but on the other hand, they didn't like it. Finally the man told us, "If you use it, I will put a lawyer onto you." I could have gone ahead, but decided not to. The German crew were very shaken by this experience, which was the only such experience during the filming; there were several families in Japan and in the arms-industry strip in the Northwest of this country where people didn't want to get into trouble by appearing in "a peace film."

Manfred Becker: I know the German family personally, and they changed after this experience. The man raised a stink when the army later used the local school during maneuvers.

DeLuca: They changed because of the film?

Becker: This is what they told me.

John Akomfrah [film- and videomaker]: You need to be congratulated for doing something quite unique. This is a film which appears to me, on a whole number of issues, to be very patient and to have listened to people who usually aren't given voice, some of them from the Third World and some from races not usually heard from in the industrialized world. I was here for only a few sections of *The Journey*, but what I saw gave me the impression that your idea was to overturn certain Eurocentric assumptions at work in the European peace movement, where nuclear apocalypse is held up as the ultimate evil which everything else has to kneel in front of. This is the first film I've seen that at least tries to work with a mixed economy within which a whole set of issues are raised, and which allows people to work out of their own priorities and skills with regard to the nuclear arms race.

I would want to add that recently in the United Kingdom a number of television programs have used precisely your strategy for making films that are tied to specific regions and support groups.

And finally a question: What argument did you use, in the Third World especially, to persuade people to participate in the film? Having tried to work in Angola, I know it's very difficult.

Seminarian: Can I add a related question? I only saw about six hours of the film, but it seemed to me that when you talked with the European families, you discussed the nuclear issue, but when you talked with the Third World families, you discussed food. Did you mean to do that?

Watkins: I traveled with a list of all the questions, and I tried—almost ritualistically—to go through *all* of them with each group, so as *not* to make such distinctions. Sometimes, in the editing, certain responses were left out, in the interest of time. And of course, different groups responded to different questions differently. The women's collective in Mozambique had seen the Hiroshima pictures, as had the Mexican family, and the Polynesians . . .

Seminarian: So *they* were the ones that took the discussion in the direction it went?

Watkins: Absolutely, and very much with the Mozambique group.

[to Akomfrah] I had a lot of discussions with the various groups and families, to see if they related to the questions I was interested in asking and to see if they wanted to be involved. But I didn't try to persuade them. I tried not to lean on them at all—that wouldn't have been productive on any level.

Ruth Bradley [director, Athens (Ohio) Center for Film and Video]: The film has an experimental cinematic *form*, but it reiterates another, conventional social form: the patriarchal family. With the exception of the Women's Collective, I see Father, Mother, Children—all over the world. And I kept hearing, "They're just like us! They're just like us!" when the families saw each other on the video. They *are* alike in what the effect would be on them of nuclear war, but they're *not* alike in terms of cultural difference.

Watkins: Well, I thought a lot about the patriarchal question. I know that's a very strong point. Obviously, I don't bring the sensitivity to this issue that a woman would, but I decided, rightly or wrongly, that since the nuclear family (a very ironic expression in these circumstances) is dominantly of this form all over the world, it would be better to deal with that and to confront it and see what would be revealed during the general dynamics of the filming.

Seminarian: As a Third World person, I come from a different position than many of those here. People all over the Third World are already under attack. To focus on the nuclear issue is to ignore what is already going on: in the West, *white* people will die in a nuclear war, but *we* are already dying.

Seminarian: I feel skeptical whether this film can work—and I also feel a tremendous excitement about the attempt. If *The Journey* does in fact succeed, I want you to be very analytical about why; if the film does not succeed, if you can't get it seen, then I hope you'll analyze what went wrong and how we might proceed from there.

Seminarian: At the beginning of the film, I was very excited by what you were attempting, but as the hours went by, I came to hate being bludgeoned by it, and I was horrified when I heard you say you *didn't* have feedback sessions with community groups—and with the teachers you hope will use the film.

Watkins: I can only reply that, horrifying though it may be, the film was made with very little money, and because of that we had tremendous time pressures.

But to be honest, time and money were not the primary considerations. The primary consideration was that, in the editing, I wanted to work with the film personally and privately. Having worked collectively as best I could before the shooting and even during the shooting, I then went inside myself, maybe at a time you would have liked me to go out.

Seminarian: I've been raising my hand for ages! I'm a former clinical psychologist and I've found over and over again that you should never give your own surveys, because when you do, you reveal, through your body language and in all sorts of ways, the answers you want. You *continually* led *your* respondents in that way.

One more statement. I'm not being mean when I say this, just brutally real—please understand that. I liken your film to radical surgery with a rusty knife without anesthesia. And I'll tell you why. I'm a professor at a small, white, conservative university. Last semester, I used a Winnie Mandela documentary about race, only a fifty-five minute film, but very painful to watch. And as a protest, my students got up and removed their seats out of the classroom. They didn't say, "We're not going to look at fifty-five minutes of this nigger bitch in South Africa"; they just moved. That was fifty-five minutes! Do you really think there is any way in the world I could get those students (who really need their consciousness raised) to sit through 14½ hours of *this?*

Watkins: I'm sorry, I can't respond to your question.

Ken Jacobs: *XCXHXEXRXRXIXEXSX* (performed in various versions since 1980), August 9, 1992

[While the titles of the Nervous System pieces are written in all capital letters, I've used conventional capitalization in the text of the discussion to enhance readability.]

Richard Herskowitz: A little background on Ken. Many of you know of him as one of the central figures in the American underground film movement of the sixties, with films like *Blonde Cobra* and *Little Stabs at Happiness* [1963]. He was involved in some of the key events in avant-garde film during that period: the trial about Jack Smith's *Flaming Creatures*, the founding of the Filmmakers' Cooperative, and of the Millennium Film Workshop. He went on to make one of the key "structural films," *Tom, Tom, the Piper's Son* [1969, revised 1971]. Also, since 1970 Ken has been a film professor at SUNY-Binghamton where he's had an enormous influence on many people, including me.

What Ken taught us was not so much how to watch experimental films, but how to watch all films experimentally. He showed us how we could play with and "re-edit" the wide variety of films he showed us *as we watched them*. That's informed all my work as a programmer.

In the past couple of decades, Ken has been much involved with the Nervous System technology you saw tonight.

Jacobs: Thank you for the kind words. To create the film you saw just now, I use identical rolls of the same film, and two stop-motion projectors. While one projector advances the film one frame at a time, the other is capable of many different kinds of movement during the performance: it can tilt up and down, and left and right. The effects on the screen depend on which two frames

are superimposed at any given movement, and on the particular differences between those frames. A propeller is mounted in front of the projectors; it moves
as I'm working and is essential for the effects I create.

John Columbus: I know a lot of things beyond the technology are on people's minds, so I might as well start the ball rolling. Maybe technically, *Cherries* is wonderful. But what about your source material? What went into that
choice? Is it a *statement?*

Jacobs: A statement? Well, I wish it *wasn't*. I guess according to the society
we live in, it would have to be a statement; any imagery of sex in public is a
statement in this society. For some of us, there was a short period of time in the
late sixties and early seventies where sex ceased to be shocking. You *are* asking
about my use of pornography, right?

Columbus: Well, of course, though we could also talk about the perceptual
visceralness of the whole performance. Why necessarily pornography? Does it
matter what your source material is?

Jacobs: It matters very much in terms of what can happen on screen. The
kinds of effects I can get depend on the character of the material . . .

Columbus: The graphic character or the content character?

Jacobs: The graphic character. Where things are in space and what kind of
movement takes place.

Herskowitz: Some of your earlier films have strong political thematic content as well. I think John wants to know how you settle on the political nature
of the pieces of film that enter your system at any given time.

Jacobs: It depends on my needs and what I'm concerned with. *Camera
Thrills of the War* [*Ken Jacobs' Theater of Unconscionable Stupidity Presents
Camera Thrills of the War*, 1981] was done during the approach of the Reagan
presidency. I had *tremendous* fears at that time; I was afraid that with Reagan
in power, apocalyptic forces in this country might actually *have* an opportunity
to achieve their goal of destroying life on Earth so it could be replaced with a
New "Christian" World. I began doing works in response to my fear. They were
cries in the dark. They reached very, very few people.

Herskowitz: Could you bring us back to your use of this particular pornographic footage?

Jacobs: I was working with a lot of very unhappy material—there was also a
work called *The Philippines Adventure* [*Making Light of History: The Philippines Adventure*, 1983], which had to do with the history of American imperialism in the Philippines—and I needed a break from all this negativity, so I chose
the porn film. [laughter, much of it sardonic] And I also wanted to get into the
potential of the Nervous System to work with rounded objects, curved volumes,
up-close; and I wanted to see if I could create a motor action in the imagery that
was appropriate to the motor action of the Nervous System itself. The Nervous
System projectors "copulate." It seemed natural to think about sex.

I wanted something as explicit as possible because I find coyness disgust-

From the French pornographic film used by Ken Jacobs in *XCXHXEXRXRXIXEXSX* (in various versions since 1980).

ing. I find beating around the bush reprehensible. So I wanted the body, and I wanted what bodies do with each other. A friend, a woman who was editing pornographic film for the Mafia, said they were throwing out some old black and white porn films, and I said, "Ideal." I got two little films and loved them both. I like the people in the piece I used tonight. I think they're very nice to each other. They seem to know what they're doing.

Jackie Pardon [artist/programmer]: One of the effects you make with the two projectors made me nauseous, especially when you sprayed the cherry scent . . .

Jacobs: I didn't do that!

Pardon: You didn't?! [laughter] Do other people complain about the strobe-like effect? I could only watch it in bits, though in some parts you created effects that didn't bother me—for example, where the imagery was like sculpture.

Jacobs: Of course it's easier on the eye not to have the strobe effect, but I'm always trying to create effects that are appropriate to the specific frames and to their position within the overall work. In *Cherries*, I need the strobing.

Seminarian: But you're not going *for* a visceral effect, right?

Jacobs: I'm not going for flicker for the sake of flicker. I have to use the flicker to get all the other effects, which I hope we can mention. Like the continuous rolling effect. And the 3-D, which is sometimes very apparent. Some of these effects are very beautiful for me—purely aesthetic satisfactions that drive me on. When I hit something that's satisfying, I stay with it and try and build on it. Martin Arnold's *Pièce Touchée* [1989], which we saw last night, doesn't introduce flicker so it's easier to stand—I understand that—and he does some beautiful things; *Pièce Touchée* is a joy. But he doesn't get quite the kinds of effects I get. He creates more surface information about a space; I create more of an illusion of space-in-depth.

Herskowitz: You also create new imagery: you create spaces where we see things that we know can't possibly be there.

Jacobs: Yes, I give you a workout. Positive and negative spaces change location. Things you *know* are forward, once you've learned to read a photograph, seem further back, and vice versa. Real, crazy illusions take place.

Alan Rosenthal [filmmaker, writer]: The first twenty minutes of this film, as we come to grips with perceiving the images, are absolutely fascinating. But after an hour, a third of the audience was outside, and I think this is a relatively sophisticated and open audience. They weren't just outside; there were a number of people saying, "Let's kill the programmer!" [laughter]

Now I know there are different perceptions of experimental film and where it's at; and some like it, some don't. Those of us who don't are trying to find out what we're missing if we're not getting it, and if we're driven out by boredom. For some of us, there was a feeling that staying in the theater another hour would not have enlarged the experience. Now, can anybody tell us what we're missing? I mean this as an open question, not as an accusation.

Seminarian: I can tell you why I left, if that will start things off. I'm really disturbed that we've spent at least twenty minutes talking about technique—and ignoring *content!* I left because I found the experience offensive and disturbing, and very violent. I'm not against violence. I think violence can be useful in movies, if it's a critique . . . but *you* think it's *fun* or something. For me to watch this is like watching a rape. Pornographic imagery has to do with women and power. I don't know if you're interested in that, but for me it was just this male gaze thing for two hours. And that's something *we* have to live with *every day!*

Jacobs: Well, it disturbs *me* that you don't want to talk about *art!* It's a very important subject that you bring up, but I think that you're stapling it onto this film. You're unable to see that in *Cherries* nobody hurts anybody else. People are engaging each other, both giving and taking pleasure. The kind of "violence" you're talking about is just the excitement of the scene—Nature *is* energetic!—but no one gets punched in the jaw, or shot . . .

Seminarian: That's not the only kind of violence!

Jacobs: No one in the film is forced to do anything!

Herskowitz: The voyeuristic gaze is a fascinating issue in connection with *Cherries*. When I first saw it ten years ago, it expanded my thinking about pornography and voyeurism. Pornography is more *how* we look at things than what we look at. When one's look is distanced, mastering, controlling, voyeuristic—that to me is a pornographic *look*. The original film was probably directed totally at a voyeuristic gaze, but in the expansion of this material, something independent of, transcendent of the original takes place. You go beyond the original intent, and something repressed in the original is liberated.

When I look at pornographic images, I look at myself looking. I see the film looking at me, looking, and at my ways of looking. *Cherries* gives me time to think about these issues. I didn't program this film [laughter], but I've recommended it to many programmers.

Jacobs: There's a problem in dealing with hot social material of any sort: it makes it very difficult for people to see the art . . . I hear a kind of *sneering* from some of you, as if *art* is some dumb, trivial thing to bring up! Art! Maybe it's worth a conversation about what art is; to me art is about whether we even come into existence . . .

Columbus: Oh, we know, artists are gods! And we all have to listen to God . . .

Jacobs: I despise the far-righteous!

Herskowitz: Please, please, let's go on.

Laura U. Marks [freelance writer]: I think there are some really interesting ways to talk about the use of pornography in this film. But I think the opposition Ken is setting up between hot social material and art is not it. And to say this is an interesting film because of the rounded objects isn't it. The reason why pornography in particular is interesting as a subject for motion study—which your film is, and which is the theme of Scott MacDonald's curating these past two days—has to do with stopping motion to investigate the body and attain a kind of mastery. Pornography is, among many other things, about a gaze that possesses.

But another interesting thing is that your film is about engaging desire and prolonging it at the same time. You took a short film and stretched it out to more than two hours. The original film's purpose was to be watched and jacked off to, but how do we deal with the prolongation of the original film? Do we jack off several times over the two hours or what? I'm not opposed to pornography, and I think your choice of the piece of porn was pretty good—the women do take pleasure, not just the man—and I think it was open to a pretty wide variety of readings. But what's also interesting is that your means have a very fundamental connection to pornography, and there's no point pussy-footing around *that*.

Jacobs: I don't understand what you're saying. If you're hopped up on the male gaze, and patriarchy, and power, I guess that's the way you'll see my film. But *Cherries* and my other work is also about becoming conscious of what exists on the screen, of *seeing* what exists.

I *don't* think I stretched a minute and a half into a two-hour masturbation festival . . .

Marks: That was a cheap shot on my part.

Jacobs: It was disgusting! *Disgusting!* Oh, you're such fools!

Columbus: Well *that* opens the dialogue!

Jacobs: I took something that was meant to be used as an abuse of the body, an abuse of even what the *camera* can do, and I transmuted it into something glorious. I took it back to life! . . .

Columbus: That's what . . .
Jacobs: SHUT UP! Don't interrupt me.
Columbus: You're such an elitist, fascist . . .
Jacobs: FUCK YOU!! You disgusting creeps!

[Jacobs walks out. After a short break, those still in the discussion space return to discussion.]

Austin Allen [filmmaker]: There's a consensus that the discussion is ending too quickly. Why leave it at this point? [laughter] Willie, do you want to start?

Willie Varela [filmmaker]: I'm sure a lot of you don't know me. I'm from El Paso, Texas. I've been making films for about twenty years. I'm going to give you a little background to position what's happened here because I think some of it has to do with a change between the generation of Ken, and Stan Brakhage and Jonas Mekas, and the generations that have come after them, for whom the social and political aspects of art—whatever form a film takes, whether it's an experimental film, a social documentary, whatever—are very important, and many times so important that they cancel out the formal aspects.

I've never met Ken Jacobs before. I'm not an apologist. But I have to say that film artists like Ken grew up having to make work in a climate that was extremely hostile; they were vilified for their work a great deal of the time, sometimes even persecuted legally for work like we saw here today.

This is the first time I've seen *Cherries*. I stayed through the whole thing, and as I watched I was trying to figure out my position on looking at this very loaded sexual material. Years ago, I too went through a period when I was interested in pornography, and at the same time, I was reading "Visual Pleasure and Narrative Cinema" by Laura Mulvey [see Mulvey, *Visual and Other Pleasures* (Bloomington/Indianapolis: Indiana University Press, 1989)] and a lot of film theory—trying to figure out what was happening in my interface with pornography, and what it would mean to a woman to be looked at in this way.

I think the response of the young woman back there was very valid. The male gaze, the exploitation of the female body, all these issues are important, and, for the generations that have come after Ken, central to their consciousness of what is seen. I myself have had to *learn* that.

However, I also see Ken's side, and recognize that he truly *was* interested in establishing a formal relationship to the material. What happened here is unfortunate because I think Ken is a great artist, and I think he had a lot to say.

Seminarian: We have to be careful not to let ideology put blinders on our brains and our sensitivities. I found it a very sexy, funny film.

R. William Rowley [filmmaker, professor at Ithaca College]: I had the experience of thinking I was looking at a zoom-in, a continuous enlargement of the frame, and then I'd look at the edge of the frame and see that in fact it wasn't changing size. Also, at certain points, those were no longer people we were watching, they were shadows. Some of us forget that, and think we're watching people.

Varela: We're watching representations of people. I don't think we can forget *that* either. I want a *frisson* where you're balancing the formal aspects with the content; that creates a unique, exquisite tension.

Rowley: There's also the tension of holding on to the imagery, recognizing it as a representation, *and* letting it become just an abstract shape for a while when the whole business of content falls away.

Seminarian: About this generational split. It's not being characterized to my satisfaction. I don't think the younger generation separates formal concerns/Art and social issues/Ideology: we see those things as woven together and quite inseparable. All of us, always, speak through the ideologies that shape us.

MacDonald: But the idea that ideology and art can't be separated is not new. I'd guess that what upsets Ken is the apparent assumption that after all these years of working with these issues, he doesn't know what he's doing. *His* assumption at a certain point in his career, and still to some degree I'd guess, is that one of the oppressive systems one has to liberate oneself from is conventional attitudes toward sexuality. Ironically, at one point not so long ago, pornography seemed to embody a *healthier* attitude about sexuality than had existed in most of the culture before porn was so widely available. Ken is coming out of a period when it was ideological and courageous to *represent* sexuality.

Seminarian: Our generation is reclaiming porn too. There's all this great, funky porn coming out right now, and there's lots of discourse about porn made by women for women, and by men for men.

Rosenthal: The question that continues to bother me, because no one's addressed it, is how we are to evaluate experimental art. It intellectually engages you while you're looking to see what the artists are playing around with. If I'm looking at a piece by Picasso or any modernist painter, I might take five or ten minutes to absorb what they're trying to do, and then I've had my pleasure. I'm not growing any more by giving it *another* five minutes. In a film like this, twenty minutes is fascinating. Then for me, there's no further growth. But a lot of people here were obviously enjoying it immensely. Maybe it's a kind of pleasure that's beyond me.

Varela: I can address that. When you see a piece like this, duration *is* important, because it provides the opportunity to go beyond your normal barriers, the normal defenses we all have, into a space where the artist wants you to be. And I think especially in this particular gathering we should be able to meet the artist more than halfway.

Rosenthal: There were people outside, at least thirty, who stayed fifty minutes to an hour. I would have thought that was enough time to find that "exquisite tension" you talked about.

Ruth Bradley: I think it's a terrific two-hour film! After twenty minutes, you've learned how to watch the film. For the next hour and a half, I tested what

I knew. I got bored at times, I got turned on at times, I fell asleep once, came back, and enjoyed the whole thing. And the last few minutes were amazing!

Seminarian: About the duration: it gives you time to ruminate. That's why I think pornography was a shrewd choice because if there's an issue we need to spend time thinking about, it's pornography. I had time to enjoy the imagery as a typical male *and* to think about how the women in the original film might have been feeling *and* to wonder if, when the lights came on, Jacobs was going to get kicked in the nuts [laughter], and how he was going to take it. I had time to think all kinds of things.

MacDonald: There are films I go to for information, knowledge, a recon-firmation that I'm intelligent, or ideologically legitimate, or whatever. But there are other films I go to to have an unusual *experience*. I don't always say to the filmmaker, the experience has to be *this* duration or I won't consider it. Sometimes I say (implicitly), I want to have the experience *you* have in mind: *you* decide the duration, and I will access it as best I can.

I don't see why the fact that a third of the people in the room are bored after an hour, which is predictable and understandable, is the crucial issue. That two-thirds of the people stay, and many of those people find it fascinating, makes the experience worth offering. In my view, everybody's justified in choosing how long they stay. If it were a matter of just *getting it*, well, I guess I can go into any commercial film, no matter how wonderful, or to any documentary, no matter how well-informed, and in fifteen minutes, I know where it's going. I could say, "*I know where it's going!*" and walk out. But I usually stay for the whole experience.

Nick Deocampo: *Revolutions Happen Like Refrains in a Song* (1987); *Memories of Old Manila* (1993); *Isaak* (1994), August 8, 1994

[Deocampo introduced his films before the screening, then answered ques-tions. I've included both his introduction and the discussion.]

Deocampo: I come here to represent the independent cinema of the Philip-pines, which is really an eighties phenomenon. Those were the dying years of the dictatorship, as well as the birth of some democratic reforms in our coun-try. The eighties were a very tough period for a lot of us young filmmakers be-cause even the movie industry was co-opted by the regime. Everything that was publicly articulated in that society was state controlled, so we had to find our own space. At that time, I was a theater arts student, but slowly I went toward cinema. I arrived in Manila thinking I would be able to *study* film; I ended up *teaching* film. My students and I made Super-8mm films, as a political move. It was the age of alternatives: alternative economies, alternative press, alternative lifestyles. For us, it was alternative cinema. We created a space within the university and then started moving on to other universities—like little monks going from one village to another, and from one island to another, preaching the Gospel of the True Cinema.

In any case, during the eighties we young filmmakers had to remain underground. We did documentaries and experimental films, without having seen the works of Warhol or Brakhage or George Stoney. When I met my first class, I had only the *Film Culture* book with Annette Michelson's essay ["Film and the Radical Aspiration," in P. Adams Sitney, ed., *Film Culture Reader* (New York: Praeger, 1970)]. It is now ten years since we started that movement and it's bearing fruit. Since I returned from New York University, I've been running a film school. We've been producing twenty-five to thirty short films a year. The biggest development is that from the little Super-8s we made ten years ago, we've gone on to 16mm, and, finally, to 35mm.

Now a few words about the three films you're going to see. They represent different periods in my "filmmaking career." The first, *Revolutions Happen Like Refrains in a Song*, is one of the films in my Super-8 trilogy I made the first part of that, *Oliver*, in 1983, at the time Aquino was killed and repression became really intense. That film was about a transvestite who supports his family by doing sex shows in the red-light district of Manila. We worked very closely together on that film: I would show him material as it was done and before the next shooting.

Then, two years after that, I made the second part of the trilogy, *Children of the Regime*, a film about child prostitution (long before anyone would talk about child prostitution). Many times I was "invited" to go to a precinct station jail to spend some nights, because we were not allowed to talk about such things, and it was a good experience seeing things from the inside. Working with the children was difficult because they were always on the run. It was one of my most difficult films. It took five years to shoot, because I too was always on the run. I had been able to document a military man who was selling protection to a gay bar and I was getting threatening phone calls. To protect the film, I shipped it out of the country, just three months before the fall of the dictatorship.

The third part of the Super-8 trilogy, which you'll see, is *really* an exercise in low-budget filmmaking. I only had ten rolls of Super-8 film, three minutes each, and went out into the streets to document the revolution, without knowing how long the revolution was going to last! Thank God I was able to cover at least four of the crucial days. Later, I thought, "Once I edit the thirty minutes, I'll have just a ten-minute film," so I dug up all the outtakes from my other films, and strung them together with my home movies and *voila!*, a film, and a trilogy.

Five or six years later, I got a grant from Channel 4 in London and was able to make a film on five centuries of art history in twenty-two minutes. You'll see that film second. And the third film, *Isaak*, was made just last December. It's 35mm, and the shortest film I've made. It was done overnight, in between trips promoting Filipino cinema. A one-night shoot, a ten-minute film. I worked for twenty-four hours and slept on the plane to Paris!

Discussion with Nick Deocampo (facing camera, left), moderated by Marlena Gonzalez-Tamrong (facing camera, right), at the 1994 Flaherty Seminar.

They're diverse works, in various gauges, with various social functions. But for those perceptive enough, there are recurring themes.

[The films are shown and the group meets for discussion.]

Seminarian: What sorts of censorship problems have you had? Your films are politically challenging and sexually-politically challenging.

Deocampo: During the time of Marcos there was heavy censorship, so we had to go underground. That term appealed to us, more than "experimental," more than "independent," more than "abstract." We identified with "underground" because we really were running from authority, and only because we ran were we successful at avoiding censorship. Ironically, my first censorship came during the time of Cory Aquino. We were all under the illusion that we were now in a democracy. I immediately fed my film to the TV station, and *that*'s where I got censored, right on screen: Oliver's ass was covered by a black dot!

That kind of deception was true in a lot of ways during the Cory Aquino years, and that's when I left for NYU. I knew I was the Master of Super-8 in all of Asia [laughter]—nobody could steal *that* crown from me. At NYU I got my introduction to Eisenstein and became an avid reader of Eisenstein.

Seminarian: I'd like to hear more about the relationship between the independent movement you spearheaded and the Philippines commercial cinema.

Deocampo: It's seldom that I make a film, because much of my time is spent in administration work and on a lot of social action. As director of a film school, my sphere is cultural production. I've studied the careers of the seventies generation—Lino Broca, Ishmael Bernard, Kidlat Tahimik—trying to see what exactly *their* solutions were to the problems of the movie industry. I think I'm posing different solutions to those problems.

The Philippines industry is very commercial. It produces 120 films a year, and we're one of the few countries in the world where a local industry film can outgross American movies, even Stallone. Filipino films make a lot of money at the box office. We are introducing the whole idea of independent cinema and education to them, and they've been responding. I used to run the film school on five hundred dollars a year from the industry. Five hundred dollars! Now, after five years, I have a million pesos, around twenty-five thousand dollars. Still, running a film school on twenty-five thousand dollars doesn't sound like NYU!

George Stoney [filmmaker]: That's what it costs to *go* to NYU!

Deocampo: Advocacy is very much a part of the creative process. At the moment, the industry, which is currently in a state of crisis, is questioning the whole validity of independent cinema, and whether it's going to be productive. The good thing is that I can out-talk any bureaucrat and any producer. I confront them in meetings and at conferences, and tell them we need to train young filmmakers if we want the industry to survive.

At the same time, I always caution everyone that we independent filmmakers should not immediately try to become part of the industry. I have studied the case of Brazil, where they made it a requirement for every feature to be shown with a domestically produced short film. Ultimately all the commercial values filtered into those short "independent" films. We want to have more options than that! We want to pluralize the modes of articulation.

I am happy that at least the industry no longer accuses us of elitism and assumes our films will only survive in academe. Not everybody likes our independent films, but we show them regularly, and an audience is growing. During December, we show *only* Filipino films, for ten days. *Isaak* and films by five of my students were presented as a package during last December and were seen by millions of people. A lot of Asian countries are now beginning to look at this model.

So my position toward the movie industry is constructive. Before I left most recently, they delegated my institute to be the training school for the whole industry. [applause] That's a big burden, but I said, "So long as you give me the right budget, we'll start training the people." Right now, they're building us a building, which we hope will be the training center for Asia. I'm going to festivals to talk to donors. In Berlin, a studio closed down, and I was able to convince them to donate three Arriflex cameras, and a Steenbeck! Wow! And everything was free! We're asking UNESCO to have training programs with us.

Patricia Zimmermann [author, professor at Ithaca College]: I wonder what kinds of "equipment" you ransack for your students from theoretical or historical paradigms around the world?

Deocampo: I throw myself into actual filmmaking, into teaching, so that these theoretical, Western questions and constructions are always deflected into praxis. I can tell a student the history of mise-en-scène, or I can grab a wicker chair and *show* the student what it is. But I *don't* want us to intellectually ghettoize ourselves. I met some of the teachers in the Beijing Film School and my god, they're teaching psychoanalysis! So why should *we* be afraid of all these theoretical models? We're beginning to introduce theory in our classes, but easy does it!

The first generation of independent filmmakers were all *personal* filmmakers (even Lino Broca, who *did* try to make a lot of institutional changes; he was a role model for lots of us), and we remember the wonderful films that they did. But did that change the structures of the movie industry? Not at all.

I thought we needed another strategy, that we must come in *as a generation* with institutional *structures*. And the first structure needed to be a film school. Our generation is beginning to affect the industry. They are now producing short films. They are now open to experimental films. They are open to animation. Philippines animation on the big screen! Can you imagine?!

What we asked for during the revolution was a democratic plurality. I'm trying to translate that into cinematic plurality.

Mani Kaul: *Uski Roti* ("A Day's Bread," 1970); *Dhrupad* (1982), August 9, 11, 1994

[L. Somi Roy, one of the programmers of the 1994 seminar, introduced Mani Kaul's films. I've included Roy's introduction and the discussion.]

Welcome to this evening's program. We're going to be showing a film by the Indian director Mani Kaul, called *Uski Roti* (the English title is "A Day's Bread"). It's a film Mani Kaul made twenty-six years ago, when he was a young man of twenty-five. He had just completed his studies at the Film Institute of India.

India, as you know, has the largest film industry in the world; its films are seen from Morocco to Indonesia (and sometimes in New York!), but the majority of the films tend to be formulaic. You all know the Indian musicals, the melodramas, and so on. The new Indian cinema started in the late sixties and early seventies, and *A Day's Bread* was one of two or three films that can be seen as the beginning of this new development (another was *Bhuvan Shome* [1969] by Mrinal Sen, who had been working with political films and was influenced by the French New Wave; and a third was *Ankur* ["The Seedling," 1974] by director Shyam Benegal. In comparison to what had been going on in the Indian film industry, most of these new Indian films were trying to be socially conscious while still appealing to a large audience.

The artistic integrity of this new Indian cinema was expressed in a couple of different ways. First, this cinema was rooted in particular regions. You have the Bengali cinema (Satyajit Ray, a precursor of the new Indian cinema, is the most famous instance), and you have cinemas from the many other regions (and languages). Shyam Benegal and other new Indian filmmakers made films in the Hindu language, which is the language of the Indian commercial cinema, but tried to deal with new themes and reach a new audience. Another precursor of the new cinema was Ritwick Ghatak, an unsung master of Indian cinema, at least in the West (and especially here in America). Ghatak was also a political filmmaker who derived his film technique from the theatrical tradition of Bengal. He became the vice principal of the Film Institute and was tremendously influential on a group of young Indian filmmakers, including Mani Kaul.

A Day's Bread caused quite a bit of controversy when it was first seen in India. It represents a departure in many different ways from what had been considered Indian film up to that point. It is a non-linear, non-narrative film based on a very short story by Mohan Rakish, who wrote in Hindi. The film does not have English subtitles, though there is very little dialogue. It's about a woman in a village in the Punjab who every day walks from the village to the highway with her husband's lunch, his daily bread. He's a bus driver who drives by a couple of times a day. He spends little time at home, and doesn't seem to care much about his wife (he has a mistress in another town, and does a lot of drinking with his buddies). One day the wife misses the bus and is distraught—after all, he provides her livelihood, and she's a traditional good Indian wife. This is when a lot of things begin to happen in her head, and the film is very much about the interior of her mind. The filmmaker starts commenting on her past in flashbacks, and she starts having fantasies.

Mani Kaul told me several things about the style of the film that I'd like to share: *A Day's Bread* is a film about time, and Mani Kaul deliberately plays with very extended shots. The film is about waiting; it is deliberately slow. Also, he used only two lenses in shooting this film: a 28mm lens and a 35mm lens—basically a wide-angle lens and a long lens. He did not employ the normal 50mm lens. At the beginning of the film, he employs the two lenses in the traditional way: that is, when you want a universal focus to bring all the action into play, you use a wide-angle lens with great depth of field, and when you want to get into more introspective material, you use the long lens and shorten the depth of field. But later on, when the flashbacks and the woman's fantasies come into play, he switches the lenses, so you're no longer sure *what* is actually happening and how much is fantasy or the filmmaker commenting on the past.

[*A Day's Bread* is shown and Kaul takes questions afterward.]

Kaul: I don't want to talk abut this film. [laughter] It's so many years ago.
George Stoney: What was the *plot?* We had no idea what was going on!

Kaul: When I made *A Day's Bread*, I wanted to completely destroy any semblance of a realistic development, so that I could construct the film almost in the manner of a painter. In fact, I've been a painter and a musician. You *could* make a painting where the brush stroke is completely subservient to the figure, which is what the narrative is, in a film. But you can also make a painting stroke by stroke so that both the figure and the strokes are equal. I constructed *A Day's Bread* shot by shot, in this second way, so that the "figure" of the narrative is almost not taking shape in realistic terms. All the cuts are delayed, though there is a preempting of the generally even rhythm sometimes, when the film is a projection of the woman's fantasies.

My way of looking at women has changed over the years, as you will see in my later films. But it's not as if I saw this woman as pathetic. Indian women are very close to the idea of tradition, and this woman's actions implied much more than her just being subservient to *him*. Really, there is no plot at all in the film, except what Somi explained.

I was living as a "paying guest" with a family at the time I made *A Day's Bread*. At a dinner with a group of people, the man in the family was explaining, "Mani Kaul has made this film where there is a woman who goes to the bus stop and waits . . . ," when his wife interrupted to say, "William, you're telling them the whole plot!" [laughter]

I must say, the idea of non-narrative has stayed with me all these years, and the closest to a conventional story I've made is a three-hour adaptation of Dostoevsky's *The Idiot* which itself has a narrative that goes haywire in terms of what we recognize as "development."

Seminarian: The film is stunning to look at. Could you talk about the process of composing the images?

Kaul: I believe the camera is not something you're *seeing* through; it's the way your body extends into life. This is what I teach my students (I should tell you that they make very different films than I make; I never encourage them to make my kind of films). I want them to understand that when I move, I move differently; and when I sit, I sit differently. You have to learn to hold the camera with *your* rhythm, and not just have an idea in your head and try to illustrate that idea. You have to understand this, even when a cameraman is physically shooting the film. We all create differently, precisely because everyone's body extends differently. Your movements are like a dance.

I sincerely believe now that I can make a film without looking through the camera. In fact, I have a project in mind where I won't allow my cameraman to look through the camera. Looking through the camera obviously was important to me when I made *A Day's Bread*, because at that time I *thought* about organizing space. Since the European Renaissance, we have been trained to understand that organizing space, and especially a sacred space—a church or a temple—is what creates a sense of attention and therefore time. But now I believe that I should in fact place myself *in time*, and into a certain quality of attention, and let the space become whatever it becomes. It doesn't interest me anymore to compose my shots, to frame them in any way. I wish to place myself in a particular sense of *time* and let *space* be, or grow. Nothing can go wrong—I know that—nothing can go wrong. When I shoot now, I have only a brief script. The film unfolds on the spot as I shoot.

Even when I am editing, my shots have mobility. In a film I will show you later there was one shot that traveled through all the reels. It was in the first reel first; then it went to the second, to the seventh, to the fifth—finally it found a place! And I know that when the shot finds a place, it has a quality of holding you. The position *is* its meaning.

Seminarian: When you were shooting *A Day's Bread*, did you mentally picture the shots and then teach the actors and the crew how to go about making those shots? Or did the specific shots come along as you rehearsed?

Kaul: With *A Day's Bread*, it was strange. I had a dream. In the dream, I saw a filmstrip lying on the floor, and on it I saw *all* the shots. So I had a very strong sense of what I was going to do.

But even at that time, locations were very important for me, as important as the actors. When I go to a certain place, like when I came here [the 1994 Flaherty Seminar was held at Wells College in Aurora, New York], immediately the location itself automatically suggests certain images and movements.

At that time, I used to *think*, then go to a location. But now I don't want to think. I don't want to think, "Now *this* is the scene; therefore she should be in the foreground and somebody should be in the background." Actually I've never done that kind of thing, not even in *A Day's Bread*.

Seminarian: Despite your unstructured, intuitive approach, you're still making feature films, which usually require a lot of organization. What kind of relationship do you have with your crew and with funders. I'm imagining you on location with everyone going crazy . . .

Kaul: No, no, no. I have a wonderful relationship with my crew; they love working with me. Really! Funders, I don't know. [laughter]

This question has been repeated for the last twenty-five years: how have I continued to raise money to make films like this? It's a big mystery. But each time, I am able to raise the money, and every year I make this kind of film. I've had no problem in finding funds. I can't explain this to you. I tell you, I know of no other similar situation, at least in my country.

[The discussion continues after the screening of *Dhrupad*. "Dhrupad" is a form of Indian classical music.]

Kaul: In *Dhrupad*, I tried to give a straightforward introduction to the music of the two musicians you see in the film. It is a music without notation. In a sense, it is not even possible to notate this music; it is too complex. There are continuously ascending and descending tones, and it is impossible to say that these tones follow this or that note. The tones are always traveling in the dissonant areas *between* notes.

I was especially interested in how the Indian musicians transmit the tradition of their music orally. A student can study this music for years and never write a sentence in a notebook. You can only learn the music by continuously listening and practicing until you begin to elaborate it in your own way. The secret of the survival of the traditions of Indian music is deeply linked with opening the disposition of the disciple, the pupil.

I'm very closely associated with the family in the film, and one day I was sitting with Ustad Zia Mohiuddin Dagar, the elder musician, and four students, who were singing a phrase that he had sung and had asked them to repeat. One by one, the four sang the phrase, and then he asked me, "What do you think?" I told him they all made mistakes: in some sense they changed the phrase that he had given them. He asked me gently, "Did you notice that they made different mistakes?" I said, "Yes, they made different mistakes." He said, "Well, the only crack through which you can look into the nature and disposition of the pupil is how he insists upon making a certain kind of mistake. Far from getting impatient with him, you should try and understand why he repeatedly insists on making *that* mistake. When he is *not* making that mistake, he is imitating me, and he's nobody. When he's making the mistake, he's himself, and you must build on *that.*"

In this music, individual musicians must express their own individual selves *as they are.* That's the secret of this tradition: if you wrote down phrases and forced people to learn only a certain way of playing, the tradition would die.

Another anecdote: Nancy Lash, an American disciple of Ustad lived in a village for five years in order to be close to Ustad's ashram. She was very devoted. Every day she wanted a lesson. She would say, "Ustad, lesson!" Ustad would say, "No, I've spoken to you today, I'm not going to speak again for fifteen days—you keep on practicing." It takes time to adapt a lesson into yourself.

Nancy had a habit, as many new students do, of plucking *chikari*—a sound you make when you complete a musical phrase—much too often. When the young students play, their playing does not have that continuous ring that you hear when great masters play, and there's a void. The student tends to play this other sound excessively, to fill the void. For some, it's very difficult to get out of this habit.

So he sat there, hearing her make this sound all the time. But he remained silent about it, waiting for *her* to realize what she was doing. After two months, she said, "Ustad, I have this bad habit." He realized that if he said, "Yes, you're playing the rhythm notes too much," her whole attention would go towards controlling this problem, and her main music would suffer. So he said, "No, no, Nancy, it's fine! There's no problem." Then next time, she says, "Ustad, I do this *too much.*" And he says, "No, no!" Every day that month she says, "I have this habit; I must get out of it!" And he says, "There's *no* problem. You don't have to get out of anything!"

Mani Kaul (facing camera) at the 1994 Flaherty Seminar.

Then, after a month, she stopped speaking about her compulsion. For fifteen days she said nothing. Finally, she asked, "Do you think I do it too much?" And he said, "Yes, I think you do." And it was corrected forever, and her main music was never disturbed.

Seminarian: Would you talk a little about the importance of meditation in preparing to play the music, or perhaps to shoot film?

Kaul: I'll tell you something, if you don't mind. This word "meditation," which is mystified in the West, has no meaning in India. There is simply a question of attention, of a quality of attention. The word *dhyan* literally means attention. There is a dichotomy between Being and this quality of attention. Being cannot free itself from certain sorrows; it cannot free itself from its past, or from problems and unhappiness, because Being is full of them. The idea of transcending them and reaching a state where there's no sorrow is all a dream. You can talk about it, but until the end of your life, your sorrows will pursue you.

However, *attention* can be free. The quality of attention can be free. The teacher transforms that quality of attention—of listening, of talking, of seeing, of feeling, of touching—until there is no sorrow, no fear, no anger, no desire. In this music, and perhaps in some of my films, one has this quality of attention.

Seminarian: I wonder if you would like to comment on the more political visions that we've been seeing in other films this week, visions that are angry at times, and that are desirous of shaking up or disbanding an established order.

Kaul: I'm very proud of the fact that I make my kind of film. But quite a few of my friends in India make political films, including films in which people are angry. I sometimes help with these films in ways I can. It would be horrible if we had to make only one kind of film. *All* that is happening is real, and *everything* desires expression. All kinds of engagements are valid and legitimate as long as they keep within a certain discipline and reach certain truths of perception. They're perfect. No problem. I enjoy films that are *completely* different from mine.

Michael Grillo: I'd like to ask about the innate cultural implications of basically a Western technology: cinema. I don't mean simply the traditional history of cinema, but rather its language: the optical system inherited from the Italian Renaissance, and the narrative system based on nineteenth century novels. Given your cultural background and the nature of what you are making, where do you run up against the limitations of these culturally loaded technologies? And how do you resist them? Somi described one instance—your use of lenses in the opposite-of-conventional way—but are there other instances where you turn this Western cultural language into your own vernacular?

Kaul: I speak English, but it's not my language, and so I am liable to make mistakes while using this language. While I'm speaking, I'm not consciously following any grammar, but there *is* a very strict grammar to English and my slightest mistake will be detected, and you'll know I don't know English completely. It is my opinion that cinema is *not* a language, whereas Indian classical music *is* a language. Why do I say that? There are strict grammatical rules concerning Indian music, and if a musician goes off, his deviation will immediately be evident. But while he sings, he's not concerned with that grammar at all, even though it is *so* strict that the slightest mistake would be detected. He goes into an intuitive singing, which is absolutely correct grammatically *and* perfectly subjective. *This* I would call a language. Cinema is nothing like that. Cinema is information, and in particular films, information is saturated or, as is true in my films sometimes, rarefied.

It is true that the camera is a product of the European principle of perspective, of convergence—which is basically an optical illusion, because in reality parallel lines *don't* converge: you can shut your eyes and walk and you won't come to a convergence point. During the Renaissance, the idea of convergence produced great work. The same is true of Western symphonic music, which is very beautiful (and in a sense, convergent), and of narrative film, which creates climactic "convergences." Earlier chronicles and epics didn't have the convergences that modern narratives do. And it is perfectly legitimate if young filmmakers would rather explore non-narrative ideas. In fact, it's a tragedy that we don't yet have an instrument that can deal with the non-narrative forms we have in our hearts.

Craig Baldwin: *Sonic Outlaws* (1995), August 9, 1995

Richard Herskowitz: It seems to me that some experimental films need experimental movie theaters. During *Sonic Outlaws*, I felt self-conscious just sitting still, quietly facing the screen, not talking back; and I'm just wondering if you've found screening venues that meet this film halfway?

Baldwin: Well, I encourage people to stand up and change seats during the film, to do whatever they want. I cut my teeth in college showing films in clubs, so I'm used to showing films in spaces where there are bodies in motion. But I don't think you need to meet the expectations of the place you go into. Just take it over. The surrealists used to do "exquisite corpse" films in Paris by going from one theater to another, creating their own montages, based on chance.

Seminarian: Tell us about your archive [one of the "themes" of the 1995 Flaherty Seminar was archiving film *in* film].

Baldwin: We started this seminar with some formal discussion about film archives in the traditional sense, and I do acknowledge them, but my project is to liquidate distinctions between official and unofficial history. I think a lot of material from pop culture *is* archival material: it represents a certain sensibility characteristic of the middle part of the century. I do collect stuff, but my "archive" comes mostly from dumpsters. Refuse is the archive of our times and the resource for what I call "cinema pauvere"—those people who are impoverished but still intent on making films. I think we live in a post-Hollywood, post-industrial society. There's so much material already *there*, in the trash (on LP records, for example, and on eight-track tapes), that it's a test of our ingenuity to take that material and redeem it, so to speak: to project new meanings into it. Even my own films become a kind of refuse. Sometimes I cut up my earlier films and rearrange them, even *after* they've come to the answer-print stage. I think that's perfectly OK, though it cuts against the whole tradition of the inviolability of the art object and the sanctity of the finished work.

John Columbus: You're an exquisite anarchist, but there *is* some organization in *Sonic Outlaws*, if only because of your use of *The Wizard of Oz* [1939] to bracket the piece. Can you say something about your organization?

Baldwin: My use of "Don't mind the person behind the curtain," which is the vocal you hear from *The Wizard of Oz*, was just a formal device to suggest that I want to expose the powers-that-be behind the media machine. It's one metaphor in *Sonic Outlaws* out of five quadrillion.

Seminarian: I've heard the phrase "culture jamming" bounced around this week, but I don't know what it means and what its ramifications are, though it seems to relate to *Sonic Outlaws*.

Baldwin: Mark Howser of Negativland claims to have invented culture jamming, but I think that's ridiculous, just more egotism; and he's already declared the end of culture jamming because it's been co-opted: there are already classes in culture jamming. The term refers to the idea that in a media-saturated environment, people are going to be taking bits and pieces from what has been done, changing them, and re-inserting them back into the cultural process. Culture jamming is different from classical resistance in that it doesn't present an oppositional argument; rather, it's art work that speaks in the language of the dominant culture, but contains a subversive message, so that when it's re-inserted into the mainstream cultural process, it becomes a kind of media virus. People see or hear the results and think, "Hold it, something's wrong here!" Hopefully, the process provokes people to question *all* received media.

Patricia Bruck [filmmaker; director, Rocky Mountain Film Center]: When I think of assemblage films, I think of a filmmaker taking found footage and editing it together, so I was puzzled when I saw in the credits that Bill Daniel edited *Sonic Outlaws*. You're listed as a director. Could you explain how you direct him to edit?

Baldwin: Bill was sitting at the flatbed but we did it together. He has good instincts, and I wanted to give him a lot of credit, so I called him "editor." I didn't know how to give myself credit so I called myself "director."

Seminarian: Could you say that the ability to *know* history combined with the inability to *make* history leads to appropriation?

Baldwin: In a lot of ways I think the language of history, the mediated version of history, is internalized. Appropriation is just a way of talking back to what we've internalized. Of course, since we do internalize so much, you can call *Sonic Outlaws* a personal film. Here, it's shown at this documentary seminar, but it's a personal expression of a culturally saturated, obsessive individual who's into talking back. I think it's healthy to be able to work with all the materials cluttering up our brains: *The Flintstones*' tune; the Shell sign; "snap, crackle, pop."

Seminarian: How many of the connections that you make between your varied sources are serendipity?

Baldwin: To a degree there is a design, especially when you're making a feature. But there is also serendipity. There's so *much* inside us that there are going to be times when things comes out perfectly. I remember Negativland saying, "We can control serendipity and exploit chance." There *is* this tension between randomness/chaos and design. We can't *totally* control what we use, like Hollywood does; we open ourselves out to the social field, the world of media. But when we *do* find something, some kind of definite correspondence, that's a magical moment. And that's what Negativland makes their art out of—and what this film tries to do. There's a certain kind of surrender in my film to social forces. Media is penetrating our bodies right now, so just *take* it, and instead of being a victim, go with the flow long enough to help redirect the flow.

Seminarian: There's a history of collaborative work in San Francisco. Have you been part of that history?

Baldwin: I know there was a group called Radio Refusés, but I wouldn't want to localize the approach I'm describing: it's an idea whose time has come.

Craig Baldwin at the 1995 Flaherty Seminar.

Art as a category, with a capital *A*, has to be liquidated. I'm part of a generation that recognizes that art has become a commodity and that the art world is just a big industry, just a way for a lot of people to establish careers and get rich by selling objects to rich people. Motion pictures *are* collaborative certainly. And when you're taking advantage of clips made by hundreds of other people before you, you have to admit to that collaboration. I think *Sonic Outlaws* and my work in general falls into the tradition of anti-art: the Dada tradition, or the Fluxus tradition, or the Situationist tradition, the Punk tradition—all of which try to attack the egoism and the careerism of people who claim to be romantic geniuses receiving inspiration from God. That's a very stupid idea, and, of course, we must wipe these people off the face of the Earth. [laughter]

Seminarian: Who were the Situationists?

Baldwin: The Situationists were very inspirational to me as I was coming up in college, especially their idea of the dissolution of category art and the diffusion of art into everyday life, and their profound skepticism about the idea of Originality and their commitment to attack the academy, to provocation. Hopefully, *Sonic Outlaws* partakes of the spirit of provocation. Of course, "Situationism" is a noun that shouldn't exist. It's an activity, a process, a general way of looking at art-making and of trying to reintegrate it into everyday life—of trying to re-use the dead culture as a means of making our lives more meaningful.

Bruce Jenkins [curator of film and video, Walker Art Center]: Though *Sonic Outlaws* is cut on film, there's an electric feel to it: in your conceptualizing the film and in your editing have you been influenced by electronic tools: nonlinear editors or time spent on the Net?

Baldwin: I certainly have and I couldn't help but be. But I want to remind everyone that editing film *is* nonlinear. I can't afford to work on an Avid, but even if I could, I wouldn't. I like film because of its plastic quality. *Sonic Outlaws* is very much a handmade film; it wears its artlessness on its sleeve; it's part of that aesthetic tradition of *not* looking for the quality image, but for the *debased* image.

To go back to your question: a lot of the material in *Sonic Outlaws* was acquired on video, and from audio tape, and radio broadcast—so, yes, there is an electronic dimension to the film.

Seminarian: Did you have earlier cuts, and how long were they?

Baldwin: Originally, it was going to be a thirty-five minute film, a twelve-hundred-foot reel; and then I got the AFI grant and one thing led to another. I didn't want to turn the film into a fanzine for Negativland (which it is to an extent); I wanted to stretch it out and talk in a meta-cultural way, not just about one group that's doing something exemplary, but about this kind of practice exploding across the culture. I just started adding on and the film grew. There was a very coarse outline on my wall, but I worked, as someone said the other day, "from the material up."

In Hollywood, everything is predetermined: you need to get *this* shot, put the people in *these* clothes under *these* lights, saying *these* lines. It might take twenty takes, or two hundred, but we'll *get* it. My process is totally the opposite: I take what I have and then try to make something *of* it, to find something *in* it. The material suggests its own form; the form grows organically from the material.

Seminarian: There's a lot of noise in *Sonic Outlaws*.

Baldwin: It *is* a noisy film, and is meant to be. In art-making some people want to refine and purify, to find a beautiful, sublime, precious moment, and I acknowledge that tradition. But it's not *my* aesthetic. What I want to do is to grate against the nervous system. Noise *is* the contemporary environment, and I think true art is a headlong embrace of this reality and an attempt to redeem it, to create an aesthetic of noise—rather than some kind of escapist, elitist, privileged retreat from our real environment.

Seminarian: At one point I started not to be able to relate to *Sonic Outlaws*, because I was thinking, "Where are the women? Where are the women?"

Baldwin: The field of culture jamming is currently dominated by males—as is rock and roll, as is experimental film. I didn't make a decision to include women in order to give a "balance"; I just gave a survey of what was happening. The Barbie Liberation Organization [a group instigated by Melinda Stone and Igor Vamos that bought Barbie dolls and GI Joe dolls, exchanged their sound components so that Barbie said GI Joe's lines and vice-versa, and returned them to the shelves of the stores] includes women. But generally, the field happens to be dominated by men—straight, white males.

Seminarian: But even the imagery you use seems male dominated.

Baldwin: It *is* an important question whether a group like the Emergency Broadcast Network [a group that modifies imagery of political figures so that they say the opposite of what they mean to say], which wants to satirize the language of power, actually transcends that language. In my view, the Emergency Broadcast Network doesn't; but Negativland does. You need to talk about each case separately. But of course, part and parcel of appropriating and re-editing imagery of white, straight political leaders is that you end up with a lot of imagery of white, straight political leaders. You remain in that same circulation of imagery. I hope the film opens up that issue.

Riyad Wadia [filmmaker, archivist]: I know this is the land of free speech but I come from a society [Wadia is Indian] that does not have such high standards of freedom, a more bureaucratic society. We're presently in a very interesting stage where America is forcing us to get into the copyright laws, into GATT [General Agreement on Tariffs and Trade], so it's very interesting for me to see that America itself seems to be opening up to this whole new concept that actually there *is* no such thing as copyright. Also, as a person running an archive, I find it very dangerous to think that my material can actually be re-made and used commercially. I don't mind if it's used aesthetically but if the artistic endeavor becomes commercial, there is a worry. Where's it all going?

Baldwin: When you say *America* wants to impose copyright laws on India, of course, you're talking about the *corporations*. The people who are represented in *this* film, and they are Americans, are anti-copyright.

Where's it all going? Despite GATT and despite the clampdown on copyrights, and the commercialization of the Internet, there's no stopping the subcultural phenomenon I've described. The paradox is that *because* these technologies exist, *because* the media is available, there is both more cultural democracy in actual practice, and at the same time, an attempt by the corporations to limit this democracy. This film finds itself at the intersection of these forces.

In any event, I don't care what's happening legally. Some people might, but I'm interested in leaving that question behind and doing my own work despite the laws. As far as I'm concerned, the situation calls for more ingenuity and more crime.

Gunvor Nelson

As a teacher, I have had to learn that there are various kinds of "good" films. What strikes me as a fascinating and enjoyable critical-cinematic work may not function as an effective critique for my students. Indeed, films that can be counted on to energize progressive, long-term critique are so rare that when I discover one, I tend to use it over and over. One such film is Gunvor Nelson's short trick-film, *Take Off* (1972); I simply cannot teach without it. As Lucy Fischer demonstrates—her *Shot/Countershot* (Princeton: Princeton University Press, 1989) begins with a discussion of *Take Off* and the early film *Fatima* (1897)—Nelson exploits/deconstructs the tradition of striptease in conventional and alternative cinema in a manner that has long-term repercussions for a good many of those who see it.

Nelson made *Take Off* at the instigation of a woman named Magda (who had an idea for a film that would create a *reductio ad absurdum* of the striptease), and in collaboration with the San Francisco stripper who called herself Ellion Ness. During the ten minutes of the film, Ness does a traditional striptease for the camera, smiling "at us" as she removes her clothing, item by item. As she nears the end of the conventional stripping routine, the mood of the film becomes somewhat ominous, but few viewers are prepared for her removal, first, of her hair, then of her legs, ears, breasts, arms, nose, and finally her head. At the end of the film her torso "takes off" into outer space and is seen flying among meteorites. For contemporary audiences, and in particular, student audiences, *Take Off* is confrontational on several levels simultaneously. First, the apparently overt exploitation of the "male gaze" during much of the film seems particularly outré in a 1990s classroom (both for those who believe in the liberation of women's bodies from male control and for those who are uncomfortable with nudity in film and in public), until the film's final destination is clear, at which point we realize that the three women who collaborated on the film have raised the specter of "the gaze" only to dismantle it. Indeed, we recognize, once Ness has in fact "taken it all off," that her smiles at the camera are not the smiles of submission to male desire that we thought they were, but smiles of complicity with her two media-guerrilla collaborators and with all those watching who are aware of the implications of a dehumanizing gaze. A second level of confrontation, which is at least as powerful now as it was in 1972, results from the decision to use a stripper who does not precisely conform to contemporary societal standards for beauty or eroticism. Most 1990s students get the point of the deconstruction of the striptease *and*, paradoxically, find themselves judging Ness "fat," though she is hardly overweight by any sane standard.

While *Take Off* may be Nelson's most usefully critical film, it is not particularly characteristic of her work, either in approach or in style (indeed, while the film seems a model of feminist collaboration, friction between Nelson and Magda during and after the shooting transformed the experience into one Nelson would as soon forget). Its tactic of luring viewers in only to confront them is far less direct than the tactics employed in other Nelson films to confront viewers; and the relatively straightforward, "goal-oriented" narrative of *Take Off* is a far cry from the complex interweaving of her mature collage films. Nelson first made a name for herself by collaborating with Dorothy Wiley on a satire of romantic media images of women, *Schmeerguntz* (the title is a nonsense "German" word Nelson's father used for "sandwich," 1966). The film juxtaposes imagery of the "ideal American woman," recycled from television and magazines, with imagery of those aspects of real women's lives relentlessly repressed in the media: menstruation, the difficulties of pregnancy, and the realities of everyday home maintenance: cleaning toilets, taking gunk out of a sink drain, and so on. Nelson and Wiley continued to collaborate: on the surrealist film *Fog Pumas* (1967); on a feature-length, personal documentary, *Five Artists BillBobBillBillBob* (1971), about Bill Wiley, Bob Nelson, Bill Allan, Bill Geis, and Bob Hudson; and on a surrealist dramatic feature, *Before Need* (1979), which was re-made in 1995.

By 1969, Nelson was also making films of her own, including *Kirsa Nicholina*, a record of a woman giving birth to a child (named Kirsa Nicholina), which is so open and matter-of-fact about the body and the experience of birth that it makes Stan Brakhage's *Window Water Baby Moving* (1959) seem nearly conventional in its melodramatic fascination with the female body-as-process. The fact that the baby is delivered at home, apparently in the company of friends, combined with the opening shots of the father and pregnant mother walking nude on the beach, the pulses of light green that punctuate the image, and the soundtrack of the father improvising a blues riff in honor of the birth make *Kirsa Nicholina* a quintessentially sixties film. More stylistically complex than *Kirsa Nicholina* but equally powerful is *My Name Is Oona* (1969), Nelson's evocation of the experience of girlhood, as she remembered it from her childhood in Sweden and as her daughter Oona (the child of Gunvor Nelson's marriage to Robert Nelson) was experiencing it in the late 1960s. Nelson's use of multilayered superimposition of both sound and image locates the innocence of childhood within a mythic context: Oona seems both real child and goddess. The soundtrack of *My Name Is Oona* stands with the soundtracks of Robert Nelson's *Oh Dem Watermelons* (1965) and Hollis Frampton's *Critical Mass* (1971) as one of the most memorable of the era.

In *Trollstenen* (1976), her feature-length portrait of her family, and *Before Need*, Nelson fashioned the approach to structure that continues to characterize her longer films. Using a wide variety of imagery—and, increasingly in recent years, a combination of animation and live action—Nelson "weaves" her various source materials together so that the finished works provide both surprise (since the variety of the imagery makes a wide range of juxtapositions possible) and continuity (since the journey through the film familiarizes us with each of the strands woven together). This structure organizes both her live-action narrative films—like *Red Shift* (1984), her exploration of the visual, auditory, and psychological textures of the evolving relationships between mothers and daughters from the morning to the evening of life—and the more obviously painterly work that has dominated her filmmaking in recent years: for example, *Light Years* (1987), *Light Years Expanding* (1988), and *Natural Features* (1990). In these more recent films, she exploits a process-approach to animation that lies somewhere between cinema and painting, and that focuses not so much on the movements of characters or objects, but on the interplay of the many layers of image and material that can inhabit the "limited" film frame.

In recent years Nelson has tended to move away from conventional filmmaking; increasingly, she uses individual images from her films as a starting point for paintings and drawings, though she does continue to make film. In quite different ways, *Time Being* (1991), Nelson's stunning farewell to her mother who lies near death in a hospital; and *Old Digs* (1993), her visual/psychic excavation of the layers of reality in and around her home in Kristinehamn, sing the beauty of decay itself.

Nelson lived and worked in the United States from the mid-1950s until 1993 (teaching for twenty years at the San Francisco Art Institute), when she returned to Kristinehamn. This interview began in January 1994, when I sent Nelson questions about *Take Off* and she replied on voice tape. In April 1995 I spoke with her in Utica about her other films. Of all the filmmakers I've interviewed, Nelson is probably the most suspicious of herself as an interviewee and of the interview process: "When I utter something, I immediately feel all the things I've *not* said, and what I *have* said inevitably takes on too much importance."

MacDonald: When did you arrive in the States?

Nelson: I went to school here in the mid-fifties, first, at Humboldt State, and then at the San Francisco Art Institute, and then at Mills College. I met Bob [Nelson] at the Art Institute, and then we went together to Mills College.

MacDonald: Were you studying art? Were you already an artist?

Nelson: Well, I had made artworks since I knew what art was. At Mills I got a Masters in painting and art history.

MacDonald: You collaborated with Bob on *Building Muir Beach House* [1961] and *Last Week at Oona's Bath* [1962], a spoof on *Last Year at Marienbad* [1961], but you didn't begin making your own films until several years later.

Nelson: I always thought filmmaking was more of a group effort, more grandiose than was relevant for me. And then I saw Brakhage's films and after that, Bruce Baillie's, and they showed me that I could make film as an individual artist.

MacDonald: Were particular Brakhage films important for you?

Nelson: *Sirius Remembered* [1959], which was originally a very dizzying experience for me. I didn't know what I saw; it was a blur of images, but *very* interesting. It *felt* important. Ten years later I saw *Sirius Remembered* again, and couldn't imagine why it had been so dizzying the first time: it was so clear and, in a way, linear. I was amazed. But of course, by that time, I'd made films myself, so that made the difference.

MacDonald: So here you were, a Swedish girl in San Francisco in the sixties. What was that experience like?

Nelson: As you know, there was an atmosphere of trying things out. All tradition was there to be changed, rules were there to be broken. I felt fortunate to be in that atmosphere, but a bit scared, though I knew I wanted more control over what I did than the seemingly happy-go-lucky Bob Nelson, William T. Wiley, and some other artists had. For them, the *moment* was valuable; you shouldn't spoil the moment. To look afterwards and see if a painting or a film was any good or not—that was less important than the explosion of what happened spontaneously in the moment. Even looking at footage after it was shot had to be done with some kind of speed, because otherwise the result might be too worked, and the magic might be gone. Coming from Europe, or maybe just because of my personality, I had a hard time with that. I wanted things to be more controlled, which you can see, for example, in *My Name Is Oona*.

MacDonald: You came from a family background very different from what

American kids were experiencing. You must have seen them as very strange, compulsively in need of a certain kind of rebellion.

Nelson: Right. Of course, I did see the need for rebellion in art, but not so much socially. Going to the performances by the Mime Troupe [San Francisco Mime Troupe] and by Steve Reich and Terry Riley felt adventurous, and I *was* adventurous in a certain way. But not against my parents, who were so far away that I didn't need to rebel against them. I have always had a good relationship with my parents. Anyway, the times were exciting, but when I look back, I know that I didn't recognize the excitement as much then as I did after it was over. You never do.

MacDonald: At the time, you don't know it *will* be over!

Nelson: Right. It was also a scary time, because of the social upheaval of the blacks, and everything else. Sometimes I wondered if it was worth staying in the United States.

Wiley and Bob and all those guys had a special kind of humor that I had difficulty understanding. It had to do with putting down their own culture, in the grossest possible way, *and*, and at the same time, wanting, even *expecting*, the benefits of the culture. And it also seemed to involve putting down those who are oppressed or weak: blacks and handicapped people—or, as I realized later, putting down common prejudiced attitudes about such people by using even grosser statements about them than prejudiced people used.

MacDonald: Like the watermelon-eating in *Oh Dem Watermelons?*

Nelson: Yes, but when these guys were in person, their humor was much grosser and more shocking than that, at least to me. At first, I couldn't differentiate between the humor and the obscenity they were attacking! *Schmeerguntz* is gross, but its aim is more straightforward; its politics are more apparent. When I finally understood their humor, I saw it was based on love and warmth for human fragility and on an awareness of complex paradoxes and absurdities. I've always been attracted to absurdities, especially Magritte absurdity, which is a quiet absurdity.

MacDonald: So how did you begin making films, and collaborating with Dorothy Wiley?

Nelson: We talked about filmmaking in the abstract for a while, but had no ideas for films, and then one day I was doing the dishes and looking at the gook in the sink and I thought, "Ooooh, here I have it: the contrast between what women 'should' look like and what they actually have to be doing." *Schmeerguntz* came out of that.

MacDonald: Bob Nelson and William T. Wiley were a team, and you and Dorothy Wiley were a team, but at no point did the four of you team up to do work.

Nelson: Right. Bob and I had been painting side by side, but had never really painted very similarly. We knew we had very different aesthetics; it wasn't natural for us to work together.

MacDonald: Though the sorts of films that the male Nelson/Wiley team and the female Nelson/Wiley team made are related: *Schmeerguntz* isn't so different from *Oh Dem Watermelons*.

Nelson: We needed to start somewhere. My natural inclinations as a painter were not very evident in the first films. And Dorothy and I needed each other to dare to do it!

MacDonald: You were both young mothers?

Nelson: Yes. She was pregnant and had one child, and I had had Oona: it was the right time for *Schmeerguntz*.

MacDonald: It really *is* a disgusting film, you know.

Nelson: I was embarrassed by it when it was finished. But when you're with small children, that *is* your world—all that shit and all that gunk. It's not a false or exaggerated picture.

There were a lot of accidents. The soundtrack worked out almost too well! When I was vomiting (in reverse: stuff was coming *into* my mouth), by accident there was this romantic voice saying, "And he kissed her again." But even though some of the accidents did add to the film, we wanted more control over what we were doing.

MacDonald: Was *Schmeerguntz* also an early reaction to the "vomit" that comes from television? My generation, here, was the first to be watching six, seven hours of TV a day, and the speed of advertising was accelerating.

Nelson: I don't remember thinking about that. I don't remember seeing much TV in those days. I can see now that the choreography in that film was more carefully thought out than is true in many first films. It was just lucky that we had such a messy subject matter because the photography is rather uneven.

MacDonald: Formally it's a perfect match!

Nelson: Yes.

In doing *Schmeerguntz*, I discovered how beautiful things *look* through the camera. Seeing a neighbor's dirty kitchen in reality, and then seeing how through the camera it became beautiful gave us a kind of euphoria. A melon or dirty dishes, seen with a lens in close-up, were translated into something else. We had so much fun looking at the world in that way. We may not have caught that experience in *Schmeerguntz*, but we *saw* it as we were making the film. The camera became like binoculars: you zero in on a small area and isolate it, and it becomes more precious *because* it's selected. That process of selection is what makes a film. I started to understand all this through *Schmeerguntz*.

We were such beginners that when we would get film back from the lab, we'd sit in the car and unroll it to see if imagery was actually there. When it was, we were astonished! It was a miracle to us that an image had created itself.

MacDonald: I can see a vestige of that in *Old Digs*, in the slice of optically printed orange in that landscape space. It creates wonder.

Nelson: Yes. Close-up lenses are wonderful, because I see not only what is depicted but worlds beyond and feelings and layers beyond or inside or behind.

MacDonald: *Fog Pumas* seems an homage to the surrealist tradition in avant-garde film.

Nelson: Early on, I had seen *An Andalusian Dog* [1929]. And surrealist painting, of course. I am a surrealist at heart. After *Schmeerguntz*, people said, "Well, now you've done a film on women; you should do a film on men!" We said, "No, we should do a film that's totally different." So we wouldn't rely on past glory [laughter]; we got a lot of attention for *Schmeerguntz*. *Fog Pumas* was much closer to my natural tendency as an artist.

MacDonald: It's also obvious that you're trying out other film possibilities: color, most obviously.

Nelson: We had a whole bunch of outdated film of different kinds—at first that seemed a problem and then we just accepted it. Later we found that one could do superimpositions. The choreography of filmmaking—the choreography in time, the dance quality of film—was natural for me from the beginning. I liked superimpositions that danced over each other and in and out of each other.

Dorothy and I filmed *Fog Pumas* together, and had the editing generally sorted out, and then she and Bill went to Europe and were gone for a long time, and I finished the film. When Dorothy finally saw it, she said, "Oh, another creepy underground film!" She said it with humor, but I think she meant it, too.

MacDonald: When you see *Kirsa Nicholina* now, does it surprise you? It's an astonishing film, even in light of Brakhage's *Window Water Baby Moving*, the avant-garde birth film everybody knows.

Nelson: Brakhage's film is wonderful.

MacDonald: His is a man's film, full of his excitement in re-discovering Jane Brakhage's body, whereas *Kirsa Nicholina* is matter-of-fact, not only about the birth itself, but about the people present in the room.

Nelson: My film is less an expression, like Brakhage's film, and more about the event.

MacDonald: There's another sort of expression in your film: implicitly you express that you were less problematized about the body than most Americans tended to be at that time.

Nelson: Probably not much less!

A friend of this couple (she was Danish, he was American; they lived across from me in Muir Beach), a more-established industry filmmaker, was asked by the couple to do the film. He came to me and said, "Can you do some shots on the beach for me because I have to be out of town; you can be second cameraman." It's not in my vocabulary to be *second* cameraman! But I did those shots, and then one day, the father, David, came by and said, "She's going to have the baby!"—it was two weeks early—"Can you shoot some film?" I drove into San Francisco, bought as much film as I could afford: five one-hundred-foot rolls. When I got back, she was already on the bed and had been in labor for quite a while.

MacDonald: The red socks are pretty funny—the one vestige of costuming.

Nelson: Just red socks! And a light blue sheet. I was unhappy about the color in the film, the redness of her body. But I like that they had a copy of Borges's *Labyrinths* lying there.

MacDonald: The friends sitting around confront the audience in a different way from *Window Water Baby Moving*, which on a certain level is very private.

Nelson: But in *Kirsa* there's just the father, the doctor, the woman who was helping her with breathing, and the doctor's wife . . .

MacDonald: And you . . .

Nelson: And me . . . that *is* quite a few! [laughter] You hear about how, in the old days, queens gave birth in front of a whole assembly of people. This birth felt more private than it looks.

Since I had so little film, I had to be very careful—I had to keep enough to get to the birth itself! Generally, it's my inclination when I see footage, to go in there and *work* it. But when this footage came back from the lab, I thought, "No, it has to stand on its own. I'm not going to do anything."

MacDonald: At what point did you add the green tinting that pulses in and out?

Nelson: Oh, that was in the lab's chemicals, or the fault of the film stock. It was not my doing.

MacDonald: Really! The green is perfect for the idea of the Natural.

Nelson: Well, I wouldn't have put it in there. I wouldn't do the soundtrack the same way now either. The mother had some kind of electrical pad that disturbed my taping, so I couldn't use the sound I had recorded, and decided on the father's singing. It's a little too much but at least it's authentic.

MacDonald: Did you shoot *My Name Is Oona* with the idea that it would have such a complex soundtrack?

Nelson: No. I had shot the picture material, and I had done some optical printing, very primitively. But I didn't understand how I was going to cut it all together. Certain sequences were done, others were not. And then I went to a Steve Reich concert where, as people came into the gallery, he would have them say their names. He had maybe twenty tape recorders set up and he would make a tape out of "My name is Gunvor," and loop it and play it on a tape recorder. All the tapes were playing simultaneously. It was all very smooth and very complex and I was taken with the piece. Later, when I was doing my soundtrack, I had Oona say, "My name is Oona" in many different ways. When Steve Reich heard I was doing this, he sent me a tape he had done with Oona a while before, saying the days of the week . . .

MacDonald: Which is in the middle of the film . . .

Nelson: Yes. Then I decided how long the film was going to be, and together with Patrick Gleeson, I finished my track. I sent the result to Steve to see if he approved of my using his idea, and he said he liked it a lot, so I made the fine cut.

MacDonald: It seems a film about you making a connection with this child and all that (familially and mythically) she represents to you.

Nelson: Well, I knew I didn't want a normal, "cute" picture of Oona. I think the world she was in and my childhood world are combined there. As a child,

Oona Nelson as mythic child, in Gunvor Nelson's *My Name Is Oona* (1969).

you're pretty secure in your known world, but the rest is very mysterious and scary; maybe there are monsters and trolls lurking out there, even if you've never seen them.

MacDonald: She reminds me of figures in John Bauer's paintings.

Nelson: Oh, very much, very much. I grew up with children's stories— "sagor" we called them—illustrated by John Bauer. They were really part of me as a child, though now his images seem a little too decorative.

MacDonald: *My Name Is Oona* begins with multilayered mysterious imagery and looping sound and then it comes out of that more mysterious passage into an everyday passage, where Oona says the days of the week and we see her caring for the horse; and at the end it slides back into the multilayered, mysterious visual space with differently looped sound.

Nelson: Sometimes, where it was complicated in the picture, I wanted it not complicated on the track and vice versa.

I'm not a "structuralist." I don't want the structure to be central: the content, the feeling, should be first. But for all my films—all my later films, at least—I do think carefully about structure though in the same way I did with *My Name Is Oona*, so that even though sometimes the structure isn't *showing*, it is *felt* underneath.

MacDonald: Your consciousness of structure is already evident in *Five Artists BillBobBillBillBob*.

Nelson: You're one of the few who's seen *that* film in these last years!

MacDonald: It has a prologue and an epilogue and within, a series of carefully arranged sections, with, however, a lot of free-form specifics.

Nelson: Right.

MacDonald: From a nineties perspective, there's a strange gender dimension to the film: certainly by 1991, there are both male artists and female artists in the homes you document, and yet the focus of the film is *entirely* on these five *guys*; everyone else and everything else is subservient to them.

Nelson: Well, we were *aware* of that. But it happened that those five men were working together, dreaming together, and had this unusual and interesting rapport. Documenting it was Dorothy's idea, and it was fine with me.

MacDonald: Did both you and Dorothy Wiley work on all parts of the film?

Nelson: I always had editing facilities so I was in charge of the editing. You know, Dorothy also did films on her own. They were more simply edited, sometimes one-shot, idea films. Have you seen them?

MacDonald: No.

Nelson: I recommend *Miss Jesus Fries on Grill* [1973]—great title, eh?—and *Letters* [1972].

MacDonald: You collaborated with two women on *Take Off*. Can you talk about the collaboration?

Nelson: *Take Off* is more removed from me than any other film I have done. It's been called a "trick-film," which it is. In a way, I was tricked into making it.

I didn't know Magda very well. She had not made films before so she didn't know what was involved. She was thinking of herself as a producer, and, of course, I don't make films with producers. Originally, I said no to her idea because it seemed too "tricky": her idea was that a stripper would take off not only her clothes, but her arms and legs and so on, going a step further than "taking it all off." Working with that idea didn't tempt me. But I don't know, I couldn't sleep that night—when I get a problem, I want to solve it—and I decided, "Well, how *could* you make that film?" Finally, I had some ideas and thought, "Well, a short, little film . . . I could make that." So I phoned Magda back; she put up the money—eight hundred dollars, I think—and the next thing was to do the research.

We didn't know about strippers or stripping, at least I didn't. Stripping was not a high art in the San Francisco area in the early seventies. I remember going to some sleazy place, but it was not at all what we had in mind; it was too raw. Somehow, Magda found Ellion Ness, who seemed like a very sweet woman and was by then semi-retired from stripping. She had done professional stripping at some fancy place, when stripping was more of a dance. She still did private parties. Anyway, Ellion seemed very interested in the film, and she didn't mind if she was made to seem ugly or whatever. At the time, she had a professional Ellion Ness costume, which was too "gangster film" for us. She offered to make her own dress, and she did. She even learned to do that rotating movement with her breasts that made the tassels on her nipples spin, for the film. She had never been filmed before.

Ellion was the one I collaborated with. Magda was a lot of fun and entertained us a lot during the filming, but troubles came later, after we had had some success with the film.

MacDonald: What reactions to the film do you remember?

Nelson: In the early seventies, when the film was just finished, it seemed as if the more militant feminist women didn't like it because they felt it furthered the same images that they were against. But in general I think that both men and women have enjoyed the film, once they've understood what I was doing with it.

Even when Ellion takes off all her clothes, and her head, her arms, she still has a core of self that nobody can touch. I felt this personally very strongly. When I was growing up, I felt that Swedish society was very restricted, but I also remember feeling that Swedish society might have all these rules and regulations on how to behave, but those were minor compared to how strong I was as a person. *That* they couldn't alter. Ellion communicated something of that feeling: she could give herself away, but still have her *self.*

MacDonald: The moment the hair comes off, viewers realize that her smiling during the previous stripping has been a smile of knowing *more* than us, rather than of being under our control. As the body is dismantled, the intelligence and the spirit become "visible."

Nelson: Most people I have shown it to have not thought that Ellion was much of a turn on, probably because she was older. Even when we were filming (it was filmed in my house in Muir Beach), Ellion missed having an audience. I was teaching at San Francisco State University at the time and my class were mostly men, so I asked them to come. It was a graduate class and I thought that they would be old enough to enjoy her. They came with a lot of still cameras, and just sat there, without clapping and hollering like a real audience. They were too cool, and she was too old for them. She had a hard time, I think.

I didn't hide signs of age or "imperfections." I go in pretty close sometimes and in a very unattractive way. *Take Off* starts off somewhat romanticized, with double exposures, and then hits harder. When she takes the pasties from her nipples, you can see how much it hurts. Those touches I *like.* But they might not be pleasing for the audience. Of course, after a third of the way into the film, the lighting is harsher, and the film develops more of a raw, staccato quality. The cutting is faster, and there's flicker: first, every foot or so, I cut in one black frame, as an introduction to the flicker, and then progressively I put in more black frames and still later clear frames. I did all this by hand, so *Take Off* is a handcrafted film.

MacDonald: In a sense, your deconstruction of the ritual of striptease is analogous to your deconstruction of the normal sequencing of frames on the filmstrip.

Nelson: All of my filmmaking is a search for ways other than the traditional of expressing myself. Deconstructing the filmstrip is just a natural.

MacDonald: You mentioned that the collaboration with Magda ended badly.

Stripper removes her breasts, in Gunvor Nelson's *Take Off* (1972).

Nelson: I felt that the film became mine once I took over the shooting and editing. At first, she wanted to contribute to the editing but didn't really know what she was doing. Her ideas were not appropriate for the filmed material. I told her I could not work with her on the editing, which she accepted. She said, "Come back to me when we think about the sound," because she probably felt she knew more about music than I did.

So when the editing was more or less finished, I phoned her and by then, she was not interested. Since she was out of the picture, I turned to Pat Gleeson, whom I knew quite well. He played synthesizer in the Herbie Hancock band. He got together with a group from the band; they looked at the film and had a lot of fun doing a rowdy music track that moved toward the abstract, which is what I told them I wanted. He gave me four different tracks and I mixed those myself to fit with the imagery. Later, Patrick also helped me with *Old Digs*.

MacDonald: So what happened with Magda?

Nelson: I finished the film, sent it to the Berkeley Film Festival, where it got first prize. Magda heard about that and became very interested again. She wanted control of the distribution, the money, everything. We had to make a contract. A lawyer had to be involved. I can't remember it all, but it went on for a year. I remember her saying at some point that I was using her as the stepping-stone to my shoddy career. [laughter] I didn't have the verbal skills to combat all the things that came at me and so I gave in, in certain ways. Finally, once we had signed the contract determining how much money she would get each year, she said, "Oh, I have an idea for another film!"

Take Off is a one-time film. If you've seen it, you've seen it. The editing is so straightforward. I found that boring.

MacDonald: For me, seeing *Trollstenen* answered a lot of questions, not just about your family background, but about your development as a filmmaker. *Trollstenen* is truly a *finished* film, made by a filmmaker in control of the medium, at least of 16mm.

Nelson: There were mistakes. It's too long, for anyone but the family. If I recut it now, I think I could make it an interesting film.

MacDonald: What was the experience of dealing with your family as a film-maker?

Nelson: I don't think I felt any pressure. They'd been so pleased with the earlier films. My mother had been *thrilled* with *Schmeerguntz*. The rest of Sweden, I don't know. I was a little embarrassed about *Trollstenen*, but later I thought, well, some people *like* looking at family albums.

MacDonald: These days when people film their families, they tend to do exposés. *Trollstenen* makes your family seem so perfect.

Nelson: That's what people have told me. But that *is* how I saw the family *at that time*.

MacDonald: In the film (and later in *Red Shift*), you seem grateful for the kind of relationship your mother and father were able to develop, and particularly grateful that your mother would *not* be a housewife.

Nelson: Sure! But *Trollstenen* is history to me now. My mother and father are both dead—and they became very different as they grew older, especially my mother—so the film is just a memory. What *they* stressed was that the strife of life *was* the beauty of life. If you think you should be given money, that things should be smooth and easy, then you're going to be disappointed. I *am* grateful to them. That I've had difficulties I don't blame on them. They gave me as much support as anybody ever has.

MacDonald: *Trollstenen* is where I first see your "mature" approach to structure: your use of a set of visual and sound motifs, parallel worlds that come and go, woven together serially to explore a certain perceptual/psychological/spiritual domestic terrain. After *Trollstenen* even the shorter films incorporate that organization.

Nelson: That's true.

MacDonald: *Before Need* develops a particularly complex version of that structure.

Nelson: From the beginning, when I was cutting *Before Need*, the older woman was the center and it was her thoughts and reminiscences we were hearing and seeing.

MacDonald: You mean the various conversations at the table are her memories of previous moments in her life?

Nelson: They *could be*—we don't say, "Yes, they are"—they just *could* be. And other things in other sections of the film could also be parts of her past. Dorothy and I sat down after seeing our new version of *Before Need, Before Need Redressed*—which is shorter, focuses more clearly on the older woman, and eliminates much of the conversation between the couples—and just mused on the strangeness of life, and the strangeness of these events in the film. The title, "Before Need," comes from the Chapel of the Chimes where the label "Before Need" is placed in a little compartment with a glass door to reserve the space for a burial urn: somebody has bought the space before they needed it and it's waiting for them!

MacDonald: The close-up dentistry adds a *Schmeerguntz*y quality.

Nelson: Otherwise the experience of the film is too distant. If you don't look at life close-up, you're not really *looking* at it. And if there's not a variety of experiences, things get pretty bland, don't they?

MacDonald: The mixture of elements in your films seems more than a desire for variety; it's as if you can't see beauty without seeing decay.

Nelson: There is beauty *in* decay—*that's* what it is. In *Light Years Expanding* the rotting apples were an investigation of how things look at different stages of decay. The more decayed and strange the apples became, the more interesting they were, and the more *beautiful*. The color of the decaying apples often takes my breath away: its incredible delicacy, its fragility. Even mountains decay. To me, it seems essential to bring in the fragile and temporary quality of life, as well as the beauty. In *Time Being*, you may be shocked to see my mother like that and so close-up, especially in contrast with the photographs you see right at the beginning, but then as the film develops, you also see the beauty of the fragile texture of her skin—or I *hope* you do. The same is true in *Red Shift*: a hand comes into the frame and pokes at my mother's aging face, trying to touch aging, to understand it, and to not be afraid of it. And then to have her smile that amazingly young, wonderful smile—I was *incredibly* happy about that.

MacDonald: *Red Shift* is about the relationships between you and Oona, and you and your mother . . .

Nelson: But that film isn't a *documentary*—for instance, most of the hostilities were based on other people's hostilities toward their parents. As I was filming, I had a list of themes—hate, jealousy, love; I don't remember the whole list—that I wanted to include. The feelings between generations cause difficulties and distances, which first comes into the film through the letters from Calamity Jane to her daughter. I wanted a contrast *and* a parallel between the incredible longing she expresses in her letters and the different experience of that same longing people can have, even when they are bumping up against each other. It's the *same* wants and needs, whether you're close or far away. How tough and strong Calamity Jane was *and*, at the same time, how vulnerable. When you're with people, close-up, it's harder to be as "sappy" as she can be in the letters. But the same feelings are there.

MacDonald: How did you decide to have Edith Kramer [Kramer is director of the Pacific Film Archive in Berkeley, California] read the letters?

Nelson: I liked the quality of her voice. Of course, I admired Edith very much, but I tested a few people and her voice was the closest to what I wanted.

MacDonald: Do you work on one film at a time?

Nelson: Most of the time, except for related films, like *Old Digs* and *Kristina's Harbor* [1993], which are two halves of the same project.

MacDonald: Do you have a film in mind from the start, or do your films just discover themselves as you work?

Nelson: I have general ideas. I knew in *Light Years* that I was going to use the Swedish landscape and I knew I was going to use animation.

MacDonald: Did you know there'd also be *Light Years Expanding?*

Nelson: No, I just generated so much good material that I either had to make a very long film or divide it into two films, which I did.

MacDonald: You use a very unusual animation technique: you don't follow an object, you move from one layer to another to another.

Nelson: In *Frame Line* [1983], I discovered I didn't want to do conventional animation. I'm not temperamentally fit to make so many drawings for one action. I move things about, as the animation camera runs at a few frames a second. Mostly, I'm filming the *process*, rather than something prepared. I'm trying for visual mysteries, and I want to use a process where accidents can surprise me. I generate a lot of material as freely and with as little worry as possible. I go in with a playful mind, knowing I can always cut things. But in the editing I want to be very, very strict. As I work, I try to maintain a certain general attitude so I don't go too far afield, and so I can focus. As artists that's what we do: narrow down the field, focus, and investigate. I think of archeological digs as close to what I do in my work.

MacDonald: You mean both the spatial "field" of the frame and the emotional "field," right?

Nelson: Right.

Christine Choy

**(and collaborators Allan Siegel,
Worth Long, and Renee Tajima)**

One of the more significant developments in recent years, at all levels of film production, has been the emergence of films from particular ethnic communities that have traditionally been left out of film history, except as fodder for stereotyping by mainstream directors. Scholars have begun chronicling not only African-American film, but Chicano film, Native-American film, and Asian-American film. For many filmmakers working out of these particular ethnic contexts, the major goals seem to be providing honest testimony about the experience of living within their particular communities and making contact with their cultural heritages. In most cases, the resulting films are "critical" primarily on the level of content: they provide cinematic representation for major dimensions of modern experience routinely ignored by the mass media. A distinguished instance of this pattern is Christine Choy's *From Spikes to Spindles* (1976), "the first film ever done on the experience of Chinese-American women," as Choy says in our interview. Choy's film bears witness to contemporary Chinese-American life in New York's Chinatown by focusing on the demonstrations that followed the police beating of Peter Yen and relates this then-current controversy to the history of the Chinese, and especially of Chinese women, in the United States. Produced by Third World Newsreel, *From Spikes to Spindles* uses a conventional mixture of narration, archival footage, talking heads, and candid on-the-street footage to bear witness to the complexity of the Chinese-American past and present and to polemicize for broader ethnic representation in American life.

From Spikes to Spindles established Choy as a significant force in the development of an Asian-American cinema, but in retrospect, it was also an early landmark in a career that evolved in an unconventional direction, toward forms of critique that often distinguish Choy's work. By the time she made *Missis-sippi Triangle* (1984), in collaboration with Allan Siegel and Worth Long (both of whom share co-director credits, though Choy is also credited as project di-rector, producer, and as one of the principal cinematographers), Choy had be-come less interested in the continuities of particular ethnic heritages than with the intersections of the multiple ethnicities that coexist within virtually any community in America: in this particular film, with the European-Americans, African-Americans, and Asian-Americans living in the Mississippi Delta re-gion. Originally conceived as an inter-ethnic project, in terms of both subject matter and production—those sections focusing on each of the three ethnic groups would be shot by a director and crew of the same or a closely related ethnicity (Choy had hoped Charles Burnett would take charge of the African-American segment, and Burnett did do some of the original research in Mis-sissippi)—the finished film is peppered with moments that provide an unusual, but quite powerful critique of conventional film expectations with regard to ethnicity.

In several instances during *Mississippi Triangle*, we hear stories of life in Mississippi spoken in the thickest good-ol'-boy southern accent imaginable, only to discover that the speaker is Chinese-American: the effect is startling and provides a memorable critique both of the Hollywood tradition of marginalizing Asian-Americans by having them speak in stereotypical "Asian-American" ac-cents, and of traditional northern assumptions about southern "good-ol'-boys." While much of *Mississippi Triangle* focuses on relatively familiar elements of the American South, Choy's sections focus on various ways in which Chinese-Americans have negotiated a personal, social, and professional space between the European-American and African-American experiences in the Delta. Her particular interest in Arlee Hen, the daughter of a Chinese-American father and an African-American mother, was so controversial among the Delta's Chinese-American community (though long the object of bias and racism, the commu-nity has its own biases as well) that some Chinese-American locals wrote let-ters to PBS asking that *Mississippi Triangle* not be broadcast.

The complex intersections of ethnicity have remained, at least for me, the most interesting and most "critically" effective dimension of Choy's prolific ca-reer, and they are central in her most conventionally successful film (receiving an Academy Award nomination for Best Feature Documentary), *Who Killed Vincent Chin?* (1988), a collaboration with Renee Tajima. *Who Killed Vincent Chin?* focuses on the case—first a criminal case and subsequently a federal civil rights case—of Chin, who was beaten to death with a baseball bat outside a Detroit bar by Ronald Ebens. Ebens murdered Chin believing he was Japa-nese and, therefore, responsible for the economic doldrums of the Detroit auto manufacturers: that is, Chin's death was a result of Ebens's inability to distin-guish between a Japanese and a Chinese person. When Ebens went free, on the grounds that the murder was self-defense, Chinese-Americans responded in protest, but the resulting civil rights trial freed Ebens a second time. For Choy the ethnic confusion at the heart of the case, and the larger context of Detroit—with its large economically disenfranchised African-American population and its various European-American communities with their own ethnic heritages—provided an opportunity to explore the relationship between ethnicity and the American Dream, and, at least implicitly, to critique the simplicity of most ethnic representations in commercial film and television.

Choy has continued to explore the intersections of ethnicity in a number of recent films, including *Yellow Tale Blues* (1990), co-made with Renee Tajima, a personal documentary about Choy's immigrant Chinese/Korean-American family and Tajima's native Japanese-American family; and *Sa-I-Gu* ("April 29th"), a 1993 documentary about Korean-Americans during the "LA Rebellion" of 1992. She lives in New York City, where in addition to producing films, she is currently the director of the Graduate Film Program at NYU.

I talked with Choy in New York City in April 1994. Since Choy has nearly always worked collaboratively, I have interviewed several of her collaborators. I spoke with Allan Siegel and with Worth Long (about *Mississippi Triangle*) on the phone. I sent Renee Tajima questions about several projects, including *Who Killed Vincent Chin?* Tajima wrote responses. The comments of these collaborators—Siegel's and Long's in interview form; Tajima's in excerpts from her letter of September 27, 1995—are bracketed within my conversation with Choy.

MacDonald: I was looking at your vita and was surprised to learn you had studied physics and architecture. How did you get into film?

Choy: Long story. I was really good at physics when I was in high school in Korea. We studied physics, chemistry, English, Chinese literature, geography, history, and Korean. But I was in love with fuckin' physics! That's why I was good at it, and I studied hard so I could get perfect scores. Actually, I was even better at Chinese language and literature. I read a lot when I was in high school. But no one really encouraged me with that.

Of course, physics also made it easier to come here from Korea. My grades were pretty high, but the Americans had no way to evaluate my level of Chinese language and literature, so they looked at my science courses.

MacDonald: You're half Chinese, half Korean, right?

Choy: Right. So I was pretty well equipped in Chinese history, geography, and language, but I had no idea about the rest of the world!

In 1967, I arrived here. They told me I was too young to be enrolled in college so I got shuffled back into high school, *Catholic* high school [the High School of the Sacred Heart in New York City], and there I improved my English and tried to learn Western civilization. Basically, I went to classes and didn't understand a word of what people were saying—except in math class. Then, in 1968, I had a physical check-up and they found a scar in my lung . . .

MacDonald: TB?

Choy: Yeah, TB. The TB germ normally takes three to six months to grow, so in order to be sure whether mine was active or nonactive, I was shipped to Grassland Hospital in Westchester County and got locked up for six months.

MacDonald: Is that how you got to Manhattanville College?

Choy: Right. At the hospital, they won't let me read; they don't want me to do this, they don't want me to do that. I'm the youngest person in the ward. Everybody just gets sucked into the television: *As the World Turns, General Hospital*. I watch the soaps and I watch people die.

I was so bored there. I did ceramics: a little angel, a little bell, a little ash-tray—they sold them at Christmas time. Actually, I kind of liked doing that, and some of the nurses thought I was good at it, and that I should be an artist.

Later, I came back to Manhattanville, where I was pretty much segregated—I didn't even have a roommate—because everybody was scared I was still infected, though the medical records said I was calcified. The kids were pretty unfriendly, with a few exceptions—especially one girl from Jamaica; she and I are still good friends. And one Chinese girl from a right-wing family from West Virginia and one girl from an Italian neighborhood. I was really miserable there.

MacDonald: Did you have family in the States?

Choy: No one. I came all by myself. I arrive at Kennedy Airport with sixty dollars in my pocket, and I wait and wait and, finally, these two girls in a flaming red sports car are there, screaming at me, saying they come from the school. It was September and I didn't know it got so cold here. I didn't know *anything* about here. The next day they took me to Macy's and I spent all sixty dollars on clothes.

Anyway, I stayed at Manhattanville for one semester plus a summer; then I transferred. Basically I told them I was born to study architecture. I don't know where I got that. I guess I figured it was something in between physics and art. The nuns helped me choose a school, and I transferred to Barnard. Barnard didn't have an architecture school, so I was taking classes at Columbia, and, of course, I couldn't keep up, my grades were terrible. But at Columbia I met Bucky [Buckminster] Fuller, who was teaching there and he had this weird idea that you should go to places in the boondocks and build geodesic domes. The following semester he was teaching in Carbondale, Illinois, and at Washington University in St. Louis. I followed him and registered at Washington University.

After babysitting for a while (it drove me crazy), somehow I got a job at HOK (Helmuth, Obada, and Kassabaum, the biggest architecture company in the Midwest): they designed Pruitt Eigo, the huge housing complex in St. Louis, where nothing worked and there was such a high crime rate that finally they blew it up. So I work there a little bit, go to school, smoke a lotta pot, drop a lotta acid, and do surrealist drawings, paintings, and sculptures. My best friend was Larry Bullard—he's married to Deborah Shaffer [documentarian whose films include *The Wobblies* (1979), *Witness to War* (1984), *Fire from the Mountain* (1987)] now: small world, right?

MacDonald: This is when?

Choy: Nineteen sixty-nine to 1971. The Vietnam War was going on, and the Washington University campus was always on strike. I was not political at all and had no idea what was happening. By this time, me and Larry and a whole bunch of other people in St. Louis—we wanted to do a Bauhaus. We had this vision that since Princeton, New Jersey, was in the country, we could get a farm and live and work in a barn there, and manufacture our own art and make a living. We decided I would be the pioneer to go and check out New Jersey. So I went to Princeton. Why Princeton? I don't know: I figured at least it's pretty. They accepted me. But there's no money. So no farms. No barns. No Bauhaus.

At Princeton, I met a bunch of radical philosophers, activists, Marxists. When the Cambodian bombing started, the whole campus shut down (we still did independent study and wrote papers); and I followed the radicals and we demanded a Third World center for minorities. We had these study groups, and we were talking about dialectical materialism, all kinds of things. I had *no* idea what it all meant. *No* idea, honestly! It was fuckin' crazy.

That summer, I went to Asia on a very cheap flight. During the war, World Airlines shipped GIs to Vietnam and back, and sometimes the flights one way or the other were empty, so they would pick up passengers in Asia and bring them here, and vice versa. To fly from San Francisco through Taiwan to Thailand was something like three hundred dollars. I flew from Thailand to Korea, stayed in Korea for about two months, and then flew back to Taiwan to catch a flight back to San Francisco.

On my way to San Francisco, I'd hitchhiked from New York. I thought it'd be fun to see America. On my way back I hitched from San Francisco to Tijuana and took a bus to Mexico City. I came back through Ajo, Arizona. What a weird place! When I came back from Asia, I brought this cough medicine, made out of pears. It's famous in Asia for coughs: everybody drinks it. So I'm crossing the border from Mexico to Arizona, and the immigration officers don't know what this pear medicine is. They hold me overnight. I looked like a hippy— long hair, sunglasses, bell-bottom pants, camera, little backpack. Finally they released me and I took the Greyhound to New York.

I was fed up with Princeton. I got a job at a place called the Urban Institute, part of Essex Community College in Newark, and somehow drifted in with this radical group. They all lived in a housing complex called Iron Bound, New Jersey. That's where Tom Hayden, Steve Friedman, and Norman Fruchter thought the Revolution was going to start. They were all SDS [Students for a Democratic Society]. A huge group of people were living in this compound when I moved in. I was working with the New Jersey chapter of the Black Panthers, leafleting in front of stores and all that. And they liked the way I drew so I did a lot of graphics for the Black Panther party newspaper, *Seize the Time*.

Elaine Brown was there, and Eldridge [Cleaver]; lots of people came in and out.

I transferred back to Columbia to continue studying architecture, and moved back to New York and worked on the Panther 21 trial and hung around with a lot of Panthers. One day, Norman Fruchter came by my house, and said, "Chris, you draw really well—what do you really want to be?" Absolutely out of the blue, I said, "I want to be a filmmaker."

MacDonald: Were you a moviegoer as a child?

Choy: When I was a kid in Shanghai, we saw a lot of movies from Russia, and from Central Europe—Czechoslovakia, Poland—and there were also Chinese domestic movies. Not that much: revolutionary stuff with heroes and heroines. Then later, in Korea, I saw a lot of movies imported from the United States, and Korea also made its own domestic films, tragic mostly (it was a good movie if you cried your butt out). When I came to the United States I had no money, no time to see movies.

So Norman told me if I wanted to learn about filmmaking, I should go check out this organization called Newsreel. At that time, Newsreel was very elite, all white. Robert Kramer was there and John Douglas, Peter Barton, Bob Mac-Kover, and Norman, who was sort of the leader of the gang. Also, Deborah Shaffer. Newsreel was up at Thirty-second Street and Seventh Avenue, next to Madison Square Garden. So I went for an interview. Oh my God, it was pretty scary. I wore a fancy outfit: I was going to a *movie* company. There was a thick door and I knocked and somebody opened the peephole and looked at me. "Who *are* you!" he said, and I said, "Norman Fruchter sent me," so they opened the door. It's Propaganda Night, and a bunch of people are sitting around watching a movie: Geri Ashur's *Janie's Janie* [1972, directed by Ashur and Peter Barton]. I'm standing in the back, thinking, "This film is a little strange!"—because it's about a working-class woman from Iron Bound, but the funny thing is that every time she talks about her experiences as a single, working mother, she points out her best friend who's a black woman, and the picture cuts to that black woman; but throughout the entire film, the black woman doesn't say a *word!* So I find that odd, and I raise my hand and say, "How come you don't allow *her* to say something?" And that just blew everybody away. Some thought that I was an agent provocateur; some thought I was correct.

I was accepted by Newsreel, but I had to have PE, political education, twice a week, and I had to clean films at night. After three months of PE, I was accepted as a member of the Newsreel Collective. Newsreel at that time had a lot of chapters. There was Boston, Washington DC, Los Angeles, San Francisco, Detroit, Vermont, Chicago, Montreal, I don't remember where else. They made films every week and traveled around in the "Blue Van": using rear projection, they showed work prints in all kinds of places.

When I arrived, the biggest talk was about *Janie's Janie* and *The Woman's Film* [1970], which was made at San Francisco Newsreel by three women [Louise Alaimo, Judy Smith, Ellen Sorin] and had become a hit. *Every* campus was dying to see that film and *The Columbia Revolt* [1969]. A lot of the Vietnam films were big hits, and Newsreel was getting a lot of films from Cuba and North Vietnam. They had a big collection of Santiago Alvarez's films.

Later on, I got promoted to head of distribution and film maintenance, and that's when I got to see all the Newsreel films. But by 1973, Newsreel was beginning to split. Among the whites, there were big fights between the haves and the have-nots. The people who came from Ivy League schools were the haves, those from City College were the have-nots. (I was in an Ivy League school, but I was Third World, so they didn't know how to classify *me*.)

MacDonald: Had you made films by this time?

Choy: Yeah. I was allowed to make my first film, *Teach Our Children* [1972], with Sue Robeson, using money from the Newsreel trust funds. We worked really cheap! The film cost something like two thousand dollars. During the time I was making that film, Newsreel split into several collectives. There was one on 72nd Street, one in Brooklyn, and Third World Collective, which I started. A National Central Committee was formed, and I was elected. There was a laboratory in Boston. We did all the processing by ourselves, underground.

MacDonald: Did the Third World Collective become Third World Newsreel?

Choy: Sort of, yeah. In 1974, all the whites left, and *that's* when I changed the name to Third World Newsreel.

It was a big mess. We were trying to unite people along color lines, so of course it didn't work. And then there was robbery: a lot of cameras got stolen by someone in the organization. Sue Robeson and I moved and started to organize it all over again. Then Larry Bullard came in, and Allan Siegel came back from the old Newsreel.

MacDonald: So around 1974, '75 you start to make films regularly?

Choy: Yeah, we had to because all the trust funds got pulled out. We were left with a bunch of films and very little equipment. A few Bolexes. No sync cameras. We didn't know what to do with the films. A lot of them never got finished, including one on the Black Panther party by Beverly Grant, *Beat of the People*.

So I had to apply for grants. In 1974, I applied to the New York State Council on the Arts [NYSCA] for ten thousand dollars to make four fuckin' films. *Four!* I think I was crazy. One of the films was *From Spikes to Spindles*, and the NYSCA people loved it: it was the first of its kind.

MacDonald: "First of its kind" in what way?

Choy: The first film ever done on the experience of Asian-American women. It was shown on ABC, Capital City, and on Channel 13, which was a big thing. But I had *no* idea what I was doing! I didn't know you can't sell a film to two different stations at the same time. And the rights were not clear. Bob Marley gave me "Stand Up, Get Up" for twenty-five dollars. The film was shot in reversal, real cheap, but it was also the first *color* film from Newsreel. It went to a lot of festivals—one of the few Newsreel films that did. It was picked up by Bill Sloan at MoMA.

There were a lot of reviews of *From Spikes to Spindles* from the Chinatown press and local people thought it was good. Now I look at it and think, "Goddamn, what a piece of junk!"

Every year after that, I applied for grants from NYSCA, and we got funding from 1974 to 1981.

MacDonald: How did *Inside Women Inside* [1978] do?

Choy: That film was also shot *really* cheap. We went to Rikers Island, and we went to Raleigh, North Carolina, to the maximum security prison where Joanne Little was held (she was accused of killing a guard in self-defense). The camera was really jerky and we had no lights. I don't know how we did it.

MacDonald: So until *Mississippi Triangle*, you made a series of formally similar documentaries . . .

Choy: With the exception of *Loose Pages Bound* [1978], which was commissioned by ABC after *From Spikes to Spindles*. I *hate* that film. It was about the Asian-American experience in the Delaware Valley. In one fuckin' hour, they wanted me to do five different nationalities: Japanese, Chinese, Korean, Cambodian, and Vietnamese! But I did it, delivered it, and then went on to make *To Love, Honor, and Obey* [1980], *Bittersweet Survival* [1981], *Mississippi Triangle*, and *Namibia: Independence Now* [1984].

MacDonald: All these were funded primarily by grants?

Choy: *Namibia: Independence Now* was funded by the United Nations. I got an all-African-American crew to go to Angola, Zambia, Botswana, Zimbabwe, Mozambique. We tried to get into South Africa, but I was not allowed in because Chinese were classified as colored (Japanese were considered white!). We did have a Japanese kid on the crew—J. T. Takagi—but she couldn't do the filming by herself. We couldn't figure out a way in. The film got done and the United Nations liked it, but there were twenty-four different countries supervising me. It was just a propaganda film for Namibia. They show it all over the world—except in the United States—so it served its function.

MacDonald: It seems very uncharacteristic of you, especially since it focuses on only one race. What interests me about your work is your mixing and scrambling of ethnic groups. At the Soviet/American Flaherty Film Seminar, you told me my paper on "global cinema" (now "transnational" is a more common term) was "shit" because—I remember *verbatim*—"You don't have to go around the world to be international, you just have to cross the street."

Choy: Right, right, right.

MacDonald: *Mississippi Triangle* is the first of your films that really speaks to that idea.

Choy: Yeah. *Mississippi Triangle* was funded by the NEH, with what was, at that time, a really big budget for me: $165,000! That film supported the entire staff of Third World Newsreel—salaries, overhead, everything!—for months.

Making that film was a big mess, too. I collaborated with Allan Siegel, who was the editor (he also edited *From Spikes to Spindles* and *To Love, Honor, and Obey*). And then we got into a big fight, because he wanted to direct.

MacDonald: Formally, it's a conventional documentary—a lot of talking heads. There are some nice formal moments: that opening shot, for example, where we think the train is moving, but then realize it's the camera. But what I find interesting and novel are those almost surreal moments where we hear this down-home southern drawl and then see this Oriental face speaking. It throws all the movie dialogue we've ever heard from Chinese-Americans into a new context, and we confront how limited our sense of ethnic experience is. I assume that these moments are the heart of the film for you.

Choy: Yes, that *was* the heart of the film. Unfortunately, things didn't work out the way I originally wanted. The film was extremely well received in Berlin; but in New York, it was disastrous! Too long. Too slow. And people literally asked me to do subtitles.

MacDonald: Because of the southern accents?

Choy: Because of the southern accents. *Mississippi Triangle* was difficult to distribute. PBS didn't want to take it in the original length [120 minutes], so we cut it to a shorter version [76 minutes]. Again, they turned it down, and they still think it should be subtitled.

So that was one problem. The second problem is that the film was originally conceptualized with a focus, but during the process of making the film, the focus got lost. Originally, my idea was not only that the finished film would talk about race relations, but that the *process* of making the film should speak to the same issues. I would direct the Chinese sections, and use an all-Asian crew—Chinese, some Japanese; Charles Burnett would direct the black sections, using an all-black crew . . .

MacDonald: He has a credit for camerawork.

Choy: Right. He did the initial research in Mississippi, and at one point was going to do the black section. Allan Siegel was going to do the white section (we weren't going to tell anyone there that Allan is Jewish).

It was almost like guerrilla filmmaking. When the Asian crew finished, we passed on the car and the equipment to the black crew in the middle of the night, and they went on to do their thing (Worth Long, not Charles, was in charge). Then they passed the equipment on to the white crew.

I wanted to have an insider point of view within each ethnic situation. Wrong! Obviously wrong! And Worth was not really a filmmaker; he was more interested in the southern black folk arts. And Allan was interested more in southern literature. *I* was interested in the day-to-day life of the Chinese people caught between blacks and whites. When the material came back, it should have had an outside editor to cut it and give it focus.

From my point of view, the narrative structure should have been built around the schizophrenia of the Delta Chinese. They bounce to the white; they bounce to the black. *That's* the film.

MacDonald: And it's also what we *don't* know about the South.

Choy: Exactly. The audience would learn something new. Allan's footage doesn't *mean* anything to me; it just drives me crazy. And there's *so much* to cover among the blacks! Worth should have focused on the blacks' relationship to the Chinese. Unfortunately, the blacks mostly talk about their relationship to the whites. And the white people: *their* focus should be the Chinese, but they have their own hang-ups.

When I first wrote the NEH proposal, it had a very sharp focus on the Mississippi Chinese. My proposal was based on research by James Loewen, who did his doctoral thesis in sociology at Harvard on the Mississippi Chinese [James W. Loewen, *The Mississippi Chinese: Between Black and White* (Cambridge: Harvard University Press, 1971); Loewen completed his dissertation in 1968].

MacDonald: For all your reservations, *Mississippi Triangle* does accomplish a lot of what you had in mind.

Choy: Well, maybe people appreciate it more now because these days we're talking multiculturalism. At that time I think it was too early for people to understand the film's dynamics. *Mississippi Triangle* grew out of my personal life. I was very close with the Black Panther party and had a lot of close black friends at Third World Newsreel. Meanwhile, I'm married to Allan, a white guy! So I *lived* that schizophrenia. When I went to a Chinese restaurant with a white, no problem; but if I'd go with a black, they don't even want to talk to me!

In Mississippi, the Chinese community *hated Mississippi Triangle*. We did a tour around the South, and in Mississippi the Chinese protested. They didn't want to deal with the black-Chinese part of their history at all, and they wanted me to focus on the success stories. They wrote a letter to PBS, asking them not to broadcast the film. The same thing happened later with *Homes Apart: The Two Koreas* [1991]: the Korean Cultural Council wrote a letter to PBS and the NEH saying tax money should not pay for that kind of film.

MacDonald: I want to get this straight: the Asian-Americans in Mississippi complained that you had focused on the *wrong* Asian-Americans?

Choy: Right. They were angry that I focused on Arlee Hen. And also on the Goons. Mr. Goon is married to a black woman (their kid is a television cameraman now), but unfortunately Mrs. Goon refused to be on camera. There are quite a few black-Chinese.

I went back three years ago and visited all those people again. Most of them are still in the same place, and they remembered me, so it was pretty interesting. The young girl who went out with the black guy had a kid and moved to Memphis. She didn't want to talk about her experiences *at all*.

[I spoke with Allan Siegel on July 27, 1995.]

MacDonald: What do you remember about the origin of the *Mississippi Triangle* project?

Siegel: I can't remember their exact chronology but there were two critical

Arlee Hen (left) in *Mississippi Triangle* (1984), directed by Christine Choy, Allan Siegel, and Worth Long.

elements. One was coming across James Loewen's book. The other was this Chinese guy from Mississippi that Chris and I met in Philadelphia when we were working on *Loose Pages Bound*. The *Mississippi Triangle* project was divided into two stages. We got a research grant and later a production grant. During the research phase of the project, the idea of breaking the project up into different teams developed more validity, at least partly because these three communities in the Delta didn't talk to each other a whole lot.

MacDonald: During the shooting, were all three of you directors, or was Chris in charge?

Siegel: All three of us worked pretty independently, as directors. I mean Chris would review the footage everyone shot but it was not from the point of view of telling us to do this or that. In fact, looking back on that project, I feel that more of that would have helped. One time in Memphis, Chris and I met with Charles Burnett (he's from Vicksburg) to screen footage and to discuss the film. There was always a lot of communication between Chris and myself, just because of our relationship, but I think the other people involved could have used more communication about the project.

MacDonald: When the shooting was done, how did the finished film develop? Chris talks about being not completely happy with the final shape of the piece. She feels it needed to focus more specifically on the Chinese-Americans in the Delta.

Siegel: Chris and I were collaborators on the editing. During the editing process, we screened one reel of the film at the Independent Feature Project Conference in New York and on the basis of that screening, the film got accepted in Berlin [the Berlin Film Festival]. Well, that was it: we were forced to come up with *something*. We had a tremendous amount of diverse material and we knew that we were not going to resort to a voice-over narration to provide a structure. But an organic structure is difficult to come by. You need time. You have to try different arrangements before you can settle on something that really works. The acceptance at Berlin drastically shortened our time frame, and that was that.

You mentioned you were also interviewing Ken Jacobs for your book. I should tell you that after I'd made my first film [*The Grain*, 1966] in Baltimore, and had come to New York, a friend of mine said, "You should take your film over to Ken Jacobs" (this was when Ken was at Millennium Film Workshop). So I did; Ken loved it and, as a result, situated me in New York. I started teaching at the Millennium, and then Ken put the film in this festival of underground film, with Bruce Conner and Bruce Baillie and all the others, a big event at the New Yorker Theater. And then he said there was a friend of his who needed someone to teach film at what was called the Free University of New York over on 14th Street. I began running the film workshop at this free university, and out of that came Newsreel.

The first Newsreel film was about the Pentagon demonstration [*Only the Beginning*, 1971]. A group of people from my Free University workshop class had gone to Washington for the demonstration to make a film about it, and Marvin Fischman was making a film about it also. Pieces from those two projects became *No Game* [1967]. There's been a tendency to create a one-dimensional picture of Newsreel, and as a result, the relationship of Newsreel to the underground film movement of that time gets minimized. For example, Jonas Mekas was a pivotal person in the early development of Newsreel.

MacDonald: What was his role?

Siegel: The first meeting of what became Newsreel took place at Anthology Film Archives, and Jonas came to the first four or five meetings. He'd come with his Nagra and record what was going on. He still has the original.

It was Jonas's style not to be an active participant, but he was an active supporter, and pushed things to happen that allowed a very divergent group of people to coalesce. You had people like Robert Kramer and Norman Fruchter, who were coming from the political filmmaking side of things. But my roots were in experimental film, as were Marvin's.

Even today, though I find a lot of experimental film difficult to deal with, I show Bruce Conner and Bruce Baillie and others. I think that's really important work and not a contradiction to the kind of filmmaker I am.

Oh, one last thing about *Mississippi Triangle*. I doubt Mira Nair would admit it, but *Mississippi Masala* [1991] came right out of *Mississippi Triangle*.

MacDonald: What's the connection?

Siegel: Chris and Mira became friends after Mira came down from Harvard. She had made one documentary, I think, and was working on another, which the Film News Now Foundation, Newsreel's foundation, had become a fiscal sponsor for. We were traveling around the South working on *Mississippi Triangle*, and Mira was coming in and out of the office, hearing all these stories about how every time we go to a motel down in Mississippi, it's run by Indians. We used to talk about how odd it is that different immigrant groups attach themselves to certain occupations in particular parts of the country. You wonder how the hell they got into *this*. I mean we figured out how the Chinese got to Mississippi, but how did the Indians get to run Mississippi motels!

So much gets left out of "film history."

[I spoke with Worth Long on August 4, 1995.]

MacDonald: I understand that you replaced Charles Burnett on the *Mississippi Triangle* project. I'm curious about how you got involved.

Long: They were working in an area where I'd done a lot of work with SNCC [the Student Nonviolent Coordinating Committee] during the sixties. Also, I'd done a film with Alan Lomax, *The Land Where the Blues Began* [1980]. When Chris and Allan asked me to be involved, I said that if we could involve Ludwig Goon (he'd worked with us on *The Land Where the Blues Began*), I'd be willing to co-direct with Allan and Chris.

MacDonald: During production how much interaction was there between the three of you?

Long: A lot of contact with Chris. In fact, Chris went on at least half of our shoots. She was the overall producer. Once you understand that, and once you understand her personality [laughter], you realize Chris was in charge. The advantage of breaking up into three groups was that Allan could go into some places, especially to the cotton brokers, and get information they would hesitate to give us. Chris could go into the Chinese communities and have people relax. And I could go into either the African-American or the Afro-Chinese communities. Some people we talked to already knew of my political work in the Delta.

MacDonald: Chris expressed reservations about the final structure of the film. She wishes she had focused the whole film more precisely on the Chinese-American community.

Long: I agree with her. *Mississippi Triangle* wasn't scripted, though there was an outline. And her outline, correctly, was to tell the story of the struggles of a Chinese minority in the Delta as it connected to a broader story of exploitation and oppression within the region. I wasn't much involved in the editing process. Allan and Chris did that. I did review the footage. We were open to doing general Newsreel footage, not just *Mississippi Triangle*. I remember one time we stopped for a day and shot material of a man on trial for his life. We knew it wasn't going into the film, but as socially conscious filmmakers we had to shoot it. Excellent footage. We also shot material about the political campaign of the first African-American with the opportunity to go to Congress from the district where we were working.

MacDonald: Who saw that material?

Long: It got archived.

Hell, you could have made three films with what we shot; but you could make one good film by braiding together material from the three teams.

MacDonald: Was *Permanent Wave* [1986] your first attempt at a dramatic fiction film?

Choy: No. Before that one, I did a black and white piece with AFI money, *White Flower Passing* [1981], about an older immigrant woman meeting a younger American-born Chinese and the clash of cultures and understanding. Pretty weird film. And then AFI gave me *more* money and I did *Permanent Wave*. After those two experiences, I thought about moving to narrative for good, so I started working on *Haitian Corner* [1987, directed by Raoul Peck], a feature narrative piece. But I hated doing it—too many people to handle. In narrative, you feel so removed, and everybody's ego is so out of control: actors and actresses, cameraperson, producers, grips. I can't really feel the subject through all that crap. They're *all* phony—they try to kiss your ass. I *hated* it!

So I finished *Permanent Wave, Monkey King Looks West* [1990], and other odds and ends, and then came *Who Killed Vincent Chin?* It took five years, 1983 to 1988, and was released in 1989.

MacDonald: It took five years because the case lasted so long?

Choy: The case lasted years and it took time to raise money. And we couldn't get Ronald Ebens to talk with us until the very end. CPB gave us a *lot* of headaches. By the time I first applied, I had already made a lot of documentaries. But they told me since I didn't have a journalism degree, I'm not eligible to do a film on this heavy-duty murder case. I brought Juanita Anderson on board—she has a journalism degree. *Then* they said I didn't have an audience: "Who's going to watch this film?" The way you secure your immediate audience is by having a television station guarantee to show your film in the area, and Detroit WTVS, Channel 56, was very good about that. The executive director, Bob Larson, was really conscientious, and came in as co-producer. And *then* the sons-of-bitches at CPB asked me *how can I be objective!* I said, "I cannot be objective! I can't change my skin!" Blah, blah, blah. So they decided, in order for us to receive CPB money, I have to take along a *white* story consultant from *Frontline*, a Mr. Dvasner. I didn't get along with *him* from Day One.

There was a sequence about mud-wrestling: these workers go mud-wrestling on their lunch hour, and they take the mud-wrestling pretty seriously. There they are, drinking their beer and singing the American national anthem. It was a *great* scene. "You can't use it," he says, "You're degrading the American working class." This Harvard graduate tells me this! He says, "You would *never* show

Chinese that way!" I said, "Bullshit!" A sequence in the film shows the Chinese gambling on mahjong. I told him, "To *you*, I'm degrading the white working class, but to the Chinese, I'm degrading the Chinese community!" Dvasner didn't like the music, either. Ultimately, I locked him out of the editing room.

That's when Peter Kinoy was editing. We went through quite a few editors. Peter Kinoy was the first; Molly Smollet was second, with Peter as supervising editor. I didn't like Peter's editing because he always argued with me. He wanted to make a propaganda film. Molly didn't know what to do with the material so I got rid of her too. And one day when I was really frustrated, Richard Schmiechen walks in (he produced *The Times of Harvey Milk* [1984], and later died of AIDS) and tells me, "Three principles: one, the editor should not argue with you about what you want to say politically; two, the editor should really love music; three, the editor should be an experimental filmmaker." And that's when I found Holly Fisher, an experimental filmmaker, with zero political orientation—or at least she didn't argue politics *with me*. She knows how to manipulate the nuances of found elements, and she's very eclectic. The first work she did for me was a scene that was shot in a sloppy way, of the girl who was on stage singing this corny Chinese song in a corny dress. Holly cut that sequence together, and I thought it was absolutely brilliant. So Holly stayed.

MacDonald: You gave her a particularly emphatic credit.

Choy: A single credit, yeah. She worked very well with me. She and Renee *hated* each other. Big problem. They fought nonstop until the end. Holly wanted to share a co-director credit with me. Renee fought that, and wanted one herself. Neither of them got it!

MacDonald: Am I right that part of what drew you to the Vincent Chin project was not only the Asian-American issue, but the fact that the events occurred in Detroit, a largely black city?

Choy: What drew me into the project was Helen Zia. There was some kind of forum at the NYU Law School, and Helen Zia came. At the time, she was president of American Citizens for Justice. To illustrate her talk, she showed a clip of local television news, about a basically open-and-shut case where this Chinese guy, Vincent, got beaten to death. The clip was poorly done. Terrible. I looked at Helen and Helen looked at me, and we remembered each other from Princeton— can you believe it? (She was a nerd at that time; I was the crazy one, so we never really spoke.) I said, "Since I'm a filmmaker, why don't I make a better clip for you to use in raising money for the case?" A little later Mrs. Chin was speaking in San Francisco. I had no money—*no* money!—and this guy from the Asian Ministry of the Presbyterian Church, Wesley Woo, gave me a thousand dollars. With that money, we got equipment from UCLA, brought it to San Francisco, crashed in someone's home, and filmed a little bit of Mrs. Chin. With that footage, I went to Detroit with Nancy Tong to interview Mrs. Chin (Nancy, who became associate producer on the film, could speak the same dialect as Mrs. Chin). I was putting the sample together when I heard about CPB, so I applied for funding.

Also, reading the court transcript of the case, I found it very interesting that no two people had the same story. It was just like *Rashomon* [1950]! That in it-self was nice to work with. And then I thought, "Why not interview Ronald Ebens?" I thought it would be a piece of cake. I'd been inside of prison, I'd been all over the place. I figured I could get to Ebens overnight. No way! He wouldn't do it, for *years!*

MacDonald: Why did he finally say yes?

Choy: After the Cincinnati trial [the federal civil rights trial], he was walk-ing down the steps of the courthouse, and I went up to him and said, "Congrat-ulations!" He was *shocked*. He looked at me, this little skinny Chinese woman in a T-shirt and shorts, and he says, "We're having a little party at a bar down the block, why don't you come." So there it was. I said, "Let's go get it!" By then, "we" were only three people—myself, Nick Doob, and Renee (Renee did all the production managing; Nick and I did sound and camera and lighting). We got to the bar, and they said, "Put the cameras down!" By this time he was familiar with the press. So I schmoozed with him. I practically sat on his lap! He was always bitching about how the press was not fair to him, how the press had drummed up the civil rights case. I said to him, "You've been bitching about what the press says about you but *you're* not saying anything. You refuse to be interviewed!" He said, "Call me in a week or two."

When I call, he says, "Come over." We scrounge every penny we can find to get to Detroit. Tape recorder isn't working. Oh my God, I was a nervous wreck. But we got him! We got him.

MacDonald: You were editing as you went, right?

Choy: We had a cut already, without the interview, but it didn't work; it was just a lot of narration. PBS kept saying, "Narration, narration, narration!" Even before the Cincinnati *trial*, fuckin' CPB is saying, "Where is our product? Cut!" I'm insisting, "*No*, I have to wait for the Cincinnati trial." They're saying, "Just put in an epilogue about what happens at the Cincinnati trial." I'm saying, "No way!" This is what pisses me off about these agencies. They didn't want me to do the fuckin' film because I don't have a fuckin' journalism degree, but they don't give a shit about the actual story! What *is* journalism, if you don't go all the way?

So I waited and waited. They stopped paying us. No money coming in. We did a big benefit in New York to raise money to cover the Cincinnati trial. And *then*, when I *did* have the complete story, *they didn't want it!* They just wanted something superficial so they could say, "We served the minority con-stituency!" Fuck 'em!

The funny thing is when the Academy Award nomination came, they sent me a telegram saying, "Congratulations! Please don't forget to mention *our* funding." I told them—right to their faces—to fuck themselves, and put their telegram on a dart board.

MacDonald: I remember being surprised you didn't win.

Choy: Hotel Terminus [1988, directed by Marcel Ophuls] won. It was politics. Every year you've got to have a Holocaust movie win an Academy Award. *The Sorrow and the Pity* [1972, directed by Marcel Ophuls] had been ineligible because of the length. At that time, feature documentaries could only be ninety minutes long. *Shoah* [1986] hadn't been eligible either. The year we went in, they changed the rules and allowed films longer than ninety minutes, and since they didn't have a *Sophie's Choice* [1982], they had to give the documentary award to *Hotel Terminus*. I mean basically it comes down to that.

And Ophuls had MGM as distributor, and of course we didn't even have a *poster*. We were penniless.

MacDonald: Actually, I figured *Vincent Chin*, which I admire, would win out of tokenism, but I'd have given the award to *Hotel Terminus*, too.

Choy: Well, even the nomination was an honor. But I think that filmically *Vincent Chin* is more interesting than *Hotel Terminus*. Filmically.

MacDonald: In what way?

Choy: It's more eclectic, there's more energy. It's more like MTV than a straight documentary. I saw *The Sorrow and the Pity* recently. *That* should have won. That was powerful.

After *Vincent Chin*, I did other collaborations with Renee Tajima: *The Best Hotel on Skid Row* [1990], which was heavily financed by HBO, and *Yellow Tale Blues*, a video—shot in film, cut in video (it was financed by New England Television). We were raising money for what we were calling *Fortune Cookies: The Myth of the Model Minority* [Tajima finished the film, now called *My America . . . or Honk If You Love Buddha*, in 1997] and still needed money (we raised $800,000!), so we did *Jennifer's in Jail* [1992] for Lifetime. A piece of shit.

After that, Renee and I mutually decided we should not work together. She went off to Los Angeles and I remained in New York and started to do smaller projects.

MacDonald: You did some good work together.

Choy: I think *The Best Hotel* was very strong. *Vincent Chin* is very strong. The concept of *Yellow Tale Blues* was interesting, but Renee's parents weren't interesting, so the film isn't either.

MacDonald: I don't agree.

Choy: You thought it was interesting?

MacDonald: Just as in *Mississippi Triangle*, it's an ethnic mix—immigrant Korean-Chinese and native Japanese-American—you rarely see in standard American film and TV.

[I asked Renee Tajima to review her involvement in the films she worked on with Choy. What follows is an edited version of her letter in response to my query.]

Tajima: In thematic terms, *Who Killed Vincent Chin?* was for me the culmination of a political agenda and of the perception of the Asian-American identity I had come to during the seventies and eighties. As a third-generation Japanese-American, I had come of age with the Asian-American arts and po-

Renee Tajima (left, under light) and Christine Choy (in scarf), during production of
Who Killed Vincent Chin? (1988).

litical movements—fueled by the battle for ethnic studies, for social, economic, and cultural justice in our communities, and against the war in Vietnam. I had been introduced to this milieu during the late sixties, when my
family left a homogenized, predominantly white Chicago suburb for Altadena—an integrated community in Los Angeles and home at one time or another to Sirhan Sirhan, David Lee Roth, and Rodney King. If my first filmmaking sensibilities had a source—other than growing up on seven-hour-days
of television, that is—it was coming of age in Altadena. The social turmoil
rocking America during the time invariably swept through the schools. Even
the children were mobilized. By the age of fourteen, I had read *The Wretched
of the Earth* [by Frantz Fanon] and *The Autobiography of Malcolm X.* By sixteen, I had already led city-wide student walk-outs over dress codes, ethnic
studies, and affirmative action for teachers. I became a cultural nationalist of
sorts. I cut neck and armholes in big bags of Asahi Premium Rice to wear over
my jeans, as was the style among young Asian-American rebels of the day. I
took a stab at playing the Japanese koto, electrified of course, although no one
could tear me away from R&B and the Doors. Toshiro Mifune and Akira
Kurosawa became my cultural heroes. I rediscovered my identity and discovered Yellow Power.

My high school was, rather absurdly, regarded as an "inner-city school" because half the students were minorities. That was my good fortune, however,
because it got me into a federally funded program for "inner city youth." The
program exposed me to a creative world I had never known before. I was as-

signed a still camera, a tape recorder, and unlimited stock to document social problems in Los Angeles, which I then edited into multiscreen slide shows. I did shows on rape, children's poverty, race—any subject for which I had a passion. Invariably, I was drawn to Little Tokyo, Chinatown, Manilatown, anywhere where Asians ruled the streets. I became captivated by the faces of the old people, the Issei, the Manong, the pioneers with paper names who came here to seek *gam saan*, the Gold Mountain.

Although I never went to film school, while an undergraduate at Harvard I did take a couple of production courses across town at MIT. I never felt comfortable as the only woman of color in the class, with Ricky Leacock proclaiming of political filmmaking, "Dahling. It's passé." At that time in the late seventies, it was dazzlingly new to us Asian-Americans. It was the first wave of Asian-American independent cinema—urgent, idealistic filmmaking—from groups like Visual Communications in Los Angeles and Third World Newsreel in New York.

The seventies were also a time when video was new and hot, and institutions were buying hardware left and right. The Harvard School of Public Health built an entire video studio, replete with Porta-Paks, none of which ever seemed to be used. Along with a group of African-American students (including Reggie "House Party" Hudlin), I organized a Third World video collective. We took over the studio and the equipment, and produced a regular program on closed-circuit television. A couple of us even found our way down to Grenada. Prime Minister Maurice Bishop was my first interview.

After graduating from college, I got my first job as a secretary to "The Mr. Bill Show," and within a short time ended up in Chinatown as the first paid staff person for Asian Cine-Vision, the organizer of the annual Asian-American International Film Festival and of Chinese Cable TV. I settled into the community of media-activist-filmmakers. We spent half of our time fighting Charlie Chan revivals and other assorted racist portrayals from Hollywood, and the other half making up for lost ground by documenting Asian-American reality.

As an Asian-American media activist, I believed that independent filmmaking served as a cultural organ of the Asian-American movement, and that the purpose of film is not only to document reality but to define an Asian-American political identity. The Vincent Chin story fit the criteria. Vincent was a Chinese-American mistaken for Japanese in the midst of a racialized trade war. He was middle-class and Americanized, yet the color of his skin defined him in the eyes of the killers. The movement for justice in this case was the culmination of the pan-Asian-American political efforts that had been building for almost twenty years: the recognition of Asian-Americans as an oppressed racial minority deserving of legal protections under civil rights law.

In making *Who Killed Vincent Chin?* I began to explore two approaches to the documentary. First, rather than look to other documentaries or journalism for inspiration, I wanted to find a literary voice. I felt that Asian-American stories could be told to broad audiences by reconstructing lives through storytelling. Although *Who Killed Vincent Chin?* has no overt narration, for its dramatic structure and fractured storytelling approach, I returned to an early influence—*Rashomon*.

The *Rashomon* approach also solved another problem for me. While I was not interested in a purely journalistic approach, I did want to get at the gray areas that shaded the Vincent Chin story. The project was originally conceived as a fifteen-minute advocacy piece, but as soon as I read the trial transcripts and took my extended research trip to Detroit, I rediscovered what every documentarian knows but sometimes doesn't want to admit. There are two sides to every story. For me, the case went to the heart of the limitations of civil rights law and the legal system itself in sorting through the narratives, the varied interpretations of fact, and the emotions, to get at the truth.

In my work, I have tried to locate the eclectic points of cultural intersection that bind us as Americans, regardless of ethnicity. Although I spent my teenage, cultural-nationalist years yearning for a return to roots, in truth, I didn't know from Japan. But I knew the Detroit sound, I knew *Breakfast at Tiffany's* [1961] and TV. This kind of cultural eclecticism is in contrast to the "roots" journeys of the 1970s which promoted racial validation by recapturing homeland traditions. I believe it is eclecticism that defines the Asian-American cultural experience, and the American experience as a whole.

For Vincent Chin and his killer, Ron Ebens, this eclecticism reverberates in Motown and Dinah Shore's exhortations to "See the USA in your Chevrolet . . ."—the same imagery of America's go-go years I remember as a child, which is used impressionistically throughout the documentary. Rather than direct illustration, these popular musical and media themes emerge organically in the film as metaphors for memories and emotion.

Another example is the use of television newsclips, which for me have always provoked drama and emotion: Walter Cronkite's announcement of President Kennedy's assassination is one of my earliest memories. For those of us who grew up on television, broadcast news, with its swelling musical introductions and urgent anchor-speak, means far more than information. An artfully done newsbreak can always send a chill down my spine. From "The President is dead" to "Magic is HIV positive"—these televised moments define my memories in the way my parents remember chasing adventure on the railroad tracks or FDR's fireside chats. So in *Who Killed Vincent Chin?* I wanted to use newsclips to signal dramatic turns in the story—with the opening logos, theme music, and all.

This is one device I really had to fight for. You'll recall the intense dichotomy between film- and videomakers at the time we were making *Who Killed Vincent Chin?* The old guard filmmakers simply hated video. Being younger, not knowing or caring about the rules, and having grown up with video and television, I had a completely different take. I don't believe film and video are interchangeable, but I do believe that video as popular collective culture, home movies, on-the-spot documentation, and the like, can be a visual and dramatic motif in films. I think problems surface when video is intermixed with film without a clear, consistent dramatic or visual purpose.

Television also influenced me in terms of the structure of *Who Killed Vincent Chin?* At that time, *Hill Street Blues* was one of my favorite shows. I was interested in its use of parallel development with several characters' stories playing out during the same hour. I felt a documentary could sustain the same kind of style, as long as there was a strong narrative spine—in this case, retracing the parallel lives of the Chin and Ebens families.

After making *Who Killed Vincent Chin?*, I (along with a thousand other young film- and videomakers) became quite obsessed with the idea of using popular media as a motif in documentary. Thus in *Yellow Tale Blues* we tried juxtaposing movie clips to our family stories in an intuitive way, and in *What Americans Really Think of the Japanese* [1990], a documentary I produced for Japanese television, I tried to integrate television and movie clips to convey the environment of popular culture in the US. My efforts in this particular work were thwarted, however, since my Japanese executive producers were nervous about my critical use of American television commercials.

In my new film, *My America . . . or Honk If You Love Buddha*, I reveal my obsession with the road movie (in fact I've developed a documentary "Road Trilogy" on American identity, of which *My America* is the first installment and *La Reunion* is the second). *My America* is an extension of the stylistic concerns I've discussed above, as well as of my thematic search for a collective and individual identity. The film is inspired by the many lives of ex-Beat, Victor Wong, who Kerouac wrote about in the novel, *Big Sur*, as well as by my own memories of a life on the road. In the narration, I recall countless vacations as a child, traveling down old Route 66 in the days when you could cross four states without ever catching a glimpse of another Asian face. Returning two decades later, I meet a cast of characters whose lives symbolize the changing face of Asian America, which has grown dramatically in size and in diversity.

What does it mean to be an Asian-American today? Similar to Wayne Wang's filmic journey through Chinatown in one of my favorite movies, *Chan Is Missing* [1982], my search in *My America* leads to these different territories—political, emotional, socioeconomic, personal—that define Asian America. It reveals a dense, complex landscape, ranging from empirical demographic data to subliminal media messages, to romance, to public policy. These varied threads are anchored in the film by the road trip, which has been a staple of the American narrative. Whereas *Who Killed Vincent Chin?* was a culmination of my political beliefs throughout the seventies and eighties—defining Asian-American as a pan-national, oppressed racial minority—*My America* represents my effort to look at the changes precipitated by post-1965 immigration and the new cultural diversity within Asian America and the United States itself.

MacDonald: I see you've actually made an avant-garde film: *Five Chapters* [1992].

Choy: That's not avant-garde! It was commissioned.

MacDonald: If I showed it in an experimental film show, it would fit perfectly.

Choy: Well, yeah. Asian Women United were putting five artists together for a show, and wanted a film for each one. They said, since you're doing something about an artist [Barbara Takanga], the filmic approach should be artistic. They gave me two thousand dollars to make the film. How am I going to make it for that? So I decided to do it MTV style and cut it in the camera. I recorded her first on the voice track (none of the soundtrack is even cut!), then I played back the soundtrack and shot the footage based on the track, timing it to the exact second. Finished!

MacDonald: It's a nice piece.

Choy: A one-day shoot! From beginning to end. It was fun. I guess it *is* pretty experimental.

MacDonald: *Sa-I-Gu*, your film about LA's Korea-town within the larger context of the riot/rebellion, is another film about ethnic intersections.

Choy: I grew up in Shanghai, but I'm not Chinese. I tried to be Chinese as much as possible when I was in Shanghai, but we were *not*, and everybody *knows* you're not. Then when we moved to Korea, I'm supposed to be Korean but I'm *not*. I tried to fit into the Korean community, but I couldn't. Then I go to Japan and the Japanese think I'm a Japanese, and I'm trying *not* to be Japanese! When you spend the first fourteen years of your life in a Communist regime, then live in a neocolonialized state, then in an advanced capitalist society, you form peculiar ways of thinking. This is reflected in all my work. I'm interested in the conflicts *between* A and B, but I'm even more interested in dealing with the conflicts that develop *within* A and *within* B as a result of the external conflicts.

Rose Lowder

For many filmmakers who mount critiques of conventional cinema, the use of "experimental" to describe their work—a term popularized by David Curtis in *Experimental Cinema* (New York: Delta, 1971)—is, at best, problematic, since it seems to suggest that their films are experiments rather than finished works. But for Rose Lowder, the term is not only acceptable, but preferable, and in exactly the meaning Curtis suggests. Her films are experiments created in the interest of exploring "the camera's ability to emulate and enhance human visual perception" (Curtis, p. 2)—some of which can *also* be considered successful finished works. Indeed, her commitment to the term is such that it provides the name for the Archives du film experimental d'Avignon, which she and her partner Alain-Alcide Sudre established in order to collect, preserve, and showcase landmark "experimental films."

Though the earliest finished work listed on Lowder's filmography is *Roulement, Rouerie, Aubage* ("Rotation, Wiliness, Paddle Wheel Unit," 1978), a lovely study of the motion of a water wheel near her home, she had begun using film to explore cinematic perception several years earlier in a series of 16mm film loops. In the twenty years since she began to conduct her own visual experiments, Lowder has devised a filmmaking procedure that usually involves working frame by frame (exceptions include *Roulement, Rouerie, Aubage* and *Couleurs Mécaniques* ["Mechanical Colors," 1979]) in accordance with precisely designed visual scores (themselves often of considerable interest) to record simple, natural processes in and around her home in Avignon. While conceiving the design for a film is usually painstaking and time-consuming, the shooting itself is generally confined to a single, intense day. Longer films combine the results of single-day enactments of several film scores.

The most memorable of Lowder's films—*Rue des Teinturiers* (1979), a visual exploration of the tiny balcony of her apartment which looks out on Rue des Teinturiers; *Champ Provençal* ("Provençal Field," 1979), a study of a peach tree in an orchard in Provence at three different times of year; *Retour d'un Repère* ("Recurrence," 1979), an evocation of a park in Avignon; *Les Tournesols* ("The Sunflowers," 1982), a study of a field of sunflowers; *Impromptu* (1989), a study of several trees and a field of poppies; and *Bouquets* (1994–95), ten one-minute explorations of Provençal landscapes—create distinct visual experiences that, in their reduction of day-long phenomena into brief, precise, intense cinematic moments, sing the potential of an ecological film aesthetic. Indeed, Lowder has kept track of every roll of film she has exposed by numbering them; only the works she puts into distribution are given titles.

I spoke to Lowder in June 1992 in Avignon, and she provided corrections and additions later. The interview was conducted in English: though Lowder has lived and worked in Avignon since 1975, she is the child of British parents and grew up in Peru. We used the French titles of her films in our conversation; they are retained throughout this volume.

MacDonald: Your first experimental film work was with film loops?

Rose Lowder: Yes. I was interested in the fact that you can see on the screen things that aren't actually on the film. A very simple way of demonstrating this is to make holes in the filmstrip with an office hole puncher. If you draw a line on a piece of transparent leader and then punch a hole in every alternate frame, the line seems to go through the hole. But if you draw the same line and then punch holes in two successive frames out of every three, the hole appears empty. For a year I explored the possibilities of these simple juxtapositions. I also tested colors to see how they could interact over a series of successive frames. What's the point of all this? There's a lot of talk about the smallest unit of cinema being the frame, but in fact, that's not the case at all. As these experiments demonstrate, pieces from different frames can make up what you're seeing on the screen. In other words, you can construct an image on the screen with bits from different frames. You can change very slightly parts of a frame or several frames—change the color, the thickness of the lines, whatever—and a completely different thing happens.

MacDonald: Even though the line actually isn't darker on the film?

Lowder: Yes, it's due to the way the mind processes images. That's how a film like *Les Tournesols* works. You're focusing on successively different flowers all over the field, and together they all look in focus. But when the images were shot, parts of every frame were out of focus.

Rue des Teinturiers works in a similar way: one frame shows the street far away. And the next frame might focus on a leaf that is very close. Those are the two pictures which are actually next to each other on the film. But when you see them projected, parts of the images are eliminated: a bright, sunlit shape in one frame might knock out a part of the bridge on the next frame. One moment we have a part of the bridge and then suddenly a piece of the bridge is missing.

MacDonald: When you were making the early loops, did you show them as gallery pieces or . . .

Lowder: No. I've never shown the loops publicly at all, except recently [1992] when I visited Robert Breer's class in New York. And once in Willem De Greef's class in Brussels as well.

I've never had access to an optical printer: I've always developed very precise scores based on what seemed to be the latent possibilities for film as an art and have shot frame by frame on the basis of these scores.

MacDonald: When you were making these early experiments, were you aware of other filmmakers who worked systematically frame by frame—Peter Kubelka, Tony Conrad, Paul Sharits?

Lowder: I certainly knew of their existence but I don't remember when I actually saw their films. I don't think it's too relevant whether I saw the films or not. What I *did* do was read about many, many films. At one point *Studio International* had a regular column, which Malcolm LeGrice and other filmmakers used to write: we were very well aware of what was happening in the United States and elsewhere. I had seen Robert Breer's *Recreation* [1956] in 1964; it predates the filmmakers you mentioned. In any case, I think too much importance is given to being first in something and not enough to studying what was achieved. The question is how well you do whatever you do.

Often it is difficult to be aware of who *was* first to do something. Sharits's work with color frames, for example, is pre-dated by Marc Adrian's work in Austria. Sharits worked with color frames in a more powerful, persistent way, but Marc worked that way earlier. Marc was friends with Kurt Kren, and together they made a film with only colored leader, called *Black Film* [1957]. Marc Adrian brought the original film to Avignon: it was put together with Scotch tape. It's very beautiful actually, though it's falling to pieces. He brought along a copy of it as well, and we showed them together: the original is much brighter than the copy, and much more interesting. In France we have quite a few filmmakers working frame by frame, with a very different sensibility from the one you have in American work, and which has largely gone unnoticed, simply because here we do not have the funding and the organizational structures that one has in North America.

MacDonald: Who do you mean?

Lowder: Cécile Fontaine, for instance, who physically moves pieces of frames from films she finds onto other pieces of film. The result is not at all like an optically printed superimposition. You actually have the original material you're re-using mixed together physically with new material, which makes for a much more vivid, tactile experience. You can have real color film and real black and white mixed together physically, which normally you can't have. Her

Successive frames from Rose Lowder's *Rue des Teinturiers* (1979).

strips of film are very beautiful to look at as art objects, quite apart from what they do on the screen.

MacDonald: Were you trained as a visual artist?

Lowder: I had early training as a painter. From the age of nine, I was in different artists' studios, different workshops because my mother thought it would be good for me. And then I went to art school in England, the Regent Street Polytechnic, at the time an extremely good art and crafts school. You had to know how to sculpt, you took theater and design, you had to produce work in all the different fields. The school closed before I had completed my studies, and I had to go somewhere else (the Chelsea School of Art).

Finally I felt I had to earn my living a little better than I had been doing until then. My father was working in commercial art. He had a couple of publicity companies and he would have liked me to work with him with the expectation of my eventually taking over, but I certainly did not want to do that. I had told him at a very young age that I didn't want to be involved with advertising. In England in the sixties, it was extremely difficult to find an interesting job. My first choice would have been to pursue my studies, but I couldn't afford that. I couldn't work in publishing without a literary degree, so I tried journalism and I tried theater—if you were a woman, they always wanted to put you in the costume department. I entered the film industry, which was another closed shop, by the back door, by applying for what they called holiday relief (taking jobs for people who were on summer vacation), and I ended up at the BBC as an assistant editor, from 1965 to 1967.

MacDonald: That was the period when Ken Russell and Peter Watkins were there.

Lowder: Yes, and Ken Loach. At the time, Loach and some others were thinking about how you could use television in a way that would be socially useful and specific as an art form.

MacDonald: That was the case with Watkins, though ironically, his most powerful BBC work, *The War Game* [1965], was released only as a film because the BBC considered it too strong for television.

Lowder: The BBC was scared stiff. I had to go to the National Film Theater to see *The War Game*. I remember being totally discouraged with the whole idea of television. If they could commission a work so superior to anything they were normally showing—and then not show it, just because the content was too critical of the society we're living in, that meant you couldn't have *any* serious thinking on television.

Watkins recently made a very long film, *The Journey* [1987], which was shown here in Avignon. It's a very honest, authentic attempt to try to come to terms with a whole set of social, cultural, and cinematographic problems. I found the film very informative and not at all boring.

MacDonald: I was one of the producers of the segments of *The Journey* that took place in upstate New York. We spent a year raising money. I hated every second of it.

Lowder: I have to do that *all the time* for the Archives, and I'm very bad at it, because I hate it, too.

MacDonald: What did you work on at the BBC?

Lowder: On all sorts of programs except for the news, which was put together by a specialized department. Editing was about the only thing women were allowed to do. I don't know how many editors there were at the BBC, but if there were five hundred, I think there were about two token women. The situation has evolved; the union has fought for women's rights, and the atmosphere has changed. I left the BBC and went to France to try to remain closer to Alain [Alain-Alcide Sudre]. The sixties had been a very interesting time to be in London, a much nicer time then, probably, than now. In fact, compared to London, we felt that France was so conservative and boring that it *had* to get better. And in fact, that's what happened. We ended up in Avignon, just because it was well connected in terms of public transportation (at the time, we didn't have a car), and the cost of living was within our means. We wanted to avoid the coast because we knew that would be much more tourist-orientated and therefore uninteresting from our point of view. At first I cleaned a school and delivered mail on my bike. Alain worked in the night wholesale market loading trucks with crates of fruits and vegetables. Finally, Alain obtained a teaching post at a school near here, where he still works.

Later Alain and I spent one year in Paris in 1975–76, a crucial year, the year when French experimental film became a movement. If you look at the list of films in the Musée national d'art moderne collection, you'll see that there is little French film in the collection before this date (with the notable exception of the Lettrist movement from the beginning of the fifties): there was hardly any French experimental work to collect! The work from the forties, fifties, and sixties is mainly American.

While we were in Paris that year, we went to all the screenings that were going on, sometimes every single night of the week, even two in one night. There were a number of different groups distributing films. I especially remember the Collective jeune cinéma and the Cooperative des cineástes, neither of which exists today. These two groups had heard of the Theater Festival of Avignon, which is one of the largest theater festivals in the world, and both groups wanted to show their films during the festival, thinking they'd get more publicity for their work—a naive idea. They approached us for that purpose. So, during the next theater festival, we found a screening space and a 16mm projector for the Collective jeune cinéma. I told them, "You have to organize everything; we can't do anything else. You'll have to ask the filmmakers if they're willing to have their films shown in the context of this theater festival, and you can divide up any money you get at the door." When the Cooperative des cineástes found out we'd made this arrangement with the Collective jeune cinéma, they were furious: they wanted us to do the same thing for them. I said, "Come the week afterwards," which is what they did. Those were the first experimental film events presented at Avignon.

We had a lot of headaches in those first years. We housed people here in this house. People slept on the floor. We didn't even have proper plumbing. We hadn't any furniture. But the events were quite successful. I saw the entire collection of films that these two organizations distributed, and I got to know the filmmakers. They found ways to come, and we found floors for them to sleep on.

After a time, it became clear to me that having filmmakers present their films wasn't always best for the work, and I realized that if we wanted to go on looking at films, it was preferable to organize regular screenings. That's what we did, for six years, with no grants whatsoever. We paid the rentals with the money that came in at the door, and made it up from our own pockets when there weren't enough people. Rather hard-going. It was Mitterand's government that was responsible for changing this, because at that point the Ministry of Culture gave the Archives, which were Alain's idea, its first grant.

Currently, we get a small sum from the government to run the Archives [this grant was eliminated in 1994]. Two-thirds goes to buy film; one-third pays for our screenings. We have to print programs, send them out; Avignon isn't close to Paris and all the films have to come from Paris. Initially, I had the naive idea that I'd not have to travel all over the place to see films, that I'd be able to see them in Avignon. Of course, that's completely impossible, because to run a good program for the public—and bearing in mind what the public in Avignon are able to see normally—you have to see most everything you program before you program it. I do take some risks. I show a few films by filmmakers whose work I already know and also some that I do not know but have reason to believe are of interest, but mostly I still need to travel to view films.

MacDonald: One of the things that struck me when I looked at *Roulement, Rouerie, Aubage*, the first film you list on your filmography, is that it's an accomplished, confident film. Were the five reels that make up *Roulement* chosen out of a larger number of reels?

Lowder: No. That's all that was shot of that water wheel. I had shot about fifteen reels before that on very similar subjects, attacking similar problems. In checking my notes, I discovered that *Roulement* is reel 21; *Rouerie* 20, 25, 26; *Aubage* 27.

MacDonald: In *Roulement*, and later in *Couleurs Mécaniques*, your choice of subject—water wheel, carousel—allows the films to continually make metaphors about the nature of the film apparatus.

Lowder: The mechanism of a water wheel *is* interesting in relation to the camera mechanism.

If you work as an artist fairly consistently, everywhere you go there's a subject for a film, perhaps a more or less interesting film, but a film. And the urgency is to try and make time to carry out at least some of the projects you conceive. For both these two subjects, which are quite near the house, I could just run home and get the camera. Actually, I thought of the water wheel film a year before I could find the time and money to make it. I can't work like Mekas used to and carry my camera everywhere. With *Couleurs Mécaniques*, I was on my bicycle taking films to the post office, and when I saw the carousel, I decided on the spot to make the film. I went home, got the six reels of film I had at that moment, and was back in five minutes.

But you see, that still meant I had to postpone mailing the films. Also, it was lucky that on that day I had enough energy to make a film. Sometimes when you run screenings, and you're struggling with authorities, you don't have the energy to do your own work, and a film doesn't get made that year. And later, when *you* are ready and able, the film can't be made because what you intended to film has disappeared. For a recent work, I wanted to film a gas station I went to—and they just dug it up. It's gone! There are dozens of gas stations but it was just the right one for the project I had in mind. And for each subject there's only a certain time of year, or hour of the day, when the light is right for what I want to do. A scientist can work full-time on what he's doing. He can concentrate. He can try something, and if it doesn't work, he can try it again. He can work on it until he *gets somewhere*. But an experimental filmmaker can't do that. You only have enough money to experiment once, and if it doesn't work, you have to stop.

MacDonald: I assume that you saw yourself in the tradition begun by the twenties European avant-garde filmmakers.

Lowder: Every country has what tends to become a traditional way of presenting the history of experimental film. In the States, the standard history begins with historical figures such as Maya Deren, and everyone reiterates that history. Such simplifications tend to restrict the context for viewing films. Deren *was* the first person to fight so forcefully for her film art as an *independent* art. That was important. It's not a question of always doing your work; you also have to work *for* the work. John Cage said that you have to make the piece of music, but you also have to make sure that it is heard.

It's fine for traditional art: there is a system. I remember Malcolm LeGrice telling me that when he went to Venice for the Biennale [a major exhibition of contemporary art], a whole group of experimental films were shown. The journalists looked at the paintings and sculpture, and the painters and sculptors didn't have to say a word. They could go off and enjoy themselves. But when the films were shown, the journalists were asking him, "Tell us about this, tell us about that." For a moment he got angry. He said, "Look, you figure out what the artists and sculptors are doing, why don't you make an effort with *this* work?"

You can pick up art magazines, dozens of them, and find out what avant-garde artists are doing, but there is virtually no equivalent body of literature to help people access experimental films. The result is that filmmakers have to go around with their work; we have to be able to write texts, we have to be able to photograph our work. There is no one to do those things for us. Of course, sometimes the result is that it gets done in a much more interesting way than if we did have people doing it for us. But it's exhausting.

MacDonald: Can we go back to the European avant-garde of the twenties? Did you see that as your context?

Lowder: Well, I think in France we saw a much wider variety of work than many American filmmakers. In a way, it's annoying that traditionally the history of experimental film in France starts with the twenties. Annoying, because the painters and sculptors who made those early films didn't see film as an independent art. [Fernand] Léger made only one film (in collaboration with Dudley Murphy), *Ballet Mécanique* [1924]. However political Léger was in his subject matter, he had absolutely no politics about trying to get his film shown. That was true of all those filmmakers: though they were very strong in their opinions about society and everything else, they didn't apply any of those ideas to trying to change the way film art was circulating. They were very *un*revolutionary from that point of view, totally traditional.

MacDonald: Of course, there was also the ciné-club movement, which was very widespread and had substantial audiences, first throughout France and then all over Europe. An artist who was making experimental films could use that network.

Lowder: But those audiences were not concerned with experimental film any more than contemporary audiences are.

Don't misunderstand me, I admire those early films. Obviously for everyone in France *Couleurs Mécaniques* recalls *Ballet Mécanique*, although the plural in the title of my film is intentional. Like many people of his time, Léger had this great admiration for machines, and even when he was filming things that weren't machines, he made them look like machines. Many people of that time were impressed by anything mechanical. The carousel in my film is mechanical but I don't focus on the mechanics at all. Contrary to Léger, I don't show the workings of the machine, I merely use them to free the object's colors for another visual purpose.

MacDonald: Also, the Léger film was more about machines as power and progress and modernity, but the machine you choose is about pleasure and play, and since it's an old-style carousel, about nostalgia.

Lowder: Although that wasn't a conscious choice at the time. I was going past this machine on my bicycle, and as I was going by, I could see immediately what you could do with it. I can't say that what came back was exactly what I had in mind, but the quality of what I had in mind does come through in places.

Most of my films leave me unsatisfied. This is what keeps me making films: you're not satisfied, and you always think you can do better. It makes you furious to not be able to do things as well as you would like to. Perhaps the title of *Rapprochements* [1979] is relevant here. "Rapprocher," the verb, means to approach, but there's also an idea, almost impossible to translate, of coming near to something that is impossible to reach. *Rapprochements* suggests you are trying to get as near to a subject as you can, but that you can never quite get there. On the other hand, many reels hold pleasant surprises; interesting things appear that you did not expect. That's another reason to keep on making films.

MacDonald: What distinguishes your films from others in which the subjects function as metaphors for aspects of the film apparatus—the room in Michael Snow's *Wavelength* [1967] or the hallway in Ernie Gehr's *Serene Velocity* [1970]—is your simultaneous interest in natural cycles. From the beginning, it's clear that you want natural process to be a major factor even in the most rigorously structured films.

Lowder: That's a definite choice. Of course, some people are more concerned with their surroundings than others. My consciousness of my environment may be a result of the fact that I was born in South America and all through my childhood, I was put in a garden and left on my own. Even as a baby, I was put in a pram underneath the avocado tree—my mother probably thought it was good for me to be outside in the fresh air. When I was looking at old photos recently, I realized that the avocado tree in one of the photos looks just like the leaves in some of my films. Then later, I had three and a half months of school holiday every year—three and a half months with nothing to do! My mother didn't watch me all the time like most modern mothers (or fathers) do. She had other things to attend to, cleaning or cooking or whatever. She'd just say, "Don't come in the house until lunch time," and you couldn't say a word to her until that hour. So you had three hours in the morning to occupy yourself constructively; you were in the middle of these tropical surroundings; the sun gradually moved and you had to move your table to stay cool. So you became visually conscious at an early age.

MacDonald: In a way, many of the films that you and I admire require of viewers the same creative, energetic effort at perception.

Lowder: Yes. They do suppose an audience able to take charge of themselves in front of what they're seeing, and then able to do something with it. That's what you always have to do when you don't have things to consume. My films are extremely anti-consumption in that sense and, for most audiences, that's the worst thing about them: they require an effort. This is probably the reason why the shorter films are shown most often. I think programmers feel no one can take more than three minutes of my work.

MacDonald: Could you talk about your choice of the one-hundred-foot roll as a structural unit, first in *Roulement*, then in *Couleurs Mécaniques?*

Lowder: One of the cameras I have now allows me to shoot a twelve-minute reel. I don't do so, for practical, down-to-earth reasons. The necessary attachment makes the camera a big thing, a heavy thing. I try to film without being noticed. I don't want to disturb the scene I film, or to be a nuisance to anyone. I don't want them to feel I'm intervening in their affairs. I'm not interested in disturbing people's personal lives. On the other hand, I don't like to be bothered. I don't like people asking me questions about what I'm doing: it's distracting. Jakobois often used to film very near some famous monument. People would think he was a tourist, and no one would bother him.

MacDonald: Not long ago, I did some research on Ralph Steiner. Steiner felt that with astute framing alone you could rediscover the world. *Couleurs Mécaniques* seems to reflect similar principles.

Lowder: This just goes back to basics. Of course, you select very carefully what you are going to do. You eliminate everything that's arbitrary. You make sure you don't do something without realizing what you're doing; you do things consciously. Then, the few things you do choose become very much more defined.

In every one of my films, the process is decided on in advance. There's never anything arbitrary. I never go out saying, "Well, I don't know if I'm going to shoot it frame by frame, or if I'm going to wave the camera over my head at twenty-four frames per second. And I never decide to do something else, half way through a reel.

MacDonald: But you build into almost every film an element which is beyond your total control.

Lowder: Although I cannot know what is going to happen on any given day, the process is always calculated for the scene *that day*. Until *Impromptu* I never calculated on one day for another day's shooting. If I didn't succeed in working out what I wanted to do in time to finish the reel that day, I abandoned it and came back another day and started again. Recently, my working methods have become more complex, often requiring several days of work to shoot one minute of film—such as in the recent *Bouquets*. I always try to get as close as I can in time and in space to the thing I'm filming, while remaining as open to it as possible.

I have shot many reels of film, and I build on my past experience, but each reel covers new ground. To me, a project isn't interesting if I know exactly what's going to happen. I could film a flower pot, but that would be cinematographically totally boring. I want the subject that I'm filming to be living its own life. One of the solutions of conventional cinema is to choose dead things and move them around. Even the actors: traditional narrative requires the actors to do exactly what they are directed to do. I *don't* want a docile subject. When everything is under control, it's dead. My filming processes are set up as a dialogue with reality.

When I first sent my reels off, I never believed that anything would be on them. I never believed that I could take a photo and actually record something. I thought you had to have special skills. Even after all this time, I always look at a reel on the bench before I put it into the projector, just to see if something is there. I look and think, "This is fantastic, you can actually see water." Sometimes there's a great disappointment, because something looks very beautiful as a strip, but projected is not interesting at all. And sometimes on the bench it doesn't look very interesting, but on the projector it is. As much as I prepare my films, each of them has become something I could not have foreseen. Obviously, there is an initial idea with enough richness to push me to do all the things you have to do in order to make film. No one is asking you to do this work, and it is a lot of work, and you have to find a way to pay the bills.

Everyone can make films when they are eighteen, but later it gets harder. There are more and more things in your life which you are obliged to do and which take you away from your filmmaking. As you get older, the initial idea has to be very intriguing.

MacDonald: Were all forty-six shots in *Rapprochements* taken the same day?

Lowder: All were taken the same day, in the same order. I sat down and filmed a black and white reel, a color reel, a black and white, a color, and so on. As you probably gathered, I used a mechanical Bolex: it goes for twenty-eight seconds, more or less, then stops, and you rewind. *Rapprochements* was the first film on which I used a tripod. I was very pleased not to have to hold my camera anymore. I like to work in good conditions; my ideal way of filming is under a shady tree.

MacDonald: Nineteen seventy-nine was a very productive year for you.

Lowder: Lots of ideas had been bubbling up during the time I didn't have a camera. And then suddenly in 1977 things got a tiny bit better financially, and I got a camera. In 1977, 1978, 1979 I made cautious, little pieces each of which gave me a certain amount of information. Also, I made a tremendous number of tests, even for *Rue des Teinturiers*. I still have the test reel for that. I filmed a tiny piece on every single point of the zoom to see which focal length would be the most suitable. The one that I liked the most was with the zoom as close-up as possible. There seemed to be possibilities there. It was a very poor lens, for a TV camera, which had been abandoned in the school next to our house, but it was the best I had.

Making *Rue des Teinturiers*, I was very tentative, in the sense that I waited for each reel to come back from the lab before I went on. A reel would come back, and according to the feelings I had about the possibilities of the reel, possibilities that weren't really carried out to the extent that I wanted to see them carried out, I planned the next reel. In each reel, I tried to develop aspects of the previous reel. Of course, each time I filmed, I was choosing a different day, interesting for different reasons. As I remember, the test reel was made in March, and the last reel in July. You can see big changes in the amount of vegetation that's visible.

MacDonald: It's a beautiful piece. It uses what would normally be considered a minimalist strategy—a tiny cityscape is filmed over and over—for anything but minimal results. When you see the space over and over at different times of day and in different seasons, your sense of the space becomes larger than the tiny porch here that you were working with. Were you choreographing the plants for the film?

Lowder: You mean putting special plants in special places? No, what you see is just what happened to be there.

MacDonald: The decision to systematically explore a space using different focus points—the approach you use in *Rue des Teinturiers*—is used again in *Champ Provençal* and in *Retour d'un Repère Composé* ["Composed Recurrence," 1981]. The immediate impact each time is a high level of visual energy in the image, something akin to what Bill Brand achieves in *Chuck's Will's Widow* [1983] with his optical printer. Was that level of energy primary in your decision to use that method?

Lowder: No. One of the reasons I started to work that way was that I had studied certain problems in perception. We have two eyes, but the camera has

Retour d'un repère (1979) : same negative used to print **Retour d'un repère composé** (1982)

Frame by frame filming procedure
Successive position of the seven focus points from near (7) to far (1), gradually extending over the filmed space :

Number of frames filmed at each focus point, a rotating system (12321) :

Interlacing of focus points

A visual transposition of a pantoun, a verse form borrowed from literary rhetorics

Rose Lowder's diagram of the system she used in making *Retour d'un Repère* ("Recurrence," 1979).

only one eye. I'd looked into the different stereo processes, which try to create volume artificially. I'm not trying to do that. If you put a camera in front of a scene and let it run normally, what you get is something which is visually poorer than if you'd been sitting looking at the scene yourself. You've got two eyes, so you experience volume; and you're aware of a lot of things which would normally be outside of the film frame: when you're seeing a film, you're in a dark room where all your other sensory input is cut off, and you're looking at one isolated little rectangle out of all there is to see. It seemed to me that if you wanted to create, not *reality*—that's not interesting at all; you might just as well *see* reality—but if you want to make a work of film art that is as rich as what one is used to in reality, you have to enrich the film image somehow. One way is to continually focus on slightly different focus points that allow you to see around the corners of things just a bit. In certain scenes in *Rue des Teinturiers*, you'll notice that at some points you can actually see through the flowering laurel tree trunk in the middle of the balcony. You are seeing *behind* it as well as *it*, because one of the focus points is giving you what is behind the laurel's trunk and another focus point is the trunk itself, and still another is in front of the trunk. Because I use all these focus points over and over, you see multiple things in the same space, which in reality is physically impossible. This gets back to the loops where you can see something on the screen that is not on the film.

MacDonald: *Champ Provençal* is one of the easiest of your films to understand . . .

Lowder: And it's shown more often, which is annoying: I suspect it's shown not because people think it's better than the other films, but because it's short.

MacDonald: But it's lovely as a précis for the later work.

Lowder: Well, it could have been much better; it could have been very good, but one of the problems was that a peach tree needs a space with a diameter of seven meters in order to grow, and I had had no experience with peach trees. It wasn't a tree that I knew. So when I went back to place the camera for the third reel, which is when the tree is at its maximum size and you have the peaches on the tree, I couldn't get the camera as close as it had been earlier. I've often felt I should remake the film correctly.

MacDonald: The overall system was the same for each of the three sections of the film?

Lowder: Not exactly the same. The more the leaves grew and the more space the tree took, the less you could see through the branches and the fewer focus points you could have. Each subsequent reel has fewer focus points and a less complex structure.

MacDonald: You continued to work with the single roll as a module until *Retour d'un Repère Composé*, in which you repeat a single module over and over.

Lowder: The film is fifty-nine minutes; the original negative is a little less than three minutes, a one-hundred-foot reel.

MacDonald: Over the years, I've heard it argued that "male" formalist work—*Serene Velocity* or *Wavelength*—tends to be characterized by an implicitly phallic directionality in the structure. Your films, and *Retour d'un Repère* and *Retour d'un Repère Composé* in particular, could be seen as providing a feminist alternative: we may learn the general contour of the structure as you cycle through the same set of images over and over, but we don't go from one clear point to another very different one. In *Materialist Film* [London, New York: Routledge, 1989] Peter Gidal suggests that your film is part of a movement toward a dispersed identity, rather than a focused identity: in other words, given Western cultural history, toward a woman's rather than a man's sensibility.

Lowder: In my film, you're not exactly sure where anything is. The film escapes simplistic definition, which is part of the project. It is also a part of my philosophy. My films don't progress along a track and arrive somewhere, because I don't think life works like that. I don't think you can plan to progress. Sometimes things get worse, sometimes they get better. You continue to work as best you can.

MacDonald: I'm correct, am I not, to say that you never see the same sequence of frames photographed at the same focus points twice in *Retour d'un Repère?*

Lowder: For the original one-hundred-foot reel that is true. Of course, even if you try to focus the same way twice, you're filming a tree that's moving around; *it's* never in the same position when you come back to it. The structure is repetitive, but it reveals a developing reality.

For the first film I made this way, *Rue des Teinturiers*, I actually looked down the lens for every single focus point. I didn't mark the lens, and it nearly killed me. I was in a terrible state after that. I had to look down the lens nearly 4,320 times! In one day! Later I found an easier way. You decide what you're going to focus on, mark the lens, and then just change your foci by putting your lens in the positions you marked. Recently, for the *Bouquet* series, I have returned to focusing independently on nearly every frame.

MacDonald: What led to the decision to expand *Retour d'un Repère*, a nineteen-minute film, into the fifty-nine-minute *Retour d'un Repère Composé?*

Lowder: Actually, there's also a double-screen version in between. When the original negative of *Retour d'un Repère* came back from the lab, I was a bit horrified because in looking at that first reel, I couldn't really see anything. It went by too fast. I thought, "Right. I'm used to working with loops, seeing things over and over." Well, you can't very usefully make a two and a half minute loop. You need a special projector set-up to do that. The easier way was to make eight copies. And that's the nineteen minutes, eight copies, one after another. Then, the thing that struck me when I looked at the imagery over and over was that every time it came around, I was seeing something else. The more you saw it, the more it evolved, and the more things there were to look at.

MacDonald: What did the two-image version accomplish?

Lowder: *Retour d'un Repère* doesn't have much color. Coming from Peru and given the kinds of colors I'm used to having around me, I get very discouraged

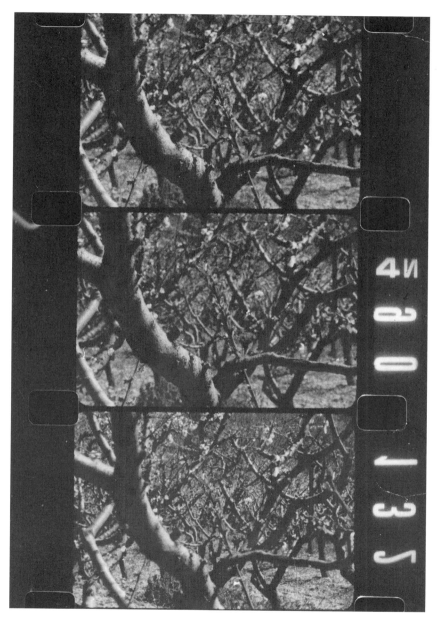

Successive frames from Rose Lowder's *Champ Provençal* ("Provençal Field," 1979).

if a film looks dull. Of course, the film was shot under several old trees and was quite dark, and the duck pond seems brown. While I was filming, I waited for those colorfully dressed people, probably tourists visiting the park, to walk through and brighten the scene. Later, I had several copies, all unsatisfactorily processed by the lab, and the possibility of using two projectors. I thought I'd try to project two copies together, one on top of the other, to see if I could make a brighter film. The coloring *is* more interesting that way, but what was more important is that that mixed version is what led to this final, long version, which I felt is as far as you can go in a certain direction.

It's also a film no one *ever* shows. It's all very well to try and do this kind of research, but it's totally useless in the sense that no one is going to see it.

MacDonald: The four parts of *Scènes de la Vie Française: Arles* [1985], *Paris* [1986], *La Ciotat* [1986] and *Avignon* [1986] remind me of extended phenakistascope imagery. You don't use the opposite sides of a disc, but you interweave two different versions of the same scene, frame by frame, so that two different times, and slightly different spaces, are superimposed on our retinas.

Lowder: That series is a direct reference to the beginning of cinema and the Lumières.

I stopped working on the *Scènes de la Vie Française* series because I was so discouraged with the results—compared to what it *could be*. The Luxembourg Gardens imagery in *Scènes de la Vie Française: Paris*, for example, was beautiful originally. It was just after a thunderstorm, when you have the most extraordinary light, but due to the process I used that's not there in the final film: between the original and the print many details are lost.

MacDonald: What you do accomplish in those films—and sometimes it has more impact than at others—is to have the same place exist within the same image, at different moments in time, simultaneously. We can see both times; and a new, filmic time is created when bits of the two moments form a new shape or movement.

Lowder: Yes, it's all a continuation of the idea that was already developing in the loops that we can experience a picture which in fact belongs to many different times, although for us, as we're seeing it, it's one time. That idea is experienced spatially in *Rue des Teinturiers*, but not so much in terms of time. In *Retour d'un Repère* time is more evident, but it becomes very pronounced in *Scènes de la Vie Française: Paris* when you see people dressed for different seasons walking through the same space, or when people are walking alongside each other and one has a shadow and the other doesn't.

Actually, I was in La Ciotat when the original Lumière films were shown there in an old theater [the Eden] dating from the time of the Lumières. They'd discovered new Lumière films no one had seen, and showed them for a whole day on an original projector, that is, at an irregular, manually generated speed which allows all sorts of things to happen which are lost when the same films are

Successive frames from Rose Lowder's *Retour d'un Repère Composé* ("Composed Recurrence," 1981).

adapted for modern projectors. And while I was there, I got the idea for a film of the launching of that huge tanker [*Scènes de la Vie Française: La Ciotat*].

MacDonald: When you talk about your films, you seem to see them as a kind of visual research. But what draws me to them is the pleasure of looking at them. Some of the films are exquisite. What is your relationship to the question of film pleasure. Does it matter to you if others find your films beautiful?

Lowder: No, not at all. One answer is that if you try to make something that looks good, you usually fail, because just looking good is not enough. Films which look good to me, look good because behind them is some very profound, essential reasoning. I never try to make a great artwork; I don't know how to do that. The kind of films I end up with, which in the end may or may not be pretty to look at, look that way because their internal structure is very complex.

MacDonald: I'm less involved with the idea of a pretty picture than with cinematic magic. When I see the trees in *Impromptu* do what they do, I can't believe my eyes.

Lowder: Every one of my reels has had a very precise project, and many of those reels do not end up being shown, because even though in theory the results should be interesting, once you've done a reel, you can see *why* it doesn't work on film. And you can then take the next step.

Les Tournesols was made to get rid of an objection a lot of people had to *Retour d'un Repère Composé, Rue des Teinturiers*, and *Champ Provençal*: "Why is the image jumping up and down all the time?" To me, the objection is irrelevant; the jumping up and down is an inevitable (and perhaps unfortunate) aspect of the way those films are made. *Les Tournesols* was made to respond to that objection: it does not jump up and down. But the only difference is that in *Les Tournesols* I used an overall pattern, so the jumping up and down is not evident because there aren't sharp divisions between areas of the frame. For some people, that overall pattern makes a connection with Van Gogh, which I *never* thought of until people brought it up. I didn't go out to make a Van Gogh film, and never imagined that I had, because the brush strokes of Van Gogh which could be taken as an equivalent "jumping up and down," are so far removed from the kind of work I had to do to make the film.

MacDonald: I'm not sure I understand the procedure you use in some of the films. In some cases you put the film through the camera more than once, right?

Lowder: *Les Tournesols* was shot frame by frame, from beginning to end in one four-hour go. The original reel of *Retour d'un Repère Composé* was shot the same way, as were *Rue des Teinturiers* and *Champ Provençal*. They're all simple, frame by frame, through-the-camera-once films. In the case of *Impromptu*, I'm still using a stationary camera, but in this case the film went through the camera many times.

MacDonald: So, in *Impromptu* you calculated the frames so that when the film went through the camera the first time only certain frames were exposed; then, the next time through, others?

Lowder: Yes. I always start by doing the simplest things and then elaborate as I go. In the case of the first tree in *Impromptu*, I just exposed one frame, left the next one black, exposed the next, left the next one black. Then I wound the film back, to exactly the same place—which can be quite difficult, depending on the camera you have: most of my work has been shot on a mechanical Bolex, which isn't too precise—and then, second time around, I exposed the second, fourth, sixth frames. That first reel ends with a bit of normal motion shot in matching light. The irony is that when the normal motion comes along, it looks more unusual than what precedes it: it looks like slow motion.

The second reel focuses on another tree, and in that case I began with some normal motion and then shifted into the frame-by-frame alternation. The third reel, the poppies, was alternate frames, though I had planned to do other things. In the middle of the process a fuse went, and I had to stop. I was furious. I knew I couldn't return to the same framing after having solved the technical problem. The last reel is more complex, also as a result of a mistake. From experience I usually know the kind of light a reel is going to need (though I've never learned to use a light meter—I don't possess one) and when I started shooting, I realized I hadn't quite the right light. I went back through the reel three or four times to add some light, and then in going back through, I started playing around with the sequence of the frames, which gave me ideas for future films: I realized you could go through the reel shooting odd numbers of frames, then leave some black, then two frames, then leave some black—things like that. And that's how I shot the poppy field in *Quiproquo* [1992]. The white tree in *Quiproquo* is done that way on a mechanical Bolex! Extremely difficult.

MacDonald: How did the sound get onto *Impromptu*?

Lowder: That was the lab—an accident, just some negative optical spacing from someone else's film. It was so funny I couldn't resist leaving some of it.

MacDonald: Is the title a result of the accidents?

Lowder: Yann Beauvais is responsible for the title. It had been several years since I'd distributed a new film—completely because of my organizational work—and he was touring French experimental films and wanted to include one of mine, so he took a copy of this film. Then other people wanted to screen it, and I thought, "Well, for once, you have a film that someone wants to see! You shouldn't stop them from seeing it—even though it's not the film you thought you were making" (It was just a beginning, some test reels for a longer film). The title refers to the fact that the film wasn't supposed to be distributed, but also to the way the sound was put on, and also to the fact that those people you see on the second reel weren't supposed to turn up. Even the way the title was put on was "impromptu." I shot some very elaborate titles, but they just didn't go with the film; the title I used was shot just to run a reel out of the camera.

MacDonald: Nearly all your films are made locally. Sometimes you go as far as La Ciotat, or the Camargue, but it strikes me that your interest in the particulars of individual frames, and individual seconds of film, is a parallel "localization" of film experience.

Lowder: It's also a practical matter. For a long time, I had no car, and went everywhere on my bicycle. I had decided since I didn't really need a car, there was no point having one. Now that I do have a car, I can go farther. I have the car for my camera, which is too sensitive for the bicycle. Cycling over rough ground in the Camargue [an island in the delta of the Rhône, famous for its marshes and wildlife] loosens all the tiny screws in the lens. Myself, I prefer the bicycle. Also, I need the car for our Archive projects. Obviously, Alain and I can't solve all the problems of experimental film in France; but we do encourage other people to program experimental film. There are many people in France who have a budget, who *could* program if they were interested. Many of them do program at art house theaters and it wouldn't be difficult for them to add experimental film. This is starting to happen—but it involves more travel for me. And in traveling, of course, I see new things to film. I enjoy looking at everything as I travel. I never take the freeway if I can avoid it. I take the smallest roads I can find.

MacDonald: But do you see your concentration in your films as a kind of cine-politics? You eat organically; you don't own a refrigerator. Is your decision to work frame by frame a kind of environmental statement?

Lowder: In opposition to big budget TV or cinema footage, yes. A developed society doesn't have to be a wasteful society. Take the example of organic farming. To survive today in France, an organic farmer has to be much more technically knowledgeable than an industrial scale farmer. The traditional farmer will be comparatively uneducated on the whole and will have technological sales representatives come along and tell him what to do, and when to do it. To reduce the number of people working on a farm, you need a tremendous amount of heavy equipment. You depopulate the countryside; you do very little manual work; and you produce a tremendous amount of food—too much, so much that you have to throw some of it away (the government pays you to throw it away so that the prices stay up). Now if you look at the organic farmer, besides having to have more education, he or she will have to do more manual work. The field will need to be dug up by hand, or by more gentle machines, three or four times. The organic system requires that people are brought back to work on the land. Actually, in organic farming, there are more pieces of machinery, but smaller, more precise, and designed to accomplish particular tasks.

As an artist—to come back to your question—it's the same choice. You can work in a very precise way and make very particular decisions about everything you do. When I worked in the industry, we sometimes had a sixty-to-one shooting ratio. I worked in one television company where I was throwing away sacks and sacks of stuff every day. In the industry, the only things that count are the ones you sell.

My ratio is one-to-one, in the sense that even what is not shown to the public is important for me. And even the work that I don't usually show sometimes gets screened. Maurice Lemaître gave me an open screening once, and I showed the reels I don't normally show, which allowed me to re-study them. Yes, my work is an ecological statement, in the sense that I do less but try to give it more attention. The film of mine that gets shown the most is not necessarily more important to me than a reel that I don't show anyone.

In the end, it's a question of balance, between what I'm doing and the kind of wealth, which is *not* material, that I'm getting from it. Commercial films can be shown for a week and if they're not popular, they disappear. Think of the millions of dollars that have gone into making the film, and the millions of hours of wasted time during the production, and the millions spent to publicize it. It's crazy!

On the other hand, while my films have not been shown as widely as some experimental films, the list of countries where they have been seen is impressive. Hardly any commercial films by known directors have as wide a range of audiences as *Les Tournesols*, a silly little film of a field of sunflowers! It's extraordinary, especially for something that cost almost nothing. I don't propose that things change all at once—that would be unecological—but hopefully things could change in an ecological direction by gradually moving toward a world that is more in the interests of everyone.

MacDonald: Oh, one last thing: I understand you have a Jack Smith story.

Lowder: Well, it's probably the story of the victim in every place that Jack Smith went. It just happened, by pure chance, that in this case it was me. No one told Yann Beauvais, who had invited Jack Smith to Paris, or me that Jack Smith was as difficult as he was. If we had known, we wouldn't have invited him, no matter how famous he was or how many good films he may have made. We're just in too poor a position to work with people like that.

Jack Smith arrived at the airport, which, as you know, is an hour and more from Paris, and Yann Beauvais asked me to cook supper while he went to fetch him. When they arrived, Jack Smith didn't seem particularly enthusiastic to see anyone. He just sat there eating. In France when you eat a meal with people, you're supposed to be sociable; no matter how badly you may be feeling that day, you show some pleasure that people have bothered to prepare a meal for you. Yann and Alain were totally bored with this unsociable character, like any Frenchman would be. I tried to be kind, and mentioned that Alain and I were from Avignon. Jack Smith immediately demanded that I find a theater for him during the theater festival. I explained that I had nothing to do with the theater festival and had absolutely no way of getting any kind of space for him, and he refused to accept this. He didn't seem to react straightaway, but later we realized he was quite angry.

Yann had paid him before his screening, just to be kind—so he'd have some money to use in Paris, and then Jack Smith started making all kinds of demands, claiming he wouldn't do the screening if Yann didn't do this or that—things that Yann couldn't possibly do: getting him a plane to Morocco . . . I don't remember. So since Yann had no money, no matter how Jack menaced him—and he menaced him the whole next day—it was to no avail. And then, Yann rang me up and said, "You can't come to the screening this evening because Jack Smith won't do the screening if you come" [on April 29, 1985, Beauvais showed *Flaming Creatures* and *Normal Love*]. I got very angry with Yann; it's the *only* time I've disagreed with the way he has proceeded, because Yann's a close friend and I've always admired the way he deals with difficult situations. He's extremely talented and devoted as an organizer. His motives were good; he was afraid that Jack Smith would be violent. Jonas Mekas has confirmed to me since that Yann was probably right.

I said to Yann, "This is absolutely ridiculous. You can't run screenings and tell people they can't come to them. We don't work like that. No matter how unimportant anyone is, they should be able to see the films. I'm coming. I'll not be obvious; I'll watch from the projection booth or something. But I'm going to see the films like anyone else." So I came and slipped into the booth. And of course, Jack Smith came into the booth and saw me and chased me around the booth until I ran out.

MacDonald: So as it turned out, you didn't see Smith's films?

Lowder: I've seen the films several times since.

Peter Hutton

Conventional overviews of film history rarely begin much before the Lumière brothers' development of the cinématographe and the Edison laboratory's development of the kinetoscope. Generally, the focus of histories of pre-cinema and early cinema has been on the development of those particular technologies that make modern filmgoing possible and on the early evolution of those economic structures of production, distribution, and exhibition that became the movie studios. However, if we see film history in its broadest sense—as a diverse set of film practices, some of which are conventional and commercial, others more fully critical—the "roots" of contemporary film practice are obviously much older and more diverse than the conventional histories of film suggest. The silent, slow-paced, meditative films of Peter Hutton reveal a commitment to the individual shot that is purposely reminiscent of the Lumière brothers' commitment to the single-shot film, the photograph-in-motion: often each individual shot in a Hutton film is separated from the next shot by a moment of dark leader. At the same time, Hutton's approach to cinema has roots in forms of the moving image that predate the cinématographe by decades: most obviously, Phillipe Jacques de Loutherbourg's Eidophusikon and Louis Daguerre's Diorama (for a description and history of these early nineteenth century entertainments, see Richard B. Altick's *The Shows of London* [Cambridge, Mass., London: Harvard University Press, 1978], chaps. 9 and 12).

The Eidophusikon and Diorama shows provided viewers with contemplative images of natural and urban scenes, in much the way that, since the early 1970s, Hutton's films have provided contemplative views of cities—most often New York, in *New York Near Sleep for Saskia* (1972), *New York Portrait, Part I* (1977), *New York Portrait, Part II* (1980), *New York Portrait, Part III* (1990);

but also Boston, in *Boston Fire* (1978); Budapest, in *Budapest Portrait (Memories of a City)* (1986); and Lodz, in *Lodz Symphony* (1994)—and of natural landscape, in *Landscape (for Manon)* (1987), *In Titan's Goblet* (1991), and *Study of a River* (1996). In fact, Hutton's commitment to depicting the Hudson Valley region (a commitment evident since Hutton began teaching film production at Bard College in Annandale-on-Hudson, New York, in 1985) locates him within another tradition with pre-cinematic dimensions: the Hudson River School of painting. Hutton's landscape imagery is often reminiscent of the landscapes of Thomas Cole (*In Titan's Goblet* is named for an 1833 Cole painting of the same name) and Frederic E. Church, not only in a literal sense—Hutton has filmed some of the very locations painted by Cole, Church, and the other Hudson River artists—but in his attitude toward landscape.

Hutton's approach to filmmaking seems a very long way from Hollywood moviemaking—not only in his choice of imagery and his meditative pacing, but in his consistent commitment to black and white and silence (few films feel as silent as Hutton's)—and even from much critical cinema. But Hutton *is* part of a distinguished and generally undervalued tradition of filmmakers who use the motion picture camera to record the familiar world in such a way as to reveal its sensual beauty and to appeal to the viewer's desire for visual subtlety, a tradition that in the United States includes such filmmakers as Ralph Steiner, Rudy Burckhardt, Nathaniel Dorsky, Larry Gottheim, and Andrew Noren. And his work seems to have had a positive impact on at least one commercially successful filmmaker, documentarian Ken Burns: "He [Hutton] has been a powerful influence on me and dozens of others" (Burns, letter to *The Independent* 20, no. 2 [March 1997], p. 7).

I spoke with Hutton in November 1995.

MacDonald: You've been making films since the late sixties. But for a long time, I just couldn't *see* your work. I would have a general sense of what other people saw, but I couldn't connect with it myself. And then about the time of *Landscape (for Manon)*—not so long ago—I not only could see them, but I found that when I included a film of yours in a program dealing with landscape or sense of place, your film would be the one people would rave about afterward. All of a sudden, there's an enthusiastic audience for your films, and not just an experimental film audience, but a much broader audience. Have you been having this experience?

Hutton: I think it depends to a large extent on how the films are contextualized. The kinds of issues I'm interested in—issues of landscape, urbanscape—are about a moment of seeing, a very removed, private glimpse of things that we're all totally familiar with. And because of that familiarity, a lot of people were dismissive of my work for a while, but over time I think some people have developed an appreciation for a film experience that is completely outside any other cinematic reference that they know, whether it's documentary, narrative, TV commercials, MTV, whatever. So many of the images of beauty that we've become familiar with in cinema are contextualized within certain ideas, certain kinds of polemic. I think some appreciate that my work is not encumbered by ideas. So much of cinema has a hidden, or maybe not-so-hidden, agenda. If there's one thing I can say about my work, it's that there is no purpose to it other than just allowing someone into my visual sensibility. I've never had any overwhelming response to my films, and I don't really expect that, because my work is relatively private and personal.

You could say, "Well, Peter's got his own agenda: he's creating these personal records of how *he* sees the world, a romanticized, overly aestheticized vision of the world that overwhelms the work." That's a current critique. But I also think many people are liberated by my work because of its lack of an overriding intent other than my reminding them of a certain kind of repose. In our manipulative, kinetic, time-is-money world, there's an appreciation for a respite from overriding intent.

MacDonald: We used to say that people went to the movies to escape their humdrum lives and have an exciting experience. But now our lives are so loaded, so layered—we all passed the "Type A" personality test ten years ago; we've become Triple-A personalities—that there's something wonderful about getting into a space where we can be *still*.

Hutton: Most people go to films to get some kind of hit, some kind of overwhelming experience, whether it's like an amusement park ride or an ideological, informational hit that gives you a critical insight into an issue or an idea. But for those few people who feel they need a reprieve occasionally, who want to cleanse the palate a bit, whether for spiritual or physiological reasons, these films seem to be somewhat effective.

I've never felt that my films are very important in terms of the History of Cinema. They offer a little detour from such grand concepts. They appeal primarily to people who enjoy *looking* at nature, or who enjoy having a moment to study something that's not fraught with information. The experience of my films is a little like daydreaming. It's about taking the time to just sit down and look at things, which I don't think is a very Western preoccupation. A lot of influences on me when I was younger were more Eastern. They suggested a contemplative way of looking—whether at painting, sculpture, architecture, or just a landscape—where the more time you spend actually looking at things, the more they reveal themselves in ways that you don't expect.

For the most part, people don't allow themselves the time or the circumstances to get into a relationship with the world that provides freedom to actually look at things. There's always an overriding design or mission behind their negotiation with life. I think when you have the occasion to step away from agendas—whether it's through circumstance or out of some kind of emotional necessity—then you're often struck by the incredible epiphanies of nature. These are often very subtle things, right at the edge of most people's sensibilities. My films try to record and to offer some of these experiences.

To go back to your original question, these days I do often get a good response from general audiences, people who don't really have much cinematic referencing but who are just struck by the beauty of images rendered in certain way.

There's also a fairly obvious quality to black and white, in terms of film history; it tends to take us back in time rather than project us forward. That also can be a bit of a reprieve for an audience, like being taken out of time and suspended in a space where there is no overt reference to daily experience. To me one of the most attractive things about cinema is the fact that you can evoke a sense of mystery, of wonder or curiosity in an environment, a landscape, a room, anyplace, by suspending time. So much of the information that we perceive in film is explained or presented to us in such a way that we can't help but rationalize it. Once someone leaves us to our own interpretive devices, we can feel a great reprieve and the opportunity to actually give something to the work. It's like sitting and looking at a painting; at first it might not grab you, but the longer you look at it, the more things reveal themselves. It might just be a formal composition that takes a while to develop, but as soon as you engage with it, you feel much more satisfied because you're actually interacting with the work. So much contemporary art is shouting at us. It doesn't allow us a sense of interaction because there's no mystery, no psychological space to really engage, no implicit invitation to enter the work and probe what is *not* said, or engage with the idea that is *not* explained. I often respond to art that speaks to me overtly, whether it's video, film, painting, installation, whatever. But my work is the opposite.

MacDonald: So far as I know, you've pretty much always worked in the way you work now. There are differences among your films, of course, but even the earliest films are presented one image at a time. You've been reasonably productive, though compared to Brakhage, who seems to explode films out of himself all the time, your production seems quite minimal—a few images a year. You talk about the viewer's experience in looking at your work as a kind of meditative reprieve in the midst of the hysteria of contemporary life. Is your *making* films an analogous experience for you?

Hutton: Oh yes, very much so. I often tell people my passion in film is just collecting images, looking through the lens and seeing things that I really respond to, and recording them. After that, I'm often in a quandary as to what to do with the images. I'm much less involved in the idea of structuring films, packaging images.

MacDonald: How much of what you collect ends up in the films that we see?

Hutton: Roughly 10 percent. There's no formula. My motto is, "Seek and you will find"; so as long as I go out with some regularity, I'm bound to come back with information. I've never gone out and brought back nothing. Some-

New York City skyscape, in Peter Hutton's *New York Portrait, Part I* (1977).

times it might be just an initial inquiry into a particular landscape or something else that looks potentially interesting, light and shadow in relationship to an architectural detail, whatever. Sometimes I quickly find something I can use. But usually it requires further investigation. I go back over and over, until I finally get it right.

When I was living in New York City, I would see potentially interesting things, but they wouldn't quite congeal cinematically so I would shoot them repeatedly. There's a shot in *New York Portrait, Part I* of these pigeons flying over SoHo. I was living in Little Italy and had observed this neighbor who would go up on his roof every day and ritually let these pigeons out of the cage. They would engage in these wonderful flying patterns. I began to see that there was a lead pigeon that would take the others on this little pattern through the sky. When I filmed these movements my imagery wouldn't look visually as significant as what I was seeing with my eyes, so I would shoot it repeatedly— until finally one day the movement of an airplane and a beautiful cloud provided the perfect backdrop for the pattern of the birds flying.

What often strikes people about my New York portraits is the fact that the moments revealed in those films are experiences that most people just don't have the time to stop and behold, because they're always moving from point A to point B. When you step away from the kinetic opera of city life and go out on an early Sunday morning, it's such a reprieve. This applies in any environment. Having the luxury to behold the simplest things can often be a revelation in itself, and it can be metaphorically transformed into meaning as well.

On the other hand, part of the pleasure of obsessively collecting imagery is that spontaneously you get fantastic stuff you've not even contemplated. For me, it's important to get out with a camera and interact with the world. Sometimes it works; sometimes it doesn't. But the act of collecting is for me the most satisfying part of filmmaking.

MacDonald: So how do the films get their final shape?

Hutton: The structuring happens over a period of time. I just digest the images, and almost subliminally the films realize a structure. Of course, I edit and project repeatedly, and often obsessively. But in terms of actually figuring out how to put one image next to the other, there's no plan. It just happens. Designing a structure that becomes a significant part of the film is the antithesis of what I do. My structures are a result of what the images tell me. It's less an intellectual than an intuitive process.

MacDonald: Sometimes there is a relatively clear structure, though. In *Landscape (for Manon)* you separate each image from the next with a moment of darkness (with one exception early in the film, and one later on, where you cut from one image to another). The moments of darkness "cleanse the palate." The film begins with relatively brief shots in which there's obvious movement. Then, in the middle of the film, the shots are longer—thirty or forty seconds—and quieter: sometimes it takes us twenty seconds of the shot to realize that there is actually movement within the image. Then right near the end the pace speeds up a bit again. *Landscape (for Manon)* is implicitly an anti-montage film: it's not a "structural" film, because the overall shape of the structure is not central in our awareness, but it certainly offers a critique of conventional editing.

Hutton: I've always tried to fight the tendency to create additive meaning, if only because it *is* such a convention. But I acquiesce to it at times, too. One part of my sensibility says, "Always defy the convention because you want to keep people guessing about where you're going." On the other hand, every now and then you acquiesce to the convention just to provide yourself with a strategy from which to then depart. You might set up a montage and then pull the rug out. I play games that way; I think all filmmakers do.

You know, there's a very simple idea behind what I do, which is to try to take people back in time, rather than forward into the future. I reference a time when there hadn't been a sophisticated history of cinema. The Lumière films are a revelation when you see them in this day and age, because there's a certain kind of innocence to how they were structured. They weren't designed either to be narrative or documentary. The Lumières were not intent on providing you with a bigger idea that results from the accumulation of images. Rather, they explored places without a lot of baggage; they responded to things as they came. That's precious to me.

Our culture is so overly sophisticated in terms of cinema: it's the most common creative language we all share. It's fun to take away those conventional gestures as a preliminary criterion for looking at a film.

MacDonald: The obvious reference of your work is to the Lumières, to the one-shot-equals-one-film approach. But in their historical context, the Lumières were probably trying to be as exciting as they could be, to sell the cinématographe. In a way, your films are the Lumières the way we wished they were, or "the Lumières do Zen."

The Lumière brothers are the film-historical background for what you do, but there is also an earlier connection, between your films and painting. Part of the reason I got into your recent landscape films is my interest in Hudson River painting, and in particular, Thomas Cole. There are moments in *Landscape (for Manon)* that are right out of Cole, not only in the sense that you're filming literally the same spaces, the same mountains that he painted (he lived in Catskill, which is only a few miles from here), but in the sense that your desire to go backwards instead of forwards in your film practice is similar to his desire to go backwards instead of forwards in his painting. Cole was painting the way things had been, as a polemic against what he saw as the overdevelopment of the American landscape.

There are also photographic analogies to your work. In *In Titan's Goblet*, it's as if you're *doing* Alfred Stieglitz. Or if I look at the New York portraits, it's as if you're *doing* Charles Sheeler photographs (and paintings). I'm assuming that when you're making imagery, you have a kind of double consciousness: you're looking at the image as part of your filmmaking; but, being aware of the history of representing cityscape and landscape, you're also providing a set of references that feeds whoever knows that tradition.

Hutton: I think that's totally accurate. I've had a lot people come up and say my films are like an art history class. I was first a sculptor and then a painter and finally a filmmaker. I bring with me what I responded to as a student and as a developing artist. When I first saw Ansel Adams's photographs, I thought how incredibly potent and poignant these frozen moments in time were. And I could say the same thing about Henri Cartier-Bresson, and a lot of photographers.

But it's the idea of bringing a sense of time into these renditions of nature that excites me about cinema. My films are a way of subtly tweaking that formal approach to beauty by allowing another language to come in: movement and transformation. On the other hand, there's often an attempt to "stop time" in my films, letting time be an overriding element that provides some small revelation about the image. Mine is an extremely reductive strategy.

MacDonald: You also reference particular transitional moments of the past. We were talking earlier about how we're all trying to play catch-up now with video art and with digital technology. We're clearly moving into a new world in which cinema is the creaky old mechanical medium. What your films do is take us back to that moment when the earliest film audiences were enthralled by

Storm in the Catskills, in Peter Hutton's *Landscape (for Manon)* (1987).

seeing photographs in motion. You're working with *that* transition at the very moment when we're all transitioning into this new space.

Hutton: If you can actually hold people captive, away from conventional manipulation, long enough to reveal that other, earlier phenomenological aspect to visual projection, *that* can be a valid revelation, too. There *is* this other kind of language in cinema that is purely phenomenological: the recorded, moving image. In our contemporary, media-influenced world, we're all struggling to interpret and negotiate the overriding cultural influence of all these new systems. As a filmmaker, if you can step out of that and appreciate the simple almost scientific implications of what this crude mechanical invention of cinema actually does, it can be a great discovery. We're always trying to rediscover things at the same time as we're discovering new ones.

My films can have an attraction because, during a proliferation of computer-generated and video-generated electronic pixel phenomena, there is a great nostalgia for the cinematic image itself, projected on a glass bead screen, and that moment when you go, "Oh, shit, this is really exquisite; I'd forgotten about this!" How beautiful that experience is! And how utterly profound it is. But how lost that reference has become in contemporary media culture.

MacDonald: Your films offer a kind of visual training. Claude Lorrain and others taught Europeans that looking at landscape was worth doing, that you could perceive landscape as a form of composition. On my drive this morning [from Utica, New York, to Annandale-on-Hudson] I was coming down into the

Hudson Valley near Albany and there was a cloud in the sky that I saw as a "Peter Hutton cloud." It was an image I would not have recognized as something to look at and be pleasured by had your films not given me that visual training.

I've been thinking recently that if it's true that we are part body and part spirit—and I believe it *is* true—and if it's also true that the spirit is eternal and the body is not, *that* must mean that the particular body we find ourselves in at this moment is the most rare and precious thing in the universe, because it will never happen again. If the soul persists, but the body does not, that makes the body much more fragile and much more special. For me, your films provide metaphors for recognizing the Now-ness of a particular body, of particular physical phenomena that will never happen again in precisely the same way. They do honor to the particular moment that we're in, as opposed to the larger theoretical, social, and psychological structures within which everything functions.

Hutton: I often think this value of my work is not really apparent until a lot of time has passed. When I made *Lodz Symphony*, I said to my Polish friends, "You know, this film is not going to make any sense to you now, but in ten or fifteen years you may well appreciate that someone actually recorded the atmosphere of this city at this particular time." Eugène Atget recorded the details of the architecture, the atmosphere, the ambiance of the streets of Paris in his time with loving care. At first, those images didn't seem to have any great value—they were too familiar—but, as time has gone on, they've increased in value. They've become miniature museums.

One other aspect of my films that is interesting to me is the influence of sculpture. I spent many years studying sculpture and making sculpture, always overtly contemplating space in a three-dimensional way. When I got into film, I very much envisioned these flat, two-dimensional projections as three-dimensional sculptures. I made an attempt at referencing space in a way that spoke of what I had learned through making sculpture. Sometimes the structures of my films are based purely on three-dimensional illusion: there will be tremendous depth, then shallow depth, then greater depth. This gives the eye something to engage with, more surface and space to wander through. I think if an image is engaging, it provides the eye with an interesting spatial map to follow.

Television has contributed to a flattening of the pictorial image, a kind of deadening of the image. I think people tend to take images much more for granted now because they're not challenged to visually engage with them. I'm interested in reminding people of the visual potential of engaging with an image, of going on a little journey within the image. Each shot becomes a film in itself, if it's choreographed in an interesting way, where you see the development of a movement and often a transformation and then the conclusion. But I realize that very few people look at film in this way. They want to be fed information, but generally they're being fed something that isn't very substantial.

MacDonald: Depth of field is certainly central in *Study of a River*. The images filmed from the ice-breaker on the river are very three-dimensional.

Hutton: What was exciting about getting back on the water was this whole dimension of movement: moving through time and space on the ships and then watching ships go through the frame itself. The river film is opening up a lot of possibilities in that regard, just because the river is constantly moving. I spent so much time doing architectural studies of cities—often very little happened other than a pigeon flying through the frame, or light or a distant figure moving—but the river is infinite. It's nice to attach yourself to something so utterly transformational. Every time I take my camera out to the river, it reveals itself in a different way, there is something I haven't noticed before: a different sense of the space, a different texture to the water, a different velocity to the wind.

MacDonald: You studied at the San Francisco Art Institute. Were particular people there formative for you?

Hutton: There were a lot of phenomenally interesting people there at the time: painters, sculptors, filmmakers. Robert Nelson, who was one of my first film teachers, I always admired very much. I never really studied with Bruce Conner, but he was around and I was certainly aware of his films: *A Movie* [1958] was a big influence on me. And we had William T. Wiley, the painter, and Bruce Nauman, the sculptor, whom I studied with briefly. Bruce Baillie fits in there at some point, even though he wasn't a teacher. His amazingly poetic rendering of image and sound was very much in evidence.

Before I went to San Francisco, I lived in Hawaii for several years. That was where I first began shipping out as a merchant seaman. A lot of my teachers were Chinese or Japanese and I got engaged in an Eastern sensibility about art, about nature, which really slowed me down a lot. It was much less about active participation than about standing back and looking. It helped me to establish a formal relationship to what I was doing, less kinetic and much more introspective.

When I came to the Art Institute, I *was* amazed by the proliferation of sixties work, from street theater to experimental film to light shows to the music, but I didn't establish a participatory relationship with it, even though at that time I did make a transition from sculpture into performance work. For a while I felt very excited about the idea of taking art out of the studio and actually participating in the culture. I'd organize fifty people, dress them up in plastic garbage bags, give them all whistles, and we'd walk through the streets to a big park where we'd create a moving figure-eight configuration—a wacky celebration of an earthquake or something. Then, someone gave me a movie camera and said, "Why don't you record one of these performances so you have a record of it." I went up on the roof of the school and filmed an event I had choreographed. When I got the film back, I was struck by how beautiful the film record of the event was, in terms of its graphic quality. And I thought, "Maybe I can just film things and not worry about creating events." From that moment, I started making films.

MacDonald: You've been a teacher as well as a filmmaker for most of your filmmaking life. You've also worked as a cinematographer on other people's films. You've worked a number of times for Ken Burns. In fact, when I found out that you knew Burns at Hampshire College, it occurred to me that one of the dimensions that gives his best work its power, is its slow pacing and his use of images of nature that run on screen longer than most documentarians would feel comfortable letting them run. It's facile to attribute this to one person, but it strikes me as something a student of your films might have responded to in your work.

Hutton: Ken was my student, but I never felt I had an overt influence on him. Jerry Leibling was probably the seminal influence on all these young kids who came out of Hampshire at the time. He was a wonderful photographer and a very compassionate humanist. When I was teaching at Hampshire, I had finished a long film about living in California: *July '71 in San Francisco, Living at Beach Street, Working at Canyon Cinema, Swimming in the Valley of the Moon* [1971]. It was a diary of my life as a student and it had a particular photographic quality, which according to Elaine Mayes who had shown the film, the Hampshire kids were knocked out by. Ken always cites this film as an early influence. He was surprised that someone could make images of familiar, everyday events in such a way that you actually developed an appreciation in looking, especially at the development in the image itself. There was a strong photographic formalism in that film and in my other films that he got off on.

MacDonald: I know you've shot films and parts of films for others. You worked on Red Grooms's *Hippodrome Hardware* [1973] and *Ruckus Manhattan* [1976], on *Born in Flames* [1983, directed by Lizzie Borden], and on several Ken Burns films. Which Burns films have you worked on?

Hutton: *The Statue of Liberty* [1985], *Baseball* [1995], and the Thomas Jefferson film [*Thomas Jefferson*, 1997], which is in progress.

MacDonald: Not *The Civil War* [1990]?

Hutton: He wanted me to do something for that, but I couldn't. He wanted to strap me into a Steadicam! Ken's a sweet kid and very generous: he always asks me if I want to do something on his films. I think he's just being nostalgic. I suspect Ken sees me as this old relic. Until I saw *The Civil War* I wasn't that interested in what he was doing, though I am impressed by the success of his work. Ken's cameraperson, Buddy Squires (who was briefly my teaching assistant at Hampshire), has an excellent eye, so it's not necessary for Ken to borrow *my* eye for his films.

Of course, the shocking thing is that often when you do work with other people, you get caught up in what you're doing and think it's really beautiful and important. Then you see the final film and they've used twenty seconds of what you shot. When other people ask you to participate in a project, you're flattered, but when you analyze their final product, you realize your contribution didn't amount to much. It's different when I work on a feature, of course. Then I'm able to have a significant influence on the look of a picture.

I just shot a feature on the Erie Canal for Phil Hartman [Hutton was director of cinematography for *Eerie* (1996)]. I was director of photography for his *No Picnic* [1986], which received the best cinematography award at Sundance. I think he decided to use me because of my being interested in recording journeys, which is something that developed out of my working on ships as a merchant seaman. That's another wonderful, romantic tradition that's gotten away from us: the travelogue. I was nurtured on the tradition of the free spirit wandering around the world, recording impressions. The experience of working on ships is something that has evaporated from the social fabric of our culture. When I was young, it was a great ticket to adventure, as well as an educational opportunity. It's so problematic now to travel in the world, for political and financial reasons.

MacDonald: It's almost a cliché to see the technological/historical connection between filmmaking and train travel. The visual sensibility I get from your films seems closer to travel by boat, where you spend long periods of time looking at a relatively unchanging but always subtly different scene.

Hutton: One of the great revelations of traveling by sea is how slow it is compared to airplane or even train travel. You can actually go backwards in time on a ship, you can sail into a storm and make no headway, no geographic progress. You are actually going backwards as you go forward. One of the exhilarating and terrifying aspects of traveling by sea is the vulnerability you feel and the fact that you're not isolated from nature, but are rather in the heart of nature itself. Sea travel can be very dangerous at times, and you confront that danger. Experientially, it can be overwhelming. And visually it is incredibly rich.

One of my great moments in traveling by sea happened one night going across the Indian Ocean en route to the Persian Gulf and encountering a storm I did not anticipate. I was up on the bow of the ship late at night, probably about three in the morning. It was completely dark: the sky was clouded up so there were no stars or moon to illuminate anything. All of a sudden I felt the temperature change. I was getting colder and colder, and then I realized it was getting even darker. It was like going into an inkwell, and I had this revelation that there were all these declensions of darkness that I hadn't been aware of. Pretty soon it started to rain and the seas kicked up rather dramatically and the mate on the bridge shined a light down and told me to come up. As I was turning around, a big wave dipped over the bow. It could have washed me over. I scurried up to the bridge and continued to observe the storm from up there. We punched through the storm and it started getting warmer, and the rain stopped, and it got lighter and lighter. It was an extraordinary experience, and so visually interesting—but too subtle to record with a movie camera. Being on the ship forced me to slow down, and allowed me to take time to look.

Valie Export

(on *Invisible Adversaries*)

Perhaps the most significant film-critical development of the 1970s and early 1980s was a function of the developing feminist awareness of the explicit and implicit sexism of mainstream cinema. This awareness led a number of women who had been identified primarily with avant-garde art not only into film production but into making feature-length melodramas that were conceived as potential alternatives to the commercial cinema's ways of telling stories about women and men. Particularly noteworthy in this development were Yvonne Rainer (*Lives of Performers*, 1972; *Film About a Woman Who . . .*, 1974; *Kristina Talking Pictures*, 1976; *Journeys from Berlin/1971*, 1980; *The Man Who Envied Women*, 1985); Laura Mulvey, in collaboration with Peter Wollen (*Penthesilea*, 1974; *Riddles of the Sphinx*, 1977; *Amy!* 1979); Sally Potter (*Thriller*, 1979; *The Gold Diggers*, 1983); and the Austrian Valie Export, whose early features—*Unsichtbare Gegner* ("Invisible Adversaries," 1976), *Menschenfrauen* (a rough translation would be "Human Women," 1979), and *Die Praxis der Liebe* ("The Practice of Love," 1984)—seemed worlds away from the films of Peter Kubelka, Kurt Kren, and Otto Mühl, which, at least in the United States, had come to represent Austrian independent film.

By the time she made *Invisible Adversaries*, Export had become a widely known avant-garde artist working in performance, multimedia, photography, and film (the best source of information on Export's career is Roswitha Mueller's copiously illustrated *Valie Export: Fragments of the Imagination* [Bloomington/Indianapolis: Indiana University Press, 1994]). Export's early films, many of them made as collaborations with Peter Weibel, were often defiantly confrontational. In *Remote . . . Remote . . .* (1973), for example, Export sits in front of a photograph of two children, removed from their parents because of abuse, and with an Exacto knife cuts into her cuticles until they bleed, periodically washing the blood off in a bowl of milk she holds between her knees. In *Mann & Frau & Animal* ("Man & Woman & Animal," 1973) Export reveals her genitals as she masturbates and orgasms using a jet of water, and as she is menstruating. And for the earlier *Tapp und Tast Kino* ("Touch Cinema," 1968) Export built a mini movie theater, which she wore over her bare chest. Accompanied by Weibel, she would venture onto crowded city streets, where passers-by would be invited to reach through the doors into the mini theater and feel her breasts. For Export, women's liberation was inconceivable without a freeing of the female body from the hypocritical social and artistic constrictions of its conventional representation.

While *Invisible Adversaries* maintains the spirit of defiance and self-exposure of the earlier films, it focuses more directly on relationships. Anna (Susanne Widl), who makes a living as a photographer, has grown alienated from the emotional/spiritual emptiness of the society around her and from the cynicism and sexism of her partner Peter (Peter Weibel), and is working to find a new psychically healthy space. Structurally, Export's first feature lies somewhere between a history of her experiments in various art forms, including a variety of new experiments performed specifically for the film; and a feature melodrama with a plot focused on the disintegrating relationship of the two lovers, a bit reminiscent of Frank Perry's *Diary of a Mad Housewife* (1970). While *Invisible Adversaries* (the title refers to Anna's fear that alien beings, "Hyksos," have been taking over the psyches of the people around her) provides no clear, positive resolution, by the conclusion of the film, it is apparent that Anna's struggle is part of a larger social movement in which many women, including other filmmakers (Helke Sander is interviewed by Anna during the film), are struggling toward more liberating, fulfilling lives. This struggle continues in Export's second feature, *Menschenfrauen*, where Anna (again played by Widl) continues to explore new possibilities, including a lesbian relationship.

In August 1995, I sent Export a series of questions about *Invisible Adversaries*. These questions were translated into German by Hermann J. Hendrich, who was also kind enough to translate Export's responses into English. I constructed a conversation from the questions and responses.

MacDonald: Before making *Invisible Adversaries*, you had made several films and you'd worked in a variety of forms of "expanded cinema," as well as in other media. What led to the decision to make a feature film, which is always a considerable undertaking?

Export: For a number of years before I made *Invisible Adversaries* I had done body performances, or body-material interactions, that analyzed the position of women in our society. In these performances and in my photo work of the sixties and seventies, I used a female body, generally my own, as a bearer of signs and symbols—individual, sexual, cultural—that could function within an artistic environment.

I was also developing my media work—video, video installation, photography, film (including several 16mm films that were expressions of inner psychic situations), and various forms of "expanded cinema," questioning the idea of media reality; and I had already begun my "discussion" with the commercial cinema, through explorations of cinematic materials and especially of the antagonistic terms: illusion/reality, image/object, recording/manipulating.

I wanted to unite my various explorations in a "larger," longer message—and in a form that could go out without me. A feature film seemed the answer.

MacDonald: How did you find funding for such an unusual project?

Export: Invisible Adversaries was one of the first projects to be funded by the Ministry for Education, Arts, and Sports. The original funding was 600,000 Austrian shillings [at the time, about $35,000], followed by another 150,000 shillings, and supplemented by 120,000 shillings that I borrowed on credit. It took me a long time to pay the loan back.

MacDonald: I want to situate *Invisible Adversaries* with regard to several film histories. First, during *Invisible Adversaries*, the narrator says (I'm using the subtitle translation), "From 1939 to 1945 Austria produced revoltingly sickly, dishonest films, known typically as 'Viennese film,' and the elite of the Berg Theater acted in them. The same crew produced after the war the popular country and folklore films. The smooth transition from Nazi Austria to the Second Republic is typical of the hypocritical mentality of the country." Did you see yourself attempting to defy and critique this "revolting" history by reinventing Austrian commercial cinema?

Export: All the critical texts spoken in *Invisible Adversaries* should be recognized as part of a long history of intellectual criticism of the cultural and political development in Austria after the Second World War. I was not ambitious at all to start a new era of Austrian commercial film, but *Invisible Adversaries* did become the first Austrian avant-garde feature film to find its way into cinemas and to get international appreciation for its cinematic and aesthetic values. Looking back now, it can be said that the film was a milestone in Austrian film history.

MacDonald: In the United States, Austrian avant-garde filmmaking tends to mean two things: first, the formal experiments of Peter Kubelka and Kurt Kren and others; and second (and to a lesser degree), the "materialactionfilms" of Mühl/Kren and the Actionist group [in the "materialactions," artists released theoretically debilitating inhibitions through often-extravagant immersions in such materials as paint, mud, feathers, blood, shit, piss; the "materialactionfilms," which document some of these performances, remain among the most shocking films in distribution (in the US through Film-makers' Cooperative in

New York City)].What connection did you have with the formalism of Kubelka, Kren, Marc Adrian, and with the materialactions?

Export: I believe that my films are different from all those you mention. I never engaged in purely formal examinations of the film material, but always considered the content of the image, which is very important for me. To some extent the films of Kubelka showed some leaning toward the tradition of the New American Cinema, whereas Marc Adrian and Kurt Kren were influenced by earlier developments in Austria in music and poetry, the Wiener Dichtergruppe, for example. The methodical inventionism of Gerhard Rühm also became a source for their cinematic approaches. When I started to make films, all this was already history.

MacDonald: In her book, Roswitha Mueller indicates that you were reacting, in part, against the sexism of the materialactions and the materialactionfilms, which tended to present the women as passive and men as active. But in the materialactionfilms in distribution in the United States, both women and men seem reasonably active in the assault on convention and taboo. So I'm a bit confused. Early in *Invisible Adversaries*, there's a brief, startling shot of a close-up of Anna's hair being pissed on, followed immediately by a shot of the faucet running water on her head. When I first saw *Invisible Adversaries*, I took that as a reference to the materialactions. Is it such a reference? To what extent *was* your body work, and *Invisible Adversaries* in particular, a gender critique of the materialactions?

Export: I criticized the women's roles in the materialactions, which had been dictated by a male artist. (Being a feminist, I did not care about the male roles.) In *my* body performances, body-material interactions, I felt much closer to the body performance scene as represented by Chris Burden or Vito Acconci.

The "pissed on" scene visualizes and expands a quotation by Claude Lévi-Strauss about certain native societies where urine is used to wash someone's hair or in ritual cleaning of the body, to demonstrate friendly relations. In *Invisible Adversaries* a number of other "quotations" have been included, from Klara Zetkin, Friedrich Hölderlin, Franz Blei, et cetera.

My work should not be understood as a critique of the materialactions, but as another artistic answer to the concept of "material action." The atmosphere of the sixties in Vienna was a progressive one, started and led by the members of the Wiener Dichtergruppe (Friedrich Achleitner, H. C. Artmann, Konrad Bayer, Rühm, Oswald Wiener). The Viennese Actionists, the media artists, some painters, and I—we were all part of this atmosphere. Naturally, I was influenced by many things happening then.

MacDonald: Is it true that you hadn't seen Don Siegel's *Invasion of the Body Snatchers* [1956] when you made *Invisible Adversaries?* What *is* the background of the Hyksos?

Export: I had not seen *Invasion of the Body Snatchers*, and had not heard about it. I learned about the Hyksos in my History of Art class in the early sixties. The Hyksos were an Asiatic tribe that moved into the Egyptian empire and usurped the southern part of Egypt. After some time they moved away—without a trace. This unexpected and massive overpowering without a longer historical consequence fascinated me. Where did they go? The only thing lasting about their presence was the "petrified" memory. So the basic idea in *Invisible Adversaries* was, "Are the Hyksos still here? Are they perhaps inside us? Did they invade *us* in order to create a degraded human being?"

MacDonald: As I remember, during the question and answer session at MoMA [in June 1995, Export presented several films as part of a retrospective of Austrian avant-garde cinema, curated by Steve Anker, and accompanied by the catalogue *Austrian Avant-Garde Cinema 1955–1993* (San Francisco, Vienna: San Francisco Cinematheque/SIXPACK, 1994)] you mentioned Michael Snow as an artist who was important to you. You and he were certainly on the same wavelength (no pun intended) in the early seventies, especially in your photographic work—the parallels are evident in his *Of a Ladder* [1971] and *Glares* [1973] and your *Ladder* [1972]. In what ways were Snow's photographs, installations, and films important to you?

Export: I learned about Michael Snow's *Of a Ladder* the same year I photographed my *Ladder*. Snow's work became very important to me because I had the feeling I had found in it my own photographic and cinematic attitudes about space and time. I would compare Snow's *La Région Centrale* with my three-projector film *Adjungierte Dislokationen* ["Adjoined Dislocations," 1973] where my body carried the documenting apparatus—two Super-8 cameras mounted so that one points in front of me and the other, to the rear—to show the movements of my body and the changes in the surrounding area, simultaneously.

One Snow work I admire very much is his book *Cover to Cover* [New York/Halifax: NYU Press/Press of the Nova Scotia College of Art and Design, 1975].

I got to know a lot of North American avant-garde films and also had information about the Happening and Performance Art scene. I saw many films when I was invited to the Underground Film Festival in London in 1970. Before that, Karl-Heinz Hein had organized a meeting of independent filmmakers in Munich, where I demonstrated my *Touch Cinema* for the second time, and showed some other films. In 1973, I was invited to the Festival of Independent Avant-Garde Film in London, where many American avant-garde films were shown.

MacDonald: Helke Sander appears in *Invisible Adversaries*. Why did you choose her in particular from among European filmmakers?

Export: I interviewed Helke Sander for my video *Wann Ist der Mensch eine Frau?* ["When Is a Human Being a Woman?" 1976], in which a number of other people appear. I took her interview into *Invisible Adversaries*, since I appreciated Helke Sander's political work very much, and I did see *Invisible Adversaries* as a political film.

MacDonald: As a woman entering the "institution" of feature filmmaking, you needed to find your way; and you reflect this in your editing experiments, which declare themselves *as* experiments, and at other moments as well. For example, the first shot of Anna and her double (her Hyksos) in the mirror has a complex impact. We can see that you're "trying" for a certain kind of mirror effect familiar from commercial movies, but we can also see that you know the shot does not work as an illusion, but more as a reference to an illusion you choose not to create.

Export: My intention in making *Invisible Adversaries*, as well as in my later filmmaking, especially *The Practice of Love* was to change perceptual structures, to put an experimental avant-garde sense of content and form into a feature film, and to find a new, innovative film "language" for myself, as well as for the recipient. I was trying to put alternative, artistic media into a discourse with conventional film.

Another intention was to find sophisticated, polyphonic, visual metaphors for various personal and psychic processes, since we are not able to reduce the multi- and polyphonic emotions created by reality, as we experience it, into single units. My inner visual representations change constantly; and the same visual contents continually receive new meanings. I have no singular identity. There is also no single, clear feminist expression.

MacDonald: At times *Invisible Adversaries* seems like a review of your previous career. There are allusions to and/or new versions of a good many performance and photographic works from the sixties and seventies [including *Körperkonifigurationen in der Architektur* ("Body Configurations in Architecture"), *Zeitgedicht* ("*Time Poem*"), *Raumsprung* ("Leap of Space"), *Ontologischer Sprung* ("*Ontological Leap*")]. There are also a number of what, so far as I'm aware, are new pieces made possible by the particular technology of cinema. I'm thinking of the "Preparation for Consumption" sequence, and the montage where Anna uses a knife to cut the fish/turtle/bread/rat/apple/bird/beetle/cake; the conversation Peter and Anna have at the coffeehouse in the park (where your repetitive, halting filmmaking expresses the state of their relationship); and the argument they have in the studio where they are accompanied by video versions of themselves.

Export: In general I was working for an audience interested in aesthetic issues, an audience that would accept an aesthetic of the avant-garde. Mainly I used new pieces, but also expanded forms of earlier work. Doesn't an artist always work on the same "vision"?—but in new forms, with other materials, using different probes, discussions, or subjects in order to search into the vision's inner core, and bring the vision into different contexts. Some of the pieces in the film developed from performances that were done explicitly for it. An example is the scene where Anna cuts some of her pubic hair in order to make a moustache.

MacDonald: In general, to what degree was directing for a feature film new for you? The acting seems reasonably effective. Had you had experience directing actors?

Export: I had had no experience whatsoever with directing.

MacDonald: A technical question: the shot that moves out from the window of Anna's apartment and pans across Vienna, with which the film begins and ends, is mysterious (and may imply the mysterious movement of the Hyksos). It seems too slow to have been made from a helicopter; how was it shot?

Export: Those shots were taken from a mobile crane. Camera, cameraman, and myself just fit into a small gondola swaying in the light wind. The crane had to be stationed on a small street in the inner city of Vienna, directly in front of the apartment building where my apartment was. The shot into my room with Anna on my bed was into my living room. Since the crane blocked car traffic, it was only allowed there from one late afternoon to the early morning of the next day, so each of the two pans could be filmed only once.

MacDonald: Peter Weibel wrote the screenplay with your assistance. To what degree are the conversations and incidents in *Invisible Adversaries* based on his and your personal experiences? Is the film personal enough to be thought of as a "new version" of *Touch Cinema*—a new, public openness not only about the body but about personal relationships?

Export: Peter Weibel wrote the script based on my concept and with me as co-writer. My ideas for this film were already established in 1972, but financing was not available until 1975. Some situations from the time he and I lived together were used in the film. In the dialogue you will sometimes find his view of things that happened between us, and sometimes mine. But I would say that such dialogue can be found in common, everyday practice. There's nothing special about our version of it.

Invisible Adversaries has become a very personal film for me, since many of my own emotions, my psychic situations, went into the film; but it is not a film about my personal relationship with Peter, since we had been separated as lovers for years.

MacDonald: Anna seems engaged in at least three levels of rebellion. First, she's rebelling against the rigidity and conformity of conventional Viennese society. Second, she's rebelling against the intellectual cynicism and lack of romance represented by Peter (she's rebelling against *his* form of rebellion). And third, she's rebelling against his sexism. At the same time, however, Anna is also optimistic: she is finding other women who share her desire to make a creative space for herself (and in some instances have been successful), and she looks forward, at least at times, to a full life. She doesn't find it during *Invisible Adversaries*, but by the time of *Menschenfrauen* the option of a lesbian relationship seems to offer one potential avenue toward fulfillment.

Export: Anna is not only reflecting the rigidity of bourgeois mentality, she confronts it in her behavior. I used Anna in order to present my critique of Viennese, or Austrian, society—especially its cultural politics.

In *Menschenfrauen* diverse models of personal relations are sketched, one of which could be a lesbian relationship. I do not see it as a fulfillment, but as a possibility of a way of life.

Valie Export on the street, presenting *Tapp und Tast Kino* ("Touch Cinema," 1968).

MacDonald: When I first saw *Invisible Adversaries*, I was fascinated and confused—confused because I couldn't separate what was *radical* from what was *Austrian*. The seemingly nonchalant, unromantic openness about the body seemed pretty shocking to me and a confrontation of the traditional romanticizing of the female body in American (and French, and Swedish . . .) commercial films. But I wasn't sure how radical this aspect of the film seemed in Austria. We Americans often hear about "sophisticated European attitudes" about the body and sexuality—and at the time of *Invisible Adversaries*, I thought that perhaps you were simply reflecting standard Austrian mores about the body. How radical did the depiction of the body in *Invisible Adversaries* seem in *Austria*?

Export: The openness about the body did not shock the audience very much, but the social and cultural statements in my film provoked considerable aggression. I was pursued by the mass media, by the Austrian courts; and to some extent I was outlawed.

MacDonald: The shots of the men flashing and masturbating (with generally limp penises!) must have seemed outrageous, especially since each of the masturbators is connected with a major institution (and, of course, a male institution): the Church, the Police . . .

Export: Those scenes were designed to provoke the institutions of the State and the Church. I had some fun directing these expressions, but there was hardly any notice in the press about them, though German television (ZDF) asked me to cut out the scene with the masturbating priest.

MacDonald: How popular was *Invisible Adversaries* in Austria and elsewhere? Was it a successful film from your point of view?

Export: *Invisible Adversaries* was shown for thirteen consecutive weeks in a regular Viennese cinema. It achieved some international festival prizes and has been shown in many international film festivals. It has been a successful film for me, since I was able to communicate my ideas with the audience. On the other hand, since the reactions were not always friendly, I had to live through all kinds of attacks, even death threats. I have boxes full of menacing letters and cassette tapes from that time. In parliament the opposition of that time raised questions about the government money spent on the film. The oppositional press asked for the resignation of the State Secretary for Education and Culture.

One of the really high points in the press was the naming of myself and Peter Weibel as the "Terrorist Pair." Ironically, in 1978 a very esteemed jury named me for the Austrian State Award on the basis of *Invisible Adversaries*. The State Secretary, however, did not dare to sign the paper, so I never received the award.

Patrick Bokanowski

(on *The Angel*)

The tradition of critiquing conventional cinema, at least in North America, has become virtually synonymous with the narrower, less expensive film gauges, especially 16mm, and less frequently, 8mm and Super-8. Mass market cinema has shown no interest in funding 35mm critiques of its methods and ideologies, and as a result, nearly all forms of counter-cinema have been financed on a smaller scale by personal investment or by government grants. This "class system" of film gauge has led at times to a fetishizing of smaller-gauge movie-making as intrinsically "purer," more ideologically correct than standard gauge. Indeed, those rare critical filmmakers (for example, Godfrey Reggio and Ron Fricke) who have chosen to face the difficulties and pressures of raising enough money to shoot in 35mm rather than consign their visions to the smaller audiences that are the nearly inevitable result of working in the smaller gauges, have often been viewed with suspicion and contempt by other critical filmmakers and by those who program and write about alternative cinema.

If we remember, however, that all that is required for a film to be "critical" is that it confront spectators with the necessity of reconsidering their definitions of cinema and their assumptions about how cinema can and should function in the world, it is obvious that 35mm film can be at least as thoroughly critical as films in the smaller gauges, if not more so. Most every contemporary exhibitor who specializes in 16mm and Super-8 can attest to the fact that in the United States the audience for overtly critical forms of film has been growing smaller ever since the heydays of Cinema 16 (the 1950s) and the New American Cinema (the 1960s). Whatever critiques are available in 16mm, 8mm, and Super-8 are experienced by that limited number of spectators who are already devotees. That is, for all practical purposes, these 16mm and Super-8 films are

262

only nominally "critiques": they *would* function as critiques if they were shown to audiences who could be surprised by their unconventional approaches, but since this is rarely the case, they remain at best *potentially* critical. On the other hand, those filmmakers energetic, imaginative, or lucky enough to find sufficient funding to make films with serious critical potential in 35mm have an opportunity to confront the conventional audience to a degree that most of the filmmakers interviewed in this volume can only fantasize about.

Of course, 35mm critical filmmaking has a distinguished history. The films of the European avant-garde of the 1920s (Hans Richter, Viking Eggeling, Luis Buñuel and Salvador Dali, Marcel Duchamp, Henri Chomette, Lotte Reiniger) were made in 35mm, as were the revolutionary films of the Russian montage school and the films of the first American avant-garde: Charles Sheeler and Paul Strand's *Manhatta* (1921), Ralph Steiner's *H2O* (1929), and the films of the collective Nykino (for example, *Pie in the Sky*, 1934). And even in recent years, many filmmakers have found ways of mounting thorough cine-critiques in 35mm: in the West, Jean-Luc Godard is the most obvious instance, though there are others—the Hungarian Belá Tarr, for example. Further, all officially sanctioned Soviet films, even the most challenging for audiences (by Sergei Paradjanov, Andrei Tarkovsky, Arthur Peleshian, Alexander Sokurov), were shot in 35mm. And there is also a tradition of filmmakers who work critically in or "near" animation: Jan Svankmajer, and the brothers Quay, Peter Delpeut (*Lyrical Nitrate* [1993])—and the Frenchman Patrick Bokanowski, whose *L'Ange* ("The Angel," 1982) is one of the most unusual 35mm feature films of recent decades.

During the seventy minutes of *The Angel*, viewers see a series of distinct sequences arranged upward along a staircase that seems more mythic than literal. Each of the sequences has its own mood and type of action. Early in the film, a fencer thrusts, over and over, at a doll hanging from the ceiling of a bare room. At first, he is seen in the room at the end of a narrow hallway off the staircase, and later from within the room. He fences, sits in a chair, fences—his movements filmed with a technique that lies somewhere between live action and still photographs. At times, Bokanowski's imagery is reminiscent of Etienne-Jules Marey's chronophotographs. Further up the stairs, we find ourselves in a room where a maid brings a jug of milk to a man without hands, over and over. Still later, we are in a room where there seems to be a movie projector pointing at us. Then, in a sequence reminiscent of Méliès and early Chaplin, a man frolics in a bathtub, and in a subsequent sequence gets up, dresses in reverse motion, and leaves for work. The film's most elaborate sequence takes place in a library in which nine identical librarians work busily in choreographed, slightly fast motion. When the librarians leave work, they are seen in extreme long shot, running in what appears to be a two-dimensional space, ultimately toward a naked woman trapped in a box, which they enter with a battering ram. Then, back in the room with the projector, we are presented with an artist and model in a composition that, at first, declares itself two-dimensional until the artist and model move, revealing that this "obviously" flat space is in fact three-dimensional. Finally, a visually stunning passage of projected light reflecting off a series of mirrors introduces *The Angel*'s final sequence, of beings on a huge staircase filmed from below; the beings seem to be ascending toward some higher realm. Bokanowski's consistently distinctive visuals are accompanied by a soundtrack composed by Michèle Bokanowski, Patrick Bokanowski's wife and collaborator. Like Robert Wiene's *The Cabinet of Dr. Caligari* (1919), Bokanowski's *The Angel* creates a world that is visually quite distinct from what we consider "reality," while providing a wide range of implicit references to it and to the history of representing those levels of reality that lie beneath and beyond the conventional surfaces of things.

My interview with Bokanowski was conducted entirely by letter. In July 1994, I sent him a list of questions in English, which Bokanowski answered in French. His answers were translated into English by my colleague at Utica College, Marie-Noëlle Little.

MacDonald: There is a community of French "experimental filmmakers": Rose Lowder, Yann Beauvais, Cécile Fontaine. Have you had much contact with this group? Who do you see as your closest colleagues in France and in Europe?

Bokanowski: Yes, yes, I have been in contact with them for about ten years now. In the beginning, when I made *La Femme Qui Se Poudre* ["A Woman Powders Herself," 1972], I did not know anything about them, not even the term "experimental film."

In those days, the few friends I had in the cinema were making cartoons, and I was learning by watching them. I thought I was an animator, but when I registered my first film in animation festivals in 1972, I was rejected. I was told, "But you don't move everything frame by frame, you don't make enough drawings. We kind of like what you do, but you don't belong to our group so you can't compete." I even had very amusing conversations with Alexander Alexeieff, whom I knew then; he would say with his very strong Russian accent, "My dearrr Patrrrrick, if you don't move everything frame by frame, you are not rrreally an animator."

To tell the truth, I don't like compartmentalization, genres, but it is difficult to do without them. In the past, the fashionable terms for such films as *Un Chien Andalou* ["An Andalusian Dog," 1929] by Luis Buñuel and Salvador Dali and *Le Sang d'un Poète* ["Blood of a Poet," 1935, by Jean Cocteau] were "films d'art et de'essai" and "avant-garde." Then, "experimental" came and slowly replaced them.

Man on staircase in Patrick Bokanowski's *L'Ange* ("The Angel," 1982).

Yes, from time to time, I do see Yann Beauvais, Miles McKane, Pip Chodorov, Rose Lowder, and also my friends from Grenoble (METAMKINE) [a collective of filmmakers, photographers, musicians, and other artists].

MacDonald: In both *A Woman Powders Herself* and *Déjeuner du Matin* [the title would appear to mean "Breakfast," but in translation the nuance is lost, 1974] one sees many elements that remain in *The Angel*—the music of Michèle Bokanowski, of course, but also your fascination with creating alternative worlds, and with working *between* animation and live action, *between* motion and stillness, and *between* two-dimensions and three-dimensions.

Bokanowski: When I was making *A Woman Powders Herself*, it looked to me like ordinary life. It was not a fantastic world but, for me, only a representation of reality. I knew very well that it was not a direct representation of the outside world. My images were very elaborate, and preconceived, but at the same time the world they created looked to me like everyday life. It was a world in which I was comfortable, my own ordinary world. *A Woman Powders Herself* reveals "the foolishness of daily gestures." I am not tempted to create fantastic worlds. That's not the point of what I'm doing. But I could not and cannot work with the immediate images produced by a camera. Modern optics handicap me: the picture they produce is too simple and not meaningful enough.

At the same time, I can be a good audience for all kinds of movies, and I get carried away. But when I *make* a film it is not possible for me to simply film an action, no matter how good the camera or the operator may be, and to be pleased with the immediate result. I can't even imagine doing a film that way. You should know that while this reaction is essential to the way I function, it is not something I really want, or plan theoretically. I just find it impossible to work with the machine as it is.

MacDonald: Am I correct in assuming that *The Angel*, which was made over a five-year period, developed in discreet sections, and that the finished film does not present the sections in the order in which they were completed?

Bokanowski: I started with "L'Homme Sans Mains" ["The Man Without Hands"], the sequence with the woman and the pitcher. Then I shot all the scenes with actors that used normal-sized sets. And afterwards, I made the minuscule or gigantic characters and the main body of special effects. At the beginning I had a "list" of all my technical "cravings," that is, things I had not tried in previous films: optical ideas, special effects, sets, certain kinds of costumes. Some ideas were suggested to me by my drawings, and I had also made lists of scenes or stories I liked and wanted to do. I assembled all those technical ideas, and while I was working on the scenario, they emerged little by little, and helped me to compose the framework for the film, which is sometimes a story and at other times a purely visual experience.

I also found inspiration in books: for example, in the works of Wilhelm Busch, who was a nineteenth-century German artist. He wrote *Max und Moritz*; it is a book known to all German children and adults, a kind of mythology. Wilhelm Busch is the father of cartoons (his work pre-dates Winsor McCay's by thirty years). What fascinates me about Wilhelm Busch is his liveliness, the freedom of his drawings and of his transitions. For example, he may show two characters in a room: in the first image, they are seated at a table; in the second, they are still there but the floor is not exactly at the same place and the walls have moved slightly; things in the background have a logic and a life of their own, independent of the characters. I found that great and wanted to do something similar, but with live actors.

Another source of inspiration for *The Angel* was the work of my friend, Lars Bo, whose engravings lie somewhere between fairy tales and fantastic stories. In his engraving *A l'Assaut du Château de l'Oeuf* ["Attacking the Castle of the Egg"], one sees a woman in a cage protected by a gigantic egg, and some men who are going to attack this castle. One does not know exactly what they are planning to do, but one can well imagine. This engraving is the source of the central part of my film, the woman in the transparent cage.

Still another source for *The Angel* is the astrology manual *360 Degrés du Zodiaque Illustrés par l'Image* ["360 Degrees of the Zodiac, Illustrated"] by Janduz, one of the books about which I used to say, "Oh la la, I am sure one could do something with *this* book." Each page corresponds to a degree of the zodiac with its positive aspect and negative aspect illustrated by a primitive drawing, beautifully done. All these vignettes, these small illustrations, have symbolic, surrealist meanings, but at the same time they are immersed in real life. It is a book which I would always read with passion. When I was working on *The Angel*, I chose a few of the degrees I liked the most (without thinking, with no logical reason): for example, the man with no hands and the fencer with the doll.

MacDonald: *The Angel* seems to proceed roughly from the demonic, or at least the troubling, toward the exalted.

Bokanowski: My method is to proceed *without* logic or psychology, which means that I did not pay any attention to the meaning, or to the progression. I was well aware that some things had to happen before others, that some were in effect more ethereal and "belonged" towards the end. But none of the crew (on those parts of the shooting when I worked with a crew) ever questioned me about the meaning. I don't really like thinking about meaning. I think meaning comes *in addition* and *on its own*. Later on, when I was doing the editing, and especially when (unfortunately) I had to send out written statements for the financing, I had to try to find words to describe what I had already shot.

And I was well aware that there are different ways to interpret the scenes and many possible meanings. Take "L'Homme au Bain" ["The Man Bathing"]. I made that section because he was a comical character I like. One could say that this guy is fanatic about purification, someone who has a compulsion for cleanliness (external? internal?). One could find such meanings, or more theatrical, or symbolic, or psychoanalytic meanings. But I don't like to have to use words.

About the overall structure of the *The Angel*, I *can* say that it is very traditional. You have a staircase, you go from the cellar to the attic. Scenes start falling into place during the dark, shapeless, not very precise starting phase; and then the more the film progresses, the more precise things become, and at the end, it reveals extremely luminous areas.

In one of the earliest stages, when I was doing the scenario, I thought that when one comes to the far top of this gigantic house, to an attic room, a last character would appear, some kind of a giant with barely discernible wings, some kind of angelic figure. He would lift the arm of a phonograph, the music would stop, and one would see all the film's scenes in still-frames. Very quickly, I disliked that character. He was impossible to film! So, I did not keep this sequence, but that character did give the film its title.

MacDonald: In the opening section with the fencer, you explore the "seam" between still photography and motion pictures in a manner that recalls Marey. Indeed, there are images where several states of a single continuous motion are captured in a single still image (later, this technique is also used with the falling pitcher in "The Man Without Hands"). Several recent books have reawakened North Americans to Marey's many accomplishments. Are you a particular admirer of his work?

Bokanowski: I was not particularly influenced by Marey. I have seen his photographs and like them a lot, but that is not what influenced me. I did not go to film school, but I did see Jean Mutschler at work as a cartoon animator, and I learned a lot from him. For me cinema started with cartoons, making "cels," drawings or photos on transparencies, and then filming them. I found that process more natural, or in any case more interesting, than just letting the camera roll.

MacDonald: "The Man Without Hands" sequence is eerie and funny at the same time. I've never seen anything like it in the cinema. But it does remind me of Dutch painting of the period of Vermeer. Should I be making a more precise identification here?

Bokanowski: What interests me the most is to vary the style of my imagery. As you have noticed, I like scenes to not have the same texture, the same appearance. I was told afterwards that the sequence you mention looked like scenes by Flemish painters. I worked on it a lot with Christian Daninos, who did the sets and masks. We had agreed on this style of imagery, which was inspired by the black and white drawing on the cover jacket of the Janduz astrology manual I mentioned earlier. Perhaps we needed this very ancient style for the atmosphere of the scene. I did not have any other reference in mind. I don't know how to explain it; it came out that way without my really thinking it through.

On the other hand, for other scenes the style was chosen beforehand. For example, the painter's studio is a reproduction of a well-known engraving by Dürer [see Albrecht Dürer, *Draftsman Drawing Portrait* (1525) and *Draftsman Drawing a Lute* (1525)]. You know, it is only when I have a lot of technical ideas that I feel like making a film. That's why for a very long time after making *The Angel*, I was not able to make other films. I had exhausted all my technical cravings; I had put *everything* into that film.

MacDonald: In the woman and pitcher section of the film, the music is particularly effective. Did you and Michèle work together through all stages of the filmmaking?

Bokanowski: For my short films, the music has always been composed once the visual editing was done, but for *The Angel* Michèle composed the themes for most of the scenes from the script, before the actual filming. One of the keys to our collaboration is that she guesses the unwritten intentions behind the script, and adds something, the same way dialogue would add something if I used dialogue. In fact, music does complete *The Angel*. But, as I remember, the creation of the music was done without any difficulties, precisely because Michèle very quickly realized what we needed. What was much less obvious was to find the exact place for the sound effects and to decide on the connections between the visual rhythms of the various sequences and the music. Sometimes, as you well know, the difference of only one frame can change the meaning or rhythm with positive or negative results.

MacDonald: The man taking the bath is reminiscent of early cinema, from Méliès to Chaplin—both because of the amusing actions and funny soundtrack, and because of the way the set is designed in relation to the camera/audience. This passage, and the one that follows (the tilted house and the reverse shot of the man waking up and getting dressed) seem a tribute to early trick-film and early comedy.

Bokanowski: Yes, I am very sensitive to the beginning of the cinema, to Chaplin's films and the music hall films that precede him. I really like silent film acting with its gestures and its improvisation. It suits my films far better than psychological acting, especially since I don't use words, but rely on masked and symbolic characters.

MacDonald: I've always been surprised that more filmmakers haven't exploited reverse. The tilted house shot gives some idea of what can be done with it. Have you done other work with reverse?

Bokanowski: Actually, one should have a good reason to use reverse imagery. In Cocteau's films reverse effects can be fantastic. For my films, once I have done the shooting, I always use an aerial-image machine [see "Aerial-image Photography" in Ira Konigsberg, *The Complete Film Dictionary* (New York: New American Library, 1989) for a description of this device] to make special optical effects. Using that machine led to ideas for scenes, as in my early film, *Déjeuner du Matin*, when the man puts on his raincoat. Seeing the material forward and reverse, I realized that at certain moments, the raincoat had an autonomous movement. The raincoat seemed to guide the actor, and not the contrary. This was the source of the scene of the awakening of the librarian. I thought it would be nice if all the clothes came towards the little guy.

MacDonald: In my teaching, I often use Edwin S. Porter's *The Dream of the Rarebit Fiend* [1907]. The librarian's waking up reminds me a good bit of Porter's film. Is it, perhaps, a favorite of yours?

Bokanowski: I don't know Porter's films, and this is the first time I have heard his name. Of course, I would like to see the film you mention.

MacDonald: The long passage in the library is very elaborate. Could you talk a bit about what went into this sequence?

Bokanowski: To build that huge set with an effect of perspective, we worked from drawings. The camera is still and the set was built in front of the lens so that the vanishing lines amplify the perspective. That set was very large but, surprisingly, not very tricky to make. Apparently simpler sets often create more problems. I have to tell you that I am not entirely satisfied with the set for the library: I find it too realistic. That's what I do not like about *The Angel* in general: the images are too traditional.

MacDonald: The library sequence is carefully choreographed.

Bokanowski: I have never wanted to use real dancers because the result would be too perfect, too aesthetic. I like normal action, played by an actor. But so much the better if he has rhythm and can go from natural movement to something with more style. In *A Woman Powders Herself*, the scene where the woman character is attacked is somewhere between theater and dance, but it was played by an actor, not a dancer.

The scene in the library with the nine librarians is something like a ballet. It

Identical librarians at work, in Patrick Bokanowski's *L'Ange* ("The Angel," 1982).

was originally to be a real ballet—choreographed by Maurice Baquet, who was superb as the chief librarian—but as it clashed with some other work he was doing, I had to direct the choreography myself. During the shooting we only had rhythms (we did not have the music), which allowed the actors to recognize that an action lasted for eight to ten beats, for example. I suppose that must be a very common procedure in the theater.

MacDonald: The shift from the library to the following sequence defines two poles in your work, at least in terms of composition. The library sequence, especially the shots at the very end, emphasizes depth of field and creates a convincing live-action world (with something like animated motion within it). The next sequence is extremely flat, as two-dimensional as anything I've seen of yours, and creates an animated world (with some sense of live-action movement within it). And this 3-D/2-D shift is reversed when the men batter down the door of the woman's space . . .

Bokanowski: If I understand correctly, you feel you are going from 3-D to 2-D to 3-D. This was not done on purpose; it just happened that way in the process. Before you mentioned it, I did not even know that it could give such an impression.

MacDonald: I'm tempted to read the sequence of the running men and the woman-in-the-box as a literal comment on traditional male/female roles, especially because of the phallic implications of that battering ram. What did you have in mind in this sequence?

Bokanowski: That is another part of the film's involuntary meaning; there-fore, it is not easy for me to speak about. Let's take "L'Homme au Sabre" ["The Fencer"]: he thrusts at a doll relentlessly. This fencer could be a desperate guy, someone aggressive against the opposite sex, as symbolized by this doll. Or the doll could represent his own inner self. But, as I've said, I don't like to talk about this level of the film at all or even to think about it. I don't like digging up all the meanings.

MacDonald: The final two sections are a kind of homage to light, light in both the physical and the spiritual sense. They seem to be a way of talking about your position and quest as filmmaker, about your part in a tradition of op-tics and in a quest for spiritual connection.

Bokanowski: The sequence with the light rays was created frame-by-frame by moving the objects. I was very much influenced by one of Michèle's pieces named *Chambre d'Inquiétude* ["Room of Unrest"]. One part of *Chambre d'In-quiétude* is called "Les Signaux" ["The Signals"]. The signals' rhythms and the music's structure really guided me, though I did not synchronize the visual events with the soundtrack.

MacDonald: At the conclusion of *The Angel*, when the light grows increas-ingly powerful, the alternation between light and darkness causes the theater space to become quite dynamic: as spectators we are *in* the world of the film. Was this part of your intent?

Bokanowski: I had no such conscious intention.

MacDonald: At various points in *The Angel* we see bits of imagery that feel a bit outside of the sequence we're seeing at the moment, but which are picked up in later sequences. Two examples are the imagery of the projector beam that we see first in the brief transitional passage after the woman-and-jug sequence (that projector beam becomes much more important at the very end) and the quick cutting of what looks to be rain falling on steps, which we see just before the man bathing, and then at greater length near the end of the film. Once we've seen the entire film, we can recognize these as foreshadowings, but they also suggest your attempt to pull the many different worlds you create during the film into a more coherent overall structure. Another way of saying this would be to suggest that these references to later (and sometimes earlier) passages in the film indicate that all the particular worlds in the film are "rooms" in the larger world of your consciousness/unconsciousness.

Bokanowski: I am amazed that you noticed all these details! What could I add to what you have observed so well?

MacDonald: In the credits, you indicate that "ce film est la suite d'études effectuées entre 1963 et 1967 sous la direction de Henri Dimier" ("this film is the result of studies made between 1963 and 1967 under the direction of Henri Dimier"). Could you talk a bit about your relationship with Mr. Dimier?

Bokanowski: Dimier, the son of an art historian, painted and knew a great many contemporary painters. He was tremendously knowledgeable about the history of procedures for creating space and perspective in painting. He could see how modern optics missed what was possible and limited and distorted the outside world. For him, the mistake was to think that photography gives a "real" document, when what it gives is only a *conventional* document—because of the way lenses are made. He had a hatred for optical lenses and conventions and struggled against them.

When I made *The Angel*, it had already been twelve years since I left his studio. Dimier did not collaborate at all on *L'Ange*, but was the first to see it finished. I brought him to the lab to see the first rough cut. He has always been the first to see my films. I put his name in the credits because I consider that all this imagery is a result of my spending four years with him, learning at his side, discovering his ideas on optics.

I did not do any painting or drawing with Dimier, but mainly photographs. I made photographic papers, sensitizing them, using procedures from the beginning of photography: bi-chromated fixers, carbon papers . . . I also tried to avoid modern optics by using pinhole cameras and by building cameras that had multiple lenses—all this while following Dimier's ideas on mixing perspectives.

I have never met a man more passionate for artistic matters than Dimier. You could come and see him day and night for just about anything regarding art, whether you had a small drawing or a small part of a film. Whatever you were working on, you could turn up a 3 a.m., knock on his door, and wake him up. He would jump up and be ready to see you: to look at what you had, to talk about it, and to celebrate afterwards if it was interesting. What was great and surprising with him was his very particular mixture of a strong sense of the rational and a desire to resort to whatever is not voluntary, to what originates in chance. He thought that we were not the ones who had ideas, but that ideas came *to* us. He would see each achievement as a metaphysical photograph of an invisible world around us, and not as a purely voluntary creation. He was a kind of sorcerer, very stable, very much at ease in his own magic—although he did not use the vocabulary of a sorcerer or a magician.

MacDonald: How was *The Angel* received in France and elsewhere?

Bokanowski: In France the film was rather well-received, considering that it is neither obvious nor easy. In 1982, it was selected for the Semaine de la Critique at Cannes, then distributed by Claude Eric Poiroux and Dominique Paini (director of the Cinémathèque Française). There was a good press review, and a few people supported the film, especially Michel Chion and Dominique Noguez. Dominique Noguez had the idea to take a copy to Japan, where the film was even better received than in France: Katsué Tomiyama has been distributing it, without interruption, for the last ten years.

MacDonald: What are you working on at present?

Bokanowski: Since 1982, I have been drawing quite regularly, almost every day. I call the drawings "yf" (which means "yeux fermés," eyes shut) because, as a matter of fact, I do start each drawing without looking at paper and then I add color or use china ink afterwards. It is a technique I love since it hinders me from using the usual conventions. I had an exhibit in Japan and my first exhibit in Paris in 1993. Overall, I have been as much into drawing as films, perhaps more. Most of the drawings are not tied to any film idea.

In 1992 I made a short film, *La Plage* ["The Beach"], and another in 1993, *Au Bord du Lac* ["By the Lake"]. I hope I have managed to create characters and spaces that are less rigid and more free than the images in *The Angel*.

Yervant Gianikian and Angela Ricci Lucchi

(on *From the Pole to the Equator*)

Few filmmakers exemplify the idea of a "critical cinema" more clearly than the Milanese collaborators Yervant Gianikian and Angela Ricci Lucchi, who see their mission as retrieving and examining the cinematic artifacts of the Italian past and critiquing them from the other end of the century these artifacts helped to introduce. That this process has generally involved slowing down the filmed material they work with, first, so they can study it frame by frame, and then, so that viewers can see it, not frame by frame, but slowly enough to profit from the painstaking examination Gianikian and Ricci Lucchi have conducted, has a specific (and local) reference: Futurism, an artistic movement that was centered in Milan and characterized by a fascination with motion and especially speed. The fact that Futurism was to become one of the pillars of Italian fascism makes a critique of it crucial, especially since, as Gianikian and Ricci Lucchi are well aware, fascist ideology is hardly a thing of the past. Indeed, their explorations of the cine-artifacts they collect are often inspired by current events reminiscent, to them, of the particular histories that produced Mussolini, Hitler, and the Turkish genocide of the Armenians (in 1915), as a result of which Gianikian lives in Italy as a second-generation Armenian immigrant.

As filmmakers, Gianikian and Ricci Lucchi have always been fascinated with the past and with memory. Among their earliest collaborations were a series of "scented films" that combined filmed images recorded at the Lombroso Museum in Turin (a collection of artifacts having to do with crime) and scents (from their own considerable collection) released using Bunsen burners during the projection of the images: "Smell is the dullest of the senses, and we began working on odors and scents as catalysts of memory, associating them with the rediscovery of the antique objects that made up our films and that already contained memories of their own" (Ricci Lucchi, interviewed by Sergio Toffetti and Daniela Giuffrida, for *Yervant Gianikian/Angela Ricci Lucchi*, a catalogue published in connection with a retrospective at the Museo Nazionale del Cinema in Turin [Florence: Hopeful Monster Press, 1992]). Since 1980 their focus has been on cinematic memory in particular: they have collected a wide variety of films, many of which they have re-photographed. Their first major work of "recycled cinema" was *Karagoez—Catalogo 9,5* (1981; *karagoez* means "shadow play") for which they re-photographed imagery recorded on Pathé Baby, the first amateur film stock (it was 9.5mm wide, with perforations in the center of the filmstrip).

Essence d'Absynthe ("Essence of Absinthe," 1981) involved re-photographing a post–World War I porn film and *Das Lied von der Erde* ["The Song of the Land"]: *Gustav Mahler* (1982) is a further exploration of the Pathé Baby materials that provides visual analogues to a T. W. Adorno essay on Mahler. But their most impressive film—still their longest (101 minutes) and their earliest with a soundtrack (of music by California musicians Keith Ullrich and Charles Anderson)—is *Dal Polo all'Equatore* ("From the Pole to the Equator," 1986), a recycling of films from the archive of early Italian cinematographer and collector Luca Comerio.

For *From the Pole to the Equator*, Gianikian and Ricci Lucchi built a special "analytic" camera:

> It is made of two elements. In the first the original 35mm runs vertically. It can accept Lumière perforations, as well as films with various degrees of shrinkage and physical decay of the emulsion. . . . The camera is run manually with a handle, because of the precarious conditions of the perforations and the continual risk of the [nitrate] material catching fire. The claw is made with two mobile teeth (instead of four). The lamps used are photographic lamps with temperatures that can be varied with a rheostat. This first part of the camera owes its existence to the transformation of a contact printer. The second camera is an air camera lined up with the first to absorb the image by back projection. It is a camera with microscope features, more photographic than cinematographic and reminds one more of Muybridge and Marey than of the Lumières. (*Yervant Gianikian/Angela Ricci Lucchi*, p. 100)

With this device Gianikian and Ricci Lucchi recorded 347,600 frames from Luca Comerio's original *From the Pole to the Equator* (the completion date is unclear; Gianikian and Ricci Lucchi estimate the late 1920s) and from various other films in Comerio's collection. The result transforms the original material—in general, artifacts of imperialism: missionaries "educating" natives, big-game hunters in Africa, British military parades in India—so that viewers not only see the original imagery and its original intent (to testify to the superiority of white, European civilization) but *see through* the imagery to the human beings looking back at these cameras from within their own complex cultures.

The haunting Ullrich/Anderson soundtrack and Gianikian and Ricci Lucchi's careful control of color—in general, the film is tinted, but several sequences are hand-painted—provide a somewhat schizoid emotional mood. The sensual beauty of *From the Pole to the Equator* simultaneously adds to our pleasure in watching and communicates a sense of what has been lost as a result of the relentless onslaught of empire. Even while detaching ourselves from the ideology implicit in the original imagery, we can hardly fail to recognize that, sitting in the theater viewing this film, we are the beneficiaries of the very political processes the film reminds us to abhor. Cinema was and remains one of the spearheads of empire. Gianikian and Ricci Lucchi allow contemporary viewers at least the illusion of entering and dismantling the forgotten artifacts of cine-imperialism, and the opportunity of becoming more alert to problematic dimensions of the cinema in our time.

The following discussion was conducted primarily in an exchange of letters, which was supplemented by conversations (with the assistance of Gabriella Massi as translator) in Milan in June of 1992, and by further letters.

MacDonald: When people ask you what kind of films you make, or what your mission as filmmakers is, how do you describe your work? Of course, you are collectors of early film imagery (and other artifacts), and you explore this imagery. Are you cine-archeologists?

Gianikian: Somebody might define us that way, but I don't like the term . . .

Ricci Lucchi: Something is missing.

Gianikian: We are interested in an ethical sense of vision. A project is usually born from our reading film images.

MacDonald: You mean from exploring the material you've collected?

Gianikian: Yes, in very controlled ways. It's something like vivisection. We write down what happens in each frame, how many frames are in each shot and sequence. We are very precise.

MacDonald: Do you *both* do this exploration?

Gianikian: I begin, but she is always following the work, so she knows everything about it. She takes part and contributes many important things. She often does other kinds of research as well. Really, we work together, but in different ways.

Ricci Lucchi: It depends on the topic, and whether I am interested. My first job is to know, very deeply, the historical time period of the material we want to explore—all the things in the world that might affect this topic.

Gianikian: For the sections on Africa in *From the Pole to the Equator*, we read all the books on the subject, all the French writers, as well as the Italians, and not only scholarship, but explorers' diaries.

MacDonald: *Karagoez—Catalogo 9,5* was your first long archival film. It developed out of the collection you found in 1977. Are you always collecting material? And do particular films develop out of particular collections?

Gianikian: It's not as conscious as that, though it is true that *Karagoez* was born from a collection of fiction films, and *From the Pole*, from a collection of documentaries. But in *Pole* we made a choice not to mix fiction with documentary. The Comerio collection included both.

We are always looking for new material, because we're always looking for new meaning, and new ways of reading imagery.

MacDonald: You used "vivisection" to describe your exploration of film imagery. Is your interest in exploring the image in such detail partly a desire to see how a fascistic way of seeing has developed in cinema in general? One could argue that popular cinema and television in general tend to be reactionary—not only in what is shown, but in the way in which viewers are asked to use their eyes. In order to watch your films, one must learn to look in a completely different way. Most popular films and TV shows simply ask you to consume images. By slowing down the process of consumption, you force us to think about that process.

Ricci Lucchi: It's not just that you *can* think about our movies; you *must* come inside each frame. We force you to think about the operations we have performed on the original material.

MacDonald: In what year did you acquire the Comerio archives?

Ricci Lucchi: After a tour in the United States in the winter of 1981, we found *From the Pole to the Equator* in an old lab in Milano.

Gianikian: At the time, I was looking for materials about travel, about exoticism and war. I was thinking about the film on Gustav Mahler [*Das Lied von der Erde: Gustav Mahler*], from the Adorno text [T. W. Adorno, *Mahler* (Frankfurt am Main: Suhrkamp Verlag, 1960)]. We had known there was an old film lab in Milano. We went there, met the man in charge of the lab, and in time we became friends. During that time, we were almost the only visitors to that lab.

We paid nearly all the money we had to get the Comerio materials. At the beginning, the man was very mysterious about Comerio, but soon we discovered he didn't know very much and didn't understand the cultural importance of the material. In 1982, he gave us some tapes—recordings of conversations with the cameramen of World War I—made for radio many years ago: the tapes included Paolo Granata, Luca Comerio's first cameraman during World War I (*granata* in Italian means "cannonball"!).

Ricci Lucchi: We continued to collect materials from the lab until 1985, when it closed. The owner of the lab (he and his wife were the only workers) was the nephew of Granata.

During fascism Granata was the most important cameraman of the fascist Institute Luce in northern Italy. Over the years, the nephew had taken over Comerio's place: the space, the films. The nephew was also a cameraman. His first shot was the hanging of the body of Mussolini in a square in Milano in 1945. The nephew remembered the last visits of Comerio to the lab.

MacDonald: How much Comerio material was at the lab?

Gianikian: The lab had many underground spaces. At the beginning it was impossible to understand how much material was there.

There was a kind of stratification of film materials, we realized later. There were early materials filmed or collected by Luca Comerio. There were fascist films shot by Paolo Granata (in which there are traces of Comerio) during the twenties, thirties and forties. And there was religious material filmed by the nephew in the fifties and sixties. The film materials were records of three different times: the time of the King, the time of fascism, and the more recent time of the Vatican.

The Comerio collection was very large: there were thousands of meters of material—documentaries from the beginning of cinema, travel films, ethnography, scientific materials, and World War I material. Except for a few rolls, there was almost no trace of the fiction films listed in Comerio's filmography. That material had disappeared, or had been collected by cinematheques. There was no interest here in the documentaries. *From the Pole* was in two cans, six hundred meters each, in a wardrobe in the room where the nephew filmed titles with the old camera Comerio used during World War I. The nephew had offered *From the Pole* to the cinematheque in Milano for a reasonable amount of money, but they wanted it only as a gift!

MacDonald: Had you known about Comerio for a long time before acquiring his films?

Gianikian: It is difficult to explain the sensation I had when I saw the two reels of *From the Pole* for the first time. The color of the tinted materials! I saw only a few meters, but it was enough. I didn't know the film was by Comerio. I didn't know who Comerio was. We discovered that every intertitle was signed by Comerio in superimposition: "Comm-Luca Comerio, Milano Cinematografia." Later we found a book, very superficial—but the filmography was useful. By juxtaposing the filmography and the images, it was possible to recover Comerio's life and travels.

In 1985, the man at the lab gave us the Comerio materials about fascism, thousands of meters of film, and also a group of stills, some signed by Comerio, of Comerio during the fascist demonstrations. By the thirties, Comerio himself was very ill and in a state of amnesia.

MacDonald: Is the original, Comerio version of *From the Pole to the Equator* still in existence?

Gianikian: It's in our home. Before the erosion wipes out the image, we hope to find a way to make a 35mm copy that's absolutely faithful to the original.

MacDonald: Tell me about his film.

Gianikian: The film is tinted positives. We think a complete negative never existed. It was an ignored film, not even mentioned in Comerio's filmography.

The original film is divided into four sections or chapters: the first begins with the intertitle, "La vita animale per perpetuarsi deve lottare E VINCERE!" ["To survive, animal life has to fight AND WIN!"].

The intertitles, almost ten minutes of the total length, were written by Gabriele d'Annunzio, the "soldier-poet."

MacDonald: When was Comerio's *From the Pole to the Equator* made?

Gianikian: We don't know the exact date. At the end of the twenties, we think, at a time when his career was almost finished. The "Cameraman of the King," the pioneer of Italian cinema, feels himself overcome by the new technology of sound. He writes letters to Mussolini, trying to find a job in the new Institute Luce, the institute for Italian fascist documentary. He may have edited *From the Pole* in the hope that it would secure him a job.

Ricci Lucchi: Comerio is not an avant-garde filmmaker like Dziga Vertov. He was a capable moviemaker, but not experimental at all. He became a proto-fascist because he wanted to make movies, and the only way to make movies was to come inside the Regime. He wanted work. There's a letter written by Comerio to Mussolini, asking to work for him at Institute Luce: he writes not as a political supporter, but as a family man looking for work.

MacDonald: How similar to what we see in your film was the original *From the Pole?*

Gianikian: There are differences in both content and technique. The Comerio film is, as I said, twelve hundred meters, 57 minutes. Our film is longer: 101 minutes (96 minutes on television).

The Comerio film is divided into four chapters. In our film there are ten sections. Of the original four chapters, we used part of the second (the South Pole material) and almost all of the third (Uganda, 1910) for two chapters in our film: the chapter about the missionaries and the chapter about the big-game hunt. The other seven sections of our *From the Pole* come from Comerio's personal archives.

The slow motion of our version is the opposite of the extremely fast movement of the original. Our slow motion changes: it is not constant for every sequence. Sometimes it changes *inside* a sequence. Slow motion becomes emphasis, the rhythm of memory.

All the materials from the archives, including those from the original *From the Pole*, are first generation prints. The definition was good enough (though in many parts the emulsion had been attacked by the mold) and the 24mm x 18mm aspect ratio of the silent frame made it possible for us to see hidden details, without losing too much definition. Sometimes we recomposed shots, as we did with several portraits of army generals and the eyes of a blind man in Tangier. Except for the animals in the first chapter, close-ups don't exist in the original *From the Pole*, or in the other material from the collection. Usually we step inside the individual frame, to get closer to it and to isolate details.

MacDonald: What about the color?

Gianikian: Sometimes we used particular filters to reinforce the original colors or sometimes to change them completely. The train material in the beginning had lost its original colors, except for some traces near the perforations. In the original *From the Pole*, the intertitles are blue and the writing is white. The name, "Comerio," is superimposed in dark blue. The original first chapter ("The Eternal Fight," the animals' struggles, which we didn't use) is tinted different colors, except for a cock fight, which is handpainted. The original "White Sphinx" chapter, about the South Pole, is blue and sepia for some animals and dark red for one or two sequences in the interior of the ship. The third chapter of the original film is generally sepia (we used various colors). In the fourth chapter of the original, which we didn't use, the colors change from sequence to sequence. In the original film, there is no use of negative; all the imagery is positive; in some cases, as you know, we print from the original negative stock that was in Comerio's cameras. We use negative symbolically.

Decay is more or less evident on all the surfaces of both the original *From the Pole* and the rest of the Comerio collection. Instead of trying to eliminate all the mold, we decided to use it as an analogue. In some sequences of the war, the decay on the film cancels out the men but not the rocks (and in some cases, the color of the mold was red). At the end of the East Africa material, we used the mold as a fade out to white—at the end of the parade of the inhabitants of the village.

MacDonald: How does your editing differ from Comerio's?

Gianikian: Each chapter of Comerio's film started with a d'Annunzio title, and each sequence or group of related sequences was preceded by an intertitle, which was illustrated by what followed. The intertitles are key in the first *From the Pole to the Equator*; they reflect the ideology of d'Annunzio and [Filippo Tommaso] Marinetti (not the young avant-garde, futurist artist Marinetti, but the older Marinetti, who went into the hierarchy of fascist power).

Our *From the Pole* is arranged according to "themes" in which elements reappear in different forms and aspects. In preparing the project, we discovered—in the original *From the Pole* and in the other materials—recurring motifs. There are parades and processions (military, religious, hunting); dances (rituals, dances of death); war landscapes (trenches, for example); crowds and other groups; and particular types of people: the priest, the warrior, the "savage," the hunter, the mystic, the traveler, the conqueror. These became the motifs in our film and they are arranged in parallels and contrasts. Elements in each of our chapters are references to elements in the next chapter. The parade of the English cavalry at the coronation of George V in one chapter parallels the mystical religious parade—the procession of the bones—in the next chapter. A contrast is evident between the African kids conditioned by a culture not theirs and the Indian kids smiling.

We reread, rewrote, re-edited the original Comerio film, overturning the original meaning and ideology. Our film was centered on the metaphor of am-

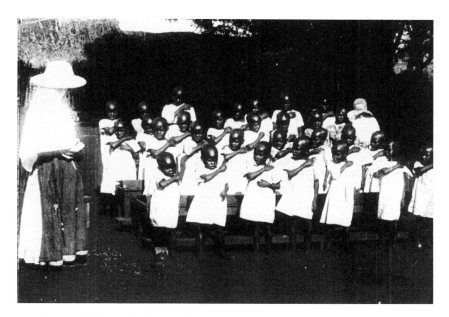

Missionaries "civilizing" African children, in Yervant Gianikian and Angela Ricci Lucchi's *From the Pole to the Equator* (1986).

nesia: the amnesia of Comerio's last years, the general "amnesia" about primitive cinema, and the desire of early audiences for exotic spectacles, which reflected their dreams of conquest and cultural pillage (their "amnesia" about early cultures). When we analyzed the frames of Comerio's film, we were irritated and disturbed by Comerio's sanctification of imperialism, colonialism and war. We wanted to make a film on the violence of colonialism as it plays itself out in different situations and spheres.

In the original *From the Pole*, the animals killing other animals in the first chapter is a "necessity of life." By applying this morality to people, it was possible (for Comerio) to justify the violence of the man who kills not only for necessity but for the pleasure of affirming his own power and will. We removed the last chapter of the original film, "Victory of Man": its images and intertitles are hymns to strength, courage, sport, war, nationalism, maternity, and religion—the last two, the Catholic blessing of the first elements. Our ending sequence, the man-rabbit-dog sequence, is the "key" to our film: it reveals violence for play, violence with no possible justification. We are not sure the shot of the man, dog, and rabbit is by Comerio. We do know that the man in the shot is [Giacomo] Puccini; the place, Torre del Lago.

MacDonald: Were you able to distinguish between what Comerio shot and what he collected?

Gianikian: Yes, though in our film we used both. A very large part of the archive is about World War I. It was shot by Comerio, the only one to have the army's permission to film the war. He lost the permission during the second part of the war; there were too many deaths in his films and the battles he recorded were often lost. The first part of the war could be seen as a game—for example, the hundreds of soldiers trying to push the enormous cannon to the top of the mountain—but later, this was not possible. At the end of the war Comerio did film the celebration of victory in Trento near the Dolomites.

In the archive, the war materials were in small reels of ten, twenty, or thirty meters or sometimes in separate sequences of less than one meter. All the positives are tinted, and some of the negatives. There is only one reel of positive, four hundred meters, edited, with intertitles (from this reel we took the war scenes with the mold damage).

We started our film by re-shooting and re-editing the war material. In our *From the Pole*, we included a shot of Mussolini on his horse entering Tripoli in 1927 (it is after the cavalry in the matte with the monument of the King on his horse). The shot is not by Comerio but by Institute Luce. We wanted to show what would be the future of the Italians.

In his filmography, we discovered that Comerio started to film in 1898. There is a short Comerio film about the funeral of King Umberto who was killed by an anarchist (Bresci) in Monza in 1900. The catalogue of the films of the Lumière brothers lists a film with this title. Monza is very near to Milano and it is possible that Comerio worked for Lumière in those years. All the Comerio films on Lumière stock are about Milano. At the turn of the century, there was only one filmmaker in Milan other than Comerio: Vittorio Calcina.

The original train material was about ninety-eight meters, exactly 5,044 frames. We excluded a section filmed, not from the train, but near the railway. There's no indication that that material is by Comerio, but perhaps it could be his *From Geeschenen to Andernatt* [1909].

We do not think Comerio traveled in the Caucasus. For our Caucasus chapter, we used two different source materials. The sequences of the train were made in Tiflis, probably in 1904, during the re-conquest of the town and of Georgia by the czarist army (we used only one sequence of the Russian cavalry with armor). For the second section, we used a separate film, of the czarist officers in white uniforms and the native men and women dancing. The place seems to be in central Russian Asia.

A very large part of the Comerio collection was about India. The material includes many different originals: some Gaumont (the English cavalry material), some Pathécolor (the handpainted materials), and some on the Italian stock, Ferrania (the travels of the cameraman with the Cook agency). Granata's nephew told us that in the last years of his career Comerio went to India. But it was impossible for us to be sure the Indian material was by Comerio. Also, before the war, Comerio visited the Middle East, and the African Mediterranean, but we don't have proof that the material on Tangier and Gondar that we use in our *From the Pole* is by Comerio.

MacDonald: I know *From the Pole to the Equator* has been seen on Italian television. In general, how widely seen are your films and what kinds of response have you gotten?

Ricci Lucchi: *From the Pole* was produced by German TV and shown on German TV also, at 10:30 at night, so there was a big audience. In Italy it was shown on Channel 3 at 1 a.m. and the audience was seven or eight hundred thousand viewers.

MacDonald: I saw *From the Pole* at the Toronto Film Festival in 1987. Everyone was rushing from one film to the next, to whatever was hot. Your film began with a packed house and, to my surprise, virtually everyone stayed though the entire film, despite its serene pace.

Ricci Lucchi: The premiere was in Rotterdam in 1987. They scheduled six screenings. At the first, there were not too many people; at the second, more; at the third, more, and so on.

MacDonald: Have you had similar experiences with other films?

Ricci Lucchi: We don't follow our films in the festivals. We like to work more than to travel.

MacDonald: Are you always working on several projects?

Gianikian/Ricci Lucchi: No. We are slow workers and like to work on one project at a time. *From the Pole* took four years. *People, Years, Life* [*Uomini, Anni, Vita*, 1990] two years, and we wanted more time for that. *People, Years, Life* was begun before the Berlin Wall came down, and was first projected *on* the Wall the night after the start of the Gulf War.

MacDonald: Suppose someone were to say, "Your work is not really film art, because it simply re-presents material that was already there." How would you respond?

Ricci Lucchi: We use ready-mades. We transform the old into the new.

Gianikian: By changing the speed, the colors, the meaning, we make the film new. By "old" and "new," we don't just mean the physical material of the film. It's a question of meanings also: the old *means* in a new way.

In our new film, *Italian Archives (No. 1)* [*Archivi Italiani (n. 1): Il fiore della razza* ("The Flower of the Race"), 1991], we consider the relationship between sport and war, as it was during fascism, but also as it is today. We started this new film when the Gulf War was *just* over. The relationship between Then and Now is always central to our films.

Elias Merhige

(on *Begotten*)

In June 1992, during a trip to Vienna to interview Martin Arnold, I discovered that the Stadtkino Theater was in the midst of a retrospective of American independent cinema, including both avant-garde film (this section of the retrospective had been curated by Steve Anker of the San Francisco Cinematheque) and of experimental narrative and documentary. The retrospective, called "Unknown Territories," was organized by the Stadtkino Theater and by Martin Arnold, Brigitta Burger-Utzer, and Peter Tscherkassky, all members of SIX-PACK, a Viennese collective that supports alternative film production and exhibition. The retrospective was accompanied by elaborate program notes, available from SIXPACK, as well as a special issue of *Blimp* (no. 20), which includes overviews by Tom Gunning, David Sterritt, and Anker). On the first evening of our stay in Vienna, Pat [Patricia O'Connor, MacDonald's wife] and I decided to fight the combination of jet lag and beer and see a bit of *Begotten* (1989), Elias Merhige's experimental narrative feature, which I had read about (the film had premiered at New York City's Film Forum in 1990) but had not seen—we were too exhausted to commit to more than ten or fifteen minutes of the film. *Begotten* begins with a long, slow, highly formal, unusually visceral sequence in extremely grainy black and white—Merhige calls the sequence "God Killing Himself"—during which a bizarre being disembowels itself, limbs flailing in agony. I found the sequence gorgeous in some mysterious way, and despite my fatigue, I knew almost immediately that nothing was going to get me out of the theater until *Begotten* was over. As I turned to Pat, who has limited patience for violence *and* for slow, formalist work, to tell her, she looked at me and said, "There's *no way* you're going to get me to leave!" That *Begotten* is Merhige's first feature makes it all the more remarkable, and the fact that it was allowed to slide quickly into obscurity, all the more frustrating (*Begotten* had a second premiere in LA early in 1995, and is now available on video).

Begotten is one of few films that effectively combines several usually distinct traditions in alternative cinema. First, it is in the tradition of the psychodrama and visionary cinema that P. Adams Sitney explores in *Visionary Film* (New York: Oxford University Press, 1974). As Mother Nature, who is born out of the death of God, struggles through one bleak landscape after another, she becomes a projection of both filmmaker and viewer mythically coming to grips with the stern realities of life. *Begotten* is also closely related to Viennese "Actionism" and the "materialactionfilms" of Otto Mühl and Kurt Kren (the group that collaborated with Merhige was called "Theatreofmaterial"), where the repressions of the psyche within society find outlet in the performers' engagement with paint, milk, blood, piss, shit. Mother Nature, like so many of the characters in the materialactionfilms, is immersed in material substances, as she drags herself and is dragged by others through Merhige's nightmare world. Finally, *Begotten* is in the tradition of films that explore the materiality of the filmstrip. The gritty, grainy textures of Merhige's images recall Ernie Gehr's *Reverberation* (1969) and Ken Jacobs's *Tom, Tom, the Piper's Son* (1969, revised in 1971). In general, *Begotten* hovers between traditions, creating an ambiguous experience that challenges viewers' sense of decency, their ability to understand, and their patience—while simultaneously providing both narrative fascination and sensual engagement with the film's remarkable chiaroscuro.

I spoke with Merhige in December of 1993, in Utica, New York, after a screening of *Begotten*. That conversation was supplemented with letters and phone calls.

MacDonald: What is, or was, the Theatreofmaterial, the group that made *Begotten*?

Merhige: While I was in school [State University of New York at Purchase] I spent a lot of time in Manhattan looking at performance. It always intrigued me when people visualized situations not just to tell a dramatic, linear story but to create some sort of otherworldly response. I'd love it when I found myself thinking, "I can't believe I'm looking at this!"

MacDonald: What performances do you remember particularly?

Merhige: A Japanese dance troupe called Sankui Juku. I was very moved by their work. I learned that they had a core group of people who worked together, slept together, ate together—did everything together. They knew each other thoroughly and not just on a professional basis. That fascinated me, and I wanted to achieve something similar. To what extent I was successful I don't know.

If you are able to bring diverse minds and talents together, it's a miracle to have them for whatever time you have them. And that's what brought me to make *Begotten* into a film, as opposed to a theater piece: I could already sense that some of the people were moving on to other things. Also, I wanted a permanent record of our work.

Specifically, the people in the Theatreofmaterial were sculptors, painters, actors. They were all in touch with modes of theatrical expression that were not conventional and were not centered around dialogue. We were interested in emotions on the fringes, emotions most directors and artists will not deal with. We wanted to give character and architecture to regions of the soul that are normally considered No Man's Land, the Unknown.

We did many exercises together—breathing exercises, for example, where we would breathe to the point of hysteria and create these moments of panic. Afterwards, we would analyze what the experience was all about. It was an intimate science.

The writing for *Begotten* was all Vision material, or whatever you want to call it, and I used those parts that scared me, or that I just couldn't understand—the parts that stuck with me for days and that forced me to wonder *where* within *me* did *this* come from? A tableau of the unknown was important to me. Then it was a matter of arranging this material as a myth. That was important, too. It began as a personal myth and ended as a collective myth, a myth of everyone involved in making the film.

At first I didn't think to bring my writing together with the group work. But in the process of working with these people, the two came together. We began to rehearse excerpts of the writings. First, I would read the material as a poet would read it; then we'd talk about it; and then we would break it down into its physical elements.

MacDonald: Did you rehearse for a long time and then shoot very intensively over a short period of time?

Merhige: Yes. The rehearsals were not so much to get the choreography perfect, but to get us all in tune with one another, so that our relationship to one another would become instinctual, as opposed to just professional. It became a tribal relationship. By the end of the four and a half months, we were so used to one another that there was nothing anyone could do or say that would be embarrassing or awkward.

It was winter at the time, and we rehearsed a lot indoors. When spring came, we made preparations to go outdoors, which in the end added a whole different element. That's when the film came together: the script began to dissolve away, to move into the distance, and the emotion of the sky and the earth and the climate mingled with the group. Another entity came out of that. And finishing the costumes—the masks—helped people get into the roles even more deeply.

MacDonald: How long did you shoot?

Merhige: About five and a half months, mostly on weekends. We really looked forward to each three-day weekend—you got the feeling that this was the most meaningful part of our lives at the time. I think that comes through in the film.

MacDonald: The opening sequence feels a little like a prologue, not just to the narrative that develops once the birth of Nature has taken place, but to your own exploration of texture, grain, light, rhythm.

Merhige: The opening twelve minutes, God killing Himself and Mother Earth's birth, were shot first. I cut that together, and it got everyone excited. I think it proved to everyone that this *was* an important film, that there really was nothing else like it, and that we were actually going to make it happen. It wasn't an intellectual reaction, it was excitement. And I really needed that because people were working for nothing—even the art director and the costume designer, both of whom were professionals. Basically, everybody worked for excellent dinners that my mother made and a place to sleep. Also, all their expenses were paid.

MacDonald: And you raised that money how?

Merhige: Raised the money? Well, first of all, I had twenty thousand dollars that my grandfather had left me for medical school. I decided I wanted to use it for this. That took care of many of the initial raw costs. I had done special effects work and had been able to accumulate some money doing that, which I put into the film. Actually, money was never a problem. What took so long was not the money, but the time involved getting the optical printer working exactly the right way for the project and getting the imagery and the sound together.

MacDonald: Once you had shot the film, what was the process?

Merhige: I would say that on the average, it took between eight to ten hours of optical work for every minute of finished film that you see.

MacDonald: Exactly what kind of work?

Merhige: Analyzing the footage, deciding on the best shots, doing tests, sending those tests off to the lab—if the lab was off that day by a degree or two, the whole relationship between the blacks and whites in a particular sequence would be changed. Often, I had to reshoot material that didn't match what had been done previously.

I worked with an optical printer that I put together myself. At different special effects places where I had worked on and off, I was able to find parts that no one else was using: a gate from an old Italian printer, an old Mitchell camera from 1936, too clumsy to use for shooting, but with perfect registration for an optical printer. I was able to mount the whole thing onto a very heavy iron rack system to keep everything steady. A machinist friend was able to machine mounts to certain specifications. Getting the whole thing working took close to eight months.

MacDonald: After the shooting?

Merhige: Yes.

MacDonald: Who have you done special effects for?

Merhige: I did one rotoscope for a Disney show I never knew the name of. Jobs like that pay very well.

MacDonald: Did you study special effects at SUNY-Purchase?

Merhige: No. I've always been able to see something in my mind and create it on film. I have a knack for translating ideas into photographic images. A lot of directors have an idea and know how to write it, but have a problem translating it visually. For me, it's more difficult to write. That's why the first ten minutes of *Begotten* were so important. After that I didn't have to explain anything.

MacDonald: You work with "material" on several levels. Of course, the characters are clothed in material, and they move through various kinds of material within the events you portray. But at what point in the process did you become involved with the material of the celluloid, in terms of texture and chiaroscuro?

Merhige: That was a part of my psyche in every stage of making the film. If I couldn't create the film the way I saw it, I didn't want to make it. I knew the style with which the images would reveal themselves was as integral as the story itself: the story wouldn't work without it.

The idea of time working on the surface of the medium itself was important to me. I wanted to create a sense that the film was going through its own trial, its own sufferings. The idea of ruins, of things falling apart—not because of the overt violence of one body against another, but through the subtle violence of time—has always fascinated me. I wanted *Begotten* to look, not as if it were from the twenties, not even as if it were from the nineteenth century, but as if it were from the time of Christ, as if it were a cinematic Dead Sea Scroll that had been buried in the sands, a remnant of a culture with customs and rites that no longer apply to this culture, yet are somewhere *underneath* it, under the surface of what we call "reality."

MacDonald: When I first saw *Begotten* in Vienna, I thought to myself—after about five minutes of the film—"I don't know where this is going and it scares the hell out of me, but there's no way I'm not sitting through it!"

Merhige: The whole idea of a movie is that you want people to *watch*. Everything about the events I'm depicting in *Begotten* is repellent. The viewer naturally wants to look away, to leave. If you verbalized the story, it would be hard to find anyone who'd say, "Oh yeah, visualize *that*—I'd really like to see *that*." But making the unpalatable palatable is the challenge. It's easy to show things that everybody is drawn to, but to show things that people are immediately repelled by *and* keep them in their seats is exciting. I hoped I could keep the audience by making the film beautiful to look at in a formal sense. I knew if I were sloppy in any stage of it—the costumes, the photography, the sound—people would leave. If *I* didn't stay with it, why should *they*?

MacDonald: The ambiguity of the plot contributes to the film's eerie violence.

Merhige: A lot of people have had trouble with the violence in the film. Of course, some people do feel that there is a ritualized necessity to what is happening, that a group is working together as a form of collective sacrifice or collective expiation of some guilt, or of sin, or of some energy that must be given form.

God killing himself, in Elias Merhige's *Begotten* (1989).

As an artist, I've always felt that violence exists on many different levels. When I see flowers or grass coming through concrete or brick walls, I know that violence has occurred. Yes, it has taken place over a long period of time, but still there is destruction, a violent display. It's always form revealing itself, form wanting itself seen and assessed. Life is always struggling for recognition from its surroundings, and it's there to validate those surroundings.

MacDonald: The journey of these characters seems endless, as does your commitment in the style. Is it fair to say that the figure we follow during *Begotten* is a metaphor for you making the film, for your dragging yourself through this process?

Merhige: Sure, but also for the viewer's experience of *seeing* the film.

MacDonald: One of the things that I think keeps the audience in the theater is that you can't quite see what you're seeing. The combination of the strange characters and actions and the dense texture creates movements and rhythms that you can't quite identify. We think, "Oh God, that looks like a rape!" but we're not sure.

Merhige: It's amazing. A member of the audience will always come up after the film and say, "You know, there were a couple scenes that I didn't understand." I'll ask the person, "Well, what do *you* think was going on?" They will invariably say *exactly* what I scripted. They've *never* misinterpreted it. There's a very peculiar and fascinating psychological process going on, of simultaneous release and repression. On the one hand, they *see* it, but on the other hand, they don't want to see it. These polarities are at odds with each other. I'm sure many people feel, "This film could mean different things to different people." And in some ways it does, but it's not like you just provide your own meaning to the material—not at all. There *is* a story being told and everybody *is* getting it, but whether you choose to talk about it is another issue.

MacDonald: Since the first time through we have no particular identifications for any of these characters at least until the credits, all we can do is see them as generic actors in some kind of primal activity.

Merhige: They are what they are on the screen, but they also function as metaphors for forces at work within our society, that seem at one moment ready to just tear our world asunder and the next moment willing to allow us a few more days. As a society, we're on a kind of precipice now, where we all feel this anxiety about where we're going. Life is simultaneously renaissance *and* imminent disaster, whether we're talking about forces of man against man, or man against nature.

MacDonald: My class [a class in horror film at Utica College] and I developed a rough allegorical plotline for *Begotten*: God (the idea of God) dies giving birth to (the idea of) Nature, or God-as-Nature; and then Mother Nature is raped, but survives and continues as best she can. These events suggest a historical overview of attitudes popular in North America and Europe during the past few centuries. Is this anything like what you had in mind?

Merhige: The fact that *Begotten* conjures the ideas outlined by your class discussion *is* the story. *Begotten* is a chrysalis made of archetypal materials, gestures, and forces that defy the "moral" and rational structure of meaning. The film is a launching pad for the mind, a "watering hole" where the imagination drinks to intoxication. The drama of *Begotten* is in the anthropomorphic rendering of forces that nobody can touch or see, but are there right at the edge of every moment—in the film, they're right at the edge of your perceptions. The twentieth-century mind has become estranged from the very foundation of creation. *Begotten* is not new; it finds its home in histories and ages when the Imagination was not fantasy, but in fact the substance of God. The historical narrative you've mentioned is the voice of the collective Imagination. This is precisely how *Begotten* works: it activates a bridge that runs between universals and individuals. In other words, *your* narrative is part of the same process that produced *Begotten*.

MacDonald: You shot *Begotten* in the Poughkeepsie [New York State] area?

Merhige: South of Poughkeepsie on construction sites, and in New Jersey and on Long Island. I befriended a few of the construction engineers and they were very helpful. During every step in the film, I found that obstacles that seemed insurmountable were overcome. I worked with some of the nicest people you could imagine, and I met amazing people as we produced the film.

MacDonald: Did you shoot the time-lapse material at the end?

Merhige: Yes.

MacDonald: At first, the viewer doesn't know what the scale is.

Merhige: Those little sprouts look like trees, and then in the next shot you see trees. The idea of perspective was very important to me in making the film. Where is up? Where is down? Is it day or night; is that the sun or the moon? There are moments in the film where I shoot a few millimeters of space, yet it looks like a canyon. And there are moments when the characters are so dwarfed by the landscape that you're wondering, "Is this animation?" At the end, when you see the farmers, they look huge, imposing, like giant mushrooms erupting out of the earth.

MacDonald: In general, how has *Begotten* been received?

Merhige: The audience's reaction to the film has been one of the most profound lessons I've ever gotten, both as an artist and as a human being. I've learned not only from people who have been very passionately in love with the film, but from people who have passionately hated the film: especially when they've written why they hated the film, they've been able to reveal all sorts of amazing stuff that I was not consciously in touch with at the time. That kind of relationship with an audience is very special and hard to describe. I love the opportunity to present *Begotten*. A lot of people last night really got what this movie is about. And what it's about is very complex. That's amazing—it really is.

When I finished the film, I felt sure it would be misunderstood and consigned to the underground again. I see it as a very serious, very beautiful work of art, but when it was first finished, I was always thinking, "What if everybody just laughs? What if they don't see *anything* in it?" There was always that possibility. The film is saying everything and it's a hairline away from saying nothing. Of course, that's its power and life: *Begotten* is *right on the edge* between snow on your television set and storytelling.

I've always felt very strongly that the film is alive, organic. I've seen it over and over again, and discover different things all the time. It's as if the film is constantly giving birth to itself, constantly metamorphosing. I figure that if I feel that way about it, then certainly other people can, too.

MacDonald: *Begotten* premiered at Film Forum in New York and showed at midnight screenings for a while, but then didn't show up in distribution. Why?

Merhige: In order to be a good distributor, you have to really understand the material you're working with. If, as the maker, you have a vision, then you need a distributor who sees similarly. Invariably, when I screened the film for distributors, they respected the film, but they couldn't put it into a niche. They couldn't say, "OK, this is a horror film, or a romantic comedy, or a musical." I think in the beginning that's what scared them the most. So I worked as its distributor and took it to a number of museums. The film did create its own publicity. In the end, there were two distributors interested in the film, but I didn't feel they were up to the job.

A distribution deal is in the works; I'm very excited about it because it involves someone who is not normally a distributor, taking the time to position the film so that it will be seen. The film should be remastered. The dub I have now is very good, but it could be better. The soundtrack was originally mixed in stereo, so there's a lot that you're not getting on the 16mm print. As a matter of fact, I almost cried when I heard what little came through on the optical track. Video would make a much better soundtrack possible, though to be perfectly honest, I never intended *Begotten* to be seen on video. For a while video repulsed me as a medium. Ideally, *Begotten* will get blown up to 35mm, in which case the integrity of the soundtrack *and* the integrity of the image would be retained.

MacDonald: Were particular films helpful to you in thinking through this project?

Merhige: *The Seven Samurai* [1957] was inspiring: Kurosawa's work in general, because of the explosiveness of each frame. I was very affected by Georges Franju's *Blood of the Beasts* [1949], which I saw at your homage to Cinema 16 at Film Forum in 1988 (I went to that program more than once), and Brakhage's *The Act of Seeing with One's Own Eyes* [1971]. And certainly *The Cabinet of Dr. Caligari* [1919]: I've always admired its obsessiveness, its creation of an obviously fictional, but somehow real town. That certainly had an effect on how *Begotten* creates its own world, a world that exists somewhere deep in the imagination and somewhere underneath our landscape . . .

MacDonald: And in a sense somewhere underneath conventional cinema?

Merhige: Yes.

Aline Mare

(on *S'Aline's Solution*)

I first saw *S'Aline's Solution* (1991) when it toured as part of the 1992 Black Maria Film and Video Festival (an annual "festival" of independent video and 16mm film that tours in the spring of each year; the festival was organized in 1980 and is run by John Columbus). I was impressed by the courage of Mare's meditations on her own saline abortion—and amazed to realize that, after decades of national debate about the morality and legality of abortion, and despite hundreds of thousands of particular instances of women struggling with their decisions to abort pregnancies, Mare's was the first video (or film) I was aware of that explored the complex emotions experienced by a woman who has chosen not to carry a pregnancy to term. That her tape focuses on saline abortion in particular, made it all the more surprising and confrontational.

S'Aline's Solution is neither apology nor polemic; it is a melodramatic meditation during which Mare attempts to make imaginative contact with the developing fetuses she has aborted. Mare intercuts between film and video imagery stolen from conventional, and often quite beautiful, explorations of the process of conception and birth—including highly magnified images of a journey through a vagina into a uterus and of a developing fetus—and her own attempts to perform as a fetus (see accompanying still from *S'Aline's Solution*). The implicit danger of Mare's topic is dramatized by her use of suspenseful music, by the eerie close-ups of the fetus's partially formed face (a face reminiscent of horror film monsters and sci-fi aliens), and, near the end, by a startling shot of a normal delivery presented in reverse, so that the baby is shoved back into the vagina.

Mare's decision to express her complex combination of guilt, sorrow, and relief in a manner that does not conform to either of the polemical, self-righteous attitudes usually expressed in the public debate over abortion, but that suggests, instead, a whistling-in-the-dark sense of humor and an implicit pride in her own sensuality, is disconcerting both for those opposed to abortion in any form and for those committed to Choice who are resistant to too close a personal "interaction" with the fetus.

I spoke with Mare on August 9, 1993, the day following a somewhat volatile discussion of *S'Aline's Solution* at the 1993 Flaherty Film Seminar (Mare was invited by John Columbus as part of a Flaherty retrospective of the Black Maria Festival).

MacDonald: When I first saw *S'Aline's Solution*, I was terrified for you as maker and protagonist in the tape. I had the same kind of reaction I do during a horror film when I've identified enough with a woman character to be frightened when she moves into the darkened space where the slasher is hiding. What I wonder is how dangerous *S'Aline's Solution* felt when you were making it.

Mare: I've always accepted the challenge of facing the forbidden. As a human being and as an artist, I'm very drawn to taboo. I'm drawn to it because I really have no choice. It's like being led in the dark, a kind of compulsive behavior. You mentioned fear: I'm instinctively drawn to the kind of beauty that is horrific. And I, myself, never get past that experience in *S'Aline's Solution*. Every time I look at the tape, and I've looked at it innumerable times, I can't leave; I *have* to look and I *can't* look. That's especially true of the perverse birthing imagery, which is so simple and yet so profound. That kind of terror is exactly what forces me to make art; the work has to have that dimension or I'm not interested.

I come out of performance. For years, I worked with Bradley Eros on work known as *Erotic Psyche*. Our collaboration mainly dealt with a kind of mythic unraveling of sexual consciousness. It was much more transformative and hallucinatory and visionary than my work is now, or was before. I broke through boundaries with Bradley and got into the world of the uncanny and forbidden. The other work that I showed yesterday [*Cassandra, Seething at the Mouth*, 1985] came from that period of performance work.

I started out working with the body—excremental kinds of imagery—and moved into a sexual zone, which was hot and heavy in New York City in the late seventies and in the eighties. I have quite a sordid history and a huge body of work to show for it. During my six years with Bradley, we made ten or twelve tapes, which were shown more in Europe than here—mostly appropriated, wild, spitting forth kind of stuff, dark and macabre.

S'Aline's Solution, too, existed first as performance and installation. For three years, I'd been haunted by these images of embryonic creatures, imagery I've stolen or appropriated from the Right. That undefined embryonic face, neither human nor animal, had haunted my nightmares, and many other people's, I'm sure.

The whole body of work is what I called "humunculus." It comes out of the Middle Ages when the alchemists were trying to create a human life form in a bottle. And that itself can be traced back further in cabalistic Jewish lore to the golem figure.

What became *S'Aline's Solution* started, of course, with myself and with experiencing, in my younger years, more abortions than I care to count. But I had always been drawn to the notion of life forms outside of the body, ghosts— "Creatures of the Imagination," I called them. And I was haunted, totally haunted. So I gathered this painful, *painful* imagery together. To *have* to make work, to be *compelled* to do it is an excruciating weight to carry.

MacDonald: What was the nature of the installation?

Mare: There were several variations, but generally I was interested in faces that were mixtures of animal and human. A lot were monkey and some were human and they were fairly indistinguishable, as they are in early developmental stages. And they were all behind glass, in glass bottles, the same as in *S'Aline's Solution*, all distorted and lit from within. And I used rock salt like crazy. I embedded myself in rock salt. Somebody told me people were referring to me as the Salt Lady.

So I did a lot of performances. The best I think were the ones where I performed in cavernous, belly-like, chemical-laboratory-looking, eerie places. I integrated slides into these performances. The slides are amazing—nothing quite as specific as on the tape, and even more terrifying, less human. That was what I was going after in all the homunculus work.

MacDonald: Did you use voice in the performances and installations? In the tape the voice both identifies you and dramatizes your attempt to deal with the complex emotions during and after abortion. I think part of what shakes people up about *S'Aline's Solution* is the sensuality in your voice as you talk about aborting the fetus. It seems part of the tape's stance that you *don't* give up your sensuality.

Mare: Well, I made the tape at the end of almost three years working with this material. I combined my voice with the imagery, first in slide format, then in a photographic installation format, and finally in the video. Producing the tape wasn't a painful process, the way works that take years are; it was spit out in three months. But in terms of the "research" involved, the real-life experience, that's not measurable in time. I think sensuality is a challenge for someone like me—how to speak a visceral language, a convulsive language, a language that seduces and repulses at the same time. I also want to sound as if I were in a trance. I do certain kinds of shamanic, trance work. I think ritual is seriously lacking from our lives. Even the communal experience of *seeing* film for me is a kind of public audience ritual that is lacking when people are home looking at movies on their little VCRs.

MacDonald: That's been my real resistance to video. I love the public experience of confronting film. This sort of transgressive work only *feels* transgressive if you're in a public space.

Mare: Basically, I agree with you. When I go to the gallery and see that little dark room for the video art, I walk right on by. And I *make* video art! We videomakers have been waiting for years for projection systems to come up to speed. Coming out of film, I've found that problem especially annoying. But then, that's another challenge.

MacDonald: One of the most interesting things you said yesterday was that you felt you unconsciously appropriated certain imagery to use in the tape so that you would *not* be able to show the finished tape in certain anti-Choice venues.

Mare: Perhaps I was protecting not just myself, but the pro-Choice movement, which I feel *so strongly* about. What has horrified me the most about my tape—and I didn't get much of this yesterday—is people saying, "There is no way we think you're pro-Choice." Even though I say over and over, "my body, my choice," my stand on abortion rights has seemed ambiguous to some women. I want people to have the option to make the decision with the full consciousness of that power and of the struggle of deciding between life and death, both of which are sacred.

MacDonald: Where have you had the most negative responses?

Mare: In San Francisco. Gay activists. Angry, female audiences. Of course, this work has gone out, and I've not always had feedback. I heard that when it toured with the Black Maria, there were some real intense discussions.

I wonder about that. *Does* the work maintain its integrity and its power if I'm not present with it? You saw it without me.

MacDonald: Well, I thought it worked very powerfully, and it was clear to me that you are pro-Choice. What stuns pro-Choice audiences, I think, is that on some level, the tape cuts through all the verbal debate and faces what it *is* we're actually talking about when we discuss abortion. That's generally been a pro-Life tactic, but I can't imagine a pro-Choice person who wouldn't agree that abortion is, at best, an unfortunate and painful option.

Mare: Well, at this point I've kind of backed off and moved on. I've let The Kitchen [a center for video production, exhibition, and distribution in New York City] handle the tape. Since Bush is out of office, I feel a breath of relief about the whole issue.

MacDonald: Who do you see as important influences on your work?

Mare: Artaud, early on. Maya Deren. Cocteau. Carolee's [Carolee Schneemann's] work is important to someone like me: she's been out there *so long*. Karen Finley has been a good friend and an important force. I've also been very influenced by French feminist theorizing about the voice of the repressed, about the privileged position women find themselves in, by being excluded from society—if you can grasp hold of that position and speak from there.

MacDonald: Your video influences?

Mare: They're vast, from Nam June Paik, whom I studied with, on. Before making video, I made silent, black and white, hand-developed structural films. I was a purist! It seems to have taken *so* long for the film community—*you're* an example—to adjust to video. Recently I assisted editing a 35mm film, and, after editing video, it seemed so prehistoric. I think video is absolutely the future, for people like me anyway. Even in earlier work video was as important as film. Bradley and I shot mostly in Super-8. And then we would blow it up or shoot it off the wall or, if we could afford to, transfer it onto video. We went back and forth between the mediums as much as possible. Nobody knew what to call it.

In my early films I did have a very tangible, sculptural kind of relationship with the film material, which I miss in video.

MacDonald: The transformation of appropriated film into video fits *S'Aline's Solution*, which is very much about the evolution and transformation of the fetus and of the woman who becomes pregnant. The one medium is inside the other, which, however—in at least once sense—gave birth to it.

Mare: Oh, that's interesting!

MacDonald: When I first saw *S'Aline's Solution*, I had just had a sigmoidoscopy. One of the weird things about having that procedure these days is that you're awake, and when they send the video camera up your anus to look at your colon, you can watch! You're simultaneously outside and inside your own body! Frankly, my video (which I didn't have sense enough to keep, damn it!) looks very much like the imagery in your tape of going through the vagina. Is any of your medical footage *of* you, or is it all appropriated?

Mare: No, none of that is me—I wish it was. I stole what I needed. I took what I could find, and I slowed it down. That's really all I did to it, other than add a layer of the personal, which that original material entirely lacks.

MacDonald: The footage of sperm and ova, and of embryos and fetuses is visually stunning. In its sensual beauty, it seems to serve a birth-at-all-costs message. But the tone of your voice and the music suggest the opposite. I was surprised to hear someone say yesterday that he wanted more of a critique of the conventional use of beauty in the birth material you use. I can't imagine a more confrontational critique than your soundtrack.

Mare: I call myself a media thief. I've appropriated film and video for so long—but I'm interested not just in stealing it, but in transforming and claiming it as mine. That's the challenge.

MacDonald: Your use of reverse to create an un-birth is startling. In general, reverse is undiscovered territory, except for Cocteau and a few others.

Mare: Backwards is fascinating and so is fast-forward. Speeding up is just as scary as slowing things down. As one ages, one is so much more aware of that.

MacDonald: I think my favorite moment in *S'Aline's Solution* is the statement, "These are dangerous times." It reverberates on so many levels. It's about

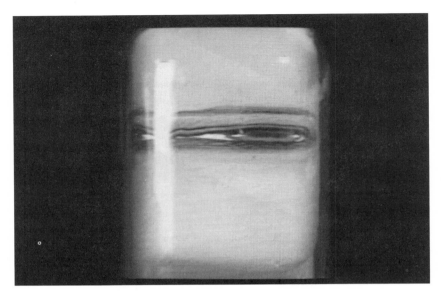

Aline Mare performing as the fetus she aborted, in *S'Aline's Solution* (1991).

abortion and about showing the tape. There are some films and videos that are scary to show, even if you didn't make them: the Otto Mühl, Kurt Kren "materialactionfilms" for example.

Mare: Those are scary fucking films!

For me, there is another extreme, of vileness and self-indulgence, which I really draw a line at, at least for myself. Like early Joe Coleman biting the heads off rats. I really want sensuality to radiate through what I do, though it's got to be dirty on some level. I've wondered about that in myself. I've wondered if that's not just an adolescent thing.

Someone asked me once, "Is that child laughing or crying?" That's an edge I'm always interested in: to laugh so hard you cry, or cry so hard you're laughing, or feel so uncomfortable that you have lapses of reality. I'll struggle again in the next work to *not* know how I feel.

MacDonald: There's an instance in *S'Aline's Solution* where you go so far as to act out the fetus; you go from a close-up of the fetus to your "fetal" face through distorting glass. It's beyond *facing* what you've done; it's *identifying* with it.

Mare: But that really is the point for me. I'm interested in getting under the skin. I appreciate all the theory in the world, but I think that to make the kind of work I make, you have to take a leap off the deep end. I don't recommend it for most people, because I, myself, have gone off the deep end and under, several times now.

MacDonald: How do you mean?

Mare: Working on the boundary between life and art is dangerous. It's not just the *issues* that are dangerous—and I am drawn to dangerous issues like rape, madness, abortion—it's being submerged in such work and taking the chance of losing your foundations. The piece I'm doing now is all about my breakdown last year. Now, I can laugh and say again, "I had to do some private research," but I don't *recommend* that kind of research. Those of us who work in this kind of area, who flirt with the darkness of our own psyches, don't always come out OK. You don't always know you're going to wake up tomorrow and be able to move on. When my work is effective, I guess it's that terrifying reality that you're picking up on.

Cauleen Smith

(on Chronicles of a Lying Spirit
(by Kelly Gabron))

In North America few groups have had as little access to filmmaking as African-American women, who were virtually invisible in film history—except, of course, as performers—until the late 1970s and Jackie Shearer's *A Minor Altercation* (1977), Julie Dash's *Four Women* (1977) and *Illusions* (1983), Ayoka Chenzira's *Syvilla: They Dance to Her Drum* (1975) and *Hair Piece: A Film for Nappyheaded People* (1984), and Kathleen Collins's *Losing Ground* (1983). In general, these filmmakers, and the younger generation that has followed in their footsteps—Zeinabu irene Davis, Cheryl Dunye, and Portia Cobb among others—have often seemed less interested in making it commercially than in providing critiques of conventional imagery of black women: even Julie Dash's box-office success, *Daughters of the Dust* (1991), makes little attempt to conform to traditional genre conventions for melodrama. Many of the critiques have taken the form of documentary, but in recent years especially, some filmmakers have begun to use approaches more akin to avant-garde filmmaking. The single most impressive instance of this tendency I am aware of is Cauleen Smith's *Chronicles of a Lying Spirit (by Kelly Gabron)* (1992).

Like some of the more recent films of Trinh T. Minh-ha, one of Smith's mentors at San Francisco State University, *Chronicles of a Lying Spirit (by Kelly Gabron)* is less a depiction of "reality" than an exploration of the implications of the mediation of history by film, television, magazines, and newspapers. Using her alter ego, "Kelly Gabron," Smith fabricates a personal chronicle of her emergence as an artist from white-male-dominated American history. Smith collages images and bits of text from a scrapbook "by Kelly Gabron" that had been completed before the film was begun, and provides the female narration *by* Kelly Gabron that, slowly but surely, makes itself felt over the male narration *about* Kelly Gabron (Chris Brown is the male voice). The film's barrage of image, text, and voice is repeated twice, and is followed by a coda. That most viewers see the second presentation of the imagery differently from the original presentation demonstrates one problem with trusting any media representation of any one individual.

In February 1994, I sent a list of questions and comments to Smith. She recorded her responses on voice tape. The transcriptions of the tape and my questions and comments were combined and edited. In the fall of 1995 Smith sent a number of revisions and additions, which were incorporated into the conversation that follows.

MacDonald: When *Chronicles of a Lying Spirit* was presented at the Flaherty Film Seminar in August 1992, it was so popular that seminar attendees demanded it be re-shown. What I think made the film so strong for that audience is its achievement in being (at least) two things at once. On one hand, it speaks from and to a particular racial heritage in a manner that is simultaneously aware of the past (both of the events of the past and of past depictions of race) and excited about the future. And, on the other hand, its visuals and soundtrack are complex and ambiguous: you avoid the clichés of traditional depictions of African-Americans by both European-Americans and African-Americans.

Smith: I had no idea that *Chronicles* was so well-received at the Flaherty. I wish I'd been there. But what you bring up about my avoiding clichéd depictions of African-Americans by both European- and African-Americans is important to me. In the mainstream media that I see produced by Afro-Americans, and even in stuff by independents, there's an inability to see ourselves for who we are. Even *we* see ourselves through a shroud of racism. Hopefully, with more and better media, we can heal, but the idea that there are only certain ways to depict black people is the real problem. Think of all the kinds of European-American characters there are. But it's rare when you see someone take a chance in casting African-Americans. Even black people have a narrow idea of what kind of story we'll like, a narrow idea of what we do, what's PC for us to do, and what's progressive.

We have such heavy weights on our shoulders in terms of our responsibility to an audience that we become blinded and revert to the same safe, tired, distorted images that have been traditionally used against us. We tend to rely on images that have become coded cultural icons, images that operate as stereotypes in the minds of a white audience. It becomes difficult for us to consider contextualizing ourselves outside of what mainstream media have permitted us in the past. Movies are coming out that are increasing the number of genres in which black actors play pivotal roles. But I constantly struggle to create ideas for interesting protagonists and to flesh them out. If you take people too far off the standard mark, they become confused and resentful, rightfully so if the character has no bottom; but if you give them what they are used to, the character suffocates in the defecation of history: as [Jean-Michel] Basquiat put it, "SOS: same old shit."

I'm lucky. Because of my background, I can see things in many different ways. I know that the fact that Afro-American culture is imitated globally says something about our diversity and our creativity and our eccentricity. One amazing thing that I'm grateful for is that our community has a huge capacity and compassion for eccentric individuals. We embrace them. So it would be refreshing for *everyone* for us to show ourselves in ways that we've never shown ourselves before. It would be a breath of fresh air. For me, it's fun to try not to be shackled by my fears of the stereotypes.

One reason why I resist theory is because theory seems to enslave the people who make it. They become prisoners of language, and get caught up in words and will talk semantics about any little thing—and just miss the point. Once we stop and analyze the semantics of a magazine cover—once we've broken it down and understand how it's working consciously, subconsciously, insidiously—can we then subvert that formula later on? It's one thing to express what's happening on a magazine cover, but *then* what are you going to do? If I can't create a formula for *practice*, then I have to leave it alone.

MacDonald: On one hand, *Chronicles* is a very political film, both issue-political and media-political, *and* it's a sensually pleasurable film. I don't know if I would have put it this way had I not seen your video, *The Message* [1993], but the viewer's experience of your physical voice in both films is similarly powerful. In fact, your voice in *Chronicles* is at least as sensual as it is in the more openly erotic *The Message.* When I think back on *Chronicles*, your saying certain sentences and phrases is what most stays with me ("I know now that the only way *I'm* going to get on TV is to make my *own* goddamn tapes and play them for my*self!*" for example).

Was your narration as one of two narrators, a "black voice" correcting the inaccuracies of a "white (male) voice," the original inspiration for the film?

Smith: My voice is not necessarily so much about correcting the white male voice as about competing for a space. Even though the gentle voice of Chris Brown, another filmmaker, is benevolent, it is still the Voice of God, the voice of authority. My voice is the buzzing fly, the annoyance you want to slap and silence. In the beginning, Chris's voice has control. It's setting the pace. But then my voice starts pushing up underneath his until it's on top, and by the end of the film, I win. I'm not *reacting* to what he's saying, I'm just setting my own pace and letting my voice rise in importance. It's *my* movie to be victorious in by just going on about my business. I'm proceeding with the truth that *I* know, and in the end, the white voice stops. The male narrator may seem to have the last word, "Sound out," but even if *he* thinks the movie is over, it continues regardless of what he says. The water just keeps going downstream without him. The life force continues.

MacDonald: Do you have a history of working with your voice artistically—your physical voice, I mean—that precedes your filmmaking?

Smith: Whenever I record sound for my films, I do it at home, alone, late at night, and that probably affects the way my voice sounds. I'm very self-conscious and I don't like to act; I can't read other people's stuff worth a damn. I've tried, because people do seem to have an interest in the quality of my voice, but I can't get it to work with other people's writing. I can't really say I work with my voice or know what I'm doing with it. I just know how I want what I write to sound, but obviously that's not unique, either. It just seems organic that my voice affects my images that way. I love color and texture; and I'm constantly drawing the viewer's eye with color and texture. I think that helps cause my voice to seem sensual.

The best way I've found to loosen up my voice is to tell jokes and laugh. I've been in a couple of plays and the other actors would be in the back going, "kuh, kuh, kuh; sah, sah, sah; ti-la-la-de-dah," over and over at different volumes. But I'd just be in the dressing room laughing at my own bad jokes. By the time I had my costume and makeup on, I'd be all warmed up. I guess that's my tip: you don't always have to be so disciplined and methodical. It's difficult for me to work within a set structure, even though I love structure. Once something is organized, once I know how it's going to go down, then I really like to bust loose within it. I like boundaries, but I don't like rules. I think that works well for someone who likes to do experimental film.

MacDonald: Your combination of the personality of your voice, and the exciting, often witty, barrage of image, sound, and visual text suggests two traditions of American avant-garde film: personal, "diary" film; and the more "postmodern" involvement with images of images and images of texts. Your voice makes the film intimate, even as the refusal of conventional cinematic movement (all that really moves are the photographs and the visual texts) refuses traditional devices for rendering commercial films "moving." Can you talk about your history as a filmgoer? How much independent film have you seen?

Smith: You know, there was this movie theater near my house that played two-dollar, mostly B movies. So I've seen a lot of those, but very little avant-garde, experimental film. I don't go see it as much as I should. I enjoy it every time I do, even though I'm also very frustrated by it and don't identify at all with the history of experimental film. Sometimes I even resent being called an experimental filmmaker because I don't like to be in a ghetto. Of course, experimental filmmakers always seem to be trying to get out of that ghetto and still maintain their identity, and I *totally* identify with that.

I'm down with X Factor [a Bay Area advocacy group for experimental media artists] in San Francisco, really down with them, because they're about getting the funding, getting the exposure, and still maintaining the integrity of being on the cutting edge of visual media. I don't feel that *I'm* on the cutting edge *technically*, because everything in my work has been done before. Everything. I don't try to do anything new—no new optical printing tricks, nothing like that. I think what makes my work refreshing is that I do an inner voice that hasn't gotten out yet.

I don't mind if my work is called "personal" or "diary," but even though there's a lot of me *in* these films, I hesitate to say that they're *about* me. And people who enjoy them understand what I'm talking about because they find *themselves* in the films. I want people to find room in my films for themselves. And in essence that's not personal and certainly not diary, because in my *diary* there's no room for anyone *but* me.

I don't even like to talk about postmodernism, even though I'm definitely a product of it. My generation [Smith was born in 1967] is postmodern in the way we can take in information on a lot of different planes at once. So I'm definitely on that wave, whether I like it or not. Plus, I love popular culture. I watch a lot of TV. I love pop almost as much as I love jazz. I have to breathe it all in.

MacDonald: Have particular filmmakers been important for your films?

Smith: I hate to say no one, because that's not true; but I'm always feeling that I need to go see more work so that somebody *can* influence me. The purpose of my making films is so different from most of the people who started out making experimental films, and who still make them, that I just get bored and disgusted. That's a terrible attitude and I've got to change. I feel the same way about having to watch *Citizen Kane* [1941]. Welles and the other canonized filmmakers don't interest me. It's not like I can *ever* follow in their footsteps, so why bother playing in their sandbox?

That's the wannabe commercial filmmaker in me talking, the filmmaker who is acutely aware that film is much more of a business than anyone cares to admit, even in the belly of the beast here in LA [Smith moved from San Francisco to LA in 1994 to begin graduate studies in the film department at UCLA]. The experimental, indie, marginal filmmaker in me is supported by the same folks everybody else admires: Maya Deren, Barbara Hammer, Carol Parrot Blue, Haile Gerima, Julie Dash. The thing that energizes me about underfunded, underexposed work is the way it blows my mind, totally expanding the cinematic possibilities.

There are some brilliant people out there, cranking out temples to the muse every day, and not just in film. I live in Hollywood. In this area, there's a gang turf tag on the street right now that's amazing. Some kid took a can of spray paint and went wild with it: the Roman numeral XVII seems to snake all over the sidewalk. I would love to make an image move the way he or she did. The things that touch me most deeply are not movies. I'm always just trying to step up to the brilliance I see everywhere (and the ugliness too).

MacDonald: In general how has *Chronicles* been received?

Smith: Surprisingly well by both black and white audiences, and I do think of those audiences as distinct in a lot of ways, and wanting to see the work for very different reasons. It got a lot of play in the San Francisco film community, which has been very supportive, enthusiastic really. On the other hand a lot of black film festivals have not been supportive. Blacklight rejected it. Black Filmmakers Hall of Fame rejected it. The National Black Programming Consortium did give it a special award. When I show the film and am present at the screening to talk about it, then people are very receptive—and anxious to discuss it, which to me is the most important thing.

I can't help but worry that I'm going to put somebody off, or that somebody is going to just think the film is shit and that I'm an incompetent—how *dare* I call myself a filmmaker? There are a lot of people I hope never see my work, because I may need something from them they won't want to give me if they believe I'm just going to take a bunch of Polaroids and bust out a soundtrack on a four-track. Black folks are looking for their Rob Reiner, their Steven Spielberg. They want to sit and be seduced and manipulated the same way that white folks get to be. It's depressing, but true: everybody is looking for *that* kind of talent.

MacDonald: Experimental film is often attacked as "elitist" by those who don't engage with it. Has *Chronicles* been attacked that way?

Smith: No one has ever called the film "elitist," to my knowledge. Many people just say it's confusing, that they didn't get it, and ask, "What did this mean? What did that mean?" Some people get angry and don't want to watch the film—I know that happens—and those are the people who are silent during discussions. But I've never really been attacked.

I decided to include a repetition of nearly the whole film in the finished film [two minutes fourteen seconds is repeated] because when I was showing it to people in the fine cut on the flatbed, the first thing they would do, before commenting on the film, was to rewind and watch it again. Finally, somebody suggested that I just play it twice. He's an experimental filmmaker, and to him this seemed a perfectly normal thing to do: just play it twice so people can get it. The repetition has often been interpreted as some sort of rebellious statement. And some people are convinced that the second, repeated sequence is different than the first. It does *feel* different because your mind takes in different things the second time.

At no point in *Chronicles* did I want to go over anybody's head. I *always* wanted to communicate. That's my purpose. And I wanted the people to know that. So if the film goes by in two minutes, fourteen seconds, and you don't get it, I'll play it again so you *can* get it. That's all. Some people get it the first time, people who can process four layers of soundtrack efficiently—something I'm sure I couldn't do!

MacDonald: Might it be fair to say that *Chronicles* is an attempt to visualize your struggle with the many heritages you are part of: your heritage as an

African-American, as a suburbanite [Smith was born in Riverside], as a film-maker, as an *independent* filmmaker, and that the multilayered nature of the film represents the complexity of the mixture of personality and cultural influence you can't help but try to come to grips with? Or to put it more simply: could we say that your film is a *clear* expression of the *ambiguity* of the experience of living and working in America?

Smith: *Chronicles* was really fun to make in part because it was truth *and* out-and-out lies combined, written history *and* oral history combined. It's my theory, I guess, that black women have always been doing incredible things throughout history and that we've been able to do these things in part because no one pays much attention to us. While you can feel—I hate to use the word—disempowered by being invisible, I think a lot of women have been resourceful in making invisibility a shield that protects them while they do and experience amazing things. *Chronicles* was an homage to all the accomplished black women in global history who are not documented anywhere.

I think it's interesting that everybody likes the line "I'm gonna make my own goddamn tapes and play them for myself." This always inspires a chuckle. No one seems to hear the hunger there. The ambition. And ambition I believe is a dangerous thing if it isn't controlled and fed steadily, and carefully. There is a layer beyond the different aspects of history and identity in the movie. How can you work when you're desperately trying to get into a whole different school of fish? Bigger, fatter, uglier fish that lead bigger, fatter, and more comfortable lives. There's a part of me that's in awe of the power of my ancestors and all that we have accomplished and survived, and there's a part of me that wants to turn into the very thing that I struggle against. If someone is going to control my image, I want to be there. But I wonder how to get there without becoming bloated and flatulent and sitting in a mansion watching myself on TV.

MacDonald: About the double naming: *Chronicles of a Lying Spirit (by Kelly Gabron)* by Cauleen Smith. How did that come about?

Smith: *Chronicles* developed out of a class assignment given by Lynn Hershman, my teacher at the time. The project was originally a performance and as part of the performance, a book was created from Polaroids I took and other materials. I liked the Polaroids so much that I decided to use them in a film, and had an opportunity to use the Oxberry [an optical printer used for 35mm and 16mm film] at San Francisco State.

The original assignment was to tell your life story twice, using the same materials both times. The first time you told the story, it was to be fiction, the second time, truth. In my film, the soundtrack creates that double sense of the materials. When I was planning the film, I thought, "If I'm going to tell a fictional version of my life, who will I be?" I decided I would be Kelly Gabron, a superhero.

Kelly is a woman traveling through many different times. She's "the Ancestor" and the culmination of all these women I talked about before. "Kelly" is a

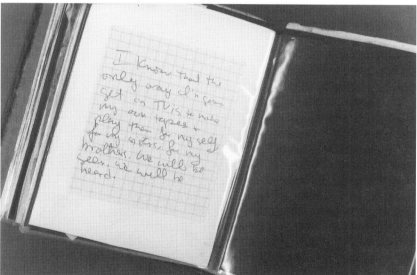

Pages of the scrapbook Cauleen Smith transformed into *Chronicles of a Lying Spirit (by Kelly Gabron)* (1992).

name I've often used when I don't want people to know my real name and "Gabron" is a distortion of Kahlil Gibran, the poet/philosopher/painter who wrote *The Prophet*. "Kelly Gabron" is an alter ego, in a sense. Of course, the whole film is by me, Cauleen Smith: Kelly's chronicles are *by me*.

Doesn't history have to be documented or written by someone even just to become history? If someone doesn't interpret it and lock it down somehow, it's like it's not really there, like it isn't real, as if I imagined what I know is real. So I couldn't just let the story of my ancestors dangle out there. I think I might have been hoping that the implication of my physical presence validated their spiritual presence. Pretty arrogant.

MacDonald: There's a long history of the use of visual text in film. *Chronicles* uses lots of visual text, but differently from most other films that do: here, the text is generally not meant to be read in the normal left-to-right way. From time to time, we read a word or a phrase as we are hearing you say it. But generally, our seeing the text is an index to your process, more than a conventional source of information. This reference to the filmmaking process is also obvious in the repetition of the first section of the film, since the viewer can't help but notice the repetition *as repetition*, and the process is evident at the end when the male narrator says "Sound out" and the sound doesn't go out, and in other ways as well. You could say that *Chronicles* is about a person-in-process, a person-as-process.

Smith: I would like to do a film where people in the audience are reading and have to be excited about the *reading* in order to find out what's happening in the movie. But in this film the text was a visual thing. It *looked* really good. So you're right about that. (All I had to do was copy on acetate the script that I had written.) And I wanted you as a viewer to know, even if you didn't have time to read, that there was a connection between what you were hearing and what you were seeing, that the juxtapositions are not random.

The film is very much about process, on very simple levels: the process of learning how to use an Oxberry, the process of understanding animation and how to do it and how not to do it, of learning to use lights and backlighting. So we have a film that was a learning process, and a processing of identity; and then we have the filmmaker continually processing the film, not even sure why people dig it, just trying to answer the questions in some kind of coherent fashion. Still processing how she wants to create and for whom. We're talking about an object/film that only lives if people watch, because for me it was one stage in a long process of continual development.

John Porter

For some film artists who have chosen to work in Super-8mm (and before that, 8mm), the use of the smallest film gauge has been political, a choice for a more democratic access to the means of production than has been possible for those working in 35mm or even in 16mm. But because the accessibility of Super-8 exhibition has never kept pace with the accessibility of Super-8 cameras (even many of those venues devoted to the exhibition of critical forms of film have refused to invest in high quality Super-8 equipment), this more democratic access to cameras has tended to produce small, "tribal" communities of small-gauge enthusiasts, devoted to that body of institutionally overlooked work that demonstrates the aesthetic viability of small-gauge production. The most interesting Super-8 work I've seen tends to reflect one of two aesthetic attitudes. The most common of these is that whatever Super-8 seems to lack in quality of image compared to the wider gauges (this distinction is itself problematic, since it has as much to do with the mediocre quality of most Super-8 projectors—specifically their use of less powerful lamps—as with the filmstrip), it allows more people to make more of the types of films that are made in 16mm and 35mm. Indeed, Super-8 may be the appropriate gauge for some of these types of film. For example, while the "diary film" developed in 16mm—Jonas Mekas's *Walden* (1969) and *Lost Lost Lost* (1976); Andrew Noren's *Huge Pupils* (1968); and Robert Huot's *Rolls 1971* (1972) are distinguished instances—Super-8, the modern, pre-video, home-movie gauge, is as least as fitting for the form's implicit domestic intimacy, as is clear in Anne Robertson's ongoing *Diary* (currently over forty hours long) and in Carolee Schneemann's two-image *Kitch's Last Meal* (presented in various versions, 1973–78).

If most Super-8 filmmakers have used the smaller gauge because it allows them the economic opportunity to make films that are as interesting as they could make in 16mm (or at least interesting enough), a few have gone further, and have produced films that would be more difficult, if not impossible, to make in 16mm or 35mm. Perhaps the earliest American filmmakers to accomplish this were George and Mike Kuchar, whose collaborative 8mm melodramas are enjoyable precisely because of the gap between their makeshift mise-en-scène and the film industry products they "imitate," a gap emphasized by their using the home-movie gauge. While the Kuchar brothers transformed the limitations of 8mm into poignant humor—that is, into "limitations"—the Canadian John Porter has gone a step further: in some of his most memorable films he has turned the "limitations" into strengths.

To date, Porter has made more than two hundred films, nearly all of them silent and most of them quite short (usually two or three minutes). These films can be grouped into three roughly distinct categories. The largest number of the films are "Condensed Rituals," as Porter calls them, made by using the time-lapse option of his Super-8 camera. They record a wide variety of personal and public events. Because of Porter's careful choice of topic and framing, many of these are inventive and revealing: *Mother and Child* (1977), for example, records a mother's nurturing of her young child, who, like most babies, is in virtually perpetual motion; *Amusement Park* (1979) transforms the rides at Toronto's Ontario Place into a visual phantasmagoria; and *Two Women* (1976) transforms everyday gestures into dance. Of course, the Condensed Rituals do not provide an experience peculiar to Super-8: time-lapsing is possible in all gauges, even if few filmmakers have used it as extensively and imaginatively as Porter has. However, the other two categories of Porter's films break new ground.

Since the very beginning of his filmmaking career, Porter has made both the "Condensed Rituals" and a series of "Camera Dances": in some instances, he creates unusual visual experiences by moving the camera in novel ways while it is recording at twenty-four frames per second; in other instances, Porter designs a space and performs in front of his time-lapsing camera. One of the most inventive and memorable of the Camera Dances is *Cinefuge*, which Porter first made in 1974—though an effect in the earlier, 16mm *Independent Filmmaking* (1974) is very similar—and has re-made several times, including a 1979 sound version used to advertise an upcoming show of his work at The Funnel (a now-defunct independent screening space in Toronto). For each version of *Cinefuge*, Porter attaches his camera to some sort of cord and, standing in a fixed position, turns so that the camera flies around him with the lens pointing at his face, which in the finished film is seen in focus and seemingly still as the world flies past him in a blur. For most viewers, *Cinefuge*, in all its versions, is a fascinating mystery. The lightweight portability of Super-8 is also imaginatively exploited in *Down On Me* (1981), for which Porter devised a means of lowering the camera from the roof of a building or from the top of several flights of stairs down to where he stands on the ground or at the base of the stairs, looking up. As the camera ascends and descends, it spins, creating kaleidoscopic mandalas.

In other Camera Dances, Porter uses techniques available to larger-gauge cameras to create lovely and magical effects and to surprise viewers' assumptions about what they're seeing. For *Angel Baby* (1979) Porter time-lapses himself from a camera mounted on the ceiling; dressed in a white outfit, lying on the floor, he moves arms and legs against a black background—creating an effect of flying reminiscent of Ed Emshwiller's *Thanatopsis* (1962). In *Firefly* (1980) Porter surprises viewers by pixilating himself [generally, "pixilation" refers to the frame by frame animation of human subjects or objects] sitting on a swing that moves left and right through and out of the frame; by editing cleverly, he produces the impression that he is flying over the top of the swing in a continuous 360 degree loop.

A final category of Porter films, one that has been developing in more recent years, involves Porter performing with the film as it is projected. The first of the performance films, *Animal in Motion* (1980) is Porter's homage to Eadweard Muybridge's *Studies in Animal Locomotion*: a simple strip of dark leader, interrupted regularly by individual frames of clear leader, is projected while Porter runs frantically back and forth in front of the screen, so that he is caught in mid-stride, again and again. For *Shootout with Rebecca* (1983), Porter dons a cowboy outfit and uses a cap-gun to challenge on-screen character Rebecca to a shootout: Porter fires at her from various spots in the theater, positioning himself so that she seems to fire back at him. Of the performance films, the most interesting are the *Scanning* films (made in several numbered variations since 1981). To make these, Porter scans an area of downtown Toronto with his handheld camera and develops the film. Then, having carefully studied his camera movements, he presents the film using a handheld *projector*, which he moves in a precise echo of the original camera movements. While his means are quite simple, the results are astonishing: it is as though we can see through the walls (and ceiling) of the theater into Toronto itself. As in the *Cinefuge* films and *Down on Me*, the *Scanning* films allow Porter to use the "low-tech" qualities of Super-8 equipment to produce effects as magical for contemporary audiences as the original, Georges Méliès trick-films must have seemed a century ago.

Many of those who chronicle and theorize film history have used Super-8's marginal economic status as a reason to ignore even the most interesting small-gauge filmmaking. I have seen no more remarkable Super-8 work than Porter's, and yet even as ambitious a chronicle and theorization of Canadian avant-garde cinema as R. Bruce Elder's *Image and Identity: Reflections on Canadian Film and Culture* (Waterloo, Ontario: Wilfred Laurier University Press, 1989) ignores Porter entirely. Porter remains active both as a filmmaker and as a

John Porter with his films and projector.

polemicist for anti-establishment film and art. A call to his answering machine always seems to provide the caller with information about current alternative media events in Toronto.

I spoke with Porter during his visit to Utica in 1993.

MacDonald: I was interested to see how much of what you would do later in Super-8 was already in the 16mm *Independent Filmmaking*, the earliest of your films I've seen. It's like a précis of your career. At what point did you know you wanted to experiment with the motion of the camera and the motion you can create, or discover, by single framing?

Porter: There's a scene in Sergio Leone's *The Good, the Bad, and the Ugly* [1967] where the camera rotates around following an actor who is running in a circle, totally blurring the background. That shot really inspired me. Also, when I was at Ryerson [Ryerson Polytechnical Institute in Toronto], still photographers were experimenting with blurred movement, which is a lot easier in still photography. To me, it was a challenge to create that same effect in film: shooting at eighteen or twenty-four frames a second, how do you get a blurred image on just one frame?

MacDonald: Is *Independent Filmmaking* in distribution?

Porter: No. I don't show it much at all. I did show it in 1977, at an open screening at Millennium Film Workshop in New York, with a voice-over I had to say live, since I couldn't play the 16mm magnetic track. I guess that was my first film performance.

MacDonald: What did you say in the voice-over?

Porter: The film starts out with images of long lineups in front of a cinema, pages of newspapers filled with movie ads, all this heavy and complicated 35mm film equipment in studios. Then the camera pulls back and you realize you've been watching all this on a film editor's viewer and that I'm the editor. I turn to the audience—at the time, my fellow Ryerson film students—and say, "Stop giving yourself the *business* and start having *fun* as an *independent* filmmaker." And then I present examples of what I consider to be fun filmmaking as opposed to industry filmmaking.

MacDonald: How long were you at Ryerson?

Porter: Five years, 1969 to 1974. At that time it was a three-year course. I failed a couple of years. They tried to kick me out once but I won my appeal. I wasn't paying attention to the academics. I wasn't passing the tests, written tests like Bruce Elder would give. I was more interested in seeing the films being shown, the films the students were making, and in making films myself. There were also art classes, sculpture classes that I really enjoyed, but of course Ryerson didn't consider those to be important subjects like film processing, lab chemistry, sound recording—courses to prepare you for the "business," which I wasn't interested in at all.

It was a real battle for me at Ryerson—about what they should be teaching me and what I should be learning. That's one of the reasons I stayed: I enjoyed that battle. I had been out of high school for three years before coming back to school. Since I was an adult, I felt I should be able to decide what I should learn, what was important to my career. Having to defend my vision helped me to clarify it for myself. I devised a plan for a "Filmmakers' Gallery," similar to The Funnel, which emerged several years later. After five years at Ryerson, I had officially completed only the second year.

I thought I might switch to the Sheridan College animation course, but I found out that they catered to all these aspiring Disney animators, and I didn't like that idea either. In 1974, I met Lotte Reiniger at the Ontario Science Center. Gerald Pratley had brought her. I took her workshop. *She* was inspiring.

MacDonald: You left Ryerson in 1974 and started producing Super-8 films. How did you support yourself?

Porter: I did odd jobs. I was a day-care bus driver and a machine operator at the same time for a while, and then a letter carrier for five years—things like that. More recently, I've worked as a bicycle courier.

I'm really proud of the period of my life right after I left Ryerson. I knew that film could be a fine art and that there should be film galleries where they could show films like mine. I tried to get support from the Canadian Filmmakers Distribution Centre, but didn't get any. I applied for a Canada Council Grant and didn't get it. Then I got the idea of showing films myself. I bought a 16mm projector and started showing films at a local community center. I called it "Autobiograph-Filmmakers Theatre." But few people came out to it. My publicity could have been better. I didn't meet any filmmakers, and I wasn't getting any encouragement, so I just gave up on that.

MacDonald: At what point did you begin to have the two series of film: the Condensed Rituals, the single-framing films; and the Camera Dances, the camera-movement films?

Porter: I bought a Braun Nizo Super-8 camera from Ron Mann in 1976 (he's a well-known documentarian now [*Comic Book Confidential* (1988) is Mann's best-known film]). That camera allows you to open the shutter all the way all the time, and it has an automatic intervalometer, so you can slow the camera down as much as you like and get longer exposures on each frame. I realized that this was just what I needed to get blurred movement for my "dance" films, but it also meant speeding up the action, which made everything I shot with that camera funny, which I didn't like. I wanted the freedom to make *serious* blurred films. In any case, it took me in another direction for a while, to the pixilated film: the idea of blurred visuals took a back seat to condensing time.

At the beginning, I was just sort of playing around, making home movies of my friends. I wasn't really inspired. There was little creativity to what I did. I did find the Santa Claus parade an interesting subject. I liked filming that crowd scene, not just the parade participants, but the audience along the route. I made that film over and over, starting in 1974. I was excited that I could record the whole Santa Claus Parade in just three minutes. For *A Day at Home* [1976], I just left the camera in a corner of the living room all day, to record the activity in the co-op house where I lived. I didn't even need to be there!

The Camera Dances are underway at this time, too. *Cinefuge* [1974] was the first Super-8 dance. The second part of *Cycles* [1976] ended up being a test for *Angel Baby* [1979]. Before any of those was *Pirouette* [1972], a 16mm film inspired partly by Norman McLaren's *Pas de Deux* [1967]. I use exactly the same lighting as McLaren did. *Pirouette* influenced *Angel Baby*. After McLaren died, they showed a lot of his test films for *Pas de Deux*. I saw that he was doing exactly the same experiments I was doing in *Cycles*: trying to get blurred movement in pretty much the same way—dressing in white against a black background, walking back and forth and spinning his arms. He ended up with that staggered step-printing effect. Years later, just before his death, he was more seriously experimenting with blurred movement.

MacDonald: Having discovered the camera's possibilities, you begin fooling the eye. In *Fog Rising* [1976] it's not just that the fog disperses: at first the image is black and white and then, once the fog disappears, we realize we're seeing a color scene.

Porter: That was accidental. In fact I'm not even sure I realized it until you just said it. A lot of what happens in those films was accidental. In *60 Winchester* [1976], for example, I just began by setting the aperture for night, and when daylight arrived, it automatically overexposed the image, creating a white-out. A similar thing happens in *Fog Rising*. In a lot of these films, I wasn't sure what was going to happen. I'd just decide on a composition and a time and start the camera.

MacDonald: You mentioned last night that *A Day at Home, Juna and I* [1976], *Two Women, O-Leo and I* [1976] and *Santa Claus Parade* [the 1976 version] were all made separately as further experiments with the intervalometer and that later you put them together for the second Toronto Super-8 Festival [1977]. Was this a prize-giving festival?

Porter: Yes.

MacDonald: Did you win a prize?

Porter: Well, in a way. They had preliminary screenings all week at some school auditorium, and then there was this last, weekend screening at a big three-hundred-seat cinema. A few films had won prizes, but the rest of the program was made up of films, including mine, that were just honorable mentions. Getting into that screening, my first with a big audience, was my prize—a *real* prize. It was so exciting. I remember listening to total strangers comment on my film without knowing that the filmmaker was sitting right next to them.

MacDonald: How does your family history play into your films? In *Landscape* [1977] we see you painting with your mother.

Porter: I don't think my family has ever understood where I'm going. But inadvertently they did influence me. My mother is a painter; my father is an engineer and scientist. I drew a lot when I was very young, and I was interested in acting. My mother enrolled me in an acting class. My father gave me a snapshot camera and a darkroom starter kit. I started immediately to do a lot of film-related still photography: narrative series, little pictorials. Then they sent me to Ryerson. My sister helped me get in. Recently, I've been making personal documentary films *about* my family.

Even to this day my mother wishes I was a painter like her, or a writer like her brother, the Canadian poet, George Johnston. I have two older sisters and when we were kids she used to take us out on her painting and drawing sessions in the country. *Landscape* was a return to those days and the last of those sessions for me, and the only one I documented. I wasn't interested in painting anymore; I was interested in filmmaking, which she thinks is a lower form of art. And I was learning to use pixilation and wanted to try it on everything. She chose the location. I tried to have as little effect in that way as possible. I just set up the camera and let whatever happened happen.

MacDonald: At the end you hold up the painting you've made, and it's within this gorgeous living image that a movie camera can make but a painting never can. It's almost a way of saying (although a viewer who didn't know your history wouldn't be conscious of this), "What I am doing is better than what *you* wanted me to do."

Porter: I do think my filmmaking is better than my painting, but it was more a way of saying, "See, I *can* paint if I want to, but I'd rather make films." Actually I showed the painting because I was proud of it. I still have it. I did still remember a bit of painting technique and she was happy that I had done something half-good in *her* medium.

MacDonald: There's a Campbell Soup can on the title card of that film.

Porter: Yeah, around then I started calling the pixilated documentaries "Porter's Condensed Rituals" after Campbell's Condensed Soup. I designed my own soup can label.

MacDonald: Your films could as easily be called "The Dance of Life," since it's clear that for you everything is a kind of dance. You're drawn to activities that have a dance aspect to them *and* the dance aspect of those activities is always contextualized by the dance you do with the camera, and sometimes with the projector. Even in *Rock Jam* [1982] and *Fireworks* [1978], where you're dealing with large crowds, dance seems to be a theme.

Porter: Once I described the Condensed Rituals as expressing both the beauty and the humor that I see in human movement, and that applies even to a large crowd scene—the movement of a crowd is as beautiful as dance is.

MacDonald: At a certain point—the first time I noticed it was in *Landscape*—you tune into the fact of movement directly toward the camera. It's a particularly dramatic way of creating motion that allows lots of things to go on on lots of planes. I'm thinking of *Fashion Show 2* [1978], *Window Cleaning* [1978], and *Fireworks*, particularly.

Porter: I did develop an interest in 3-D. I collect 3-D toys. I always wanted to make 3-D films, like Lenny Lipton. He had identical twin Super-8 cameras and I've never been able to manage that. But I was never satisfied with what he did in 3-D. He never experimented very much with it.

MacDonald: In *Fireworks* the three-dimensionality in the space you choose is pretty astonishing. Also, *Fireworks* seems to encapsulate an aesthetic principle of yours. The most exciting moment is not the actual big city fireworks . . .

Porter: Yes, those look almost like normal speed . . .

MacDonald: But the fireworks that the spectators themselves set off waiting for the "real" ones.

Porter: Yes! The smoke that's coming out of that crowd!—it's like the people are on fire!

I began to make a distinction between time-lapse and pixilation. Pixilation is a form of single framing or animation; time-lapse is more like getting a time exposure on each frame. Time-lapse is a form of pixilation, but pixilation isn't necessarily time-lapse. It's a personal distinction I make in order to identify the techniques. I use "time-lapse" because it's close to "time exposure"—and easier to say than "pixilation with time exposures."

MacDonald: When Pat [Pat O'Connor, MacDonald's wife] and I first saw *Mother and Child*, we were struck by its effectiveness in communicating how exhausting young children can be.

Porter: Of course I couldn't have known that until after I made the film! When I showed it to the mother, she was screaming with laughter. She told me, "That's just the way it is!" Her positive reaction meant a lot to me, and other mothers react the same way.

MacDonald: It's like a Madonna and Child but in the workaday world, the opposite of those serene Renaissance Madonnas and children.

Porter: Both *Mother and Child* and *Landscape* were conscious attempts to refer to classic painting and to make something serious and beautiful. But even they were funny because of the pixilation.

MacDonald: Well, audiences laugh during *Mother and Child*, but I think they're laughing in recognition of what the film reveals: the mother's labor and patience is something most industry films ignore.

You keep returning to certain subjects—portraits, crowd scenes of particular kinds (amusement parks, parades)—the way many painters do. You do studies.

Porter: I find I'm often using that analogy to explain the way I work, since a lot of filmmakers *don't* work that way.

At the end of 1979, with *Christmas*, I was really winding down the Condensed Rituals series. I had done so many of them (at least a hundred) and I was tired of tracking down all these big events. Also, I felt that with the second half of *Amusement Park*, I'd taken time-lapse to the limit. I have shot some other pixilated films over the years since then—I was really happy with *Drive-In Movies* [1981]—and I'd like to film a professional golf tournament sometime. But by 1979 I was heavily involved with The Funnel, and getting a lot of inspiration and encouragement to work more with my Camera Dances, which I thought were a much rawer, more anarchistic way of making films.

Up until The Funnel I wasn't getting any opportunity to show or distribute: nobody showed or distributed Super-8. I was getting all of my satisfaction out of shooting. Then when The Funnel started up, I could think about having shows, and about how to show my films, how to package them. In 1979 my volume of shooting went down. That's partly because the Camera Dances required more preparation than the Condensed Rituals, but also because I was showing more.

MacDonald: When did your involvement with The Funnel begin?

Porter: In September of 1977. I wasn't very involved at first but I went to some of their open screenings. A lot of filmmakers got interested in The Funnel through the open screenings. I showed the Condensed Rituals, and the people there were very encouraging, very inspiring.

MacDonald: Who else was involved at that time?

Porter: Ross McLaren was the main founder, though not the only founder. I remember him being supportive of my work. Tom Urquhart, who was not a filmmaker but an aficionado and a very positive-minded person, was there all the time. And Frieder Hochheim, who had been at Ryerson with me—he's the one who told me about The Funnel.

MacDonald: Was The Funnel part of a larger independent film scene in Toronto?

Porter: Sometimes there were showings in bars or studios or small galleries, that people set up themselves, but The Funnel was such a fine theater that I tended to show there. The Art Gallery of Ontario sometimes showed local experimental film, but not Super-8. The annual Toronto Super-8 Film Festival was very corporate and not very artistic.

Filmmakers were coming to the Funnel from New York, Europe, and all over. But I was particularly inspired by other local filmmakers: Ross McLaren and Jim Anderson early on, and, later on, Sharon Cook. And Fast Würms, which was a trio that did totally anarchistic Super-8 films and installation work—sticking pins in the projector gate to slow down the film, really destroying the film while showing it.

At The Funnel, we were within the narrow field of personal film, but we wanted to be very broad in our treatment of the field. We wanted to provide personal film artists with exhibition *and* production *and* distribution facilities, all under one roof, and in most formats. We didn't show 35mm, but we did show 16mm, Super-8, regular-8, performance art, video, and we had installations in the gallery: film artists could show paintings and sculpture. We had a darkroom for photographers. We knew that many personal film artists work in several media at the same time, all related to film, and we wanted to make room for all those possibilities.

I also learned about performance art at The Funnel, and that's when I did *Animal in Motion*, my first conscious film performance piece. That then led me into the projector as a creative tool.

MacDonald: Speaking of *Animal in Motion*, had you been interested in Muybridge for a while?

Porter: Oh yes. Remember, I was a still photographer before I made films, and I was fascinated by those early pioneers.

MacDonald: In your view what led to the demise of The Funnel?

Porter: It was internal politics, for one thing. The membership structure had been very closed, which I always thought was important. Originally, to become a member you had to be voted on by the board. We specifically wanted to screen out industry types. We had learned from experience that when you put film artists looking toward the industry together with personal film artists, the industry types, who are much more ambitious, tend to dominate. They need more expensive equipment and more time to use it, so their needs crowd out ours. Personal artists can be very quiet and unambitious. They need a place of their own. By 1986, some of us at The Funnel thought we could open up the membership: after ten years, people knew enough about our biases, and we had established a strong enough foundation and profile that some of us felt we could afford to be more democratic. That became a big issue.

Personally, I wanted The Funnel to be much more aggressive in its fight against the Ontario censor board, which would have put the theater at risk, but I thought that was fine. We were a strong group and could survive, even without a theater. The censor board had made life miserable for us for years.

These issues came to the forefront as a desire for some significant changes in policy. What I would call the "old guard" did not want to change and wouldn't budge, although they were a minority. As a result, a lot of the newer people, plus some of the old guard (including myself), just weren't interested in hanging around there as much.

Later, those who stayed decided they wanted a new space, a bigger space, closer to downtown, but because so many members had lost the level of spirit that they had had early on when we built the first theater and later when we renovated it, they couldn't handle this big move. They took on a huge space with a huge rent and did a lot of work to build the new theater, but there were only a few of them to do all that work. They did build it, but it took a long time and was very taxing, and I think they lost some funding because of mismanagement. They had to give up the theater after only a year. It must have been very disheartening.

MacDonald: I'd guess many viewers find the Camera Dances your most interesting work. The 1974 version of *Cinefuge* is a remarkable film.

Porter: Yeah, I was pretty happy with that one.

MacDonald: But *then* you decided to redo that film, using different means. There are two different versions using wires. *Cinefuge 3* [1977] is beautiful, color-wise, and very elaborate and complex. And then, still not satisfied, you came back to the idea and made the version you show most often: the advertisement for the show at The Funnel, which includes two versions shot at different times and spliced together. Among other things, the *Cinefuge* films (and some of the other Camera Dances) are unusually dynamic self-portraits. You're always in the middle of the image, in focus, while the world flies through the frame at high speed. I can't help but read the image as a metaphor for your sense of yourself and your life—trying to hold steady in the midst of

John Porter (with Judith Miller) filming the 1979 version of *Cinefuge*.

fast-moving forces. The effect reminds me of Keaton, who creates a cinematic world where anything can move into or out of the frame.

Porter: That's a good observation—myself steady in this whizzing world. I'd never thought about that in connection with *Cinefuge* but always in connection with the Condensed Rituals. After looking at all of the Condensed Rituals, I saw myself as this slow-moving person in a chaotic world.

I *was* interested in self-portraiture in still photography, but not so much in film. The fact that the *Cinefuge* films are self-portraits is just a product of the fact that with this technique the filmmaker has to be in front of the camera. If somebody else were in the camera's view, it would have been somebody else making the film I was feeling.

MacDonald: But the magic of it is that we realize it *is* indeed *you* creating the amazing image we're seeing, *as we see it*. It's a clear image, and yet, at least for a while, I'd guess, most viewers can't figure out how you're doing what you're doing.

Porter: As far as the history of that idea goes, I often talk about being inspired by that scene in *The Good, the Bad, and the Ugly* I mentioned earlier. But I was trying to choreograph the image, and that's why I wasn't satisfied with it initially: the first versions were so out of control.

MacDonald: The one on the tripod is very much in control.

Porter: Yes, but then I could only do a circular movement parallel to the ground, or a forward or backward walking movement. I wanted to have the camera moving on its own axis, and parallel to the ground in ways I *could* control. In one case, I went even further than using just wires. I asked a friend who made model balsa-wood airplanes to design and build wings for my camera. The plan was that the camera would be mounted between the wings inside a metal cylinder with wires I would control with a plunger. While the camera was spinning around *me*, I wanted it also to be able to spin head over heels *inside* the wings. I wanted to be able to control all these different movements and then choreograph a dance and shoot it. But the process was taking so long and involved so many factors that finally I ended up going back to the first *Cinefuge*, the one with the white rope, realizing that it was not only much easier to shoot that way, but that the very fact that the camera was out of control made for a more exciting film.

MacDonald: Michael Snow's *La Région Centrale* [1971] used a device like the one you describe.

Porter: In a way, yes, but that was a big, complex device and created very different effects from what I wanted.

I had the wings for a long time, though I never ended up using them. In general, I still wasn't sure then that what I was doing was serious filmmaking, but I *was* almost obsessed with the idea of getting the camera to fly. I also made a film about building the wings: *Wings* [1977].

MacDonald: At the beginning of the 1977 version of *Cinefuge*, the camera spins around you while you remain right-side up; but later it spins around you *and* you spin on an axis around the lines, sometimes clockwise, sometimes counterclockwise.

Porter: I had a little stabilizer, a piece of cardboard like an airplane tail, taped to the side of the camera to keep it level. Removing it made the camera spin on its axis. The change in the spinning from clockwise to counterclockwise is a function of the increasing tension on the string; it was out of my control.

MacDonald: A lot of the Camera Dances move toward the abstract, a result of the way the camera spins in response to gravity. Some films (*Down on Me*, and *Soarin'* [1981], for example) create circling, centered, mandala-shaped imagery that reminds me of Jordan Belson and the Whitney brothers. I wonder if you see a spiritual dimension in your acceptance of what the world gives the camera and what the camera gives the world?

Porter: No. I have friends who are into spiritual things and I appreciate spirituality, but I'm not interested in trying to understand it at all. I don't consider it part of my work, unless it's in a totally accidental, maybe subconscious way.

MacDonald: Often I get the sense that you see the camera and projector as toys, rather than as technological responsibilities you're required to "live up to."

Porter: I'd had that feeling about the camera as far back as 1974.

MacDonald: In recent years you've done some amazing performance pieces with the Super-8 projector. On one level, these pieces are quite simple, but they're also magical; audiences find them astonishing.

Porter: I love panoramas. I've made a lot of them in still photography, and many of my condensed rituals are panoramic views. A couple of other film-makers at The Funnel were working on similar ideas. Ross McLaren created a composite panorama on microfiche from the frames of a 16mm film. Anne Walters from Chicago came to The Funnel and hung a Super-8 projector from the ceiling by a rope so she could project her 360 degree panorama film around the room on the walls.

My first *Scanning* film in 1981 was just the flat image of the front of The Funnel building projected on the movie screen with a handheld projector. I've made five variations. The one I show now is the most recent and most complex, projecting on all the walls and the ceiling, and turning the projector upside down. I still plan to do a much longer, more complex version. This year I mounted a small screen onto the projector for an added dimension in the *Scanning* series.

MacDonald: Most of your recent work has involved one or another kind of performance. Why is that?

Porter: I've always been a performer. I was an actor before I started photography or filmmaking, but I hated memorizing lines. I've decided that film itself, being a theatrical medium, is a performance medium. I always consider the presentation of my films a performance. I like to be there in person to project the originals, and talk during them like live narration.

MacDonald: I know from talking with you that you have very strong feelings about what, in a general sense, film ought to be and what it oughtn't be. In a sense, you've designed your life as a way of demonstrating how to function as a filmmaker. For you, what *is* filmmaking at its best? What is it at its worst?

Porter: Well, I would say that film *shouldn't* be one way. Commercial films can be film at its best. But that's an almost entirely different medium than mine: I've chosen film as a visual art. I *would* like to see the medium I've chosen as well-respected as any other type of film or art. I've always enjoyed fighting for the underdog, and I've come to enjoy this "battle" of trying to show that Super-8 and personal film is just as important as commercial film and should receive just as much public funding.

MacDonald: If you could conceptualize an ideal Toronto film exhibition scene, what would it be?

Porter: Well, personal film would be all over the place. Right now, there's not enough personal film being made to supply what I would envision, but I've learned from experience that when you provide a good place to *show* work, more good work gets made by more people. So it would be shown in galleries, especially large galleries like the Art Gallery of Ontario, which has a curator of contemporary art *and* a separate film programmer. I think film, video, and performance art should be treated equally with painting and sculpture. Film or art curators and critics should be qualified and active in *all* art media. There should be smaller galleries that just show film, just as some smaller galleries just show painting.

MacDonald: Of course, then you get into that inevitable issue that film is not an object that appreciates in value, and galleries are businesses.

Porter: The commercial film industry makes a lot of money from videos. Galleries could sell videos or charge admission. There are possibilities.

At The Funnel we were government funded, and we would join these national art or film organizations. But we felt sort of lost between art and film. There is a national organization of artist-run galleries and then there's a national organization of film co-ops. They're separate. They don't get together. We found we were always having to argue with the art people that film is an art, and we'd always have to be arguing with the film co-op people that the personal art we were producing was serious film. We were never taken seriously by either side. It was very frustrating. It's natural for film and art to be *together*.

There are government departments that fund what is generally considered art—painting and sculpture—and different departments fund film. The funding bodies have a prejudice against small format and the blending of media. You can apply to the film department for a film grant or to the performance department for performance. I'd like to be able to apply to the theater department for a film performance piece or just a film piece, or to the dance department for a film piece, because I consider film to be dance. But no, you can't do that. And you have to be judged by conventional film artists—not necessarily industry filmmakers, but people who work only in conventional ways.

There are young artists in Toronto working in regular-8 now. That really excites me, especially one of the artists, Linda Feesey, who all of a sudden appeared on the scene with a whole body of really strong, radical work on regular-8 [8mm]. It excites me because here all these years we've been arguing with places like the Canadian Filmmakers Distribution Centre and the Art Gallery of Ontario to distribute or show Super-8. They haven't even got used to Super-8 yet and *now*, if they want to be contemporary—the way they claim to be— they'll have to start showing old *regular*-8. I love the irony of that.

Raphael Montañez Ortiz

One of the distinctive dimensions of the current film-historical moment is the intersection of two different cultural projects: the ongoing development of that area of independent cinema and video usually called "avant-garde" and the flowering of a range of ethnically based, independent film and video. While these projects have a good bit in common—both provide a set of critiques of conventional commercial film and television—makers in these two areas often evince as much suspicion of each other as camaraderie. Those familiar with the long history of avant-garde media are troubled by the fact that media artists working out of an ethnic context often seem unaware of the broad range of experimentation that has already occurred: what is trumpeted as "new" is sometimes just another instance of an approach that's become virtually traditional. On the other hand, those using film and video to come to terms with particular ethnic heritages or with the intersections of different ethnic heritages recognize that whatever traditions of experimentation have been developed by "avant-garde" film and video artists, a serious engagement with issues of race and ethnicity has never seemed central to those traditions. Indeed, from an ethnic standpoint the avant-garde has not been noticeably more open or aware than mainstream film, a point dramatized by the fact that notable contributions to American avant-garde cinema by African-Americans, Asian-Americans, and Latinos have sometimes been ignored by historians of the avant-garde.

Raphael Montañez Ortiz is a case in point. Ortiz has been making notable contributions to American film culture since the late fifties, though he is better known for his "Destructionist" performances and assemblages (the best source of information about this work is Kristine Stiles's *Raphael Montañez Ortiz: Years of the Warrior 1960 / Years of the Psyche 1988* [New York: El Museo del

Barrio, 1988]) and for his role in establishing New York's El Museo del Barrio in 1969. Ortiz's engagement with his other art activities (and with activities related to his complex, largely Hispanic heritage) has tended to keep him away from the major institutions devoted to avant-garde film, while his wildly experimental approach can frustrate those who prefer to bear witness to marginalized ethnic heritages in simple, direct, "realistic" ways. For me, his work has become a symbol of the potentially productive relationship between two separate attempts to critique contemporary mass media culture.

That Ortiz is not well known, especially among "film people," is also a function of his tendency to work outside conventional understandings of art, and, especially in recent years, at the intersections of various media technologies: the works that are the focus of our interview are neither films, nor videos, nor computer art, nor laser art—though each of these four technologies is a crucial dimension of the process that produces the works. On one level, Ortiz's refusal to function within one particular arena of aesthetic history and influence parallels his ethnic heritage. As a "slum kid" who grew up on the Lower East Side, a member of the first Hispanic family in his neighborhood, Ortiz developed outside the centers of social power, "with no resources for anything beyond working at the Educational Alliance and the Henry Street Settlement" (organizations in Lower Manhattan that provide educational and cultural opportunities for youth). And even his own particular "Hispanic" heritage can hardly be described simply: Ortiz's roots reach back through Puerto Rico not only to Portugal and Spain, but to Ireland and to the indigenous Yaqui people of northern Mexico.

Ortiz made his first films when he was a student at Pratt Institute in Brooklyn during the late 1950s, and from the very beginning he declared himself an innovator. Though much of the earliest work is lost, several films from 1958 remain, including *Cowboy and "Indian" Film, Newsreel*, and *Henny Penny: The Sky Is Falling*. The first two are mini-landmarks in what has come to be called "recycled cinema" (William C. Wees is the leading chronicler of recycled cinema, also called "found footage film": see his *Recycled Images* [New York: Anthology Film Archives, 1993]).

Finished the same year as Bruce Conner's influential *A Movie, Cowboy and "Indian" Film* and *Newsreel* are, at once, related to Conner's work and distinct from it. Like Conner, Ortiz did not have the economic means to shoot his own footage. In order to satisfy his desire to make movies, he bought inexpensive 16mm prints of films that were widely available in local drugstores and camera stores, and re-edited them. Conner's method in *A Movie* was to accept the literal actions occurring within individual shots, but to change their impact by arranging the shots into an entirely new and imaginative continuity. Ortiz's method combined his developing fascination with his Yaqui heritage and an interest in the Dadaist tactic of appropriating found objects: "I would chop the films up with the tomahawk and put them into a medicine bag. I would shake it and shake it, and for me the bag would become a rattle, and I would chant with it. . . ." When he felt comfortable with his ritual, he would reach into the medicine bag, pull out pieces of chopped-up film, and randomly splice them together.

As a result of this unconventional process, the continuity of the films Ortiz worked with (Anthony Mann's *Winchester '73* [1950], in *Cowboy and "Indian" Film*; a Castle Films newsreel in *Newsreel*) is utterly shattered. Images are presented in every possible permutation: right-side up and forward, upside down and in reverse, and so on. And not only do the successive images follow each other with no implication of their original continuity, but as a result of the random re-editing, the sound we hear with any given image bears no particular relation to it. Further, Ortiz includes not only the imagery that was part of what the original film audiences saw in theaters, but bits of Academy leader and even the informal notations written on the strip of 16mm leader that preceded the Academy leader.

While Conner's *A Movie* creates a grim, though generally entertaining vision of modern life, Ortiz's *Cowboy and "Indian" Film* and *Newsreel* are not entertainments. For Ortiz, the ethnic ramifications of the Western were (and remain) offensive, since the genre tended to reconfirm a vision of North American history that was disastrous for the indigenous peoples and problematic for many Hispanics. His cinematic response was not irony but a physical attack on the cultural artifact that represented the suppression of the indigenous and the Hispanic in history and within himself. By editing the shards of *Winchester '73* and the Castle Films newsreel into montages that emphasize the distance between the original films and what we're seeing, Ortiz announces his distance from the enterprise of conventional cinema and all that it represents.

And yet, Ortiz's destruction of the Western and the newsreel does have a constructive dimension beyond his refusal to accept a set of oppressive conventions. Indeed, this constructive dimension of Ortiz's Destructionist art was to fuel his outrageous performance work during the sixties and more recent decades, as well as the digital/laser/video deconstructions that have occupied him since 1985. It is evident even in the grotesque *Henny Penny: The Sky Is Falling* (Ortiz has also called it *Chicken Little*). Only the imagery of *Henny Penny*—a series of handheld 8mm images of a chicken slaughterhouse in Brooklyn leading to a series of extended close-ups during which chickens are partially decapitated, thrown into metal funnels to be bled and twitch in the throes of death—dates back to 1958; the current sound is from a later performance during which Ortiz "cleaned" a piano with a chicken, killed the chicken and destroyed the piano with an axe, then walked around the performance space scattering feathers on the audience. For most viewers of practically any ideological bent, the close-up killing of the chickens would seem little more than a visual assault. But more was involved. The conventional, capitalist cinema's function has been to provide adult nursery rhymes that help audiences believe that essentially all is well with the world, regardless of what is actually going on, as a means of maintaining the film industry's economic viability. Ortiz's unpleasant little film is the opposite: it's a "life reflex," a clinging to reality in the interest of psychic health. The chickens' very real spasms are a metaphor for the "spasm" caused by this filmmaker's interruption of the smooth, passive predictability of our usual cinematic pleasure. What Ortiz did with random, montage editing in *Cowboy and "Indian" Film* and *Newsreel*, he does with a continuous, unflinching gaze in *Henny Penny: The Sky Is Falling*. The sky *is* falling for the chickens and for the viewers.

During the 1960s, Ortiz was centrally involved with performance work, little of it incorporating film, though in general his approach remained close to the early film work. Often, Ortiz would devise a ritualized process that would lead to the destruction of objects that encoded problematic elements of the larger culture. For a time, he became well known for chopping up pianos with his axe, and his various Destructionist performances had considerable influence. In the introduction to *The Primal Scream* (New York: Dell, 1970, p. 9), Arthur Janov describes how one of his patients, a college student, transformed Janov's approach to therapy by describing how he had seen a performance during which Ortiz enacted the trauma of a child who has lost his parents, by spasmodically tearing off his clothes, gorging himself with milk, vomiting it up, and releasing what Janov would later call "the primal scream." Could Ortiz's destruction of pianos be a source for The Who's and Jimi Hendrix's destruction of guitars?

Though the violence in Ortiz's performances was always symbolic, always "violence" with the fundamentally constructive purpose of eliminating real violence, by the 1970s, even the symbolic violence he worked with was becoming more gentle, as is clear in the video *Past Life Regression* (1979) where Ortiz directs several people into past life regressions during which their contact with previous lives sometimes expresses itself in "spasms" of laughter. And by the 1980s, his discovery of the possibility of using the new digital, laser, and video technologies as a means of ritually shredding—deconstructing and reconstructing—moments from conventional cinema allowed him to devise an almost sedentary process for responding "violently" to the overt and implicit psychic violence promoted and marketed by the media.

Using his Apple computer, along with a Deltalab Effectron II sound effects generator, he began to deconstruct and reconstruct tiny excerpts from classic films on laser disks, and to record the results on video. He has made dozens of these "digital/laser/videos," many of which are arresting, provocative, and suggestive. In some cases, a single excerpt from one film is reworked. In *Dance No. 1* (1985), for example, Ortiz reveals how the original "choreography" of a moment in *Citizen Kane* (1941)—specifically, the arrival of Kane, Leland, and Bernstein at the *Inquirer* office to take over from Mr. Carter—obscures the essential nastiness of what is actually occurring and allows viewers to identify

Raphael Montañez Ortiz performing *Piano Destruction Concert* in 1967.

with and take pleasure in the workings of class privilege and power. In other digital/laser/videos, excerpts from several films are interwoven so as to create a meta-film that has impact as a discrete work *and* implicitly comments on the film history exemplified by the excerpts. *My Father's Dead* (1991), for example, combines brief excerpts from *High Plains Drifter* (1973, directed by Clint Eastwood; Ortiz uses less than a second of an explosion), *Quest for Fire* (1981, directed by Jean-Jacques Annaud; Ortiz uses two shots from the sequence where the Rae Dawn Chong character uses the "missionary position" for the first time during sex), and *Excalibur* (1981, directed by John Boorman; Ortiz uses the shot where Uryen's daughter Morgana has a psychic realization that her father has been murdered). There is no space here to suggest the many possible readings of Ortiz's excerpting and editing these moments from three mythic stories; but in general, *My Father's Dead* is Ortiz's way of responding to his (and our) inheritance of a patriarchal film industry: the video declares both his patrimony and his psychic and technological independence.

Ortiz and I talked in January and February 1994, refining the resulting interview by phone and mail.

MacDonald: You've worked as an artist in various media, periodically returning to film. What were your earliest film experiments?

Ortiz: When I was about nine years old, I had one of those Lone Ranger rings that you could look at Long Ranger filmstrips with. I used to belong to this gang—all kids belong to some sort of gang, a sandlot gang or whatever—and we used to meet in the basement of a church, where some of us were altar boys. A couple of the guys were mischievous, delinquent types, and they came in one night with a box full of films they said they'd found in the backyard of a photography studio. In the box were all these 8mm porno films. And guess what! The 8mm films fit into the Lone Ranger ring perfectly. So I spent hours sliding them through the ring, looking at them frame by frame. I spent weeks piecing together each story. I guess that was the beginning of my whole notion of working frame by frame.

And I remember Coney Island arcades. You put in the nickel, you turned the crank, and all these single frames became a movie. I spent a lot of time looking at that effect. I was really turned on by it. I think I was a filmmaker in a past life or something. So, all of that came together with my desire to draw and paint, and led finally to some photography and film courses at Pratt in the mid-fifties.

I enrolled in the Architecture Program at Pratt in January 1955. And I became familiar with the Western tradition and reactions against it from within, like Dada. For me, Pratt was the opportunity to (finally) have the resources to make film. I was a slum kid with no resources for anything beyond working at the Educational Alliance and the Henry Street Settlement, with whatever was available there in terms of art. I learned how to play the piano a little bit down at the Settlement, and how to shoot pool, play the harmonica, and, of course, how to play basketball. And I was always interested in theater.

So I had all those interests in kinetic kinds of performance by the time I got to Pratt. Making films seemed natural. Also, at that time, I was getting to know what my grandfather was all about and to understand the North American indigenous connection in our family roots.

MacDonald: Specifically what is your indigenous connection?

Ortiz: My grandfather is half Yaqui—then it was just called the geegee culture. There was this whole side of our family that we didn't talk too much about. But as I did the research, I found out that *his* father was Irish, and his mother was full-blooded Yaqui. I developed a romantic connection with all that. I explored the visionary culture of my Yaqui ancestors in peyote rituals. Peyote was legal then. In those years, the Yaqui peyote ritual was my means to discover the psychic, shamanic, cultural-root resources necessary for making film.

It was during a number of peyote rituals in 1956 that my visions connected up with cowboy-and-Indian movies, which led to *Cowboy and "Indian" Film*. Peyote ritual visions also led to *Henny Penny: The Sky Is Falling*. When I returned to Pratt in 1960, I submitted these works for credit and received it.

There were cowboy-and-Indian movies all over the place in those years. Remember? If it wasn't Cochise, it was some Comanche uprising, and the cavalry coming to the rescue. I went through the usual stage of cheering the cavalry. And one day I'm sitting there, thinking, "What am *I* doing cheering the cavalry?!" There was a whole cultural revolution going on: things were happening in the Afro-American community, in the Hispanic community, and in the indigenous community. I felt connected with all of it.

This spilled over into whatever aesthetic concerns I had as a student. I was reading philosophy, taking a psych course, looking into anthropology, and exploring my identity. I made the link between Dada and the whole shift out of the more formalist kind of art that had been happening in Western culture before it, and looped that into the notion of indigenous ritual. And that relationship between Dada and ritual came to bear on my problem solving as an artist.

I had always been fascinated with ritual. For a while, I was the Shabbes Goy [a non-Jew who does tasks forbidden to Jews on the sabbath] at the local temple, lighting lights and watching the rabbis during the high holy days. And that *fascinated* me. I had always been looking into ritual, and its sacred context, so later it was easy for me to look for the sacred context in art.

First, I worked with objects. I did a whole series of pieces, using shoes, flower pots, anything I got my hands on. I ritualized, deconstructed, sacrificed, released the spirit from these things. It was all a wonderful experiment. I was experiencing my roots in a process which was entirely relevant to my life.

MacDonald: Are *Cowboy and "Indian" Film* and *Newsreel* parts of a series of films? How much filmmaking were you doing?

Ortiz: Those were films I "finished." But there were other films—about sixteen—that I sacrificed, released the spirits from.

MacDonald: The film recycled in *Cowboy and "Indian" Film* is *Winchester '73*, directed by Anthony Mann.

Ortiz: Yes, with Jimmy Stewart. Little 8mm and 16mm films were for sale in tourist shops. I'd wander around these shops and pick up films. I'd look through old newsreels and see what I wanted to purge. I found a number of cowboy-and-Indian films, a number of touristy films—some of the Statue of Liberty, some ferry boat footage—and some old newsreel footage. I took one film on golf and made hundreds of holes in the filmstrip with a punch.

MacDonald: Does that still exist?

Ortiz: Yes, but it's not in good shape.

Of course, in the process of my personal life, I found myself falling in love and leaving a film here or a painting there—it was part of the courtship process. So there's no way I can locate a lot of the early stuff. When I was having my retrospective at El Museo del Barrio [1988], I was trying to track down some of the people. I found five films. Two punch films, *Henny Penny: The Sky Is Falling, Cowboy and "Indian" Film*, and *Newsreel*.

MacDonald: Did you consciously choose that particular newsreel with the nuclear explosions and the Pope? Bob Breer also satirized Pope Pius XII, in *Un Miracle* [1954; see Breer's comments on *Un Miracle* in *A Critical Cinema 2*, p. 20].

Ortiz: I was interested in the fact that that newsreel included footage of the Nuremberg trials, of the Pope, of war and death. It allowed me to have the Pope blessing the bomb, as a comment on the Catholic collaboration with the Nazis. For me, making the film was a way to purge all this, to release the good from the evil. I was always looking for a ritual way of moving into these self-contained structures that protected the lies or sins. That's what drove me.

MacDonald: Even in those early films, you seem to be using different ways of dealing with different kinds of information. In *Cowboy and "Indian" Film* the editing is slow enough that we can identify the stars, and can get a sense of what the movie was, before it was chopped up. The editing of *Newsreel*, however, is so fast that it approaches flicker: it's more a tommy-gun barrage of imagery.

Ortiz: That had to do with the rhythms I wanted to create. I've always been very conscious of drum rhythm. I could play congas, and I was familiar with the various kinds of drumbeat: the African, the Latin, and the indigenous, which is more repetitive—the harmonics change more gradually so it sustains itself over longer periods of time.

I would chop the films up with the tomahawk and put them into a medicine bag. I would shake it and shake it, and for me the bag would become a rattle, and I would chant with it. I was always trying to find some process, some activity, that would connect what I was doing with the indigenous sacred. I was imitating indigenous ritual to find my place in it. When I had chanted long enough, and felt comfortable with my ritual, *then* I would reach into the medicine bag, pull out pieces of chopped-up film, and randomly splice them together.

Pope Pius XII blesses the Bomb, in successive frames from Raphael Montañez Ortiz's *Newsreel* (1958).

MacDonald: It's an interesting way of turning things inside out. In *Winchester '73* indigenous people are "contained" by the military arm of a very limited world view.

Ortiz: Yes, I could change the time, the space, the whole linearness of the original, which was also a part of what I needed to change in *my* image as well: I was locked into a very linear, and hurtful, notion of my worth.

MacDonald: Paradoxically, you come to grips with your *spirituality* by recognizing the *material* dimension of moviemaking. In *Cowboy and "Indian" Film* it's not just the images that are chopped up and reconstructed, but the leader.

Ortiz: Yes. I was interested in that whole universe. For me, every bit of the celluloid contained the life of what that film was about.

MacDonald: You later became famous for attacking things with your axe. Were these films your first chopping performances?

Ortiz: Yes. And then I moved on to the piano, which was an important object for me. Sound is a crucial part of indigenous ritual, and the drumming sounds of the pianos that resonated when I chopped them apart were an expansion of their voice, so to speak. For at least a moment they had an indigenous voice.

MacDonald: Seeing several decades of your work in a short time, I can see a lot of continuity. Yesterday, when I was looking at *Henny Penny: The Sky Is Falling*, I was thinking that after the chickens' throats are cut and they're thrown into the funnels to be bled, their twitching suggests both the spasms of people undergoing past life regression in *Past Life Regression* and the "spasms" you create in excerpts from classic films in the digital/laser/videos.

Ortiz: Yes! That's a clinging to life. It's a positive thing, a life reflex, like a heartbeat.

MacDonald: Spasm (in the literal and metaphoric sense) is what most behavior training in Western culture tries to control or eliminate. The culture conspires to create, as often as possible, this appearance that everything is working smoothly. Conventional film encodes this desire in its commitment to smooth continuity.

Ortiz: You know, a lot of the lighting that we use *seems* to be a constant flow of radiation. But in fact, it has a flicker, a pulse. My work tries to get at the pulse of life that we've lost sight of, lost touch with. I want to get in tune with it again, to reveal it, to become part of it. I was really excited when this surfaced in me. It was a revelation, like discovering the heartbeat and that the blood circulated. I became interested in getting out of the passivity of perception that I felt in myself and then in bringing my revelation to others.

MacDonald: *Henny Penny* was shot in 1959. But the sound on the current tape version is from a performance you did in London some years later. When did the sound and image get put together?

Ortiz: Two or three years ago. There were times when I played it silent because there is something very powerful about the imagery without sound.

Later, in my performances, when I introduced the Santeria ritual, a ritual involving animal sacrifice that bridges the several cultures that came together in the Caribbean, I played tapes of chicken-cackling sounds while the film was showing. And then recently I was interested in seeing what would happen if I put one of the sixties performances on the soundtrack. Hitting the piano with a chicken, instead of an axe, was an extension of that earlier work.

MacDonald: Who saw your early films?

Ortiz: I heard about this place way over in the East Village, a basement where Jonas Mekas was showing experimental films [I assume Ortiz means the Charles Theater, at Avenue B and 12th Street]. I took my films there and showed them. I met Jonas and a whole group of crazy filmmakers. Andy Warhol is the only one I remember.

MacDonald: Speaking of crazy artists, at the 1966 Destruction in Art Symposium in London, you met Otto Mühl, Hermann Nitsch, and the other Viennese "Destructionists." How did you come to be at that conference?

Ortiz: I was there with Al Hanson—we were the American contingent. Al and I had gone to Pratt together. Al had called from Europe and said, "Hey, they're doing this thing over in London; it's right up your alley: you know, you're always running around destroying something, dancing around something while it's burning. You should come to London!" So I called Gustav Metzger, the organizer. I told him about my work, and he said by all means to come. I had the typical aggressive American attitude about going to England. You know, when Bob Dylan went to England, he seemed real tough, New York tough. And the English folk singers were blown away. I had this fantasy, as an American ritual destruction artist, that I'd go to London and just blow them away, the way he did.

I arrived early and worked pretty closely with Metzger, doing the PR part of the conference. I helped design events that would be news, to draw attention to the symposium. Metzger was really excited about it. This is all before the Vienna group arrived. For my first event, I bought a chair at one of those men's clubs where everybody goes in to read the newspaper. I planned to arrive and when somebody was sitting in the chair, I'd tell him to get off the chair. It was *my* chair. Then I'd start an argument with the chair and I'd battle with it and destroy it right there in the club. Then I'd carry the chair down to Africa Center, a big meeting hall where we were exhibiting work.

MacDonald: Taking the chair apart is certainly more humane than attacking the people who use the chair. Since it's a chair in a men's club, it encodes that whole space. Is it fair to say that at that point, you picked an icon from the culture and destroyed it *in lieu of* doing real damage? In a sense, the recent digital pieces are similar: you find a moment in a film that encapsulates a certain cultural way of looking at things and then take it apart as a means of venting your frustration with it and as a way of moving *through* it into something else . . .

Ortiz: And that something else is, for me, the sacred context. The path back to the sacred is ritual; ritual is what allows us to cross from dislocation to an affirmation of life. Read the Bible or any sacred literature. We see that as the culture evolves spiritually, it moves from human sacrifice (in ancient cultures throughout this planet) to animal sacrifice and then to the notion finally of crucifying one's *imperfection* rather than oneself or someone else. Sacrificing yourself or other people is the primal error, the dislocation from the sacred. For me, relocating art within the sacred context is always in service of the affirmation of life. In fact, once that was clear to me, everything fell into place. My destruction of objects can be worded as simply as you have worded it: there is certainly a displacement—I kick the chair instead of kicking somebody—but there's more metaphysics involved. My destruction work is linked to the larger notion of sacrifice within mystical philosophies, which for me is a more authentic root.

MacDonald: The word "root" is useful because you don't just take an object or a sequence from a film and destroy it; you destroy its original impact by looking at, and *through*, its original elements. There's more than just anger in the work, there's a seeking for meaning, an attempt to turn the problem into a solution.

Ortiz: You could call it a counterphobic reaction to passivity in the face of one's sense of worth being overwhelmed. The counterphobic reaction is the reaching out. When you have a sense of not having any more breath, you gasp. For me, that spasmodic reaction is the struggle of Eros over Thanatos.

By the way, at the London symposium I also organized a film which would burn, frame by frame, as it was shown. The projector would stop on each frame, play it, burn it out. Amazing.

MacDonald: What film did you use?

Ortiz: A war film. *The Red Badge of Courage* [1951, directed by John Huston], I think. That was my way of releasing Thanatos energy, and also a way of speaking about Armageddon. Another artist was running the projector, while I had the audience exploding paper bags and throwing them all over the place.

And then there was going to be a Santeria, which I had announced. But the people at the gallery couldn't find a live chicken for the ritual sacrifice. All they could come up with was a parakeet! Well, once people had heard about what I was going to do—*sacrifice an animal*—they called the police, who arrived in the middle of all this. I tried to explain Santeria. But they said, "No, it's not possible. You can't do that." So I said, "Well, okay," and went out into the street, followed by the whole audience (it was a storefront gallery). I had the cage with the parakeet and I said, "I'll free the parakeet. I'll sacrifice my sacrifice." They said, "No, you can't do *that*. We don't know what will happen to the bird." I saw this child in the crowd and gave her the cage and said, "It's yours." At the end of the year, the *Sunday Herald*, one of the London newspapers, awarded me the Tweety Pie Award.

At this point in the conference, Hermann Nitsch was busy organizing one of his lamb rituals—buying the carcass, the five gallons of blood. He showed some films with brains and livers and people's laps covered with blood, and their penises tied with string around the waist in an aboriginal sort of way. Everybody was getting upset and the police wanted to confiscate the film footage and take everybody's name and so on. Ultimately, there was a trial and I think the Destruction in Art Symposium was fined.

I was going all over the place doing piano concerts with the axe and attracting a lot of attention. It was real competitive between me and the Vienna group. My feeling was that they were still not dealing with the issue of destruction within a *ritual* context, within a *spiritual* context.

Nitsch and I did become friends. We shared a sense of mystery about archaic rituals and how they fit into culture—whether it's ancient Celtic rituals or indigenous American rituals.

Of the Destructionists at the conference, I found Otto Mühl the most intelligent.

MacDonald: What did you find particularly interesting about him?

Ortiz: Behavior as ritual was something he had always been fascinated with. We had long conversations. He was very wise about the roots of art. I would tell him about shamanics. He made a lot of people very angry by defying social etiquette and taboos, which ultimately got him into a lot of trouble.

MacDonald: I understand you visited him in prison.

Ortiz: Yes. His imprisonment was a whole, complicated series of events that developed when a very wealthy publisher paid people to come forward to make statements about what happened in the commune. The publisher felt that his son wouldn't leave because of brainwashing.

Otto was head of that community for so long—always elected. I was there for a number of the elections.

MacDonald: Secret ballots?

Ortiz: Oh, no! Open community elections. He would be elected by 99 percent. They had twelve houses, twelve families. And each of the families elected members to head the families. It was all very biblical. Women were elected as important women, men were elected as important men, children were elected as important children, adolescents were elected as important adolescents. The whole structure was broken down into democratically elected leadership, which constantly fluctuated. *But* they always came back to Otto. I think after a while he regretted that he was constantly elected. After about the tenth time he was hoping some other person would win. At least, that's what he told me. But they were always looking to Otto. He was so empowered that inevitably his own personal, psychic difficulties didn't have time to get resolved and they became part of his leadership, and they were problematic enough to build a case to "get him."

MacDonald: When you say his "difficulties," what do you mean?

Ortiz: He was so busy with this huge community. Everyone had time for their analyst but him. As a result, the community became the place where he acted out all his unresolved hang-ups. I don't excuse any of it. I think that it was unfortunate that no one spoke to him sooner, confronted him sooner and more directly about these violations. When I was there before one of the elections, I suggested that he have a funeral, that he ritually die. Then someone else would have to take his place. But they just wouldn't let go of him. And, in the end, the leader had to be "killed."

MacDonald: In her catalogue of your Museo del Barrio show, Kristine Stiles includes a picture of the Destructionist group. I don't know how I would have felt about it at the time, but today, my reaction is, "Wow, what a male group!"—especially compared with Fluxus, which included many women.

Ortiz: Yes. The Lollipop Gang was the only exception. They were three women and two men who had a giant lollipop full of incendiary material.

MacDonald: How did you end up with Johnny Carson on *The Tonight Show?*

Ortiz: I'd just come back from the Destruction in Art Symposium, and a guy from *The Village Voice* was writing about what I was doing. He interviewed me about what had happened in London, and something got published. Anyway, this guy had contacts and evidently mentioned my name to one of the people who select the guests. And I was selected. I was brought in and interviewed, and I did a piano concert. So there I was on the Johnny Carson Show.

MacDonald: I remember your appearance! I remember the conflict your chopping up the piano caused in me. But I don't remember what you talked about.

Ortiz: Carson talked to me about the symposium. I mentioned a number of pieces I'd done, and I mentioned the Yoko Ono piece that I had participated in in London.

MacDonald: Which piece?

Ortiz: Her *Cut Piece* [see *Grapefruit* (New York: Simon and Schuster, 1964)] where she sat in a meditative pose and people came up and cut pieces of her clothing off. Her audience became, with time, less polite: reaching and grabbing and cutting until finally she was nude. And then she held up a sign saying, "My Nudity is the Scar of My Soul," or something like that. Someone came forward with a blanket and wrapped it around her and that was the end. That was a strong piece. To me, it was the only one of her pieces that was relevant to the Destruction in Art Symposium. I found the rest of her work to be lightweight, frilly, Fluxus stuff.

MacDonald: So you described some of these works . . . and then?

Ortiz: I dedicated the piece to Glenn Gould, and bashed the piano. Carson enjoyed the piece so much, he replayed it on another show. But he didn't include me in the Best of Carson video he just put out!

Soon after that appearance there was a cartoon in *The New Yorker* of a guy up on a stage bashing a piano with a baseball bat. There were other TV appearances too.

MacDonald: In your tape about past life regression, women make an appearance, but in a context very different from your earlier work.

Caption: "I don't like this tampering with the score. He should be using an axe." The *New Yorker* cartoon spoof of Ortiz's "piano concerts." Drawing by Ed Fisher; © 1968 The New Yorker Magazine, Inc.

Ortiz: That transformation is also linked to my fascination with the indigenous. Within indigenous culture, the patriarchal visionary context is about spasm on the level of BLOOD and NOISE and THUNDER. But within the matriarchal tradition, the dream is the place for revelation. Unlike men, women don't have to go up to the mountaintop and starve to death or freeze to death, they don't need to go to extremes of deprivation or of pain in order to achieve revelation. No. They take a nap and dream. Inner vision work became important to me when I realized there are more subtle forms of deconstruction: the destruction of the ego, of normal consciousness, in dreaming. Falling asleep and moving into the dream state is another form of sacrifice. Children don't want to go to sleep; they don't want to sacrifice their connection with the waking world.

So I learned to recognize the importance of the dream. That then created an important link for me in my relationship with women, and I wanted to make that more subtle, matriarchal form of revelation central.

A lot of things are always happening simultaneously, Scott. It's not like I stop one thing and move on to another. As I was learning about dreams, the piano performances were still happening. I had released myself from the Santeria, the sacrifice of the chickens: just covering the piano with feathers was finally enough.

MacDonald: There's also a change in mood. For most audiences, the spasms of the dying chickens in *Henny Penny* would be very unpleasant, even horrible. But, in *Past Life Regression*, the spasms are very different: they lead to laughter. It's *funny* to be in touch with this level of oneself.

Ortiz: But there is a consistency, as you've said: there's always the spasm.

MacDonald: It's been very interesting for me to examine the evolution of the digital/laser/video work. I want to talk about at least some of the specific pieces, but I have a general question first. Until recently, film was thought of as the ultimate technological medium, and yet it's also become a cliché to say that its primary popular use has been to reinforce cultural patterns that were around long before film. Some have said it's a twentieth-century medium devoted to a nineteenth-century vision. Is it fair to say that for you the new technologies you work with—digital, laser, video—have provided you with a means of overturning the mechanical technology of cinema, and investing it with what you might define as a twentieth- (or twenty-first-) century vision?

Ortiz: At the simplest level, when we talk metaphysically, we say, "Well, you're thinking too materialistically, you've got to think more spiritually." For me popular films contain what continues to be *a* way of seeing the world. They're part of the self-perpetuating notion that we can have complete control, that we can put things in a certain order and they will remain in that order forever. What I saw as basic to ritual was that that is definitely *not* the case. It's a very Western notion that once we're solidly formed, that's it; that's who we are. Ritual was about deconstructing the self, ages before the term "deconstruction" was invented. Ritual is about destroying notions of our solidity. As we in the West became more and more materialistic and less spiritual, we saw ourselves as creating things that were more and more lasting.

For me, film is one of the places where our culture most believes it has established what this culture means, what it is about, and where it should be going. It communicates these assumptions in the resonance between us and that information on the screen, at the nervous-system level. I found a way to re-mystify that experience and, in the process, relocate it back into the sacred, by releasing the whole notion of its containing, and being contained by, a vision of a stable, solid world with meanings cemented into place. I found other meanings submerged in that cement that allowed me to relocate the more conventional meanings into the context of the infinite—the infinity of possible meanings.

What I tried to do in a simpler way with my axe long ago, I do now with this alchemical machine, the computer, which provides a shamanic context within which I can move the medium of film into the electrical space of the sacred and transmute it.

MacDonald: You can really see the impact of ritual in *The Kiss* [1985]. The original filmic sources for some of your pieces are immediately identifiable, but I don't recognize the sequence you work with in *The Kiss*.

Ortiz: It's from *Body and Soul* [1947, directed by Robert Rossen]: the scene when the boxer visits the studio of the artist who wants to do his portrait. On the way out he quickly kisses her and she pushes him out the door. For me, there was something interesting in the tension between them, between body and soul.

MacDonald: In conventional movies the kiss is so inevitable, so automatic that it gets disconnected from passion. By slowing the kiss down and forcing it into a new ritualized format, you re-endow it with a powerful energy. By reversing the sequence, the man enters the "body" of the house, goes "down the hallway," to the door where they kiss. You transform the sequence back into a spasm—a sign of the passion with which the spiritual expresses itself in love, which is what made the gesture of kissing interesting and important in film originally.

Ortiz: That's what's interesting about relocating something back into the sacred: there *is* this whole reversal. Within deconstruction—this shredding things apart—a whole other perception is revealed. Some hidden, submerged truth suddenly rises, like a phoenix from the ashes.

MacDonald: In another 1985 piece, *Dance No. 1*, you use film material that any film lover would recognize from *Citizen Kane*. It's a very dramatic moment in the film, when Kane, Leland and Bernstein come into the *Inquirer* office to take over. The ritual here is that you are doing to Welles's film what Kane is doing to Mr. Carter, *but* from the point of view of someone "outside" the class that both Kane and Carter share. You (digitally) "come in" and throw their world into a spasm.

Ortiz: And in the process reveal their "dance," which is what allows us to forget what's really going on in that scene. For me, this funny moment in the film hid something cruel that needed to be exposed. In *Dance No. 1* you experience Carter's humiliation *and* how he is pulled into the dance. We (and he) forget his humiliation as he's dancing.

MacDonald: What is the excerpt you explore in *What Is This?* [1985].

Ortiz: *What Is This?* is from an old forties movie on an air raid warden. I don't remember the title. But I remember air raids. The air raid wardens used to put gauze on all the windows with some funny wallpaper glue because a bomb blast would splinter the glass. So in the film, here's Pop, the local warden. He's brought home part of the bomb demonstration he does to help people prepare. It's lying on the table. He's sitting in the living room, puffing on his cigar, reading the paper. Mom's knitting. It's the typically happy American family. Norman Rockwell. For me, there was something else happening there, which had another emblematic meaning. It was in the curiosity this young woman is experiencing about the device on the table. And that becomes a perfect metaphor for her mother's sense of her daughter's awakening sexuality as somehow *dangerous* . . .

MacDonald: It's a bomb!

Ortiz: It's a bomb. What will this young girl *do* with the whole patriarchal system that's represented by the bomb? As I explored that material, shredded it digitally, the whole sexual dimension just unraveled.

MacDonald: You have the daughter make very sexual sounds.

Ortiz: Exactly. That was part of the ritual of the awakening. And, of course, the repression of this very curiosity, Wilhelm Reich would say, is ultimately the cause of war.

MacDonald: Is that explosion image from the same movie?

Ortiz: Yeah.

MacDonald: On one level, it's a metaphor for your process: your film is a "bomb" that explodes this *image* of reality.

Dance No. 6 [1985] is from *King Kong* [1933], the moment when the filmmakers and sailors search the boat for the missing Ann Darrow. Your recycling of the sequence is reminiscent of Muybridge. And it provides another metaphor for your process: Miss Darrow has been stolen by a monster just as, in a sense, you've stolen this segment of the film, you monster.

Raw Oysters [1991] is from *The Magnificent Ambersons*?

Ortiz: Right. I combine the part where the son is putting on his pants, with the shot where the sister is being dressed by the maid and the shot where George as a boy is punching out the guy who's bad-mouthing the family. About a second here, a half second there, a quarter second there. I'm dealing with a lot of archetypal, psychological metaphors. Here's this little boy, dressed like a little girl (you're not quite sure), punching this grandfather figure. I'm dealing with issues of identity and the whole notion of the power of the mother and the father, and of old people. As children we always sense a mystery in old people. I remember when I was very young and was told to kiss grandma, I was always terrified that when I kissed her, I would get all wrinkled like her.

And there's all the things that raw oysters conjure up: they're like a seminal, erotic substance. There's the whole notion of oysters as aphrodisiacs. It all seemed related to me.

You know, there's a loop between all this film material and myself. It's not just out there in a vacuum. I remember as a kid looking forward to putting on long pants so I didn't have to be a little baby, and wanting to have my hair cut so I would look like a boy—having to wrestle with my mother's wanting to have a little girl and my own intuitive desire for my own identity as a boy. I'm also working to relocate *myself* into a sacred space where I can deconstruct all of the dislocation inside me that comes out of our being immersed in a powerful (cultural, familial) context that forces us into a kind of passivity as we're formed.

The one thing I look for as I'm composing a piece, moving forward and back through imagery and sound during the process of deconstruction, is the right moment at the right speed. I live with all of the possibilities, until finally I find the ratio where the meaning unfolds. It might take me a month, or six months.

When I find that ratio, it's like those time-lapse films where you see flowers budding, some at *just the right speed*. I'm always looking, looking, looking, for that perfect speed. I start dreaming like that! These pieces of footage all end up as parts of my dreams.

MacDonald: There's also the question of image and the sound. You always work with both.

Ortiz: For me, they're absolutely related; they're woven together as a fabric.

MacDonald: In *The Briefcase* [1992] we think, at first, that we're on the verge of being able to understand what the characters say. But finally we realize we're seeing the sequence backwards, so we never quite understand. In other pieces we can understand what's being said. That's true in *If You Don't Want It Any More* [1987].

Ortiz: Sometimes just the image will come together and reveal itself, and later I work with the sound. But when it happens together with sound and image, it's phenomenal. I have to go through thousands, millions of possibilities. I give myself up to it. I'm there working, just chanting and chanting the passage, until finally it's a prayer, a ritual within which whatever I'm relocating relocates and reveals itself.

MacDonald: Do you work at these pieces one at a time?

Ortiz: Sometimes I'm working on two or three over a period of months.

MacDonald: *Mr. Marechal Have You Seen This Photograph?* [1992] can be read as comment on the process viewers engage in as they watch. Three different images are included; all seem to be about trying to find something underneath the surface of things. In the shot from *Grand Illusion* [1937, directed by Jean Renoir] the officer in charge is trying to read the different layers on a map. There's also an obscure shot of what looks like a drill coming through a ceiling . . .

Ortiz: That's from the film about the air raid warden again, the same sequence we talked about in connection with *What Is This?* That's the bomb coming through the ceiling.

MacDonald: And there's a shot of the girl, though in *this* context, we don't know what she is looking at. We're trying to make sense of the individual images, *and* we're trying to discover the connections between them.

Ortiz: We need to relocate ourselves within what has dislocated us. I reconstruct things in reverse as a way of re-walking the path and in the process *un*-making what has been made, in order to *re*make it in a more completely humane form, and in order to allow the audience to discover a new understanding.

MacDonald: Is it fair to say that in the digital/laser/videos, you see yourself as the person who helps us relocate ourselves spiritually, rather than, as in conventional film and TV, the person who helps us forget we are dislocated.

Ortiz: Exactly. At least, that's my hope. We sense the dislocations in our consciousness, but we're distracted from them, by media above all. We think everything is fine until some real event happens that dislocates us from that precarious illusion. Then we're in free fall and can't ground ourselves anywhere.

We are only fragments. When we begin to put all the fragments together, then we sense ourselves being healed, and we begin to sense the revelation, and then we *know*.

Film and TV are counterphobic, and that's the problem right now. When film and TV avoid the phobic, the dislocated, then you get the fantasy of violence, the smooth, seemingly rational spectacle of violence. The notion of sacrifice is lost, and destruction cannot be a transcendental process that leads to an affirmation of life. The nihilism becomes "*an*nihilism."

MacDonald: So all there ever is is more revenge, instead of healing.

Ortiz: There can never be a retribution that moves one into grace. Retribution only moves one into further retribution.

MacDonald: Tell me if this is correct: when you're making a digital/laser/video piece, you spend a lot of time looking at particular passages, and "chanting" them, exploring them. This preparatory work is like sketching. But when you decide to make a work, you re-chant what you've been exploring in a pre-arranged order.

Ortiz: Yes. Except for the bricolage pieces where several separate elements come together, after I've made them individually.

MacDonald: That always happens later?

Ortiz: Well, not always. At this point there's so much in the "library," that when I'm working on one piece, I'll sometimes get a flash to other footage I've deconstructed. That for me is another link and I accept it—and I may see *another* connection. The deconstructed footage has its own integrity, its own continuum. And several of these discontinuous continua then link together.

MacDonald: It's possible to interpret *My Father's Dead* by accepting that we don't know where the excerpts are from and just making what sense we can of a child saying, "My father's dead!"; an explosion; and an image of two primitive beings fucking. On the other hand, since the video disks that are available to you are almost inevitably of relatively well-known films, a person like me whose business is to study film almost inevitably tracks down the original sources. Now that I've tracked them down, there is a whole other level on which I can explore *My Father's Dead*. If it were possible to get video disks of lesser-known films, would you do that? Or do you want the viewer to know that the excerpts are from relatively interesting and sometimes important films? And does the original context play a part in your using the passages you do?

Ortiz: It does play a part, but mostly on the id level. The movie itself is an "id-ish" realization. It's a dream. I'm going into the dream and underneath it, to reveal its *inner* workings.

MacDonald: Would I be correct in assuming that you find the three films excerpted in *My Father's Dead—Excalibur, Quest for Fire*, and *High Plains Drifter*—particularly interesting?

Ortiz: Well, they're an important part of our collective unconscious.

MacDonald: Are they *more* important in our collective unconscious than other films, or are all films equal in this sense?

Ortiz: I believe that all are equally part of the societal unconscious, but some of them access certain particular aspects of it effectively. And in a sense, I'm ritually tracking my connections to these aspects.

MacDonald: So an individual piece like *My Father's Dead* is (for lack of a better term) a model of the relationship of your unconscious to the larger unconscious of the culture?

Ortiz: Right. Which many of us are similarly linked to.

MacDonald: What are you interested in de- and reconstructing these days?

Ortiz: I'm becoming more and more interested in finding those situations in films where bias is expressed (the way that for a long time I've found the moments where there's dance) and exposing them. I think I've done some of that already. In *Beach Umbrella* [1985], I exposed the insidious hostility that's built into some of the cartoon characters in *The Three Caballeros* [1945]. As soon as you focus in on that brief passage I used, you can unravel how it encodes the hostile, shit role we men are acculturated into, that we suffer through life with. The scene becomes a kind of rape. Moments like that happen so quickly that they get absorbed in the larger story and we don't consider their implications. But in that one fragment, there is a whole story. Unraveling *those* stories is the challenge for me.

It's amazing how much goes on underneath the surface in all areas of our lives. We always stop at the red and go at the green (and on the yellow we're supposed to slow down, but we go faster): what are the psychosomatic implications of that pattern; how does it link up with our sense of race, of politics? In *pushAnn pushAnn* [1986], I was challenged to discover the minimal amount of visual information that we then *internally* unravel. I think that what we consciously see and what we internally, unconsciously unravel are two very different things. You know the notion of the magician whose hand is quicker than the eye? Conventional, linear media are always making things disappear into our unconsciousness without our realizing it. To what extent can we work that in reverse and, using a minimal amount of "normal" media information, make its real implications reappear?

MacDonald: I think this kind of work is particularly important right now. Years ago, racism was more overt. Now everybody pretends that we're all past the racist stage. The only way you know racism is there—and it's clearly *there*—is in quiet, coded little phrases, or in the subtle tones in people's talk, especially in their hunger to tell others that their anger at ethnic others is *not* an instance of racism. Racist attitudes have gone underground—they've become privatized—and conventional film confirms the process.

Ortiz: You can see that in a film like *Mo' Money* [1992, directed by Peter McDonald], where the African-American community turns on itself, not in the old, obvious Oreo cookie sense, where someone is African-American on "the outside," European-American on "the inside," but within the class structure. In *Mo' Money* the person being made fun of, seen as spurious and inauthentic, is the African-American who has been educated enough to run a computer and organize information for a credit card company. The boyz-from-the-'hood-type underclass guy is the hero in the film. The encoded notion is that being educated is something we *don't* want for African-Americans, that it's a weakness for them to learn to problem solve on a more complex level. That serves the interest of bias. I want to do more with that kind of moment.

I think that my working with films is just an extension of the Dadaist idea of the found object—though, for me, as I've said, it also relates to indigenous culture's animism, the ability to find spirit in the stone. We filmmakers, or media artists I should say, can spend lifetimes going through the warehouses of film and exploring the realities within those realities. We can recontextualize and humanize them.

People have understandable anxieties about the computer working against the role of the artist as a humanizer. As a culture, we have often chosen to dehumanize invention, which is central to the creative and artistic process, and to allow it to become deformed. That in itself isn't even unnatural. Nature itself includes poison ivy and poison mushrooms, floods and locusts, things that lead, from the human point of view, to a great deal of inhumanity. So perhaps it's a tragic flaw that a certain amount of psychosomatic deformation is inevitable in any process of representation and communication. We can see film as a universe of creation within which such elements exist, and we need to take time—before we spend *all* our energy making new films that include the *same* kinds of deformation—to reexamine what's been created so far, so that its deformations become clear, and so creation can move on in a way that understands these deformations, and can aid in undoing the damage they cause, and finally can create new paths that lead toward the humanity that we all pay lip service to.

I'm reminded of indigenous people saying, "How could you get lost in this little part of the woods." And you say, "But I don't know where I am!" And they say, "But you just moved thirty feet." They can name each tree and all the little plants, and so they can orient themselves. It's the same with our media consciousness: at this point we're lost; all the trees look the same, and we don't even *see* the little plants.

The laser (I realized some fifteen years ago) is important because when you operate with video in the normal way, with videotape, there's just no way to get out of a linear context. Ultimately, when you want to look at a videotape, you can only see it front-to-back. With the laser, you punch the directory and access any frame you want. Electronic media can replicate the holographic openness of actual consciousness. Fifteen years ago, when I first started working this way, my colleagues considered it bizarre. For me, it was a fantastic new universe, like the mixture of cartoon and familiar figurative reality in *Cool World*

[1992, directed by Ralph Bakshi] and *Who Framed Roger Rabbit?* [1988, directed by Robert Zemeckis]. I was suddenly *inside* film.

I can see that some of my work is still caught up in the familiar, conventional space-time, and is no more or less profound than the material I'm working with. But at other times, when I really let go of the familiar ego attachment to more linear time and space and move into the holographic sense of things, something profound does seem to happen.

Martin Arnold

It is a commonplace of film history that the development of narrative, and in particular, extended melodramatic narrative, by D. W. Griffith and others, transformed the makers of pre-cinema and early cinema into "primitives"—or at best "pioneers"—whose discoveries became merely means to an end. The idea that motion study (à la Eadweard Muybridge's photographs and zoopraxiscope demonstrations; and the Lumière brothers' extended cinematographic gazes on everyday and exotic sights) and magic (à la Méliès's "trick-film" and its many contemporaries) might exist as filmic ends-in-themselves, outside of narrative development, seems to have become untenable, at least in the popular mind. And yet, motion study and magic have remained crucial elements in the history of critical forms of cinema. Indeed, for many independent filmmakers of recent decades, the determination to critique industry filmmaking has been related to a fascination with those "primitive" approaches to cinema "left behind" as the industry developed. In the case of the young Austrian independent Martin Arnold, motion study and magic have been central tactics for deconstructing and refashioning conventional Hollywood visual and auditory gestures.

For *Pièce Touchée* (1989) and *Passage à l'Acte* (1993), Arnold used a homemade optical printer to analyze, respectively, the visual motion in an eighteen-second shot from *The Human Jungle* (1954, directed by Joseph M. Newman) and the visual and auditory motion in a brief passage from *To Kill a Mockingbird* (1962, directed by Robert Mulligan). In *Pièce Touchée* a man, apparently a husband, comes home and is greeted by a woman, apparently his waiting wife. While Muybridge seems to have believed his photographs analyzed the motion of "reality," Arnold is well aware that *Pièce Touchée* explores a Hollywood cliché that is, at most, only a pretense of reality: a cinematic gesture that polemicizes a culturally approved relationship between the genders. Arnold uses his optical printer to lay bare the gender-political implications of the husband's arrival *and* to transform this gesture, which has become nearly invisible to most viewers, into a phantasmagoria of visual effects that would make any trick-film director proud. *Passage à l'Acte* focuses on a domestic scene in which a father demands that his young son not leave the dinner table until his sister has finished eating. Again, Arnold lays bare the politics of a conventional media moment, in this case transforming the original scene into a breathtaking mechanical ballet accompanied by a soundtrack that hovers somewhere between rap music sampling and stuttering. Indeed, stuttering—and limping, its visual counterpart—are as Arnold explains, two of his central fascinations.

My decision to interview Arnold may seem strange, given the fact that only two short films were in distribution at the time we talked (*Pièce Touchée* is fifteen minutes; *Passage à l'Acte*, twelve). But the visual and auditory accomplishments of these films, the amount of thought that seems encoded within them, and their considerable usefulness for those who teach cinema studies fueled my interest in talking with Arnold.

Our interview began in the fall of 1991 with an exchange of letters; Arnold and I talked in person in Vienna in June 1992, and we subsequently refined the conversation in a further exchange of letters. We are much indebted to Thomas Korschil for his assistance with translation.

MacDonald: The two areas of Austrian independent film I'm most aware of are the formalist work of Peter Kubelka and Kurt Kren, both of whom worked frame by frame, but not as animators; and the "materialactionfilms" of Otto Mühl and Kren. Kubelka's films, especially those he did before *Unsere Afrikareise* ["Our African Journey," 1966], seem a background for your work.

Arnold: I grew up with the Peter Kubelka films. I started attending his lectures when I was eighteen. In many ways Kubelka influenced me: his frame by frame thinking, his structural thinking. Kubelka wanted to advance towards the unexplored essences of the medium. He wanted to make the most filmic film. The central focus of Kubelka's thinking is what is happening between the frames. Therefore, he also tries to work against representation in the single frame: on one hand the very short temporal units he uses in his early films cause the individual frames to fuse; on the other, the images themselves are already graphically abstracted. In *Adebar* [1957, the title refers to a Viennese café] silhouettes are dancing, and in *Schwechater* [1958, the title refers to a brand of beer] the drinking models are hardly discernible after Kubelka's printing processes. In *Arnulf Rainer* [1960, Arnulf Rainer is a painter], as you know, there is no image at all in the traditional sense.

I work with feature film scenes, with popular cinema, so for my work the image itself is also very important, because the imagery doesn't only show certain places, actors and actions; it also shows the dreams, hopes and taboos of the epoch and society that created it.

Kubelka became a member of the international film community at a time when a strong belief in progress was still widespread, be it concerning the most filmic film, the most liberal sexuality, the most ideal model for society, or the newest technology. This way of thinking suffered severe damage in the early eighties (at the latest). The much-praised technologies have turned the world into a radioactive dump. Today, nobody believes in the idea of free sexuality in the wake of AIDS. The idea of social emancipation led to the dictatorships of the former Eastern Bloc countries and thus proved itself wrong. And if somebody talks about the most filmic film today, he too will be confronted with skepticism.

In the eighties, people paused and questioned why the paradigms of progress and emancipation had failed so utterly in so many respects. The issue is no longer what should be, but what is and was.

But Kubelka, and Kren too, did the right thing for *that* epoch: they filmically explored the possibilities of knowledge about art and expression inherent in their time. And both made very good films.

I am influenced not so much by Kubelka's films, but more by his frame by frame thinking. And Kubelka is only one influence among many.

MacDonald: *Pièce Touchée* is a remarkable film. How did it develop? What gave you the idea to focus on that one shot?

Arnold: A friend of mine, Walter Jaklitsch, used scenes of old movies to demonstrate a computerized projector to me. He had constructed it in such a way that it could project images at any speed from two to twenty-five frames per second. I remember looking at a scene from *The Human Jungle* that took place in the kitchen: while the couple is talking, the man is reaching into a drawer to get out a knife. At a projection speed of four frames per second, the event was thrilling; every minimal movement was transformed into a small concussion. We were convinced that we were watching a crime story and expected him to threaten her with the knife. To our surprise though, we found out that he was not "the murderer," but the husband preparing a sandwich. I owe Walter a lot!

At that time, I already intended to work with the possibilities of optical printing. Walter sensed my excitement and gave me the roll of film. At home I went through it with a magnifying glass and decided to start my optical printing experiments with the eighteen-second shot I used in *Pièce Touchée*, without ever having seen it projected.

My decision to use that particular shot was very intuitive. That representation of a man and a woman and a time and a space was a small universe that I wanted to observe in detail. Probably I also sensed that it is especially interesting to observe those things which we (falsely) think we have seen a million times. The husband coming home and the wife waiting for him are familiar images to everyone, especially because that scenario is used in all genres of conventional cinema. Every male Hollywood hero at some point returns home to his waiting wife—whether he has just shot a few dozen Indians or arrested illegal alcohol distillers in the Chicago of the thirties. Beyond that, the entering and leaving of rooms is itself a central impulse in conventional narrative cinema of the fifties. It is the simplest way to signal a change of place.

I also found formal factors that I was impressed by. When I discovered the quick pan at the end of the shot, I immediately thought of amplifying it in both the forward and backward directions, in order to destroy the calmness of the previously symmetrical composition. The structure of space in conventional narrative cinema is as much at a deadlock as the structure of gender, and because of that I felt great pleasure in thoroughly shaking up that space.

At the beginning, I tried out certain forward and backward movements. Naturally most of the material produced was trash, but I repeatedly corrected and expanded the more promising passages. In that manner I was able to feel my way towards an end product. Also, I continued to search through the original footage for all manner of implications and possibilities. I wanted to see what the actors were doing, what the camera was doing, what the light was doing, which shadows would appear when and where, and so on.

I was never tempted to exercise any kind of conceptual art: that is, to think up an abstract system into which I would fit the images.

MacDonald: How long did you work on *Pièce Touchée?*

Arnold: I worked on it very intensely for one and a half years. Using an optical printer I made myself—very simple and very fragile—I photographed 148,000 single images and wrote down the sequences of the frames in a two-hundred-page score. I learned to think movies forwards, backwards, flipped and upside down.

MacDonald: *Pièce Touchée* asks that the viewer investigate a bit of film the way a scientist investigates a cell—though you're more playful than most scientists in your presentation of your "findings": your exposure of the gender implications is as theoretically aware as it is entertaining. The woman in the shot is still, passive, waiting for the man; and when he arrives, his movement causes her to move. When the door begins to open, her head begins to move in the same direction, and when his hand closes the door, her head swings the same way. It's as if she's a puppet attached to him by strings.

I've heard you described as a film theorist; what theorizing—by you or others—do you see as particularly relevant to *Pièce Touchée* and its exploration of gender?

Arnold: I am not a film theorist and I did not try to filmically translate any theory of gender politics.

And your comparison with the scientist is only partly true. I suppose I do use the optical printer as a kind of microscope. But concerning the cell, the comparison is problematic: a cell is something natural, whereas a shot from a movie is an artifact, it comes from an industry which supplies people with pictures and stories that move them.

MacDonald: I'll switch analogies. In my view, your film combines the strategies of the earliest filmmakers and pre-cinematic explorers of movement. Like Muybridge, you do a "motion study" of a social artifact (Muybridge studied the way people conventionally moved; you study the way people conventionally move *in film*); like the Lumières, you explore the possibilities of a single shot (though a single shot from a film, rather than from "reality"), and like Méliès, you use your apparatus, the optical printer, to transform conventional motion into magic. While Méliès, and the approaches he inspired, was later incorporated into the history of conventional narrative, you transform conventional narrative back into magic. It's like a revenge on film history.

Arnold: I like the expression "revenge" in this context. When I look at the history of humankind, at my own history, and also at film history, I can think of a lot of things I would love to take revenge for. But a revenge on the history of humankind is impossible; the revenge on one's own history is called psychoanalysis and touches upon the early enemies only in one's own head—and with film history it is also difficult. As an independent filmmaker, you fight in a very small army; lonely and badly armed, you compete against the star wars systems of Warners and Metro.

With respect to my relation to early cinema: your comparisons are certainly flattering, but I have never seriously thought about these relations myself. To establish such relationships is the task of the theoretician; an artist who indulges in such comparisons is presumptuous.

I like the idea that people inscribe themselves into different kinds of materials, all forms of human representation and expression, from ancient cave painting to sculpture to computer art. Film is such a "space of inscription."

When you look at a strip of film you will at first see a regular sequence of rectangular frames that represent a three-dimensional space. Those are the tracks the camera left behind; the apparatus inscribed itself onto the material. If you look more closely "into" the frame, you will see tracks of the people and objects that were in front of the camera at the time of the recording. In amateur films an individual inscribes himself into the material with his family; in commercial-narrative movies an industry inscribes its actors, modes of representation, and stories into the material. It is here that the tradition of representation is being written, and those cultural idols, Man and Woman, and their ideal life together are being established.

Into the original strip of film I used to make *Pièce Touchée*, the society of the fifties had inscribed some of its codes of representation and a lot of its social norms (above all, those concerning gender). And all this was and is apparent in a couple of frames: it is not necessary to watch the complete movie to recognize the obvious and not-so-obvious messages inscribed in it.

But I approached the material very openly: at first I was interested above all in the strong sensual effect that is created by running the film forward and backward. I had the impression that the movements on the screen were extending to the body of the spectator. During the projection of my first sketches I was repeatedly rocking in my chair, as if *I* were attached to the figures by strings.

Many people experience *Pièce Touchée* as very erotic; I've been asked again and again why it's so sexual. I think that this impression originates on a formal level, as the product of that irregular vibration. The representation of genders adds to this and channels this instinctive mood. In the beginning I was surprised myself about the multiplicity of possible ways to influence meaning. Naturally this led me to search the original material for those aspects of the imagery that create particular meanings. It was fascinating to see that minuscule shifts of movement could cause major shifts in meaning. But also, the sensuality and energy of a work of art always work on a level where it is not yet (or not anymore) possible to talk about "representation." Forms, colors, contrast, and rhythms don't affect the spectator in the realm of language and logic; they communicate on deeper levels: I would situate the discourse they take part in in the unconscious.

MacDonald: You do more than discover what's in that shot: you transform it.

Arnold: It was fascinating to see the moments in *Pièce Touchée* where certain events are *created* just by the forward and backward movement. An example is the "sequence of the kiss," when the woman is endlessly blinking her eyes while he is massaging the back of the chair and swinging his hips. In the original shot there is no blinking; she has her eyes closed much longer; and he just takes his hand off the chair.

The game of producing new meanings is introduced in a less lascivious way right at the beginning. We see two frames repeated over and over, showing a motionless woman in an armchair. After longer observation, one might notice that one of her fingers is rendered out of focus. As a third and fourth frame are added, the finger starts to move and the spectator is inclined to attribute a certain meaning to it. We see a "trembling" finger, which ultimately becomes a "beating" finger. Movement enters the picture, meaning is seen.

MacDonald: In that opening moment, the man turns the hall light off, and you work with the relevant frames until, finally, his gesture of turning off the light becomes a flicker—a reference, I assume, to a basic element of cinema technology and to those "structural filmmakers," including Kubelka, who have explored flicker in their work. In North America and in England, critics (and some filmmakers) have seen a schism between filmmakers who explore the mechanical/chemical bases of cinema (Ernie Gehr, Tony Conrad, Paul Sharits) and a later generation who explore the issue of gender (Yvonne Rainer, Laura Mulvey/Peter Wollen, Sally Potter). Often, the assumption is that these two

Successive frames from Martin Arnold's *Pièce Touchée* (1989).

approaches are in conflict. I've always assumed both approaches mean to lay film bare, and confront conventional cinema and conventional audiences. *Pièce Touchée* combines both investigations: it's very much about the mechanics of cinema *and* about its gender (and other) politics.

Arnold: I go back to the term "inscription." I think that in the sixties, avant-garde film was concerned with inscription into the material, whereas in the eighties it was concerned with inscription into the tradition of representation.

In any case, I don't see any contradiction between the two approaches. The politics of cinema don't begin where gender roles are stereotyped (or challenged). Representing the world in linear perspective (in German: *Zentralperspektive*, "central perspective") through the optics of the camera is already an ideological undertaking, in which not only the object, but a certain view of this object is being portrayed. The optics of the camera construct a world the way certain humans see it, a world in which they can experience themselves as its center. This is already a politics of representation.

If we go a step further and consider the dominant practice of the cinematic apparatus in society, we are again confronted with political ventures. There are ideologies for telling stories and for presenting time and space. In classical narrative cinema the rules for representing temporal and spatial sequences are predetermined precisely. What was once called "realism" in cinema does not develop on its own. It is forced into being by a multitude of prohibitions and restrictions. Of course, there are similar phenomena of exclusion on the narrative level: certain stories are told, others not.

The cinema of Hollywood is a cinema of exclusion, reduction, and denial, a cinema of repression. In consequence we should not only consider what is shown, but also that which is not shown. There is always something behind that which is being represented, which was not represented. And it is exactly *that* that is most interesting to consider.

In my childhood, Hollywood's love and crime stories instilled in me great expectations of adulthood. I absolutely wanted to be a part of that exciting world. When I grew up, I was tremendously disappointed. Was the disappointment caused by the fact that Hollywood's male heroes spend more time kissing and shooting than do real-life people? Was it the pleasure received from Hollywood's stories, which in contrast to those of real life, always have a definite beginning, a definite end, and a definite meaning? Or was it just the voyeuristic opportunities Hollywood gave me to intrude into the private living quarters of strangers to watch their most intimate emotions? There is no one answer to the question of what constituted the attractiveness of cinema during my childhood. But one thing is for sure: I owe to it my current use of that apparatus.

Of course, theories that film artists themselves attribute to their work are to be taken with a grain of salt. In the sixties some filmmakers attempted to get to "the essence of film," the "ultimate elements" of the medium. On one hand, it is necessary, of course, to deal with the elements of the apparatus one works with. Through this exposition one can advance its creative potentials and contribute to an understanding of the possibilities of the medium. But if one describes the film exclusively, "essentially," as a set of mechanical, physical, and chemical variables, then one curtails the object to be defined. Film *is* all of that, but a lot more too! It is also *essential* to look at what film actually *is* in society.

And yes, the hall-light passage *is* a joke on structural filmmaking. I had a lot of fun confronting "flicker," a holy relic of avant-garde film, within the earthbound reality of a narrative movie, to send the "essential" film-thinking into a filmic living room, where obviously little essential thinking is happening.

MacDonald: Was the location of the eighteen-second shot within *The Human Jungle* important to you?

Arnold: The husband has just come home from a gangster chase. He's the inspector who pursues a killer of blondes. It is very late. His wife has already been waiting for hours, and in the following kitchen shot she admonishes him to work less and to care more about her. It is not a key scene, and the setting isn't representative, because the major part of the plot takes place at the police station and in nocturnal (studio-) Chicago.

MacDonald: Why the title *Pièce Touchée*? "Touchée" in English means a concession to an opponent for a point well made.

Arnold: Literally translated, "Pièce Touchée" means "touched piece," but this French term also stands for a rule in international chess competitions. If you touch a figure, even if it is just by chance, your competitor may say, "pièce touchée," which means that you have to move that piece. The German equivalent is *berührt/geführt* ("touched/conducted"). I like all of the associations of this phrase, not only those connected with gender, but those connected with the mode of production: I "touched" and "conducted" my snippet of film very often (148,000 times) to make *Pièce Touchée*.

MacDonald: I assume the film uses the sound of the optical printer as the accompaniment to the visuals. This sound seems to function in a variety of ways. In a general sense, it suggests that the imagery you appropriated—that is, the actions of the man and the woman—are products of the industry, of a machine or a set of machines/technologies. But I wonder if it doesn't go further still. At times, the man and woman seem to "dance" to *your* rhythm. It's clear that you controlled their motions so that from time to time they would be "in sync" with the sound *you* chose. Is this a way of suggesting, "confessing," your own inevitable complicity with the "machinery" of representation as it has developed in the industry? After all, without the industry, you'd have no film.

Arnold: The sound in *Pièce Touchée* does *not* originate from an optical printer. One hears a very narrowly laid loop which reproduces the sound of the door being opened, distorted in recording. Of course, I was aware of the fact that the sound is suggestive of projectors, blimped cameras, and in the case of *Pièce Touchée*, of an optical printer.

The choice of this sound was formalist. I only started to deal with the sound after the picture had already been completed, and at first I wavered between two extremes, sync sound and silence. Sync sound turned out to be impossible, because of the very small measures of time I had used for the picture. The qualities of a sound are hardly audible at lengths of a twelfth or a twenty-fourth of a second. At that level, every sound becomes a peeping noise and adds a childish, seemingly sarcastic tone to visual events. After the first trials with sync sound, I realized that I had to save that concept for my next project, where I could create the sound along with the picture from the beginning. As you know, that's what I did in *Passage à l'Acte*.

As a silent film, I did not like *Pièce Touchée*. I believe that silence in cinema confers a certain monumentality on the events on the screen. And further, "no sound" never equals silence. At screenings of silent movies the audience produces its own sounds and thus highlights the events by blowing their noses, coughing, and moving about in their seats. After silence had been eliminated as a possibility, I tried to work with sound loops of simple variations. In fact, I tried to construct different loops for the different parts of the film. But in the face of the very complex picture track, these loops looked like a "very ambitious try," at best.

Well, what remained was the most simple loop, a repetition of a small piece of the original soundtrack, but without its referential or representative character. I produced a few loops like that, listened to them along with the picture and finally decided on the one that at least in part conveys aspects of sync sound: it's the sound of the door opening. Although the sound, with its complete simplicity, is not comparable to the picture, I believe that it conveys a kind of tension that goes along perfectly with the tension of the picture.

MacDonald: *Passage à l'Acte* is an interesting expansion of *Pièce Touchée* in its foregrounding of sync sound. But it's also different in the sense that you use an image from a film that many more people will recognize immediately. I recognized Gary Merrill in *Pièce Touchée* when I first saw it, but had no idea what film the shot was from. *To Kill a Mockingbird* is popular, one of Gregory Peck's major films, a multiple Oscar winner. It will be recognized instantly. What do you do in terms of permissions?

Arnold: Nothing. You can't get old film material in Europe as easily as you get it in the United States. I decided to use what I could get, a scene from a stolen German print of *To Kill a Mockingbird*. Sometimes I am afraid there may be consequences, but I'm not making money with my films, or I'm making so little that I can't imagine anyone will be interested. When I decided to use the scene from *The Human Jungle*, I tried to find out who had the European rights. I located a distributor who told me on the phone that he didn't have the rights anymore, but that it was completely senseless for me to waste my time: as long as no one was getting poorer or richer, who would care? But before he said that, he did ask three times if I was making advertisements.

MacDonald: Have you been working on *Passage à l'Acte* since finishing *Pièce Touchée?*

Arnold: No. It was very hard to work for a year after *Pièce Touchée*. I did a promotional tour for that film—mailings to festivals, festival visits.

Then I tried to work with image and sound in another scene from *The Human Jungle*, but I didn't feel comfortable with sound at that point.

MacDonald: How did you choose this particular scene from *To Kill a Mockingbird?*

Arnold: I had two interests in the scene. First, I wanted another domestic moment. Second, because I wanted to integrate sync sound into my repetitive patterns, the scene had to have a certain density on the auditory level: to put it simply, it had to be loud and eventful. At this point, it was already clear to me that in *Passage à l'Acte* I would not work with a single shot only, but with a whole scene. I was interested in how my forward and backward repetitions would work on the cuts, especially with shot/countershot patterns. Moreover, I felt challenged to coordinate the actions of a whole group of people.

Those points of departure soon merged into the idea of choosing a scene of a family at the dinner table, where the family, home, and gender theme could pair best with my formal ambition to work with repetitions of sounds. There would be a lot of clatter and scraping at the table, the shrill voices of the kids, and the lower voices of the grown-ups who "educate," that is, repeat certain orders to furnish the kids with a decent behavioral repertoire. However, even if you know generally what you want, and are determined to rip films off instead of buying them, it's not easy to get your hands on the right scene. I taped a lot of things from TV, and finally chose the scene from *To Kill a Mockingbird*—a scene that is not vital for the narrative structure of the original movie and which does not have anything to do with the central theme of racism. The race issue made *To Kill a Mockingbird* famous, and I would have been afraid to use a scene where, for example, the black man is on trial. I wouldn't want to play around with that material. In any case, the scene I chose is a family scene, not different from many other family scenes, where parents and children are sitting at a breakfast table eating.

It's true, as you've said, that if somebody knows *To Kill a Mockingbird*, he could associate the rest of the film to what I am doing. But that wasn't my intent. I did go through a phase during which I was uncertain about this issue, since some writers I am acquainted with brought it to my attention. When the film was finished, the same people began to talk about the "family" as a matter of fact—the visual impression of my film was evidently stronger than their "better knowledge" of the original source.

MacDonald: I don't know the phrase "passage à l'acte."

Arnold: In spite of evident differences, *Passage à l'Acte* and *Pièce Touchée* have quite a few things in common. The two snippets are similar to each other. Both are scenes from classical Hollywood cinema, which show scenes of everyday family life. And I manipulate both pieces in continuously repeated forward and backward movement. I wanted to express these common aspects with another French title. This time, I found my title in a dictionary for psychoanalysis and psychiatry.

"Passage à l'acte" has several levels of meaning. In common usage, it means "transition into action." In slang it means something like "just do it." In psychoanalysis it is a (dated) expression for impulsive actions that are not explainable within the usual system of human motivations, the impulsive actions of violent characters. The English term "acting out" is only partly congruent with the concept.

MacDonald: I don't know anyone who has explored film sound quite the way you do. In the sixties there was a tradition among many avant-garde filmmakers of making silent film as a reaction against commercial movies on the very problematic assumption that film was, essentially, a *visual* medium. Of course, some avant-garde filmmakers have worked in complex and subtle ways with the connections between sound and image: Bruce Conner in *Cosmic Ray* [1962] and other films; Kubelka in *Our African Journey*; Larry Gottheim in *Mouches Volantes* [1976], *Four Shadows* [1978], *Mnemosyne, Mother of Muses* [1986]; Morgan Fisher in *Standard Gauge* [1984]; Su Friedrich in *The Ties That Bind* [1984] and *Sink or Swim* [1990]. But except for Frampton's *Critical Mass*, I don't know predecessors for your work with sound. Do you?

Arnold: I think I have been influenced not so much by American film as by contemporary American music. Hip-hop, for example, is full of sampled phrases that are being repeated for longer or shorter durations. Often, turntables are used to move records forward and backward. Such techniques are also used in more complex forms of contemporary American music—John Zorn, for example. Christian Marclay cuts up old records and puts the parts together in new ways. He also employs obstacles which make the needle jump forward and backward.

By the way, recently I listened to a popular program on Austrian radio in which amateur inventors had the chance to talk about their work. An ice cream vendor, who is also crazy about records, called in. He had invented a frozen record; he filled the pressing mold with water, and with certain (I am sure very elaborate) techniques he froze it in his freezer. A great idea: can you imagine how it feels when Marilyn Monroe's "I'm Through with Love" melts away on your turntable?

I myself began to put together a tape of "scratched dreams" two months ago. A friend of mine let me use her teenage record collection. Back then she had listened to her favorite passages over and over again lifting the needle and putting it back within the same song. In doing so she had scratched those passages so severely that now the needle gets stuck, endlessly repeating certain grooves: "Dream lo-lo-lo-lo-ver where are you-u-u-u. . . . " Thus the psyche of a young girl has engraved its desires into the record—now a document situated

Successive frames from Martin Arnold's *Passage à l'Acte* (1993).

somewhere between the unconscious of a single person and popular culture. This is a good example of how an individual can inscribe herself into popular culture and shift its messages towards collapse.

But let's get back to our topic. There was also a strong tendency towards radical new interpretations in the music of the eighties. Here, too, something is being transformed; "musical meanings" are being shifted, be it in John Zorn's ingenious interpretations of jazz giants like Ornette Coleman, Kenny Dorham, and Sonny Clark, or in the case of some guys from the "Nato" label putting "Running Bear & Little White Dove" through a musical meat grinder with a lot of humor.

MacDonald: You discover many sounds one would normally not hear, and you discover what new sounds you can build out of those. What was the process?

Arnold: For *Passage à l'Acte* I transferred the sound from the 16mm print of the scene onto magnetic film, to separate it from the picture. That way it was possible to discern on the editing table what was happening at which frame of the picture and of the soundtrack, and how long the different picture and sound events were.

On the level of the soundtrack my manipulations lead to a strong "equalization" of simple sounds and language. Through the continuous repetitions, the background sounds appear to be much louder than in the original narrative structure; the mechanism of selection which normally favors perception of language seems to be disengaged. Noise and language become sound events of equal value and importance. But this is not only due to repetition, but also to the fact that the forward and backward manipulations not only undermine parts of the structure of language but make a previously unstructured sequence of noises appear to be structured. Since the noises now follow a certain order, language loses its sovereignty, its special status, which it gains exactly because its sequence of sounds is structured.

Moreover, the phrases heard in *Passage à l'Acte* are such clichés that nothing personal is being expressed. Who is it that's talking? Society's norm speaks through language and language speaks itself, and apart from that, nobody speaks! In the film we don't experience people determining the conversation, but the conversation determining the people. This is the same way in life: we did not invent language ourselves. Through the acquisition of language, our entrance into symbolic order and thus into societal order is accomplished. And there is no escape from language (and society) except for becoming mad. This holds true for us as well as for the protagonists of *Passage à l'Acte*, though they are evidently treated worse: they are not only victims of the order of family, society, and language, they are *also* victims of the order of Hollywood cinema, and, in my hands, of independent cinema as well.

MacDonald: What draws you to the optical printer?

Arnold: In a certain sense the optical printer is an apparatus that works against the camera. The camera produces images in quick sequence in order to reproduce movement. With the optical printer one proceeds from the single image, from the "brick" of the reproduction of movement, to a novel movement. The decisive question here though is, what kind of movement should be produced?

In *Pièce Touchée* and *Passage à l'Acte* I work with a more-or-less continuous forward and backward motion. I start with frame x, go forward to frame $x + 1$ and then from $x + 1$ back again through x to $x - 1$. In *Pièce Touchée* I am not skipping any frame. In *Passage à l'Acte*, I do skip frames (every second frame within the backward movement) but in a way that the forward and backward motion remains intact. If I had chosen a different process, there might have been jumps in the motion. Both methods would be based on the apparatus of the optical printer and would lead to a restructuring of the original material. However, the filmic products would be very different. With the second procedure, I would break up the filmstrip and thus visualize, primarily, one of the technical possibilities of the optical printer. The actual movements of the actors would drift into the background, disappear behind the demonstration of the machine, since the abrupt movements of a machine have only a slight equivalent in human motion. But with my procedure in *Pièce Touchée* and *Passage à l'Acte*, there *is* an equivalent. We are familiar with stepping forward and backward in life: taking "two steps forward and one step back" is associated with insecurity. When a body trembles, we perceive anxiety or nervousness. My filmic interventions infuse the characters' actions with tic-like twitchings, that once in a while become so dominant as to seemingly create new actions out of themselves. The same holds true in *Passage à l'Acte* with respect to sound. If you play a word backwards, then the tape player as a machine will become audible. But if I play a word forward repeatedly, varying where I start, then something happens that we know from life. The repetition of words and sentences confers an "insisting character" on them; one can associate them with litanies and orders. The repetition of syllables produces the impression of stuttering.

Recently Maureen Turim wrote a text about *Pièce Touchée* ["Eine Begegnung mit dem Bild" ("An Encounter with the Image"), in Alexander Horwath, Lisl Ponger, Gottfried Schlemmer, *Avantgardefilm* (Vienna: Wespennest, 1995), pp. 301–307] in which she describes the tapping of the finger in the beginning of the film as a symptom—at first a symptom of the woman, then a symptom of the apparatus, and finally a symptom of the viewer. I liked that a lot and it also made me question my own associations with symptoms like tics and stuttering, both of which fascinate me. My apparatus produces movement through breaks, and thus has a "tic" itself. I reinforce that tic by letting the apparatus run forward and backward. It lets me enter into these different worlds and take viewers and listeners with me.

Psychoanalysis suggests that in the case of a tic, the movement that is actually acted out is superimposed over an opposite or at least different movement, which had to be repressed as a consequence of censored wishes, ambivalences, and aggressive urges. Stunted to a rudiment, they vainly try to overcome the manifest action. Something similar is true for the phenomenon of stuttering: a message that is in conflict with what actually is being said wants to be expressed.

To put it in general terms: in the symptom, the repressed declares itself. Hollywood cinema is, as I said earlier, a cinema of exclusion, denial, and repression. I inscribe a symptom into it, which brings some of the aspects of repression to the surface, or, to say it in more modest words, which gives an idea of how, behind the intact world being represented, another not-at-all intact world is lurking. Maybe this is the revenge on film history you mentioned earlier.

Ken and Flo Jacobs

Not only has Ken Jacobs been a productive filmmaker for forty years, but he has fought doggedly for independent cinema. In 1963, he and his wife, Florence, and Jonas Mekas were arrested for showing Jack Smith's *Flaming Creatures* [1963] in a case that helped to topple New York State's censorship regulations. In 1966 he established the Millennium Film Workshop in New York City, at St. Marks Church in Washington Square, where, as Howard Guttenplan remembers, Jacobs hosted open screenings on Friday nights: "Ken was a brilliant teacher and a very perceptive and provocative person when talking about films and related matters" (*Millennium Film Journal*, nos. 16–18, 1986–87, p. 9: this special Twentieth Anniversary issue includes a wealth of information about the history of the Millennium Film Workshop). In 1969, Larry Gottheim brought Jacobs to the State University of New York at Binghamton to teach, and for a time they made Binghamton a center for avant-garde filmmaking that inspired a generation of students, several of whom have had substantial impact on the field, including Steve Anker, Alan Berliner, Dan Eisenberg, Amy Halpern, Richard Herskowitz, Jim Hoberman, Ken Ross, Rene Shafransky, and Phil Solomon.

As a filmmaker, Jacobs has made substantial contributions to at least three major critical film trends. During the late 1950s and early 1960s, often in collaboration with Jack Smith, he developed what would later be called "trash film": with no money but plenty of chutzpah, Jacobs would film Smith, dressed up in makeshift costumes as he performed anarchic, gender-bending melodramas on lower Manhattan streets, sometimes with neighborhood children. The resulting films—*Saturday Afternoon Blood Sacrifice* (filmed in 1957; sound added, prints made 1964), *Star Spangled to Death* (shown in various "incomplete" versions from 1958 to 1960), *Little Stabs at Happiness* (shown in various versions, 1958 to 1960), *Blonde Cobra* (shown in various versions, 1958 to 1963)—confronted both the commercial cinema and those approaches to critical filmmaking current in the late 1950s and early 1960s. Looking back, they seem prescient of some of Andy Warhol's films and of John Waters's trash melodramas of the late 1960s and early 1970s.

With *Soft Rain* (1968) and in particular, with *Tom, Tom, the Piper's Son* (presented in various versions, 1969–71), Jacobs reestablished himself, as one of the most influential "structural filmmakers." (Since the publication of *Visionary Film* in 1974, P. Adams Sitney's problematic but widely used term has been much debated; its relevance for *Tom, Tom, the Piper's Son* has always been limited.) In the films of this period, Jacobs turned his full attention to an exploration of the mechanical/chemical, and spatio-temporal bases of the film experience, and of the viewers' ways of seeing and understanding film imagery. In *Tom, Tom, the Piper's Son* Jacobs provides a rigorous and extensive exploration of the original Biograph one-reeler, *Tom, Tom, the Piper's Son* (1905), revealing a wide range of visual territories within the early short's narrative action.

Finally, in *Tom, Tom, the Piper's Son* and in other, more recent films and film performances, Jacobs has been a major contributor to "recycled cinema," the tradition of using earlier films as the raw material for new works of film art, a tradition that begins with Esther Shub and Joseph Cornell (for whom Jacobs worked, briefly, in the 1950s)—and, in recent years, has become a, if not *the*, dominant critical procedure in independent film and videomaking. Except for *Tom, Tom, the Piper's Son* Jacobs's most noteworthy contributions to "recycled cinema" have come in the long series of cine-performance works that have dominated Jacobs's creative activities since the early 1970s. Jacobs has devised several ways of creating new spaces and times from filmstrips he has accumulated over the years, but the most important of these is what he calls "the Nervous System," a set-up of two analytic 16mm projectors (the analytic projectors Jacobs has worked with can be run, forward or backward, at 1, 2, 4, 6, 8, 12, 16, and 24 frames per second) mediated by a propeller that spins in front of the two lenses, and allows Jacobs to create a wide variety of visual effects, including 3-D, which are usually accompanied by one or another form of recycled sound (Jacobs describes his method, in relation to *XCXHXEXRXRXIX-EXSX* ["Cherries," with an X—as in X-rated—before and after each letter], at the beginning of his volatile discussion with the Flaherty Seminar audience, included in the "At the Flaherty" chapter of this volume). The titles of the Nervous System pieces are written in capital letters; to enhance the readability of the interview I have used conventional capitalization.

For a number of years, I resisted interviewing Jacobs for extra-cinematic reasons: mainly, a rebellion against the seemingly hierarchical family structure he and Flo had chosen. My excitement about the Nervous System work, and especially *Two Wrenching Departures* (performed in various versions since 1989), overcame my resistance, along with a determination to confront this issue in our interview. Our discussions began in September 1993, and continued in January and June of 1994. Flo Jacobs was an active participant throughout these discussions.

MacDonald: So at what point did you start making film?

Ken Jacobs: I really wanted to make film when I was a teenager. But I had no money.

MacDonald: Was your family poor?

Ken Jacobs: I had broken from my family. I had a grandmother and an uncle in Williamsburg [a section of Brooklyn]. I could always go there to eat something, though it meant walking over the Williamsburg Bridge to their place and walking back again. For years I was dead broke and hungry, not willing—as they say these days—to get with the program.

MacDonald: What's your first memory of a camera in your hand?

Ken Jacobs: I was about eighteen, visiting my father. I stole his Kodak magazine camera. I was shocked when I looked through the viewfinder, at the chasm between what I had in my head and what I could see. I didn't know how to reconcile it, how to get what I wanted out of this little box. Later, I went into the Coast Guard, and when I came out, I had saved money and bought a Bell & Howell 16mm camera. I resumed some contact with my father, whom I hadn't seen in years, and returned his camera. I hadn't used it. It was tainted—that's a big problem with stealing. I do steal a lot in my filmmaking now, but I don't feel the same way about that. I feel I collaborate—though often without permission from the people who made the pictures and sounds I use!

I tried a few things with the Bell & Howell, made some stabs. I was working on a film of the Third Avenue El when I saw Stan's film [Stan Brakhage, *The Wonder Ring*, 1955]. Being as young as I was, I felt the Third Avenue El had now been covered, so I dropped the project and began to make a film about pigeons in New York as an angelic presence. That didn't go very far. Eventually, I did complete shooting and editing a film about Orchard Street. I stayed with that project up to the point where I needed a soundtrack and money to print. The person I asked to do the sound refused, and I couldn't raise any money.

During the period after not being able to complete the film [*Orchard Street* was released, without sound, in 1965], I was working in a Marlboro bookstore (a big chain of stores which vanished like the A & P), and a poet who worked there said he knew people who were interested in film, including a composer. We worked it out for me to go over to his place and show *Orchard Street* to the composer. When I got there, it wasn't just the composer, it was a party—a slew of people. I was shaken.

After I showed the film, people snubbed the film and me. For them, it just wasn't avant-garde. Gary Goodrich, the actor, was at the party (he recited some of Edith Sitwell's *Facade*, stunningly; he and his beautiful girlfriend came over and said that the film was very good and I shouldn't judge it by the reaction of that crowd. But the main response I remember—I got it either from Adolfas Mekas (he and Jonas were there; Jonas recited poetry, in Lithuanian) or more likely from this friend of theirs, Edouard de Laurot, a crazy mean guy—was a tongue-lashing. He compared my film unfavorably to a recent British short [perhaps Lindsay Anderson's and John Fletcher's *O Dreamland*, 1953] that showed people at a fair eating ice cream in close-up and how loathsome they were. Why hadn't *I* done things like that?

Now viewers like *Orchard Street* and its embrace of people. At the time, I did know what I was doing. I wasn't naive. I wanted to get Orchard Street, without commenting on it. And I definitely didn't want to make distorted, low-angled monstrosities out of the people there. What I've got now is a cut-down version of what I showed at that party.

So, things didn't work out with the musician at the party, and I was not sure enough of myself at the time to not be affected by this crowd. That, and a broken marriage engagement, wounded me and I didn't film for a while.

I had hoped that *Orchard Street* would help me raise money for a feature I'd scripted. That hope had been shot down, but it made me totally free. I began shooting in another way, a go-for-broke way, just to *my* taste, or *my* own fantasy, without any consideration of where things would go afterwards and what kind of audience I would have.

I began filming Jack Smith as a white-faced mime, very influenced by *Children of Paradise* [1944, directed by Marcel Carné]. *Saturday Afternoon Blood Sacrifice* came out of having fun with Jack, Bob Fleischner, and other friends. I was staying at Jack's place, a block and a half away from here [Ken and Flo Jacobs live on Chambers Street in Lower Manhattan]. I had half a roll of film left after *Saturday Afternoon Blood Sacrifice*. Precious film! I shot the half-roll of Jack alone in an airshaft space to the side of the building. It became *Little Cobra Dance*. When that came back from the lab, it was a revelation for both of us. It had been done in a very offhand way, very quickly, and it was *alive*. What I'd been doing before was painstaking, relatively stiff, but it had given me the tools to work in this fresh way. I had developed control of my brush. I had learned to look through this crazy, little, detached rectangle and actually conceive an image.

Little Cobra Dance instigated my way of working for years, through *Star Spangled to Death*.

MacDonald: Did you go to alternative screenings often? Later on, you founded the Millennium Film Workshop and your students founded the Collective for Living Cinema.

Ken Jacobs: Cinema 16 was tremendously important to me, a revelation. It was about the only place you could see interesting work, except occasionally at the Museum of Modern Art. I didn't go as often as I would have liked, not having the price of a membership, which sounds ludicrous since Cinema 16 was very cheap. But I was *that* broke.

MacDonald: Were specific screenings particularly important to you?

Ken Jacobs: They were *all* important to me: the diversity of what Amos Vogel showed was important. One film does come to mind immediately, a film about mentally ill children, rocking back and forth [*Grief*, 1949, a documentary by Dr. Rene A. Spitz, shown at Cinema 16 in January 1954]. I used that later in *Star Spangled to Death*, presenting my characters as children rocking back and forth, isolated from each other while in close physical proximity.

MacDonald: Did you meet filmmakers at Cinema 16?

Ken Jacobs: No, I didn't. I wasn't always happy with the Cinema 16 audience. *The Wonder Ring* was on a program about the Third Avenue El [In January 1959, Cinema 16 presented "The Third Avenue El (as Seen by Three Film Artists)"; the program included *The Wonder Ring*, Henry Freeman's *Echo of an Era* (1958), and Kit Davidson's *Third Avenue El* (1958), and was followed by Buster Keaton's *The General* (1926)]. The other two movies about the El were terrible, and then Brakhage's gem comes on. And the audience (which I saw mostly as people looking to pilfer the films, use bits in advertising) hated it, talked during it, *booed* it! Usually I just endured the audience, but this time I got into a verbal fight with them. At the time, I was not only hotheaded, I could be physical. I don't think that happened then, but it happened a lot of times.

I didn't know anything about Brakhage; *The Wonder Ring* was my first Brakhage film. Later on—probably a couple of years later, 1962 or so—Flo and I, who were now together, first saw *Window Water Baby Moving* [1959] and other films.

MacDonald: *Little Stabs at Happiness* seems a seed for what came to be two different traditions. It's one of the first American films to declare its materiality by including perforations and flares, which became a standard tactic for many filmmakers. And the presentation of Smith prefigures the trash film approach that Warhol and John Waters developed in the late sixties.

Ken Jacobs: Remember, *Little Stabs* is preceded by *Star Spangled to Death*, which is hours long and full of perforations, misprints, et cetera.

MacDonald: There are, or were, various versions of *Star Spangled to Death*, right?

Ken Jacobs: Well, no. It has been seen in different versions through the years, just because I was trying to raise money for it with parts I had already done. I made shorter versions people could sit through—the original was meant to test human tolerance.

MacDonald: How long was the complete film?

Ken Jacobs: Four hours at least. To many people, it could look like a form-less jumble. Which it's not. For me, form is only interesting to the extent that it verges on formlessness, to the extent that it challenges incoherence. That's the drama. *Star Spangled* was an extreme example.

About 1964 the Bleecker Street Cinema showed *Venom and Eternity* [a.k.a., *Treatise on Drivel and Eternity*, Jean Isadore Isou, 1951]. I was so impressed, and so unhappy: "Somebody's been there before me!"—though it was a very different film from *Star Spangled*.

I had pretty silly reactions when I saw precedents for my films, even if they were precedents for minor aspects of what I'd done. That was especially true when Pop Art emerged, which made me feel that what I'd done was no longer going to be seen as original. Pop Art chilled much of my interest in completing *Star Spangled to Death*.

MacDonald: What was your objection to Pop Art?

Ken Jacobs: I was interested in social indictment, and I was disgusted and angry that with few exceptions Pop Art was going *with* society, was making salable products from sending up its cultural icons. *My* humor was wrathful, destructive; and Pop Art was making the differences in cultural strata very comfortable. Acceptable. It was a way of feeling superior to the mass culture monstrosity that was engulfing us *and* a lesson in how one could skate on it, get off on it, rather than be offended by it.

MacDonald: I mean, exactly how did you see Pop Art impinging on *Star Spangled to Death?*

Ken Jacobs: One obvious instance is that I cut out my use of American flags in the film because the Pop Artists had co-opted the flag. Now I wish I'd been able to just carry through with what I wanted to do. But vanity, some simplis-tic idea of originality, made anything that appeared similar to what I was doing seem threatening, and caused me to shrivel further into my essentiality. I can see now that my reaction was dumb.

I remember going to Cinema 16 when they were showing Ron Rice's *The Flower Thief* [1960; Cinema 16 showed *The Flower Thief* on April 25, 1962]. By this time I'd edited a lot of *Star Spangled* and there were even a few people who could see value in what I was doing. There's a crowd at the Fashion In-dustries Auditorium to see *The Flower Thief* and I can't get in! I don't have any money and the guy at the door won't let me in! People are walking out one after the other, so I keep getting *glimpses* of the film through the door, and I'm re-ally shocked and in pain because texturally it looks very similar to what I've been doing. It looks like it has my open-air, street quality and the anti-arty roughness I've been going for. And I'm devastated. I'm saying to the guy at the door, "Look, *they* don't want to see it; the place is emptying! Let me in!" Schmuck! Asshole! (I saw *The Flower Thief* a year or two later and didn't think much of it, and don't now, but it did have a breakthrough quality then.)

I really went into depression. I didn't have the money to assemble a sound print. I didn't even have the money to eat. *No money!* No *source* of money. I'd spent *everything* on the film. I just felt trapped. Ironically, it was possible to *shoot* film, especially on outdated stock, very cheaply at the time. A couple of labs were wonderfully cheap, absurdly cheap, and people in labs have always been very nice to me and have often done things for me for next to nothing. But still I had to eat, I had to pay the rent. I had to . . . but often didn't. I wanted to feel like a somebody walking around in the world I despised, but I couldn't.

MacDonald: Were you a beatnik?

Jacobs: No! But I was closer to the Beats than to the hipsters. I remember meeting Cassavetes and seeing him as a hipster type. I hated him on the spot. I saw a slickster, a guy on the make.

MacDonald: Did you continue to feel that way after you saw his films?

Ken Jacobs: I either matured or softened or broadened and later on did appreciate, grudgingly, *Faces* [1968] and, more so, *Husbands* [1970].

MacDonald: Tell me more about the evolution of *Star Spangled to Death*.

Ken Jacobs: What a story! I started it in the fifties, right after *Saturday Afternoon Blood Sacrifice* and *Little Cobra Dance*. It was the freshness and the quickness of this new approach that turned me on. Jack and I had been doing a lot of zany street theater, playing with the chance events of life. Dangerous! A kind of malicious amusement would bubble up in one of us and we would take the risks. A friend, Alan Becker, said, "Why don't you film this?" Fired by Alan's suggestion, I began to record what we were doing and to shape it for the camera.

Eventually, I had this long, impossible film and no expectation of it being shown anywhere. Which was all right. Something demands to be done and you do it. You obey: "I hear, Oh Master, I obey." One will learn *afterwards* what kind of accommodation society can make with such cultural mutants. I kept adding to it into 1960, 1961. And sometime in 1961 or 1962 the Charles Theater began showing independently made films.

MacDonald: I don't know about the Charles Theater.

Ken Jacobs: It was a regular movie house on the Lower East Side, quite a ways over [Twelfth Street and Avenue B] that had days when they would show what later became known as "Underground Film." The Charles Theater was very important, in that until the Charles Theater, most of us working independently hadn't known that other people were making films. It was similar to Kerouac's *On the Road* coming out and all the isolates around the country—and maybe around the world—discovering that there were other freaks and outsiders living lives similar to their own.

I knew of Stan Vanderbeek through a mutual friend, and I had seen a marquee he'd put up somewhere in the West Village advertising "Underground Film." I was very pissed off with that marquee: I had been using that expression, too, and out of my boundless egotism and vanity, I thought "Underground Film" was *my* term! I couldn't figure out how the hell it got up on a marquee. I'd used the term politically . . .

MacDonald: Relating back to the French Underground in World War II?

Ken Jacobs: Yeah. Resistance. Occupation. Jack and I would deface posters in the subway, which I called "counter-desecration." At one point, I wanted to make kits for people to attack posters. We had discovered some things you could do with the posters, erasing and adding things. We had a lot of fun. While there was no hope of a real revolution, there could be this playful revolution— a mischievous, little-boy revolution.

Anyway, the Charles Theater: one night a week they invited filmmakers to bring a film, and they'd put it on. Nobody would screen it beforehand, nobody would decide what to show. It was absolutely wonderful, utopian, and usually there was a pretty good audience. There were all kinds of films in the most perfect sequence: irrational, beyond any curator's imagination.

MacDonald: Who was in charge?

Ken Jacobs: Two guys [Walter Langsford and Edwin Stein] who were very haughty and impossible to speak with. The Charles Theater hadn't been doing well for years, but somehow they were able to take this gamble. They would show normal Hollywood films most of the week, and then there would be a night of selected independent films, and then this open night.

I get there one night and show *Little Stabs*, the silent camera-originals with records—pretty much the music you hear in the film—and Jonas [Mekas] is in the audience. Later, I get a postcard (I have no telephone at the time): Jonas is working with Jerome Hill, who is making some money available to obscure, emerging filmmakers. He gives me the money to make sound-composite prints of *Little Stabs* and *Blonde Cobra*! Amazing!

MacDonald: How much has the color changed over the years? When I talked to Jonas about the early footage in *Lost Lost Lost* [1975; the early footage was shot in 1949, soon after Mekas's arrival in the United States], he felt that the imagery had aged well, that the decay of the color had improved the imagery.

Ken Jacobs: We like the *original*, but it's hard now to make good prints. We tend not to like the crummy prints we get now: they lend the films an artistic ethereality I hate. I went to Turin years ago and they showed a copy of one of the oldest prints, which they'd gotten from the London Film-Makers' Co-operative, made when it was still possible to get Kodachrome prints. It had such solidity, sharpness, and color density. It's holding up through all these years.

MacDonald: So you had shot up to four hours of *Star Spangled* material in the late fifties and performed the piece with records, but didn't have money to make prints . . .

Ken Jacobs: *At least* four hours. It included appropriations, entire found films, and other pieces of films.

Flo Jacobs: Making a print was complicated because there was color, black and white, reversal, and negative.

Ken Jacobs: It came out of a collage aesthetic; it's a movement towards order arguing *with* order every inch of the way.

MacDonald: So when you presented it, you showed the original?

Ken Jacobs: Yes. Some sections. I do have a print of the sections photographed on negative. *Star Spangled* is a raging, careening monster. It was willing to include the boring, which I must say, is part of what impressed me about *Venom and Eternity*: it also intended, in part, to bore.

As I say in *Little Stabs at Happiness*, things became bitter between Jack and me, bitter enough after a while for me not to want to work with his image. Much of *Star Spangled* was a glorifying portrait of Jack, and later I didn't want to present him in that light. Also, I felt the film was coming out way after it should have, and its innovation wouldn't be recognized. Money finally became available at the other end of the decade—in 1969, when I began working for SUNY-Binghamton. But by that time my mind was elsewhere and I no longer had the charge for it; its *necessity* had waned in me, beyond my resentment that the wherewithal to complete the film hadn't been available ten years earlier.

MacDonald: *Two Wrenching Departures* is an homage to those early days. Why did you choose the particular material you did? Obviously, you had many hours of work to chose from.

Ken Jacobs: It's odd, but it isn't like I made decisions. At least, I didn't make them in terms of should I use this or should I use that? The early section of people in the street comes from *Saturday Afternoon Blood Sacrifice*, the rest from *Star Spangled to Death*. But decisions about exactly what to use were made very deep in my head, and I just got the results: this, this, this, this. Similarly with the sound—I don't remember ever getting into any question about it. And I don't remember any kind of questioning about the title. It just happened. I was very disturbed, still am, about Jack and Bob [Fleischner] dying, especially about my close witnessing of Bob's death.

MacDonald: How do you mean?

Ken Jacobs: At the hospital, I met Bob's sister for the first time and got a sense of his family background. And learning where Bob had come from, I realized the enormity of what he had achieved, given what he had been up against, which he never could explain, I'm sure, even to himself. That was probably true of Jack, too. A few relatives appeared after Jack died, given by Jack the task of handling his estate. Judging from what Jim Hoberman says, Jack's family was pretty offended by Jack and totally unsympathetic to his work—which is grim, because they became the owners of everything he left behind. Of course, he had shunned them for many years. A thorough suicide was Jack. Irving Rosenthal recalls him saying that he *should* get AIDS.

MacDonald: I know you and Smith had a falling out, but were you close to Fleischner all this time?

Ken Jacobs: It's hard to call it "close" because as a friend Bob was inadequate in many ways. He was like a relative—a chance connection—you care for. One acknowledged his limits. That was true of Jack, too. You didn't want to be with either of these people if you were going through some kind of hell, because they couldn't meet you there, they couldn't be in contact. I think Jack was embarrassed by any kind of emotion—like you were imposing on him. Why bleed around *him?* If anything, his response would be to make you bleed more.

MacDonald: Did you have much to do with Jack after the falling out in 1961?

Ken Jacobs: We were always off and on, even before 1961. A lot of it was my fault, too. There were periods when we saw each other daily, worked together, hung out, *really* hung out—and then something would happen, a shift in the atmosphere and things would explode. It would take a period of staying away from each other, then we would just resume as if nothing had happened. We did that for six or seven years. And a lot of it was fun, great fun. A lot of stunts, and some wonderful conversations.

Occasionally, Jack would be in a state where he could listen and I could go into some of the things I was thinking about, and in those interludes, I think he received these thoughts very profoundly. Not that he would have so much to say, but it would land, and my isolation would let up for a moment. Especially ideas about art.

MacDonald: What kinds of things would you agree on?

Ken Jacobs: He had his own understanding of things, which was often very surprising to me. He was the first person I ever met who voiced deep feeling for black and white, revering von Sternberg. And similarly, he appreciated the atmospheric photography of film noir, which was still developing when we met. He liked the Andrews Sisters and Judy Canova—people I couldn't *begin* to fix my attention on. I remember him saying, "I have nostalgia for the forties. I'm sure no one ever told you that!" This is like the mid-fifties! Nostalgia for the forties took a *gift* for nostalgia, because it was such a seedy, dry, dumb period, culturally. But that turned my mind to the idea of nostalgia. I hadn't realized it, but I suffered nostalgia for the thirties.

There were things Jack knew about Hollywood, trivial things, which he took very much to heart. Everybody knows about his thing for Maria Montez. She was no longer a convincing movie fantasy to him: he saw her for what she was, but he could empathize with her narcissistic self-delusion. She was a drag queen who happened to be female. He was deep in admiration of all the Dan Duryea films. Hollywood was concocting a crazy imagery of life that Jack could appreciate, while I had written it all off. Jack helped me realize its mythic value, and that much good work had come out of Hollywood.

I had, at that time, no capacity for "camp" humor—none. It took me a while to catch up with "camp," to be able to go with *Blonde Venus* [1932] and not see it solely as stupid, dishonest, racist. Good God, the operatic nonsense of it! Were they kidding? For me, von Stroheim was the master, and *Greed* [1924]

Jack Smith in *Blonde Cobra* (1963).

was everything. Partly through Jack, I came to see *Blonde Venus* as a flight of a certain kind of corny fantasy, a mass-produced but genuine fantasy, that could engage very deeply, could be taken personally . . . as Jack took it. The absurdities weren't absurd to him—he grandly encompassed them—and he could impart some of that to me. Jack could *talk* about a von Sternberg.

When I met Jack, his hope was to become a fashion photographer. He had made movies as a teenager, wonderful pure-faith movies, trying to recreate Hollywood Arabia in backyards in Ohio. I had a film of his called *The Saracens* for a long time and then gave it back. A wonderful, miniature Hollywood movie. You know, the neighbors' clotheslines visible over Ohio Arabia. It was so blind in its pure faith in the fantasy. I mean Jack wasn't seeing *the film* at all, just the fantasy that the film indicated and made accessible to him.

And in New York, before I met him, he had shot, in 16mm color, this poor girl (with terrible skin, the lights burning her up), trying to make her his Maria Montez, in this lily pond he had built with bricks and junk in a loft on Twenty-sixth Street. It was absurd. Blind. His sincerity was beautiful, but also awful.

He did do wonderful photography in the late fifties, much better I think than what I saw by him years later, when I think he had lost his eye. I don't know why that work didn't become valuable when photography began to become salable gallery merchandise. It's inexplicable to me that they aren't among the most valued photographs. They're so evocative! I hope nothing has happened to them. I keep a few.

I can see now how the photographs developed into the atmosphere of *Flaming Creatures*.

MacDonald: So what was the final falling out?

Ken Jacobs: In 1961, we had had one of our periodic blow-ups, and I went away for the summer, hoping to make some money working at this and that. I ended up out of money in Provincetown. Hans Hofmann had a studio in Provincetown that he would let people use. He had been my painting teacher. He was a great artist, and very important to me. Mostly by accident, I ended up at his studio. Flo had come down from the Rhode Island School of Design to make money doing street portraits of people. The day after I got there, I met Flo and her friend, Alice. I had one dollar. I latched on to their lives. And things went swimmingly. I got over my current anger at Jack and sent him a postcard saying, "It's great here. Come on up." And one day, without warning, Jack appears with a trunk of theater gossamers! He's hitchhiked with this huge theater trunk! Unbelievable! Jack did the inconceivable. He *was* inconceivable.

I had my camera and a little bit of film and I began filming what became *The Death of P'town* [1961] with Jack as the Fairy Vampire. I have one roll of that. We tried showing it around to get money to buy more film. People were amused, but no money.

Provincetown already had a large homosexual population. And Jack came out that summer. No question he had had homosexual experiences before, but in Provincetown he made it into an identification for himself. And when he did, he projected—I will take *no* responsibility for this; it was a bum rap—disapproval and estrangement from us. We neither condemned him, nor disapproved, nor cut him out. But he flipped.

At the same time, I think he was interested in Flo, and very torn and jealous. Flo cared for him. They had been very tight that summer. One time, we were in bed in this little bungalow and Jack wanted to come in. We couldn't let him come in at the moment. And he just went insane. I think there was some kind of feeling of the child being forced from the parents' bedroom. He and I had been doing all kinds of things together that summer—poetry, theater—and it all just became snarled, and more and more bitter. By the end of the summer, it was real bad. I don't think I saw him again until it was necessary to record sound for *Blonde Cobra*. We made one or two attempts after that to socialize. Impossible.

Flo Jacobs: Later, we were also very angry with Jack for the *Flaming Creatures* episode. We were arrested for showing the film, and he treated us like dummies who had invited arrest. We were involved with the trial for probably a year, but Jack never acknowledged us. He acted as if he had no connection to what took place. He was disgusting.

MacDonald: How exactly were you involved in that screening?

Flo Jacobs: Ken was the theater manager and I was the ticket seller (Jerry Sims was the ticket taker), when it was shown at the St. Mark's Theater on Third Avenue. Jerry Sims got off because he denied knowing what was on the screen.

Ken Jacobs: He claimed he never turned around to see what was playing behind him!

Flo Jacobs: And the projectionist ran out of the theater . . .

Ken Jacobs: We've never seen him since!

MacDonald: So just you two were arrested?

Flo Jacobs: Jonas came down and insisted on being booked.

Ken Jacobs: Poet Diane DiPrima called up Jonas and told him what was happening. He came rushing over and told the cops, "I booked the theater!" That was very wise because Jonas was a name then, with his mind-rattling column in *The Village Voice*. He made the incident an event that got noticed.

Flo Jacobs: We lived on Long Island for the summer, and we had to come in for the trial days, and it just went on and on. Once in awhile Jack would appear in the back . . .

Ken Jacobs: Very disdainful . . .

Flo Jacobs: As if what we were doing was ridiculous. The whole thing was awful. We were never even allowed to speak in court. It went all the way to the federal Supreme Court. Up until then you had to submit a written transcript of a film's sound to the New York State Censor Board. They'd look at it and give you a license that you were supposed to put in front of the film to show that it had been approved. Other underground films ignored the procedure, like Gregory Markopoulos's *Twice A Man* [1963], but *Flaming Creatures* was a film the Censor Board felt they could make an issue of. The State gave Kenneth and Jonas six months in the workhouse, but suspended the sentence. The Supreme Court decided they couldn't pass judgment on the film and that was the end of the censorship laws. And then by 1967 there was legal pornography!

MacDonald: I want to come back to *Two Wrenching Departures*. The first section of Fleischner dancing down the street doesn't remind me so much of your other work, but when the door opens and Jack and these other people explode out the door, I'm reminded of *Tom, Tom, the Piper's Son*, especially in your dedication to frieze as opposed to a now more-conventional focus on a single character.

Ken Jacobs: One of the first Nervous System pieces I did was the door opening in *Tom, Tom, the Piper's Son*: it was called *Hell Breaks Loose* [*The Impossible: Chapter Three, Hell Breaks Loose*, 1980].

MacDonald: All through the remainder of *Two Wrenching Departures* you reveal great admiration for Jack's sensibility. At times he's a romantic figure. The passage where he seems to tumble through the street in that elaborate outfit is awe inspiring. And, at other moments—when we see him through the bars of the fire escape—he seems like a goofy teenager . . .

Ken Jacobs: But he's *more* than *goofy*; he's also ferocious and sad. There are many, many things going on there . . .

MacDonald: And then, when the visuals end, we sit in the dark listening to Jack recite "The Biggest Tits in High School," which is frightening. It's almost like a punch line. Whatever respect you've given Jack in the body of the film is recontextualized when you make clear that there's this other very terrifying person behind the person you've revealed.

Ken Jacobs: That's right.

I should tell you how the shot of Jack in front of the tobacco store, the one you describe as awe inspiring, was made. We were walking down the street together and Jack's got this outfit on and we're making shots. I get this idea and say to Jack, "I'd like you to tumble along the street and sprawl in front of this store." No discussion. He just goes over and does it. One shot and we continue. Just like that. Between envisioning the shot and having shot it, less than five minutes lapsed.

The scene with the bars of the fire escape is actually a clump of shots. During the shooting of *Star Spangled to Death*, I needed reaction shots. So I said, "Okay Jack, I'm doing reaction shots. The camera's on you: react." I didn't ask for any reaction in particular. Jack was "on" almost all of the time: he was ready at a moment's notice to direct himself in his ongoing personal movie.

MacDonald: That's a particularly beautiful part of *Two Wrenching Departures*. When his face is not moving, it's as if we're seeing a photograph and then when he moves, it feels magical.

Ken Jacobs: And his "reacting" works perfectly in *Two Wrenching Departures* with what's happening in the sound from *The Barbarian* [1933, directed by Sam Wood]. Jack moves into a very sinister, cruel, sadistic stance, just as we hear the Sheik whipping Diana. I don't know how sadomasochistic Jack was in his actual sex life, but there were certainly sadistic elements in his psychological life, in the shocking things he could find funny, for example.

The early Dada and surrealist artists often got off on cruelty. They rebelled against their natural sympathies. At one point, I had a very hard time drawing a line between myself and whatever else was out there, a hard time not feeling everything *so much*. I over-empathized; Jack was the opposite. He had a capacity for cruelty that astonished me, and that I wasn't a good audience for.

MacDonald: I've noticed that your career "dissolves" from one kind of work to another, to another . . . all of which are related, but also different. There's the period of *Star Spangled to Death* and *Little Stabs at Happiness*, which dissolves to the period of *The Sky Socialist* [1965; revised, 1988] and *The Winter Footage* [1965; revised, 1984], which include skeletal plots and characters reminiscent of your earlier work, but combined with a developing exploration of 3-D. A formal interest and a narrative interest are happening at the same time. Then there's another dissolve into more rigorously formal work—*Window* [1964], *Airshaft* [1967] and *Soft Rain* [1968]. That period culminates in *Tom, Tom, the Piper's Son*. And then, most recently, there's the Nervous System.

Ken Jacobs: I guess that's true. Even in *Star Spangled to Death*, there is an interest in movement and composition, but I didn't do much towards making depth palpable, so I guess there is a jump.

MacDonald: The first place it's obvious is in *Window*.

Ken Jacobs: Yes.

MacDonald: Because there people are eliminated, or at least are outside the frame, and you're focusing on texture and shape and . . .

Ken Jacobs: I was excited about the zoom lens. It was the first time I could afford one. It was a German lens, a gem, a Schneider-Variagon with its own reflex-viewer, that attached to a Bolex regular-8 camera. The importer in New Jersey let me keep changing the lens until I was satisfied. They were more than decent.

MacDonald: Does the shift into more rigorously formal work also have to do with your becoming a teacher?

Flo Jacobs: Ken, *I* know one of the reasons for the change! I've heard you say that your hand movement had become too automatic, and you wanted resistance. You started making films on a tripod so that you didn't become too . . .

Ken Jacobs: Glib. As Flo says, I had to do something that pulled me out of my habits of operation. I had come to feel I was repeating myself.

MacDonald: When Keaton first got a camera, the first thing he did was take it apart and put it back together, so he could understand this new tool. When I looked at *Soft Rain* again (which I vividly remember seeing at a symposium at SUNY-Binghamton in—I think—1972 as part of what was for me a life-changing program [the program included *Soft Rain, Barn Rushes* (Larry Gottheim, 1971), *Serene Velocity* (Ernie Gehr, 1970), and *The Act of Seeing with One's Own Eyes* (Stan Brakhage, 1971)], I realized that it's about being inside the camera, inside the space you're "in" when you're looking through a camera. And about the real world outside the camera, as movie screen. It's as if you're doing the Keaton thing, implicitly "taking your equipment apart."

Ken Jacobs: You noticed! Ditto *Airshaft*. And you've moved me to remember the split that was in my mind then between a concern with formal involvement and a whole other impulse, an autobiographical impulse, combined with a need to be socially effective. At a certain point I was able to bring these two things together—in *my* mind at least: by the late sixties, I had come to feel that formal development *was* social development. A formal film experience changed minds *operationally* and caused them to behave differently in society.

Flo Jacobs: When I first met you, you were as hateful of propaganda on the Left as on the Right. You said that Eisenstein's work had been totally absorbed by the advertising industry and had become repulsive to you, though you could admire the invention of his original contributions. I remember that *Airshaft* was shown as part of a protest against the war in Vietnam. When Jonas asked you about it, you said, "This film is for people who couldn't make war." You told him it was a political film.

Ken Jacobs: It was antiwar by being pro-peace, pro-serenity.

Flo Jacobs: Yes. And most of the rest of the stuff in that program had the same aesthetic development as advertising, except it was against things we were against.

MacDonald: What was this program?

Ken Jacobs: In 1967, we—Flo and I and some others—invited people to bring in antiwar films up to three minutes long.

Flo Jacobs: And as they came in, we just strung them together. There was an enormous amount of stuff. Ken called it "For Life, Against the War."

Ken Jacobs: Later, a selected compilation was made, but I didn't participate in that. I thought everything should be included.

Flo Jacobs: People booed *Airshaft*. They were also very hostile to Jonas's film, a beautiful film, *The Bill of Rights* [1967], made by photographing really close to the page.

Ken Jacobs: There was a huge audience at NYU. The program went on for hours and hours.

Flo Jacobs: But it was so normal! It was like a giant Crest toothpaste ad, except that these were advertisements against the war.

Ken Jacobs: Some were very clever and very skillful, and the audience picked up on that. But we were asking people to think further, to *feel* further. *Airshaft* invited people into another state of mind, what I thought was a post-war state of mind, a sensibility beyond war.

MacDonald: Do you know Hemingway's story, "Big Two-Hearted River"?

Ken Jacobs: No.

MacDonald: That's a story about war, where the war is never mentioned. Knowing firsthand the horrors of war, Nick, the protagonist, is much more sensitive to the beauty of simple things.

Ken Jacobs: That's *exactly* my approach in *The Sky Socialist*, which is about the Holocaust: the big signifier is that Flo is a stand-in for Anne Frank. But it's not a *lesson* in what the Holocaust was (I hate that word, "Holocaust," by the way); it doesn't pretend to *explain* and it doesn't attempt to get you to feel it again. It's very far from both the great *Shoah* [1986, directed by Claude Lanzmann] and the dismal *Schindler's List* [1994, directed by Steven Spielberg]. It *doesn't* give you information. Understand? It accepts those events as facts, and it's addressed to people who also know the facts. I don't want to play a violin and make them *feel* war. I don't want to encourage people to enjoy that kind of agony. *The Sky Socialist* attempts to help us love the world better. It attends to life.

Flo Jacobs: I feel that film needs intertitles . . .

Ken Jacobs: Yes, it's too obscure.

MacDonald: You began teaching at SUNY-Binghamton in 1969, right?

Ken Jacobs: Yes, Larry Gottheim and some students, including Jim Hoberman, came to a film festival at St. Lawrence University in Canton, New York, where I was a judge, and later I was invited to do a week-long seminar in Binghamton, which went well and led to the students petitioning to have me hired. I agreed, but only if they established a *cinema* department—Larry was in the English Department at the time. Amazingly, they complied.

I was totally naive about teaching. I'd never gone to college. I thought you worked *at least* forty hours a week at your teaching, and I threw myself into it with a missionary zeal. Believe it or not, I was shocked to discover that these relationships with students that we were developing, which seemed like *life* relationships to me, tended to come to an end at graduation. I couldn't believe it when people left!

Flo Jacobs: And there were Oedipal reactions, too. A lot of those.

I'd been far less excited than Ken about going to Binghamton. I remembered living in Albany during World War II, until I was six years old. I had to learn to run fast, to get away from kids who wanted to beat me up "for killing Jesus"! And Binghamton had a long history of anti-Semitism; in the twenties it had been a center for Klan activity.

Ken Jacobs: Anti-Semitism came at us in 1973, during a scandal that resulted from the students' decision to show *Shadows of Forgotten Ancestors* [1964, directed by Sergei Paradjanov], along with my short film *Nissan Ariana Window* [1969]. Binghamton has a sizable Ukrainian community that, I was told, had emigrated from the Carpathian Mountain territories where *Shadows* had been filmed. When the screening was announced, a church group considered bringing parishioners to see the film. But they wanted to preview it first—which I was against, though the students agreed to their demand. *Shadows* was judged OK, but then they asked to see the short film that was going to be shown before it. Well, in *Nissan Ariana Window* you see Flo nude and pregnant. The priests decided this was pornography, and the students agreed to show the short *after Shadows*. After the grand opera of *Shadows*, people are going to see my little, silent, meditative film? Impossible. At my insistence, the students decided to show *Nissan Ariana Window* first, following it with an intermission (for those who wanted to skip the short and then come in) and then *Shadows*. The church said this was unacceptable but the students stuck to this program.

The night of the screening, the parishioners show up, and some of them go into the theater to see both films. In the middle of my film, a priest comes in and begins berating the parishioners by name! And I see grown people get up like chastised children and, heads hanging, leave the screening. Grotesque!

And there's a tumult in the lobby. I step out and one woman from the church, who worked as a secretary at SUNY, turns to me in a fury and says, "Go back to New York City! This was a nice place before you Jews got here!"

The local newspapers were full of the incident for months. They never interviewed us, but the *Flaming Creatures* arrest was written up; we were pornographers!

Flo Jacobs: We have a thick file of things that were written about us. There were threatening calls. We kept our curtains closed. It was a very isolating and depressing experience, partly because we got so little support from our colleagues.

Ken Jacobs: Even from people you'd have thought would come to our defense! Though, surprisingly enough, that was the semester I got tenure.

As you know from experience, for a while Binghamton was a very exciting place for film. Peter Kubelka taught there, and Ernie Gehr and Klaus Wyborny (Heinz Emigholz came as a student) and Nicholas Ray, and we had visiting filmmakers every two weeks. In those days, the state universities had much deeper pockets; we could do what we wanted.

MacDonald: *Tom, Tom, the Piper's Son* is so unconventional that there's no way *not* to know that you're asking for an entirely different way of experiencing film . . . and, by implication, life.

Ken Jacobs: I'm beyond diatribe by the time of *Tom, Tom*. I've plunged into a new territory with new possibilities.

MacDonald: How did *Tom, Tom* develop? I've assumed that you worked on particular sections for long periods of time, and slowly accumulated the film.

Ken Jacobs: I was teaching at St. Johns University and getting deep into the presentation of film by way of projector play. I didn't have the analytic projectors I have now, but I did have this old, versatile Kalart-Victor. I could slow it down; I could stop it, I could go back and forth.

I'd read about these "paper prints" at the Library of Congress and rented some to show to my class . . .

Flo Jacobs: But before he showed films to his class, they would be delivered to our house so he could get to know them. And as he's looking at them, he's toying with them, not the way he does now with the Nervous System, but more like, "Wow! Watch me make this guy go backwards!"

Ken Jacobs: Gradually, step by step, I began playing with these films as a kind of performance. And then I'd have friends over and do it for them. At the end of one performance, my painter friend John Koos came up to me—where I was standing by the projector with my back against the wall really pooped, but also thoughtful and dizzy, trying to sort things out—and said, "Ken, that was wonderful. You should be filming it." I said, "I've been *thinking* about that"—that's exactly what I *had* been thinking about. He grabbed me by the shoulders and said, "*Do it!*"

Actually making *Tom, Tom* was a long procedure.

MacDonald: Did you work with other films before you decided on *Tom, Tom?*

Ken Jacobs: No . . .

Flo Jacobs: There were other films on that reel, but *Tom, Tom* was the one that Ken was always attracted to . . .

Ken Jacobs: It popped my eyes out! But it was the longest time before I could grasp *any* narrative order to it—I mean dozens of viewings before there was even a *pig* there. It was the welter of commotion that fascinated me, and then the hide-and-seek thing of picking out people, objects, events. And it was so beautiful, so beautiful.

When *Tom, Tom* first came out, there was interest in it for formal reasons: "Structural Film" was in the air then. But the work didn't exist only in that area for me. It was very spooky and very psychologically crucial. There's a thread of anxiety that runs through much of the film, which I met up with in my early twenties. As I was completing my Coast Guard stay in Alaska, I got into a very bad anxiety state. And I can see a reflection of what I experienced in the film. We think of ourselves as entities in relation to other entities. But how much of all this is just a whirling of energy, and the energy itself just a whirling of space? I was on thin ice in Alaska and the film is on thin ice all the time. The thin ice of this membrane of emulsion that dissolves, breaks up, threatens to fall apart. It's a perilous journey.

Joseph Campbell was very much with me when I was working on *Tom, Tom*. I had read *The Hero with a Thousand Faces* and a lot of it tallied with what I learned from my experiences in that anxiety state. In the Coast Guard, I was surrounded by people who were heedless, driven, full of force, and unself-critical in their being. My own energy was inhibited both by kindness and fastidiousness. I didn't want to mix in, and I was in terrible danger of being overwhelmed. I came back together not through psychiatry, but by attempting to get back to work, and then to my surprise, by *getting* back to work, back to art-making.

Tom, Tom, the Piper's Son was still one more investigation beyond appearances, which of course is very perilous. The film finally gets back to appearances, and hugs appearances, adores them—after the terror of slipping away into disintegration, into pure energy, noise and dust—just as I gratefully hugged appearances once I returned from *my* disintegration.

MacDonald: It makes a lot of sense to me that you were drawn to this particular moment of early cinema because of its frequent combination of documentation and obvious fabrication. In the original *Tom, Tom*, we see a real bird come out of an obviously paper barn. That's very similar to *Saturday Afternoon Blood Sacrifice* when bizarrely costumed people do events in the middle of an obviously real street.

Ken Jacobs: I have a couple of sources for that. One was a photograph that appeared in *Life* magazine when I was a teenager, people wearing sheets over their heads and bodies and doing odd things. But the people's shoes showed under the sheets, and the shoes were so mundane, so *non*surreal. That juxtaposition knocked me out, and set me off into playing between fantasy and the commonplace. What you're describing persisted all the way through *Star Spangled to Death* and *The Sky Socialist*. Pitting these dimensions against each other, forcing them together, fusing them, interested me very much.

MacDonald: What exactly was your filming procedure for *Tom, Tom?*

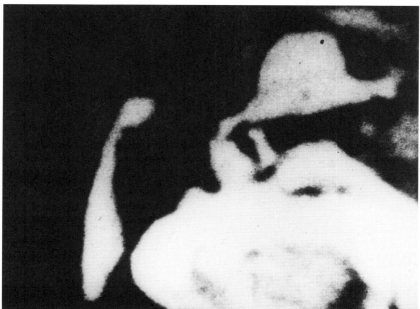

Abstracted carnival performers in Ken Jacobs's *Tom, Tom, the Piper's Son* (1969, revised 1971).

Flo Jacobs: He used a translucent screen: the projector was on one side and the camera on the other side.

MacDonald: You can see the light of the projector, particularly in the section where the film slides through the gate.

Ken Jacobs: Exactly. I've always been amazed when people think I used optical printing. To me, it's so clearly a projector.

Flo Jacobs: Around the time of *Tom, Tom*, "expanded consciousness" was in the air, and tripping. A lot of people saw *Tom, Tom* as an extension of that.

Ken Jacobs: Which did *not* make me happy! What *isn't* interesting on drugs?

My experience is that most well-meaning analyses of art assume the basic cogency of the art object. But the ultimate experience of art is fragmented. Art blows you into a million pieces and brings you back together for another hit. The work may have an order, but that order is just the recipe for stimulating a disorienting experience.

All in all, the filming of *Tom, Tom* was a real pleasure. I still look at the original, of course, and say, "Gee, why didn't I do *that*? Why didn't I get *that*?" And I actually thought at the time, "Well, okay, *this* film on *Tom, Tom* is done; now I'll start another one."

MacDonald: That's implicit in the experience. You and Flo mentioned the other day that the overall structure of the film echoes the way you used to teach: you and the class would see a film; and then you'd do an analysis; then you'd see the film again. But what strikes me is that when I see the original *Tom, Tom* the second time in your film, I *don't* think, "Oh, now I've *seen Tom, Tom*; I've had a systematic investigation of every detail." It's more like I've gone through a long film experience that reveals a tiny bit of what could be virtually an infinite investigation.

Ken Jacobs: That *is* implied, yes. Flo is always saying to me, "Don't eat so fast!" Usually, we consume our films too fast. We take them twenty-four frames a second, and go from one to the next. I'm interested in chewing and tasting, really slowing down the process of consuming, so that the experience is actually delectable. I want to see how much flavor is possible.

MacDonald: Starting with *Tom, Tom*, you begin to recycle material made by others; but what you do with that material is not "postmodernist"; that is, you don't decode the way in which the sociopolitical history has formed the imagery and the way it's put together. That may be some of what's going on in your *Tom, Tom*, but primarily you transform material used for one kind of experience into a different experience . . .

Ken Jacobs: To savor more of what is, and was, actually there, and to augment it and embellish it in various ways, to *play* it. The original material is my score. I honor the score, but like any musician, I bring who I am and the technique I've developed to my interpretation of the score, to my re-presentation/representation of it.

Earlier in life, after my faith in personality had been demolished by my reading and my thinking, I needed to restore that faith in order to go on. "Faith" is the right word, too. Personalities took on tremendous value for me—these very strong original presences, like Jack Smith, brought me back into intercourse with fellow beings, and reinforced myself as an entity, rather than as just something for other energies to impact upon, and shatter. The most important thing about *Star Spangled to Death* was the presentation of *personalities*. And I felt these personalities could be even more evident if I gave them half-assed roles to play in a half-assed way. I did *not* want the "actors" to "lose themselves" in the roles, but rather to keep the roles at arm's length, to *play* with them.

MacDonald: And later as you gained confidence both as a person and as a filmmaker, you could take a score like the original *Tom, Tom* and just wail on your own?

Ken Jacobs: That's right. By that time I was long-practiced at asserting myself. I had all the makings of a personality. I had hung in there, and was ready to risk a force-meets-force countermove.

MacDonald: How many Nervous System pieces are there?

Flo Jacobs: *The Impossible*, which has five sections [made from 1975–80], *Camera Thrills of the War* [*Ken Jacobs' Theater of Unconscionable Stupidity Presents Camera Thrills of the War*, 1981], *The Whole Shebang* [1982], *Cherries* [*XCXHXEXRXRXIXEXSX*], *Making Light of History: The Philippines Adventure* [1983].

Ken Jacobs: And there are pieces that were worked up to some extent but never shown publicly. And there's *Two Wrenching Departures*.

Flo Jacobs: *The Subcinema* [1990], which, like *The Impossible*, has several parts is related—though it doesn't use the Nervous System itself.

MacDonald: I think one reason why the Nervous System work has not been written about much . . .

Ken/Flo Jacobs: Tell us! Tell us!

MacDonald: That it's easier to write about something you can hold on to. Last night during your performance of *Cherries* I was writing notes as fast as I could; but, of course, once you're making notes, you're thinking "What is it that I just saw and how do I describe it?" and you're out of the experience. Your eye, ear, and mind are no longer drenched in the process.

Ken Jacobs: I forbid my students to take notes the first time they see a film.

MacDonald: But that's much less a problem with a normal film than with *Cherries*, where every performance is so evanescent. I've been to three presentations of *Cherries* and I'd be hard-pressed to write accurately about it other than in the most general way.

Ken Jacobs: But people have been writing about theater and dance for centuries.

MacDonald: But in theater they can go buy the play; in music, the score. There's a precise notation. I'm neurotic about being accurate, but how can I be

Ken and Flo Jacobs and the Nervous System apparatus.

accurate about pieces that are not only evanescent, but always new—since you improvise a good bit during your performances.

Ken Jacobs: I see what you mean. To hear music seriously, I have to listen to it over and over again and absorb the score. But what can I do! I feel that presenting work where the audience can't get a direct sense of the performance labor itself is like coming with a condom. I want the immediate contact. I want them to hear the tape recorder, I want them to hear that there's a guy *working* behind them. Today you can listen to a violinist on CD and maybe hear the music better than in a concert hall. But many people still prefer to go to the concert hall to experience visually the producing of the sound.

MacDonald: When I first saw *Two Wrenching Departures*, you did a fine performance, but I had never seen a long Nervous System piece before, so it was all new, and I didn't know where I *was* in the length. The second time through, at the 1992 Flaherty, I had as good a time as I've ever had in a movie theater. It felt like Saturday afternoon when I was nine years old, at a horror film with my friends, in a theater where the seats were wired for some kind of tingle-o-rama.

Ken Jacobs: Can this tape recorder record our smiles? That's sure better than somebody talking about the piece as "laborious"! Well, a lot of people don't want to meet up with a film *experience*; that might interfere with their political program!

Do you feel that the reminders of process in *Two Wrenching Departures* or *Cherries* are a problem?

MacDonald: Not at all. In fact, one of the things that happens in those pieces is that we can't help turning around to try and see the device—something most of us haven't done since we were kids in a movie theater for the first time, turning around to look at the projector beam.

Ken Jacobs: Oh wonderful! Right! With *Cherries* in particular, I want the audience to hear the projectors. I want the projectors to be among the "voices of the night."

Flo Jacobs: In the section of sound before the imagery starts, a narrator says, about the frogs, "So mighty a call from so small a creature," and then the sound of the frogs' mating call fades out and the projector motor comes on . . .

Ken Jacobs: And you hear one projector, then the other. I'm realizing, more and more, that *Cherries* is a mating act *between the projectors*.

MacDonald: It occurred to me last night that for you the sexuality in the porn clip you work with is a metaphor for the film experience, rather than vice versa.

Ken Jacobs: [Laughter] That's right! I mention in the program notes that the Nervous System is two stop-motion projectors that have a kind of congress. The fusion of their "DNA" is what produces these "bodies" of work.

MacDonald: How did the Nervous System apparatus develop?

Ken Jacobs: That's a long story. I'd never had any respect for what I'd seen in 3-D movies, so it never turned me on to do a film in 3-D. From studying twentieth-century painting, I had become very alert to the tension between 2-D stasis and 3-D dynamics. By chance, I came upon some cheap 3-D spectacles that promised to allow you to see TV in 3-D. The people who designed them didn't want you to know that all they were sending you was a piece of gray plastic, so they complicated it up so much that it hardly worked, but every so often there was the ghost of a 3-D phenomenon—I remember a ticker-tape parade in particular—and I became fascinated, though Flo kept telling me to get our dollar back. We needed every dollar.

So I took the glasses apart and tried to figure out what made the 3-D happen and eventually clarified it to myself. Some years passed and in 1969 I made what is now called *Globe* [shot in 1969, released in 1971] . . .

Flo Jacobs: It was *Excerpt from the Russian Revolution* then. Jonas saw it and gave Kenneth this book called *Eye and Brain* by R. L. Gregory, and Ken discovered that what he'd been investigating was called the Pulfrich pendulum effect, and that the piece of plastic was the Pulfrich filter . . .

Ken Jacobs: Pulfrich was blind in one eye, but he figured all this out! He learned that if you swing the pendulum as it would normally swing in a clock and put the filter over one eye, the pendulum would appear to circle in that direction, and if you put the filter over the other eye, it would circle in the other direction. So I began to work with the Pulfrich effect. I also got very involved in doing 3-D shadow plays . . .

Flo Jacobs: We had done shadow plays in 1965 with one light source, but

From 1896 Lumière brothers tracking shot, recycled by Ken Jacobs in *Opening the Nineteenth Century: 1896* (1990).

then he started using two light sources, and the people in the audience would wear Polaroid spectacles so that the shadows in space took on volume . . .

Ken Jacobs: And color . . .

Flo Jacobs: For example, we were behind the shadow-play screen, and we might hit a clear balloon up towards the screen. The balloon would seem to float out over the audience's heads, and they could not understand how the balloon wasn't actually above their heads . . .

Ken Jacobs: We had people out in front of the screen bouncing actual balloons in the audience's vicinity, so they never knew which was a real balloon and which was a 3-D shadow. We did these performances for years. Some were incredible, but it just wouldn't take off—I suppose because we're both so utterly inept at PR. I was very dismayed that when performance art began to get hot, we weren't being called on to do shadow play. We spent months shaping pieces that would only have a couple of performances, or one performance.

Flo Jacobs: A lot of people were needed for the shadow-play performances. I think that's part of the reason why Kenneth started working with two projectors. Then he didn't have to call upon a whole crew. Of course, even in 1965 he was doing things with two projectors.

Ken Jacobs: Yes, for *The Apparition Theater of New York* [1965], which was highly cinematic. We did that piece here, and in Canada, and once in London; and I did it in August of 1982 in Colorado, with students.

All right, back to 1975. I was up at SUNY-Binghamton, and Dan Barnett was teaching there that semester, and one day I described an idea for something to do with two projectors and 3-D, and he was fired up. He made himself available to me, which was great because I needed assistance. In 1975, we did *The Impossible: Chapter One, Southwark Fair*, which is the first tableau in *Tom, Tom, the Piper's Son*: the people gathered in the market (it's based on the Hogarth etching of Southwark Fair). At some point *The Impossible* was shown at the Whitney, and I did it at Anthology Film Archives on Wooster Street.

Jonas had a very odd reaction to these early 3-D pieces: he said he enjoyed them more when the spectacles were off. With the spectacles off, what I'm after is gone! So that was Jonas's particular perversity. Later, he wrote that he liked films where you put the film in the projector and it runs through normally. That was cinema, and all this expanded cinema stuff was contrivance. [See Mekas, "On Ken Jacobs, or Images and Sound in Space," in *Movie Journal* (New York: Collier, 1972), pp. 384–85, for the June 4, 1970, *Village Voice* review of this performance.] Jonas was my strongest supporter originally. He took a lot of us out of total obscurity, and at least gave other people who wrote on film the problem of whether to deal with us or not. But when Jonas knocked this work, I think he gave a lot of people the opportunity to say, "I don't have to deal with that, thank god!" And that's what happened—for years and years afterward. It wasn't until sometime late in the eighties when I was doing *The Philippines Adventure* at the Whitney as part of the Biennial—John Hanhardt has always been supportive—that Jonas said it was one of the greatest things he'd ever seen.

Generally, the dearth of reviewing was the killer. After a program at the Whitney with a tiny audience—most of whom came in, looked for a moment, and walked out—a friend of ours, who loves us, told us that this was self-defeating, that I had elected self-defeat by choosing to do these pieces, that I should go back to making discrete works and revive my reputation, because I had clearly been written off. That was very painful. This person meant no malice, and it seemed that, yeah, he was right. After that, I didn't work at new pieces as readily as I had before, but I couldn't help but persist in it—I was fascinated by the work!—so a lot of the results just took place at home.

So one thing led to another, and by the time I first did *Cherries* in 1980, I had developed a sliding shutter that shuttled rapidly back and forth, alternating the image and creating a sort of stereopticon depth, more like flat contours arranged in space. But that original shutter device wasn't adequate for the piece. I needed voluptuous space, rounded bodies.

At that time, there was another artist in New York working with 3-D—Alphons Schilling.

MacDonald: I was just going to ask you about him! Years ago I brought students into the city to several events sponsored by the New York State Council on the Arts (Jonas and Anthology Film Archives were involved). One of the options that weekend was to visit Alphons Schilling's studio.

Ken Jacobs: We were good friends at the time and each other's best audience. I'd look at his stuff at his studio and go, "Wow!" And he'd come to my place and look at my stuff and go, "Wow!" We *needed* each other because nobody else—including Flo sometimes—was capable of seeing the phenomena we could see. Later on, it turned out that our son Aza was exceptionally able to see 3-D; that probably had something to do with his inheriting my dyslexia.

Flo Jacobs: When we had to start learning about dyslexia, we discovered that sometimes people compensate for the problem by being extra sensitive spatially.

Ken Jacobs: A more-than-ordinary proportion of visual artists are dyslexic.

MacDonald: During that visit to his studio, I remember Schilling explaining that to have the kind of 3-D he wanted—not the planar 3-D that you see in stereopticons, but 3-D with volume—you have to have motion. I remember ocean waves . . .

Ken Jacobs: He made a *great* piece called *Lebensraum* sometime around 1979, or maybe earlier—a one-camera 3-D film! And he made paintings in 3-D. Alphons became very bitter, crazy bitter, because this stuff just didn't penetrate. Nothing was reviewed. The same kind of thing was happening to him that was happening to me. We were up against people who were passing judgment on the work with no development in seeing work like this. They were coming to it with their defenses up, and very few were willing to build up a discernment. It wasn't enough to say, "Oh, yes, I see the 3-D"—that's the least of it. Neither of us was just trying to get the "Wow! 3-D!" response, which is very easy. We could *do* things in this 2-D/3-D territory. Together, we became very good complainers, let me tell you, but I think he was even better than me! More explosive.

MacDonald: More explosive!?

Ken Jacobs: I think of myself as tempered.

MacDonald: Oh yeah? [laughter]

Ken Jacobs: Alphons was violent. He saw himself as a genius, and he perceived his inferiors coming into the money . . .

Flo Jacobs: He was involved with painting and galleries, and you have a different expectation when you're in that world.

Ken Jacobs: At some point in the fifties I'd been able to get these 3-D projectors, when there'd been a craze to project 3-D slides. I sold Alphons one of them. He said later that one morning he woke up with an idea for a shutter device that would work like the Pulfrich filter but people wouldn't have to wear the filter. He set this propeller up in front of the 3-D projector, putting slides in, and began to get these effects, and I thought it was *wonderful. Wonderful!* He showed it at the Collective and in a couple of galleries. He wouldn't show finished works so much as do demonstrations of this device. He was trying to teach the audience a little bit about what this was. Among these very pedagogical statements that he would flash up on the screen was one I loved, something like, "These are not only two points of view in space, but two points of view in time."

Well, that related to what I was doing. I was working with two points of time—different frames, in a series of frames—and in a sense I was deriving space *out of* time . . .

Flo Jacobs: You had already done *Hell Breaks Loose*, which uses the shuttling device, and *Southwark Fair*.

Ken Jacobs: At some point during this period Alphons says to me, "Why aren't you using the propeller?" and I say, "It's yours. *You* found it. *You* develop it." And he says, "That's ridiculous! Use it!"—knowing that I would take it to a different place from where he wanted to go: I wouldn't be staying with the stereo slides, but would work with the two stop-motion projectors from school I was using at that time. So I thanked him and thought, "Wow, this is really camaraderie!" A colleague in the arts is a gift . . .

Flo Jacobs: And so *The Impossible: Chapter Four* was called *Schilling* [1980] . . .

Ken Jacobs: Like *Hell Breaks Loose*, this piece used material from *Tom, Tom, the Piper's Son*, but it proclaimed the gift of the spinning shutter from Alphons.

MacDonald: You know, in the early phenakistascopes, the sophisticated ones, and in other, related devices, there were two discs, one spinning the opposite way from the other, to keep the image from stretching. That device is built into movie projectors.

Ken Jacobs: Is that so?

MacDonald: What you've done is externalize a device that got internalized during the development of cinema technology. You reverse "progress" and use the original "problem" for creative ends.

Ken Jacobs: Oh, marvelous. So they defeated the stretching effect . . .

MacDonald: And you *un*defeated it!

Ken Jacobs: What you say really excites me, because I've been saying that what I've been doing was possible before film. I knew there was that double-disc device, but I didn't know it was about not stretching the image.

When I began to modify the original propeller that Alphons gave me, through trial and error I began to come to another set of configurations and—gradually, nonscientifically—to develop the one I use now, which is the richest in possibilities. I have other propellers that do certain very interesting things, but it's always been a problem to switch propellers during a show.

So to get back to Alphons, I presented *Schilling* in 1980 at the Collective and then at the Museum of Modern Art. I wrote notes for MoMA crediting him—I've always done that. And then, at a New Year's Eve party, Flo comes over to me and says, "Alphons is calling you a crook." I said, "What about?"

Flo Jacobs: He was saying that he'd meant Kenneth could only use the propeller in the studio.

Ken Jacobs: My getting the show at MoMA had burnt him up. There was "his" effect, but I was using it in a different way and finding more things in it . . .

Flo Jacobs: Later, we got a phone call from his lawyer who said that he had patented the propeller.

Ken Jacobs: Alphons had a scientific background. He was far better read in optics and physics than I. He said he was more of a scientist and that I was more of a showman, as if my using the device in a theatrical work was a cheapening of this pure scientific finding . . .

Flo Jacobs: The patent lawyer who phoned for Alphons said he would allow Ken to use the device, but that every time Ken did a performance, he had to pay Alphons.

Ken Jacobs: Finally, we found out he had no legal hold on the propeller, and I disregarded him.

But I felt like the early filmmakers threatened by Edison. It was sad: here was this professional envy and jealousy coming at me while there were *no fucking rewards* for the work I was doing! A wonderful situation! Very depressing.

Let's come back to the present. When I called to tell you about this series of shows at Anthology, I was ready to say good-bye to the Nervous System. It had become too painful. The Flaherty experience was particularly depressing.

I figured I would paint, I would work in photography, and in sound. There are people I respect who consider the Nervous System pieces good work. Peter Kubelka saw *Cherries* and said, "Bravo!" And Peter is hard to please. Fred Worden was very supportive, and Mark McElhatten, and later on, David Schwartz. John Hanhardt recognized that the work was valuable enough to present at the Whitney; but after the MoMA show, over ten years passed before I got another invitation to MoMA. And in Binghamton we had Maureen Turim . . .

Flo Jacobs: No, don't . . .

Ken Jacobs: It's significant. Maureen comes out with this book, *Abstraction in Avant-Garde Film* [Ann Arbor, Mich.: UMI Research Press, 1985], and doesn't deal with my work at all. My god, she was in my department! And I realized that someone this ambitious would only make themselves vulnerable by this kind of omission if I were critically *dead*.

You know, many filmmakers are half crazy about this kind of thing. Brakhage has gotten the most writing and acknowledgment, and even he's had to outgrow this kind of heartbreak.

MacDonald: Some of the resistance to your work, including mine, has been a result of consternation about the nature of your relationship with Flo. In the late seventies, when I was just starting this interview project, I wrote to you and didn't get a response. A year or so later, we were at the Collective, sitting next to each other in the same row, and, Flo, you leaned over and apologized for not getting back to me. This was at a time when many of us were working to become more aware of gender inequities. My first thought when *Flo* apologized was that I didn't want anything to do with either of you. You seemed to have just the sort of hierarchical relationship I was trying to avoid: Ken gets to be the famous artist, and Flo gets to apologize for whatever *he* doesn't do. It's not so unusual for independent filmmakers (especially during certain periods) not to include credits, but Ken's decision not to include credits has the effect of rendering your contributions invisible—something that would be almost inconceivable in the supposedly less-progressive Hollywood industry.

Now, I do know that at the end of recent Nervous System performances, Ken wants you to stand up and be acknowledged for your contribution, but it's clear you don't want to be acknowledged. Do you consider yourself a collaborator on Ken's work?

Flo Jacobs: Absolutely not.

MacDonald: You seem always to have been a part of the process of the films and, during the Nervous System performances you always work along with Ken. So in what sense are you *not* a collaborator?

Flo Jacobs: Well, I do collaborate in the sense that I value the work. I think I know when the work is alive and when it's not. Sometimes calamities happen or the audience is so unreceptive that it's practically like hitting your head against the wall. I'm there so there *is* one audience member who can receive the work.

Ken Jacobs: Basically I'm doing the work for *it*, not for the audience, but it's helpful to know that Flo sees what I'm doing. Talking to her helps me formulate my thoughts. I "think" to her, and in many ways I direct what I do to her.

Flo Jacobs: But I don't consider this *my* work. I consider my work painting.

MacDonald: Are you an active painter?

Flo Jacobs: No. I do mostly watercolors right now because there isn't enough room here to do anything else, but I don't work enough.

MacDonald: I guess the suspicion would be . . .

Ken Jacobs: Be candid . . .

MacDonald: That you support Ken in ways that he doesn't support you. During the seventies, many people recognized the unfairness of the woman always being there as the sounding board and general support for the man, when men so rarely function that way for women. Not that I can pretend to have left this pattern behind: it's very important to me to have Pat as a witness and a support, and I have to admit, I'm less likely to be there for her.

Flo Jacobs: But that *isn't* the case with Ken and me. It absolutely isn't! And if there *is* an imbalance, I make allowances. He is earning the money we need, and I respect that. If he's not supporting me as much as I'm supporting him, it's because he has an insatiable appetite for accumulation, which *is* difficult. He's better recently, but it's still difficult.

Ken Jacobs: Say what I accumulate; otherwise I sound like Citizen Kane.

Flo Jacobs: Books, records, projection devices, cameras, machinery that will eventually turn into something that could be used to produce visual imagery. I do wish that *he* had a place and *I* had a place; and that we had a separate place for family stuff. Here it's been a three-ring circus, especially when the kids are around. It's not really that Ken doesn't support me, but I have had to be a little more organized than he is to keep things running.

My life is not really organized for making art. If it were, I'd have to say, "I can't deal with all this; I'm just going to deal with myself." And I don't really want to do that. But I'm not sacrificing 100 percent of what I want to do for myself. Maybe it's 20 percent. But *this* life is also something I really want. I want our kids to be healthy; I want them to prosper and to have a lot of intellectual stimulation, which this life has provided.

I knew when I connected up with Ken that there'd be a lot of combustion. In a way I left art school because of meeting Jack and Ken. After knowing *them*, I couldn't believe my teachers. Art school felt like careerist thinking and I wanted something else.

MacDonald: Ken, is there anything you'd like to add about this collaboration issue?

Ken Jacobs: Well, *I* acknowledge Flo as a collaborator, regardless of what *she* says. At the talk the other night, I tried to induce Flo to stand so people could know how important she's been to me. But she wouldn't face the audience. It has to do with her particular personality, and I'd be abusing her, forcing her away from her character, if I said, "Flo, you *must* stand up. You *must* be acknowledged!"

On the other hand, I *am* the filmmaker. I do what I want to do. I've never deferred to Flo in any kind of aesthetic decision. I listen to her carefully and no one has greater weight in my mind, but I'll do things that she doesn't like. For instance, the soundtrack to *Globe* . . .

Flo Jacobs: There's this tracking past suburban houses in the snow and you see the hills of Binghamton in deep, deep space. And he put sound from the record *The Sensuous Woman* on the soundtrack!

Ken Jacobs: Flo objects to it every time she hears it.

Flo Jacobs: I acknowledge the piece is perfect. I just hate it.

Ken Jacobs: You're *supposed* to hate it. It's a set-up. I'm putting those things there *to be* hated, but in a complex way.

As much as possible I'll have Flo look at what I'm doing. I'm always asking, "What do you think of this? Do you like this?" I don't know how I could have continued without her ability to see and value what I'm doing through long stretches when nobody else was supportive. Flo's a super helpmate at work, and organizationally, I'm very dependent on her. *She* apologized to you for my not writing because I'm almost beyond apologizing. You wouldn't put a one-legged man in the hundred-yard dash. It's wrong to expect apologies from me. I'm not constituted that way. In many ways, I wish I were, but I'm not.

Flo Jacobs: You know, when I met Amy Taubin in the early seventies, she said, "Marriage is dead" . . .

Ken Jacobs: *Her* marriage *was* dead . . .

Flo Jacobs: She meant the *idea* of marriage was passé. She liked the idea of everybody being independent and taking care of themselves. But there are other good ways to live, and ours is one.

Ken Jacobs: Over the years we've built up a wonderful labyrinth of conversation. I'm sorry that people think I cheat Flo in some way. I live in a state of constant appreciation of my wife.

MacDonald: The four parts of *The Subcinema* [1990] seem an investigation of ways of "doing" space. *Chronometer* is almost holographic. You cause a two-dimensional filmstrip to take on the illusion of three-dimensional substantiality. *Opening the Nineteenth Century: 1896* plays with Renaissance perspective and lens design, the conventional space of film. During *Phonograph* we're *inside* a space in the dark, hearing rain on a tin roof. And the final section, *Better to Be Frightened Than to Be Crushed*, explores multiple layers of texture. Is this what you had in mind?

Ken Jacobs: Well, let's say that I have the issue of space in mind all the time. I wasn't conscious of what you describe; these pieces just felt good together. By the way, even the intermission in *The Subcinema* is part of the piece. It's an unsung fifth section. I'm always very careful to consider the music I play during intermissions. I think *The Subcinema* is very well shaped. Each section pulls the audience towards the next, though there's no particular intellectual point to be deduced from my going from *Chronometer* to *Opening the Nineteenth Century: 1896*. It's just that after *Chronometer*, the audience is in a state where they can best experience *Opening*. And *that* puts them in a state where they can perceive *Phonograph*. And so on.

Flo Jacobs: The darkness of *Phonograph* prepares the focus on the soundtrack in *Better to Be Frightened Than to Be Crushed*.

Ken Jacobs: During the intermission, I play this Weimar Republic Euro-jazz to suggest that we're going into Hitler-time. That's implicit in [Edgar J.] Ulmer's *The Black Cat* [1934], which provides the soundtrack for *Better to Be Frightened*, and I relate *that* to the Black Nationalist fascism going on right now. The piece ends with racist talk by Leonard Jeffries from the radio.

MacDonald: What exactly is it that we see in *Chronometer?* I assume it's a strip of 35mm film and that slowly the frame we're seeing moves, but I couldn't see what's in the frame.

Ken Jacobs: You saw a performance where the nude woman in that image wasn't all that clear. A very sweet guy, Mike at the Chambers Camera Store, said to me, "I've got something for you." It was a box of 35mm still-negative strips of nude cuties, which I'm sure he shot himself on weekends. I'm using one of those strips—after storing it for a decade or so.

MacDonald: Is the original strip of the nude black and white?

Ken Jacobs: Yes. There is color in the projected piece but it's prismatic, maybe a lens aberration.

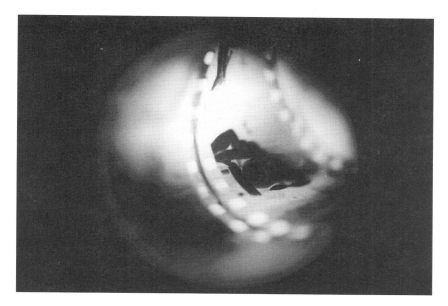

The nude in Ken Jacobs's *CHRONOMETER*, the opening section of *THE SUBCINEMA* (1990).

MacDonald: I found it a wonderfully sensual piece, even without knowing what I was looking at.

Flo Jacobs: He uses narrow sticks to pull things around so that different sections of the filmstrip are in focus. It's an improvisation and always different.

MacDonald: You know, even though I'm researching your work, I can never force myself out of my seat to come back and actually watch you do what you do.

Ken Jacobs: Good!

Many years ago, I named this series of works *The Impossible*. I don't think people realize how impossible what they're seeing *is*. Once something is there in front of you, you take it for granted. And if I *ever* did the impossible, I did it in *Chronometer*.

MacDonald: *The Subcinema* can be approached as a kind of meta-film-history. In *Chronometer* we're looking at stills of a nude, which is reminiscent of Muybridge . . .

Ken Jacobs: Yes, though Muybridge objectifies women while holding desire at bay. I'm inviting desire in. In *Chronometer* I want the woman to be narcis-sistically displaying herself, being alluring, inhabiting cinema the way a beau-tiful woman can inhabit cinema.

MacDonald: Am I right that in *Opening the Nineteenth Century: 1896* we see exactly the same footage forward and right-side up, then backward and upside down?

Ken Jacobs: Yes. The imagery is a collection of what were supposedly the first traveling shots by the Lumière company. The material switches directions, and you switch your filter from one eye to the other, halfway through. In the original sequence there were movements to the right and to the left, but the 3-D effect only works when the filter is in front of the eye that corresponds to the direction of the movement, that is, so that when the filter is over the right eye, the foreground figures move in that direction. Some images are turned upside down to maintain the direction.

The second pass *is* the same images in the same order, but the whole film is turned upside down and inside out: it ends with what was the first shot of the film, and whatever was upside down the first time is now right-side up and vice versa. The film is entirely symmetrical. Recently we've been toying around with train whistles. Right now there's a train whistle at the very beginning, and another one halfway through, which is a signal to the audience to switch the filter to the other eye. We'll see if that stays.

MacDonald: To get back to the overall design of *The Subcinema*: in *Opening the Nineteenth Century: 1896*, we've gone from Muybridge to the Lumières. Sound comes in in *Phonograph*; and finally we hear a Hollywood film. Are you tracing the development of film's fascistic potential?

Ken Jacobs: Wow. I wasn't aware of that progression. But Ulmer himself is warning us about fascism.

Flo Jacobs: When Ken releases the dialogue from the imagery, the dialogue is recognized as shocking. The original imagery keeps it contained . . .

Ken Jacobs: Within the horror movie, within the genre. Of course, I love many movies (though I hate more movies than I can find to love), but I wasn't trying to make a statement about the social control of movies in the final section of *The Subcinema*. I value *The Black Cat* and I'm attempting to make its message clearer to people. But I like what you're saying about Muybridge, Lumière, and the coming of sound. When you say it, it sounds familiar, but I know I didn't concern myself very much with that; I concerned myself with the work itself as an *experience*.

Sally Potter

Sally Potter is that unusual filmmaker who has made both a successful commercial feature, *Orlando* (1992), and films that must be identified with the formalist avant-garde. Indeed, the considerable distinctions among the films produced during the several phases of Potter's filmmaking life have regularly surprised those of us who have followed her career, in something like the way the eternally young Orlando continually surprises the contemporary film viewer who watches his/her remarkable journey through four hundred years of British history. And yet, as varied as Potter's films seem, during each of the several phases of her career, Potter has confronted many of the same fundamental issues and in ways that, in retrospect, seem to transcend the more obvious distinctions among these phases.

Potter began making films as an adolescent, when an uncle loaned her an 8mm camera. At first, she made improvisational "film poems" that were shown mostly to family and friends. By her late teens, she was conducting formal explorations in 8mm and 16mm, most notably of the possibilities of multiscreen presentation. In *Play* (1971), for example, she filmed six children—actually, three pairs of twins—as they play on a sidewalk, using two cameras mounted so that they recorded two contiguous spaces of the sidewalk. When *Play* is screened, two projectors present the two images side by side, recreating the original sidewalk space, but, of course, with the interruption of the right frame line of the left image and the left frame line of the right image—that is, so that the sidewalk space is divided into two filmic spaces. The cinematic division of the original space is emphasized by the fact that the left image was filmed in color, the right image in black and white. Indeed, the division is so obvious that when the children suddenly move from one space to the other, "through" the frame lines, their originally continuous movement is transformed into cinematic magic. Potter's "play" with multiple image informs several of her most accomplished films of the late 1960s and early 1970s, including the most elaborate of her multiscreen pieces, *Combines* (1972), produced in collaboration with Richard Alston and the London Contemporary Dance Theatre.

Combines used three, contiguously mounted screens to present seven separate sequences, most with musical accompaniment. These sequences—sometimes using one of the three screens, sometimes two, and in a single instance all three—introduced the live dance company, provided five entr'actes, plus a conclusion that accompanied the audience's exit from the theater. Instead of focusing on the "seam" between the contiguous filmic spaces, *Combines* created magic in its transitions between the filmic representations of performance and the live performance itself. *Combines* was presented for several weeks at the Place Theatre in London. It remains impressive today, though of course, since it was so intimately related to a specific group of performers working together at a particular moment, we can no longer experience its original energy.

Combines was the culmination and conclusion of the first phase of Potter's filmmaking career: she didn't make another film until *Thriller* (1979), seven years later. In the interim, she "trod the boards," first, with Richard Alston's innovative dance company, Strider (Potter was a founding member), and later with Jacky Lansley, with whom she formed Limited Dance Company in 1974. In addition, Potter presented solo theatrical performances and appeared in large-scale theatrical presentations, including *Mounting* (1977), *Death and the Maiden* (1977), and *Berlin* (1977), all with Rose English. While none of this work involved Potter working as a filmmaker, it did, in a general sense, prepare the way for *Thriller* and *The Gold Diggers* (1983), both of which incorporate performance into cinematic examinations of gender politics as they have traditionally functioned in the performing arts (including cinema) and in society at large.

Thriller is a distinguished instance of what Laura Mulvey has called "scorched earth" feminist cinema: that is, Potter refuses virtually all the pleasures of commercial movies, and especially the convention of exploiting women as erotic objects. Indeed, the traditional sacrifice of women for pleasure is the subject of *Thriller*, which critiques the gender (and class) politics of two texts: Puccini's opera *La Boheme* (1896) and Hitchcock's *Psycho* (1960). Potter's film simultaneously critiques and exploits the suspense thriller genre. In its minimalist mise-en-scène (the film takes place entirely within a bare attic space), its anti-illusionist tactics (there is no conventional narrative development at all: action occurs in narration, in photographs, in tableaux), and its choice of a black woman (Colette Laffont) as protagonist, *Thriller* undercuts the genre. And yet, on another level, *Thriller is* a thriller. Mimi, who is the "same" Mimi who dies in *La Boheme* only to be reincarnated by Potter, investigates the reasons for her death in the opera: *why* was it necessary to sacrifice *her?* Her questioning is frequently accompanied by the passage of Bernard Herrmann's music for *Psycho* that prepares the way for Norman's murder of Marion Crane. Of course, Mimi/Laffont represents Potter's own questioning of the relationship of the sacrifice of women and the film audience's pleasure. The bare attic in *Thriller* is not only an allusion to Mimi's garret in Puccini's opera, but a metaphor for Potter's attempt to "clear out all distractions and start from scratch" in her examination of the way women function within narrative entertainments.

Potter's investigations in *Thriller* continue in *The Gold Diggers*, though in the more elaborate form of a 35mm feature. Basically, *The Gold Diggers* expands on the "good girl"/"bad girl" distinction between Mimi and Musette, the central female characters in *La Boheme*. At the conclusion of *Thriller*, Mimi realizes that the plot of the male-centered opera kept the two women from knowing each other and from understanding their sisterhood: "We never got to know each other. Perhaps we could have loved each other." Written by Potter, Rose English, and Lindsay Cooper, *The Gold Diggers* focuses on a rich white woman (Julie Christie) and a working-class black woman (Colette Laffont) as they slowly find their way to each other and in the end, ride off into the sunset. As the women journey, unknowingly, toward each other, they explore a series of symbolic landscapes and cityscapes, familiar from a variety of commercial film genres. Ultimately, Potter's decision to abjure the obvious narrative and spatial continuity of conventional cinema (along with the exploitive use of women as erotic objects) and to replace traditional forms of pleasure with the less cinematically conventional pleasures of intellectual investigation and formal sensuality—the exquisite chiaroscuro of Babette Mangolte's cinematography, most obviously, and the memorable voices of Christie and Laffont—kept *The Gold Diggers* from achieving anything like the audience Potter had hoped for. Indeed, the film was so unsuccessful that it threatened to end Potter's career, and brought its second phase to a close: it would be nine years before she completed another feature film.

Before Potter would have the opportunity to direct *Orlando*, she would need to prove she could communicate with a broader audience than had been willing to support *The Gold Diggers*. This she did in *The London Story* (1986), a hilarious spoof of the spy thriller; and in two documentary video projects for the UK's Channel 4: *Tears, Laughter, Fears and Rage* (1986), a four-part piece on human emotions, and *I Am an Ox, I Am a Horse, I Am a Man, I Am a Woman* (1988), a one-hour piece on women in modern Soviet cinema. In the meantime, she worked (often with Tilda Swinton, who plays Orlando) on the script for *Orlando*, which finally went into production in 1991. *Orlando* was/is a successful film both aesthetically and commercially, and in its use of Orlando's frequent acknowledgment of the audience's presence, it is virtually revolutionary. Though it is a common gesture in various forms of live performance, characters within a film narrative rarely make eye contact with the audience. Indeed, the gesture is so unusual in film that the exceptions are quite memorable (and almost always part of comedy): Oliver Hardy's exasperated glances at us, for example, and Groucho Marx's asides to the viewer. Instances where a character in a non-comedy makes eye contact with the viewer are particularly rare. Memorable exceptions occur in Godard's *Breathless* (1959) and in several of Peter Watkins's films—*The War Game* (1965), *Punishment Park* (1971), *Edvard Munch* (1974), and *The Journey* (1987)—where eye contact between characters and viewer is a fundamental figure of style, and an extension of Watkins's polemic: a Watkins character will look at us, often from the midst of personal agony, as if to say, "I know *you* can do something to avoid what's happening to me; *you've* got time to watch a movie." Another exception is Babette Mangolte's *The Cold Eye (My Darling, Be Careful)* (1980), an attempt at a "first-person" film: all the characters speak directly to the camera/protagonist. In *Orlando*, Orlando's glances at the camera become, as Potter herself has suggested, "a golden thread" that connects the audience with the character, allowing "the spectacle and the spectator . . . [to] become one through the release of laughter" (Potter, "Introduction" to the screenplay of *Orlando* [London, Boston: Faber and Faber, 1994], p. xiii). By creating the illusion of an unusually intimate relationship between Orlando and the audience, Potter has found a novel and effective way of responding to the debate about the exploitive, voyeuristic "male gaze" that has been so important in film studies since Laura Mulvey published her "Visual Pleasure and Narrative Cinema" in 1975 (in *Screen* 16, no. 3): our personal intimacy with Orlando causes us to experience him/her, not as an object to be gazed at, but as a complex, sensual friend with whom we empathize, especially during moments of personal disappointment or happiness and during episodes where Orlando-as-woman is the victim of gender discrimination by patriarchal British society.

I spoke with Potter in New York in October of 1994 and subsequently in London in November.

MacDonald: When I first saw *Orlando*, it occurred to me that Orlando's transformations in time and of gender are a little bit like the transformations you've gone through as a filmmaker. From my perspective, you keep reappearing every few years with something that, at least at first, seems radically different from whatever you've done before. Was that a conscious connection that you made with the novel?

Potter: Well, I like the idea of falling asleep and waking up as if the past almost didn't exist. To the public eye, I do disappear and reappear.

MacDonald: Maybe it's to the American public eye?

Potter: No. It's true here, too. But to myself I am a continuum, though I do a lot of twisting and stepping sideways. Two days ago, I was dancing the tango in Buenos Aires for a week, and here I am talking with you about films and filmmaking. I'm not interested in consciously repeating myself, although in my work, as in most people's work, you can trace repetitive things.

There was something about the story of *Orlando* that completely gripped my imagination when I first read it, and continued to grip my imagination through the necessary ambivalence that you enter into when you work on a project for a long period of time. After the first year or so of writing the adaptation, I began to loathe *Orlando*, to detest Woolf's writing. That inevitable love/hate engagement with a work needs to be balanced by something at the core which can sustain you through the ambivalence about the project you've entered into, and return you, in the end, to a state of love.

The idea of being able to emerge into a continual present, which means we are positively saying good-bye to a past, was the sustaining principle that I discovered. It's difficult because I think most of us are embedded in our pasts. Being on the precipice of the present, as Orlando is, is a dangerous place to be, but a very exciting one.

MacDonald: I know you come out of dance and theater and music. Are you still working in those areas, or do you see yourself now as Sally Potter, filmmaker?

Potter: I see myself as Sally Potter, 100 percent filmmaker, who is also from time to time Sally Potter, 100 percent musician or 100 percent dancer. It's not about being half one thing and half another. But the primary channel for me has always been cinema. That's where I started as a fourteen-year-old and that's where I still am. But cinema in itself involves other forms; as a filmmaker, it's good to have, for example, a vibrant sense of musicality (a feeling for the invisible and the nonliteral worlds, which is what music is) and of dance (movement, after all, is the essence of cinema).

MacDonald: What happened when you were fourteen?

Potter: My uncle lent me an 8mm camera.

MacDonald: What kinds of films did you make with it?

Potter: I probably thought of them as little poems. At the time, I wrote a lot of poetry. These were visual poems. I loved the idea of editing in the camera so they were quite carefully composed but nonetheless improvised.

My very earliest 8mm films were done in the company of my uncle and his then companion, Sandy Daley (she later made *Robert* [Mappelthorpe] *Having His Nipple Pierced*, 1970), in a sort of expanded family situation. They were independent-film aficionados, and they gave me as a young teenager, a fourteen-year-old, the status of an artist doing her work, which was the most incredible gift! They gave me respect. I'd written my own plays when I was ten, and had put on shows for audiences at eleven, so I was obviously already on my track. But they gave me a wonderful push.

MacDonald: Did you become part of an 8mm scene? Did *Jerk* [1969] get shown around?

Potter: By the time I got to *Jerk*, I'd already decided that I was going to be a filmmaker. Definitely. No doubt whatsoever. I made the announcement at school, to a lot of scoffing. So I certainly had clarity about it. I made *Jerk* when I was seventeen; it was a serious work as far as I was concerned. I suppose I'd already joined the Co-op [the London Film-Makers' Co-operative] by then. *Jerk* was shown there and in underground film festivals, and it was shown in Holland. Later on, I took *Play* [1971] and *Jerk*, and perhaps other films, to a few film festivals around Europe.

To be frank, I always felt like a loner, an outsider. I never felt part of a community of filmmakers. I was often the only female, or one of few, which didn't help. I didn't have a buddy thing going, which most of the men did. They also had rather different concerns, more hard-edged structural concerns.

MacDonald: Who are you thinking of?

Potter: Peter Gidal. And all the heroes, Hollis Frampton *et al.*—all of whose work I saw a lot of.

I was probably more eclectic in my taste than many of the English structural filmmakers, who took an absolute prescriptive position on film. Most of them had gone to Oxford or Cambridge or some other university and were terribly theoretical. I left school at fifteen. I was more the hands-on artist and less the academic. The overriding memory of those early years is of making things on the kitchen table by myself—although I did have a companion, Mike Dunford, who was in *Jerk*, and who did the color separation stuff in *Combines*.

MacDonald: *Hors d'Oeuvres* [1971] was the quintessential kitchen table film?

Potter: Yes. The original material was generated on 8mm and projected on a little ground glass screen, about one foot across. A 16mm camera was on the other side filming. Mike operated the projector. Everything was done by hand and mostly the film was edited in the camera. I was just exploring the texture of film, and the possibility of making optical effects in a very manual way. I was asking basic questions. What *is* film space and film time? What *is* the frame? What is it for? *Black and White* [1969], where people push against the edge of the frame, and *Play*, the two-screen film where people move between the frames, were questioning that one issue.

I was also beginning to ask the question, which the other people in the Co-op at this time were not, what is performance on film? To me now, *Hors d'Oeuvres* seems very stifled and stilted in a way that I was probably a little embarrassed by, even at the time. But if I look with a slightly more compassionate eye at my twenty-one-year-old self, I can see that I was working on some serious things.

MacDonald: Were there particular films that fed you at that point?

Potter: Well, I had already seen *Mister Hulot's Holiday* [*Les Vacances de Monsieur Hulot*, 1953, directed by Jacques Tati] at least a dozen times, and a lot of the great American musicals. In my teens, I went to film societies and gobbled up Eisenstein and the Russians, and a lot of early cinema. By the time

I was seventeen, I was watching anything the Film-Makers' Co-op had, from Warhol's stuff to *Wavelength* [Michael Snow, 1967]. At that point in London, the Arts Laboratory had started (the Co-op was attached to it for a while). For a very low price you could sit on a mattress, and watch Underground Film, as it was known then, all day long. And I loved Godard and Truffaut. I was totally eclectic. I gobbled up whatever there was.

MacDonald: Of the early films *Combines* seems to be the most elaborate.

Potter: I was a dance student at a school attached to the London Contemporary Theatre. I became friends and colleagues with Richard Alston, and was in his dance company, Strider. He saw my early films and was interested, so we decided to collaborate.

MacDonald: Did you work together throughout the development of this piece? Was the choreography done knowing there would also be film?

Potter: Yes. I would film some stuff and show it to him and that would give him an idea for some choreography, or he would show me some choreography and I would think of a way to work with it filmically.

MacDonald: And how long did *Combines* run?

Potter: A short time. For a season.

MacDonald: There are so many things that work nicely in it; it's a shame it can't be redone.

Potter: Right, because the same people aren't there, and the whole thing was about the relationship with the real people on the stage and those same people on screen. But there are bits of it that still work in their own right.

MacDonald: In the United States, experimental filmmakers usually fit one of two patterns: either they make narrative, proto-conventional films that are different enough from commercial movies to be called "experimental," but are on some level, training exercises for conventional filmmaking (whether the filmmakers ultimately make it into commercial filmmaking or not); or they make defiantly noncommercial work that has no likelihood of breaking even. The filmmakers in this second group either stop making films at a certain point or continue to make unconventional experimental films for a lifetime. The number of people who have gone from making truly experimental films to making conventional or proto-commercial films is small. J. J. Murphy is virtually the only American instance I can think of. But I can think of several instances here in Britain: you and Peter Greenaway and Derek Jarman, most obviously.

When you were making the early films, was the idea of being a commercial filmmaker hovering in the back of your mind? Or was that the last thing you would have considered at that point?

Potter: I don't recall a fantasy of being a commercial filmmaker exactly. On the other hand, I also don't remember that I thought of these little 8mm films you've been seeing, as substantially different than anything I might go and see in the cinema. They were just smaller and concentrated on one tiny facet of filmmaking. That's why I gave them very modest titles like "Hors d'Oeuvres" and "Play." I knew they were fragments within the total possibilities of cinema.

MacDonald: I guess the distinction I would draw is that in two-screen films like *Play* or *Black and White*, the whole focus is the moment when a figure moves from the one image to the one projected next to it. Clearly, you're interested in surprising the audience by causing the impossible to happen. In most conventional films, such effects would have a narrative justification . . . though I suppose the dinosaurs in *Jurassic Park* are, in a sense, a much larger, more expensive version of jumping from one "frame" to another.

Potter: You're exactly right. The concerns I had at the time were the concerns of an artist falling in love with her medium, a breathless thrill about the most basic elements of filmmaking.

And also it was a question of what elements of cinema were at my disposal at that point. A lot of the early films, after the very early 8mm work, and *Combines* in particular, are about editing, because that was something I could do which didn't cost money. So much of an aesthetic comes out of the person grappling with the means of production available at the time.

The transition to thinking about storytelling in relation to film came much, much later for me. I remember it as a very difficult moment. For years, especially in performance work, I'd been passionately committed to the idea of the non-narrative use of time—to all the uses of time that are *not* about storytelling.

MacDonald: The earlier films are more about space than about time.

Potter: Exactly. And about jumping in and out of synchronicity, or in and out of what you think of as real time. I was interested in tricking, and then retricking, and re-tricking again, your perceptual processes.

By the time I got to *Combines*, I had some command of this sort of visceral trickery, and was interested in going further—specifically, into dance. You can't really film the experience of dancing, at least not directly. You may get the surface of it, but you don't get anything that resembles the incredible feeling in the body that dance gives you. In *Combines*, I was trying to find an editing equivalent to that.

I've jumped around. Your question is not something I've thought much about, particularly in comparison with other filmmakers.

MacDonald: Let me ask it in a different way. If somebody had walked up to you in the late sixties or early seventies and said, "Hey, Sally, I can give you the opportunity to make a half-hour story film in 35mm," would you have wanted to do it?

Potter: Oh, I'm sure I would have. I'm sure I would have found it terrifying, but that would have been the next thing to grapple with.

Of course, I'm sure I would have done things with the storytelling—you know, turn it around, turn it inside out. Around about that time, I was seeing films like *The Saragossa Manuscript* [1964, directed by Wojciech Has] or *Last*

Year at Marienbad [1961, directed by Alain Resnais], which I would have thought of as storytelling films but which were doing extraordinary things with storytelling and with time.

I certainly remember a lot of frustration with the fact that I was working with images that were, relatively speaking, drained of content. And I remember knowing that content was something that was going to come later. That was my big argument with most of the structural filmmakers at the time. I thought this notion of the designified image was a load of bullocks, to put it in the vernacular. I never thought there could be an entirely designified image. But when I look back, there's something very appealing about this kind of bony concentration on the building blocks of cinema, and I often wonder how people could go straight into narrative filmmaking without that experience.

MacDonald: I suppose you could say that your early interest in two-screen, three-screen, four-screen film experiences was implicitly a hunger to go beyond what was economically possible, rather than to adjust to those early limitations and build a filmmaking career from within them.

Potter: Yes. *Black and White* is in my mind because we've just seen it. I can trace in it the beginning of my exploration of cinematic space in later films. *The Gold Diggers* was all about characters trapped in cinematic time and space.

I can also see the early films as images of *myself*: I was a filmmaker trapped in the austerity of my possibilities at the time and faced with the challenge of doing something with nothing. How do you transform something very limited into something with a metaphysical dimension? How could you expand the limits, the possibilities of what was there? Of course, many painters at that time were preoccupied with similar issues, with the idea of going beyond the edge of the frame.

MacDonald: Babette Mangolte once told me in connection with *What Masie Knew* [1975] that a filmmaker can put any sequence of events together and automatically we'll make them into narrative [see *A Critical Cinema*, pp. 283–84]. Seeing your early films, now that I know the later trajectory of your career, it's probably automatic that I find the "narrative" of your development as a filmmaker. Those jumps of people from one image into a contiguous, but separate image, something the viewer knows is impossible, is similar to what happens in *Orlando*: *Orlando* is the narrative version of the formal trick of *Black and White* and *Play*, just a different version of an ongoing fascination with the moment of transformation. And that connection is even evident in the retinal collages of *Jerk*, where two faces "impossibly" become one face.

Potter: I think the key word in my work *is* transformation. That's been the basic principle in all of the films.

MacDonald: So, having produced a body of film work and a general approach, you became a choreographer.

Potter: Yes. That's where I got my major training as a director of people. Film is so expensive and I was so poor that most of my work experience in my twenties was as a performer and as a performance artist. I had a small company called Limited Dance Company. And I was in several touring bands. I trod the boards! Show business! But the avant-garde end of show business.

MacDonald: Did you go to art school at any point?

Potter: I went to art school for a year, and what I got from it above all was life drawing, a sense of draftsmanship and composition within the frame, which has been a passionate engagement ever since. My experience was pragmatic, never academic. I learned from being out there and working.

I'd been fed by the sensibility of independent cinema, so I suppose it was only a matter of time until I returned to it. I thought of *Thriller* as the first of my films that was not so much an *hors d'oeuvre*, but a main course. I'd delivered plenty of "main courses" in live work before then.

MacDonald: In *Thriller* you decided to clear out the whole attic, and start from scratch. You use *La Boheme* and *Psycho* as your central texts. I assume that you meant to comment on *la boheme* of London in the sixties and early seventies, suggesting that the opera was as relevant in terms of gender politics then as it was a century earlier. Was the choice of *La Boheme* and *Psycho* also an attempt to explore "High Art"/"Pop Art" vis-à-vis gender politics?

Potter: That's about fifteen questions in one! Let me do some unraveling. *Thriller* was filmed in the top-floor attic of the house where I was living, which was a squatted house. The squatting movement in London at that time developed a politics around taking over empty houses to live in. Heathcote Williams, who was Nick Greene, the poet, in *Orlando* was one of the original poetic squatters. Squatting wasn't just a pragmatic solution. It was about economics and ownership and a whole set of issues.

There's a subtext in *La Boheme* about the poverty of artists, and the romanticization of the poverty of artists and the notion of artists living in garrets. There I was, living in a garret in a squat with no money, with my friends and other people working in art, who also had no money. And I mean *really* no money. We scrounged around trying to get grants of a hundred pounds to do something or other, and we sometimes got it, and we survived and were fine.

But there is an essential difference, in my opinion—and this was one of the things I was looking at then—between the kind of poverty that somebody working in a sweatshop might have and the poverty of squatting artists, because for artists there is usually an element of choice. You can talk about the economic oppression of artists, but it's not inherent in the artist's life: you can be either poor or rich at certain points, which forces you to make, or not to make, certain compromises. The other kind of poverty is rooted in class oppression.

MacDonald: A sweatshop person cannot apply for a grant.

Potter: You can't apply for a grant. And you don't have the option that *maybe* in five years you're suddenly going to make more money, as a result of sacrifices you're making now. There isn't a future. There isn't even an imagined way out.

So I got interested in different kinds of poverty and what they meant, along with the fact that in operatic narratives and many other forms of narrative, the female role adds a second romanticization, as in the case of Mimi in *La Boheme*. Not only is she an instance of working-class poverty, but also her role in relation to illness and death is a further romanticization of another kind of poverty: the male character is really about life and the female character is about death. I got interested in decoding the politics of those very, very familiar stories, while at the same time tapping into what was so moving and so profound about the music that surrounds these stories, and even about the stories themselves. After I'd listened to *La Boheme* a thousand times, I could still find myself moved to tears at the end of the death scene, not by the heroine's victimization, but perhaps by the melancholy and the loss within relationships that's captured in that incredible music.

MacDonald: Did you feel the same way about *Psycho?* When I saw *Psycho* the summer it came out, the loss of Marion Crane (and Janet Leigh) was my most powerful movie experience to that point.

Potter: There is the loss, yes, but there's also that incredible musicality in *Psycho* from the very first image. *Psycho* has one of the most *brilliant* scores by Bernard Herrmann.

It's true, *La Boheme* is supposedly "high art" and *Psycho* "low," but these distinctions were for me, not worthy of contemplation.

MacDonald: You mention in your introduction to *Orlando* that you were part of an aesthetic movement that was decoding the way in which stories were told in film. Were you much involved with other people making feminist cinema in the seventies? On some level *Thriller* responds to the critiques developed in Yvonne Rainer's *Film About a Woman Who . . .* [1974] and Laura Mulvey and Peter Wollen's *Riddles of the Sphinx* [1977].

Potter: I hadn't seen *Film About a Woman Who . . .* (so its use of *Psycho* was entirely a coincidence) or *Riddles of the Sphinx*, though I knew Laura and Peter. I always felt my roots more in the live work I'd come out of. In retrospect, things may seem related, but I think the wellspring at the time is much more intuitive. I probably would have felt much more directly influenced by *Psycho*, let's say, than by structural film, though I'd been somewhat involved in the structuralist movement.

I suppose *Thriller* was my way of synthesizing various interests—the emotional, the analytical; dance, theater; movies and opera—in an incredibly austere way. These days, I'm much less interested in reference and cross-reference and much more interested in making something which is *itself*, and doesn't only refer to other strands in the arts. Then, I was trying to find *the* most condensed way of expressing complicated ideas. Near the end of *Thriller*, an anonymous hand passes a book into the frame and Mimi reads from the introduction to the book, which is a structuralist text. That image is asking, "What function does theoretical and analytical work have in understanding my life?

Mimi (Colette Laffont) in Sally Potter's *Thriller* (1979).

Mimi's life? Cinema? What is the correct relationship between the complexities of theory and complexities of the image?" And the answer, in my film, is laughter.

MacDonald: *Thriller* is full of paradox. On one level, it eliminates all the elements of conventional thrillers. It doesn't allow us to empathize with or to enjoy the sacrifice of the woman (although it asks that we remember taking such enjoyment). But on another level it *is* a thriller: we're in this attic without all these things that in a conventional film make us feel secure. And there are moments that are very creepy: the image of the woman in the doorway, for example, though, unlike most thrillers, it's the woman *appearing*, rather than her disappearing, that creates the creepiness. It's as if you were making the opposite of a thriller *and* a thriller at the same time.

Potter: Absolutely. Even the making of *Thriller* was a thriller for me. It was a passionate and terrifying journey to try and make a film out of what seemed like nothing, out of a bunch of clues. Just as Mimi is the detective looking into her own death, I felt as if I were a detective looking into the meaning of this work I was trying to construct. Even the word "thriller," and its evocation of the thrill of the chase was important to me. And the thrill of the image, and the sense of some barely graspable truth that was embedded in the bones of the idea. I certainly *wasn't* interested in mystification for its own sake, which a film of that ilk can slip into very easily; I was interested in the pursuit of clarity.

MacDonald: How did you decide on Colette Laffont as the central character and narrator?

Potter: She was a performer I'd known and liked. I loved her voice, adored her laugh. And she's black, of course, and I was very interested in putting a black, female voice in the center. Normally, such a voice would be peripheral, and she might be stereotyped as an object; here she becomes the subject. I don't think I could have rationalized it that way at the time. I've always found casting to be very intuitive, and for *Thriller* I just wanted that particular combination of people. Later, I came to realize more and more of the implications.

MacDonald: You also flip the general tendency of film history to worship light, by having this "dark" woman bring enlightenment into the darkened theater.

Potter: Perhaps, but black people are often cast as representing issues that have to do with being black. It's a double burden: if you're there at all, you have to come carrying a flag. I was interested in casting a black character who was dealing with issues that were not necessarily directly to do with being black, and who had the authority to be at the center of all the issues.

MacDonald: Did you tour a lot with *Thriller?* Was it well received?

Potter: *Thriller* was well received and it led to an invitation from the BFI [British Film Institute] to submit a proposal, which is how *The Gold Diggers* started. Yes, I did tour a lot with it, and I learned a lot from doing so.

MacDonald: Like what?

Potter: Like what I'd *done*. The act of being questioned or scrutinized forces you to analyze and articulate what you've done in a way that's not necessary to do at the time you're making the work, at least not in quite the same way. And I learned from people's responses, what *they* were getting from it. I was rooted in live performance where the feedback from the audience is immediate. On stage, if something is working or not working, you can immediately adjust the timing. Especially in an improvised performance—and I was very interested in the discipline of improvisation—you simply change what you're doing to meet the needs of the audience. In film you can't do that. But if you travel with the film, you get a feeling for how it works in all these different countries and environments: you discover the bits that work, the bits that don't; where people get bored, where they don't; what people seem to be picking up, what they're rejecting.

MacDonald: How much did the responses vary? Were British audiences for *Thriller* different from American audiences?

Potter: I found, and this has continued with all my films to this day, an absolute miracle of sameness, of remarkably similar responses in different countries. A lot of people came to meet *Thriller* in a way that at the time I found nothing short of miraculous. And then there'd be people who drew a complete blank, who did not have a clue what I was up to. For me, that was par for the course at the time, the expected. I never used the word, "avant-garde," but I thought of myself as working on the knife edge of accessibility and inaccessibility, and proudly so.

MacDonald: The first time I saw *Thriller*, I was completely befuddled. But it was the kind of befuddlement that annoys me, where three or four years later, I was still trying to "get it."

The Gold Diggers was your first 35mm project. Having more money for *The Gold Diggers* allowed you to foreground more completely the whole issue of economics, which is certainly there in *Thriller* very clearly, but here is the central subject—especially the connection between women not being paid, or being underpaid, for their labor and the surplus men accumulate as a result of this underpayment, a surplus that allows them to control society. What strikes me is how this idea works out filmically in *The Gold Diggers*. While *Thriller* refers to commercial work, it's obviously not a commercial film. But *The Gold Diggers* seems to be an attempt to be both a commercial entertainment *and* an avant-garde critique, simultaneously. I'm curious about the thinking that went into the project, and I'm curious as to how well it worked. The film was a very hard sell in the United States, I'm sure.

Potter: It was the toughest experience of my working life, and even thinking about it is still surrounded by painful emotion. It was a collaborative script with Rose English, who also designed the film, and Lindsay Cooper, who wrote the score. And it was never a finished script. It was always a collection of images, and ideas, and some dialogue, and so on. I'd made *Thriller* by accumulating a bunch of material and shooting the images, but then actually constructing the film in the cutting room. I was treating it as substance to be shaped, like clay. I wrote all the voice-over in the cutting room and recorded it later.

Having had the experience of *Thriller*, which had worked on its own terms, I tried to make that procedure the blueprint for how to work on *The Gold Diggers*, which was, of course, a vastly different situation. I had a crew and a cast, a schedule and money. I had a kind of script, but not what I would now think of as a script. I expected that I would accumulate these scenes, and then construct the film in the editing room.

My conscious intention was to try to make something following on from *Thriller*, but which went wider—something that still dealt with myriad, complex ideas, something that was exploring the idea of narrative from within, in a nonlinear way, but that made conscious links between economics and representation—all the preoccupations that had already been there in *Thriller*, but which could be worked with on a larger scale and hopefully made more accessible. I think I failed almost entirely in that quest. It was the hardest physical shoot and the hardest edit, much harder than anything I'd ever done. And the experience of going out with it once it was finished was very painful.

MacDonald: Why was it a hard physical shoot?

Potter: Oh, Iceland was so cold. I could hardly move, it was so cold. I had a very inexperienced crew, because I'd decided to have an all female crew and half the people hadn't even been on a film set before. *I* was very inexperienced: I'd never worked with a crew, so I didn't know what I could expect or not expect. As you can imagine, the insecurity was running pretty high. It was much more money than I'd had before, but a very low budget for what the film was, and the schedule was tight.

And when it was time to cut the film, I'd never cut anything on 35mm. I was an entirely self-taught editor, and didn't even know the most rudimentary things a properly trained-up beginning editor would know. I've always learned everything on the job. It was one horrendous mistake after another.

MacDonald: Did having Julie Christie involved, with her considerable career in the industry, create a lot of pressure for you?

Potter: Oh, that was one of the luxurious aspects of *The Gold Diggers*! And I don't want to be unduly negative about the experience. My relationship with all the cast was incredible. That was the one area of ease for me. By that time, as a result of my performance work, I *was* a relatively experienced director of people; I suppose you could say that that was an area in which I *was* trained— unlike many filmmakers, who are experienced with the technology, but haven't a clue what the performer is going through or what you're really asking a performer to do. No, Julie was fantastic and no pressure at all.

It's just that the film set itself an impossible task. We could have made it at least 300 percent more accessible, had we conceded certain narrative conventions. For example, if the two central characters had met each other in a realistic space, whether it was in the ballroom or in the computer center, and *then* entered into a kind of fantasy, so you could easily distinguish what was real and what was not, that would have allowed an audience to accept the nature of the journey. But we were deliberately making that not the case: the boundaries between what was real and nonreal were invisible and irrelevant. This was *cinematic* space we were occupying and therefore you could go left, right, up, down, backwards, forwards, without regard for the conventions of reality.

The audience who saw Julie Christie's name and went in expecting to see a 35mm feature film, and who had never seen an underground film before (that is, the majority of the film audience and even of film critics in most countries) were totally baffled. And *furious*, because they felt they'd been led up the garden path. Some independent filmmakers, who were expecting something even more unraveling, felt I had made too many concessions. So *The Gold Diggers* was caught in a bind.

It had its fans and it *still* has its fans: I get letters from people saying that it changed their lives, which I find extraordinary. But it was the greatest baptism by fire *and* the greatest learning experience of my life—for which I am profoundly grateful. But I think the film was a monumental failure.

Ruby (Julie Christie), as performer (on the left of the stage) and as spectator, in Sally Potter's *The Gold Diggers* (1983).

MacDonald: Was the choice of Babette Mangolte to do the cinematography an attempt to provide visual pleasure as a way of compensating for the conventional narrative pleasures you withheld.

Potter: Yes. I felt she had exactly the background that I needed: she was a seeing eye who understood completely the power of imagery in its own right.

MacDonald: I teach conventional film for the most apart, but my research is primarily into more critical forms of film. I relate to *The Gold Diggers* because it's so obviously right in the middle, between the two traditions. It's loaded with references to commercial film history. I don't mean just your casting of Julie Christie, but the shack, which is right out of Chaplin's *The Gold Rush* [1925] and D. W. Griffith's *Birth of a Nation* [1915]. And there are all these shadowy film noir streets. The film references enough genres to implicitly reference all genres. But even this was probably lost on much of the audience.

Potter: Yes, absolutely.

MacDonald: How did you get Julie Christie involved in the project?

Potter: I phoned her up. It did take a bit of convincing. As you've suggested, I wanted to work with somebody who occupied an iconic space in the culture. And her face *is* charismatic. I think she was intrigued because at that point she herself was asking a lot of questions.

MacDonald: She always exuded a detachment from the commercial manipulation of her as an actress.

Potter: She's extremely intelligent and was quite extraordinarily generous to me and to those working on the film. She said she really enjoyed it, that it was a liberating experience for her; but she taught *us* a lot by her professionalism and her spirit of adventure.

MacDonald: I heard a rumor that *The Gold Diggers* was going to be shown at Lincoln Center last year, and then at the last minute you pulled it . . .

Potter: It wasn't really last minute. I'd already decided that I didn't want it to be tacked onto the opening of *Orlando*. I wanted *Orlando* to stand on its own.

MacDonald: Were you afraid *The Gold Diggers* would drag *Orlando* down?

Potter: Not exactly. It goes back to your first question about my eliminating the past and awakening with a new identity. For me, *The Gold Diggers* was somewhere I *had been*, and I wanted *Orlando* to have an opportunity to meet a new audience who knew nothing about me, and wouldn't interpret *Orlando* through *The Gold Diggers*. I like the idea of each film being treated as if it were the first.

But also, to be completely honest, I had had some really difficult, painful critical responses to *The Gold Diggers*, and I needed at least the illusion of a completely fresh start.

MacDonald: I was disappointed because the Walter Reed Theater has spectacular projection, and I've never seen *The Gold Diggers* in 35mm.

Potter: The first time I saw *The Gold Diggers* projected in 16mm, I nearly died. I felt as if all the work that had gone into creating this pristine 35mm image might as well never have existed. I even wished that I'd never allowed it to go onto 16mm, though I didn't have the contractual power to prevent that. I suppose most of those few who have seen it have seen it on 16mm.

MacDonald: Let's get into the specifics a bit. One of the constants in the film is the fictional space of the alley: at one end you see Julie Christie as a Madonna/idol being carried by a group of men, and at the other end you see the gold bricks being carried. The fact that these two images are the "opposite ends of the same street" has many implications, one of which is the idea of money being made in early Hollywood through the "deification" of women.

Potter: There is apparently a ceremony somewhere in Spain where a Madonna is carried around the streets to the final port of call: a bank! Obviously, the subtext of the whole film is the role of the female star in relation to money, and the question of what a star is in relation to the larger history of icons, and what icons are as a form of value that is circulated. I was trying to find an image that made a parallel between the literal circulation of money in an economic system and the circulation of iconic images in the imagination. On a very crude level, stars equal cash; and on more subtle levels, I wanted to deal with the ways in which we carry valued images in our heads.

MacDonald: I suppose one of the most condensed forms of that relationship is the early Renaissance images of the Virgin, surrounded by gold leaf.

Potter: Exactly. In recent years, I've gone into churches in Russia, poverty-stricken churches with the bricks falling off the wall, but the images of the Virgin are absolutely dripping in silver, gold, and diamonds. So I was trying to make a parallel between these very primal images of the Virgin and "virgin soil," and "virgin elements," and money.

Of course, alchemy, the attempt to find the secret of transforming base matter into gold, is behind everything in *The Gold Diggers*. The alchemist is always trying to find the matter *behind* the matter, the same as the physicist does now, but in a different, quite literal way. The motif of the icon at one end of the alley and the gold at the other was an attempt, as almost all the images in that film were, to find a kind of poetic, condensed image that would evoke layers of meaning. I hesitate to use the word "metaphor," which tends to say this image equals that meaning; my imagery was never meant to be as literal as that. I was trying to *distill* ideas and thoughts and feelings into one image, just as a poet will try to find a combination of two or three words that suggests any number of meanings.

For me it was an attempt to respect the viewer's intelligence. I meant to *open* a door—but for viewers who weren't tuning in, it seemed like a double-door closing. After a screening in Australia, people were shouting at each other across the auditorium. One half was yelling, "IT'S SHIT"; the other half was yelling, "NO, IT'S NOT!" I had this incredible feeling of dangerous aesthetics, which when I think about it now, I feel proud of. Risks *were* taken.

MacDonald: You mentioned the problem of shooting in Iceland. Did you want to shoot in a location that looked like the American West, but definitely wasn't?

Potter: Well, of course, the whole film exists in fictitious cinematic space. I'd been to Iceland once before, as a musician, and I found it to be magical—"The Land of Ice and Fire" is what they call it—which of course is the alchemical mix, the elemental mix. So yes, I wanted to evoke the idea of the frontier West, the prospectors, and so on, and yet to be not quite there, just as the city streets are sort of film noir, but not quite.

MacDonald: I cannot understand the words Colette Laffont sings at the end, though I get the drift of the song. If *The Gold Diggers* were a Trinh Minh-ha film, that might be a conscious choice . . .

Potter: It's technical inadequacy on my part. The mix is wrong: the voice was too low in relation to the instruments. It's frustrating because unlike the convention for songs in film, which is that you don't need to understand every word, this song is very densely written and all the lyrics need to be understood.

MacDonald: What did you learn from the problems you had with *The Gold Diggers?*

Potter: What I did not understand before *The Gold Diggers* was the function of a script. I had come out of an aesthetic where you work things out as you go, or in the cutting room. The idea of drawing up a blueprint in advance and working from that was a complete bafflement to me. What I learned from *The Gold Diggers* is that the function of the script is really to imagine the whole film in all its detail as if it already exists by the time you start to shoot. And *then* you can, and probably should, be ready to throw the script away, because the circumstances will always teach you how to do things better, or the actors will or the lighting will—something will—and you can improve the script and make it come to life. But even if something *doesn't* improve the script and you just follow the blueprint as if it's a diagram, a film will still get made and will hang together.

Before *The Gold Diggers* I didn't know what a pressured, scheduled shoot was like and what kind of thinking you have to do as a director while you're shooting. It's a different kind of thinking from what I used to do when time wasn't an issue.

There were other things to learn, too—like what can you expect of an audience that hasn't spent years at the Co-op watching films? What can you expect them to find interesting and exciting? *I* found it very interesting and exciting to see how long I could stretch a line of characters walking up a mountain while a riddle is being stated; but what was excitingly stretched for me was, for the audience, boring. I'm not the kind of filmmaker, and I don't think I ever was really, who doesn't care about courting an audience's attention. I *am* interested in taking an audience with me. I want to communicate. I want to share the same heartbeat. So I had to learn those lessons.

MacDonald: I assume you saw yourself as the ship's welder we see at the beginning and end of the film, trying to construct a new "ship" of cinema?

Potter: Something like that.

MacDonald: You mentioned in the introduction to the *Orlando* script that you had already begun working on that script in 1984.

Potter: I started thinking about *Orlando* immediately after finishing *The Gold Diggers*.

MacDonald: So you're dealing with the pain of what for you was a disaster, while you're beginning to conceptualize a major new project (it's certainly hard to imagine doing *Orlando* on a small budget). And soon after you begin this new project, you do two documentaries for TV and the spy spoof, *The London Story*, which is about as far from *The Gold Diggers* as you can get in one leap. Were the documentaries and especially *The London Story* attempts to demonstrate that you *could* indeed entertain? Were these films conscious means to an end?

Potter: Yes, though it probably was not quite as calculated as that. Listen, the day I finished *The Gold Diggers* I was ready to start a new film. The learning curve had been vertical. I felt, "Now I've done my training, please let me start!"

The making of *The Gold Diggers* had been difficult in the way that any important learning experience is difficult. But the *reaction* to *The Gold Diggers* made me feel seriously in danger of not being able to do my life's work. And I'm somebody who is on earth to do my life's work. The real possibility that I wouldn't be able to proceed took me into a state of almost unbearable frustration and despair. When I tried to get things started, one door after another was slammed in my face: "Oh, *she's* the one who made *The Gold Diggers*."

Finally, I decided that I had to make a film. And it had to be quick because *The Gold Diggers* had taken so long. I had the idea for *The London Story* on New Year's Eve, and I said, "This is going to be on the screen in three months." Then I started to raise money for it and everybody said no. So I did the whole thing literally on credit cards and deferred payments.

I decided it had to be a racy little narrative, with the kind of timing I'd learned from live work. It was like a whole bunch of little reversals from the way I'd been accustomed to work on film. *The London Story was* on the screen in three months. Immediately after it was done, the BFI, who had turned it down as an idea, bought it. They had been completely negative about the project beforehand, like everybody else. So the result was entirely pleasurable, the exact reverse of the experience of *The Gold Diggers*.

I loved every minute of making the film. It took something like five days to shoot and ten days to edit. I remember coming home every night and falling on my bed, saying to myself, "I'm happy!" and reminding myself just how passionately in love with the process of filmmaking I was. It was a small film but it was important for me at the time.

MacDonald: It's got some laugh-out-loud moments.

Potter: I was weeping with laughter during rehearsals.

MacDonald: Your documentary about Soviet women filmmakers, *I Am an Ox, I Am a Horse, I Am a Man, I Am a Woman*, was made during the same period. There's a certain defiance in the film, not just on the level that you're focusing on women and not men, but in your not mentioning Eisenstein, Pudovkin, and Vertov and the period of the twenties and thirties, which is what most people in the West know about Soviet cinema.

Potter: Well, this project was not initiated by me, but by Sian Thomas and Renny Bartlett, who had already done considerable research for it. They were my tour leaders on my first trip to the Soviet Union at the end of 1983. I had wanted to be in Red Square on New Year's Eve of 1984, for George Orwell's sake. And that's where I was, as the snow came tumbling down. Since then I've been in Russia just about every year. I was there before and after *perestroika*. It became a very important place for me and an important experience for any number of reasons, from treading on the soil where a revolution had taken place to being in a country where two thousand people turn out for a poetry reading, to being around these wonderful crumbling film studios where Tarkovsky and Eisenstein and others have been.

Anyway, I was asked to make *I Am an Ox* at the Moscow Film Festival, the first one after *perestroika*. It was an extraordinary, unique time of transition, especially for a child of the Cold War. I remember watching perhaps a hundred films as research for this project in a small, cold basement theater—scratchy film after scratchy film that had never been seen in the West. I could not *believe* what I was seeing. The project, as it had been set up by Sian and Renny, was very specific: it was about women in Soviet cinema, and I got very interested in the *function* of the female characters in these films as representing the nation, which seems to be the case in many Third World cinemas, as well. It's a very different function for women from what we see in Western film; it puts a different perspective on the meaning of female characters. Of course, I was looking at the work of female directors as well.

MacDonald: How did they choose you for this project?

Potter: We had this common love of Russia, and they liked my other work. I had taken *Thriller* with me on the first trip. A bunch of filmmakers (Jon Jost was along) were traveling around, visiting studios, meeting our opposite numbers, and showing our films to Russian audiences, who were *completely* baffled by what they were seeing. Of course, there was no equivalent to our work. Our "opposite numbers" were people working in the studios making vast films. There was no independent cinema culture in the Soviet Union at that point. There was no need for it.

All the stereotypes that I'd had, that we'd all had I think, about filmmakers in Russia dealing with this heavy censorship flipped right over. I began to realize that it was the filmmakers in the West who were dealing with censorship, economic censorship. Many filmmakers in the West were silenced by never getting to make films at all. In Russia, most filmmakers who had been through film school got to make films. The films weren't necessarily shown, but they got to make them. The political censorship they were dealing with was very overt, whereas in the West the censorship was covert. All my definitions of "independence," "mainstream," "censorship," "voice," "culture," and the role of the artist were totally shaken up.

MacDonald: Orlando picks up on something that I'm sure many of us have loved in the movies, but few directors have really explored. When Chaplin walks onto the screen at the beginning of *The Kid* [1921], he looks at the camera as if to say, "*I'm* ready; are *you* ready?" I've always thought that Oliver Hardy gets too little credit for Laurel and Hardy: for me, it has always been Hardy's intimate look at the camera that makes me laugh. You talk about Orlando's looks at us in your introduction to the screenplay as a "golden thread." And it is a remarkable gesture, that—among other things—defeats the whole debate about "the male gaze" by simply having the character on the screen create a relationship with us that informs everything that happens and everything we see. How did you decide on this tactic?

Potter: It came relatively late in the script, as a solution to an unrealized part of what I felt could be happening. Of course, in performance work, this sort of thing happens all the time: you look out from the stage, you directly engage the audience. And there are plenty of examples in cinema.

MacDonald: Not *so* many.

Potter: But key ones, especially in comedy. Comedy is *about* complicity; it's about saying *you*, the audience, and *I*, the performer, we understand each other in relation to what we're looking at. In *Orlando* I was searching for an essential innocence and connectedness that is outside of time. In the voice-over, right in the beginning, the narrator says that when Orlando was born, "it wasn't privilege he sought, but company." "Company" is a loose word, but it's about connectedness. We're born and we die alone, but we're *here* to connect. Certainly that's part of the essence of cinema: creating a state of connectedness. So it's a simple, structural device for making that link easily, and, also, it's a way of making very simple jokes, like Groucho did with a flicker of an eye.

There's a tendency for a "historical drama" to become a spectacle. I've always said that *Orlando* is *not* a costume drama, *not* a period film, no matter how much it may appear so: it's really about the present moment. And, of course, as soon as you look into the lens, you're in the present. So it was trying to interweave the present and the apparent past through that look. I don't know how one arrives at these kinds of solutions. They just seem to arrive by themselves. Tilda used to say that you earn your luck. We tried out things and rejected them, tried and rejected, tried and rejected, and then suddenly (finally!) eye contact seemed to be the key.

MacDonald: Well, it's a wonderful stroke of whatever it is! And it has so many reverberations. All my life, when I've been so drunk or so stoned that I can't *believe* what I've done to myself, I always end up in a bathroom looking

Orlando (Tilda Swinton) and Shelmerdine (Billy Zane), nineteenth-century lovers in Sally Potter's *Orlando* (1992).

into a mirror and making contact with this *self* that seems to look back at me and say, "Here you are, again!" In your film, the character's looks at us *are* a way of having us make contact with the character, but it's also like making contact with yourself as a character in the drama of your own experience.

By having Orlando's glance and statement to us ["that is, I"] interrupt the opening moment of the film, you create a new kind of viewer: there's no point during the rest of the film when we're not waiting for that contact to be reestablished. You've created the essence of friendship. When you're with a friend in a social situation, and some jerk is doing or saying something annoying, you just . . .

Potter: Exchange a look, yes.

MacDonald: When I heard you had made *Orlando*, I reread Woolf's novel. I have to say I was again disappointed in it. There are a lot of interesting dimensions to the book, especially the idea of having the character go through these impossible transformations, but the articulation of the changes in the novel doesn't really work for me. I think it's a case where the film adaptation of a pretty interesting novel (written by a great novelist) does a better job of doing what the novel wants to do, than the novel does. Do you feel that way?

Potter: Do I feel that my film is better than the novel? Oh, I don't think I would say *that*—although I would hope my film has its own life. An adaptation which is slavish to a text, trying to make the novel "come alive," is doomed to a sort of literary stultification. An adaptation has to be a transformation. I was much more interested in what I interpreted as the core of the book, in the *spirit* of what Woolf was trying to do. But I'm only too well aware that the film only exists because she wrote that book. I could have made another film which dealt with some of the same themes, but instead I adapted what she did and made it cinematic, and changed things which didn't work for me. But anyway, I always thought it was one of her *more* interesting books, and I guess I'm in the minority about that. I did find myself enraged by aspects of it: the smugness, the class assumptions, the idea of history as a series of kings and queens and the upper classes.

But there are things I absolutely love about the book. Just the sheer daring of the essential idea, which is to create a character who lives for four hundred years and changes sex! I could kiss Virginia Woolf's feet for that alone. I understood at the start that I had to be really hard on the book, in order to give it a chance of working as a film, and I *was* really hard on her.

MacDonald: One of the moments where I think the film succeeds better than the novel is in the transformation of gender. It's such a radical idea, so difficult to be convincing about in writing, that Woolf must frame the transformation with all this mock-mythological material, pages and pages of buildup. In the film you can just have Tilda Swinton reveal herself as a woman, so when she looks at us and says, "Same person, different sex," it's true in a way that can only be suggested in the novel.

Potter: My God, that was a difficult scene to shoot. I re-shot it four times. It had to have a quality of absolute simplicity and brightness; and we had to see Orlando's body and yet it had to be a non-exploitative moment.

MacDonald: Have people argued that, in order to say there's *no* difference, you reveal Orlando/Tilda Swinton in precisely the way that film history has revealed women in order to *demonstrate* the difference? I take it that that paradox is at the heart of the film.

Potter: People seem to be pretty accepting of that moment, actually. There's a tenderness that's made possible by the relationship that's been established between Orlando and the camera. And throughout the film, there was so much care about where the camera was placed.

The issues to do with men and women in the film reflect the gradual transformation of my own ideas, subsequent to *Thriller* and *The Gold Diggers*. *Orlando* ends up being a film about female experience, but I think it starts out as a film about male experience, and in sum total it's about human experience—though "human" is a difficult word to use because it's so woolly. But we don't have a more precise one for the state of being alive, whether you're a man or a woman. I think the viewer feels the *humanness* of that moment.

MacDonald: As difficult as it may have been to shoot, in the film the transformation feels very natural. The same is true of the shifts through the centuries.

Potter: In the film, I can just cut! It's so beautiful! See, that's something I learned from *The Gold Diggers*: you can just cut to the next thing. You don't have to spend a lot of time getting people in and out of doors, getting them to sit down in a chair. And, providing you have set up a code at the very beginning of the film that tells the audience, "*This* is the kind of film that we're in; will you come with me?" you can jump a hundred years in a single cut. That's why I decided that Orlando had to look into the camera in the first couple of minutes and the various paradoxes had to be set up right away, so people would know what realm they're in.

MacDonald: Probably the most significant single change you make between the novel and the film is in the events leading up to the transformation of gender. In the film, and unlike the novel, there's a clear connection between what happens before the gender change and the change itself: Orlando is told by Archduke Harry that the wounded youth she's concerned about is "not a man, he is the enemy." She immediately leaves the battle, and the transformation occurs that night.

Potter: In the book, Woolf was able to be arbitrary, to play with arbitrariness in a rather arch way. I think the point she was making is that the difference of sex *is* arbitrary, and she as the author could be God and just decide arbitrarily that Orlando was now a woman. But the Godliness of the author is not in the film; my presence is not the same.

Also, it seemed to me that because I was stretching credibility already, I had to make each step credible on its own terms, and in human terms also. So there is a reason for the change, however flimsy it might appear if you try to analyze it. The reason why somebody would change sex is that they've reached the point past which they cannot go and will not go. They're in a corner. And if you think about it in the widest possible context, the most extreme point that men have to face, or that the masculine role has to face, is to kill or be killed. Men are almost always the defenders, the soldiers, whatever, which is something that in 99 percent of cultures, women haven't got to face. So it seemed to me that that could be the logical zenith point at which Orlando would say no to being a man.

Plus I wanted to change Orlando's relationship to class and the exoticism of Virginia Woolf's Orient. In the film, Orlando is pushed to the extreme of his sex and of his class—by fighting a territorial battle in a colonial outpost of Britain—something he no longer wishes to do.

MacDonald: A friend of mine commented that *Orlando* is not strictly feminist because Orlando is a male for 60 percent of the film and a female for only 40 percent. Did you consider making it 50–50?

Potter: No, that's much too schematic. I did chart all the scenes to see where exactly the proportioning of the sex change was falling, and in earlier drafts it was more exactly at 50 percent, but some of the later scenes were dragging and earlier scenes seemed too compressed. I had worked schematically earlier. In

Combines, the editing sequences were divided mathematically, as I remember, because I was trying to work with the fundamental principles of harmony. Later, for *The Gold Diggers*, I divided up the scenes, saw where things fell in time according to the mathematical principles of the golden section, and discovered that on the screen it doesn't work. You don't necessarily register the moment where things fall schematically in the narrative, as you do in something like *Combines*, where the cut itself is the rhythm: narrative transforms your sense of time.

So when I got to *Orlando*, I knew that those kinds of schematic plans weren't really the key.

MacDonald: At the end, when we have the nineties incarnation of Orlando, and she comes out of the publisher's office (where we realize that other characters—the Heathcote Williams character, for example—have also been undergoing their own transformations and living forever, too), she gets onto the motorcycle and drives through an area of London under construction. In a conventional romantic sense, it's an unattractive area. I assume what you're suggesting is that for women, this is a new world, with possibilities that weren't there before. But like the boat in *The Gold Diggers*, it's still under construction, and it brings with it the loss of a certain comfortable beauty that has impeded progressive change all along.

Potter: I think that's fair.

MacDonald: I'd extend this idea into the final scene, where the child is playing with the video camera. Do you feel the same way about the coming of video, that it's liberating on one level but . . .

Potter: But less precise: when you whiz around with a pan, you get electronic stripes (which I found very beautiful actually), because the tape records so much less information than is chemically recorded on the filmstrip in 35mm.

I'm intrigued by the collision of the electronic and the chemical worlds. For the younger generation, the electronic is primary. And it *is* possible for a five-year-old to make a video. I don't think video replaces film yet, but since I was dealing with the present, it seemed sensible to have a little dialogue between video and film.

MacDonald: When you were making your early "poetic" films, were you influenced by the gestural handheld camerawork Stan Brakhage and Jonas Mekas became famous for? When I first saw the handheld video material at the end, it struck me, on one hand, as a parallel to the technological world under construction suggested by the skyscrapers, and on the other hand, as a reference to the rebellion against technology represented by "personal" filmmakers in the fifties and sixties.

Potter: I did do some of that whizzing-around, handheld camerawork in my earliest films, though here I wasn't thinking so much of my own work as about a more general reference to a loose, subjective cinema. That video camerawork stands out because everything else in *Orlando* is so constructed and so chore-

Orlando's gaze at the viewer, the "golden thread" of Sally Potter's *Orlando* (1992).

ographed, though ironically the video material was as constructed as every-thing else—to look unconstructed. The little video camera was, in fact, held by Alexei Rodionov, who was down on his knees moving around in the grass.

MacDonald: Was Tilda Swinton always your choice for Orlando? I know you were in contact with her very early on in the script.

Potter: Yes, she was. Of course, when I contacted her, I hoped we would be in production within six months. As it turned out, it was four years, so we had a long time to build a relationship and work together and discuss the script and the part, and to build up a common language so that, when we were on the shoot, a flicker of an eyelash was all we needed to communicate with each other. It was an extraordinary experience really.

MacDonald: At the end, the publisher asks Orlando, "How long have you been working on this book," and Orlando looks at us: *we know* it's been several centuries! Were you referring to the *Orlando* project?

Potter: That *was* a little joke for myself, yes.

MacDonald: I'm curious about the general reception of *Orlando*. Recently I've heard people talking about it in conjunction with *The Piano* [1993, directed by Jane Campion]. Have you heard this particular pairing?

Potter: When I was first being interviewed about *Orlando*, a lot of people would ask what I thought of *The Piano*. Or people would come up to me and say, "You're Sally Potter! I just saw *The Piano*!" as if there were a connection. Maybe there's something in the films themselves that causes people to link them, beyond the fact that they happened to be made at the same time, by women directors. I don't find it worrisome. I'm an enormous fan of Jane Campion's work and of her as a person, and I'm happy about being bracketed with her, rather than with many others, and I hope she would feel the same. It's an exciting moment for both of us; we've become visible in a way that transcends the ghetto principle.

MacDonald: What did *Orlando* finally cost? And, in the end, how well did it do financially?

Potter: For a few weeks, it was the commercial number one in Britain—above the big American blockbusters. And it was altogether an exceptional success. *Orlando* did well for an English film anywhere in the world (it's been distributed in forty countries). And certainly for a independent, small-company film, it did exceptionally well. But, of course, on the relative scale of *Jurassic Park*, it's peanuts.

The film cost two and a quarter million pounds, approximately four million dollars. It was originally budgeted at seventeen million dollars, and it's the same film. I didn't cut anything but the cost. In a sense, it's the same principle that was at work in my early films, just more money was involved. It was exactly the same feeling squeezing thirty-nine minutes of projected film time out of a hundred thirty pounds, and squeezing four hundred years of costumes and three continents out of four million dollars. Both projects push at the financial limits.

MacDonald: At the end of *Orlando* you thank Michael Powell. Did you work with him at some point? Or were you paying your respects to his films?

Potter: I did want to thank him for his body of work. But it was several things. I met Michael Powell and Emeric Pressberger after a screening of *Gone to Earth* [1950] in London. I was just a face in the crowd, but I was so moved by the film and by their presentation that I went up to thank them, and they both took the care to spend a minute or two with me and to give me little bits of advice, which made me vow that every time I was ever at a screening of my own film and someone I didn't know came up to me, I would take care to make contact with them—because this one minute sustained me for something like a year afterwards. I think I really made *Tears, Laughter, Fears and Rage* so that I could get to know Michael Powell. And he took an interest in *Orlando*. I met with him on several occasions, once or twice with Tilda, and he was just fantastically encouraging. He had no idea who I was. He hadn't seen anything that I'd done. But from the very first moment, at a point when everyone but *everyone* was rejecting the idea that I could ever make *Orlando*—it was impossible, infinitely too expensive, nobody would ever be interested, et cetera, et cetera—he just looked me in the eyes and said, "Yes, you'll do it, and it will be great." He had a calm, encouraging confidence that was infinitely sustaining and extraordinarily generous.

MacDonald: There's also a dedication to Beatrice Quennell.

Potter: That's my grandmother. She was an actress. Both my grandmothers were actresses, but I didn't know the other one. Hunny, as Beatrice was called, was an incredibly important figure to me as I was growing up. She was a great encourager. I think everybody needs at least one person who says yes to them as they're growing up, and she always said yes to the artist in me. She died before *Orlando* was made, but I continued to feel her presence, and I love her very much. I just wanted to thank her.

MacDonald: What are you working on now?

Potter: There was an absolute explosion after I finished doing the press tour of *Orlando*, which seemed to take a minimum of four hundred years and was, in fact, one year of my life. I got back to my table and sat down and thought, "Now what?" I reached for my pencil and there was this wild explosion of ideas that had accumulated over the endless period of focusing on *Orlando*. Gradually, I've narrowed the ideas down to a few.

MacDonald: Are these projects you don't want to talk about at this point?

Potter: Basically, yes.

MacDonald: One last question, one that I recognize is absolutely none of my business, though it is suggested by the films. At the end of *Thriller*, the Colette Laffont character looks at Rosetta and says, "We could have loved each other." This has many levels of meaning, one of which is literal. That moment and the transformation in *Orlando* lead me to ask . . .

Potter: What my sexual identity is?

MacDonald: Yes, though actually, I don't know *anything* about your personal life, even whether you have children . . .

Potter: I don't have children. I'm reluctant to talk about sexual identity, for the opposite reason than you might think. You see, I think everything that I need to say about sexual identity is in *Orlando*. I'm not somebody who thinks my own sexual identity is a key to understanding the work, but I would say that my own sexual history is as complex as Orlando's. I don't have a singular sexual identity. For some years, I have had a close relationship with a man, but that's precisely the reason why I don't like to announce my sexual identity. If I were a lesbian at this point, it might be important to say so, but to say I'm heterosexual feels almost as if I'm making a homophobic statement. In reality, it doesn't make the slightest bit of difference, because I'm more interested in the idea of claiming identities and then throwing them away, and of melting identities, as gender melts in *Orlando*. At the time when I made *Thriller*, there were probably many meanings to the statement you mentioned: one was about female friendship and the tragedy of how women are divided against each other. But so are men divided from each other. The fear of homosexuality can mean that men, including gay men, are prevented from achieving closeness and connectedness. There's something about the way stories set people in polarized positions—the bad girl, the good girl; the villain, the hero—so that they, and you, have to choose one or the other. You can't bring together your own complexity and your polymorphous desire. It seems to me that the natural condition is to be unconditionally connected to all other life. But we live in unnatural and constructed times in which we're divided into bits and groups.

This is a very long-winded answer to what appears to be a simple question.

MacDonald: But it's useful, because it's at the heart of the device that makes *Orlando* work: it doesn't matter who Orlando is looking at when she looks at the camera; anyone can make connection with her/him.

Potter: The look is a search for the essential eye and an essential connection, not for a particular sexual identity. But you know we also have Quentin Crisp cast as Queen Elizabeth; and there are references to Virginia Woolf's relationship with Vita Sackville-West (though the film goes further away from Vita Sackville-West than the book did, for reasons of class). There's a way in which the gay/lesbian/queer sensibility provides a much wider and more courageous, cutting-edge frame of reference for thinking about the connectedness between beings, than the heterosexual frame of reference has tended to provide. Because heterosexuality is "the norm," it's also invisible, whereas because the same sex connection is not "the norm," it's up for scrutiny. Therefore, people who are gay tend to be in many ways more advanced in their thinking. The camp sensibility is about complicity: you and I can see that all this masculinity/femininity stuff is really a dressing up of an essential self. They're identities that we can choose or not choose.

You know, I feel I can't even begin to do justice to the complexity of this subject, which is why I can't make a simple statement like "I'm a lesbian" or "I'm a heterosexual," because for me at this point, neither is a freeing statement. Also, while you need a man and a woman for reproduction—it doesn't necessarily have to be a man and a woman in a relationship, but at least it takes a sperm and an egg—there are many forms of relationship, other than reproduction, both sexual and social. You don't have to construct your whole life around reproduction, whether you have children or don't have children. And you don't have to reduce same-sex closeness to the sexual component for it to be infinitely valuable and meaningful. Many other forms of relationship, including friendship, are undervalued.

I can see a parallel between questions of sexual identity and of national identity. I'm English, but not English. There are times in the history of nations when it's important to claim your national identity—for example, when you've been oppressed by others—but claiming your national identity with a dominant nation like England is often a kind of destructive patriotism.

MacDonald: What's the part of you that's not English?

Potter: I don't *feel* English. I grew up in England, but I don't identify with the image of England in the world. My father was an anarchist. I grew up in a left-wing household that thought of itself as outside Englishness, that thought of itself as international, that would identify with exactly those countries that England had oppressed during its own imperialist history. I often feel more at home in Moscow than I do in London and I'm not Russian. But then the question comes up: "Well, what *does* it mean to be Russian or English? What *is* a national identity?"

MacDonald: It's fascinating that you, of all people, would choose to work with *Orlando*, which seems as English a novel as you can get.

Potter: It *is* as English a novel as you can find, but that's another of these paradoxes about identity. You pick it up, you examine it, you claim it, you find out how it's formed you and how it's formed others—and then you throw it away.

MacDonald: It's interesting the parts we pick up and don't pick up. I'm half German, a quarter Scottish and a quarter English; but for some reason, I identify with the Scottish part.

Potter: Why not? It's like what we talked about earlier about my being 100 percent filmmaker and occasionally 100 percent singer. You're totally Scottish *and* totally English *and* totally American at the very least, and at the core of it, you're a unique individual who, like everyone else, should be free to roam anywhere on earth.

Filmography

In the following listing, the title of each film (and video) is followed by the year in which the piece was completed; the format (generally film or video, and the film gauge in which the piece was shot); the length to the nearest quarter minute; and whether the piece is black and white and/or color, silent or sound. Primary rental sources are indicated in parentheses, often using the following abbreviations:

BFI (British Film Institute, 21 Stephen St., London W1P 1PL)

CC (Canyon Cinema, 2325 3rd St., Suite 338, San Francisco, CA 94107)

CFDC (Canadian Filmmakers Distribution Centre, 67A Portland St., Toronto, Ont., M5V 2M9)

FACETS (video only, 1517 W. Fullerton Ave., Chicago, IL 60614)

FMC (Film-makers' Cooperative, 175 Lexington Ave., New York, NY 10016)

FR (First Run, 153 Waverly Place, New York, NY 10014)

LC (Light Cone, 27 rue Louis-Graille, 75012 Paris, France

LFC (London Film-Makers' Co-operative, 42 Gloucester Ave., London, NW1)

MoMA (Museum of Modern Art, Circulating Film Program, 11 W. 53rd Street, New York, NY 10019)

NFB (National Film Board of Canada, in New York: 1251 Avenue of the Americas, 16th Floor, New York, NY 10020)

TWN (Third World Newsreel, 335 38th St., 5th Floor, New York, NY 10018)

WMM (Women Make Movies, 225 Lafayette St., Suite 207, New York, NY 10012)

Martin Arnold

O.T. (i.e., *Ohne Titel*, "Untitled"). 1985. 16mm; 10 minutes; color; silent.

O.T.-2. 1986. 16mm; 10 minutes; color; silent.

Pièce Touchée. 1989. 16mm; 15 minutes; black and white; sound (CC, CFDC, FMC, LC).

Passage à l'Acte. 1993. 16mm; 12 minutes; black and white; sound (CC, CFDC, FMC, LC).

Jesus Walking on Screen. 1993. 35mm; 1 ¹/₂ minutes; color; sound (SIXPACK, Neubaugasse 36, 1070 Vienna, Austria).

Stadtraum Remise. 1994. 35mm; ¹/₂ minute; color; sound (SIXPACK).

Brain Again. 1994. 35mm; 1 minute; color; sound (SIXPACK).

Don't. 1996. 35mm; 3 minutes; black and white; sound (SIXPACK).

Life Wastes Andy Hardy. 1996. 16mm; ? minutes; black and white; sound.

Craig Baldwin

Flickskin. 1976. Super-8mm; 8 minutes; color; sound.

Stolen Movie. 1977. Super-8mm; 12 minutes; color; sound.

Wild Gunman. 1978. 16mm; 20 minutes; color; sound (CC).

RocketKitKongoKit. 1986. 16mm; 30 minutes; color; sound (CC).

Tribulation 99: Alien Anomalies under America. 1991. 16mm; 48 minutes; color; sound (CC).

¡ O No Coronado! 1992. 16mm; 40 minutes; color; sound (CC).

Sonic Outlaws. 1995. 16mm; 87 minutes; color; sound (Baldwin, 992 Valencia St., San Francisco, CA 94110).

Jordan Belson

Transmutation. 1947. 16mm; c. 3 minutes; black and white; silent (lost).

Improvisation #1. 1948. 16mm; c. 3 minutes; black and white; silent (lost).

Bop-Scotch. 1952. 16mm; 3 minutes; color; sound.

Mambo. 1952. 16mm; 4 minutes; color; sound.

Caravan. 1952. 16mm; 3 ¹/₂ minutes; color; sound.

Mandala. 1953. 16mm; 3 minutes; color; sound.

Raga. 1958. 16mm; 7 minutes; color; sound.

Seance. 1959. 16mm; 4 minutes; color; sound.

Allures. 1961. 16mm; 9 minutes; color; sound.

LSD. 1962. 16mm; 6 minutes; color; sound.

Re-entry. 1964. 16mm; 6 minutes; color; sound.

Phenomena. 1965. 16mm; 6 minutes; color; sound.

Samadhi. 1967. 16mm; 6 minutes; color; sound.

Momentum. 1968. 16mm; 7 minutes; color; sound.

Cosmos. 1969. 16mm; 7 minutes; color; sound.

World. 1970. 16mm; 7 minutes; color; sound.

Meditation. 1971. 16mm; 8 minutes; color; sound.

Chakra. 1972. 16mm; 8 minutes; color; sound.

Light. 1973. 16mm; 8 minutes; color; sound.

Cycles (co-made with Stephen Beck). 1975. 16mm; 10 minutes; color; sound (CC).

Music of the Spheres. 1977. 16mm; 10 minutes; color; sound.

Infinity. 1979. 16mm; 8 minutes; color; sound.

Pisces/Blues (part of *Synchronicity Suite*). 1980. 16mm; 12 minutes; color; sound.
Apollo's Lyre (part of *Synchronicity Suite*). 1980. 16mm; 12 minutes; color; sound.
Seapeace (part of *Synchronicity Suite*). 1980. 16mm; 11 minutes; color; sound.
Eleusis/Crotons (part of *Synchronicity Suite*). 1980. 16mm; 10 minutes; color; sound.
The Astronaut's Dream. 1981. 16mm; 7 minutes; color; sound.
Moonlight. 1981. 16mm; 6 minutes; color; sound.
Fireflies. 1981. 16mm; 6 minutes; color; sound.
Apollo. 1982. 16mm; 10 minutes; color; sound.
Imagery made for *The Right Stuff* (1983, directed by Philip Kaufman). 1982–83. 35 mm; c. 120 minutes; color; silent.
Quartet. 1983. 16mm; 11 minutes; color; sound.
Fountain of Dreams. 1984. 16mm; 12 minutes; color; sound.
Northern Lights. 1985. 16mm; 7 minutes; color; sound.
Thoughtforms. 1987. 16mm; 10 minutes; color; sound.
Samadhi and Other Films. 1989. Video; 22 minutes; color; sound (FACETS).

Patrick Bokanowski

La Femme qui Se Poudre ("A Woman Powders Herself"). 1972. 35mm; 18 minutes; black and white; sound (CC, LC).
Dejeuner du Matin (apparently "Breakfast," but in translation the nuance of the French is lost). 1974. 35mm; 12 minutes; color; sound (Bokanowski, 362 rue d'Avron, 75020 Paris, France).
L'Ange ("The Angel"). 1982. 35mm; 70 minutes; color; sound (FR, LC).
Television de Chambre ("Chamber Television"—as in chamber music). 1984. 35mm; 40 seconds; color; sound.
La Part du Hasard ("The Role of Chance"). 1984. 16mm; 54 minutes; color; sound (Bokanowski).
La Plage ("The Beach"). 1992. 35mm; 13 minutes; color; sound (CC, LC).
Au Bord du Lac ("By the Lake"). 1993. 35mm; 6 minutes; color; sound (CC, LC).

Charles Burnett

Several Friends. 1969. 16mm; 45 minutes; black and white; sound.
The Horse. 1974. 16mm; 14 minutes; color; sound; (Burnett, 4534 S. Presidio Dr., Los Angeles, CA 90008).
Killer of Sheep. 1977. 16mm; 87 minutes; black and white; sound (TWN).
My Brother's Wedding. 1983. 35mm; minutes; color; sound (Burnett).
To Sleep with Anger. 1990. 35mm; 101 minutes; color; sound (Samuel Goldwyn).
The Glass Shield. 1995. 35mm; 108 minutes; color; sound (Swank, 201 S. Jefferson Ave., St. Louis, MO 63103–9954).
When It Rains. 1996. 35mm; 13 minutes; color; sound (Burnett).

Christine Choy

Especially in her first years as a filmmaker, when she was involved with the production/distribution organization, Third World Newsreel, Choy functioned in various capacities in collaboratively made films. The collective nature of Third World Newsreel Productions makes precise indications of the contributions of individuals difficult to assess with confidence: often many people worked on many aspects of particular films in a production hierarchy much more loosely defined than is usually the case with either industry features or individually produced avant-garde films. This listing includes only those films Choy is credited as producing and/or directing, or co-producing and/or co-directing, even when she contributed in other ways to the films (and even when others also made major contributions). For example, in *Homes Apart: Korea*, Choy is listed as co-producer and co-director, but she was also narrator, interviewer, and one of several cinematographers. And Choy has done cinematography and editing for a good many films not listed here.

Teach Our Children (co-director, with Susan Robeson). 1972. 16mm; 35 minutes; black and white; sound (TWN).

Generation of the Railroad Builder (director). 1975. Video; 40 minutes; black and white; sound.

Fresh Seeds in the Big Apple (producer/co-director, with Allan Siegel). 1975. 16mm; 45 minutes; color; sound (TWN).

From Spikes to Spindles (producer/director). 1976. 16mm; 50 minutes; color; sound (TWN).

North Country Tour (director). 1977 (unfinished). 16mm; 30 minutes; color; sound.

The History of the Chinese Patriot in the U.S.A. (director; made for Peoples Republic of China). 1977. 16mm; 60 minutes; color; sound.

A Dream Is What You Wake Up From (producer). 1978. 16mm; 60 minutes; color; sound (Pennsylvania State University, AV Services, University Park, PA 16802).

Loose Pages Bound (producer/director). 1978. 16mm; 60 minutes; color; sound.

Inside Women Inside (producer/co-director, with Cynthia Maurizio). 1978. 16mm; 28 minutes; color; sound (TWN).

To Love, Honor, and Obey (director/co-producer, with Marlen Dann). 1980. 16mm; 55 minutes; color; sound (TWN).

Bittersweet Survival (producer/co-director, with J. T. Takagi). 1981. 16mm; 27 minutes; color; sound (TWN).

Go Between (producer/director). 1981. 16mm; 30 minutes; color; sound.

White Flower Passing (producer/director). 1981. Video; 20 minutes; color; sound.

Mississippi Triangle (producer/co-director, with Allan Siegel, Worth Long). 1984. 16mm; 120 minutes/79 minutes; color; sound (TWN).

Fei Tien: Goddess in Flight (director). 1984. 16mm; 23 minutes; color; sound (TWN).

Chronicle of Hope: Nicaragua (director). 1984. 16mm; 50 minutes; color; sound (TWN).

Namibia: Independence Now (director). 1984. 16mm; 55 minutes; color; sound (TWN).

Permanent Wave (director). 1986. 16mm; 20 minutes; color; sound (TWN).

Haitian Corner (co-producer, with Renee Tajima). 1987. 16mm; 90 minutes; color; sound (ZDF Television, Germany).

Who Killed Vincent Chin? (director/produced by Renee Tajima). 1988. 16mm; 90 minutes; color; sound (Filmmakers Library, 124 E. 40th St., New York, NY 10016).

Monkey King Looks West (director). 1990. 16mm; 46 minutes; color; sound (Filmmakers Library).

Yellow Tale Blues: Two American Families (co-producer, with Renee Tajima/co-director, with Renee Tajima). 1990. 16mm; 30 minutes; color; sound (Filmmakers Library).

The Best Hotel on Skid Row (co-producer, with Renee Tajima/co-director, with Renee Tajima). 1990. 16mm; 47 minutes; color; sound (HBO).

Homes Apart: The Two Koreas (co-producer, with J. T. Takagi/co-director, with J. T. Takagi). 1991. 16mm; 56 minutes; color; sound (TWN).

Special Olympics International (one segment; co-director, with Renee Tajima). 1991. 16mm; 10 minutes; color; sound (ABC).

Jennifer's in Jail (producer/co-director, with Renee Tajima). 1992. Video; 60 minutes; color; sound (Lifetime).

Five Chapters (producer/director). 1992. 16mm; 11 minutes; color; sound (Choy, Institute of Film and Television, Tisch School of the Arts, N.Y.U., 721 Broadway, 10th Floor, New York, NY 10003–6807).

Sa-I-Gu (co-producer, with Elaine H. Kim, Dai Sil Kim Gibson/co-director, with Dai Sil Kim Gibson). 1993. Video; 41 minutes; color; sound (Choy).

Galaxy Glass Room (executive producer of seven 30-minute segments). 1993. Video, 210 minutes; color; sound.

Made in New York (producer/director). 1994. Video; 5/10/15-minute versions; color; sound (Greater Blouse and Undergarment Association).

Out in Silence (director). 1994. 16mm; 30 minutes; color; sound (Filmmakers Library).

Not a Simple Story (director). 1994. 16mm; 7 minutes; color; sound (Filmmakers Library).

Letter to Mom (director of a segment of Program 1: "Community"). 1994. Video; 9 minutes; color; sound (PBS).

Ain't Nothing But a She Thing (director of eleven 3-minute episodes). 1995. Video; 33 minutes; color; sound (MTV).

In the Name of the Emperor (co-producer, with Nancy Tong/co-director, with Nancy Tong). 1995. 16mm; 52 minutes; color; sound (NFB).

Nick Deocampo

Oliver. 1983. Super-8mm; 45 minutes; color; sound (Deocampo, 66 Rosario Drive, Cubao, Quezon City, Philippines; Fax: 63–2-722–8628).

Children of the Regime. 1985. Super-8mm; 50 minutes; color; sound (Deocampo).

Beyond the Mainstream. 1986. Video; 45 minutes; color; sound (Deocampo).

Revolutions Happen Like Refrains in a Song. 1987. Super-8mm; 50 minutes; color; sound (Deocampo).

Homage. 1987. Super-8mm; 30 minutes; color; sound (Deocampo).

A Legacy of Violence. 1990. Video; 50 minutes; color; sound (Deocampo).

Let This Film Serve As a Manifesto for a New Cinema. 1990. Super-8mm; 30 minutes; color; sound (Deocampo).

Ynang Bayan: To Be a Woman Is to Live at a Time of War. 1991. 16mm; 60 minutes; color; sound (Deocampo).

Tuklas Sining: Philippine Cinema from 1960 to the Present. 1992. Video; 30 minutes; color; sound (Cultural Center of the Philippines, Roxas Blvd., Manila, Philippines).

Tuklas Dining: Philippine Literature during the Spanish Period. 1992. Video; 30 minutes; color; sound (Cultural Center of the Philippines).

Memories of Old Manila. 1993. 16mm; 22 minutes; color; sound (Channel 4, London, UK).

Continuing Lives: Women of the Bases (producer). 1993. Video; 10 minutes; color; sound (Channel 4, London, UK).

Isaak. 1994. 35mm; 10 minutes; color; sound (Deocampo).

The Sex Warriors and the Samurai. 1995. 16mm; 26 minutes; color; sound (Channel 4, London, UK).

Private Wars. 1995. 16mm; 62 minutes; color; sound (Deocampo).

Valie Export

In *Valie Export: Fragments of the Imagination* (Bloomington/Indianapolis: Indiana University Press, 1994), Roswitha Mueller includes a detailed, annotated description of Export's film and video work up through 1989 as well as her work in other media. The following listing focuses on film, video, and a wide range of practices—installations, environments, multimedia events—that I have listed as "expanded cinema." For further information about work not in distribution in the US and about work completed since 1987, contact Export, Kettenbrückengasse 21/3, A-1050, Vienna, Austria.

Menstruationsfilm ("Menstruation Film"). 1967. 8mm; 3 minutes; color; silent.

Ars Lucis. 1967–68. Expanded cinema.

Abstract Film No. 1. 1967–68. Expanded cinema.

Ohne Titel No. 2 ("Untitled No. 2," co-made with Peter Weibel). 1968. Expanded cinema.

Der Kuss ("The Kiss," co-made with Peter Weibel). 1968. Expanded cinema.

Ohne Titel xn ("Untitled xn," co-made with Peter Weibel). 1968. Expanded cinema.

Ein Familienfilm von Waltraud Lehner ("A Family Film by Waltraud Lehner"). 1968. Expanded cinema.

Instant Film (co-made with Peter Weibel). 1968. Expanded cinema.

Valie Export (co-made with Peter Weibel). 1968. Expanded cinema.

Wor(l)d Cinema: Ein Sprachfest ("Wor(l)d Cinema: A Festival of Languages," co-made with Peter Weibel). 1968. Expanded cinema.

Gesichtsgrimassen ("Facial Grimaces"). 1968. 8mm; 1 minute; color; sound.

Ansprache Aussprache ("Speak to, Speak out"). 1968. Expanded cinema.

Splitscreen—Sopipsismus. 1968. Expanded cinema.

Tapp und Tast Kino ("Touch Cinema"). 1968. Expanded cinema.

333. 1968. Expanded cinema.

Ping Pong. 1968. Expanded cinema.

Vorspann: Ein Lesefilm ("Cast and Credits: A Film to Be Read"). 1968. 16mm; 12 minutes; color; sound.

Auf+Ab+An+Au ("Up+Down+On+Off"). 1968. Expanded cinema.

Proselyt ("Proselyte"). 1969. Expanded cinema.

Eine Reise ist eine Reise Wert ("A Journey Is Worth the Trip," co-made with Peter Weibel). 1969. 8mm; 8 minutes; color; silent.

Das Magische Auge ("The Magical Eye," co-made with Peter Weibel). 1969. Expanded cinema.

Tonfilm ("Sound Film"). 1969. Expanded cinema.

Split Reality. 1970. Expanded cinema/video.

Eros/ion. 1970. Expanded cinema.

Facing a Family. 1971. Expanded cinema/video.

Stille Sprache ("Silent Language"). 1971–72. Performance by Export.

Interrupted Line. 1971–72. Expanded cinema.

Touching (1970). 1973. Expanded video; 2 minutes.

Hauchtext: Liebesgedicht (1970) ("Breath-text: Love Poem"). 1973. Expanded video; 3 minutes.

Die süsse Nummer: Ein Konsumerlebnis ("The Sweet One: A Consumer Experience"). 1973. Video; 10 minutes; color; sound.

Sehtext: Fingergedicht ("Sight Poem: Finger Poem"). 1973. Video; 2 minutes; color; sound.

Hyperbulie ("Hyperbole"). 1973. Video (of body performance by Export); 8 minutes; color; sound.

Asemie ("Asemia"). 1973. Video (of body performance by Export); 9 minutes; color; sound.

Adjungierte Dislokationen ("Adjoined Dislocations"). 1973. 16mm/8mm (3 screens); 10 minutes; black and white; sound.

Mann & Frau & Animal ("Man & Woman & Animal"). 1973. 16mm; 12 minutes; color; sound.

. . . Remote . . . Remote. . . . 1973. 16mm; 12 minutes; color; sound.

Body Politics. 1974. Video (of performance by Export); 2 minutes; color; sound.

Raumsehen und Raumhoren ("Seeing Space and Hearing Space"). 1974. Video (of performance by Export); 20 minutes; color; sound.

Schnitte ("Cuts"). 1976. Video; 10 minutes; color; sound.

Wann Ist der Mensch eine Frau? ("When Is a Human Being a Woman?"). 1976. Video; 15 minutes; color; sound.

Homoter II. 1976. Video (of performance by Export); 10 minutes; color; sound.

Unsichtbare Gegner ("Invisible Adversaries"). 1976. 16mm; 112 minutes; color; sound (FACETS).

Delta: Ein Stuck ("Delta: A Piece"). 1977. Video (of performance by Export); 19 minutes; color; sound.

I[(Beat) It]. 1978. Video (of performance by Export); 9 minutes; color; sound.

Restringierter Code ("Restricted Code"). 1979. Video (of performance by Export); 10 minutes; color; sound.

Menschenfrauen ("Human Women"). 1979. 16mm; 100 minutes; color; sound (FACETS).

Das Bewaffnete Auge ("The Armed Eye"). 1982. Video; 3 parts, each 45 minutes; color; sound.

Syntagma. 1983. 16mm; 18 minutes; color; sound.

Die Praxis der Liebe ("The Practice of Love"). 1984. 35mm; 90 minutes; color; sound (FACETS).

Tischbemerkungen—November 1985 ("Table Quotes—November 1985"). 1985. 16mm; 45 minutes; color; sound.

Die Zweiheit der Natur ("The Duality of Nature," co-made with F. Praschek). 1986. Video; 2 minutes; color; sound.

Ein Perfektes Paar oder die Unzucht Wechselt Ihre Haut ("A Perfect Pair, or, Indecency Sheds Its Skin"). 1986. Video; 12 minutes; color; sound (distributed as part of *Seven Women—Seven Sins* by WMM).

Yukon Quest (co-made with Elly Forster, Ingrid Weiner, Oswald Weiner). 1986. Video; 45 minutes; color; sound.

Mental Images, oder de Zugang der Welt ("Mental Images, or, The Gateway to the World"). 1987. Digital work; minutes; color; sound.

Aktionkunst International ("Actionism International")—interviews with Vito Acconci, Jean Baudrillard, Karen Finley, Dick Higgins, Allan Kaprow, Otto Mühl, Gina Pane, Mark Pauline, Gerhard Rühm, Carolee Schneemann, Wolf Vostell). 1989. Video; 73 minutes; color; sound.

Yervant Gianikian and Angela Ricci Lucchi

A complete, annotated filmography of Gianikian/Ricci Lucchi's films up through 1991 is included in *Yervant Gianikian/Angela Ricci Lucchi*, (Florence: Hopeful Monster Press, 1992), pp. 53–128, a catalogue on the occasion of a retrospective of their films at the Museo Nazionale del Cinema in Turin in 1992. Many of their early films were screened with the accompaniment of particular scents (the specifics are indicated in italics after the designation of film gauge).

Erat-Sora. 1975. 8mm (rose scented); 10 minutes; color; silent (Gianikian/Ricci Lucchi, via Lazzaro Palazzi 19, 20124 Milano, Italy).

Wladimir Propp—Profumo di Lupo ("Wladimir Propp—Wolf Smell"). 1975. 8mm (scented with raspberry); 10 minutes; color; silent (Gianikian/Ricci Lucchi).

Del Sonno e Dei Sogni di Rosa Limitata al Senso Dell'Odorato ("Of Sleep and of Rose Dreams Limited to the Sense of Smell"). 1975. 8mm (scented with lily of the valley and wintergreen); 10 minutes; color; silent (Gianikian/Ricci Lucchi).

Alice Profumata di Rosa ("Alice Scented with Rose"). 1975. 8mm (scented with rose); 10 minutes; color; silent (Gianikian/Ricci Lucchi).

Klinger e il Guanto ("Klinger and the Glove"). 1975. Super-8mm (disguised scents); 5 minutes; color; silent (Gianikian/Ricci Lucchi).

Catalogo della Scomposizione ("Scomposition Catalogue"). 1975. 8mm (scented with naphthalene); 10 minutes; color; silent (Gianikian/Ricci Lucchi).

Non Cercare il Profumo di B N L ("Do Not Look for the BNL's Perfume"). 1975. 8mm (scented with basil, nutmeg, and lavender); 10 minutes; color; silent (Gianikian/Ricci Lucchi).

Catalogo Comparativo ("Comparative Catalogue"). 1975. 8mm (scented with natural and artificial essences); 10 minutes; color; silent (Gianikian/Ricci Lucchi).

Stone-Book. 1975. 8mm (scented with essence of wood); 10 minutes; color; silent (Gianikian/Ricci Lucchi).

Cataloghi—Non e Altro Che Gli Odori che Sente ("Catalogues—It Is No More Than the Smells She Senses"). 1975. 8mm (scented with violets and strawberry); 10 minutes; color; silent (Gianikian/Ricci Lucchi).

Dal 2 Novembre al Giono di Pasqua ("From the 2nd of November until Easter Sunday"). 1975–76. 8mm (scented with incense); 10 minutes; color; silent (Gianikian/Ricci Lucchi).

Cesare Lombroso/Sull'Odore del Garofano ("Cesare Lombroso/Scent of Carnation"). 1976. 8mm (scented with carnation); 10 minutes; color; silent (Gianikian/Ricci Lucchi).

Di Alcumi Fiori Non Facilmente Catalogabili ("Of Some Not Easily Classifiable Flowers"). 1976. 8mm (scented with artificial scents); 10 minutes; color; silent (Gianikian/Ricci Lucchi).

Cataloghi—Non e Altro Che gli Odori Chi Sente ("Catalogues—It Is No More Than the Odors He Senses"). 1976. 16mm (scented with violets, strawberry, and wintergreen); 27 minutes; color; silent (Gianikian/Ricci Lucchi).

Catalogo N. 2 ("Catalogue No. 2"). 1976. 8mm (scented with vanilla); 20 minutes; color; silent (Gianikian/Ricci Lucchi).

Profumo ("Perfume"). 1977. 8mm (scented with various scents and odors); 27 minutes; color; silent (Gianikian/Ricci Lucchi).

Catalogo N. 3—Odore di Tiglio intorno la Casa ("Catalogue No. 3—Lime Scent around the House"). 1977–79. 8mm; 12 minutes; color; silent (Gianikian/Ricci Lucchi).

Un Prestigiatore/Una Miniaturista ("A Conjurer/A Miniaturist"). 1978. 8mm (scented with musk and camphor); 10 minutes; color; silent (Gianikian/Ricci Lucchi).

Millenunanotte ("One Thousand and One Nights"). 1979 (unfinished). 16mm (scented with jasmine); 120 minutes; black and white; silent.

Karagoez et les Bruleurs d'Herbes Parfumes ("Karagoez and the Burners of Scented Herbs"). 1979. 8mm (scented with damask-rose and bitter almonds); 16 minutes; color; silent (Gianikian/Ricci Lucchi).

Catalogo N. 4—Une Due Tre: Immagini. Un Due Tre: Profumi ("Catalogue No. 4—One Two Three: Images. One Two Three: Perfumes"). 1980. 16mm (scented with acetate of amyl-propyl-methyl); 18 minutes; color; silent (Gianikian/Ricci Lucchi).

Karagoez—Catalogo 9,5. 1981. 16mm; 56 minutes; color; silent (MoMA).

Essence d'Absynthe ("Essence of Absinthe"). 1981. 16mm; 15 minutes; color; silent (Gianikian/Ricci Lucchi).

Das Lied von der Erde: Gustav Mahler. 1982. 16mm; 17 minutes; color; silent (Gianikian/Ricci Lucchi).

Dal Polo all'Equatore ("From the Pole to the Equator"). 1986. 16mm; 101 minutes; color; sound (MoMA).

Ritorno a Khodorciur: Diario Armeno ("Return to Khodorciur: Armenian Diary"). 1986. Video; 80 minutes; color; sound (Gianikian/Ricci Lucchi).

Frammenti ("Fragments"). 1987. 16mm; fifty-two separate 3-minute films; color; sound (Gianikian/Ricci Lucchi).

La Più Aamata Dagli Italiani ("The One the Italians Love Best"). 1988. Video; 90 minutes; color; sound.

Passion. 1988. 16mm; 7 minutes; color; silent (Gianikian/Ricci Lucchi).

Uomini, Anni, Vita ("People, Years, Life"). 1990. 16mm; 70 minutes; color; sound (MoMA).

Interni a Leningrado ("Interiors in Leningrad"). 1990 (unfinished). 16mm; c. 60 minutes; black and white/color; sound (Gianikian/Ricci Lucchi).

Archivi Italiani (n. 1): Il Fiore della Razza ("Italian Archives (No. 1): The Flower of the Race"). 1991. 16mm; 25 minutes; color; sound (Gianikian/Ricci Lucchi).

Archivi Italiani (n. 2) ("Italian Archives (No. 2)"). 1991. 16mm; 12 unedited fragments, 20 minutes; color; silent (Gianikian/Ricci Lucchi).

Giacomelli—Contact. 1993. 35mm; 13 minutes; black and white; sound (Gianikian/Ricci Lucchi).

Animali Criminali ("Criminal Animals"). 1994. 16mm; 7 minutes; color; silent (Gianikian/Ricci Lucchi).

Diario Africano ("African Diary"). 1994. 16mm; 7 minutes; color; sound (Gianikian/ Ricci Lucchi).

Aria. 1994. 35mm; 7 minutes; color; sound (Gianikian/Ricci Lucchi).

Prigioniere della Guerra ("Prisoners of War"). 1995. 16mm; 62 minutes; color; sound (Gianikian/Ricci Lucchi).

Lo Specchio di Diana ("Diana's Looking Glass"). 1996. Video; 27 minutes; color; sound (Gianikian/Ricci Lucchi).

William Greaves

Greaves has had such a varied, productive career, and has worked on so many film projects, that a complete review of his activities, or even a complete filmography, is beyond the scope of this volume. For example, of the roughly eighty films Greaves worked on at the National Film Board of Canada (NFB) in the 1950s (primarily as an editor), only four are listed below. Greaves has provided a selected filmography for *A Critical Cinema 3*—though it will be obvious from our interview and from this listing that a thorough documentation of Greaves's career is needed. In some instances the length of films is approximated. Much of Greaves's work has been on sponsored projects. In the filmography, after the title, I indicate Greaves's specific contributions (in parentheses) to each film and, when relevant, the sponsoring organization.

Emergency Ward (director/writer/editor; NFB). 1958. 16mm; 30 minutes; black and white; sound (NFB).

Four Religions: "Christianity" (director, one of four segments; NFB). 1959. 16mm; 15 minutes; black and white; sound (University of Minnesota, Film & Video, 1313 Fifth St. SE, Suite 108, Minneapolis, MN 55414).

Smoke and Weather (director/writer/editor; NFB). 1959. 16mm; 20 minutes; black and white; sound (NFB).

Putting It Straight (director/writer/editor; NFB). 1959. 16mm; 15 minutes; black and white; sound (NFB).

Roads in the Sky (producer/writer; International Civil Aviation Organization). 1962. 16mm; 28 minutes; color; sound.

Cleared for Takeoff (producer/director; United Nations Television). 1963. 16mm; 28 minutes; black and white; sound (University of Illinois, Film Center, 1325 South Oak St., Champaign, IL 61820).

Wealth of a Nation (producer/director/writer; US Information Agency). 1964. 35mm; 25 minutes; black and white; sound.

The First World Festival of Negro Arts (producer/director/writer; USIA). 1966. 16mm; 20 minutes; Sepia-toned; sound (Greaves, 230 W. 55th St., New York, NY 10019).

Beauty and Fashions of the Women of Senegal (producer/director/writer; USIA). 1967. 16mm; 15 minutes; color; sound.

Still a Brother: Inside the Negro Middle Class (producer/director/editor/cameraperson; National Educational Television). 1968. 16mm; 90 minutes; black and white; sound (University of Michigan, Film Video Library, 400 Fourth St., Ann Arbor, MI 48103–4816).

In the Company of Men (producer/director/writer/editor; Newsweek). 1969. 16mm; 52 minutes; black and white; sound (Greaves).

Black Journal (executive producer/co-host, with Lou House (a.k.a., Walid Siddiq); NET). 1968–70. Broadcast television; series of twenty 60-minute programs; color; sound.

The Job Interview (producer/director/writer; US Department of Labor). 1970. 16mm; 20 minutes; color; sound.

On Liberty (director; WGBH Boston). 1970. Broadcast television; 60 minutes; color; sound.

Choice of Destinies (producer/director/writer; WNBC New York). 1970. Broadcast television; 60 minutes; color; sound.

Symbiopsychotaxiplasm: Take One (producer/director/writer; USIA). 1971. 16mm; 70 minutes (revised to 74 ¹/₂ minutes, 1994); color; sound (Greaves).

Ali, the Fighter (a.k.a., *The Fight of the Champions*) (producer/director/writer; WNBC New York). 1971. 35mm; 90 minutes; color; sound (Greaves).

To Free Their Minds (director; Dillard University). 1971. 16mm; 34 minutes; color; sound (University of Colorado, Academic Services, Box 379; Boulder, CO 80309).

On Merit (producer/director/writer; US Civil Service Commission). 1972. 16mm; 23 minutes; color; sound.

EEOC [US Equal Employment Opportunity Commission] *Story* (producer/director/writer; EEOC). 1972. 16mm; 38 minutes; color; sound.

Voice of La Raza (producer/director/writer; EEOC). 1972. 16mm; 54 minutes; color; sound (Eastern New Mexico University, Film Library, Portales, NM 88130).

Struggle for Los Trabajos (producer/director/writer; EEOC). 1972. 16mm; 38 minutes; color; sound (Iowa State University, Media Resources Center, 121 Pearson Hall, Ames, IA 50011).

Childhood Schizophrenia (producer/director/writer; Ittleson Foundation). 1973. 16mm; 20 minutes; black and white; sound.

A Matter of Choice (producer/director/writer; US Department of Health, Education and Welfare). 1973. 16mm; 30 minutes; color; sound (Kent State University, Audio-Visual Resources, 330 Library Building, Kent, OH 44242).

Someone Who Cares (producer/director/writer; US Department of Labor—Job Corps). 1973. 16mm; 30 minutes; color; sound.

Power vs. the People (producer/director/writer; EEOC). 1973. 16mm; 36 minutes; color; sound.

Nationtime: Gary (producer/director/editor; Dillard University). 1973. 16mm; 90 minutes; color; sound.

From These Roots (producer/director/writer; Schomburg Center for Research in Black Culture). 1974. 16mm; 29 minutes; black and white; sound (Greaves, MoMA).

Opportunities in Criminal Justice (producer/director/writer; National Urban League). 1975. 16mm; 35 minutes; color; sound.

A Nation of Visitors (producer/director/writer; USIA). 1975. 16mm; 20 minutes; color; sound.

The Hard Way (producer/director/writer; US Department of Health, Education and Welfare). 1976. 16mm; 25 minutes; color; sound.

The Marijuana Affair (producer/director; Film Jamaica Productions). 1976. 35mm; 90 minutes; color; sound.

Just Doin' It (producer/director; Corporation for Public Broadcasting). 1976. 16mm; 30 minutes; color; sound.

In Search of Pancho Villa (producer/director/writer; Anthony Quinn). 1978. 16mm; 15 minutes; color; sound.

Your Housing Rights (producer/director/writer; US Housing and Urban Development). 1979. 16mm; 25 minutes; color; sound.

Where Dreams Come True (producer/director/writer; NASA). 1979. 16mm; 30 minutes; color; sound.

Getting to Know Me (director; Children's Television International). 1980. 16mm; five 30-minute dramatic films; color; sound.

A Piece of the Pie (producer/director/writer; Exxon). 1981. 16mm; 30 minutes; color; sound.

Bustin' Loose (executive producer; Universal Pictures). 1981. 35mm; 94 minutes; color; sound (FACETS).

Space for Women (producer/director/writer; NASA). 1981. 16mm; 30 minutes; color; sound.

Booker T. Washington: The Life and Legacy (producer/director; National Park Service). 1983. 16mm; 30 minutes; color; sound (University of Minnesota).

Space for Security (producer/director/writer; NASA). 1983. 16mm; 30 minutes; color; sound.

No Time for Privacy (producer/director/writer; American Cancer Society). 1983. 16mm; 25 minutes; color; sound.

A Plan for All Seasons (producer/director/writer; Social Security Administration). 1983. 16mm; 40 minutes; color; sound.

Frederick Douglass: An American Life (producer/director/co-writer; National Park Service). 1985. Video; 30 minutes; color; sound (State University of New York, Buffalo, Media Library, 24 Capen Hall, Buffalo, NY 14260).

Fighter for Freedom (producer/director/writer; National Park Service). 1985. 16mm; 18 minutes; color; sound.

On the Wings of Diversity (producer/director/writer; National Center for Neighborhood Enterprises). 1986. Video; 30 minutes; color; sound.

Beyond the Forest (producer/director/writer; Indian Red Cross). 1986. 16mm; 25 minutes; color; sound.

Golden Goa (producer/director/writer; Government of India). 1986. 16mm; 40 minutes; color; sound.

Black Power in America: Myth or Reality (producer/director/writer; Corporation for Public Broadcasting). 1986. 16mm; 60 minutes; color; sound.

Take the Time (producer/director/writer; American Cancer Society). 1987. 16mm; 18 minutes; color; sound (University of Minnesota).

The Deep North (producer/director/writer; WCBS, New York City). 1988. 16mm; 60 minutes; color; sound.

That's Black Entertainment (director/host; Skyline Entertainment). 1989. Video; 60 minutes; color; sound.

Ida B. Wells: A Passion for Justice (producer/director/writer). 1989. 16mm; 53 minutes; color; sound (Greaves).

Tribute to Jackie Robinson (producer; Jackie Robinson Foundation). 1990. Video; 18 minutes; color; sound.

Resurrections; Paul Robeson (producer/director/writer; pilot for Black Entertainment Television). 1990. 16mm; 60 minutes; color; sound.

Peter Hutton

In Marin County. 1970. 16mm; 10 minutes; color; sound (CC).

July '71 in San Francisco, Living at Beach Street, Working at Canyon Cinema, Swimming in the Valley of the Moon. 1971. 16mm; 33 minutes; black and white; silent (CC; Freunde der Deutchen Kinemathek (FDK), Welserstrasse 25, Berlin D10777, Germany).

New York Near Sleep for Saskia. 1972. 16mm; 10 minutes; black and white; silent (CC, FDK).

Images of Asian Music (A Diary from Life 1973–74). 1974. 16mm; 33 minutes; black and white; silent (CC, FDK).

Florence. 1975. 16mm; 8 minutes; black and white; silent (CC).

New York Portrait, Part I. 1977. 16mm; 15 minutes; black and white; silent (CC, FDK).

Boston Fire. 1978. 16mm; 7 minutes; black and white; silent (CC, FDK).

New York Portrait, Part II. 1980. 16mm; 15 minutes; black and white; silent (CC, FDK).

Lenin Portrait. 1983. 16mm; 12 minutes; black and white; silent (Hutton, Bard College, Annandale-on-Hudson, NY 12504).

Budapest Portrait (Memories of a City). 1986. 16mm; 30 minutes; black and white; silent (CC).

Landscape (for Manon). 1987. 16mm; 18 minutes; black and white; silent (CC, FDK).

New York Portrait, Part III. 1990. 16mm; 15 minutes; black and white; silent (CC, FDK).

In Titan's Goblet. 1991. 16mm; 10 minutes; black and white; silent (CC, FDK).

Architecture of Berlin. 1993. 15 minutes; black and white; silent (CC).

Lodz Symphony. 1993. 16mm; 20 minutes; black and white; silent (CC, FDK).

Study of a River. 1996. 16mm; 16 minutes; black and white/color; silent (CC, FDK).

Ken Jacobs

Completion dates for early Jacobs films are sometimes misleading. For example, *Little Stabs at Happiness* and *Blonde Cobra* were for all practical purposes finished, and were presented publicly, years before money was available to make sound prints. The dates in this filmography, however, refer to these final versions.

Jacobs has made films and two other general kinds of work relating to cinema: what he calls "cine-theater" works (performances employing film projection and/or various kinds of shadow play); and "Nervous System" works (works employing the "Nervous System," two analytic projectors, usually mediated by one of several propellers of Jacobs's own design, with which he explores previously recorded film imagery frame by frame, creating a variety of 2-D and 3-D experiences). Many of the Nervous System works are presented for years, in continually evolving versions; the date of completion for a Nervous System piece indicates when Jacobs began to perform the piece.

The titles of the Nervous System and cine-theater works have varied over the years. Jacobs approved the titles that appear in this listing. Contact Jacobs for these works at 94 Chambers St., New York, NY 10007.

Orchard Street. 1956. 16mm; c. 15 minutes; black and white; sound (Jacobs).

Saturday Afternoon Blood Sacrifice: TV Plug: Little Cobra Dance. 1957. 16mm; 9 minutes; black and white; color (Jacobs).

Star Spangled to Death. 1958–60. 16mm; various versions of various lengths from 120 minutes to 240 minutes; black and white/color; sound (Jacobs).

Death of P'town. 1961. 16mm; 7 minutes; color; sound (Jacobs).

Little Stabs at Happiness. 1963. 16mm; 15 minutes; color; sound (FMC).

Blonde Cobra. 1963. 16mm; 33 minutes; black and white/color; sound (FMC, MoMA).

Baud'larian Capers. 1963. 16mm; 20 minutes; black and white/color; silent, with 3 minutes of musical accompaniment (Jacobs).

We Stole Away. 1964 (unfinished). 8mm; c. 90 minutes; color; silent (Jacobs).

Window. 1964. 16mm; 12 minutes; color; silent (FMC).

Lisa and Joey in Connecticut, January '65: "You've Come Back" "You're Still Here." 1965. 16mm; 28 minutes; color; sound (Jacobs).

Naomi Is a Vision of Loveliness. 1965. 8mm; 4 minutes; color; silent (Jacobs).

The Big Blackout of '65: Chapter One, "Thirties Man." 1965. Cine-theater work.

The Apparition Theater of New York. 1965. Cine-theater work.

Airshaft. 1967. 16mm; 4 minutes; color; silent (FMC).

Soft Rain. 1968. 16mm; 12 minutes; color; silent (FMC).

Tom, Tom, the Piper's Son. 1969 (revised 1971). 16mm; 115 minutes; black and white/color; silent (FMC).

Nissan Ariana Window. 1969. 16mm; 14 minutes; color; silent (FMC).

Globe (previously known as *Excerpt from the Russian Revolution*). 1969. 16mm (uses the Pulfrich filter to create 3-D); 22 minutes; color; sound (FMC).

Restful Moments. 1970. Cine-theater work, using 2-D and 3-D shadow play.

A Good Night for the Movies (II): 4th of July by Charles Ives by Ken Jacobs. 1972. Cine-theater work.

Urban Peasants. 1974. 16mm; 60 minutes; black and white/color; sound (FMC, MoMA).

A Man's Home Is His Castle Films: The European Theater of Operations. 1974. Cine-theater work.

"Slow Is Beauty"—Rodin. 1974. Cine-theater work, using 2-D and 3-D shadow play.

THE IMPOSSIBLE: Chapter One, SOUTHWARK FAIR. 1975. Nervous System performance.

The Boxer Rebellion. 1975. Cine-theater work, using 2-D and 3-D shadow play.

Flop: 4th of July. 1976. Cine-theater work.

"Air of Inconsequence." 1977. Cine-theater work, using 3-D shadow play.

The Doctor's Dream. 1978. 16mm; 23 minutes; black and white; sound (FMC, MoMA).

Ken Jacobs at the Console Performing "Stick to Your Carpentry and You Won't Get Nailed." 1979. Cine-theater work.

THE IMPOSSIBLE: Chapter Two, 1896. 1979. Nervous System performance.

THE IMPOSSIBLE: Chapter Three, HELL BREAKS LOOSE. 1980. Nervous System performance.

THE IMPOSSIBLE: Chapter Four, SCHILLING. 1980. Nervous System performance.

THE IMPOSSIBLE: Chapter Five, THE WRONG LAUREL. 1980. Nervous System performance.

XCXHXEXRXRXIXEXSX (Cherries). 1980. Nervous System performance.

KEN JACOBS' THEATER OF UNCONSCIONABLE STUPIDITY PRESENTS CAMERA THRILLS OF THE WAR. 1981. Nervous System performance.

Audio-Optical Vaudeville. 1982. Cine-theater work.

THE WHOLE SHEBANG. 1982. Nervous System performance.

MAKING LIGHT OF HISTORY: THE PHILIPPINES ADVENTURE. 1983. Nervous System performance.

The Winter Footage. 1984. 16mm (shot on 8mm in 1964–65); 42 $^1/_2$ minutes; color; silent (FMC).

Audio-Optical Vaudeville. 1984. Cine-theater work.

Perfect Film. 1985. 16mm; 21 $^3/_4$ minutes; black and white; sound (FMC).

Jerry Takes a Back Seat, Then Passes Out of the Picture. 1987. 16mm (shot on 8mm in 1975); 13 minutes; black and white/color; silent (FMC).

The Sky Socialist. 1988. 16mm (shot on 8mm in 1964–65); 90 minutes; color; silent, with 2 minutes of sound (Jacobs).

TWO WRENCHING DEPARTURES. 1989. Nervous System performance.

THE SUBCINEMA: CHRONOMETER. 1990. Performance using slide projector, film-strip, propeller; c. 25 minutes.

THE SUBCINEMA: OPENING THE NINETEENTH CENTURY: 1896. 1990. 16mm (uses the Pulfrich filter to create 3-D); 9 minutes; black and white; silent (Jacobs).

THE SUBCINEMA: PHONOGRAPH. 1990. Sound piece; c. 15 minutes.

THE SUBCINEMA: BETTER TO BE FRIGHTENED THAN TO BE CRUSHED. 1990. 16mm; c. 60 minutes; black and white/color; sound.

Keaton's Cops. 1991. 16mm; 23 minutes; black and white; silent (Jacobs).

NEW YORK GHETTO FISHMARKET 1903. 1992. Nervous System performance.

BI-TEMPORAL VISION: THE SEA. 1994. Nervous System performance (uses the Pulfrich filter to create 3-D).

The Georgetown Loop (1903 American Mutoscope and Biograph Co./arrangement by Ken Jacobs). 1995. 16mm (2 projectors, 2 images); 10 minutes; black and white; silent (Jacobs).

Disorient Express (1906 Miles Bros./arrangement by Ken Jacobs). 1995. 16mm (2 projectors, 2 images); 24 minutes; black and white; silent (Jacobs).

THE MARRIAGE OF HEAVEN AND HELL (A FLICKER OF LIFE). 1995. Nervous System performance.

FROM MUYBRIDGE TO BROOKLYN BRIDGE. 1996. Nervous System Performance.

Mani Kaul

Kaul's Indian films are in Hindi. Kaul can be contacted at Cinemaya, B90, Defence Colony, New Delhi, India 110024; fax: 91–11–4627211.

Uski Roti ("A Day's Bread"). 1970. 35mm; 110 minutes; black and white; sound.

Ashad Ka Ed Din ("A Monsoon Day"). 1971. 35mm; 143 minutes; black and white; sound.

Duvidha ("Of Two Minds"). 1973. 35mm; 82 minutes; color; sound.

The Nomad Puppeteers. 1974. 35mm; 18 minutes; color; sound.

Picture Stories. 1977. 35mm; 18 minutes; color; sound.

Arrival. 1979. 35mm; 20 minutes; color; sound.

Satah se Uthta Aadmi ("Arising from the Surface"). 1980. 35mm; 144 minutes; color; sound.

Desert of a Thousand Lines. 1981. 35mm; ? minutes; color; sound.

Dhrupad. 1982. 35mm; 72 minutes; color; sound.

Mati Manas ("Mind of Clay"). 1985. 35mm; 80 minutes; color; sound.

Before My Eyes. 1988. 35mm; 20 minutes; color; sound.
Siddeshwari. 1989. 35mm; 92 minutes; color; sound.
Nazar ("The Gaze"). 1990. 35mm; ? minutes; color; sound.
The Idiot. 1991. 35mm; minutes; color; sound.
The Cloud Door. 1994. 35mm; 26 minutes; color; sound.

Hara Kazuo

Hara has worked in various capacities on films by Kei Kumai, Shohei Imamura, Shinsaku Himeda, and others. The following listing is of films he has directed.

Sayonara CP. 1972. 16mm; 82 minutes; black and white; sound (Hara, Shisso Production, #502 Kaizuka Bldg., 1–3413–502 Shinjuku, Shinjuku-ku, Tokyo 160, Japan).
Kyokushiteki Erosu Koiuta ("Extreme Private Eros: Love Song"). 1974. 16mm; 92 minutes; black and white; sound (Hara).
Rekishi Ha Kokoni Hajimaru "Onna Tachi Ha Ima" ("Women Now: 'History Begins Here'"). 1975. Broadcast television (TBS, Japan); ? minutes; color; sound.
Yuki Yukite Shingun ("The Emperor's Naked Army Marches On"). 1987. 16mm; 122 minutes; color; sound (Kino, 333 W. 39th St., #503, New York, NY 10018).
A Dedicated Life. 1994. 35mm; 157 minutes; color; sound (Hara).

Rose Lowder

Roulement, Rouerie, Aubage ("Rotation, Wiliness, Paddle Wheel Unit"). 1978. 16mm; 15 minutes; black and white/color; silent (CC, FMC, LC).
Parcelle ("Particle"). 1979. 16mm; 3 minutes; color; silent (CC, CFDC, FMC, LC).
Couleurs Mécaniques ("Mechanical Colors"). 1979. 16mm; 16 minutes; color; silent (CC, FMC, LC).
Rue des Teinturiers. 1979. 16mm; 31 minutes; color; silent (CC, FMC, LC).
Champ Provençal ("Provençal Field"). 1979. 16mm; 9 minutes; color; silent (CC, FMC, LC).
Retour d'un Repère ("Recurrence"). 1979. 16mm; 19 minutes; color; silent (FMC, LC).
Rapprochements. 1979. 16mm; 23 minutes; black and white/color; silent (LC).
Certaines Observations ("Certain Observations"). 1979. 16mm (2 projectors, 1 screen); 14 minutes; color; silent (LC).
Retour d'un Repère Composé ("Composed Recurrence"). 1981. 16mm; 59 minutes; color; silent (FMC, LC).
Les Tournesols ("Sunflowers"). 1982. 16mm; 3 minutes; color; silent (CC, CFDC, FMC, LC).
Les Tournesols Colores ("Colored Sunflowers"). 1983. 16mm; 3 minutes; color; silent (CC, LC).
Scènes de la Vie Française: Arles ("Scenes of French Life: Arles"). 1985. 16mm; 21 minutes; color; silent (LC).
Scènes de la Vie Française: Paris. 1986. 16mm; 26 minutes; color; silent (CC, LC).
Scènes de la Vie Française: La Ciotat. 1986. 16mm; 31 minutes; color; silent (CC, LC).

Scènes de la Vie Française: Avignon. 1986. 16mm; 11 minutes; color; silent (CC, LC).
Impromptu. 1989. 16mm; 8 minutes; color; sound (CC, LC).
Quiproquo. 1992. 16mm; 13 minutes; color; sound (CC, LC).
Three in One (a.k.a. 3̲). 1994. 16mm (3 screens); 5 minutes; color; silent (LC).
Bouquets 1–10. 1994–95. 16mm; 11 ½ minutes; color; silent (CC, LC).

Aline Mare

Mare has worked in film and video, in performance (often with Bradley Eros), and in installation; and she has been employed in various capacities on music videos, commercials, commercial features, and, in one instance, an IMAX film. The following listing includes only discrete films and videos.

Mater. 1980. 16mm; 15 minutes; black and white; silent (Mare, 540 Alabama St., #209, San Francisco, CA 94110).
D.B. 1981. 16mm; 10 minutes; black and white; silent (Mare).
Venus to Penis (co-made with Bradley Eros). 1983. Super-8mm and video; 15 minutes; black and white/color; sound (FMC).
Psyche Psychosis. 1984. Super-8mm; 7 minutes; black and white/color; sound (FMC).
Cassandra, Seething at the Mouth. 1985. Super-8mm; 7 minutes; black and white/color; sound (FMC).
Pyrotechnics (co-made with Bradley Eros). 1986. Super-8mm; 10 minutes; color; sound (FMC).
Electromorphic (co-made with Bradley Eros). 1987. Super-8mm and video; 12 minutes; color; sound (Eros).
S'Aline's Solution. 1991. Video; 9 minutes; color; sound (The Kitchen, 512 W. 19th St., New York, NY 10011).
The Book of Flesh. 1996. Video; 28 minutes; color; sound (Mare).

Elias Merhige

Implosion. 1983. Super-8mm; 48 minutes; black and white; sound.
Spring Reign. 1984. 16mm; 8 minutes; black and white/color; sound.
A Taste of Youth. 1985. 16mm; 5 minutes; black and white; sound.
Begotten. 1989. 16mm; 78 minutes; black and white; sound (Henry Rosenthal, Complex Corporation, 535 Stevenson St., San Francisco, CA 94103; World Artists Home Video, P.O. Box 36788, Los Angeles, CA 90036–0788).

Gunvor Nelson

Some of Nelson's films have been shown publicly and subsequently revised; I have listed the date when Nelson considers the film to have been in its final state.

Building Muir Beach House (co-made with Robert Nelson). 1962. 16mm; 3 minutes; black and white; silent.
Last Week at Oona's Bath (co-made with Robert Nelson). 1962. 16mm; 2 minutes; black and white; silent.

Schmeerguntz (co-made with Dorothy Wiley). 1966. 16mm; 15 minutes; black and white; sound (CC, CFDC).

Fog Pumas (co-made with Dorothy Wiley). 1967. 16mm; 25 minutes; color; sound (CC).

Kirsa Nicholina. 1969. 16mm; 16 minutes; color; sound (CC).

My Name Is Oona. 1969. 16mm; 10 minutes; black and white; sound (CC, CFDC, MoMA).

Five Artists BillBobBillBillBob (co-made with Dorothy Wiley). 1971. 16mm; 70 minutes; color; sound (CC).

Take Off. 1972. 16mm; 10 minutes; black and white; sound (CC, CFDC).

One & the Same (co-made with Freude). 1973. 16mm; 4 minutes; color; sound (CC).

Moons Pool. 1973. 16mm; 15 minutes; color; sound (CC).

Trollstenen. 1976. 16mm; 120 minutes; color; sound (CC).

Before Need (co-made with Dorothy Wiley). 1979. 16mm; 75 minutes; color; sound (CC),

Frame Line. 1983. 16mm; 22 minutes; black and white; sound (CC).

Red Shift. 1984. 16mm; 50 minutes; black and white; sound (CC).

Light Years. 1987. 16mm; 28 minutes; color; sound (CC).

Light Years Expanding. 1988. 16mm; 25 minutes; color; sound (CC, LC).

Field Study #2. 1988. 16mm; 8 minutes; color; sound (CC).

Natural Features. 1990. 16mm; 30 minutes; color; sound (CC).

Time Being. 1991. 16mm; 8 minutes; black and white; silent (CC).

Kristina's Harbor. 1993. 16mm; 50 minutes; color; sound (CC).

Old Digs. 1993. 16mm; 20 minutes; color; sound (CC).

Before Need Redressed (co-made with Dorothy Wiley). 1994. 16mm; 42 minutes; color; sound (CC).

Raphael Montañez Ortiz

The following listing includes only films, videos, and "digital/laser/videos." For a documentation of Ortiz's many other kinds of work—art objects, performances, environments—see Kristine Stiles, *Raphael Montañez Ortiz: Years of the Warrior 1960 / Years of the Psyche 1988.* New York: El Museo del Barrio, 1988.

The listing is chronological according to year, but—in the case of the digital-laser-videos—alphabetized within individual years (Ortiz usually works on several digital-laser-videos simultaneously over a period of months). In North America, Ortiz distributes his work on 3/4-inch and 1/2-inch video; he can be reached at 315 Harper Place, Highland Park, NJ 08904. In Europe, Oritz's distributor is 235 Media (Spichernstrasse 61, D-50672 Cologne, Germany; Fax: 02–21–52–27–41). 235 Media has some work Ortiz does not, and vice versa. The early films are currently available on video only.

Cowboy and "Indian" Film. 1958. 16mm; 2 minutes; black and white; sound.

Golf. 1958. 16mm (with holes punched into frames); 20 minutes; black and white; sound.

Henny Penny: The Sky Is Falling (a.k.a. *Chicken Little*). 1958. 8mm; 7 minutes; black and white; silent (sound added to video version c. 1990).

Newsreel. 1958. 16mm; 1 3/4 minutes; black and white; silent.

Sports Gems. 1959. 16mm (with holes punched into frames); 9 minutes; black and white; sound.

Piano Destruction Concert, London, England. 1966. 16mm; 4 ½ minutes; black and white; sound.

Destruction Room, Judson Church. 1967. 16mm; 4 ½ minutes; black and white; sound.

Past Life Regression. 1979. Video; 26 minutes; color; sound.

Beach Umbrella. 1985. Video; 7 ½ minutes; black and white; sound.

Bridge Game. 1985. Video; 12 minutes; black and white; sound.

Dance No. 1. 1985. Video; 3 ¾ minutes; black and white; sound.

Dance No. 2. 1985. Video; 2 ½ minutes; black and white; sound.

Dance No. 3. 1985. Video; 4 ¾ minutes; black and white; sound.

Dance No. 4. 1985. Video; 3 ¾ minutes; black and white; sound.

Dance No. 5. 1985. Video; 9 minutes; black and white; sound.

Dance No. 6. 1985. Video; 2 ¼ minutes; black and white; sound.

The Kiss. 1985. Video; 6 minutes; black and white; sound.

The Kiss, Version II. 1985. Video; 4 ½ minutes; black and white; sound.

What Is This? 1985. Video; 9 ¼ minutes; black and white; sound.

Back Back Back Back. 1986. Video; 7 minutes; black and white; sound.

Couplett. 1986. Video; 20 ½ minutes; black and white; sound.

Good and Evil. 1986. Video; 20 ¼ minutes; black and white; sound.

Man Has Man Has Always. 1986. Video; 3 ¼ minutes; color; sound.

pushAnn pushAnn. 1986. Video. 3 ¼ minutes; black and white; sound.

You Bust Your Buns. 1986. 5 ½ minutes; color; sound.

Chamber Music Group, No. 1. 1987. Video installation; three tapes of 30 minutes for three separate monitors; color; sound.

Christ. 1987. Video; 3 ½ minutes; color; sound.

If You Don't Want It Anymore. 1987. Video; 3 ½ minutes; black and white/color; sound.

They Bombed the Speak. 1987. Video; 5 ¾ minutes; black and white; sound.

Welcome. 1987. Video; 5 ½ minutes; color; sound.

Election Promises. 1988. Video; 7 ¼ minutes; black and white; sound.

Mischievous Shadows. 1988. Video; 3 ½ minutes; black and white; sound.

Shadow Boxing. 1988. Video; 3 minutes; black and white; sound.

Expulsion from the Garden. 1991. Video; 4 minutes; black and white; sound.

Gonna Get Me a Gal. 1991. Video; 3 minutes; black and white; sound.

Here's Looking at You Kid. 1991. Video; 3 ¾ minutes; black and white; sound.

My Father's Dead. 1991. Video; 3 ¾ minutes; color; sound.

Now You've Done It. 1991. Video; 3 ¼ minutes; black and white; sound.

Raw Oysters. 1991. Video; 6 minutes; black and white; sound.

The Briefcase. 1992. Video; 13 minutes; black and white; sound.

The Drowning. 1992. Video; 3 ¾ minutes; color; sound.

If We Believe That Man's/Womyn's Soul Has Not Reached Its Fulfillment . . . Is It Right . . . Is It Wise . . . to Tamper with the Problem? 1992. Video; 6 ½ minutes; black and white/color; sound.

Mr. Marechal Have You Seen This Photograph? 1992. Video; 5 ¾ minutes; black and white; sound.

Our Thoughts Are Made of Clay: Horse Women of the Apocalypse. 1992. Video; 7 ¾ minutes; black and white; sound.

That's the Way I Feel About Him. 1992. Video; 3 ¹/₄ minutes; black and white; sound.

Dance No. 22. 1993. Video; 7 ¹/₄ minutes; black and white; sound.

Elvis: The Premonition. 1993. Video; 4 ¹/₂ minutes; color; sound.

Fred and Ginger. 1993. Video; 6 ³/₄ minutes; black and white; sound.

Gonna Get Gonna Get Gonna Get a. 1993. Video; 8 minutes; black and white; sound.

Send Him to the Capital. 1994. Video; 7 ¹/₄ minutes; black and white; sound.

Slam Dance. 1994. Video; 8 ³/₄ minutes; black and white; sound.

Kiss Number Also. 1994. Video; 6 ¹/₄ minutes; color; sound.

Behind It All. 1995. Video; 20 ³/₄ minutes; black and white/color; sound.

Rag Time. 1995. Video; 6 minutes; black and white; sound.

You Were Right. 1995. Video; 26 minutes; black and white; sound.

The Critic. 1996. Video; 11 ¹/₄ minutes; black and white/color; sound.

The Conversation. 1996. Video; 12 minutes; black and white/color; sound.

Ring Ring Rag-Time. 1996. Video; 11 ¹/₄ minutes; black and white/color; sound.

That's Too Much. 1996. Video; 4 ¹/₂ minutes; black and white; sound.

Humpty Dumpty Piano Destruction Concert (documentation of performance at the Whitney Museum of American Art, December 19, 1996). 1996. Video; 39 minutes; color; sound.

Arthur Peleshian

Gornyi Patrul ("Mountain Vigil"). 1964. 35mm; 10 minutes; black and white; silent.

Zemlya Ludei ("Country of Human Beings"). 1966. 70mm; 10 minutes; black and white; sound.

Nachalo ("The Beginning"). 1967. 35mm; 9 minutes; black and white; sound.

My ("We"). 1969. 35mm; 30 minutes; black and white; sound.

Obitateli ("The Inhabitants"). 1970. 70mm; 10 minutes; black and white; sound.

Vremena Goda ("The Seasons"). 1975. 35mm; 30 minutes; black and white; sound.

Nash Vek ("Our Century" or "Our Age"). 1982/1990. 35mm; 50 minutes (1982), 30 minutes (1990); black and white; sound.

Konets ("The End"). 1992. 35mm; 10 minutes; black and white; sound.

Zhizn ("Life"). 1993. 35mm; 10 minutes; color; sound.

John Porter

Many of Porter's films are made, shown, and subsequently expanded. My listing only indicates the most recent year of completion. All films are available from Porter, 11 Dunbar Rd., Toronto, Ont., M4W 2X5, Canada.

Sandbox. 1968. Super-8mm; 3 minutes; color; silent.

Home. 1969. 16mm; 2 ¹/₂ minutes; black and white; sound.

Subway Station, 1969. 16mm; 2 minutes; black and white; sound.

Exercise. 1969. 16mm; 1 minute; black and white; silent.

Park in the City. 1970. 16mm (2 projectors); 3 minutes; black and white; sound.

Albatross. 1970. 16mm; 3 minutes; black and white; sound.

Belt Line. 1970. 16mm; 3 minutes; black and white; sound.

Tobogganing. 1971. 16mm; 3 minutes; black and white; sound.

Streetcar. 1971. 16mm; 3 minutes; black and white; sound.
Keep on Dancing. 1971. 16mm; 2 minutes; black and white; sound.
Canoe Trip. 1971. Super-8mm; 10 minutes; color; silent (destroyed).
Toronto Rock Groups. 1972. Super-8mm; 17 minutes; color; silent.
Raccoon & Crowd. 1972. 8mm; 3 minutes; color; silent.
Pirouette. 1972. 16mm; 2 ¹/₂ minutes; black and white; sound.
Singing Om. 1972. 16mm; 2 minutes; black and white; sound.
Morning Sounds. 1972. 16mm; 2 minutes; black and white; sound.
Gee, This Is an Exciting School. I Hope Someday to Be a Famous Movie Director! 1972.
    16mm and Super-8mm (3 projectors); 30 minutes; black and white; sound.
Greg Backwards. 1973. 16mm; 3 minutes; black and white; sound.
Cube Rotation. 1973. 16mm; 3 minutes; black and white; sound.
Independent Filmmaking. 1974. 16mm; 3 minutes; black and white; silent.
Odds & Ends. 1974. Super-8mm; 20 minutes; color; silent.
Al's Rock Group. 1974. Super-8mm; 10 minutes; color; silent.
Blues Festival. 1974. Super-8mm; 3 minutes; color; silent.
Baseball. 1974. Super-8mm; 53 minutes; color; silent.
Bus Route. 1974. Super-8mm; 14 minutes; color; silent.
Soap Box Derby. 1974. Super-8mm; 20 minutes; color; silent.
Cinefuge 1. 1974. Super-8mm; 3 minutes; color; silent.
Santa Claus Parade. 1974. Super-8mm; 10 minutes; color; silent.
Eedie's TD Show. 1975. Super-8mm; 5 minutes; black and white; silent.
CN Tower. 1975. Super-8mm; 2 minutes; color; silent.
Passers-by Balcony. 1975. Super-8mm; 3 minutes; color; silent.
Pole Painting. 1975. Super-8mm; 4 minutes; color; silent.
Power Shovel. 1975. Super-8mm; 7 minutes; color; silent.
Winchester Hotel Day. 1975. Super-8mm; 3 minutes; color; silent.
Bruce's Sound Test. 1975. Super-8mm; 3 minutes; color; sound.
Cabbagetown Festival. 1975. Super-8mm; 3 minutes; color; silent.
Cabbagetown. 1975. Super-8mm; 3 minutes; color; silent.
Juna vs. Joshua. 1975. Super-8mm; 2 minutes; color; silent.
Eedie, Al & Larry. 1975. Super-8mm; 13 minutes; color; silent.
Santa Claus Parade. 1975. Super-8mm; 13 minutes; color; silent.
Paulette. 1976. Super-8mm; 3 minutes; black and white; silent.
60 Winchester. 1976. Super-8mm; 3 minutes; black and white; silent.
Fog Rising. 1976. Super-8mm; 1 minute; color; silent.
A Day at Home. 1976. Super-8mm; 3 minutes; color; silent.
Juna and I. 1976. Super-8mm; 2 minutes; black and white; silent.
Two Women. 1976. Super-8mm; 2 minutes; color; silent.
O-Leo and I. 1976. Super-8mm; 3 minutes; color; silent.
Waiting. 1976. Super-8mm; 13 minutes; color; silent.
Cycles. 1976. Super-8mm; 3 minutes; color; silent.
Hockey. 1976. Super-8mm; 3 minutes; color; silent.
Passing Streetcars. 1976. Super-8mm; 3 minutes; color; silent.
St. Lawrence Market. 1976. Super-8mm; 3 minutes; color; silent.
Jensen & Walker. 1976. Super-8mm; 5 minutes; color; sound.
Santa Claus Parade. 1976. Super-8mm; 6 minutes; color; silent.

Around the Corner. 1977. Super-8mm; 3 minutes; color; silent.
Cinefuge 2. 1977. Super-8mm; 3 minutes; color; silent.
New York Apartment. 1977. Super-8mm; 3 minutes; color; silent.
Eedie. 1977. Super-8mm; 1 minute; color; silent.
Wedding Reception. 1977. Super-8mm; 3 minutes; color; silent.
The Dishes. 1977. Super-8mm; 3 minutes; color; silent.
Leaving 107 King. 1977. Super-8mm; 3 minutes; color; silent.
Streetcar. 1977. Super-8mm; 3 minutes; color; silent.
Queen Street. 1977. Super-8mm; 3 minutes; color; silent.
Roof Views. 1977. Super-8mm; 7 minutes; color; silent.
Yonge Street. 1977. Super-8mm; 3 minutes; color; silent.
Sam Smart Day. 1977. Super-8mm; 3 minutes; color; silent.
Adelaide & Parliament. 1977. Super-8mm; 3 minutes; color; silent.
Mother and Child. 1977. Super-8mm; 2 minutes; color; silent.
O-Leo and Huck. 1977. Super-8mm; 3 minutes; color; silent.
Landscape. 1977. Super-8mm; 1 minute; color; silent.
Halloween Ball. 1977. Super-8mm; 1 minute; color; silent.
Wings. 1977. Super-8mm; 2 minutes; color; silent.
Circus Rehearsal. 1977. Super-8mm; 3 minutes; color; silent.
Moscow Circus. 1977. Super-8mm; 4 minutes; color; silent.
High School Mosaic. 1977. Super-8mm; 4 minutes; color; silent.
Queen's Tattoo. 1977. Super-8mm; 3 minutes; color; silent.
Cinefuge 3. 1977. Super-8mm; 7 minutes; color; silent.
CNE Rides. 1977. Super-8mm; 7 minutes; color; silent.
Santa Claus Parade. 1977. Super-8mm; 3 minutes; color; silent.
Watching TV. 1977. Super-8mm; 3 minutes; color; silent.
Family Christmas. 1977. Super-8mm; 3 minutes; color; silent.
Square Dance. 1978. Super-8mm; 7 minutes; color; silent.
Fashion Show Reject. 1978. Super-8mm; 3 minutes; color; silent.
Fashion Show 1. 1978. Super-8mm; 5 ¹/₂ minutes; color; silent.
Fashion Show 2. 1978. Super-8mm; 2 minutes; color; silent.
Owen Sound Tour. 1978. Super-8mm; 13 minutes; color; silent.
Elements Concert. 1978. Super-8mm; 6 minutes; color; silent.
Shriners Circus. 1978. Super-8mm; 8 minutes; color; silent.
O-Leo Jumping. 1978. Super-8mm; 3 minutes; color; silent.
Bay Street. 1978. Super-8mm; 3 minutes; color; silent.
Highlanders Ball. 1978. Super-8mm; 1 minute; color; silent.
Studio Self-Portrait. 1978. Super-8mm; 3 minutes; color; silent.
Time-Lapse Dance. 1978. Super-8mm; 2 minutes; color; silent.
Clouds. 1978. Super-8mm; 2 minutes; color; silent.
Seagulls. 1978. Super-8mm; 3 minutes; color; silent.
Studio Shots. 1978. Super-8mm; 3 minutes; color; silent.
May Parades. 1978. Super-8mm; 1 ¹/₂ minutes; color; silent.
Highland Games. 1978. Super-8mm; 3 minutes; color; silent.
C.U.F.F. Festival. 1978. Super-8mm; 2 minutes; color; silent.
Window Cleaning. 1978. Super-8mm; 3 minutes; color; silent.
Fireworks. 1978. Super-8mm; 2 minutes; color; silent.

Band Spectacular. 1978. Super-8mm; 7 minutes; color; silent.
Scarborough Parade. 1978. Super-8mm; 3 minutes; color; silent.
Canada Day Parade. 1978. Super-8mm; 2 minutes; color; silent.
Orange Parade. 1978. Super-8mm; 2 minutes; color; silent.
Drum & Bugle Corps. 1978. Super-8mm; 7 minutes; color; silent.
Police Games. 1978. Super-8mm; 2 minutes; color; silent.
Caribana Parade. 1978. Super-8mm; 3 minutes; color; silent.
Tartan Tattoo. 1978. Super-8mm; 4 minutes; color; silent.
Warriors Day Parade. 1978. Super-8mm; 3 minutes; color; silent.
Musical Ride. 1978. Super-8mm; 1 minute; color; silent.
Labour Day Parade. 1978. Super-8mm; 3 minutes; color; silent.
Eedie's "30 × 12." 1978. Super-8mm; 3 minutes; color; silent.
Bubbles. 1978. Super-8mm; 3 minutes; color; silent.
Days. 1978. Super-8mm; 2 minutes; color; silent.
Window Toys. 1978. Super-8mm; 2 minutes; color; silent.
Santa Claus Parade. 1978. Super-8mm; 3 minutes; color; silent.
Funnel Footage. 1978. Super-8mm; 3 minutes; color; silent.
Son of Funnel. 1978. Super-8mm; 3 minutes; color; silent.
Post Office. 1978. Super-8mm; 3 minutes; color; silent.
Studio Circling. 1978. Super-8mm; 2 minutes; color; silent.
Ice Follies. 1979. Super-8mm; 3 minutes; color; silent.
Stock Exchange. 1979. Super-8mm; 2 minutes; color; silent.
Funnel Audience. 1979. Super-8mm; 7 minutes; color; silent.
Amusement Park. 1979. Super-8mm; 6 minutes; color; silent.
Angel Baby. 1979. Super-8mm; 2 minutes; color; silent.
Dave Anderson. 1979. Super-8mm; 2 minutes; color; silent.
Lydia Lunch & Harbinger. 1980. Super-8mm; 3 minutes; color; silent.
Parachute. 1980. Super-8mm; 3 minutes; color; sound.
Dream Factory. 1980. Super-8mm; 7 minutes; color; silent.
Firefly. 1980. Super-8mm; 3 minutes; color; silent.
Gail Swinging. 1980. Super-8mm; 3 minutes; color; silent.
Goal Slow. 1980. Super-8mm; 3 minutes; color; silent.
Party. 1980. Super-8mm; 2 minutes; color; silent.
Eedie Swinging. 1980. Super-8mm; 2 minutes; color; silent.
Passover 1. 1980. Super-8mm; 7 minutes; color; silent.
Passover 2. 1980. Super-8mm; 5 minutes; color; silent.
Chuck. 1980. Super-8mm; 3 minutes; color; silent.
Foldes at Al's Stag. 1980. Super-8mm; 3 minutes; color; sound.
Al & Ette Wedding. 1980. Super-8mm; 30 minutes; color; sound.
For John. 1980. Super-8mm; 3 minutes; color; sound.
Post Office. 1980. Super-8mm; 3 minutes; color; silent.
Animal in Motion. 1980. Super-8mm (with performance by Porter); 1 minute; color; sound.
Revolving Restaurant. 1981. Super-8mm (with performance by Porter); 3 minutes; color; silent.
Scenic Elevators. 1981. Super-8mm; 2 minutes; color; silent.
Cinefuge 4 & 5. 1981. Super-8mm; 4 minutes; color; sound.
Headbanging. 1981. Super-8mm (with performance by Porter); 3 minutes; color; sound.

Head-Dancing. 1981. Super-8mm; 2 minutes; color; sound.
Toy Catalogue 1. 1981. Super-8mm; 5 minutes; color; sound.
Swinging. 1981. Super-8mm; 2 minutes; color; silent.
Down On Me. 1981. Super-8mm; 4 minutes; color; silent.
Bicycle. 1981. Super-8mm; 3 minutes; color; silent.
Scanning 1. 1981. Super-8mm (with performance with Super-8mm projector by Porter); 3 minutes; color; silent.
Soarin'. 1981. Super-8mm; 2 minutes; color; silent.
Fashion Show 3. 1981. Super-8mm; 7 minutes; color; silent.
Harbinger. 1981. Super-8mm; 7 minutes; color; sound.
Drive-In Movies. 1981. Super-8mm; 7 minutes; color; silent.
Moon Eclipse. 1981. Super-8mm; 3 minutes; color; silent.
Royal Wedding. 1981. Super-8mm; 17 minutes; color; sound.
Tom's Weekend. 1981. Super-8mm; 3 minutes; color; silent.
Tom's Trampoline. 1981. Super-8mm; 1 minute; color; silent.
T.V. People. 1981. Super-8mm; 2 minutes; color; sound.
My Trip to Europe. 1981. Super-8mm; 37 minutes; color; sound.
Devo. 1981. Super-8mm; 2 minutes; color; silent.
Greg and Guitar. 1981. Super-8mm; 3 minutes; color; silent.
Funnel on TV. 1981. Super-8mm; 10 minutes; color; sound.
Ross's Film Class. 1982. Super-8mm; 3 minutes; color; silent.
Tour of a Cat House. 1982. Super-8mm; 6 minutes; color; sound.
Exams. 1982. Super-8mm; 3 minutes; color; silent.
Fifth Column. 1982. Super-8mm; 7 minutes; color; sound.
Scanning 2. 1982. Super-8mm (with performance with Super-8mm projector by Porter); 3 minutes; color; sound.
Scanning 3. 1982. Super-8mm (with performance with Super-8mm projector by Porter); 2 minutes; color; silent.
Rock Jam. 1982. Super-8mm; 13 minutes; color; silent.
Funnel Benefit. 1982. Super-8mm; 5 minutes; color; sound.
Collaboration Mural. 1982. Super-8mm; 3 minutes; color; silent.
Slow Dancing with Guy Fox. 1982. Super-8mm (with performance by Porter); 7 minutes; color; sound.
Famous Scenes from Funnel Films. 1982. Super-8mm; 3 minutes; color; sound.
Christmas. 1982. Super-8mm; 15 minutes; color; silent.
Martha's Balloon Ride. 1982. Super-8mm; 6 minutes; color; silent.
Drawing Group. 1983. Super-8mm; 5 minutes; color; silent.
Scanning 4. 1983. Super-8mm (with performance with Super-8mm projector by Porter); 4 minutes; color; silent.
Shootout with Rebecca. 1983. Super-8mm (with performance by Porter); 3 minutes; color; sound.
Hallowe'en's Kittens. 1983. Super-8mm; 13 minutes; color; sound.
Beach Party. 1983. Super-8mm; 15 minutes; color; silent.
Cycle Circle. 1983. Super-8mm; 7 minutes; color; silent.
Hot Rod Truck Pull. 1983. Super-8mm; 7 minutes; color; silent.
Scanning 5. 1983. Super-8mm (with performance with Super-8mm projector by Porter); 3 minutes; color; silent.

Attack of the UFO. 1983. 16mm; 1 minute; color; sound.
Chroma Living. 1983. Super-8mm; 13 minutes; color; silent.
Way to Go Argos. 1983. Super-8mm; 1 minute; color; silent.
Family Portrait. 1983. Super-8mm; 7 minutes; color; sound.
Dave Anderson at YYZ. 1984. Super-8mm; 3 minutes; color; silent.
Ghost Goes Gear. 1984. Super-8mm; 3 minutes; color; sound.
Fireworks '84. 1984. Super-8mm; 3 minutes; color; silent.
Fashion Show 4. 1984. Super-8mm; 4 minutes; color; silent.
Trampoline Festival. 1984. Super-8mm; 7 minutes; color; silent.
My Trip to Sudbury. 1984. Super-8mm; 23 minutes; color; sound.
Window Water Bobby Moving. 1984. Super-8mm; 3 minutes; color; sound.
Variety Lights. 1984. Super-8mm; 4 minutes; color; silent.
Daily Double Dick Van Dyke. 1985. Super-8mm (performance with 3 projectors by
    Porter); 4 minutes; color; sound.
Uncensored Movies. 1985. Performance by Porter with 16mm and Super-8mm film,
    video; 60 minutes; color; sound.
Hamilton Homes. 1985. Super-8mm; 9 minutes; color; sound.
Urban Underground. 1985. Super-8mm; 10 minutes; color; sound.
Dot's Cottage. 1985. Super-8mm; 3 minutes; color; silent.
Seven Year Itch at The Funnel. 1985. Super-8mm; 7 minutes; color; sound.
Marathon Run. 1985. Super-8mm; 3 minutes; color; silent.
A Trip around Toronto Harbor. 1986. Super-8mm; 2 minutes; color; silent.
Ellen's Cottage. 1986. Super-8mm; 9 minutes; color; sound.
On the Waterfront. 1986. Super-8mm; 15 minutes; color; silent.
Kauffmann Christmas. 1987. Super-8mm; 7 minutes; color; sound.
Toronto Homes. 1987. Super-8mm; 7 minutes; color; sound.
Calendar Girl. 1988. Super-8mm; 3 minutes; color; sound.
Toy Catalogue 2. 1989. Super-8mm; 15 minutes; color; sound.
Picture Pitcher. 1989. Super-8mm; 4 minutes; color; sound.
Pleading Art. 1989. Super-8mm; 3 minutes; color; sound.
Wallpaper Films (a series, co-produced with Fifth Column). 1983–90. Super-8mm; 50
    minutes; black and white; live sound.
The Secret of the Lost Tunnel. 1992. Super-8mm; 3 minutes; color; sound.
Shovelling Snow. 1992. Super-8mm; 3 minutes; color; sound.
CineCycle. 1992. Super-8mm (with performance by Porter); 5 minutes; color; sound.
Carousel Cycle. 1992. 35mm film sculpture; continuous; color; silent.
Oh, My Heart. 1992. Super-8mm (with performance by Porter); 3 minutes; color; silent.
3 Speed Gear. 1993. Super-8mm; 3 minutes; color; sound.
Magic Lantern Cycle. 1993. Super-8mm (with performance by Porter); 3 minutes;
    color; silent.
Thomas Highway. 1993. Super-8mm; 3 minutes; color; sound.
Vac/All. 1993. Super-8mm (with performance by Porter); 3 minutes; color; sound.
Symptom Hall Shadowplay. 1993. Super-8mm (with performance by Porter); 5 minutes;
    color; sound.
The List of Bicycle Messenger. 1994. Super-8mm; 4 minutes; color; sound.
Jewison, Superstar. 1995. Super-8mm; 4 $^1/_2$ minutes; color; sound.
On the Street Where She Lived. 1995. Super-8mm; 3 minutes; color; sound.

222 Loop. 1995. Super-8mm; 1 minute; color; silent.
Toy Catalogue 3. 1996. Super-8mm; 60 minutes; color; sound.

Sally Potter

In the 1960s, Potter made a number of 8mm films that may be lost. This listing begins with the earliest film currently in her possession, though the disorder in her archives makes a complete listing of the late 1960s and early 1970s films impossible at present.

Jerk. 1969. 8mm; 3 minutes; black and white; silent.
Black and White. 1969. 8mm (2 projectors, 2 screens); ? minutes; black and white; silent.
The Building. 1970. 8mm (2 projectors, 2 screens); c. 7 $^1/_2$ minutes; black and white/color; silent.
Play. 1971. 16mm (2 projectors, 2 screens); 15 minutes; black and white/color; silent.
Hors d'Oeuvres. 1971. 16mm; 10 minutes; black and white/color; silent.
Daily. 1971. 8mm (2 screens and live performance); c. 10 $^1/_2$ minutes; color; silent.
Combines. 1972. 16mm (3 projectors, 3 screens, with live choreography by Richard Alston for the London Contemporary Dance Theatre); 20 minutes; black and white/color; live music.
Thriller. 1979. 16mm; 35 minutes; black and white; sound (Arts Council of England, 14 Great Peter St., London SW1P 3NQ; BFI; WMM).
The Gold Diggers. 1983. 35mm; 90 minutes; black and white; sound (BFI, WMM).
Tears, Laughter, Fears and Rage. 1986. Video; four 60-minute shows; color; sound (Channel 4, London, UK).
The London Story. 1986. 35mm; 15 minutes; color; sound (BFI, WMM).
I Am an Ox, I Am a Horse, I Am a Man, I Am a Woman (in USA: *Women Filmmakers in Russia*). 1988. Video; 60 minutes (USA version: 51 minutes); color; sound (WMM).
Orlando. 1992. 35mm; 93 minutes; color; sound (Electric Pictures, in UK; New Yorker, 16 W. 61st St., New York, NY 10023; SONY Pictures Classics, in USA).

Cauleen Smith

Daily Rains. 1980. 16mm; 12 minutes; color; sound (Smith, 7518 West Norton Ave., Apt. 1, West Hollywood, CA 90046).
Chronicles of a Lying Spirit (by Kelly Gabron). 1992. 16mm; 5 $^1/_2$ minutes; color; sound (CC).
The Message (Sapphire Tape #1). 1993. Video; 3 $^1/_2$ minutes; color; sound (Smith).
Still Lives of Divinity and Redemption (Sapphire Tape #2). 1996. Video; 10 minutes; color; sound (Smith).

Peter Watkins

A filmography for Watkins up through 1987 is included in *A Critical Cinema 2.* Additions to it are as follows:

The Media Project. 1991. Video; 120 minutes; color; sound (Watkins, Siltadarzio skg. 3–12, Vilnius, 2001, Lithuania).
The Freethinker. 1994. Video; 270 minutes; color; sound (Watkins).

Bibliography

While the preceding filmographies are as complete and up-to-date as I am able to make them, the scope of this volume does not allow for an equally thorough bibliography of this field. The following selected bibliography means only to provide an entry into the discourse on critical cinema in general and on those interviewed for *A Critical Cinema 3*.

General References

A Critical Cinema and *A Critical Cinema 2* include listings of general references. The following is an addendum to them. Books listed in the individual filmmaker bibliographies are given in shortened form if they are cited in full in the General References section.

Alexander, William. *Film on the Left: American Documentary Film from 1931 to 1942*. Princeton: Princeton University Press, 1981.

Arnold, Martin, and Peter Tscherkassky, eds. *Austrian Avant-Garde Cinema, 1955–1993*. San Francisco/Vienna: San Francisco Cinematheque/SIXPACK film, 1994. A catalogue for a traveling exhibit of Austrian avant-garde film curated by Steve Anker.

Barnouw, Erik, and Patricia R. Zimmermann, eds. *The Flaherty: Four Decades in the Cause of Independent Cinema*. A special issue of *Wide Angle* 17, nos. 1–4 (1995–96).

Blimp Film Magazine (Austrian), no. 16 ("Found Footage Film," June 1991) and no. 20 ("Unknown Territories: American Independent Film," Summer 1992).

Bonet, Eugeni, ed. *Desmontaje: Film, Vídeo/Apropiación,, Recielaje* ("De-montage: Film, Video/Appropriation, Recycling"). Valencia: Institut Valencia d'Art Modern, 1993. A catalogue for a traveling exhibition of recycled cinema, curated by Eugeni Bonet (includes essays by Yann Beauvais, Bonet, Catherine Elwes, Joel Katz, William C. Wees, and John Wyver).

Canyon Cinema Film/Video Catalogue 7. San Francisco: Canyon Cinema, 1992. Compiled by Melanie Curry and Heather Mackey.

Cripps, Thomas. *Slow Fade to Black: The Negro in American Film, 1900–1942*. London, Oxford, New York: Oxford University Press, 1977.

Diawara, Manthia, ed. *Black American Cinema*. New York, London: Routledge, 1993.

Film Culture. 1955–Present. Available through Anthology Film Archives, 32 Second Ave., New York, NY 10003.

Gever, Martha, John Greyson, and Pratibha Parmar, eds. *Queer Looks: Perspectives on Lesbian and Gay Film and Video*. New York, London: Routledge, 1993.

Hausheer, Cecilia, and Christoph Settele, eds. *Found Footage Film*. Lucern: VIPER/ zyklop, 1992.

Heresies: A Feminist Publication on Art and Politics.

Horak, Jan-Christopher, ed. *Lovers of Cinema: The First American Film Avant-Garde, 1919–1945*. Madison: University of Wisconsin Press, 1995.

Horwath, Alexander, Lisl Ponger, and Gottfried Schlemmer, eds. *Avantgardefilm: Österreich. 1950 bis Heute* ("Austrian Avant-Garde Film: 1950 to the Present"). Vienna: Wespennest, 1995.

James, David E., ed. *To Free the Cinema: Jonas Mekas and the New York Underground*. Princeton: Princeton University Press, 1992.

Klotman, Phyllis Rauch, ed. *Screenplays of the African American Experience*. Bloomington, Indianapolis: Indiana University Press, 1991.

Light Cone Catalogue. Paris: Light Cone, 1994. Compiled by Yann Beauvais, Jennifer Lou Burford, Pip Chodorov, and Miles McKane.

Lowder, Rose, ed. *The Visual Aspect: Recent Canadian Experimental Film*. Avignon: Archives du film experimental d'Avignon, 1991. A catalogue for a touring exhibition of Canadian experimental films curated by Rose Lowder.

MacDonald, Scott. *Avant-Garde Film/Motion Studies*. New York/Cambridge: Cambridge University Press, 1993.

———, ed. *Cinema 16: Documents toward a History of the Film Society*. Two special issues of *Wide Angle* 19, no. 1 (January 1997) and no. 2 (April 1997).

———. *Screen Writings: Scripts and Texts by Independent Filmmakers*. Berkeley, Los Angeles, London: University of California Press, 1995.

Millennium Film Journal. 1977–Present. Available at 66 E. 4th St., New York, NY 10003.

Mulvey, Laura. *Visual and Other Pleasures*. Bloomington, Indianapolis: University of Indiana Press, 1989.

Noriega, Chon A., and Ana M. Lopez, eds. *The Ethnic Eye: Latino Media Arts*. Minneapolis, London: University of Minnesota Press, 1996.

Peterson, James, ed. *Dreams of Chaos, Visions of Order: Understanding the American Avant-Garde Cinema*. Detroit: Wayne State University Press, 1994.

Reid, Mark A., ed. *Redefining Black Film*. Berkeley, Los Angeles, Oxford: University of California Press, 1993

Schobert, Walter, ed. *The German Avant-Garde Film of the 1920s*. Munich: Goethe Institute, 1989.

Sitney, P. Adams, ed. *Modernist Montage: The Obscurity of Vision in Cinema and Literature*. New York: Columbia University Press, 1990.

Small, Edward S. *Direct Theory: Experimental Film/Video as Major Genre*. Carbondale, Edwardsville: Southern Illinois University Press, 1994.

Starr, Cecile, ed. *Film Society Primer*. Forest Hills, NY: American Federation of Film Societies, 1956.

Stauffacher, Frank, ed. *Art in Cinema*. New York: Arno, 1968. A catalogue for a symposium on avant-garde film at the San Francisco Museum of Art, 1947.

Steven, Peter, ed. *Jump Cut: Hollywood, Politics and Counter-Cinema*. New York: Praeger, 1985.

Testa, Bart. *Back and Forth: Early Cinema and the Avant-Garde*. Toronto: Art Gallery of Ontario, 1992.

Voorhuis, Nelly, ed. *A Passage Illuminated: De Amerikaanse Avant-Garde Film 1980–1990*. Amsterdam: Stichting Mecano, 1991. A catalogue for a series of programs of American avant-garde film (includes articles by Paul Arthur, Manohla Dargis, Tom Gunning, and Nelly Voorhuis).

Wees, William C. *Light Moving in Time: Studies in the Visual Aesthetics of Avant-Garde Film*. Berkeley, Los Angeles, Oxford: University of California Press, 1992.

———. *Recycled Images: The Art and Politics of Found Footage Film*. New York: Anthology Film Archives, 1993.

Weiss, Andrea. *Vampires and Violets: Lesbians in Film*. New York: Penguin, 1992.

Willis, Holly, ed. *Scratching the Belly of the Beast: Cutting-Edge Media in Los Angeles, 1922–1994*. Los Angeles: Filmforum, 1994. A catalogue for a series of programs of film and video (includes articles by Terry Cannon, Albert Kilchesty, Morgan Fisher, Shea Castleman, O. Funmilayo Makarah, Todd Boyd, James M. Moran, and Michael Nash; an interview with John Whitney by Maureen Furniss; and extensive program notes).

Zimmermann, Patricia R. *Reel Families: A Social History of Amateur Film*. Bloomington, Indianapolis: Indiana University Press, 1995.

Martin Arnold

Claus, Phillip. "Tanz mit Fundstücken" ("Dance with Artifacts"). In *Gegenschub* ("Countershot"), ed. Peter Illetschko. Vienna: Verlag, 1995.

Tscherkassky, Peter. "The Analogies of the Avant-Garde." In Hausheer and Settele, *Found Footage Film*, 27–35.

Turim, Maureen. "Eine Begegnung mit dem Bild" ("An Encounter with the Image"). In Horwath, Ponger, Schlemmer, *Avantgardefilm*, 301–307.

Craig Baldwin

Baldwin, Craig. "Statement." In Hausheer and Settele, *Found Footage Film*, 92–93.

———. *Tribulation 99: Alien Anomalies under America*. New York: Ediciones la Calavera, 1991.

Bonet, Eugeni. "Appropriation Is Theft." In Bonet, *Desmontaje: Film, Vídeo/ Apropiación,, Recielaje*, 136–155.

"Crazy Baldwin and the Other Cinema." *Wide Angle* 14, nos. 3–4 (1992): 130–135 ("San Francisco" issue, edited by Jeanne Hall).

Fox, Michael. "Take the Image and Run: Craig Baldwin's Outlaws Push the Edge of Fair Use" (an interview with Baldwin and Alan Korn). *The Independent* 18, no. 10 (December 1995): 32–35.

Stephens, Chuck. "Craig Baldwin: No-Budget Visionary." *The Independent* 17, no. 2 (March 1994): 32–33.

Tyner, Kathleen. "Pushing the Envelope with *RocketKitKongoKit*," *Cinematograph*, no. 4 (1991): 28–36.

Wees, William C. *Recycled Images*, 23–25.

Jordan Belson

Curtis, David. *Experimental Cinema*, 75–77. New York: Delta, 1971.

Igliori, Paola, ed. "3 October 1994: [Interview with] Jordan Belson." In *Harry Smith: American Magus*, 19–29. New York: Inanout Press, 1996.

James, David E. *Allegories of Cinema*, 127–136. Princeton: Princeton University Press, 1989.

LeGrice, Malcolm. *Abstract Film and Beyond*, 82–84. Cambridge, MA: MIT Press, 1977.

Renan, Sheldon. "The West Coast Abstract School" and "Jordan Belson." In *An Introduction to the American Underground Film*, 93–96, 116–118. New York: Dutton, 1967.

Stephenson, Ralph. *The Animated Film*, 67–68. London, New York: Tantir/Barnes, 1973.

Wees, William C. *Light Moving in Time*, 130–136.

Youngblood, Gene. "The Cosmic Cinema of Jordan Belson." In *Expanded Cinema*, 157–177. New York: Dutton, 1970.

Patrick Bokanowski

Bokanowski, Patrick, with the Groupe Art Toung in discussion. "Styles d'Image Cinematographique" ("Styles of the Film Image"). *Revue & Corrigee*, no. 8 (Spring 1991): 22–25.

Ishaghpour, Youssef. "De Derrière le Miroir" ("The Back of the Mirror"). In *Cinema Contemporain*, 318–331. Paris: Editions de Différence, 1986.

Kermabon, Jacques. "Portrait: Patrick Bokanowski." *Bref*, no. 20 (February–April 1994): 17–19.

Langlois, Gérard. "L'Image Standard en Question" ("Questioning the Standard Image"). *Cinema Pratique*, no. 137 (May–June 1975): 46–49, 80.

Noquez, Dominique. *Le Cinema, Autrement* ("The Other Cinema"), 280–281. Paris: Editions du Cerf, 1987.

Ostria, Vincent. "Patrick Bokanowski." *Cahiers du Cinema*, no. 478 (April 1994): 10–11.

Charles Burnett

Burnett, Charles. "Inner City Blues." In Jim Pines and Paul Willemen, *Questions of Third Cinema*, 223–226. London: British Film Institute, 1989.

———. Screenplay for *Killer of Sheep*. In Klotman, *Screenplays of the African American Experience*, 91–118.

Masilela, Ntongela. "The Los Angeles School of Black Filmmakers." In Diawara, *Black American Cinema*, 107–117.

Reid, Mark A. *Redefining Black Film*, 128–133.

Reynaud, Bérénice. "An Interview with Charles Burnett." *Black American Literature Forum* 25, no. 2 (Summer 1991): 323–334.
Sharp, Saundra. "Interview with Charles Burnett." *Black Film Review* 6, no. 1 (1990): 4–7.

Christine Choy

Abbe, Elfrieda. "Interview with Christine Choy." *Angles* 3, no. 1 (1996): 7–9.
Agosta, Diana, and Barbara Osborn. "If I Ever Stop Believing. . . . " *Heresies 16* (Fall 1983): 68–72.
Dittus, Eric. "Mississippi Triangle: An Interview with Christine Choy, Worth Long, and Allan Siegel." *Cineaste* 14, no. 2 (1985): 38–40.
Harris, Valerie. "Power Exchange 1: Chris Choy" (an interview). *Heresies 8* (1979): 24–27.
Millner, Sherry. "Third Word Newsreel: Interview with Christine Choy." In Steven, *Jump Cut*, 158–165.
Renov, Michael. "Newsreel: Old and New—Towards an Historical Profile." *Film Quarterly* 51, no. 1 (Fall 1987): 20–33.

Nick Deocampo

Deocampo writes regularly for *Movement*, the magazine published by the Mowelfund Film Institute (of which Deocampo is director) in the Philippines.

Berry, Chris. "On Questions of Difference." *Cinemaya* [India], no. 23 (Spring 1994): 40–43.
Cantrill, Arthur, and Corinne Cantrill. "Nick Deocampo: Independent Filipino Cinema" (an interview). *Cantrills' Filmnotes*, nos. 59–60 (September 1989): 5–10.
———. "Philippine Independent Film and the Mowelfund Film Institute." *Cantrills' Filmnotes*, nos. 61–62 (May 1990): 4–6.
Deocampo, Nick. "Homosexuality as Dissent/Cinema as Subversion: Articulating Gay Consciousness in the Philippines." In Gever, Greyson, and Parmar, *Queer Looks*, 395–402.
———. "The Radical Impulse." *Cinemaya*, nos. 28–29 (Summer 1995): 42–47.
Gonzales-Tamrong, Marlina. "Introduction to Nick Deocampo." In Barnouw and Zimmermann, *The Flaherty*, 339–340.
Reyes, Manny. "Independent in Spirit." *Cinemaya*, nos. 28–29 (Summer 1995): 47–51.
———. "Saved by Mowelfund." *Cinemaya*, no. 27 (Spring 1995): 41–42.

Valie Export

Cornwell, Regina. "Interactive Art: Touching the Body in the Mind." *Discourse* 14, no. 2 (Spring 1992): 203–221.
Export, Valie. "About *Invisible Adversaries*." *Idiolects*, nos. 9–10 (Winter 1980–81): 14.
———. "Aspects of Feminist Actionism." *New German Critique*, no. 47 (Spring–Summer 1989): 69–92.

————. "The Real and Its Double: The Body." *Discourse* 11, no. 1 (Fall–Winter 1988–89): 3–27.

Kiernan, Joanna. "Films by Valie Export." *Millennium Film Journal*, nos. 16–18 (Fall–Winter 1986–87): 181–187.

Mueller, Roswitha. *Valie Export: Fragments of the Imagination*. Bloomington, Indianapolis: Indiana University Press, 1994.

Prammer, Anita. "Avant-Garde—die Lust des Geistes: Anita Prammer im Gespräch mit Valie Export" ("Avant-Garde—The Mind's Desire: Anita Prammer in Conversation with Valie Export"). In Horwath, Ponger, Schlemmer, *Avantgardefilm*, 174–187.

————. *Valie Export*. Vienna: Frauenverlag, 1988.

Weibel, Peter. "Women Working" (a review of *Invisible Adversaries*). *Camera Obscura*, nos. 3–4 (Summer 1979): 219–224.

Yervant Gianikian and Angela Ricci Lucchi

The most useful source of information (in English) about Gianikian and Ricci Lucchi is *Yervant Gianikian/Angela Ricci Lucchi*, the catalogue published by the Museo Nationale del Cinema in Turin in 1992. It includes an interview with Gianikian and Ricci Lucchi by Sergio Toffetti and Daniela Gürffrida; articles by Alberto Farassimo, Janis Crystal Lipzin, and Michel Hommel; and an annotated filmography through 1991.

Bellour, Raymond. "L'Arrière-monde." *Cinémathèque* (Autumn 1995): 6–11.

MacDonald, Scott. *Avant-Garde Film/Motion Studies*, 112–121.

William Greaves

Greaves, William. "A Black Filmmaker Remembers Louis de Rochemont." *Film Library Quarterly* 12, no. 4 (1979): 13–15.

————. "Black Journal: A Few Notes from the Executive Producer." *Television Quarterly* 8, no. 4 (Fall 1969): 66–72.

————. "The First World Festival of Negro Arts: An Afro-American View." *The Crisis* 73, no. 6 (June–July 1966): 309–314, 332.

————. "100 Madison Avenues Will Be of No Help." *New York Times*, August 9, 1970.

————. "A Statement." In Barnouw and Zimmermann, *The Flaherty*, 21, 128–134.

————. "*Symbiopsychotaxiplasm: Take One*: Director's Early Notes Prior to and during Production in the Spring of 1986"; "Transcript of Excerpt from *Symbiopsychotaxiplasm: Take One*"; "Program Notes for *Symbiopsychotaxiplasm: Take One*." In MacDonald, *Screen Writings*, 31–48.

Knee, Adam, and Charles Musser. "William Greaves, Documentary Film-making, and the African-American Experience." *Film Quarterly* 45, no. 3 (Spring 1992): 13–25.

Reid, Mark A. *Redefining Black Film*, 126–127.

Peter Hutton

Burns, Ken. "Ken Burns' Vision of Peter Hutton" (a letter). *The Independent* 20, no. 2 (March 1997): 7.

Grindon, Leger. "The Films of Peter Hutton." *Millennium Film Journal*, nos. 4–5 (Summer–Fall 1979): 175–178.

Gunning, Tom. "The Image and Its Eclipse: The Films of Peter Hutton." *Spiral*, no. 4 (July 1985): 7–10.

Hoberman, J. "Peter Hutton: A Tale of Two Cities." *Artforum* 25, no. 2 (October 1986): 93–97.

Jost, Jon. "Image Conscious." *American Film* 11, no. 3 (December 1985): 72–73.

Ken Jacobs

Arthur, Paul. "Creating Spectacle from Dross: The Chimeric Cinema of Ken Jacobs." *Film Comment* 33, no. 2 (March–April 1997): 58–63.

Boone, Charles. "Memorials in Slowed Time: Morton Feldman, Composer / Ken Jacobs, Filmmaker." *Cinematograph*, no. 5 (1993): 58–62.

Ehrenstein, David. *Film: The Frontline/1984*, 34–42. Denver: Arden Press, 1984.

Gunning, Tom. "Doctor Jacobs' Dream Work." *Millennium Film Journal*, nos. 10–11 (Fall–Winter 1981–82): 210–218.

―――. "Looking Backward: Ken Jacobs Presents the Past." In Vincent Grenier, Kathy Dieckmann, John Pruitt, eds., *Ten Years of Living Cinema*, 53–55. New York: Collective for Living Cinema, 1981.

Hanlon, Lindley. "Kenneth Jacobs, Interviewed by Lindley Hanlon [Jerry Sims Present], April 9, 1974." *Film Culture*, nos. 67–69 (1979): 65–86.

―――."Recycling Cinema: Urban Peasants by Ken Jacobs." *Millennium Film Journal*, no. 6 (Spring 1980): 117–120.

Hanlon, Lindley, and Tony Pipolo. "Interview with Ken and Flo Jacobs." *Millennium Film Journal*, nos. 16–18 (Fall–Winter 1986–87): 26–53.

Hoberman, J. *Vulgar Modernism*, 187–189. Philadelphia: Temple University Press, 1991.

Jacobs, Ken. "The Day the Moon Gave Up the Ghost." *No Rose* 1, no. 1 (Winter 1976): 14–20.

―――. Statement in "Recollections." In Barnouw and Zimmermann, *The Flaherty*, 33.

MacDonald, Scott. "The Millennium after Twenty Years: An Interview with Howard Guttenplan," *Millennium Film Journal*, nos. 16–18 (1986–87): 9–10.

Marks, Laura. "Here's Gazing at You." *The Independent* 16, no. 2 (March 1993): 26–31.

Matturri, John. "Ken Jacobs on Theater of Embarrassment." *Idiolects*, no. 8 (Spring 1980): 12–16.

Mekas, Jonas. *Movie Journal*. New York: Collier, 1972. Includes reviews of many Jacobs works (see Mekas's index).

Mendelson, Lois, and Bill Simon. "Tom, Tom, the Piper's Son." *Artforum* 10, no. 1 (September 1971): 46–52.

Schwartz, David, ed. *Films That Tell Time: A Ken Jacobs Retrospective*. Catalogue for a retrospective at the American Museum of the Moving Image, October 20—November 15, 1989. Includes Tom Gunning, "Films That Tell Time: The Paradoxes of the Cinema of Ken Jacobs"; an interview with Jacobs (and Flo Jacobs), by David Schwartz and Tom Gunning; and an essay "Is Tom Gunning for Me?" detailed program notes, and selected other writings by Jacobs.

Solomon, Phil. "*XCXHXEXRXRXIXEXSX*." *Cinematograph*, no. 5 (1993): 54–57.

Testa, Bart. *Back and Forth: Early Cinema and the Avant-Garde*, 7–21. Toronto: Art Gallery of Ontario, 1992.

Wees, William. *Recycled Cinema*, 5–11.

Worden, Fred. "Ken Jacobs' *Chronometer*." *Cinematograph*, no. 5 (1993): 52–53.

Mani Kaul

Cinemaya (India), no. 31 (Winter 1995–96). A special issue on Mani Kaul.

Hara Kazuo

Sinkler, Scott. "Made in Japan: Upholding the Japanese Independent Tradition." *The Independent* 16, no. 9 (November 1993): 20–25.

Rose Lowder

Beauvais, Yann. Program notes for a retrospective of Lowder's films at the Cinéma du musée, Musée national d'art moderne/Centre Georges Pompidou, February–March, 1987.

Cartwright, Lisa, and Peter Gidal. "Rose Lowder's *Composed Recurrence*." *Millennium Film Journal*, nos. 16–18 (1986–87): 176–179.

English, William. "Three Aspects of French Experimental Film: Interviews with Yann Beauvais and Rose Lowder and Alain-Alcide Sudre." *Millennium Film Journal*, nos. 23–24 (Winter 1990–91): 102–116.

Gidal, Peter. *Materialist Film*, 136–143. London, New York: Routledge, 1989.

Lowder, Rose. "Distribution in France: An Account and Some Considerations Concerning Experimental Film." *Independent Eye* 12, no. 2 (Winter 1991): 22–25.

———. "Le Film Experimental en Tant qu'Instrument de Recherche Visuelle: Contribution des Cinéastes Expérimentaux à une Démarche Exploratoire" ("Experimental Film As an Instrument of Research: The Contribution of Filmmakers to an Experimental Approach"). Ph.D. dissertation, University of Paris and Nanterre, 1987.

———. Program notes for the regular presentations of the Archives du film experimental d'Avignon, 72 rue des Lices, 8400 Avignon, 1977–Present.

———. "Switzerland: Signs of Activity and an Important Yearly Event in Lucerne." *Independent Eye* 12, no. 2 (Winter 1991): 16–28.

———, ed. *The Visual Aspect: Recent Canadian Experimental Films*. Avignon: Editions des archives du film experimental, 1991. Catalogue for a French traveling show of Canadian Avant-Garde film, October–December 1991, curated by Lowder. Includes Lowder's "Introduction: The Visual Aspect," 9–10, and "Another Level of Perception," 57–76.

Aline Mare

Durant, Mark. "A Call across the Unknowing." *Artweek* 20, no. 2 (January 14, 1989): 6–7.

Hartouni, Valerie. "Fetal Exposures: Abortion Politics and the Optics of Allusion." *Camera Obscura*, no. 29 (May 1992): 131–151.

Zimmermann, Patricia. "Fetal Tissue: Reproductive Rights and Activist Amateur Video." In Michael Renov and Erika Suderburg, eds., *Resolutions: Contemporary Video Practices*, 304–332. Minneapolis, London; University of Minnesota Press, 1996.

Elias Merhige

Gunning, Tom. "New Horizons: Journeys, Documents, Myths and Counter Myths." *Blimp*, no. 20 (Summer 1992): 12–13 (originally published in Voorhuis, *A Passage Illuminated*).

Gunvor Nelson

Fischer, Lucy. *Shot/Countershot: Film Tradition and Woman's Cinema*, 26–31. Princeton: Princeton University Press, 1989.
Kitchen, Diane. "In and Around the Making of *Red Shift*." *Cinematographe*, no. 1 (1985): 72–84. Includes excerpts from Kitchen's journal made during the making of *Red Shift* and an interview with Nelson.
Vogel, Amos. *Film As a Subversive Art*, 259–262. New York: Random House, 1974.

Raphael Montañez Ortiz

MacDonald, Scott. "Media Destructionism: The Digital/Laser/Videos of Raphael Montañez Ortiz." In Noriega and Lopez, *The Ethnic Eye*, 183–207.
Noreiga, Chon. "On Curating." In Barnouw and Zimmermann, *The Flaherty*, 293–304.
Stiles, Kristine. *Raphael Montañez Ortiz: Years of the Warrior 1960/Years of the Psyche 1988*. New York: El Museo del Barrio, 1988. Catalogue for a retrospective of Ortiz's work at El Museo del Barrio, March 26–May 22, 1988. Includes an annotated listing of writings by and about Ortiz, including his many Destructionist manifestos.

Arthur Peleshian

Pigoullié, Jean-François. "Peleshian: Le Montage-Movement." *Cahiers du Cinema*, no. 454 (April 1992): 30–34.

John Porter

Fleming, Martha. "Filming Buildings/Building Films." *Parachute*, no. 25 (Winter 1981): 15–19.
Porter, John. "Artists Discovering Film/Post-War Toronto." *Vanguard* 13, nos. 5–6 (Summer 1984): 24–26.
———. "Consolidating Film Activity." *Vanguard* 13, no. 9 (November 1984): 26–29.
Rist, Peter. "John Porter: Super-8 Idealist." *Vanguard* 15, nos. 3–4 (April–May 1986): 30–33.
Tuer, Dot. "Fragile Imprints/Mediated Resistances." *C*, no. 6 (June 1990): 14–19.

Sally Potter

Chaimowicz, Marc. "Women and Performance in the UK" (an interview with Sally Potter). *Studio International*, no. 192 (July 1976): 33–35.
Ehrenstein, David. *Film: The Front Line/1984*, 119–127. Denver: Arden Press, 1984.
English, Rose, Jacky Lansley, and Sally Potter. *Mounting*. Oxford: Museum of Modern Art, 1977. Text-image catalogue to accompany performances in May 1977.

Kaplan, E. Ann. *Women and Film*, 142–170. New York, London: Methuen, 1983.
Kopjec, Joan. "*Thriller*: An Intrigue of Identification." *Ciné-Tracts*, no. 11 (1981): 33–38.
Mellencamp, Patricia. *Indiscretions*, 150–172. Bloomington, Indianapolis: Indiana University Press, 1990.
Potter, Sally. *Orlando* (the screenplay). London, Boston: Faber and Faber, 1994.
———. "Sally Potter on *Thriller*." *Camera Obscura*, no. 5 (Spring 1980): 99.
Weinstock, Jane. "She Who Laughs First Laughs Last." *Camera Obscura*, no. 5 (Spring 1980): 100–110.

Cauleen Smith

Gibson, Linda. "Cauleen Smith: Media Griot." *The Independent* 17, no. 2 (March 1994): 38–39.
White, Jerry. "The Many Layers of Cauleen Smith." *Black Film Review* 8, no. 2 (Summer 1994): 6.

Amos Vogel

In the years after Cinema 16 closed, Vogel became a regular commentator on independent film. He established the "Independents" column in *Film Comment*, supplying regular reviews to the bimonthly from July-August 1971 through September-October 1981. Beginning in March 1971 and continuing into 1975, Vogel supplied approximately sixty columns to *The Village Voice*.

Dobi, Stephen J. "Cinema 16: America's Largest Film Society." Ph.D. dissertation, New York University, 1984.
MacDonald, Scott. "Amos Vogel and Cinema 16." *Wide Angle* 9, no. 3 (1987): 38–51.
———. *Cinema 16: Documents toward a History of the Film Society*.
Vogel, Amos. "Amos Vogel on Cinema 16." *The Independent* 7, no. 8 (September 1984): 15–17.
———. "Cinema 16 and the Question of Programming." In Starr, *Film Society Primer*, 54–58.
———. *Film As a Subversive Art*.
———. "Thirteen Confusions." In Gregory Battcock, ed., *The New Cinema*, 124–138. New York: Dutton, 1967.

Peter Watkins

A selected Watkins bibliography through 1991 is included in *A Critical Cinema 2*.

MacDonald, Scott. *Avant-Garde Film/Motion Studies*, 169–188.

Index

Compositor:	Impressions Book and Journal Services, Inc.
Text:	Times Roman
Display:	Helvetica
Printer and Binder:	Malloy Litho